谨以此书献给郑权在天之灵

郑 权
(1935年10月—2020年5月)

1982年5月,美国宾州州立大学

1987年5月上海科学技术大学30周年校庆,郑权与共事同事及7241班部分学生的合影
前排左起:陈小珠、潘仲雄、黄育仁、郑权、颜珍棣、孙秀妹
后排左起:周宗直、徐鸿明、朱天顺、沈龙弟、王翼飞、董炳华

左起：韩伯顺、柯寿仁、郑权、涂仁进的合影

1988年第三次中国运筹学会全国代表大会暨学术年会在安徽九华山召开
会议期间，郑权（左）与天津南开大学史树中的合影

郑权与G. Galprin的合影（1990年7月，加拿大蒙特利尔）

郑权与陈巩的合影

2001年12月，美国普林斯顿大学

郑权与探望他的学生们共进午餐（2016年5月，亲和源对面农家乐酒店）
前排左起：蔡建平、王翼飞、涂仁进、郑权、周建新、谢志刚
后排左起：梁泽亮、彭建平、张亦芃、许伟静、韩伯顺、姚奕荣、张丽苹、纪令克、陆钦雯

郑权获国家教委科技进步二等奖证书

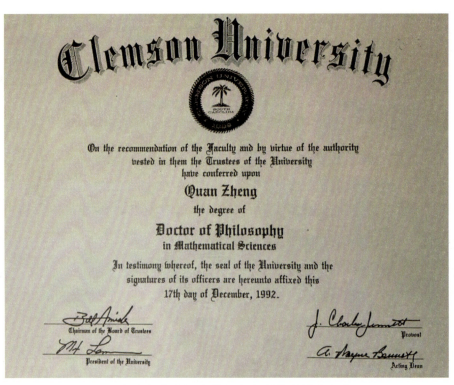

1992年郑权获美国克莱姆森大学数学博士学位

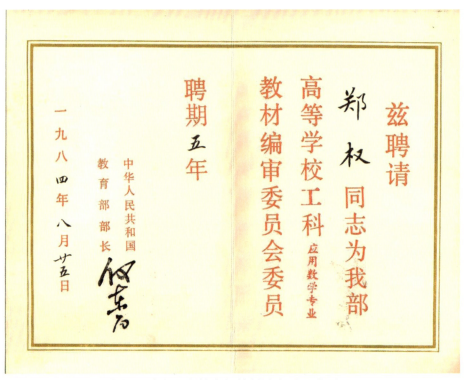

郑权应聘为国家教育部教材编审委员会委员

上海市劳动模范和先进工作者证明

上海市社会保险事业基金结算管理中心：

　　兹有原上海科技大学（单位）郑权同志（身份证号：310104193510301810），被授予1979年度上海市劳动模范荣誉称号。

　　特此证明。

上海市劳动模范评选委员会
办公室
2010年8月11日

郑权获上海市劳模的证明

郑权同志：

　　经中国数学会运筹学会12月9日常务理事会推荐并通过，特聘请您担任运筹学杂志编委。

　　现把运筹学杂志的主编、付主编及编委的名单，以及运筹学杂志的编辑方针、读者对象等有关事项附于后，请您在百忙的工作中给运筹学杂志积极撰写和推荐稿件，为办好杂志，促进运筹学在我国的发展作出贡献。

中国数学会运筹学会
1980·12·17·

郑权应聘为《运筹学杂志》副主编的证明

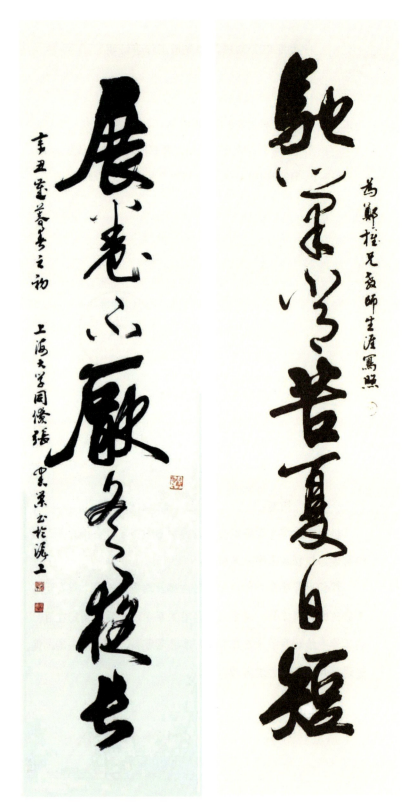

为郑权兄教师生涯写照：驰笔当苦夏日短，展卷不厌冬夜长

辛丑岁暮春之初，上海大学同僚张宪荣书于沪上

数学家郑权

——科研和教育的拓耕者

涂仁进 编

上海大学出版社

图书在版编目（CIP）数据

数学家郑权：科研和教育的拓耕者/涂仁进编. — 上海：上海大学出版社，2021.11
ISBN 978-7-5671-4398-2

Ⅰ.①数… Ⅱ.①涂… Ⅲ.①郑权－传记 Ⅳ.①K826.11

中国版本图书馆CIP数据核字(2021)第235397号

责任编辑　黄晓彦　韩伯顺
封面设计　缪炎栩
技术编辑　金　鑫　钱宇坤

数学家郑权

科研和教育的拓耕者

涂仁进　编

上海大学出版社出版发行
（上海市上大路99号　邮政编码200444）
(http://www.shupress.cn　发行热线021-66135112)
出版人：戴骏豪

*

上海颛辉印刷厂有限公司印刷　各地新华书店经销
开本787×1092 1/16　插页8　印张25.5　字数621千
2021年12月第1版　2021年12月第1次印刷
ISBN 978-7-5671-4398-2/K·246　定价：160.00元

版权所有　侵权必究
如发现本书有印装质量问题请与印刷厂质量科联系
联系电话：021-56152633

序

  郑权教授去世已有一年多了。这一段时间,特别是在这次编辑这本纪念册的过程中,我听到和看到了他生前的同事和好友对他的真情回忆,从而对郑权教授在学术研究与服务和学科交流与建设多方面的重要贡献,有了更多的了解,也对他更加敬佩。

  我很早以前就曾听运筹学前辈说起郑权教授,但是十分遗憾没有机会与他见过面,聆听他的教诲和得到他的指导。1985年我从大学毕业以后,便到中国科学院应用数学研究所读研究生,导师是韩继业研究员。记得在论文选题的时候,韩先生就提到了郑权教授在全局优化的创新工作,在国内乃至国际上都是非常有影响的。不过,我最终还是选择了跟韩先生做非光滑优化和非线性优化算法的收敛性证明。后来,堵丁柱教授从美国回到所里,开设了组合优化的讨论班,我的研究兴趣便被吸引到这个方向了。不过,研究方向不是韩先生的排序方向,而是网络优化。我博士毕业以后,就一直从事组合优化方向的研究和教学,对非线性优化的了解和关注就逐渐少了。

  记得当年我读研究生时,有了一点研究结果,韩先生就鼓励我写成了一篇短文,随后投到了《运筹学杂志》上。1988年论文发表以后,我当时非常兴奋,毕竟这是我的第一篇学术论文。受此鼓励,我在1989年和1990年又先后在《运筹学杂志》上发表了两篇论文。当20多年以后,我以中国运筹学会理事长的身份担任了《运筹学学报》主编,才了解到这本中国运筹学会主办的期刊的历史。1980年,中国数学会下属的运筹学会成立,中国数学会理事长华罗庚先生兼任理事长。华先生建议办一个运筹学方面的杂志,以推动国内运筹学的研究和交流。郑权教授时任上海科学技术大学数学系教授,他与张连生教授一起积极推动该校办刊。经过他们的努力,1982年《运筹学杂志》创刊,由越民义先生任主编、郑权和管梅谷两位教授任副主编,这是我国第一份关于运筹学综合性期刊,无疑对我国运筹学的发展起到了非常重要的推动作用。此外,在著名数学家、复旦大学苏步青和谷超豪两位先生的关注与支持下,1987年1月,郑权教授与时任上海科学技术校长郭本瑜教授一起主持创办了《应用数学与计算数学学报》,郭本瑜教授为主编,郑权教授兼任副主编。在20世纪80年代,郑权教授在创办这两个期刊的过程中都发挥了非常重要的作用,充分体现了他的学术眼界之远,科研水平之高,工作能力之强。

  郑权教授依靠他在基础数学方面坚实的基础,经过多年的钻研,与庄松林院士一起创立了求总体极值点的积分型方法及其相应的理论基础,并将其应用于实践中。他们一直与上海光学仪器研究所合作,应用该方法,克服经典光学透镜自动设计的问题,成功地提出了一种"带迭代序列的蒙特卡洛总极值的求解"方法,在自动光学设计领域取得了突破;论文发表在《应用数学学报》的创刊号上,该方法用到其他的优化问题也都有非常好的效果。在半个世纪前的"文革"中,郑权教授等能取得这样的科研成果确是难能可贵的。

  此外,浙江大学为解决光学干涉滤波器多层膜系自动设计中的瓶颈问题,郑权教授与庄松林院士合作，最终成功地发展了基于总体极值优化方法的"抗反射宽带光学薄膜的优化设计"方法。他自称自己方法是"野路子"。其实，这恰恰反映了他不迷信传统和经典，敢于创新和突破的科学精神，值得我们年轻的科研人员和师生学习。

郑权教授在其学术生涯中，持之以恒，求真务实。他不仅具备扎实的数学理论功底，更是致力于将数学理论应用于解决工业中的实际问题，通过实践反馈而推进数学理论的发展。他在研究中不仅注重于夯实所提方法的数学理论基础，而且还编制计算程序包，再应用于解决工业与工程中的实际问题，不断改进算法理论的构架。在20世纪80年代，我国的科研条件和环境还十分落后，但是他能在研究中应用这种系统性的方法，是不多见的。他也因此在科研和教学中都能取得突出成果，先后荣获上海市重大科技成果二等奖、上海市劳动模范、国家教委科学技术进步二等奖等奖励和荣誉。

在郑权教授逝世一年之际，我们年轻一代要学习和发扬他在学术研究中"顶天立地，自主创新，不断进取"的科学精神和品质，为我国早日成为创新型强国作出自己的贡献，这也是对郑权教授的最好纪念。

胡晓东
中国科学院数学与系统科学研究院
2021 年 8 月 12 日

目　录

郑权先生小传 ……………………………………………………………………… (1)

上篇　论文选

一个求总极值的方法 ………………………………………………………………… (5)
一类不连续函数及其总极值问题 …………………………………………………… (18)
无限维空间中总极值的有限维逼近 ………………………………………………… (29)
关于丰满极小点存在性的注记 ……………………………………………………… (39)
Discontinuous Robust Mappings are Approximatable ……………………………… (43)
On Existence of Robust Minimizers ………………………………………………… (57)
Upper Robust Mappings and Vector Minimization: An Intergral Approach ……… (65)
Integral Global Minimization: Algorithms, Implementations and Numerical Tests
　………………………………………………………………………………………… (83)
Robust Analysis and Global Optimization ………………………………………… (111)
Global Minimization of Constrained Problems with Discontinuous Penalty Function
　………………………………………………………………………………………… (121)
Finite Dimensional Approximation to Solutions of Minimization Problems in Functional
　Spaces ……………………………………………………………………………… (140)
Solution and Control of PDE VIA Global Optimization Methods ……………… (157)
Automatic Design of Optical Thin-film Systems-merit Function and Numerical
　Optimization Method …………………………………………………………… (176)
Vector Minimization of Upper Robust Mappings ………………………………… (189)
Optimality Conditions for Global Optimization (I) ……………………………… (202)
Optimality Conditions for Global Optimization (II) ……………………………… (215)
Integral Global Optimization Method for Solution of Nonlinear Complementarity Problems
　………………………………………………………………………………………… (230)
Robust Analysis and Global Minimization of A Class of Discontinuous Functions (I)
　………………………………………………………………………………………… (241)
Robust Analysis and Global Minimization of A Class of Discontinuous Functions (II)
　………………………………………………………………………………………… (261)
Minimax Methods for Open-loop Equilibra in N-person Differential Games Part III:

Duality and Penalty Finite Element Methods ……………………………………（282）
A Method for Approximating Solutions of Multicriterial Nonlinear Optimization Problems ………………………………………………………………………（298）

下篇　忆郑权

复旦同学忆郑权

缅怀郑权教授……………………………………………………陶宗英（315）
从一次班级活动的照片说起………………………………………邹　悦（316）
与郑权共同创作歌曲事宜…………………………………………尚汉冀（317）
四个复旦毕业生在"上工"………………………………………俞丽和（319）

上大（上工、科大）同事忆郑权

忆上海工学院时期的郑权………………………………………程沅生（321）
深切缅怀郑权教授………………………………………………沈海华（322）
忆郑权教授………………………………………………………汤生江（324）
深切缅怀郑权教授………………………………………………张荣欣（326）
运筹先驱　丰碑永存……………………………………………盛万成（327）
我们怀念郑权教授 …………………………………许梦杰、李志良（329）
丰碑永在…………………………………………………………朱国勇（331）
难以忘却的记忆…………………………………………………邬冬华（333）
追思我的挚友郑权教授…………………………………………陈明仪（336）

学生的回忆

数学思维比数学运算更重要……………………………………汤德祥（338）
我终生的导师——郑权教授……………………………………孙世杰（340）
深切怀念老师郑权教授…………………………………………周建新（342）
忆郑老师二三事…………………………………………………尹小南（344）
郑权老师…………………………………………………………谢志刚（345）
纪念我的导师郑权教授…………………………………………鲁习文（358）
我的一些回忆……………………………………………………张晓东（362）
纪念恩师郑权教授………………………………………………宋学锋（364）
我的成功离不开恩师的栽培……………………………………戴万阳（366）
缅怀恩师郑权先生………………………………………………方敖大（367）
尊其师, 效其行 …………………………………………………刘逸明（369）
怀念导师郑权教授………………………………………………姚奕荣（370）
纪念我的导师郑权先生…………………………………………彭建平（371）
刻骨师恩伴风雨，一朝教诲益终身……………………………梁泽亮（374）
缅怀郑权先生……………………………………………………陈　熙（376）

朋友的回忆

怀念好友郑权教授……………………………………………庄松林(378)
记与郑权老友共处和合作的几件事……………………………胡毓达(379)
深深怀念老师与挚友郑权教授…………………………………蒋百川(381)
深切怀念郑权教授………………………………………………潘星辰(384)
与郑老师相识之点滴……………………………………………金玉华(385)

亲属的回忆

深情怀念郑权弟弟………………………………………………郑　栋(386)
怀念我的郑权叔叔………………………………………………郑　敏(388)
相惜相知六十年…………………………………………………涂仁进(390)

感恩与鸣谢………………………………………………………………(396)

郑权先生小传

郑权，教授、博士生导师，最优化理论及运筹学与控制论领域的先驱者，在国内外相关学科领域皆享有声誉的数学家。

郑权先生1935年生于上海，1960年毕业于复旦大学数学系，1992年获美国克莱姆逊大学数学系博士。大学毕业后先后在上海工学院、上海科技大学任教。1994年这两校与其它一些院校合并为上海大学。

先生一生致力于数学理论研究并注重解决实际问题，又通过实践的总结与反馈，进一步推动理论的发展进步。20世纪七八十年代，先生正式创立的"积分型总体极值的最优化理论与计算方法"，从奠定其理论基础到编制计算程序包，再到应用于解决光学仪器优化设计等工业实际问题，不断改进算法理论的构架，使之体系逐渐完整。先生与国内外不同领域的许多学者共同出版了多部学术专著和译著，其中代表性专著包括：*Integral Global Optimization*：*Theory*, *Implementation and Applications*（Springer-Verlag，1988）；*New Theory of Continuous Games*（NP Research Publication，1990）；*Global Solutions in Optimal Control and Games*（NP Research Publication，1991）；《应用薄膜光学》（上海科学技术出版社，1984）等；更多的则是他自己独立发表的论文。俄语和法文译著则有《泛函分析》（高等教育出版社，1982）和《最优化理论与算法》（高等教育出版社，1982）等；本书从他所发表的百余篇论文中选载了21篇代表性论文结集出版。

郑权

郑权先生终生勤奋治学，诲人不倦。他怀着满腔热忱，孜孜不倦地把自己对教学与科研的理想倾注到教书育人之中。在20世纪七八十年代，在上海科大数学系，他呕心沥血地推动专业学科发展：从设立教研室，到创立硕士点，再到创立博士点。他启发、培养学生创新，鼓励并尊重学生发展个人的研究兴趣与方向。在教学和科研过程中，先生特别重视国际学术动态和学术交流，他不仅用英文授课，也要求学生用英文写作和报告论文。他邀请国内外知名专家教授来校作学术报告，与研究生共同探讨相关学术问题。从而开拓了学生的学术视野，培养了他们的创新精神。郑权先生严谨的治学态度、启发式的教学风格成为同仁们学习的榜样，也成了学生们毕业后步入社会为人处事的一种宝贵的精神力量。多年来，郑权先生陆续培养出一批优秀学生，他们后来都成为应用数学相关领域中的佼佼者，为数学的理论和应用作出了很多重要贡献。

1981年间，由于郑权先生在计算数学专业最优化理论与计算领域中的开创性工作，使得上海科学技术大学数学系争取到了承办中国数学会运筹学会创建全国性运筹学专业学术期刊《运筹学杂志》的机会，并使该杂志得于1982年正式出版。该杂志的名誉主编是著名数学家华罗庚先生，主编是越民义研究员，郑权先生是副主编兼编委。他为此倾注了大量的时间与心血，除了协调组稿，还亲自承担审稿。1983年郑权教授出任数学系主任后，他始终如一地直接指导着期刊的进展（注：1997年《运筹学杂志》已经改刊为《运筹学学报》）。1987年《应用数学与计算数学学报》正式出版。著名数学家苏步青为创刊题词，该学报名誉主编是谷超豪院士，主编是上海科学技术大学郭本瑜校长，郑权先生兼任副主编。此后，期刊与学报作为平台，拓展了师生的学术视野，极大地促进了教学和科研的发展，提高了上海科大数学系的知名度，为学术交流、引进和培养人才奠定了坚实的基础。

由于郑权先生的贡献，他受到诸多奖励。其中包括上海市重大科技成果二等奖(1979)、上海市劳动模范(1979)、加拿大科技理事会国际科学交流奖(1986)、国家教委科学技术进步二等奖(1987)等。

郑权先生于2020年5月9日在美国乔治亚州哥伦布市圣弗兰西斯医院病逝，享年84岁。

上 篇
论 文 选

一个求总极值的方法*

1 引言

考虑 m 维欧氏空间 $\mathbb{R}^m$ 中区域 G 上的连续函数

$$f(x)=f(x^1,x^2,\cdots,x^m), \tag{1.1}$$

若有一点 $x^*\in G$,存在一个以 x^* 为中心 $\delta>0$ 为半径的领域 $O(x^*,\delta)$,使不等式

$$f(x^*)\leqslant f(x) \tag{1.2}$$

对于一切 $x\in O(x^*,\delta)$ 均成立,则称 x^* 是函数 $f(x)$ 在 G 上的局部极小值点,$f(x^*)$ 是局部极小值. 若不等式(1.2)对于一切 $x\in G$ 均成立,则称 x^* 是函数 $f(x)$ 在 G 上的总极小值点,$f(x^*)$ 是总极小值. G 中所有总极小值点全体,构成了总极小值点集.

在生产和科学技术中遇到大量的求总极值问题,然而,现有的求极值的最优化数值方法,大都只能考虑求局部极值问题.

在本文,提出一种求总极值迭代解的构思模型,这个迭代模型可以用统计试验方法具体实现. 我们给出了具有迭代过程的随机搜索方法(称它为统计试验最优化方法). 自从 Brooks[1]引进了用随机搜索方法求总极值之后,不少人对此作了评述[2,3],还论证了随机搜索方法不及均匀格点搜索[4]. 然而,对维数 m 较大的情形,这两个方法所需的计算量都大得难以实现. 我们在引进了迭代过程后,就使计算量剧减,在一定程度上克服这种困难,使得求总极值有可能实现. 经过实算表明,这个算法是可以实际运用的.

本文是以前一些文章[5,6]中提出的方法的进一步分析和提高. 下面,我们先对构思模型进行理论分析,在此基础上,给出用统计试验方法实现这个模型的算法,并对这个算法进行统计分析,估计总运算量,最后介绍几个应用方法的实算例子(由于克服了局部极值,这些实例,在所讨论的领域中,结果都比通常得出的要好得多).

2 总极值与总极值点集

给出一个常数 c_0,使水平集

$$H_0=\{x\mid f(x)\leqslant c_0, x\in G\} \tag{2.1}$$

非空,上式右端的记号表示在 G 中满足关系式 $f(x)\leqslant c_0$ 的点的全体. (下面所用的实变函数、测度和泛函分析知识可在一般教科书[7]中找到.)

设 G 是闭区域,若 H_0 有界,则 H_0 是 $\mathbb{R}^m$ 中的紧集,$f(x)$ 在 H_0 上达到极小. 由于对 $G-H_0$ 上的点,$f(x)>c_0$,故这个极小必是总极小值. 于是,我们只需在 H_0 上讨论 $f(x)$ 在 G 中

---

* 本文合作者:蒋百川、庄松林,原文发表于《应用数学学报》,1978,1(2):161-174.

总极小问题.

引理 2.1 若 $\mu(H_0)=0$,其中 $\mu(H_0)$ 表示集合 H_0 的勒贝格测度,则 c_0 就是 $f(x)$ 的总极小值,H_0 就是 $f(x)$ 的总极小值点集.

证明 若不然,设有 $\bar{x}\in G, f(\bar{x})<c_0$,由函数的连续性,必存在一个邻域 $O(\bar{x},\delta)$,对于 $x\in O(\bar{x},\delta), f(x)<c_0$. 因此,$O(\bar{x},\delta)\subset H_0$. 但是,这将导致 $\mu(H_0)\geqslant\mu(O(\bar{x},\delta))>0$,与 $\mu(H_0)=0$ 相矛盾.

于是,设 $\mu(H_0)>0$. 构造 $f(x)$ 在 H_0 上的均值

$$c_1=\frac{1}{\mu(H_0)}\int_{H_0}f(x)\mathrm{d}\mu, \tag{2.2}$$

则

$$c_1\leqslant\frac{1}{\mu(H_0)}\int_{H_0}c_0\mathrm{d}\mu=c_0. \tag{2.3}$$

一般,由 c_k 构造水平集

$$H_k=\{x\mid f(x)\leqslant c_k, x\in G\} \tag{2.4}$$

及均值(若 $\mu(H_k)=0$,由引理 2.1,H_k 已是极值点集,c_k 是总极值,因此,可设 $\mu(H_{k+1})>0$)

$$c_{k+1}=\frac{1}{\mu(H_k)}\int_{H_k}f(x)\mathrm{d}\mu, \tag{2.5}$$

并且

$$c_{k+1}\leqslant\frac{1}{\mu(H_k)}\int_{H_k}c_k\mathrm{d}\mu=c_k, \tag{2.6}$$

$k=1,2,\cdots$. 从而得到了一个单调下降的数列 $\{c_k\}$ 及一个单调的集序列 $\{H_k\}$. 由于 $c_k\geqslant f(x^*)(k=1,2,\cdots)$,故 $\{c_k\}$ 有下界,设

$$\lim_{k\to+\infty}c_k=c^*, \tag{2.7}$$

$$\prod_{k=1}^{\infty}H_k=H^*. \tag{2.8}$$

引理 2.2 设单调下降数列 $\{c_k\}$ 的极限为 c,则水平集

$$H_k=\{x\mid f(x)\leqslant c_k, x\in G\}$$

也单调,它们的极限集为 H_c,即 $\prod_{k=1}^{\infty}H_k=H_c$,其中

$$H_c=\{x\mid f(x)\leqslant c, x\in G\}. \tag{2.9}$$

证明 因为 $c\leqslant c_k$,即知 $H_c\subset H_k$ 对一切 k 成立,故 $H_c\subset\prod_{k=1}^{\infty}H_k$. 反之,对于任一个 $x\in\prod_{k=1}^{\infty}H_k, f(x)\leqslant c_k$ 对一切 k 成立,令 $k\to\infty$,取极限后得 $f(x)\leqslant c$,即 $x\in H_c$,因而证明了 $H_c=\prod_{k=1}^{\infty}H_k$.

定理 2.1 若 $f(x)$ 是区域 G 上的连续函数,则均值序列的极限 c^* 是 $f(x)$ 在 G 上的总极小值,水平集序列的极限 H^* 是 $f(x)$ 的总极小值点集.

证明 用反证法证明. 设有 $\bar{x}\in G, f(\bar{x})<c^*$. 由于 $f(x)$ 在区域 G 上的连续性,存在 $\eta>0$ 及 $\bar{x}$ 的一个领域 $O(\bar{x},\delta)$,对于 $x\in O(\bar{x},\delta)$,

$$f(x) < c^* - \eta. \tag{2.10}$$

由(2.10)可知,$O(\bar{x}, \delta) \subset H_k, k=1, 2, \cdots$. 另外,由于 $c_k \to c^*$,故对于任一个 $\varepsilon > 0$,存在 N,当 $n \geqslant N$ 时

$$0 \leqslant c_n - c_{n+1} < \varepsilon. \tag{2.11}$$

然而

$$\begin{aligned}\mu(H_n) c_{n+1} &= \int_{H_n} f(x) \mathrm{d}\mu = \int_{H_n - O(\bar{x}, \delta)} f(x) \mathrm{d}\mu + \int_{O(\bar{x}, \delta)} f(x) \mathrm{d}\mu \\ &\leqslant c_n [\mu(H_n) - \mu(O(\bar{x}, \delta))] + (c^* - \eta) \cdot \mu(O(\bar{x}, \delta)) \\ &\leqslant c_n \mu(H_n) - \eta \mu(O(\bar{x}, \delta)).\end{aligned}$$

故得

$$(c_n - c_{n+1}) \cdot \mu(H_n) \geqslant \eta \cdot \mu(O(\bar{x}, \delta)).$$

最后推出

$$c_n - c_{n+1} \geqslant \eta \cdot \frac{\mu(O(\bar{x}, \delta))}{\mu(H_0)}. \tag{2.12}$$

上式中不等号右端是一个和 n 及 ε 无关的正数,从而得出与(2.11)式矛盾. 故 c^* 是 $f(x)$ 在 G 上的总极小值.

由引理 2.2 得知,$\prod_{k=1}^{\infty} H_k = H_{c^*}$,但是 c^* 是总极小值,对于 $x \in G, f(x)$ 不能小于 c^*,故

$$H_{c^*} = \{x \mid f(x) = c^*, x \in G\} = H^* \tag{2.13}$$

是总极小值点集(非空).

推论 2.1 H^* 是闭集.

推论 2.2 若存在某个 k,$f(x)$ 是 H_k 上的凸函数(局部凸性),则 H^* 是连通凸集.

实际上,$H^* \subset H_k$,$f(x)$ 也是 H^* 上的凸函数. 若 $x, y \in H^*$,对于 $\alpha > 0, \beta > 0, \alpha + \beta = 1$,

$$f(\alpha x + \beta y) \leqslant \alpha f(x) + \beta f(y) = c^*. \tag{2.14}$$

但上式只能成立等号,即联结 x 与 y 的线段上的点都落在 H^* 中,H^* 是连通凸集.

推论 2.3 若存在某个 k,$f(x)$ 是 H_k 上的严格凸函数,则 H^* 只包含一个点.

例 求 $f(x) = |x|$ 在 $(-1, 1)$ 上的总极小.

解

$$c_1 = \frac{1}{2} \int_{-1}^{1} |x| \mathrm{d}x = \frac{1}{2}, \quad H_1: \left[-\frac{1}{2}, \frac{1}{2}\right], \quad \mu(H_1) = 1.$$

一般,

$$c_k = \frac{1}{2} \cdot c_{k-1} = \left(\frac{1}{2}\right)^k, \quad \mu(H_k) = 2 \cdot \left(\frac{1}{2}\right)^k, \quad k = 1, 2, \cdots.$$

$c_k \downarrow 0, \mu(H_k) \downarrow 0$,区间套 H_k 收缩为原点,即得 $f(x) = |x|$ 的总极小值点.

容易想到,为了迫近总极值和求出总极值点值,不一定严格地取均值序列,但这种序列与均值序列有密切的关系. 它们的极限是一样的.

定理 2.2 单调下降数列 $\{c_k\}$ 的极限 c 是 $f(x)$ 在 G 上总极值的充要条件为

$$c_k - m_k \to 0, (k \to \infty), \tag{2.15}$$

其中 m_k 是均值

$$m_k = \frac{1}{\mu(H_{k-1})} \int_{H_{k-1}} f(x) \mathrm{d}\mu,$$

$$H_{k-1}=\{x\mid f(x)\leqslant c_{k-1}, x\in G\}, \quad \mu(H_{k-1})>0, \quad k=1,2,\cdots.$$

证明 **必要性** 由均值 m_k 的定义可知
$$c\leqslant m_k\leqslant c_{k-1}, \quad k=1,2,\cdots.$$
令 $k\to\infty$ 得知,$c_{k-1}-m_k\to 0$,即 $c_k-m_k\to 0$.

充分性 设 c^* 是 $f(x)$ 在 G 上的总极值,由于 $\mu(H_k)>0$,故 $c_k\geqslant c^*$.设 $c_k\to c$,$c_k-m_k\to 0$ 成立,而 c 不是总极值,这时必有 $c>c^*$.令
$$H_c=\{x\mid f(x)\leqslant c, x\in G\},$$
则 H_c 非空,且 $\mu(H_c)>0$(不然,若 $\mu(H_c)=0$,由引理 2.1,c 已是总极值了).这时
$$m_k-\frac{1}{\mu(H_c)}\int_{H_c}f(x)\mathrm{d}\mu=\frac{1}{\mu(H_{k-1})}\left(\int_{H_{k-1}}f(x)\mathrm{d}\mu-\int_{H_c}f(x)\mathrm{d}\mu\right)$$
$$+\left(\frac{1}{\mu(H_{k-1})}-\frac{1}{\mu(H_c)}\right)\int_{H_c}f(x)\mathrm{d}\mu.$$

由引理 2.2,$H_k\to H_c(k\to\infty)$,又因 $\mu(H_k)$ 有界,$f(x)$ 有界,故知
$$\frac{1}{\mu(H_c)}\int_{H_c}f(x)\mathrm{d}\mu=\lim_{k\to\infty}m_k=c,$$
又因,当 $x\in H_c$ 时 $c-f(x)\geqslant 0$,由此推得,$f(x)=c$ 在 H_c 上几乎处处成立,但 $f(x)$ 在 G 上连续,故知在 H_c 上 $f(x)=c$ 处处成立,这导致与 $c>c^*$ 矛盾,即证 c 就是总极小值.

下面来考虑收敛判别准则.

设数列 $\{c_k\}$ 单调下降趋于 c,水平集
$$H_k=\{x\mid f(x)\leqslant c_k, x\in G\}$$
非空,测度 $\mu(H_k)>0$(由引理 2.1,若 $\mu(H_k)=0$,H_k 已是总极小点集了).

定理 2.3 单调下降数列 $\{c_k\}$ 的极限 c 是 $f(x)$ 的总极小值的充要条件为,当 $k\to\infty$ 时,方差序列
$$\sigma_k^2=\frac{1}{\mu(H_k)}\int_{H_k}(f(x)-c_{k+1})^2\mathrm{d}\mu \tag{2.16}$$

趋于 0.这时,$\prod_{k=1}^{\infty}H_k$ 就是总极小点集.

证明 **必要性** 设 c 是总极小值,则
$$\sigma_k^2\leqslant\frac{1}{\mu(H_k)}\int_{H_k}(f(x)-c)^2\mathrm{d}\mu+\frac{1}{\mu(H_k)}\int_{H_k}(c-c_{k+1})^2\mathrm{d}\mu$$
$$\leqslant(c_k-c)^2+(c-c_{k+1})^2\to 0 \quad (k\to\infty)$$

由引理 2.2,$\prod_{k=1}^{\infty}H_k$ 是总极小点集.

充分性 设在条件成立时 c 不是总极小,令
$$H_c=\{x\mid f(x)\leqslant c, x\in G\},$$
由引理 2.1,$\mu(H_c)>0$.下面来证明
$$\lim_{k\to\infty}\sigma_k^2=\frac{1}{\mu(H_c)}\int_{H_c}(f(x)-c)^2\mathrm{d}\mu. \tag{2.17}$$
$$\sigma_k^2-\frac{1}{\mu(H_c)}\int_{H_c}(f(x)-c)^2\mathrm{d}\mu=\frac{1}{\mu(H_k)}\int_{H_k-H_c}(f(x)-c_{k+1})^2\mathrm{d}\mu$$

$$+\frac{1}{\mu(H_k)\mu(H_c)}\int_{H_c}[\mu(H_c)(f(x)-c_{k+1})^2-\mu(H_k)(f(x)-c)^2]\mathrm{d}\mu \quad (2.18)$$

由引理 2.2 可知 $H_k \to H_c(k\to\infty)$，故 $\mu(H_k)\to\mu(H_c)(k\to\infty)$，(前面已假设 H_0 有界)由于 (2.18)式右端被积函数一致有界，故当 $k\to\infty$ 时，两个积分都趋于 0. 即(2.17)式成立.

设 $f(x)$ 在 G 上的总极小值为 $c^*=f(x^*)$，则 $c^*<c$. 故存在 $\eta>0$ 及 x^* 的一个邻域 $O(x^*,\delta)$，对 $x\in O(x^*,\delta)$，$f(x)<c-\eta$. 这时

$$\frac{1}{\mu(H_c)}\int_{H_c}(f(x)-c)^2\mathrm{d}\mu \geq \frac{1}{\mu(H_c)}\int_{O(x^*,\delta)}(f(x)-c)^2\mathrm{d}\mu$$
$$\geq \frac{\eta^2\cdot\mu(O(x^*,\delta))}{\mu(H_c)}>0.$$

由(2.17)式得出与条件 $\lim_{k\to\infty}\sigma_k^2=0$ 相矛盾.

定理 2.4 对于前面构造的均值序列，若有某个足标 k，$c_k=c_{k+1}$，或 $\mu(H_k)=\mu(H_{k+1})$，则 $f(x)\equiv$ 常数.

证明 先证若 $c_k=c_{k+1}$，则 $\mu(H_k)=\mu(H_{k+1})$，$\mu(H_{k-1})=\mu(H_k)$. 前一个式子显然成立，现证后一个. 令 $\Delta H_k=H_{k-1}-H_k$，则

$$c_k\mu(H_{k-1})-c_{k+1}\mu(H_k)=\int_{\Delta H_k}f(x)\mathrm{d}\mu. \quad (2.19)$$

由于 $c_k=c_{k+1}$，上式左边又可表为

$$c_{k+1}\mu(\Delta H_k)=\int_{\Delta H_k}c_{k+1}\mathrm{d}\mu, \quad (2.20)$$

由此

$$\int_{\Delta H_k}(f(x)-c_{k+1})\mathrm{d}\mu=0. \quad (2.21)$$

当 $x\in\Delta H_k$ 时，$f(x)-c_{k+1}\geq 0$，这时或 $\mu(\Delta H_k)=0$，即已证明 $\mu(H_{k-1})=\mu(H_k)$，或在 ΔH_k 上 $f(x)\equiv c_{k+1}$. 由定义 $\Delta H_k=H_{k-1}-H_k=\{x|c_k<f(x)\leq c_{k-1}\}$，$\Delta H_k$ 必是空集，也证明了 $\mu(H_{k-1})=\mu(H_k)$.

再证，若 $\mu(H_k)=\mu(H_{k+1})$，则 $c_k=c_{k+1}$，$c_{k+1}=c_{k+2}$. 后一个式子显然成立，现证前一个. 设 $c_k>c_{k+1}$，由于 $f(x)$ 的连续性，存在一个测度为正的小邻域 $O(x,\delta)\subset\Delta H_k=\{x|f(x)\leq c_k,f(x)>c_{k+1}\}$. 从而与 $\mu(H_k)=\mu(H_{k+1})$ 相矛盾.

利用前面的结果，若 $c_k=c_{k+1}$，可推得 $\mu(H_k)=\mu(H_{k-1})$，$\mu(H_k)=\mu(H_{k+1})$，从而又得 $c_{k-1}=c_k,c_{k+1}=c_{k+2}$. 以此类推，可知 $f(x)\equiv$ 常数. 若 $\mu(H_k)=\mu(H_{k+1})$，则 $c_k=c_{k+1}$，从而也可推知 $f(x)\equiv$ 常数.

令

$$\frac{c_{k+1}-c^*}{c_k-c^*}=c(f,k), \quad (2.22)$$

$$\frac{\mu(H_{k+1})-\mu(H^*)}{\mu(H_k)-\mu(H^*)}=h(f,k), \quad (2.23)$$

它们分别表示函数 $f(x)$ 的均值序列向总极小值收敛的速率和水平集序列向总极小值点集收缩的速率. 由上面的定理可知：

推论 2.4 $c(f,k)=1$ 或 $h(f,k)=1$ 对其中某一个 k 成立的充要条件是 $f(x)\equiv$ 常数. 对于不恒等于常数的连续函数 $c(f,k)<1,h(f,k)<1(k=1,2,\cdots)$.

由此可见，按这种模型实现的求总极小值法，相当于线性收敛，随着迭代次数的增加，它们都按几何级数收敛.

3 统计试验实现

上述的迭代构思模型，归结为计算均值序列 $\{c_k\}$ 和水平集序列 $\{H_k\}$. 求均值相当关于 m 求积分，求水平集一般则更为复杂，应用统计试验方法，可以实现这个构思模型. 下面我们给出这个构思模型的一个具体实现方法，用到的统计试验法知识，可在[14]中查到.

考虑 $f(x)$ 是 m 维长方法

$$G=\{x\,|\,a^i\leqslant x^i\leqslant b^i, i=1,2,\cdots,m\} \tag{3.1}$$

上的连续函数. 预先给出两个正整数 kM 和 t，kM 是首次投点数，t 叫做统计指标.（下面，我们将对统计指标的性质和取法作进一步分析）.

迭代过程：

1. 产生 H_0

设 $\xi=(\xi^1,\xi^2,\cdots,\xi^m)$ 是 m 个相互独立的标准伪随机数（即 ξ^i 是 $(0,1)$ 上的均匀分布，$i=1,2,\cdots,m$）. 令

$$x^i=a^i+(b^i-a^i)\xi^i, i=1,2,\cdots,m, \tag{3.2}$$

即对 $x=(x^1,x^2,\cdots,x^m)$ 作随机抽样，得一系列 $x_j, j=1,2,\cdots,M$. 计算 $f(x_j)$.

随机投点后，比较函数值大小，产生接受集 W. 接受集 W 中包含 t 个点，它们对应于按大小排列成序的 t 个函数值集 $FV[i], i=1,2,\cdots,t$. 随着投点数增加，FV 中的 t 个函数值不断由小的代替，接受集 W 中对应函数值的 t 个点也不断更新.

所得到的 W 就可以看成是水平集 H_0 的近似表现. 令 FV 中 t 个函数值的最大的一个为 c_0，$FV[1]=c_0$，则对于 $x\in W, f(x)\leqslant c_0$. 另外，$FV$ 中函数值的平均

$$c_1=\frac{1}{t}\{FV[1]+FV[2]+\cdots+FV[t]\}, \tag{3.3}$$

可以看成是 H_0 上函数均值的近似代表.

2. 产生新的搜索区域

要使计算过程能继续下去，形成迭代过程，应产生 H_0 上的均匀分布，再进行随机投点. 然而，H_0 的结构复杂，它的近似代表 W 也很复杂，直接产生 H_0 上的均匀分布有困难. 为此，可以对接受集 W 中的随机子样进行统计处理，产生一个包含 W 的 m 维长方体：

$$D_1=\{x\,|\,a_1^i\leqslant x^i\leqslant b_1^i, i=1,2,\cdots,m\}, \tag{3.4}$$

然后再产生 D_1 上的均匀分布. 由接受集 W 产生新搜索区域的具体办法将在后面讨论. 由构造可见，$D_1\subset D$.

3. 迭代过程的继续

在 D_1 中随机投点，令

$$x^i=a_1^i+(b_1^i-a_1^i)\xi^i, i=1,2,\cdots,m. \tag{3.5}$$

计算函数值 $f(x)$. 如第一步所述那样，产生包含 t 个点的接受集 W 及按大小次序排列的 t 个函数值集 FV. 投点数不断增加，FV 中的 t 个函数值不断变小，W 中的点不断更新，直到 FV 中的最大函数值 $FV[1]\leqslant c_1$ 为止. 这样得到的 W 是 H_1 的近似表现，FV 中函数值的平

均值为 c_2 的近似值. 如第二步中所述,由这个接受集 W 再产生包含它的 m 维长方体 D_2. 这个过程继续下去,我们得到了一个单调下降的均值序列 $\{c_k\}$ 及单调的 m 维长方体序列 $\{D_k\}$.

4. 迭代解

用每次迭代的 FV 中最小值 $FV[t]$ 作为这次迭代的近似解. 也可以用 $f(\bar{x})$ 作为近似解,其中 $\bar{x}$ 是接受集 W 中的点的某种统计平均.

5. 收敛判别

由定理 2.2 可知,用 FV 中函数值的方差

$$D_f = \frac{1}{t-1} \sum_{i=1}^{t} (FV[i] - \overline{F})^2, \quad \overline{F} = \left(\sum_{i=1}^{t} FV[i]\right)/t, \tag{3.6}$$

是否满足预先给出的要求来判断是否终止计算. 也可以用新搜索区域 D_k 的体积(或边长)是否满足预先给定的要求作为是否终止计算的判据.

4 算法的统计分析

4.1 新搜索区域的确定与统计指标

我们先来讨论由接受集 W 产生包含水平集 H 的 m 维长方体 D(即后次迭代的新搜索区域)的方法.

接受集 W 是水平集 H 的近似表现,根据算法的构造,W 中的点可以看成是 H 上的均匀分布随机变量的 t 个子样,由随机变量各分量的独立性,这些子样的各坐标分量能分别处理,用来产生包含 H 的 m 维长方体的各边. 因此,我们先对单个变元进行分析.

设 ξ 是 (a,b) 上的某种分布,分布函数为 $F(y)$,其中端点 a、b 是未知的. 我们可以用 ξ 的 t 个随机子样 $\xi_1, \xi_2, \cdots, \xi_t$ 构成的统计量对 a、b 进行估计. 不失一般性,令 $a=0, b=1$,记

$$\eta_0 = \min\{\xi_1, \xi_2, \cdots, \xi_t\}, \tag{4.1}$$

$$\eta_1 = \max\{\xi_1, \xi_2, \cdots, \xi_t\}, \tag{4.2}$$

则 η_0, η_1 的分布函数 $\phi_0(y), \phi_1(y)$ 分别为

$$\phi_0(y) = \begin{cases} 0, & y \leq 0 \\ 1-(1-F(y))^t, & 0 < y < 1 \\ 1, & y \geq 1 \end{cases} \tag{4.3}$$

$$\phi_1(y) = \begin{cases} 0, & y \leq 0 \\ (F(y))^t, & 0 < y < 1 \\ 1, & y \geq 1. \end{cases} \tag{4.4}$$

由于 η_0, η_1 的均值为

$$M\eta_0 = \int_0^1 (1-F(y))^t dy$$

$$M\eta_1 = 1 - \int_0^1 (F(y))^t dy.$$

故 η_0, η_1 并不是两个端点的无偏估计. 如果函数 $f(x)$ 是一元单峰函数,则 ξ 是均匀分布,对于复杂的多元多峰函数,ξ 是比较复杂的. 为了简单起见,考虑 ξ 是均匀分布,则

$$M\eta_0 = \frac{1}{t+1}, \quad M\eta_1 = \frac{t}{t+1},$$

故

$$\zeta_0 = \eta_0 - (\eta_1 - \eta_0)/(t-1) \tag{4.5}$$

$$\zeta_1 = \eta_1 + (\eta_1 - \eta_0)/(t-1) \tag{4.6}$$

是端点的无偏估计. 另外, $D\eta_0 = D\eta_1 = t/(t+1)^2(t+2)$ ($D\eta$ 表示随机变量 η 的方差), 因此, 用这二个估计量, 其随机误差 $\sim 1/t$. 对于一般情形, 我们仍用(4.5)和(4.6)作为端点估计.

我们确定新的搜索区域 D, 要求函数的总极值点不逸出区域 D. 总极值点逸出区域 D 的概率与函数的构造性态有关, 也与所取的统计指标 t 有关.

为了进一步分析, 还必须考虑函数总极值点在水平集中不对称的性态, 即所谓偏畸程度. 设总极值点为 x^*, 我们用 x^* 与区域中心的距离同区间总长度之比的二倍

$$\delta = 2 \frac{\left| x^* - \frac{a+b}{2} \right|}{(b-a)} \tag{4.7}$$

来描述. 若主峰对称, 则偏畸程度 $\delta = 0$, 偏畸程度的极限是主峰为端点, 这时 $\delta = 1$. 下面略作一些数量分析. 不妨设 $a = 0, b = 1$. 设主峰偏右, 则主峰逸出右端的概率为

$$P\{\zeta_1 < (1+\delta)/2\}. \tag{4.8}$$

由(4.6)和(4.4)式, 可以算出 ζ_1 的分布函数, 从而算出不同的 δ 和 t 时总极值点 x^* 逸出的概率, 但计算比较繁杂. 下面我们主要考虑渐近估计.

由(4.4)式可知, 主峰逸出右端的概率小于 γ^t, 其中 $\gamma = F((1+\delta/2))$. 主峰逸出左端的概率更小(假设主峰偏右). 总之, 逸出概率 q 满足下列关系式:

$$p \leq 2 \cdot \gamma^t, \quad \gamma = F((1+\delta/2)). \tag{4.9}$$

因此, 只要 $\delta \neq 1$, 则 $F((1+\delta/2)) < 1$, 当统计指标很大时, 逸出概率将变得很小.

4.2 总投点数的渐近估计

设初始投点区域的体积为 V_0, 经过一次迭代后新的搜索区域的体积为 V_1, 其中 V_1 是包含水平集 H_1 的最小 m 维长方体的体积. 我们称比值

$$\alpha_1 = V_0/V_1 \tag{4.10}$$

为这次迭代中投点区域的体积收缩率(简称收缩率), 设 H_1 的体积为 V_{H_1} 则称比值

$$\beta_1 = V_{H_1}/V_1 \tag{4.11}$$

为这次迭代的投点效率. 当我们在 V_0 个投了 k_{M_1} 个点后, H_1 中接受了 t 个点, 按照分布的均匀性,

$$\frac{k_{M_1}}{V_0} = \frac{t}{V_{H_1}} \tag{4.12}$$

或

$$k_{M_1} = \frac{\alpha_1}{\beta_1} t. \tag{4.13}$$

于是, 经过 k 次迭代后, 体积收缩为

$$V_k = V_0 / \prod_{i=1}^{k} \alpha_i, \tag{4.14}$$

其中 $\alpha_1, \alpha_2, \cdots, \alpha_k$ 是各次迭代的收缩率, 设每次迭代的投点数为 $kM_1, kM_2, \cdots, kM_k$, 经过 k

次迭代后,总投点数 N 为各次投点数的总和

$$N = kM_1 + kM_2 + \cdots + kM_k = \sum_{i=1}^{k} \frac{\alpha_i}{\beta_i} t. \tag{4.15}$$

设在各次迭代中收缩率和投点效率满足条件

$$1 < \alpha_0 \leqslant \alpha_i \leqslant \alpha, \quad 0 < \beta_0 \leqslant \beta_i, \quad i = 1, 2, \cdots, \tag{4.16}$$

则得

$$N \leqslant k \cdot \alpha/\beta_0 \cdot t. \tag{4.17}$$

(4.17)式中的 k 与 t 由问题的要求和精度来确定. 设我们要求在逸出概率不大于 q_0 的条件下, 由初始体积 V_0(设为 1)收缩为体积 V_ε(设为 ε)的小区域, 这时总的体积收缩率为

$$V_0/V_\varepsilon = \frac{1}{\varepsilon} = \prod_{i=1}^{k} \alpha_i. \tag{4.18}$$

若取

$$k = \frac{\ln \frac{1}{\varepsilon}}{\ln \alpha_0}, \tag{4.19}$$

则总体积收缩率 $\geqslant \frac{1}{\varepsilon}$. k 是迭代次数,它应取整数,因此,严格地讲 k 应取(4.19)式中右端的整数部分加 1,由于下面是讨论渐近性态,故就简单地取(4.19)式.

下面再讨论逸出概率与 t 和 k 的关系. 设各次迭代各坐标方向的 γ 的最大值为 γ_0, $\gamma_0 = \max F((1+\delta/2))$,则经 k 次迭代后逸出概率 q_0 有下面的估计式:

$$q_0 \leqslant 1 - (1 - 2\gamma_0^t)^{mk}. \tag{4.20}$$

因此,若取

$$t = \frac{\ln(1 - p_0^{mk}) - \ln 2}{\ln \gamma_0}, \tag{4.21}$$

则经过 k 次迭代后逸出概率小于 q_0, 其中 $p_0 = 1 - q_0$ 是置信概率, 它是在计算前预先给出的小于 1 的数. 把(4.19)和(4.21)代入(4.17),得

$$N \leqslant \frac{\alpha}{\beta_0} \cdot \frac{\ln \frac{1}{\varepsilon}}{\ln \alpha_0} \frac{\ln(1 - p_0^{\frac{\ln \alpha_0}{m \ln \frac{1}{\varepsilon}}}) - \ln 2}{\ln \gamma_0}. \tag{4.22}$$

由于

$$\lim_{\varepsilon \to \infty} \frac{\ln(1 - p_0^{\frac{\ln \alpha_0}{m \ln \frac{1}{\varepsilon}}}) - \ln 2}{\ln \ln \frac{1}{\varepsilon}} = -1, \tag{4.23}$$

故证得总投点数的渐近估计.

定理 4.1 在上面所述条件下,当 $\varepsilon \to 0$ 时总投点数满足下列估计式

$$N \leqslant c \ln \frac{1}{\varepsilon} \cdot \ln \ln \frac{1}{\varepsilon}, \tag{4.24}$$

其中

$$c \approx \frac{\alpha}{\beta \ln \alpha_0 \ln \frac{1}{\gamma_0}}. \tag{4.25}$$

(4.25)式中,当 $\alpha = \alpha_0 = \alpha_i (i=1,2,\cdots,k)$ 时,若取 $\alpha = e$ 时达极小,故若每次迭代时收缩

率 $\alpha \approx e = 2.71828$ 时,总投点数可望较少.

下面同栅格法和随机投点法[1]作比较. 这两种算法所需总投点数为

$$N = c' \cdot \frac{1}{\varepsilon}. \qquad (4.26)$$

上式常数 c',在栅格法中 $c'=1$,在随机投点法中 $c' = \ln\frac{1}{1-p_0}$,可见本文所述方法在收敛阶上有本质改进. 但是,本方法的常数 c 与函数性态有关,一般要比前二种方法大得多. 下面我们对影响 c 的投点效率和偏畸率作一些讨论.

4.3 提高投点效率的转轴变换

从(4.24)和(4.25)可见,要减少运算量,必须提高投点效率. 投点效率是与函数性质有密切关系的一个量. 对一元函数,若水平集是凸集,则投点效率为1,然而对多元函数,即使水平集是凸集,投点效率也可能很低,对于多峰函数,水平集可能不是连通集,投点效率可能更低,因此,提高投点效率对减少运算量,有效地运用这个算法,显得十分重要.

当函数的水平集是扁长倾斜的区域时,我们采用转轴变换来提高投点效率,取得良好的效果. 在得出接受集 W 后,可以用最小二乘法或其他方法定出接受集 W 的"轴",再用正交化过程,使之建立一个新的坐标系. 设新旧坐标系之间的变换阵为 T,则在新的坐标系下,接受集 W 中的点 x 变换为 $y = T^{-1}x$,由此可以定出新坐标系中投点区域. 之后,我们就在新的坐标系中随机投点,计算函数 $f(x) = f(Ty)$.

以 Rosenbrock 函数[2]

$$f(x_1, x_2) = \alpha(x_2 - x_1^2)^2 + (1 - x_1)^2 \qquad (4.27)$$

为例. 我们取初始搜索区域为 $-5 \leqslant x_1 \leqslant 5, -5 \leqslant x_2 \leqslant 5$,搜索体积为100. 若取 $\alpha=10$,当体积缩为 10^{-10} 时,计算函数约4000次,采用转轴变换后,计算函数减少为940次. 若取 $\alpha=100$,当搜索体积缩为 10^{-10} 时,计算函数11250次,采用转轴变换后,减少到1420次. (极值为 $f(1,1)=0$.)

值得指出,在[15]中用随机搜索方法考虑同一函数(4.27),α 取100,初始搜索区域为 $-1.2 \leqslant x_1 \leqslant 2, -1 \leqslant x_2 \leqslant 2$,经过16384次函数计算,求得最小点为 $x_1 = 1.0103, x_2 = 1.0213$. 由这个实例来看,计算量符合(4.24)、(4.26)的估计.

4.4 函数的偏畸率

在(4.25)式里,常数 c 中还包含了与函数偏畸率有关的一项 $\frac{1}{\ln\frac{1}{\gamma_0}}$,$\gamma_0 = \max F((1+\delta/2))$,当 $\gamma_0 \to 1$ 时,它将趋于无穷. 若函数总极值在区域边界达到,γ_0 可能达到1,逸出概率很大,上述方式须作修改. 另外,若总极值点集不是连通域,则随着搜索区域的收缩,$\gamma_0 \to 1$,这时必须会扔掉一些总极值点. 然而,通常我们处理的是单主峰极值问题,或者只需找到一个主峰就达到要求. 用上述方法,以较大的概率扔掉尖陡的峰,保留平坦的峰,这样所得的极值具有较高的稳定性.

对于一般只有一个总极值点的函数,在极值点附近展开为幂级数,舍掉高阶项,因此,当函数趋近总极值点时,它接近于二次函数,函数的偏畸率较小.

在上述分析中,我们引进了投点效率,偏畸率等一些比较直观的概念,对于复杂的函数是很不容易确定下来的. 在解决实际问题时只须考虑统计指标,往往是经过一些试验来定出统计指标. 我们在实算中, 统计指标取得并不太大, 所以, 一般实际问题, 只要计算几千次函数, 已大致能达到使用要求.

5 应用举例

我们用上述方法对一些实际生产和科学技术问题进行了实算, 得到不少有用的结果[8-12]. 下面, 我们选二个典型例子来说明算法的应用情况和实际效果.

5.1 光学多层薄膜的自动设计

多层薄膜的光学性能用其反射率表示, 反射率是各层膜的折射率、膜厚及使用波长 λ 的复杂的函数. m 层薄膜的反射率为

$$R[\lambda] = \left|\frac{\eta_0 - Y}{\eta_0 + Y}\right|^2, \qquad Y = c/B,$$

$$\begin{pmatrix} B \\ c \end{pmatrix} = \left\{\prod_{r=1}^{m} \begin{bmatrix} \cos\delta_r & i\sin\delta_r/\eta_r \\ i\sin\delta_r \cdot \eta_r & \cos\delta_r \end{bmatrix}\right\} \begin{pmatrix} 1 \\ \eta_{m+1} \end{pmatrix},$$

$$\delta_r = \frac{2\pi x_r n_r \cos\theta_r}{\lambda},$$

$$\eta_r = \begin{cases} n_r \cos\theta_r & (s \text{ 波}) \\ n_r/\cos\theta_r & (p \text{ 波}), \end{cases} \quad r = 1, 2, \cdots, m+1. \tag{5.1}$$

其中 λ 是入射光的波长, n_r 是各层膜的折射率, n_0 是入射介质的折射率, n_{m+1} 是衬底(如玻璃)的折射率, θ_0 是入射角, θ_r 是各层的折射角, 由折射定律

$$n_0 \sin\theta_0 = n_r \sin\theta_r \tag{5.2}$$

定出, x_r 是各层膜的几何厚度.

光学多层薄膜的设计任务是选取适当的层数、各层膜的折射率和膜厚, 以获得要求的特征. 所谓自动设计, 就是用计算机选取设计参数, 使得在使用波段上设计反射率 $R[\lambda]$ 和目标反射率 $RD[\lambda]$ 的偏差达到极小, 这就构成了评价函数

$$F = \|R - RD\|, \tag{5.3}$$

其中 $\|\cdot\|$ 是按实际需要确定的各类模. 自动设计就是使评价函数(5.3)达到极小的最优设计.

我们用统计试验最优化方法对减反膜、高、低通光学滤波器、中性分光镜、消偏振分光镜等一系列光学多层薄膜进行了自动设计, 获得不少新的结果[9]. 下面举三层减反膜(即 $RD \equiv 0$)的设计为例.

要求设计一个在 $400\text{m}\mu$ 到 $700\text{m}\mu$ 这可见光波段上工作的宽带减反膜, 由空气垂直入射, 基底玻璃折射率为 1.75, 对各层膜厚和折射率同时选优.

若初始搜索区域取 $a = (70\text{m}\mu, 200\text{m}\mu, 70\text{m}\mu, 1.35, 1.35, 1.35)$, $b = (170\text{m}\mu, 300\text{m}\mu, 170\text{m}\mu, 2.35, 2.35, 2.35)$, a, b 中前三个参数表示各层膜的厚度的优选范围, 后三个参数表示各层膜的折射率优选范围. 在 $400\text{m}\mu$ 到 $700\text{m}\mu$ 等间隔取 16 个波点, 采用平方膜

$$F = \sum_{\lambda=1}^{16} (R[\lambda])^2. \tag{5.4}$$

经搜索得到的最优点, 其膜厚结构接近 $\lambda/4 - \lambda/2 - \lambda/4$ 型, 评价函数值极小为 $F_{\min} = $

0.000303.

如果改变中间层膜厚的初始搜索区域,取 $a=(70\mathrm{m}\mu,70\mathrm{m}\mu,70\mathrm{m}\mu,1.35,1.35,1.35)$, $b=(170\mathrm{m}\mu,170\mathrm{m}\mu,170\mathrm{m}\mu,2.35,2.35,2.35)$,采用同样的评价函数,则得到的最优结果接近 $\lambda/4-\lambda/4-\lambda/4$ 型,$F_{\min}=0.000147$.

再扩大膜厚的搜索区域,设初始搜索区域取 $a=(70\mathrm{m}\mu,70\mathrm{m}\mu,70\mathrm{m}\mu,1.35,1.35,1.35)$,$b=(300\mathrm{m}\mu,300\mathrm{m}\mu,300\mathrm{m}\mu,2.35,2.35,2.35)$,也采用(5.4)式评价,所得最优结果接近 $\lambda/4-\lambda/2-\lambda/2$ 型,$F_{\min}=0.000044$.

在以往的宽带减反膜的设计方法中[13],只讨论 $\lambda/4-\lambda/2-\lambda/4$ 及 $\lambda/4-\lambda/4-\lambda/4$ 两种类型的膜系,我们的计算表明[12],这两种膜系只能对较低折射率的基底玻璃(1.50~1.65)有较好的效果,而对较高折射率基底玻璃,减反射效果显得很差.但是,在一个实际镜头中大量采用的光学玻璃是高折射率的,从而产生困难.现在我们获得的新结构,反射率大都为 0.1%~0.2%,最大反射率仅 0.3%,减反射性能良好,上述困难满意地得到克服.

从这个例子可以看出,在较小的结构参数范围中搜索,我们得到的是局部极值,在更大范围内搜索,我们可以越过局部极值,获得总极值.

附带指出,微波匹配滤波器与光学减反膜之间有完全类似的对应形式,所以,用这个方法设计微波滤波器,同样是很有效的.

5.2 在环状光学位相滤波器中的应用

中心点亮度是评价光学系统质量优劣的指标之一,它是有象差时衍射图案中最大亮度与无象差时最大亮度之比.设通光孔是半径为 1 的圆孔,则光学系统的中心点亮度为

$$S.D.=\frac{1}{\pi^2}\left|\int_0^1\int_0^{2\pi}\exp\{ikW\}\rho\mathrm{d}\rho\mathrm{d}\theta\right|^2, \tag{5.5}$$

其中 $W=W(\rho,\theta)$ 是光学系统的波象差,$k=2\pi/\lambda$,λ 是光波波长.$S.D.$ 越大,系统质量越好,对无象差系统,$S.D.=1$,一般系统,$S.D.\leqslant 1$.若在光瞳处置一个位相滤波器,则可以大大提高光学系统的质量,这种技术是所谓切趾技术(Apodization)中的一种.

设所加的位相滤波器的位相变化函数为 $F(\rho,\theta)$,此时,

$$S.D.=\frac{1}{\pi^2}\left|\int_0^1\int_0^{2\pi}\exp\{ik(W+F)\}\rho\mathrm{d}\rho\mathrm{d}\theta\right|^2. \tag{5.6}$$

显然,若取 $F(\rho,\theta)=-W(\rho,\theta)$,则 $S.D.=1$,象质达到理想,然而,要制作一 $W(\rho,\theta)$ 的滤波器,在工艺上难于实现.为此,可以考虑采用环状位相滤波器,即

$$F(\rho,\theta)=\begin{cases} c, & a_{2i-2}\leqslant\rho<a_{2i-1}, \\ 0, & a_{2i-1}\leqslant\rho<a_{2i}, \end{cases} \quad i=1,2,\cdots,m. \tag{5.7}$$

其中 c 表示位相推移量,a_i 是光瞳半径分割系数.于是

$$S.D.=\phi(c,a_0,a_1,\cdots,a_{2m}). \tag{5.8}$$

现在的问题归结为选取参数 $c,a_i(i=1,\cdots,2m)$,使(5.8)式中 $S.D.$ 达到极大,同时满足下列 $m(2m+1)$ 个约束

$$a_0=0, \quad a_{2m}=1, \quad a_i\leqslant a_j, \quad i<j,j=1,2,\cdots,2m. \tag{5.9}$$

上面给出的模型是一个较复杂的有约束最优化问题,可以用统计试验最优化方法求解.我们对许多系统进行了计算,都得到了合理的结果[11].下面我们举一个简单的例子.

设一个系统的波象差为

$$W(\rho)=-2\rho^2+2\rho^4.$$

取 $\lambda/4$ 的位相膜组成环状滤波器,在不加位相滤波器时,$S.D.=0.19474$,系统的中心点亮度太小,已无法使用. 经加环状滤波器后,$S.D.=0.81346$,中心点亮度有显著改善,系统已能使用.

我们初始选环数 $m=3$,经 12 次迭代后得 $a_0=1.0, a_1=0.904, a_2=0.429, a_3=0.411, a_4=0.411, a_5=0.020, a_6=0$. 从这个结果可以看出,最后产生了并环现象. 即可以减少位相环的环数. 经分析,这种并环现象在光学上也是合理的. 我们从计算的中间结果中可以清楚地看到渡过多峰和并环的过程.

参考文献

[1] Brooks, S. H. A discussion of random methods for seeking maxima [J]. *J. Opr. Res. Soc. Am.*, 1958, 6:244—251.

[2] Wilde, D. J. Optimum seeking methods [M]. 1964.

[3] Spang, H. A. A review of minimization technique for non-linear function [J]. *SIAM Rev.*, 1962, 4:343—365.

[4] Anderssen, R. S., Loomfield, P. B. Properties of the Random Search in global optimization [J]. *J. O. T. A.*, 1975, 16:383—398.

[5] 上海科技大学计算数学专业. 最优化及有关非线性问题的统计试验解法[R]. 上海科技大学科技资料,1974(3).

[6] 上海科技大学计算数学专业,一个求总极值的方法[R]. 上海科学技术大学科技资料,1976(3).

[7] 江泽坚、吴智泉. 实变函数论 [M]. 北京:人民教育出版社,1961.

[8] 上海科大四系、上海照相机二厂. 镜头涂单层膜的最优化问题 [J]. 照相机工业,1974(2).

[9] 郑权、蒋百川. 光学减反膜的自动设计 [J]. 电影光学,1975(1).

[10] 郑权、蒋百川. 用统计试验最优化法自动设计光学多层薄膜 [J],电影光学,1976(2).

[11] 庄松林、郑权、蒋百川. 环状位相滤波器补偿光学系统象差的切趾效应[J]. 光学仪器情报,1976(6).

[12] 蒋百川、郑权. 摄影镜头减反膜的设计[J]. 仪器制造,1976(5).

[13] Cox, J. T., Hass, G. Anti-reflection coatings, in physics of thin films, Vol. 2, ed. G. Hass and R. E. Thun.

[14] 张建中. 蒙特卡洛方法[J]. 数学的实践和认识,1974(1,2).

[15] Соболъ, И. М., Статников, М. А. Пронина испытание ЛП-поиска на некоторых тествых функциях. «Проблемы случайного поиска», 1973, 2:213.

一类不连续函数及其总极值问题*

1 引言

在经济学理论、统计学和计量经济学中,出现不少求不连续函数极值的问题. 但是,以导数和凸性为基础的最优化理论和方法,排除了研究这类极值问题的可能性. 其实,在数学学科本身,也有兴趣研究和描述不连续函数极值点的性态和求解这类极值问题. 例如,求函数

$$f(x)=\begin{cases} x+\left[\sin\left(\dfrac{1}{x}\right)\right], & x\neq 0, \\ -1, & x=0 \end{cases}$$

的极小,其中$[y]$表示y的整数部分. 容易看到,$f(x)$有无限多个不连续点,而总极小本身是一个第二类不连续点. 但还有一些函数,例如,

$$f(x)=\begin{cases} 1, & x\neq 0, \\ 0, & x=0, \end{cases}$$

是不能用其余的点去判定极值点 0 的性质的.

在这篇文章中,我们采用测度和积分途径去研究一类不连续函数的总极值问题. 我们将讨论这类函数的性质,给出最优性条件及算法. 最后还给出两个数值例子. 这些理论和方法在经济学和统计学中的应用,将另文发表.

2 丰满集

在这一节中,我们将引进丰满集概念并讨论丰满集的性质. 为了对丰满集的结构有更清楚的了解,我们还给出直线上丰满集的构造. 这些研究将成为以后讨论的基础.

设 X 是一个拓扑空间,G 是 X 的一个子集.

定义 2.1 拓扑空间 X 中的子集 G 叫做丰满集,如果

$$\mathrm{cl}(\mathrm{int}\, G) = \mathrm{cl}\, G. \tag{2.1}$$

其中 int G 表示 G 的内点集,cl G 表示 G 的闭包.

开集显然是丰满集,闭集可能是丰满的,也可能不是丰满的. 例如在平面上的一点是闭集但不是丰满的. 非空丰满集的内点集非空. 若不然,$\mathrm{cl}(\mathrm{int}\, G)=\emptyset\neq \mathrm{cl}\, G$.

下面我们将进一步考虑丰满集的性质.

命题 2.1 G 是丰满集的充要条件为对于任一点 $x\in \mathrm{cl}\, G$ 和它的任一邻域 $O(x)$,

$$O(x)\cap \mathrm{int}\, G\neq \emptyset. \tag{2.2}$$

---

* 原文发表于《高等学校计算数学学报》,1985,(1):31—43.

证明 设 G 是丰满集,$x\in$ cl G. 这时 $x\in$ cl(int G). 因此,对于点 x 的任一个领域 $O(x)$, $O(x)\cap$ int $G\neq\varnothing$.

如果条件(2.2)成立但 G 不是丰满集,则存在一点 $x\in$ cl $G\backslash$cl(int G). 但(2.2)导致 $x\in$ cl(int G). 从而导致矛盾.

下面引进丰满点的概念.

定义 2.2 点 $x\in G$ 叫做 G 的丰满点,如果对于 x 的任意领域 $O(x)$,恒有
$$O(x)\cap \text{int } G\neq\varnothing.$$

如果 x 是 G 的丰满点,且 $G\subset G_1$,则 x 也是 G_1 的丰满点.

命题 2.2 集 G 是丰满集的充要条件为 G 中的每一点都是丰满点.

证明 由命题 2.1 可知,cl G 中的每一点都是丰满点. 反之,设 $x\in$ cl G,则对于 x 的任意领域 $O(x)$,$O(x)\cap G\neq\varnothing$. 设 $y\in O(x)\cap G$,即 y 是丰满点,则对于 y 的任意领域 $O_1(y)$, $O_1(y)\cap$ int $G\neq\varnothing$. 但 $y\in O(x)$,而 $O(x)\cap O_1(y)$ 本身也是 y 的邻域. $O(x)\cap O_1(y)\cap$ int $G\neq\varnothing$. 因此 $O(x)\cap$ int $G\neq\varnothing$. 由命题 2.1 可知 G 是丰满集.

由命题 2.1 可知,cl G 中的点都是丰满点,故得

推论 2.1 如果 G 是丰满集,则 cl G 也是丰满集.

命题 2.3 集 G 是丰满集的充要条件为
$$\partial G=\partial \text{int } G, \tag{2.3}$$
其中 $\partial G=$cl$G\backslash$int G 表示 G 的边界.

证明 设 G 是丰满集,则
$$\partial \text{int } G=\text{cl}(\text{int } G)\backslash\text{int}(\text{int } G)=\text{cl}G\backslash\text{int } G=\partial G.$$

反之,如果(2.3)成立,则
$$\partial \text{int } G=\text{cl}(\text{int } G)\backslash\text{int}(\text{int } G)=\text{cl}(\text{int } G)\backslash\text{int } G$$

因此
$$\partial G=\text{cl}G\backslash\text{int } G=\text{cl}(\text{int } G)\backslash\text{int } G.$$

于是 cl $G=$ cl(int G).

命题 2.4 设 G 是丰满集,D 是开集,则 $G\cap D$ 仍是丰满集.

证明 设 $G\cap D\neq\varnothing$,否则命题自然成立. 假设 $G\cap D$ 不是丰满集,即 cl(int($G\cap D$))$\subsetneqq$ cl($G\cap D$). 故存在一点 $x\in$ cl($G\cap D$),但 $x\bar\in$ cl(int($G\cap D$)). 因此,存在 x 的一个领域 $O(x)$,使得 $O(x)\cap$ int($G\cap D$)$=\varnothing$,或者
$$O(x)\cap \text{int } G\cap D=(O(x)\cap D)\cap \text{int } G=\varnothing. \tag{2.4}$$
但是 $O(x)\cap D=O_1(x)$ 也是 x 的一个邻域而 G 是丰满集. 由命题 2.1,$O_1(x)\cap$ int $G\neq\varnothing$. 这与(2.4)相矛盾.

注 两个丰满集的交不一定是丰满集.

推论 2.2 设 G 是丰满集,D 是闭集,则 $G\backslash D$ 是丰满集.

证明 由 $G\backslash D=G\cap D^C$ 及命题 2.4 即可得证,因为 D^C 是开集.

命题 2.5 设 $G_k,k=1,2,\cdots$ 是丰满集,则 $\bigcup\limits_{k=1}^{\infty}G_k$ 仍是丰满集.

证明 因为 $G_k,k=1,2,\cdots$ 是丰满集,则对于任意 n,
$$\text{cl}\left(\bigcup_{k=1}^{n}G_k\right)=\bigcup_{k=1}^{n}\text{cl }G_k=\bigcup_{k=1}^{n}\text{cl}(\text{int }G_k)=\text{cl}\left(\bigcup_{k=1}^{n}\text{int }G_k\right)\subset\text{cl}\left(\text{int }\bigcup_{k=1}^{n}G_k\right).$$

现在设 $x \in \mathrm{cl}\left(\bigcup_{k=1}^{\infty} G_k\right)$,则对于 x 的任意邻域 $O(x)$,

$$O(x) \cap \bigcup_{k=1}^{\infty} G_k \neq \varnothing.$$

譬如说,$y \in O(x) \cap \bigcup_{k=1}^{\infty} G_k$. 即,对于某个 N,$y \in \bigcup_{k=1}^{N} G_k$. 由此推出

$$y \in \mathrm{cl}\left(\bigcup_{k=1}^{N} G_k\right) = \mathrm{cl}\left(\bigcup_{k=1}^{N} \mathrm{int} G_k\right) \subset \mathrm{cl}\left(\mathrm{int}\left(\bigcup_{k=1}^{\infty} G_k\right)\right).$$

于是

$$O(x) \cap \mathrm{cl}\left(\mathrm{int}\left(\bigcup_{k=1}^{\infty} G_k\right)\right) \neq \varnothing.$$

所以

$$x \in \mathrm{cl}\left(\mathrm{cl}\left(\mathrm{int}\left(\bigcup_{k=1}^{\infty} G_k\right)\right)\right) = \mathrm{cl}\left(\mathrm{int}\left(\bigcup_{k=1}^{\infty} G_k\right)\right).$$

可见

$$\mathrm{cl}\left(\bigcup_{k=1}^{\infty} G_k\right) \subset \mathrm{cl}\left(\mathrm{int}\left(\bigcup_{k=1}^{\infty} G_k\right)\right).$$

另一方面,下面的关系始终成立

$$\mathrm{cl}\left(\mathrm{int}\left(\bigcup_{k=1}^{\infty} G_k\right)\right) \subset \mathrm{cl}\left(\bigcup_{k=1}^{\infty} G_k\right).$$

故证得

$$\mathrm{cl}\left(\mathrm{int}\left(\bigcup_{k=1}^{\infty} G_k\right)\right) = \mathrm{cl}\left(\bigcup_{k=1}^{\infty} G_k\right),$$

即 $\bigcup_{k=1}^{\infty} G_k$ 是丰满集.

下面讨论在实轴上丰满集的构造.

显然,开区间和非退化的闭区间都是丰满集. 半开半闭区间是开区间和闭区间之和,它也是丰满集. 令人惊奇的是丰满集中还包含某些点,它不包含在任何区间之中.

定义 2.3 在实轴上的丰满集 G 中的点 x 叫做奇异丰满点,如果它不包含在任何 G 中的区间之中.

例 2.1 设 $G = \left(\bigcup_{k=1}^{\infty}\left(\frac{1}{2k-1}, \frac{1}{2k+1}\right)\right) \cup \{0\}$. 则 G 是实轴上的丰满集,而 0 是 G 的奇异丰满点.

命题 2.6 对于实轴上丰满集 G 的每个奇异丰满点 x,存在一个两两不相交的区间序列 $\{J_n\}$,使得 x 是 $J_n, n=1,2,\cdots$ 的端点的公共极限. 此外,G 的奇异丰满点至多可列个.

证明 设 $x \in G$ 是奇异丰满点. 取 $\delta_1 > 0$,则 $B_{\delta_1}(x) \cap \mathrm{int} G \neq \varnothing$,其中 $B_{\delta_1}(x) = (x-\delta, x+\delta)$. 设 $y_1 \in B_{\delta_1}(x) \cap \mathrm{int} G$. 找出包含 y_1 并包含在 G 中的最大的区间 J_1. 因为 x 不能是 J_1 的端点,所以存在 $\delta_2 > 0 (\delta_2 < \delta_1)$,使得 $B_{\delta_2}(x) \cap J_1 = \varnothing$. 这时,$B_{\delta_2}(x) \cap \mathrm{int} G \neq \varnothing$. 设 $y_2 \in B_{\delta_2}(x) \cap \mathrm{int} G$ 且再找出包含 y_2 并包含在 G 中的最大区间 J_2. 这时 $J_1 \cap J_2 = \varnothing$,不然就和构造方式相矛盾. 存在 $\delta_3 > 0 (\delta_3 < \delta_2)$,使得 $B_{\delta_3}(x) \cap J_2 = \varnothing$,同时有 $B_{\delta_3}(x) \cap J_1 = \varnothing$. 重复上述过程即找到了 J_3,以此类推. 我们找到了一个两两不相交的区间序列 $\{J_k\}$. 这些区间中有

无穷多个在点 x 的左边或右边. 取一子区间无限序列, 它们都在 x 的一边. 不妨仍记为 $\{J_k\}$. 这时 $J_{k+1} \subset B_{\delta_k}(x), k=1,2,\cdots$. 因此, 它们的端点 a_k 和 $b_k, k=1,2,\cdots$ 都趋于 x.

令 $D = \left(\bigcup_{k=1}^{\infty} J_k\right) \cup \{x\}$, 则 $G \backslash D$ 仍是丰满集. 实际上, 可以证明 $G \backslash D = G \backslash \mathrm{cl}\, D$, 这时, 由推论 2.2 可知 $G \backslash D$ 是丰满集. 现在假设它们不相等, 即存在 $z \in G \cap \mathrm{cl}\, D$ 但 $z \bar{\in} D$. 因为 $z \in \mathrm{cl}\, D$, 则存在 $\{z_n\} \subset D$ 使得 $z_n \to z$. 这时, 或者 $\{z_n\}$ 包含在有限个区间之中, 这时 z 是某区间中的点或这区间的端点, 但 $z \bar{\in} G$, 所以这端点也包含在这区间中从而与 $z \bar{\in} D$ 相矛盾. 或者 $\{z_n\}$ 包含在无限多个区间中, 但这时 $z_n \to x$, 也与 $z \bar{\in} D$ 相矛盾.

现在设 $x_1 \neq x$ 是 G 的另一个奇异丰满点. 令 $\rho = |x_1 - x|$. 因为 $J^k \subset B_\rho(x), k \geq k_0$, 所以 x_1 也是 $G \backslash D$ 的奇异丰满点. 重复上述过程, 我们得到另一个两两不相交的区间序列, 它们的端点趋于 x_1. 以此类推.

不同的奇异丰满点对应于不相交的区间序列. 下面我们将看到, 丰满集中的区间数至多可列个. 因此, 奇异丰满点个数也是至多可列个. 证毕

命题 2.7 实轴上非空丰满集 G 是可列个区间之和, 也可能再包含可列个 G 的奇异丰满点.

证明 实轴上的区间都是丰满集, 可列个区间之和也是丰满集. 设它们的和是 G_1. G_1 中的点都是 G 的丰满点, 再加上余下的奇异丰满点成为 G. 因此, G 中的点都是丰满点, 即 G 是丰满集.

反之, 设 G 是实轴上的非空丰满集, 则 $\mathrm{int}\, G \neq \varnothing$. 对于任一点 $x \in \mathrm{int}\, G$, 存在一个包含 x 并包含在 G 内的最大区间 $J(x)$. 按照构造, 如果 $x' \in \mathrm{int}\, G$, 但 $x' \bar{\in} J(x)$, 则有 $J(x) \cap J(x') = \varnothing$. 由于在直线上两两不相交的区间至多是可列个, 故若令 $G_1 = \bigcup_{x \in \mathrm{int}\, G} J(x)$, 则 G_1 为至多可列个两两不相交的区间之和, 而且 $\mathrm{int}(G \backslash G_1) = \varnothing$.

按此构造, 余下的点都是奇异丰满点. 若不然, 设有丰满点 $z \in G \backslash G_1$, 它是某区间中的点, 则 $\mathrm{int}(G \backslash G_1) \neq \varnothing$. 再根据命题 2.6, 这些奇异丰满点至多可列个.

3 上丰满函数

设 $f: X \to \mathbb{R}$ 是一个 Hausdorff 空间 X 上的实函数. 在这一节中我们将考虑一类不连续函数以及它与第二节中所讨论的丰满集的联系.

定理 3.1 函数 f 叫做上丰满函数, 如果对于任意的实数 c, 集合
$$H_c^0 = \{x \mid f(x) < c\} \tag{3.1}$$
是丰满的.

上半连续函数是上丰满函数, 从而连续函数是上丰满的.

命题 3.1 设 f 是丰满函数, g 是上半连续函数(对于除法, g 是下半连续函数), 则下列函数是上丰满的.

(1) αf $(\alpha \geq 0)$;

(2) $f + g$;

(3) $f \cdot g$ $(g(x) > 0,$ 对于所有的 $x \in X)$;

(4) f/g　($g(x)>0$,对于所有的 $x\in X$).

证明 (1) 如果 $\alpha=0$,则 αf 连续. 设 $\alpha>0$. 对于任意的实数 c,集合
$$\{x\mid \alpha f(x)<c\}=\{x\mid f(x)<c/\alpha\}$$
是丰满的,故 αf 是上丰满函数.

(2) 把所有的有理数排序:$r_1,r_2,r_3\cdots$. 容易证明,对于任意的实数 c,
$$\{x\mid f(x)+g(x)<c\}=\bigcup_{k=1}^{\infty}\{x\mid f(x)<r_k\}\cap\{x\mid g(x)<c-r_k\}. \tag{3.2}$$

实际上,设 $x\in\bigcup_{k=1}^{\infty}(\{x\mid f(x)<r_k\}\cap\{x\mid g(x)<c-r_k\})$,则至少有一个足标 k 使得 $x\in\{x\mid f(x)<r_k\}\cap\{x\mid g(x)<c-r_k\}$. 因此 $f(x)+g(x)<r_k+c-r_k=c$. 设 $f(\hat{x})+g(\hat{x})<c$. 令 $f(\hat{x})=a,g(\hat{x})=b$ 则 $c-(a+b)=2\eta>0$. 因为有理数在实轴上是稠密的,我们可以找到一个有理数 r_k,使得 $0<r_k-a<\eta$. 由此推出 $f(\hat{x})=a<r_k$ 和 $g(\hat{x})=b=c-a-2\eta<c-r_k$. 因此 $\hat{x}\in\{x\mid f(x)<r_k\}\cap\{x\mid g(x)<c-r_k\}$. 这就证明了(3.2). 对于任意的 $k=1,2,\cdots,\{x\mid f(x)<r_k\}$ 是丰满集,$\{x\mid g(x)<c-r_k\}$ 是开集,从而 $\{x\mid f(x)<r_k\}\cap\{x\mid g(x)<c-r_k\}$ 是丰满集. 作为可列个丰满集之和,集合 $\{x\mid f(x)+g(x)<c\}$ 是丰满集.

(3) 对于任意的实数 c,类似地可证
$$\{x\mid f(x)g(x)<c\}=\bigcup_{k=1}^{\infty}\left(\{x\mid f(x)<r_k\}\cap\left\{x\mid g(x)<\frac{c}{r_k}\right\}\right). \tag{3.3}$$
故 $\{x\mid f(x)\cdot g(x)<c\}$ 是丰满的.

(4) 因为 $f(x)/g(x)=f(x)\dfrac{1}{g(x)}$,其中 $\dfrac{1}{g(x)}>0$ 且上半连续,故由(3)可知 f/g 是上丰满函数.

例3.1 单调函数 f 是上丰满的,因为对于任一个实数 c,集合 $\{x\mid f(x)<c\}$ 是半无限区间. 因此,一元分布函数是上丰满的. n 元分布函数 F 也是上丰满的. 对于任意的实数 c,令 $H_c^0=\{(x_1,\cdots,x_n)\mid F(x_1,\cdots,x_n)<c\}$,并设它非空. 设 $(y_1,\cdots,y_n)\in H_c^0$,则 $(-\infty,y_1]\times(-\infty,y_2]\times\cdots\times(-\infty,y_n]\subset H_c^0$ 因此,对于 $(y_1,\cdots,y_n)$ 的任意邻域 $O(y),O(y)\cap\prod_{k=1}^{n}(-\infty,y_k)\neq\varnothing$ 但 $\prod_{k=1}^{n}(-\infty,y_k)\subset\text{int}H_c^0$,因此 $O(y)\cap\text{int}H_c^0\neq\varnothing$. 即 y 是 H_c^0 的丰满点,从而证明了 H_c^0 是丰满集.

例3.2 函数
$$f(x)=\begin{cases} \sin\dfrac{1}{x}, & x\neq 0, \\ \alpha, & x=0 \end{cases}$$
是下半连续的,若 $\alpha\leqslant -1$;当 $\alpha\geqslant -1$ 时,则 f 是上丰满函数.

例3.3 令
$$f_1(x)=\begin{cases} 1, & x\leqslant 0, \\ 0, & x>0 \end{cases} \quad \text{和} \quad f_2(x)=\begin{cases} 0, & x<0, \\ 1, & x\leqslant 0, \end{cases}$$
则 f_1 和 f_2 都是上丰满函数,但是
$$f_1(x)+f_2(x)=\begin{cases} 1, & x\neq 0, \\ 0, & x=0 \end{cases}$$

不是上丰满的.

下面引进函数的上丰满点的概念.

定义 3.2 点 x 叫做函数 f 的上丰满点,如果存在 x 的一个开邻域 $O(x)$,使得对于任意 c,$H_c^0 \cap O(x)$ 是丰满集.

命题 3.2 函数 f 是上丰满函数的充要条件是它在每一点 $x \in X$ 处是上丰满的.

证明 如果 f 是上丰满的,则 H_c^0 对任意 c 是丰满的. 因此 $H_c^0 \cap O(x)$ 是丰满的. 即 f 在任一点 x 处上丰满.

设 X 中的任一点 x 都是 f 的上丰满点,我们来证明,对于任意 c,H_c^0 是丰满集. 对于任意的 c 及 $x \in H_c^0$,因 f 在 x 处上丰满,故存在一个开邻域 $O(x)$ 使得 $H_c^0 \cap O(x)$ 是非空丰满集,从而 x 是 $H_c^0 \cap O(x)$ 的丰满点,故 x 也是 H_c^0 的丰满点,这就证明了 H_c^0 是丰满集,而 f 是上丰满函数.

我们已经看到,两个上丰满函数之和可能不是上丰满的. 但是,由命题 3.2,我们可以考虑一点附近的性态. 如果它们没有共同的不连续点,则两个上丰满函数之和仍然是上丰满的. 同样可以考虑乘积和商的情形.

注 我们考虑上丰满函数是为了处理极小问题. 如果用 $\{x \mid f(x) > c\}$ 代替 $\{x \mid f(x) < c\}$,则可以类似地考虑下丰满函数以处理极大问题.

4 总极值的最优性条件

设 f 是在 Hausdorff 空间 X 上的实函数. 在下面的讨论中,我们始终假设:

(A_1) f 是上丰满函数;

(A_2) f 是下半连续函数,并且存在一个实数 α,使得水平集 $\{x \mid f(x) \leqslant \alpha\}$ 是非空紧集.

假设(A_2)保证了 f 的极小存在,并且

$$\min f(x) = \min_{x \in H_\alpha} f(x). \tag{4.1}$$

因此,不妨假设对于任意 $c > \alpha$,H_c 也是紧集.

我们用测度和积分理论来建立总极值的最优性条件,并设 (X, Ω, μ) 是一个测度空间,它具有下列性质:

(M_1) Ω 是一个 Borel 域,即任意开集都可测;

(M_2) 非空开集的测度为正;

(M_3) 紧集的测度有界.

下面的引理给出一个最优性充分条件:

引理 4.1 设 f 是上丰满函数,水平集 $H_c = \{x \mid f(x) \leqslant c\}$ 非空. 如果 $\mu(H_c) = 0$,则 c 是 f 的总极小值,H_c 是其总极小点集.

证明 设 c 不是总极小值而 $\hat{c} < c$ 是总极小值. 令 $2\eta = c - \hat{c} > 0$,则 $H_{c-\eta}^0 = \{x \mid f(x) < c - \eta\}$ 是非空丰满集. 因此 $\mathrm{int} H_{c-\eta}^0 \neq \emptyset$. 于是

$$\emptyset \neq \mathrm{int} H_{c-\eta}^0 \subset \mathrm{int} H_c.$$

但是

$$\mu(H_c) \geqslant \mu(\mathrm{int} H_c) > 0,$$

从而导致矛盾.

注 由引理 4.1 可知,如果,$c > \bar{c} \min f(x)$,则 $\mu(H_c) > 0$.

下面将引进一个函数在其水平集上的均值、方差、修正方差和高阶矩的概念. 这些概念和下面的最优性条件,是[2]和[3]的推广.

定义 4.1 设 $c > \bar{c} = \min f(x)$,则称

$$M(f,c) = \frac{1}{\mu(H_c)} \int_{H_c} f(x) \mathrm{d}\mu,$$

$$V(f,c) = \frac{1}{\mu(H_c)} \int_{H_c} (f(x) - M(f,c))^2 \mathrm{d}\mu,$$

$$V_1(f,c) = \frac{1}{\mu(H_c)} \int_{H_c} (f(x) - c)^2 \mathrm{d}\mu,$$

$$M_m(f,c;a) = \frac{1}{\mu(H_c)} \int_{H_c} (f(x) - a)^m \mathrm{d}\mu, m = 1, 2, \cdots$$

分别为 f 在其水平集 H_c 上的均值、方差、修正方差和中心为 a 的第 m 阶矩.

由引理 4.1 可知,$\mu(H_c) > 0$,这些定义有意义. 下面我们将只讨论均值的性质和定义,其余的可以用类似于[2]和[3]的方式去讨论.

引理 4.2 均值具有下列性质.

(1) $\bar{c} \leqslant M(f,c) \leqslant c$, 对于 $c > \bar{c}$;

(2) $M(f,c_1) \leqslant M(f,c_2)$, 对于 $c_2 \geqslant c_1 > \bar{c}$;

(3) $\lim\limits_{c_k \downarrow c} M(f,c_k) = M(f,c)$, 对于 $c > \bar{c}$.

证明 只证(3). 容易看出 $H_c = \bigcap\limits_{k=1}^{\infty} H_{c_k}$, 所以 $\lim\limits_{k \to \infty} \mu(H_{c_k}) = \mu(H_c)$. 故

$$\left| \frac{1}{\mu(H_{c_k})} \int_{H_{c_k}} f(x) \mathrm{d}\mu - \frac{1}{\mu(H_c)} \int_{H_c} f(x) \mathrm{d}\mu \right| \to 0 \quad (k \to \infty).$$

当 $c = \bar{c}$ 时,$\mu(H_{\bar{c}})$ 可能为 0, 定义 4.1 无意义. 因此我们用极限过程来定义这些概念.

定义 4.2 设 $c \geqslant \bar{c}$,则称

$$M(f,c) = \lim_{c_k \downarrow c} \frac{1}{\mu(H_{c_k})} \int_{H_{c_k}} f(x) \mathrm{d}\mu, \tag{4.2}$$

$$V(f,c) = \lim_{c_k \downarrow c} \frac{1}{\mu(H_{c_k})} \int_{H_{c_k}} (f(x) - M(f,c))^2 \mathrm{d}\mu, \tag{4.3}$$

$$V_1(f,c) = \lim_{c_k \downarrow c} \frac{1}{\mu(H_{c_k})} \int_{H_{c_k}} (f(x) - c)^2 \mathrm{d}\mu, \tag{4.4}$$

$$M_m(f,c;a) = \lim_{c_k \downarrow c} \frac{1}{\mu(H_{c_k})} \int_{H_{c_k}} (f(x) - a)^m \mathrm{d}\mu, m = 1, 2, \cdots \tag{4.5}$$

为 f 在其水平集 H_c 上的均值、方差、修正方差和中心为 a 的第 m 阶矩.

由于 $\{M(f,c_k)\}$ 是递降有下界序列,极限存在并且不依赖于 $\{c_k\}$ 的选取,因此定义有意义. 由引理 4.2 的(3)可知,当 $c > \bar{c}$ 时,定义 4.2 与定义 4.1 一致. 此外,引理 4.2 对于 $c \geqslant \bar{c}$ 也都成立.

定理 4.1 设假设 (A_1) 和 (A_2) 成立,则下列命题等价:

(1) 点 $\bar{x}$ 是 f 的总极小点而 $\bar{c} = f(\bar{x})$ 是其总极小值;

(2) $M(f,c) \geqslant \bar{c}$, 对于 $c > \bar{c}$;

(3) $M(f,\bar{c})=\bar{c}$;

(4) $V(f,\bar{c})=0$;

(5) $V_1(f,\bar{c})=0$;

(6) $M_{2m-1}(f,c;0)\geqslant(\bar{c})^{2m-1}$,对于 $c>\bar{c}$ 及某个正整数 m;

(7) $M_{2m-1}(f,\bar{c};0)=(\bar{c})^{2m-1}$ 对于某个正整数 m;

(8) $M_{2m}(f,\bar{c};M(f,\bar{c}))=0$,对于某个正整数 m;

(9) $M_m(f,\bar{c};\bar{c})=0$,对于某个正整数 m.

证明 只证(1)与(9)等价. 设 $\bar{c}$ 是 f 的总极小值,则 $f(x)\geqslant \bar{c}$ 故对于 $c>\bar{c}$

$$M_m(f,c;\bar{c})=\frac{1}{\mu(H_c)}\int_{H_c}(f(x)-\bar{c})^m\mathrm{d}\mu\geqslant 0,$$

因此 $M_m(f,\bar{c};\bar{c})\geqslant 0$. 现在假设 $M_m(f,\bar{c};\bar{c})=2\eta>0$. 由定义 4.2,对于递降数列 $\{c_k\}$,存在正整数 K_0,使得对于 $k>K_0$,

$$\frac{1}{\mu(H_{c_k})}\int_{H_{c_k}}(f(x)-\bar{c})^m\mathrm{d}\mu>\eta. \tag{4.6}$$

但是在 H_{c_k} 上 $\bar{c}\leqslant f(x)\leqslant c_k$,因此 $(f(x)-\bar{c})^m\leqslant(c_k-\bar{c})^m$,故由(4.6)可得

$$(c_k-\bar{c})^m\geqslant\frac{1}{\mu(H_{c_k})}\int_{H_k}(f(x)-\bar{c})^m\mathrm{d}\mu>\eta>0. \tag{4.7}$$

令 $k\to\infty$,由上式导致矛盾 $0\geqslant\eta>0$.

(9)→(1). 设 $M(f,\bar{c};\bar{c})=0$,但是 $\bar{c}$ 不是总极小值,而 $\hat{c}<\bar{c}$ 是总极小值. 令 $2\eta=\bar{c}-\hat{c}>0$. 这时 $\mu(H_{\bar{c}})$ 和 $\mu(H_{\bar{c}-\eta})$ 都为正. 此外,当 $x\in H_{\bar{c}-\eta}$ 时 $f(x)\leqslant\bar{c}-\eta$. 当 m 是奇数时

$$(f(x)-\bar{c})^m\leqslant-\eta^m,\quad \forall x\in H_{\bar{c}-\eta}, \tag{4.8}$$

$$(f(x)-\bar{c})^m\leqslant 0,\quad \forall x\in H_{\bar{c}}. \tag{4.9}$$

于是

$$M_m(f,\bar{c};\bar{c})=\frac{1}{\mu(H_{\bar{c}})}\int_{H_{\bar{c}}\setminus H_{\bar{c}-\eta}}(f(x)-\bar{c})^m\mathrm{d}\mu$$
$$+\frac{1}{\mu(H_{\bar{c}})}\int_{H_{\bar{c}-\eta}}(f(x)-\bar{c})^m\mathrm{d}\mu$$
$$\leqslant -\eta^m\frac{\mu(H_{\bar{c}-\eta})}{\mu(H_{\bar{c}})}<0, \tag{4.10}$$

这与条件(9)相矛盾. 如果 m 是偶数(4.8)和(4.9)不等式变向. (4.10)式变为

$$M_m(f,\bar{c};\bar{c})\geqslant\eta^m\frac{\mu(H_{\bar{c}-\eta})}{\mu(H_{\bar{c}})}>0, \tag{4.11}$$

也与条件(9)矛盾. 证毕.

5 算法和数值例子

取一实数 $c_0>\min f(x)$,则根据引理 4.1, $\mu(H_{c_0})>0$. 令

$$c_1=M(f,c_0),$$

则

$$\min f(x)\leqslant c_1\leqslant c_0.$$

一般,令
$$c_{k+1}=M(f,c_k), \quad k=0,1,2,\cdots. \tag{5.1}$$

我们得到递减均值数列
$$c_0 \geqslant c_1 \geqslant \cdots \geqslant c_k \geqslant c_{k+1} \geqslant \cdots \geqslant \bar{c} \tag{5.2}$$

和递减水平集序列
$$H_{c_0} \supset H_{c_1} \supset \cdots \supset H_{c_k} \supset H_{c_{k+1}} \supset \cdots \tag{5.3}$$

它们都有下界,因此都存在极限.

定理 5.1 设条件(A_1)和(A_2)成立,则极限 $\bar{c}=\lim\limits_{k\to\infty}c_k$ 是 f 的总极值而 $\overline{H}=\bigcup\limits_{k=1}^{\infty}H_{c_k}$ 是其总极值点集.

证明 因为 $\lim\limits_{k\to\infty}c_k=\lim\limits_{k\to\infty}c_{k+1}=\bar{c}$,(5.1)式取极限后得
$$\bar{c}=M(f,\bar{c})$$

由定理 4.1 可知 $\bar{c}$ 是 f 的总极小值.

设 $x\in\overline{H}$,则对于任意的 $k, f(x)\leqslant c_k$.令 $k\to\infty$ 得 $f(x)\leqslant\bar{c}$.但 $f(x)\geqslant\bar{c}$.因此 $\overline{H}=\{x|f(x)=\bar{c}\}$.即 $\overline{H}$ 是 f 的总极小点集.

由定理 5.1 和最优性条件,我们给出求总极值的算法如下:

第 0 步:任取一点 x_0,使得 $c_0=f(x_0)>\min f(x)$;给定精度 $\varepsilon>0; k:=0$;

第 1 步:计算均值 $c_{k+1}:=M(f,c_k)$;令 $H_{c_{k+1}}:=\{x|f(x)\leqslant c_{k+1}\}$;

第 2 步:计算方差 $VF:=V_1(f,c_k)$;

第 3 步:如果 $VF\geqslant\varepsilon$,则 $k:=k+1$;转第 1 步,否则转第 4 步;

第 4 步:$\hat{c}\Leftarrow c_{k+1}; \hat{H}\Leftarrow H_{c_{k+1}}$;停机.

这个算法是实际下降的,即我们有下列定理:

定理 5.2 设假设(A_1)和(A_2)成立.如果 f 在 H_{c_k} 上不是常数,则 $\{c_j\}$ 和 $\{H_{c_j}\}, j\geqslant k$ 严格下降.换言之,如果存在一个 k 使得 $c_k=c_{k+1}$ 或 $H_{c_k}=H_{c_{k-1}}$,则 f 在 H_{ck} 上是常数.

证明 如果 $c_k=c_{k+1}$,则显然 $\mu(H_{c_k})=\mu(H_{c_{k+1}})$.下面证明 $\mu(H_{c_k})=\mu(H_{c_{k-1}})$.令 $\Delta H_k=H_{c_{k-1}}\setminus H_{c_k}, \Delta H_k^0=\{x|c_k<f(x)<c_{k-1}\}$,则
$$c_k\mu(H_{c_{k-1}})-c_{k+1}\mu(H_{c_k})=\int_{\Delta H_k}f(x)\mathrm{d}\mu.$$

因为 $c_k=c_{k+1}$,故
$$c_{k+1}\mu(\Delta H_k)=\int_{\Delta H_k}f(x)\mathrm{d}\mu.$$

或者
$$\int_{\Delta H_k}(f(x)-c_{k+1})\mathrm{d}\mu=0. \tag{5.5}$$

设 $\hat{x}\in\Delta H_k^0, a=f(\hat{x})>c_k$,令 $c_k-a=2\mu$,则存在一个开邻域 $O(\hat{x})$ 使得 $f(x)>c_k+\eta, \forall x\in O(\hat{x})$.但由于 ΔH_k^0 是丰满集,$O(\hat{x})\cap\mathrm{int}\Delta H_k^0\neq\varnothing$.因此存在一个非空开集 $O\subset O(\hat{x})\cap\Delta H_k^0$.但这将导致下式与(5.5)矛盾
$$\int_{\Delta H_k}(f(x)-c_{k+1})\mathrm{d}\mu\geqslant\int_O(f(x)-c_{k+1})\mathrm{d}\mu\geqslant\eta\cdot\mu(O)>0.$$

如果 $\mu(\Delta H_k\setminus\Delta H_k^0)>0$,而 $\Delta H_k-\Delta H_k^0=\{x|f(x)=c_{k-1}\}$,则由(5.5)可知

$$\int_{\Delta H_k} (f(x)-c_{k+1})\mathrm{d}\mu = (c_{k-1}-c_{k+1})\cdot \mu(\Delta H_k)=0. \tag{5.6}$$

这时,或者 $\mu(\Delta H_k)=0$,或者 $c_{k-1}=c_{k+1}$,这时也有 $\mu(\Delta H_k)=0$.

如果 $\mu(H_{c_k})=\mu(H_{c_{k-1}})$,则

$$c_{k+1}=\frac{1}{\mu(H_{c_k})}\int_{H_{c_k}} f(x)\mathrm{d}\mu = \frac{1}{\mu(H_{c_{k-1}})}\int_{H_{c_{k-1}}} f(x)\mathrm{d}\mu = c_k.$$

于是,从 $c_k=c_{k+1}$ 或 $H_{c_k}=H_{c_{k-1}}$ 可知 $\mu(H_{c_k})=\mu(H_{c_{k-1}})$,从而可知 $c_{k+1}=c_{k+2}$,以此类推,$c_k=c_{k+1}=c_{k+2}=\cdots$,$H_{c_k}=H_{c_{k+1}}=H_{c_{k+2}}=\cdots$,故 $f(x)$ 在 H_{c_k} 上是常数 c_k.

给定 $c_0>\min f(x)$,令 $c_1=M(f,c_0)$,但由于计算 $M(f,c_0)$ 时产生误差 Δ_1,得 $d_1=c_1+\Delta_1$.在下次迭代时用 d_1 代替 c_1,令 $c_2=M(f,d_1)$.但是也产生计算误差 Δ_2,得 $d_2=c_2+\Delta_2$,以此类推,得一序列 $\{d_k\}$.因为 $M(f,d_k)\leqslant d_k$,所以 $\{d_k\}$ 是递降的.设 $\lim d_k=\bar{d}$.现在的问题是误差是否会积累?在什么情况下 $\bar{d}$ 仍是总极小值?

定理 5.3 设假设 (A_1) 和 (A_2) 成立.设 $\{d_k\}$ 是一递降数列,$\lim\limits_{k\to\infty} d_k=\bar{d}$.令

$$c_k=M(f,d_{k-1}),\quad \Delta_k=d_k-c_k,\quad k=1,2,\cdots, \tag{5.7}$$

则 $\bar{d}$ 是 f 的总极小的充要条件为

$$\lim_{k\to\infty}\Delta_k=0. \tag{5.8}$$

证明 设 $\lim\limits_{k\to\infty}\Delta_k=0$,则 $\lim\limits_{k\to\infty} c_k=\lim\limits_{k\to\infty} d_k=\bar{d}$.由 (5.7) 取极限后得

$$\bar{d}=M(f,\bar{d}),$$

故 $\bar{d}$ 是 f 的总极小.反之,设 $\bar{d}$ 是 f 的总极小,则

$$\lim_{k\to\infty} d_k=\lim_{k\to\infty} M(f,d_{k-1})=\lim_{k\to\infty} c_k=\bar{d},$$

故 (5.8) 成立.

上述算法可以用 Monte Carlo 方法来实现,实现的方法与[1]并无实质差别.

例 5.1 求 $f(x,y)=2(x^2+y^2)-[x^2+y^2]$ 的总极小.

这个函数有有限个不连续圆周(其上都是局部极小点).总极小在 $(0,0)$,$f(0,0)=0$.

取初始搜索区域为 $D=\{(x,y)\mid -10\leqslant x\leqslant 10, -10\leqslant y\leqslant 10\}$.经过 30 次迭代,计算函数 1310 次,求出 $\hat{x}=-3.48\cdot 10^{-10}$,$\hat{y}=8.19\cdot 10^{-11}$,$f=2.56\cdot 10^{-10}$ 及 $VF=0.90\cdot 10^{-25}$.

例 5.2 求下列函数的极小

$$f(x)=\begin{cases} 1+n\sqrt{\sum_{i=1}^n |x_i|}+\mathrm{sgn}\left(\sin\left(\dfrac{1}{\sqrt{\sum_{i=1}^n |x_i|}}-0.5\right)\right), & x\neq 0, \\ 0, & x=0. \end{cases}$$

这个函数的总极小(原点)是一个第二类不连续点,在其周围有可列个不连续的超曲面.但它是一个下半连续的上丰满函数.(A_1) 和 (A_2) 成立.可以用前法求极值.

例如,取 $n=5$.初始搜索区域为 $D=\{x=(x_1,\cdots,x_5)\mid -1\leqslant x_i\leqslant 1, i=1,\cdots,5\}$.经过 100 次迭代,总计算函数次数 $N_f=4962$,求得 $\hat{x}=\{-8.93\cdot 10^{-14}, 7.21\cdot 10^{-14}, -3.01\cdot 10^{-13}, 6.57\cdot 10^{-13}, 3.05\cdot 10^{-14}\}$,$\hat{f}=7.27\cdot 10^{-6}$ 及 $VF=3.57\cdot 10^{-12}$.

注 上述计算都是用携带式微计算机 Osborn 01 完成的. 该机字长为 8 位, 可见此算法不因字长短而积累误差.

参考文献

[1] 郑权, 蒋百川, 庄松林. 一个求总极值的方法[J]. 应用数学学报, 1(1978), 161—174.
[2] 郑权. 关于总极值的最优性条件[J]. 高等学校计算数学学报, 3(1981), 273—275.
[3] 郑权. 高阶矩与总极值的最优性条件[J]. 运筹学杂志, 1(1982), 73—74.

无限维空间中总极值的有限维逼近*

变分学、最优控制、微分对策等问题,要求考虑无限维空间中的总极值问题,但实际计算中只能得出有限维空间中的解. 本文利用积分型总极值途径和变测度的思想,给出了最优性条件,算法及从有限维过渡到无限维的收敛性,最后还给出构造变测度序列的两个例子.

1 引言

设 U 为可分 Frèchet 空间,S 为 U 中的子集,J 为 U 上的实函数,考虑下列求极小问题:
$$c^* = \inf_{u \in S} J(u). \tag{1.1}$$
如果集合
$$H^* = \{u \in S | J(u) = c^*\} \tag{1.2}$$
非空,则还要找出 H^*.

在本文中我们对总极值点存在性问题不作进一步讨论. 如果

(A) 存在一个常数 $b > c^*$,使得
$$H_0 = \{u | J(u) \leqslant b\} \tag{1.3}$$
为非空紧集,J 为下半连续函数,S 为闭集,则总极值点集 H^* 非空.

此外,上述条件还可推出 $J(u)$ 有下界
$$J(u) \geqslant M, \forall u \in U. \tag{1.4}$$

在实际计算中我们很难找出无限维空间中的总极值 c^* 及总极值点集 H^*,而只能求出它们的有限维逼近
$$c_k^* = \inf_{u \in S^k} J(u), \tag{1.5}$$
其中 S^k 为 S 的子集,通常 S^k 还嵌入一个有限维空间中,我们希望找出构造 S^k 的方法,使得 c_k^* 趋于 c^*,从而找出总极值点,本文将利用积分型总极值途径,推广[1]和[7]中的变测度方法来讨论该问题,找出用有限维空间中的总极值去逼近无限维空间中总极值的条件.

在第 2 节中将考虑测度序列的 Q-收敛,第 3 节中讨论变测度的均值、方差和高阶矩,及由它们描述的最优性条件;第 4 节中讨论构造 S^k 和变测度 μ_k 的条件和方法,并证明 $c_k^* \to c^*$. 在第 5 节中给出两个构造 S^k 和 Q-测度序列的例子,它们已经应用于解最优控制和微分对策问题上[4,5].

---

* 原文发表于《应用数学与计算数学学报》,1991,5(1):78—89.

2 Q-测度和测度序列的 Q-收敛

设 U 为 Hausdorff 空间，Ω 为 U 中的子集构成的 σ-域，μ 为 (U,Ω) 上的测度. 如果(i)所有 U 中的开集可测；(ii)非空开集的测度为正，(iii)紧集的测度有限，则称 (U,Ω,μ) 为 Q-测度空间，引进 Q-测度空间并考虑由它定义的积分，目的在于导出最优性条件并构造积分型算法. 我们假设

(R) S 为丰满集，J 为 S 上的丰满函数.

我们称 S 为 U 中的丰满集，如果
$$\mathrm{cl}\, S = \mathrm{cl}\, \mathrm{int}\, S. \tag{2.1}$$
我们称 J 为 S 上的丰满函数，如果对于任意的实数 c，集合
$$\{u \in S \mid J(u) < c\} \tag{2.2}$$
为 U 中的丰满集. 由于非空丰满集的内点非空，故非空可测丰满集的测度为正. 由此可证，如果 $c > c^* = \min_{u \in S} J(u)$，则 $\mu(H_c \cap S) > 0$. 关于丰满集和丰满函数的讨论，参见[6,7].

设 $(\Omega_1, U_1, \mu_1), \cdots, (\Omega_k, U_k, \mu_k), \cdots$ 为测度空间，(Ω, U, μ) 为 Q 测度空间，其中 U_k 为 U 的子空间，$\Omega_k = \{A \cap U_k \mid A \in \Omega\}$. 如果对于任一开集 $G \subset U$，
$$\mu_k(G \cap U_k) \to \mu(G), \quad k \to \infty \tag{2.3}$$
则称测度序列 $\{\mu_k\}$ Q-收敛于 μ，并记为 $\mu_k \xrightarrow{Q} \mu$.

注 1 在[1]和[6]中我们定义在紧空间 U 上的测度序列的 Q-收敛，这里我们并不要求 U 为紧空间

注 2 由于我们的目标为处理无限维空间中的最优化问题，为此，(U,Ω) 上的测度为有限测度.

注 3 设 G 为非空开集，由于 $\mu_k(G \cap U_k) \to \mu(G)$，所以存在 k_0，使得 $\mu_k(G \cap U_k) > 0, \forall k \geq k_0$（$k_0$ 与 G 有关），所以，在实际讨论中，我们将考虑序$\{\mu_k\}$ 中的测度均为 Q-测度.

在下面的讨论中，我们假设

(M) $\mu_1, \cdots, \mu_k, \cdots$ 为 (U,Ω) 上的有限 Q 测度，$\{\mu_k\}$ Q-收敛于 Q.

注 4 由于 U 本身为开集，并且 $\mu(U) < +\infty$，所以
$$\mu_k(U \cap U_k) = \mu_k(U_k) \to \mu(U), \quad k \to \infty. \tag{2.4}$$
设 F 为 U 中的闭集，则 $U \setminus F$ 为开集
$$\mu_k(U_k \cap U) - \mu_k(F \cap U_k) = \mu_k((U \setminus F) \cap U_k) \to \mu(U \setminus F) = \mu(U) - \mu(F).$$
故对于任一 U 中的闭集 F，
$$\mu_k(F \cap U_k) \to \mu(F). \tag{2.5}$$
关于测度序列的 Q-收敛，下列定理成立. 虽然这里的定义和[1]中的有些不同，但是证明方法没有多大变动.

定理 2.1 设 $(U_1, \Omega_1, \mu_1), \cdots, (U_k, \Omega_k, \mu_k), \cdots$ 和 (U, Ω, μ) 为有限 Q-测度空间，U_k 为 U 的子空间，$k = 1, 2, \cdots$，则下列命题等价.

(1) 对于 U 上的任一有限下半连续函数 J，$\int_{U_k} J \mathrm{d}\mu_k \to \int_U J \mathrm{d}\mu$；

(2) 对于 U 上的任一有限上半连续函数 J，$\int_{U_k} J \, d\mu_k \to \int_U J \, d\mu$；

(3) 对于 U 中的任一开子集 G，$\mu_k(G \cap U_k) \to \mu(G)$；

(4) 对于 U 中的任一闭子集 F，$\mu_k(F \cap U_k) \to \mu(F)$.

3 变测度均值、方差和高阶矩　最优性条件

在这一节中，我们推广[1]和[6]中的变测度模型，考虑约束集 S^k 也变化的情形. 设 S 为 U 中的子集，J 为 U 上的函数. 假设我们构造 S 中的子集 S^k，它是 U 的子空间 U_k 中的子集，J 限制在 U_k 中也是其中的函数. 我们暂不考虑怎样构造 U_k 和 S^k 及测度 μ_k 的方法，先考虑在假设 (A)，(R) 和 (M) 下，当 $\{\mu_k\}$ Q-收敛于 μ 时的收敛性态.

设 $c > \min\limits_{u \in S^k} J(u)$，我们分别称

$$M(J, c; S^k; \mu_k) = \frac{1}{\mu_k(H_c \cap S^k)} \int_{H_c \cap S^k} J(u) \, d\mu_k \tag{3.1}$$

$$V(J, c; S^k; \mu_k) = \frac{1}{\mu_k(H_c \cap S^k)} \int_{H_c \cap S^k} (J(u) - M(f, c; S^k; \mu_k))^2 \, d\mu_k, \tag{3.2}$$

$$V_1(J, c; S^k; \mu_k) = \frac{1}{\mu_k(H_c \cap S^k)} \int_{H_c \cap S^k} (J(u) - c)^2 \, d\mu_k, \tag{3.3}$$

$$M_m(J, c; S^k; a; \mu_k) = \frac{1}{\mu_k(H_c \cap S^k)} \int_{H_c \cap S^k} (J(u) - a)^m \, d\mu_k, \quad m = 1, 2, \cdots \tag{3.4}$$

为 J 在水平集 $H_c = \{u \mid J(u) \leq c\}$ 上关于测度 μ_k 及约束集 S^k 的均值、方差、修正方差和（中心为 a 的）m 阶矩，在 (A)，(R) 和 (M) 条件下，上述定义有效.

首先讨论均值、方差和高阶矩在变测度方法中的收敛性态. 通常我们考虑

$$c_k \geq c_k^* = \min_{u \in S^k} J(u), \quad c_k \downarrow c \geq \min_{u \in S} J(u) = c^*. \tag{3.5}$$

引理 3.1　设 $c \geq c^*$，$c_k \geq c_k^*$、$c_k \downarrow c$. 如果 $\mu_k \xrightarrow{Q} \mu$，并且

$$\mu_k(S^k) \to \mu(S), \tag{3.6}$$

则

$$\lim_{k \to \infty} \mu_k(H_{c_k} \cap S^k) = \mu(S \cap H_c). \tag{3.7}$$

证明　首先指出，由于 $S^k \subset S$，

$$0 \leq \mu_k(S \cap U_k) - \mu_k(S^k) = (\mu_k(S \cap U_k) - \mu(S)) + (\mu(S) - \mu_k(S^k))$$

故由 $\mu_k \xrightarrow{Q} \mu$ 及条件 (3.6) 可知

$$\mu_k(S \cap U_k) - \mu_k(S^k) \to 0. \tag{3.8}$$

其次证明

$$\lim_{k \to \infty} \mu_k(H_{c_k} \cap S \cap U_k) = \mu(H_c \cap S). \tag{3.9}$$

由于 $H_c \subset H_{c_k}$，及 $\mu_k \xrightarrow{Q} \mu$，

$$\mu_k(H_{c_k} \cap S \cap U_k) \geq \mu_k(H_c \cap S \cap U_k) \to \mu(H_c \cap S),$$

故
$$\liminf_{k\to\infty}\mu_k(H_{c_k}\cap S\cap U_k)\geqslant\mu(H_c\cap S).$$
设 $k\geqslant j$,则 $H_{c_k}\subset H_{c_j}$,所以,对于任意但固定的 $j\leqslant k$,
$$\mu_k(H_{c_k}\cap S\cap U_k)\leqslant\mu_k(H_{c_j}\cap S\cap U_k),$$
$$\limsup_{k\to\infty}\mu_k(H_{c_k}\cap S\cap U_k)\leqslant\lim_{k\to\infty}\mu_k(H_{c_j}\cap S\cap U_k)=\mu(H_{c_j}\cap S).$$
再令 $j\to\infty$,我们得到(由 μ 的连续性)
$$\limsup_{k\to\infty}\mu_k(H_{c_k}\cap S\cap U_k)\leqslant\mu(H_c\cap S).$$
从而证明了(3.9)中极限存在,并等式成立.

最后可得,当 $k\to\infty$ 时
$$|\mu_k(H_{c_k}\cap S^k)-\mu(S\cap H_c)|$$
$$\leqslant|\mu_k(H_{c_k}\cap S^k)-\mu_k(H_{c_k}\cap S\cap U_k)|+|\mu_k(H_{c_k}\cap S\cap U_k)-\mu(H_c\cap S)|\to 0,$$
其中第 1 个式子趋于 0 是由于(3.8)及
$$0\leqslant\mu_k(H_{c_k}\cap S\cap U_k)-\mu(H_{c_k}\cap S^k)=\mu_k(H_{c_k}\cap(S\cap U_k\setminus S^k))$$
$$\leqslant\mu_k(S\setminus S^k)\cap U'_k)\to 0.$$

定理 3.1 设对于极小化问题(1.1)和(1.5)条件(A),(R)和(M)成立.则在引理 3.1 的条件下,下列式子成立:
$$\lim_{k\to\infty}M(J,c_k;S^k;\mu_k)=M(J,c;S;\mu),\tag{3.10}$$
$$\lim_{k\to\infty}V(J,c_k;S^k;\mu_k)=V(J,c;S,\mu),\tag{3.11}$$
$$\lim_{k\to\infty}V_1(J,c_k;S^k;\mu_k)=V_1(J,c;S;\mu),\tag{3.12}$$
$$\lim_{k\to\infty}M_m(J,c_k;S^k;c_k;\mu_k)=M_m(J,c;S;c;\mu),m=1,2,\cdots\tag{3.13}$$

证明 先证当 $c>c^*$ 时(3.10)成立.由于 $\mu(H_c\cap S)>0$ 及引理 3.1,我们可假设 $\mu_k(H_{c_k}\cap S^k)>0$.这时
$$M(J,c_k;S^k;\mu_k)-M(J;c;S;\mu)$$
$$=\frac{1}{\mu_k(H_{c_k}\cap S^k)}\int_{H_{c_k}\cap S^k}J(u)\mathrm{d}\mu_k-\frac{1}{\mu(H_c\cap S)}\int_{H_c\cap S}J(u)\mathrm{d}\mu$$
$$=\left(\frac{1}{\mu_k(H_{c_k}\cap S^k)}-\frac{1}{\mu(H_c\cap S)}\right)\int_{H_{c_k}\cap S^k\cap U_k}J(u)\mathrm{d}\mu_k$$
$$+\frac{1}{\mu(H_c\cap S)}\left(\int_{H_c\cap S^k\cap U_k}J(u)\mathrm{d}\mu_k-\int_{H_c\cap S\cap U_k}J(u)\mathrm{d}\mu_k\right)$$
$$+\frac{1}{\mu(H_c\cap S)}\left(\int_{H_c\cap S\cap U_k}J(u)\mathrm{d}\mu_k-\int_{H_c\cap S}J(\mu)\mathrm{d}\mu\right)=I_1+I_2+I_3.$$
其中
$$|I_1|\leqslant\left|\frac{1}{\mu_k(H_{c_k}\cap S^k)}-\frac{1}{\mu(H_c\cap S)}\right|\cdot A\mu_k(H_{c_k}\cap S^k),$$
$$|J(u)|\leqslant\max(|M|,c_1),\quad\forall u\in S\cap H_{c_k},\quad\mu_k(H_{c_k}\cap S^k)\leqslant\mu_k(U).$$
由引理 3.1 可知,当 $k\to\infty$ 时,$I_1\to 0$.
$$|I_2|\leqslant\frac{1}{\mu(H_c\cap S)}2A|\mu_k(H_c\cap S^k)-\mu_k(H_c\cap S)|$$

$$\leqslant \frac{1}{\mu(H_c \cap S)} 2A|\mu_k(H_{c_k} \cap S^k) - \mu(H_c \cap S)| + |\mu(H_c \cap S) - \mu_k(H_c \cap S \cap U_k)|.$$

由引理 3.1 及 $\mu_k \xrightarrow{Q} \mu$ 可证当 $k \to \infty$ 时，$I_1 \to 0$.

I_3 是当约束集合不变化时的变测度均值的收敛性，利用[1]中的定理即知当 $k \to \infty$ 时 $I_3 \to 0$.

当 $c = c^*$ 时，对于任意的 k，由于在 H_{c_k} 上 $J(u) \leqslant c_k$，故

$$M(J, c_k; S^k; \mu_k) = \frac{1}{\mu_k(H_{c_k} \cap S^k)} \int_{H_{c_k} \cap S^k} J(u) \mathrm{d}\mu_k \leqslant c_k.$$

所以

$$\limsup_{k \to \infty} M(J, c_k; S^k; \mu_k) \leqslant \lim_{k \to \infty} c_k = c = c^*. \tag{3.14}$$

另一方面，

$$M(J, c_k; S^k; \mu_k) \geqslant c_k^* \geqslant c^*,$$

故

$$\liminf_{k \to \infty} M(J, c_k; S^k; \mu_k) \geqslant c^*, \tag{3.15}$$

因此，(3.10)中极限存在，并且

$$\lim_{k \to \infty} M(J, c_k; S^k; \mu_k) = c^* = M(J, c^*; S; \mu). \tag{3.16}$$

最后的等式成立是利用了有约束极小的总极值的均值条件，参见[2]和[7].

下面来证明(3.13)成立. 当 $c > c^*$ 时，其证明类似于均值情况. 当 $c = c^*$，并且 m 为奇数时，证明也类似于均值的证明. 现设 $m = 2r$ 为偶数. 先考虑 $r = 1$ 情形. 由于

$$V_1(J, c_k; S^k; \mu_k) \geqslant 0, \quad k = 1, 2, \cdots$$

故

$$\liminf_{k \to \infty} V_1(J, c_k; S^k; \mu_k) \geqslant 0. \tag{3.17}$$

我们来证明 $\limsup_{k \to \infty} V_1(J, c_k; S^k; \mu_k) = 0$. 假设不成立，则存在一个子序列（我们仍用同样记号）$V_1(J, c_k; S^k; \mu_k) \to 2\eta > 0$. 故存在 N，当 $k \geqslant N$ 时

$$V_1(J, c_k; S^k; \mu_k) > \eta. \tag{3.18}$$

由于 J 在 $H_{c_1} \cap S$ 上有下界，故存在 $g \geqslant 0$，使得

$$J(u) + g \geqslant 0, \forall u \in H_{c_1} \cap S. \tag{3.19}$$

这时

$$V_1(J, c_k; S^k; \mu_k) = \frac{1}{\mu_k(H_{c_k} \cap S^k)} \int_{H_{c_k} \cap S^k} (J(u) - c_k)^2 \mathrm{d}\mu_k$$

$$= \frac{1}{\mu_k(H_{c_k} \cap S^k)} \left[\int_{H_{c_k} \cap S^k} (J(u) + g)^2 \mathrm{d}\mu_k + \int_{H_{c_k} \cap S^k} (g + c_k)^2 \cdot \mathrm{d}\mu_k \right.$$

$$\left. - 2(g + c_k) \int_{H_{c_k} \cap S^k} (J(u) + g) \mathrm{d}\mu_k \right] > \eta$$

由此可得

$$(c_k + g)^2 + (g + c_k)^2 > 2(g + c_k) \cdot (g + c_k^*) + \eta \geqslant 2(g + c_k) \cdot (g + c^*). \tag{3.20}$$

在上式中令 $k \to \infty$ 后得

$$(c^* + g)^2 + (g + c^*)^2 \geqslant 2(g + c^*)(g + c^*) + \eta$$

从而导致矛盾:$0 \geqslant \eta > 0$,因此,当 $c = c^*$ 时,(3.12)中极值存在并等于 0. 但由总极值的方差条件,c^* 为总极值的充要条件为 $V(J, c^*; S, \mu) = 0$. 从而证得,当 $c = c^*$ 时
$$\lim_{k \to \infty} V_1(J, c_k; S^k; \mu_k) = 0 = V_1(J, c^*; S; \mu).$$

当 $m = 2r(r > 1)$ 时,$M_m(J; c_k; S^k; c_k; \mu_k) \geqslant 0$,故
$$\liminf_{k \to \infty} M_m(J; c_k; S^k; c_k; \mu_k) \geqslant 0.$$

另一方面,
$$M_m(J; c_k; S^k; c_k; \mu_k) = \frac{1}{\mu_k(H_{c_k} \cap S^k)} \int_{H_{c_k} \cap S^k} (J(u) - c_k)^{2m} \, \mathrm{d}\mu_k$$
$$\leqslant A^{2(r-1)} \frac{1}{\mu_k(H_{c_k} \cap S^k)} \int_{H_{c_k} \cap S^k} (J(u) - c_k)^2 \, \mathrm{d}\mu_k$$
$$= A^{2(r-1)} V_1(J, c_k; S^k; \mu_k) \to 0, \text{当 } k \to \infty \text{ 时}.$$

其中 $|J(u) - c_k| \leqslant A, \forall u \in H_{c_1} \cap S$. 从而证明了
$$\lim_{k \to \infty} M_m(J, c_k; S^k; c_k; \mu_k) = 0 = M_m(J; c^*; S; c^*; \mu_k).$$
在最后式子中我们用到了总极值的高阶矩充要条件.

上述定理实际上还给出了用变测度描述的总极值的充要条件.

定理 3.2 在定理 3.1 的条件下,$c^*(c_k \downarrow c = c^*)$ 为 J 在 S 上总极小值的充要条件为下列条件之一成立.

1) $\lim\limits_{k \to \infty} M(J, c_k, S^k; \mu_k) = c^*$,
2) $\lim\limits_{k \to \infty} V(J, c_k; S^k; \mu_k) = 0$,
3) $\lim\limits_{k \to \infty} V_1(J, c_k; S^k; \mu_k) = 0$,
4) $\lim\limits_{k \to \infty} M_m(J, c_k; S^k; c_k; \mu_k) = 0, m = 1, 2, \cdots$.

4 变测度方法

在上一节中我们讨论了变测度最优性条件,其中要求(3.6)成立. 在这一节中,我们先给出满足这个要求的条件,利用这个条件,给出变测度算法,并证明它导致收敛于总极值.

定理 4.1 如果 $S^k \subset S \cap U_k, \mu_k \xrightarrow{Q} \mu$ 如果
$$\mu_k(S^k) \geqslant \mu(S), k = 1, 2, \cdots \tag{4.1}$$
则 $\mu_k(S^k) \to \mu(S)$.

证明 由(4.1)可知
$$\liminf_{k \to \infty} \mu_k(S^k) \geqslant \mu(S). \tag{4.2}$$
另一方面,因为 $S^k \subset S \cap U_k$
$$\mu_k(S^k) \leqslant \mu_k(S \cap U_k) \quad k = 1, 2, \cdots$$
由 $\mu_k \xrightarrow{Q} \mu$ 推出
$$\limsup_{k \to \infty} \mu_k(S^k) \leqslant \limsup_{k \to \infty} \mu_k(S \cap U_k) = \lim_{k \to \infty} \mu_k(S \cap U_k) = \mu(S) \tag{4.3}$$
合并(4.1)和(4.3)即证得

$$\lim_{k\to\infty}\mu_k(S_k)=\mu(S).$$

注 初看条件(4.1)似乎难以实现,因为 $S^k\subset S\cap U_k$,但在实际构造中是常常这样做的,条件(4.1)提供一个构造满足收敛条件的途径. 见第 5 节中的例子.

下面给出变测度算法. 取 $S^1\subset S$,S^1 在所在的子空间上丰满(例如可取 S 在一维子空间上的投影),取 $c_1>\min\limits_{u\in S^1}J(u)$. 构造 Q-测度 μ_1 满足(4.1),这时 $\mu_1(H_{c_1}\cap S^1)>0$. 令

$$c_2=M(J,c_1;S^1;\mu_1).$$

取 S^2,使得 $S^1\subset S^2\subset S$,S^2 在所在子空间上丰满. 构造 Q-测度使得(4.1)成立. 要使这过程继续下去,我们还要证明.

引理 4.1 $\mu_2(H_{c_2}\cap S^2)>0.$

证明 若 $c_2=c_1$,则 $\mu_2(H_{c_2}\cap S^2)>0$,若不然,c_2 是 J 在 S^2 上的总极值,但

$$c_1>\min_{u\in S^1}J(u)\geqslant\min_{u\in S^2}J(u)=c_2,$$

从而导致矛盾.

现设 $c_2<c_1$. 如果 $\mu_2(H_{c_2}\cap S^2)=0$,则 c_2 是 J 在 S^2 上的总极值,

$$J(u)\geqslant c_2,\forall u\in S^2$$

由于 $S^1\subset S^2$,故

$$J(u)\geqslant c_2,\forall u\in S^1. \tag{4.4}$$

因为 $\mu_1(H_{c_1}\cap S^1)>0$,故存在 $\varepsilon>0$,使得 $0<\varepsilon<c_2-c_1$,并且

$$\mu_1(G_\varepsilon\cap S^1)>0,$$

其中

$$G_\varepsilon=\{u\,|\,c_2+\varepsilon<J(u)\leqslant c_1\}. \tag{4.5}$$

这时,

$$\begin{aligned}c_2&=M(J,c_1;S^1;\mu_1)=\frac{1}{\mu_1(H_{c_1}\cap S^1)}\int_{H_{c_1}\cap S^1}J(u)\mathrm{d}\mu_1\\&=\frac{1}{\mu_1(H_{c_1}\cap S^1)}\left(\int_{H_{c_1}\cap S^1/G_\varepsilon\cap S^1}J(u)\mathrm{d}\mu_1+\int_{G_\varepsilon\cap S^1}J(u)\mathrm{d}\mu_1\right)\\&\geqslant\frac{c_2}{\mu_1(H_{c_1}\cap S^1)}(\mu_1(H_{c_1}\cap S^1)-\mu_1(G_\varepsilon\cap S^1))+(c_2+\varepsilon)\frac{\mu_1(G_\varepsilon\cap S^1)}{\mu_1(H_{c_1}\cap S^1)}\\&=c_2+\varepsilon\frac{\mu_1(G_\varepsilon\cap S^1)}{\mu_1(H_{c_1}\cap S^1)}>c_2,\end{aligned}$$

也导致矛盾.

用 c_2 代替 c_1,则我们可以构造 S^3 和 μ_3,使得 $\mu_3(H_{c_3}\cap S^3)>0$,等等. 故对于任意 k,由 c_k 构造 S^k 和 μ_k,使得

$$S^{k-1}\subset S^k\subset S. \tag{4.6}$$

并构造 Q-测度 μ_k,使得

$$\mu_k(S^k)\geqslant\mu(S). \tag{4.7}$$

令

$$c_{k+1}=M(J,c_k;S^k;\mu_k). \tag{4.8}$$

用此算法,我们得到一个单调递降序列

$$c_1 \geqslant c_2 \geqslant \cdots \geqslant c_k \geqslant c_{k+1} \geqslant \cdots \tag{4.9}$$

及集合序列 $H_{c_k} \cap S^k = \{u \in S^k | J(u) \leqslant c_k\}$.

注 由于 $\mu_k(H_{c_k} \cap S^k) > 0, k = 1, 2, \cdots$ 可知

$$c_k > c_k^* = \min_{u \in S^k} J(u).$$

定理 4.2 $\lim\limits_{k \to \infty} c_k = c^* \min\limits_{u \in S} J(u).$ (4.10)

$$\emptyset \neq \bigcap_{n=1}^{\infty} \mathrm{cl} \bigcup_{k=n}^{\infty} (H_{c_k} \cap S^k) \subset H^*.$$

证明 由算法构造可知,$c_k \geqslant c_k^* \geqslant c^*$,并且 $\{c_k\}$ 为递降数列,故极限

$$\lim_{k \to \infty} c_k = \hat{c} \geqslant c^*$$

存在. 在(4.8)中令 $k \to \infty$ 得

$$\hat{c} = \lim_{k \to \infty} c_{k+1} = \lim_{k \to \infty} M(J, c_k; S^k; \mu_k) = M(J, \hat{c}; S; \mu).$$

由定理 3.2 可知 $\hat{c}$ 是 J 在 S 上的总极值,即 $\hat{c} = c^*$.

因为 $H_{c_k} \cap S^k \subset S$,故 $\bigcup\limits_{k=n}^{\infty} (H_{c_k} \cap S^k) \subset S$,又因 S 假设为闭,故 $\mathrm{cl} \bigcup\limits_{k=n}^{\infty} (H_{c_k} \cap S^k) \subset S$,从而

$$\bigcap_{n=1}^{\infty} \mathrm{cl} \bigcup_{k=n}^{\infty} (H_{c_k} \cap S^k) \subset S.$$

此外,设 $u \bigcap\limits_{n=1}^{\infty} \mathrm{cl} \bigcup\limits_{k=n}^{\infty} (H_{c_k} \cap S^k)$,它为 $H_{c_k} \cap S^k$ 中元素构成的收敛子序列 $\{u_{k_i}\}$ 的极限 $\lim\limits_{n \to +\infty} u_{k_i} = u$. 但是,$J(u_{k_i}) \leqslant c_{k_i}$,由 J 的下半连续性可知.

$$J(u) \leqslant \lim c_{k_i} = c^*,$$

即 $u \in H^*$,最后,由于我们假设 $H_{c_k} \cap S^k$ 为非空紧集,故

$$\bigcup_{k=n}^{\infty} (H_{c_k} \cap S^k) \neq \emptyset,$$

从而证明了

$$\bigcap_{n=1}^{\infty} \mathrm{cl} \bigcup_{k=n}^{\infty} (H_{c_k} \cap S^k) \neq \emptyset.$$

注 自然要问,H^* 是否等于

$$\bigcap_{n=1}^{\infty} \mathrm{cl} \bigcup_{k=n}^{\infty} (H_{c_k} \cap S^k),$$

即 H^* 中任一元素是集合 $H_{c_k} \cap S^k$ 中元素组成的收敛子序列的极限. 这个问题还有待证明.

推论 4.1 令 $c_k^* = \min\limits_{u \in S^k} J(u)$ 及 $H_k^* = \{u \in S^k | J(u) = c_k^*\}$,则

$$\lim_{k \to \infty} c_k^* = c^*,$$

$$\emptyset \neq \bigcap_{n=1}^{\infty} \mathrm{cl} \left(\bigcup_{k=n}^{\infty} H_k^* \right) \subset H^*$$

注 在推论 4.1 中 c_k^* 和 H_k^* 与测度 μ_k 的取法无关(只要存在这样变测度序列即可). 在应用中,常取一个固定的 k,求出 c_k^* 及 H_k^* 作为 c^* 及 H^* 的逼近.

5 例子

在前面的讨论中,我们要求 $\{S^k\}$ 和 $\{\mu_k\}$ 满足某些条件,并假设它们存在. 到目前为止,我们还没能证明对于任何给定的约束子集 S(或满足某种条件的 S)都可以构造出 $\{S^k\}$ 和

$\{\mu_k\}$. 下面给出两个例子：一个是在最优控制中的，一个应用于微分对策中，对它们的约束子集分别构造$\{S^k\}$和$\{\mu^k\}$。

例 5.1 设 $U=l^2, S=\{u\in l^2\mid \|u\|\leqslant M\}$，其中 M 是给定的常数。在最优控制中表示控制 u 的能量有界。

令
$$S^k=\{u\in S\mid u=(a_1,\cdots,a_k,0,\cdots)\}, \tag{5.1}$$

即 S^k 包含的 S 中的元素，它的 $k+1, k+2,\cdots$ 分量全为 0，显然
$$S^k\subset S^{k+1}\subset S, k=1,2,\cdots \tag{5.2}$$

令 μ 为 l^2 上的非退化 Guass 测度[9]，它是一个 Q-测度。设 D 为 l^2 中的一个可测子集。令
$$\hat{D}^k=\{u\in l^2\mid u=(a_1,\cdots,a_k,b_{k+1},\cdots), \text{其中}(a_1,\cdots,a_k,a_{k+1},\cdots)\in D\}, \tag{5.3}$$

即 $\hat{D}^k$ 和 D 在 $\mathbb{R}^k$ 上的投影相同。$\hat{D}^k$ 显然是 l^2 中的可测集（根据 μ 的构造要求）。现在我们定义 $\mu_k(D)$ 为
$$\mu_k(D)=\mu(\hat{D}^k). \tag{5.4}$$

我们指出，由构造可得
$$S\subset \hat{S}^k. \tag{5.5}$$

实际上，设 $u=(a_1,\cdots,a_k,a_{k+1},\cdots)\in S$。$\|u\|\leqslant M$，即 $\sum_{i=1}^{\infty}a_i^2\leqslant M^2$，从而可知 $\sum_{i=1}^{k}a_i^2\leqslant M^2$，即
$$(a_1\cdots,a_k,0,\cdots)\in \hat{S}^k,$$

从而推出 $u\in\{u\in l^2\mid(a_1,\cdots,a_k,b_{k+1},\cdots)\}=S^k$。于是
$$\mu_k(S^k)=\mu(\hat{S}^k)\geqslant\mu(S). \tag{5.6}$$

最后还要证明测度序列 $\{\mu_k\}$ Q-收敛于 μ，设 F 是 l^2 中的任一闭集，则
$$F\subset \hat{F}^k, k=1,2,\cdots \quad F\subset\bigcap_{k=1}^{\infty}\hat{F}^k. \tag{5.7}$$

假设存在 $u\in\bigcap_{k=1}^{\infty}\hat{F}^k, u=(a_1,\cdots,a_k,\cdots), u\notin F$，则至少存在一个足标 k_0，使得 $(a_1\cdots,a_{k_0-1},a_{k_0},\cdots)\notin F$。不管 $a_{k_0+1},\cdots$ 取什么值，这就导致 $u\notin\hat{F}^{k_0}$。因此
$$F=\lim_{k\to\infty}\hat{F}^k=\bigcap_{k=1}^{\infty}\hat{F}^k.$$

由测度 μ 的连续性可知，
$$\mu_k(F)=\mu(\hat{F}^k)\to\mu(F), \quad k\to\infty \tag{5.8}$$

即 $\{\mu_k\}$ Q-收敛于 μ。

例 5.2 给定 $\{b_k\}$ 满足条件 $b_k>0, k=1,2,\cdots, \sum_{k=1}^{\infty}b_k=M$。例如，可取
$$b_k=\frac{1}{2^k}k=1,2,\cdots,$$

即满足上述要求。令
$$S=\{\{a_k\}\mid |a_k|\leqslant b_k, \quad k=1,2,\cdots\}, \tag{5.9}$$

它是 Fréchet 空间 $U=\prod_{k=1}^{\infty}\mathbb{R}_k$ 中的一个凸紧集（Keller 空间），由于它的内点非空，故 S 是

个丰满集. 令

$$\rho_k(t) = \begin{cases} \dfrac{1}{2b_k}, & -b_k \leqslant t \leqslant b_k, \\ 0, & \text{其他}. \end{cases} \quad (5.10)$$

设 B^n 是 $\mathbb{R}^n$ 中的 Borel 可测集, B_n 为以 B^n 为底的柱形集, 令 Ω 为这些柱形集产生的最小 σ-域, 则我们有一个可测空间 (U, Ω). 令

$$\mu_n(B^n) = \int_{B^n} \rho_1(t_1) \cdots \rho_n(t_n) \mathrm{d}t_1 \cdots \mathrm{d}t_n \quad (5.11)$$

则我们得到一组协调测度. 由 Kolmogorov 测度扩张定理[8], 得到一个测度 μ, 它是 S 上的 Q-测度.

设 D 为 U 中的任一可测子集, 令

$$\hat{D}^k = \{u = (a_1, \cdots, a_k, b_k, \cdots) \mid \text{其中}(a_1 \cdots, a_k, a_{k+1}, \cdots) \in D\}, \quad (5.12)$$

即 $\hat{D}^k$ 是以 D 在 $\prod_{i=1}^{k} \mathbb{R}_i$ 上的投影为底的柱形集, 令

$$\mu_k(D) = \mu(\hat{D}^k). \quad (5.13)$$

令

$$S^k = \{u \in S \mid u = (a_1, a_2, \cdots, a_k, 0, \cdots)\}. \quad (5.14)$$

$S^k \subset S^{k+1} \subset S$, 并且是 $\prod_{i=1}^{k} \mathbb{R}_i = \mathbb{R}^k$ 上的丰满集, 显然, 由定义.

$$S \subset \hat{S}^k,$$

并且,

$$\mu(S) = \mu(\hat{S}^k) = \mu_k(S^k). \quad (5.15)$$

我们可用与例 5.1 类似的方法证明 $\mu_k \xrightarrow{Q} \mu$, 从而得到满足第 4 节中所要求的 $\{S^k\}$ 和 $\{\mu_k\}$.

参考文献

[1] 郑权. 积分型求总极值的变测度算法[J]. 高校应用数学学报, 1988, 2, 281—288.

[2] Zheng Quan. Optimality Conditions for Global Optimization (Ⅰ)[J]. Acta Mathematicae Applicatae Sinica, 1985, 2, 63—78.

[3] Zheng Quan. Optimality Conditions for Global Optimization(Ⅱ)[J]. Acta Mathematicae Applicatae Sinica, 1985, 3, 118—134.

[4] E. Galperin, Q. Zheng. Integral Global Optimization Method for Differential Games with Application to Pursuit-Evasion Games [J]. International Journal, Computer Mathematics with Applications, Vol. 1, No. 1—3, 1989, 209—243.

[5] E. Galperin, Q. Zheng. Variation-Free Iterative Method for Global Optimal Control [J]. International Journal of Control, 1989, Vol. 50, No. 5, 1989, 1731—1743.

[6] Zheng Quan. Robust Analysis and Global Minimization of a Class of Discontinuous Functions (Ⅰ) [J]. Acta Mathematicae Applicatae Sinica, 1990.

[7] Zheng Quan. Robust Analysis and Global Minimization of a Class of Discontinuous Functions (Ⅱ) [J]. Acta Mathematicae Applicatae Sinica, 1990.

[8] Ash, R. B. Real Analysis and Probability [M]. Academic Press, New York, 1972.

[9] N. N. Vakhania, Probability Distributions on Linear Spaces [M]. North Holland, New York, 1981.

关于丰满极小点存在性的注记[*]

1 总极小点的存在性

设 X 为拓扑空间,S 为 X 的子集,$f:X\to\mathbb{R}^1$ 为实值函数.考虑极小化问题:求 f 在 S 上的总极小值

$$c^* = \min_{x\in S} f(x)$$

及总极小点集

$$H^* = \{x\in S: f(x)=c^*\}.$$

如果函数 f 有下界,则 f 在 S 上有下确界 c^*,但其总极小点集 H^* 也可能是空的.本文考虑当 $S=X$ 时总极小点集非空性条件.

如果

$$f \text{ 为下半连续和下紧的,} \tag{1.1}$$

则总极小点集 H^* 非空.条件(1.1)中下紧的意思为:存在一个实数 c,使得水平集 $H_c=\{x:f(x)\leqslant c\}$ 为非空紧集.条件(1.1)中对函数 f 下半连续的要求并不过分,但下紧的条件还是比较强的.

如果

$$X \text{ 为有限维 Banach 空间,} f \text{ 为下半连续及强制的,} \tag{1.2}$$

则 H^* 非空.在条件(1.2)中强制的意思为:$\lim\limits_{\|x\|\to\infty} f(x)=+\infty$.这里空间为有限维的条件起很关键的作用.

当空间为无限维时,如果

$$X \text{ 为自反 Banach 空间,} f \text{ 为弱下半连续及强制的,} \tag{1.3}$$

则 $H^*\neq\varnothing$.

条件(1.2)或(1.3)对有界函数不适用.另一类是近似极小点的存在性定理[2]:

$$(X,d) \text{ 为完备度量空间,} f \text{ 有下界及下半连续,} \tag{1.4}$$

则对于任意的 $\varepsilon>0$,存在 $x_e\in X$,使得对于所有的 $x\in X$,

$$f(x_e)<c^*+\varepsilon, \text{ 及 } f(x)\geqslant f(x_e)-\varepsilon d(x_e,x). \tag{1.5}$$

还有一种极小点存在定理[3],它把紧条件加到函数自身上,有较大的优越性.

$$X \text{ 为 Banach 空间,} f\in C^1, \text{并满足 Palais-Smale 条件,} \tag{1.6}$$

则存在 $x^*\in X$ 使得

---

[*] 本文合作者:史树中,庄德铭.原文发表于《运筹学杂志》,1994,13(1):77—80.

$$f(x^*)=c^*, \text{并且} df(x^*)=\theta, \tag{1.7}$$

其中 Palais-Smale 条件是指:对于任意的 $\{x_n\}\subset X$,

$$\text{由 } f(x_n) \text{有界及} df(x_n)\to\theta \text{推出}\{x_n\}\text{有收敛的子序列}. \tag{1.8}$$

2 丰满极小点

除了条件(1.6)外,(1.1)~(1.4)中之一只保证了 H^* 非空. 但 H^* 的非空性不能保证极小点的可逼近性[4],也就无法把它们求出来. 这里可逼近性的意思是:f 的连续点集 C 在 X 中稠密,对于任意 $x_0\in X$ 存在序列 $\{x_a\}\subset C$ 使得

$$x_a\to x_0 \text{ 并且 } f(x_a)\to(x_0). \tag{2.1}$$

例如,设 $X=\mathbb{R}^1$,

$$f(x)=\begin{cases} x^2, & x\neq 0, \\ -1, & x=1. \end{cases}$$

条件(1.1)~(1.4)都满足,但其极小点 $x^*=0$ 是不可逼近的.

丰满函数一定是可以逼近的;反之,如果 X 是完备距离空间,则可逼近函数也是丰满的. 拓扑空间 X 中集合 D 是丰满集,若

$$\text{cl int}D=\text{cl}D, \tag{2.2}$$

其中 int$D$ 表示 D 的内点集,cl$D$ 表示 D 的闭包. 一点 $x_0\in D$ 是 D 的丰满点,若 $x_0\in$ cl int$D$. 集合 D 为丰满集的充分必要条件为 D 中每一点都是 D 的丰满点. 函数 $f:X\to\mathbb{R}^1$ 称为在 $x_0\in X$ 处丰满,如果对于任意 $\varepsilon>0$ 及 $y_0=f(x_0)$ 的邻域 $U(y_0)=(y_0-\varepsilon,y_0+\varepsilon)$,点 x_0 是 $f^{-1}(U(y_0))$ 的丰满点. 若 f 在 X 中的每一点处丰满,则 f 在 X 上丰满,或对于任意的开集 $G\subset X$,$f^{-1}(G)$ 为丰满集. 在上例中的函数 f 在 $x_0=0$ 处不丰满. 关于丰满集和丰满函数的讨论可参见文献[7—8].

定义 2.1 点 $x^*\in X$ 称为 f 的丰满极小点,若

$$f \text{ 在 } x^* \text{处丰满,并且} f(x)\geqslant f(x^*), \forall x\in X. \tag{2.3}$$

因此,把丰满性的要求添加到极小点的存在性条件上,就成为丰满极小点存在性的条件.

命题 2.1 设 X 为拓扑空间,$f:X\to\mathbb{R}^1$ 为下半连续丰满函数及下紧,则存在丰满总极小点.

命题 2.2 设 X 为有限维 Banach 空间,f 为下半连续丰满函数,并满足强制条件,则存在丰满总极小点.

命题 2.3 设 X 为自反 Banach 空间,f 为丰满弱下半连续函数,并满足强制条件,则存在丰满总极小点.

命题 2.4 设 (X,d) 为完备度量空间,f 为有下界的下半连续丰满函数,则对于任意 $\varepsilon>0$,存在 $x_\varepsilon\in X$,使得对于任意 $x\in X$,

$$f(x_\varepsilon)<c^*+\varepsilon, \text{及} f(x)\geqslant f(x_\varepsilon)-\varepsilon d(x_\varepsilon,x),$$

并且 x_ε 是 f 的丰满近似极小点.

3 一个丰满极小点的存在定理

Palais-Smale 条件(1.6)确保了丰满极小点的存在性,然而,附加在 f 上的解析条件太

强,不能处理一般的连续函数,更不能处理不连续的目标函数极小点的存在性.下面,我们把它修改为适合丰满分析框架的条件.

定理 3.1 设 X 为距离空间,f 为有下界的下半连续丰满函数,C 为 f 的连续点集. 若对于任一序列 $\{x_n\}\subset C$,

$$\text{由 } V_1(f,f(x_n))\to 0 \text{ 推出 } \{x_n\} \text{ 有收敛子列} \tag{3.1}$$

则存在丰满总极小点 x^* 使得

$$x_n\to x^* \text{ 并且 } f(x_n)\to f(x^*)=\min_{x\in X}f(x). \tag{3.2}$$

注 这里,我们用到了修正方差 $V_1(f,c)$ 的概念. 当 $c>c^*=\inf\limits_{x\in X}f(x)$ 时,它定义为

$$V_1(f,c)=\frac{1}{\mu(H_c)}\int_{H_c}(f(x)-c)^2 d\mu, \tag{3.3}$$

其中 $H_c=\{x:f(x)\leqslant c\}$ 为水平集,μ 为 X 上的 Q-测度. 当 $c=c^*$ 时,可以用极限过程

$$V_1(f,c)=\lim_{c_n\downarrow c}V_1(f,c_n)$$

来延伸其定义. 点 $x^*\in X$ 为 f 的总极小点,$c^*=f(x^*)$ 为总小极值的充分必要条件为

$$V_1(f,c^*)=0. \tag{3.4}$$

关于修正方差的讨论可参见文献[7—8].

定理 3.1 的证明 设 $c^*=\inf\limits_{x\in X}f(x)$ 为下界,则对于任意 n,存在 y_n,使得

$$f(y_n)<c^*+\frac{1}{2n}.$$

又由于 f 的丰满性,存在 $x_n\in C$(C 为 f 的连续点集),使得

$$f(x_n)<f(y_n)+\frac{1}{2n}<c^*+\frac{1}{n}. \tag{3.5}$$

此外,我们还不妨假设 $\{f(x_n)\}$ 是递减的. 于是我们取到了点列 $\{x_n\}\subset C$,使得

$$f(x_n)\downarrow c^*=\inf_{x\in X}f(x). \tag{3.6}$$

由总极值的充要条件可知

$$V_1(f,f(x_n))\to 0. \tag{3.7}$$

从而由(3.1)推出存在收敛子序列,不妨仍记为 $\{x_n\}$,即存在 $x^*\in X$,使得 $x_n\to x^*$. 下面我们来证明 x^* 就是丰满总极小点. 首先,由于 c^* 是总极小值,故

$$f(x^*)\geqslant c^*.$$

又由于 f 的下半连续性,对于任意 $\varepsilon>0$,存在一个 x^* 的领域 $U(x^*)$ 使得

$$f(x)>f(x^*)-\varepsilon, \forall x\in U(x^*).$$

因 $x_n\to x^*$,故存在正整数 N,当 $n>N$ 时,

$$f(x_n)>f(x^*)-\varepsilon.$$

在上式中令 $n\to\infty$,由(3.6)得知

$$c^*\geqslant f(x^*)-\varepsilon.$$

再由 ε 的任意性可知 $f(x^*)\leqslant c^*$. 从而推出

$$f(x^*)=c^*=\min_{x\in X}f(x).$$

此外,由假设 f 在 x^* 处丰满,x^* 也是 f 的丰满极小点.

条件(3.1)比 Palais-Smale 条件弱. 如果 $f\in C^1$,并满足 $f(x_n)$ 有界及 $df(x_n)\to 0$ 的点

列 $\{x_n\}$,不一定导致 $V_1(f,f(x_n))\to 0$. 所以,Palais-Smale 条件要求更多的点列有收敛子序列. 定理的结论当 $f\in C^1$ 时是与(1.7)一致的,因为 $V_1(f,c^*)=0$ 是充要条件,当 $f\in C^1$ 及 X 为 Banach 空间时可推出必要条件 $\mathrm{d}f(x^*)=0$. 当然,此定理最大的优越性还在于对目标函数 f 的要求,它可以是不连续函数. 关于这种定理的进一步推广和应用,将在文[6]中讨论.

参考文献

[1] J. Aubin and I. Ekeland. *Applied Nonlinear Analysis* [M]. Wiley-Interscience, New York, 1983.

[2] I. Ekeland. *Non-convex minimization problems* [J]. Bull. Amer. Math. Soc. (N. S.), 1(1979), 443—473.

[3] R. S. Palais and S. Smale. *A generalized Morse theory* [J]. Bull. Amer. Math. Soc., 70(1964), 165—171.

[4] S. Shi, Q. Zheng and D. Zhuang. *Discontinuous robust mappings are approximatable*. preprint.

[5] S. Shi, Q. Zheng and D. Zhuang. *Set-valued mappings and approximatable mappings* [J]. J. Math. Aual. & Appl., 183(1994), 706—726.

[6] S. Shi, Q. Zheng and D. Zhuang. *Existence of robust minimizers*. preprint.

[7] Q. Zheng. *Robust analysis and global minimization of a class of discontinuous functions* (I) [J]. Acta Mathematicae Applicatae Sinica (English Series), 6:3(1990), 215—223.

[8] Q. Zheng. *Robust analysis and global minimization of a class of discontinuous functions* (II) [J]. Acta Mathematicae Applicatae Sinica (English Series) 6:4(1990), 317—337.

Discontinuous Robust Mappings are Approximatable*

Abstract: The concepts of robustness of sets and functions were introduced to from the foundation of the theory of integral global optimization. A ste A of a topological space X is said to be robust iff cl A=cl int A. A mapping $f: X \to Y$ is said to be robust iff for each open set U_Y of Y, $f^{-1}(U_Y)$ is robust. We prove that if X is a Baire space and Y satisfies the second axiom of countability, then a mapping $f: X \to Y$ is robust iff it is approximatable in the sense that the set of points of continuity of f is dense in X and that for any other point $x \in X$, $(x, f(x))$ is the limit of $\{(x_a, f(x_a))\}$, where for all a, x_a is a continuous point of f. This result justifies the notion of robusteness.

1 Introduction

The concepts of robustness of sets and functions were proposed in [10]–[12] for establishing the theory of integral global optimization and for weakening the requirement of continuity of the objective function in the global optimization problems. Until now, the importance of this concept has not been sufficiently addressed and affirmed. This paper will show that the nature of a discontinuous robust mapping is its "approximatability", which is the essence of numerical analysis.

The main goals of numerical analysis are to provide effective approximation procedures for solving equations, which may be algebraic, differential or those deduced from optimization, calculus of variations, optimal control and so on. A general problem of solving equations may be formulated as follows:

$$\text{to find } \bar{x} \in X \text{ such that } f(\bar{x}) = \bar{y}, \qquad (1.1)$$

where X and Y are two sets, $f: X \to Y$ is a map and $\bar{y} \in Y$ is given. An effective approximation procedure or an algorithm for solving this equation is a rule of constructing a sequence $\{x_k\}$ such that $\{x_k\} \to \bar{x}$ and $y_k = f(x_k) \to \bar{y}$. Therefore, X and Y should be two topological spaces in order that the two limits are well defined; and usually f is assumed to be continuous at $x = \bar{x}$. Surely if $f(\bar{x})$ is not assumed to be related in any way to the valuse of f near $\bar{x}$, it is impossible to propose an algorithm to produce an approximate solution to the equation (1.1). For example, suppose that $X = Y = \mathbb{R}$, $\bar{y} = 0$ and

---

* In collaboration with Shi S. Z., Zhang D. M. Repainted from Transaotionsof the American Iuathematical Socieoy, 1995, 347(12):4943—4957.

$$f(x) = \begin{cases} 1, & \text{if } x \neq 0, \\ 0, & \text{if } x=0. \end{cases} \qquad (1.2)$$

Then the solution $\bar{x}=0$ cannot be approximated by using the value of f near $\bar{x}$.

However, many problems from both theory and applications do require solving an equation of a discontinuous mapping. Examples include the likelihood functions and the expected utility functions when the probability distributions possess discontinuities. For such examples one often attempts to reduce the problem to one of continuous mappings. For instance, there exist several works ([1],[5],[9]), in which minimization problems of discontinuous functions are treated by combining smoothing techniques with conventional optimization methods. But these methods are complicated.

In our opinion, the continuity of f is not indispensable for designing an algorithm to solve the equation (1.1). A more reasonable concept for numerical analysis should be the approximation. In fact, many discontinuous mappings are "approximatable". We consider the following examples:

Example 1.1 $X=Y=\mathbb{R}, \bar{y}=0$ and

$$f(x) = \begin{cases} 1, & \text{if } x<0, \\ x, & \text{if } x \geq 0. \end{cases} \qquad (1.3)$$

Example 1.2 $X=Y=\mathbb{R}, \bar{y}=0$ and

$$f(x) = \begin{cases} 1, & \text{if } \sin(1/x)<0, \\ \sin(1/x), & \text{if } \sin(1/x) \geq 0, \\ 0, & \text{if } x=0. \end{cases} \qquad (1.4)$$

In Example 1.1, f is only right-continuous at $\bar{x}=0$; in Example 1.2, f is not even one-sidedly continuous at $\bar{x}=0$. Nevertheless, for these two functions, the approximation to $\bar{x}$ is possible, because there always exists a sequence $\{x_k\}$ of points of continuity of f such that.

$$\lim_{k \to \infty} x_k = \bar{x} \quad \text{and} \quad \lim_{k \to \infty} f(x_k) = f(\bar{x})$$

and it is possible to approximate points of continuity of f.

It is natural to define an approximatable mapping $f: X \to Y$ by the approximatability of all the points $(x, f(x))$ in the graph of f. The first aim of this paper is to prove that any approximatable mapping is robust, and that under some mild hypotheses, the converse is also valid. This amounts to saying that in a suitable setting the concept of robust mappings is actually equivalent to that of approximatable mappings. This affirmation greatly justifies the notion of robustness.

The outline of the paper is as follows. We first give the definitions of robust mappings and of approximatable mappings (Section 2). In Section 3, we prove our main theorem: a robust mapping is approximatable under the conditions that X is a Baire space and Y satisfies the second axiom of countability. In Section 4, we suppose that X is a complelte metric space and Y is a real separable Banach space and show that all bounded robust (approximatable) mappings from X to Y can be divided into many "Banach spaces of bounded robust (approximatable) mappings", the intersection of which is the Banach space of bounded continuous mappings. In Section 5, we discuss the rpbust functions, which were stated by Zheng [10]−[13] and Zheng-Zhuang [15], but only for the upper topology on $\mathbb{R}$. Our main theorem implies that a robust function for the natural topology on $\mathbb{R}$. is just an approximatable function. However, we can also prove that any "upper robust function" (i. e. robust function in the sense of [10]−[13]) has the dense set of points of continuity. Section 6 contains some concluding remarks.

2   Robust Mappings and Approximatable Mappings

The concept of robust sets was proposed in [10]−[12]. We recall the definition.

Definition 2.1   Let X be a topological space and A be a subset of X. A is said to be *robust* iff
$$\text{cl } A = \text{cl int } A, \tag{2.1}$$
where cl A is the closure of A and int A is the interior of A. A point $x \in A$ is said to be a *robust point* of A iff $x \in \text{cl int } A$. If x is a robust point of A, then A is said to be a *semi-neighbourhood* of x.

The concepts of robust sets, robust points and semi-neighbourhoods are extensions of those of open sets, interior points and neighbourhoods, repectively. Any open set of X, including the empty set, is robust. Any interior point of A is a robust point of A. Any neighbourhood of x is a semi-neighbourhood of x. A set $A \subset X$ is robust iff all its points are robust points of A or A is a semi-neighbourhood of all its points. If A is a semi-neighbourhood of x and $A \subset B$, then B is also a semi-neighbourhood of x.

Any union of robust sets is robust, but the intersection of two robust sets may not be robust unless one of them is open. Similarly, and union of semineighbourhoods of x is also a semi-neighbourhood of A, but the intersection of two semi-neighbourhoods of x may not be a semi-neighbourhood of x unless one of them is a neighbourhood of x.

Recall that a set $A \subset X$ is *nowhere dense* iff int cl $A = \varnothing$. Then we have

Proposition 2.1   *Any robust set or its complement can be represented by the union of an open set and a nowhere dense set.*

Proof. From the definition (2.1), for a robust set A, int A and A have the same boundary: $\partial A = \partial \text{int } A$, which is nowhere dense. Obviously, A is the union of int A and a set $F \subset \partial A$. The complement of A is the union of the complement of cl A and $\partial A/F$. □

Remark 2.1   Recall ([6],[7]) that a closed (respectively, open) set $A \subset X$ is said to be *regular* iff $A = \text{cl int } A$ (respectively, $A = \text{int cl } A$). The complement of a regular closed set is a regular open set and vice versa. By Definition 2.1, $A \subset X$ is robust iff its closure is regular or the interior of its complement is regular.

A set $A \subset X$ is said to be *of the first category* iff it is the union of a countable family of nowhere dense sets. A set $A \subset X$ is said to be a G_δ set iff it is the intersection of a countable family of open sets. A set $A \subset X$ is said to be an F_σ set iff it is the union of a countable family of closed sets. A set $A \subset X$ has the *Baire property* iff it can be represented as a G_δ set plus (or an F_σ set minus) a set of the first category. By Proposition 2.1, any robust set and its complement have the Baire property.

Definition 2.2 Let X and Y be two topological spaces and $f: X \rightarrow Y$ be a mapping. f is said to be *robust at* $x \in X$ iff for any neighbourhood $U_Y(y)$ of $y = f(x)$, $f^{-1}(U_Y(y))$ is a semi-neighbourhood of x or x is a robust point of $f^{-1}(U_Y(y))$. f is said to be *robust* iff f is robust at every $x \in X$ or for any open set U_Y of Y, $f^{-1}(U_Y)$ is robust in X.

The concept of robustness for a mapping is an extension of that of continuity. Any continuous mapping is robust, but a robust mapping may be discontinuous (see Example 1.1—1.2).

Remark 2.2 Recall ([6],[7]) that a mapping $f: X \rightarrow Y$ has the *Baire property* iff for any open set U_Y of Y, $f^{-1}(U_Y)$ has the Baire property. By Definition 2.2, any robust mapping has the Baire property. □

The following proposition shows that the uniform convergence preserves the robustness of mappings.

Proposition 2.2 *Let X be a topological space, $Y = (Y, D)$ be a metric space and $f_\delta: X \rightarrow Y$, $\delta \in \Delta$ be a net of mappings. Suppose that all f_δ are robust at $\bar{x} \in X$ and a mapping $f: X \rightarrow Y$ satisfies*

$$\lim_\delta \sup_{x \in X} d(f_\delta(x), f(x)) = 0. \quad (2.2)$$

Then f is also robust at $\bar{x}$.

Proof. We have to prove that for $\bar{x} \in X$ and for any ε-neighbourhood of $\bar{y} = f(\bar{x})$

$$U_\varepsilon(\bar{y}) = \{y \in Y \mid d(y, \bar{y}) < \varepsilon\} \quad (\varepsilon > 0),$$

$f^{-1}(U_\varepsilon(\bar{y}))$ is a semi-neighbourhood of $\bar{x}$. It suffices to show that there exists a semi-neighborhood $V(\bar{x})$ of $\bar{x}$ such that

$$\forall x \in V(\bar{x}), \ d(f(x), f(\bar{x})) < \varepsilon \quad (2.3)$$

From (2.2), using standard $\varepsilon/3$ argument, we can easily verify that (2.3) holds. □

Now we propose the definition of an approximatable mapping.

Definition 2.3 Let X and Y be two topological spaces and $f: X \rightarrow Y$ be a mapping. Suppose that S is the set of points of continuity of f. Then f is said to be *approximatable* iff

1. S is dense in X;
2. for any $\bar{x} \in X$, there exists a net $\{x_a\} \subset S$ such that

$$\lim_a x_a = \bar{x} \text{ and } \lim_a f(x_a) = f(\bar{x}).$$

Theorem 2.1 *Any approximatable mapping is robust.*

Proof. Let $f: X \rightarrow Y$ be an approximatable mapping. We show that for any open set U_Y of Y, $f^{-1}(U_Y)$ is a robust set of X. In fact, if $x \in f^{-1}(U_Y)$ is a continuous point of f, then x must be an interior point of $f^{-1}(U_Y)$, because $f^{-1}(U_Y)$, as the inverse image of a neighbourhood of $f(x)$, is a neighbourhood of x. On the other hand, if $\bar{x} \in f^{-1}(U_Y)$ is not a continuous point of f, then by the definition of approximatable mapping, there exists a net $\{x_\alpha\} \subset S$ such that $\lim_\alpha x_\alpha = \bar{x}$ and $\lim_\alpha f(x_\alpha) = f(\bar{x})$, where every x_α is a continuous point of f. Since U_Y is a neighbourhood of $f(\bar{x})$, for α sufficiently large, $f(x_\alpha) \in U_Y$, and then, x_α is an interior point of $f^{-1}(U_Y)$. Hence, $\bar{x}$ is a cluster point of the interior of $f^{-1}(U_Y)$. That is to say that $\bar{x}$ is a robust point of $f^{-1}(U_Y)$. Thus, $f^{-1}(U_Y)$ is a robust set of X. □

The simplest example of a discontinuous approximatable mapping is a robust piecewise continuous mapping in the following sense:

Definition 2.4 Let X and Y be two topological spaces. A mapping $f: X \to Y$ is said bo be *robust piecewise continuous* iff there exists a "robust partition" of X, i. e.
$$X = \bigcup_{i \in I} V_i \quad \text{and} \quad \forall i \in I, i \neq j, V_i \cap V_j = \emptyset,$$
where for any $i \in I$, V_i is robust in X, and for any $i \in I$, the restriction of f in V_i is continuous.

Obviously, when Y is a metric space (even a uniform space), the uniform convergence also preserves the robust piecewise continuity of mappings. Notice that if in its definition the partition of X is not required to be "robust", then a piecewise continuous mapping may not be robust.

A mapping whose points of continuity form a dense subset of the domain may not be approximatable.

Example 2.1 Let $X = Y = \mathbb{R}$ and
$$f(x) = \begin{cases} \sin(1/x), & \text{if } x \neq 0, \\ \alpha, & \text{if } x = 0. \end{cases} \tag{2.4}$$
Then f is approximatable iff $\alpha \in [-1, 1]$.

An approximatable mapping can possess a dense set of points of discontinuity as illustrated in the following example.

Example 2.2 Let $X = Y = [0,1]$, $\{r_k\}$ be the set of all rational numbers in $[0,1]$ and $\alpha_k > 0, k = 1, 2, \cdots$, with $\sum_{k=1}^\infty \alpha_k = 1$. Then the function
$$f(x) = \sum_{r_k < x} \alpha_k$$
is a left-continuous monotone function from $[0,1]$ to $[0,1]$ and discontinuous at every rational point in $[0,1]$.

3 Main Theorem

Recall that a topological space is asid to be a *Baire space* iff no nonempty open set in the space is of the first category; a topological space is said to satisfy the *second axiom of countability* iff it has a countable base (of open sets). Then we have

Theorem 3.1 *Assume that X is a Baire space and Y satisfies the second axiom of countability. Then a mapping $f: X \to Y$ is robust iff it is approximatable. In this case, the set D of points of discontinuity of a robust mapping is always of the first category.*

In addition, *if Y is a separable metric space, then D is an F_σ set of the first category.*

The proof of this theorem is based on the following four propositions.

Proposition 3.1[4]   *Let X and Y be two topological spaces and $f: X \to Y$ be a mapping. Assume that Y has a base $\{U_a\}_{a \in A}$. Then the set D of points of discontinuity of f can be represented by*

$$D = \bigcup_{a \in A} f^{-1}(U_a) \setminus \text{int } f^{-1}(U_a). \tag{3.1}$$

Proof. If x is a discontinuous point of f, then there exists an open neighbourhood $V(y)$ of $y = f(x)$ such that x is not an interior point of $f^{-1}(V(y))$, i.e. $x \in f^{-1}(V(y)) \setminus \text{int } f^{-1}(V(y))$. Since $\{U_a\}$ is a base of Y, we can suppose that $U_a \subset V(y)$ for some a. Hence, $x \in \bigcup_{a \in A} f^{-1}(U_a) \setminus \text{int } f^{-1}(U_a)$. Conversely, if for $x \in X$, there exists $a \in A$ such that $x \in f^{-1}(U_a) \setminus \text{int } f^{-1}(U_a)$, then x is not an interior point of the inverse image of an open neighbourhood U_a of $f(x)$, and so f is not continuous at x. □

Proposition 3.2   *Let X be a topological space, $Y = (Y, d)$ be a metric space and $f: X \to Y$ be a mapping. The set D of points of discontinuity of f is an F_σ set in X.*

Proof. Suppose that for any $x \in X$, $\{V_\beta(x)\}$ is a base of neighbourhoods of x. Define the oscillation function $\omega: X \to \mathbb{R}_+$ of f as follows:

$$\forall x \in X, \quad \omega(x) = \lim_\beta \sup_{x_1, x_2 \in V_\beta(x)} d(f(x_1), f(x_2)).$$

It is easy to verify that ω is a upper semi-continuous function, i.e. for $c \geq 0$, $\omega^{-1}([c, +\infty))$ is closed in X. Since

$$D = \{x \in X \mid \omega(x) \geq 1/n, \text{ for some } n \geq 1\} = \bigcup_{n=1}^\infty \omega^{-1}([1/n, +\infty)),$$

it is an F_σ set. □

Proposition 3.3   *Let X and Y be two topological spaces, Y satisfy the second axiom of countability and $f: X \to Y$ be a mapping. If for each open set U_Y of Y, $f^{-1}(U_Y)$ is the union of an open set and a nowhere dense set in X, then the set of points of discontinuity of f is of the first category.*

Proof. Since Y has a countable base, we can suppose that $\{U_k\}_{k=1,2,\ldots}$ is a base of Y. According to Proposition 3.1, the set of points of discontinuity of f is

$$D = \bigcup_{k=1}^\infty f^{-1}(U_k) \setminus \text{int } f^{-1}(U_k).$$

From the assumptions of the proposition, $f^{-1}(U_k) \setminus \text{int } f^{-1}(U_k)$ is nowhere dense. Hence, D is of the first category. □

Proposition 3.4   *Let X and Y be two topological spaces, $f: X \to Y$ be robust and $S \subset X$ be the set of points of continuity of f. If S is dense in X, then f is approximatable.*

Proof. We have to show that for any $x \in X$ and $y = f(x) \in Y$, there exists a net $\{x_a\} \subset S$ such that

$$\lim_a x_a = x \quad \text{and} \quad \lim_a f(x_a) = f(x). \tag{3.2}$$

Suppose that $\{V_\beta(x)\}$ and $\{U_\gamma(y)\}$ are open neighbourhood bases of x in X and of y in Y, respectively. Then for any β and γ, $f^{-1}(U_\gamma(y)) \cap V_\beta(x)$ is a nonempty robust set in X; in

particular, its interior is nonempty. Since S is dense in X, we have that
$$\forall \beta, \gamma, \quad \exists x_{\beta\gamma} \in f^{-1}(U_\gamma(y)) \cap V_\beta(x) \cap S.$$
Set $\alpha = (\beta, \gamma)$ and $x_\alpha = x_{\beta\gamma}$. Then (3.2) holds, where $\alpha = (\beta, \gamma) \succ \alpha' = (\beta', \gamma')$ is defined by $V_\beta(x) \subset V_{\beta'}(x)$ and $U_\gamma(y) \subset U_{\gamma'}(y)$. □

Proof of Theorem 3.1. From Propositions 2.1 and 3.3, the set D of points of discontinuity of f is of the first category. Since X is a Baire space, the set of points of continuity of f, $X \backslash D$, is dense in X. Joining this up with Propositions 3.2 and 3.4 proves the theorem. □

The following two examples show that the assumptions on X and Y in Theorem 3.1 are indispensable.

Example 3.1 Let $X = \{r_k\}$ = set of all the rational numbers in $[0,1]$ with the induced topology by $[0,1]$ (so X is not a Baire space), $Y = [0,1]$ and $\alpha_k > 0, k = 1, 2, \cdots$, with $\sum_{k=1}^{\infty} \alpha_k = 1$. Then the function
$$f(x) = \sum_{r_k < x} \alpha_k$$
is robust, but discontinuous at every point in X.

Example 3.2 Let $X = \mathbb{R}$ *and* $Y = \mathbb{R}^\mathbb{R}$ with the product topology. Y can be identified with a space of all functions $g(\cdot): \mathbb{R} \to \mathbb{R}$ with the topology of the pointwise convergence. This topological space has no countable base. Let $f: X \to Y$ be defined as follows.
$$f(x)(z) = g_x(z) = \begin{cases} 1 & \text{if } z \geq x, \\ 0 & \text{if } z < x. \end{cases}$$
The sets of the following form in Y constitute a base of the open neighbourhoods of $y = f(x)$:
$$U(y; z_1, \cdots, z_k; \varepsilon) = \{h(\cdot) \in Y \mid |g_x(z_i) - h(z_i)| < \varepsilon, i = 1, 2, \cdots, k\}$$
where $z_i \in \mathbb{R}$, $i = 1, 2, \cdots, k$ and $\varepsilon \in (0, 1)$. Since
$$f^{-1}(U(y; z; \varepsilon)) = \{x' \in \mathbb{R} \mid |g_{x'}(z) - g_x(z)| < \varepsilon\}$$
$$= \begin{cases} (z, +\infty), & \text{if } z < x, \\ (-\infty, z], & \text{if } z \geq x, \end{cases}$$
we have that
$$f^{-1}(U(y; z_1, \cdots, z_k; \varepsilon)) = \{x' \in \mathbb{R} \mid |g_{x'}(z_i) - g_x(z_i)| < \varepsilon, i = 1, \cdots, k\}$$
$$= \begin{cases} (\max_i z_i, +\infty), & \text{if } \max_i z_i < x, \\ (-\infty, \min_i z_i], & \text{if } \min_i z_i \geq x, \\ (z_i, z_{i+1}], & \text{if } z_i < \cdots < z_i < x \leq z_{i+1} < \cdots < z_k \end{cases}$$
in which x is a robust point. Hence, f is a robust mapping from X to Y.

$f: \mathbb{R} \to \mathbb{R}^\mathbb{R}$ is continuous at $x \in \mathbb{R}$ iff
$$\forall z \in \mathbb{R}, \lim_{x' \to x} g_{x'}(z) = g_x(z).$$
Since we have always that
$$\forall x \in \mathbb{R}, \limsup_{x' \to x} g_{x'}(x) = 1 \quad \text{and} \quad \liminf_{x' \to x} g_{x'}(x) = 0,$$

f is discontinuous at all $x \in \mathbb{R}$.

Remark Recall ([3],[4],[6]) that a mapping $f: X \to Y$ is said to be *of the first Baire class* iff for every open set U_Y of Y, $f^{-1}(U_Y)$ is an F_σ set. When $X=Y=\mathbb{R}$, every function from $\mathbb{R}$ to $\mathbb{R}$ of the first Baire class is measurable. A classic theorem says that under the hypotheses in Theorem 3.1, the set of points of continuity of a mapping of the first Baire class is a dense G_δ set. However, a robust mapping may not be of the first Baire class and vice versa. For instance, the function in (1.2) is of the first Baire class, because it is lower semi-continuous and every l.s.c. function is of the first class; an example of a nonmeasurable robust real function (then, it is impossible to be a function of the first Baire class) is as follows.

Example 3.3 Let $X=[0,1]$ and $C \subset [0,1]$ be a Cantor-type set with positive Lebesgue measure, which is a nowhere dense perfect set (no isolated points and closed). Then $X \setminus C$ is open. Take a non-measurable subset C_1 of C. Such a subset exists [6]. Divide X into two disjoint robust parts A_1 and A_2 such that $C_1 \subset A_1 \setminus \text{int } A_1$ and $C \setminus C_1 \subset A_2 \setminus \text{int } A_2$. Then A_1 and A_2 are also nonmeasurable. The characteristic function of A_1:

$$\chi_{A_1}(x) = \begin{cases} 1, & \text{if } x \in A_1, \\ 0, & \text{if } x \notin A_1, \end{cases}$$

is piecewise continuous, but nonmeasurable. The construction of A_1, A_2, C_1 and C_2 is similar to that in [14].

4 Banach Spaces of Bounded Robust Mappings

In this section, we assume that X is a complete metric space and Y is a real separable Banach space. Then the hypotheses in Theorem 3.1 hold and all the robust mappings from X to Y are approximatable. We will discuss the construction of the set of all the bounded robust mappings in this setting.

Since Y is a real Banach space, we can consider linear operations for mappings from X to Y. If $f: X \to Y$ is robust, then for any $\lambda \in \mathbb{R}$, λf, defined by

$$\forall x \in X, \quad (\lambda f)(x) = \lambda f(x),$$

is also robust. But, if f_1 and f_2 are robust, then, in general, $f_1 + f_2$, defined by

$$\forall x \in X, \quad (f_1 + f_2)(x) = f_1(x) + f_2(x),$$

is not necessarily robust.

Example 4.1 Let $X=Y=\mathbb{R}$,

$$f_1(x) = \begin{cases} 1, & \text{if } x > 0, \\ 0, & \text{if } x \leq 0, \end{cases}$$

and

$$f_2(x) = \begin{cases} 1, & \text{if } x < 0, \\ 0, & \text{if } x \geq 0. \end{cases}$$

Then f_1 and f_2 are robust. But

$$(f_1+f_2)(x)=\begin{cases}1, & \text{if } x\neq 0,\\ 0, & \text{if } x=0,\end{cases}$$

is not robust.

This example is typical. By the same idea we can claim that for any discontinuous robust mapping f, there always exists another discontinuous robust mapping g such that $f+g$ is not robust.

In this section, we will look for a condition for the robustness of the sum of two robust mappings, or a condition under which a family of robust mappings becomes a linear or Banach space.

Definition 4.1 Let $S\subset X$ be dense in X,

$$c_S=\{\{s_k\}\subset S|\ \exists x\in X, \lim_{k\to\infty}s_k=x\}$$

and $A_S:X\backslash S\to c_S$ such that for any $x\in X\backslash S$, $A_S(x)=\{s_k(x)\}$ satisfies $\lim_{k\to\infty}s_k(x)=x$. If $f:X\to Y$ possesses the following property:

1. f is continuous at each point $s\in S$;
2. for any $x\in X\backslash S$ and $A_S(x)=\{s_k(x)\}\subset S$, $f(x)=\lim_{k\to\infty}f(s_k(x))$; then we say that f belongs to the (S,A_S)-class. The set of all the mappings of the (S, A_S)-class is denoted by $F_{(S,A_S)}(X,Y)$.

Obviously, each mapping of an (S, A_S)-class is robust (approximatable) and each robust mapping belongs to a certain (S, A_S)-class, but not uniquely. Any continuous mapping belongs to all the (S, A_S)-classes and, in particular, all the continuous mappings from $F_{(X,A_X)}=F_{(X,\emptyset)}=C(X,Y)$.

Proposition 4.1 1. *If f_1, $f_2\in F_{(S,A_S)}(X,Y)$, then for any λ_1, $\lambda_2\in\mathbb{R}$, $\lambda_1 f_1+\lambda_2 f_2\in F_{(S,A_S)}(X,Y)$.*

2. *If $\{f_n\}\subset F_{(S,A_S)}(X,Y)$ and for a mapping $f:X\to Y$,*

$$\lim_{n\to\infty}\sup_{x\in X}\|f_n(x)-f(x)\|=0,$$

then $f\in F_{(S,A_S)}(X,Y)$.

The proof is elementary.

Set

$$B_{(S,A_S)}(X,Y)=\{f\in F_{(S,A_S)}(X,Y)|\sup_{x\in X}\|f(x)\|<+\infty\}. \tag{4.1}$$

Then Proposition 4.1 means that defining the norm $\|f\|=\sup_{x\in X}\|f(x)\|$, $B_{(S,A_S)}(X,Y)$ is a Banach space. $B_{(S,A_S)}(X,Y)$ includes the Banach space of bounded continuous mappings from X to Y, denoted by $B_C(X,Y)$, as a closed subspace. On the other hand, each bounded robust mapping from X to Y belongs to some $B_{(S,A_S)}(X,Y)$. Denoting the set of all the bounded robust mappings from X to Y by $B_R(X,Y)$, we have that

$$\bigcup_{(S,A_S)}B_{(S,A_S)}(X,Y)=B_R(X,Y) \text{ and } \bigcup_{(S,A_S)}B_{(S,A_S)}(X,Y)=B_C(X,Y) \tag{4.2}$$

Furthermore, if for two dense sets S_1 and S_2 in X and for two mappings $A_{S_1}:X\backslash S_1\to c_{S_1}$ and $A_{S_2}:X\backslash S_1\to c_{S_2}$, we have that

$$S_1\subset S_2 \quad\text{and}\quad \forall x\in X\backslash S_2, A_{S_1}(x)\subset A_{S_2}(x),$$

then it follows that
$$B_{S_1, A_{S_1}}(X, Y) \supset B_{S_2, A_{S_2}}(X, Y).$$
However, any $B_{(S_1, A_S)}(X, Y)$ is not maximal with respect to the partial ordering of set inclusion, because for any $B_{S, A_S}(X, Y)$, it is easy to construct another $B_{(S', A'_{S'})}$ which contains $B_{(S, A_S)}$ as a proper subclass.

Let $M(X, Y)$ be the set of *all* Banach spaces of bounded robust mappings from X to Y. We can define the set inclusion as a partial order relation in $M(X, Y)$. This partial order in $M(X, Y)$ is inductive, i. e. each totally ordered subset of $M(X, Y)$ has a maximal element, which is the completion of the union of all the elements (considered as the subsets of $B_R(X, Y)$) of this totally ordered subset. Thanks to Proposition 2.2, it is easy to show that the uniform limit of a sequence of bounded robust mappings is also a bounded robust mapping. Hence, by Zorn's lemma, $M(X, Y)$ possesses maximal elements, which are the "maximal Banach spaces" in $B_R(X, Y)$. Denote these "maximal Banach spoaces" of bounded robust mappings from X to Y by $B_{M\delta}(X, Y)$, $\delta \in \Delta$. Then we have that
$$\bigcup_{\delta \in \Delta} B_{M\delta}(X, Y) = B_R(X, Y) \quad \text{and} \quad \bigcup_{\delta \in \Delta} B_{M\delta}(X, Y) = B_C(X, Y).$$
If $B_{M\delta_1}(X, Y) \neq B_{M\delta_2}(X, Y)$, then they will not be included in each other.

It is interesting to investigate the quotient space of $B_{(S, A_S)}$ to $B_C(X, Y)$. Even for $X = [0, 1]$, $Y = \mathbb{R}$ and $X \setminus S$ a singleton, the quotient space $B_{(S, A_S)}([0, 1], \mathbb{R})/B_C([0, 1], \mathbb{R})$ is not trivial.

Finally, if Y is a separable Banach algebra, then any $B_{(S, A_S)}$ is also a Banach algebra by defining
$$\forall x \in X, \quad (f_1 f_2)(x) = f_1(x) f_2(x).$$
The similar conclusion for the "Banach algebras of bounded robust mappings" also holds.

5 Robust Functions

Now we assume that X is a Baire space and $Y = \mathbb{R}$. In this case, the robust mappings become the "robust functions", which have a set of points of continuity dense in X and are approximatable at their points of discontinuity. However, it is not necessary to only consider robust functions with respect to the natural topology of $\mathbb{R}$. In fact, in Zheng [10]–[12], for the application to the global minimization problem, a robust function is always defined for the "upper topology" of $\mathbb{R}$, which means that all the open sets have a form of $(-\infty, c)$, $c \in \mathbb{R}$. To distinguish robust functions with respect to the diverse topologies of $\mathbb{R}$, we propose the following definitions.

Definition 5.1 Let X be a topological space and $f: X \to \mathbb{R}$. f is said to be *robust* (respectively *upper robust* or *lower robust*) at x iff for any $\varepsilon > 0$, $f^{-1}((f(x) - \varepsilon, f(x) + \varepsilon))$ (respectively, $f^{-1}((-\infty, f(x) + \varepsilon))$ or $f^{-1}((f(x) - \varepsilon, +\infty))$) is a semi-neighbourhood of x. f is said to be a *robust function* (respectively, *upper* or *lower robust function*) iff f is robust (respectively, upper or lower robust) at all $x \in X$; or for any a, b

$\in \mathbb{R}$ (respectively, $c \in \mathbb{R}$), $f^{-1}((a, b))$ (respectively, $f^{-1}((-\infty, c))$ of $f^{-1}((c, +\infty,))$ is robust in X.

The concepts of robustness, upper robustness and lower robustness for a function are extensions of continuity, upper semi-continuity and lower semicontinuity. Any continuous (respectively, upper or lower semi-continuous) function is robust (respectively, upper or lower robust), but a robust (respectively, upper or lower robust) function may not be continuous (respectively, upper or lower semi-continuous). In addition, an upper robust and lower semi-continuous (respectively, a lower robust and upper semi-continuous) function is robust, but an upper and lower robust function may not be robust, because the intersection of two semi-neighbourhoods may not be a semi-neighbourhood.

Example 5.1 Let $X = \mathbb{R}$ and f be defined by

$$f(x) = \begin{cases} 1, & \text{if } x > 0, \\ 0, & \text{if } x = 0, \\ -1, & \text{if } x < 0. \end{cases}$$

Then f is neither upper or lower semi-continuous nor robust, but is both upper and lower robust.

From Proposition 2.2, we obtain

Proposition 5.1 *Let X be a topological space and $f_\delta : X \to \mathbb{R}$, $\delta \in \Delta$, be a net of functions. If all the functions f_δ are robust at $\bar{x} \in X$ and a function $f : X \to \mathbb{R}$ satisfies*

$$\limsup_{\delta} \sup_{x \in X} |f_\delta(x) - f(x)| = 0, \tag{5.1}$$

then f is also robust at $\bar{x}$.

Proposition 2.2 is not applicable for the upper or lower robustness of functions, because $\mathbb{R}$ with the "upper" or "lower" topology is not a metric spce, not even a Hausdorff space. But it is obvious that Proposition 5.1 is also valid for upper or lower robust functions. However, for these two cases, we can modify the concept of "uniform convergence" and the following proposition is valid:

Proposition 5.2 *Let X be a topological space, $f_\delta : X \to \mathbb{R}$, $\delta \in \Delta$, be a net of functions and all the function f_δ be upper (respectively, lower) robust at $\bar{x} \in X$. If for a function $f : X \to \mathbb{R}$ and for all $x \in X$, we have uniformly*

$$\liminf_{\delta} f_\delta(x) \geq f(x) \quad (resp. \; \limsup_{\delta} f_\delta(x) \leq f(x)) \tag{5.2}$$

and

$$\lim_{\delta} f_\delta(\bar{x}) = f(\bar{x}), \tag{5.3}$$

then f is also upper (respectively, lower) robust at $\bar{x}$.

Proof. We have to show that for $\bar{x} \in X$ and any ε-"upper neighbourhood" of $\bar{y} = f(\bar{x})$, $U_\varepsilon(f(\bar{x})) = (-\infty, f(\bar{x}) + \varepsilon)$ ($\varepsilon > 0$), $f^{-1}(U_\varepsilon(f(\bar{x})))$ is a semineighbourhood of $\bar{x}$. Thus, we need to show that there exists a semi-neighbourhood of $\bar{x}$, $V(\bar{x})$, such that

$$\forall x \in V(\bar{x}), \quad f(x) < f(\bar{x}) + \varepsilon. \tag{5.4}$$

From (5.2), using standard $\varepsilon/3$ argument, we can verify easily that (5.4) holds.

In the case of the lower robust functions, the proof is similar. □

Proposition 5.3 *Let X be a topological space, $f_\gamma: X \to \mathbb{R}$, $\gamma \in \Gamma$, be a family of functions and all the function f_γ be upper (resp., lower) robust at $\bar{x} \in X$. If for a function $f: X \to \mathbb{R}$ and for all $x \in X$, $f(x) = \inf_{\gamma \in \Gamma} f_\gamma(x)$ (resp., $f(x) = \sup_{\gamma \in \Gamma} f_\gamma(x)$), then f is also upper (resp., lower) robust at $\bar{x}$.*

Now we apply Theorem 3.1 to the case of robust functions.

Theorem 5.1 *Let X be a complete metric space, $f: X \to \mathbb{R}$ be a function on X and S be the set of points of continuity of f. Then f is robust iff f is approximatable, i.e. S is dense in X and for any $x \in X \setminus S$ there exists a sequence $\{s_k(x)\} \subset S$ such that $\lim_{k \to \infty} f(s_k(x)) = f(x)$. In this case, S is a dense G_δ set in X.*

Although $\mathbb{R}$ with the upper or lower topology is not a Hausdorff space, the second axiom of countability is valid. So, replacing the continuity by the upper or lower semicontinuity, a similar theorem for an upper or a lower robust function is also valid. However, we can prove a stronger theorem as follows.

Theorem 5.2 *Let X be a complete metric space, $f: X \to \mathbb{R}$ be a function on X and S be the set of points of continuity of f. Then f is upper (respectively, lower) robust iff S is dense in X and for any $x \in X \setminus S$, there exists a sequence $\{s_k(x)\} \subset S$ such that $\limsup_{k \to \infty} f(s_k(x)) \leq f(x)$ (respectively, $\liminf_{k \to \infty} f(s_k(x)) \geq f(x)$). In this case, S is a dense G_δ set in X.*

Proof. Consider an upper robust function f. Let $\{r_k\}$ be the set of rational numbers in $\mathbb{R}$. We prove that

$$D = \bigcup_{i \neq j} f^{-1}((r_i, r_j)) \setminus \text{int } f^{-1}((r_i, r_j)) \tag{5.5}$$

is of the first category. It suffices to show that $f^{-1}((a,b)) \setminus \text{int } f^{-1}((a,b))$ is of the first category for any $a, b \in \mathbb{R}$.

Since f is upper robust, $f^{-1}([c, +\infty)) = X \setminus f^{-1}((-\infty, c))$ is the complement of a robust set. From Proposition 2.1, it is the union of an open set and a nowhere dense set. Hence,

$$f^{-1}((a,b)) = f^{-1}((-\infty, b)) \cap f^{-1}((a, +\infty))$$

$$= f^{-1}((-\infty, b)) \cap \left(\bigcup_{n=1}^{\infty} f^{-1}([a + (1/n), +\infty))\right)$$

$$= V \cap \left(\bigcup_{n=1}^{\infty} [O_n \cup T_n]\right),$$

where V is a robust set, O_n is open and T_n is nowhere dense, $n = 1, 2, \cdots$. Thus, we have that

$$f^{-1}((a,b)) = \bigcup_{n=1}^{\infty} [(V \cap O_n) \cup (V \cap T_n)] = \bigcup_{n=1}^{\infty} (V_n \cup T'_n), \tag{5.6}$$

where V_n is robust (maybe empty) and T'_n is nowhere dense, $n = 1, 2, \cdots$; and

$$f^{-1}((a,b)) \setminus \text{int } f^{-1}((a,b)) \subset \bigcup_{n=1}^{\infty} (V_n \setminus \text{int } V_n) \cup T'_n. \tag{5.7}$$

The right side of this inclusion is obviously of the first category, and so is the left side. The G_δ-ness of S is a consequence of Proposition 3.2. □

In Example 2.1, if $a \geqslant -1$, then f is upper robust; and if $a \leqslant -1$, then f is lower robust.

Finally, the discussion of the last section is suitable to the robust functions, but not to the upper or lower robust functions. If f is upper (respectively, lower) robust, then only for any $\lambda \geqslant 0$, λf is also upper (respectively, lower) robust, but for any $\lambda \leqslant 0$, λf is lower (respectively, upper) robust. However, we have the similar conclusion for the upper or lower robustness of the sum of two upper or lower robust functions.

6 Conclusions

The initial motivation to introduce the robustness of a set or of a function ([10]—[12]) is to enlarge the class of objective functions and of constraint sets of global optimization problems. This paper demonstrates that the concept of robustness is essential for numerical analysis. We show that if X is a complete metric space and Y has a countable base, then a robust mapping $f: X \to Y$ is precisely an approximatable mapping. For the problem of solving equation (1.1), we only need Y to be a metric space (Y, d), which may not have a countable base. This is because the problem is equivalent to the following problem:

$$\text{to find } \bar{x} \in X \text{ such that } d(f(\bar{x}), \bar{y}) = 0. \tag{6.1}$$

If $f: X \to Y$ is a robust mapping, then it is obvious that the function $x \to d(f(x), \bar{y})$ from X to $\mathbb{R}_+$ (having a countable base) is also robust, and so, approximatable. Notice that the problem (6.1) is a global minimization problem.

In Zheng [10]—[12], for a global minimization problem, the objective function f is always assumed to be lower semi-continuous and "upper robust" (according to our definition). Now we know that it is equivalent to assume that f is l.s.c. and robust, or f is a l.s.c. approximatable function. In general, a l.s.c. function is not approximtable. (1.2) is a typical example.

In Chew-Zhen[2], Zheng[11] and other works, a theory of integral global optimization is presented. In this theory, we require an objective function to be integrable and robust. In general, a robust function may not be integrable. Now we know that the set of points of discontinuity of a robust function is always an F_σ set of the first category. When X is $[0, 1]^k$, it is reasonable to assume that this F_σ set of the first category is a Lebesgue null set, and then a robust function becomes a Riemann integrable function. In particular, when $k=1$, a robust function will be topologically equivalent to a Riemann integral function [6, Theorem 13.3]. This situation is very favourable to the theory of integral global optimization.

In the applications of integral global optimization, we often require the sum of two robust functions to be robust. Before this paper, we only knew that it suffices to require one of the functions to be continuous. Now we have indeed a necessary and sufficient condition for the robustness of the sum of two robust functions; that is, they must possess the same property of discontinuity.

In [2], [11] and others, a Monte Carlo implementation of the integral global minimization algorithm was also proposed. It is shown that the global minimizers can be obtained with high probbility. Due to the stochastic nature of Monte Carlo implementation, one would suspect that some global minimizers may be lost during the course of computation. However, according to our computation experiences over the past twenty years, we can always find global minimizers even for discontinuous functions [2], [16]. The main theorem of this paper could give a new theoretical explanation of our method, but it would be the subject of another paper.

The main results in this paper can be generalized to the case of set-valued mappings. The reader is referred to [8] for details.

References

[1] L. V. Batuchtin and L. A. Maoboroda. *Optimization of discontinuous functions*, "Nauka", Moscow 1984.

[2] Soo Hong Chew and Quan Zheng, *Integral global optimization: Theory. implementation and applications*. Lecture Notes in Econ. and Math. Sys., vol. 298, Springer-Verlag, 1988.

[3] G. Choquet, *Outils topologiques et métriques de l'analyse mathématique*, Centre de Documentation Universitaire et S. E. D. E. S. Réunis, Paris-V, 1969.

[4] ___. *Lectures on analysis*, Vol. 1, Benjamin, 1969.

[5] I. V. Mayurova and R. G. Strongin, *Minimization of multi-extremum function with a discontinuity*. U. S. S. R. Comput. Math. and Math. Phys. 1984, 24:121—126.

[6] J. C. Oxtoby, *Measure and category*, 2nd ed., Springer-Verlag. 1980.

[7] Z. Semadeni. *Banach spaces of continuous functions*, Polish Scientific Publishers. 1971.

[8] Shuzhong Shi, Quan Zheng and Deming Zhuang. *Set-valued robust mappings and approximatable mappings*. J. Math. Anal. Appl. 1994, 183:706—726.

[9] I. Zang. *Discontinuous optimization by smoothing*. Math. Oper. Res. 1981,6:140—152.

[10] Quan Zheng, *Robust analysis and global minimization of a class of discontinuous functions* (I), Acta Math. Appl. Sinica (English Ser.) 1990,6:205—223.

[11] ___. *Robust analysis and global minimization of a class of discontinuous functions* (II), Acta Math. Appl. Sinica (English Ser.) 1990, 6:317—337.

[12] ___. *Robust analysis and global optimization*, Comput. Math. Appl. 1991, 21:17—24.

[13] ___. *Global minimization of constrained problems with discontinuous penalty functions* (to appear).

[14] ___. *Discontinuity and measurability of robust functions in the integral global minimization*, Comput. Math. Appl. 1993, 25: 79—88.

[15] Quan Zheng and Deming Zhuang, *Integral global optimization of constrained problems in functional space with discontinuous penalty functions*, Recent Advances in Global Optimization (C. A. Floudas and P. M. Pardalos, eds.), Princeton Univ. Press, 1991.

[16] Q. Zheng. B. Jiang and S. Zhuang, *A method for finding global extrema*, Acta. Math. Appl. Sinica 1978, 1:161—174. (Chinese)

On Existence of Robust Minimizers*

Abstract: The concepts of robustness of sets and functions were proposed for the theory of integral global optimization. A robust minimizer of a nonlinear minimization problem can be approximated by a sequence of points at which the objective function is continuous. In this paper, we discuss the existence of robust minimizers. With the integral global optimality conditions, we extend the Palais-Smale condition to establish the existence results of robust minimizers for nonlinear programs whose objective function may be discontinuous.

1 Introduction and Preliminaries

Let X be a topological space, S a subset of X and $f: X \to \mathbb{R}^1$ a real valued function. Consider the following minimization problem: Find the minimum values of f over S

$$c^* = \inf_{x \in S} f(x)$$

and the set of global minimizers:

$$H^* = \{x \in S: f(x) = c^*\}.$$

If the objective function f is bounded below, then f has the infimum c^* over S. However, the set H^* of global minimizers may be empty. In this paper, we will study conditions for non-emptiness of the set of global minimizers.

The existence of global optimal solutions is a fundamental question in optimization theory. It is Weierstrass who proved the celebrated existence theorem using compactness arguments: a continuous real-valued function attains its minimum and maximum on a compact set. This classical theorem has been generalized to various cases. In this section we summarize several existence results for minimization problems.

It follows directly from the definition of lower semicontinuity and from the Weierstrass theorem that a lower semicontinuous function attains its minimum on a compact set. Based on this fact, we have immediately the following standard results concerning the existence of global minimizers.

Recll a real-valued function $f: X \to \mathbb{R}^1$ is said to be *inf-compact* if there is a real number $c > c^*$ such that the level set $H_c = \{x \in X: f(x) \leq c\}$ is a non-empty compact set.

---

* In collaboration with Shi S Z, Zhuang D M. Repainted from *C. A. Floudas and P. M. Pardalos (eds.), State of the Art in Global Optimizanon*, 1996, 47—56.

Proposition 1.1 *If f is lower semi-continuous and inf-compact then the set of minimizers H^* is not empty.*

For many practical optimization problems, while the requirement of lower semicontinnity in the above proposition is moderate, that of inf-compact is demanding.

Now assume that X is a normed space, $f: X \to \mathbb{R}^1$ a real valued function. f is said to be *coercive* if
$$\lim_{\|x\| \to \infty} f(x) = +\infty.$$
Note that when f is coercive, the level set $H_c = \{x \in X: f(x) \leqslant c\}$ is bounded for all real number c. If f is also assumed to be lower semi-continuous then H_c is a closed and bounded set, which is compact when X is finite dimensional. Thus:

Proposition 1.2 *If X is a finite-dimensional normed space, f is lower semi-continuous and coercive then the set of minimizers H^* is not empty.*

The renowned Eberlein-Smulian Theorem states that in a reflexive space, any weakly closed bounded set is weakly compact. Based on this theorem, we immediately arrive the following two propositions:

Proposition 1.3 *If X is a reflexive Banach space, f is weakly lower semi-continuous, coercive, and bounded from below, the set of minimizers H^* is not empty.*

Proposition 1.4 *Let X be a closed, bounded and convex subset of a reflexive Banach space. f be a convex and lower semicontinuous real-valued functional on X, then the set of minimizers H^* is not empty.*

Let f be a continuous differentiable functional on a Banach space. We say that f satisfy the following *Palais-Smale* condition if for each sequence $\{x_n\} \subset X$,
$$\begin{cases} \{f(x_n)\} \text{ is bounded} \\ df(x_n) \to \theta \end{cases} \Rightarrow \begin{array}{l} \text{the sequence } \{x_n\} \text{ possesses} \\ \text{a convergent subsequence.} \end{array} \qquad (1.1)$$

Proposition 1.5 *If X is a Banach space, $f \in C^1(X)$ is bounded from below, and satisfies the Palais-Smale condition, then the set of minimizers H^* is not empty.*

The Palais-Smale condition is important because it places the "compactness" condition onto the objective function f itself. It has very extensive application in many areas.

2 Approximatable Functions and Robust Minimizers

In optimization practice, we not only need to know the existence of optimal solutions but also need to find these solutions numerically. It is for this reason that we introduced the concept of approximatable functions in [6,7]. Recall that a function $f: X \to \mathbb{R}^1$ is said to be approximatable if the set C of points of continuity of f is dense in X, and for each $x_0 \in X$, there is a sequence $\{x_\alpha\} \subset C$ such that
$$x_\alpha \to x_0 \quad \text{and} \quad f(x_\alpha) \to f(x_0). \qquad (2.1)$$
The existence results discussed in the previous section, with the exception of Proposition 1.5, do not ensure the approximatablility of minimizers. For example, let $X = \mathbb{R}^1$ and

$$f(x) = \begin{cases} x^2, & x \neq 0, \\ -1, & x = 0. \end{cases} \tag{2.2}$$

It is easy to see that f and X satisfy every condition in these propositions. However, the global minimizer $x^* = 0$ is not approximatable.

Recall that a set D in a topological space X is said to be robust if

$$\text{cl int } D = \text{cl } D, \tag{2.3}$$

where int D denotes the interior of D and cl D the closure of D. Locally, a point $x_0 \in D$ is said to be a robust point of D if $x_0 \in \text{cl int } D$, or if there is a net of point $\{x_a\} \subset \text{int } D$ such that $x_a \to x_0$. Thus, a set D is robust if and only if each point of D is a robust point of D. A function $f: X \to \mathbb{R}^1$ is said to be a robust function on X if for each open set $G \subset X$, the inverse image $f^{-1}(G)$ is a robust set. Locally, f is said to be robust at $x_0 \in X$ if for any $\varepsilon > 0$ and a neighbourhood $U(y_0) = (y_0 - \varepsilon, y_0 + \varepsilon)$ of $y_0 = f(x_0)$, the point x_0 is a robust point of $f^{-1}(U(y_0))$. For more details of robustness of sets and of functions see [8-10]

The importance of the concepts of robustness is emphasized by the fact that a robust function is always approximatable. Moreover, when the space X is a complete metric space, the approximatability and the robustness of f are equivalent [6,7].

In the above example, the function f is not robust at $x_0 = 0$. Indeed, by taking $\varepsilon = 0.5$, we obtain the inverse image of an open set $f^{-1}((-1.5, 0.5)) = \{0\}$, which is not a robust set.

The example suggests that a non-robust minimizer is not desirable if we are interested in finding optimal solutions numerically. This motivates the following definition:

Definition 2.1 A point $x^* \in X$ is a robust minimizer if

$$f \text{ is robust at } x^* \text{ and } f(x) \geqslant f(x^*), \quad \forall x \in X. \tag{2.4}$$

By adding the appropriate robustness requirements to the proportions in the previous section, we obtain sufficient conditions of the existence of robust minimizers.

Proposition 2.1 *If X is a topological space, $f: X \to \mathbb{R}^1$ is lower semicontinuous, robust and inf-compact, then there exist robust minimizers of f in X.*

Proposition 2.2 *If X is a finite dimensional Banach space, f is lower semicontinuous, coercive and robust, then there exist robust minimizers of f in X.*

Proposition 2.3 *If X is a reflexive Banach space, f is weak lower semicontinuous, coercive and robust then there exist robust minimizers of f in X.*

Proposition 2.4 *Let X be a closed and convex subset of a reflexive Banach space, f be a convex, lower semicontinuous and robust real-valued functional on X, then there exist robust minimizers of f in X.*

Since a continuous function is always robust, the conclusion of Proposition 2.5 can be strengthened as:

Proposition 2.5 *If X is a Banach space, $f \in C^1(X)$, bounded from below, and satisfies the Palais-Smale condition, then there exist robust minimizers of f in X.*

3 A New Existence Theorem of Robust Minimizers

The proposition 2.5 ensures the existence of global robust minimizers. However, the analytic requirements on the objective function f is quite demanding. For example, this proportion does not apply to continuous objective functions. In this section we will modify the Palais-Smale condition to establish a much more general existence theorem of robust minimizers which is applicable even to optimization models with discontinuous objective functions.

Let X be a metric space, $f: X \to \mathbb{R}^1$ a real-valued function bounded from below. Let $c^* = \inf_{x \in X} f(x)$, let $c > c^*$ be a real number. We recall the concept of modified variance of f with respect to c.

Definition 3.1 The modified variance of a function f with respect to c is defined as

$$V_1(f,c) = \frac{1}{\mu(H_c)} \int_{H_c} (f(x) - c)^2 d\mu, \tag{3.1}$$

where μ is a Q-measure defined on X and H_c is the level set of f with respect to $c: H_c = \{x: f(x) \leq c\}$

Note that, when $c = c^*$, the definition of $V_1(f,c)$ can be extended by a limit process:
$$V_1(f,c) = \lim_{c_n \downarrow c} V(f,c_n)$$

The modified variance plays an important role in the integral global optimization. In particular, the following optimality condition was established in [8—10].

Theorem 3.1 *Let (X, Ω, μ) be a Q-measure space, $f: X \to \mathbb{R}^1$ a measurable realvalued robust function on X. Then $c^* = \inf_{x \in X} f(x)$ is the infimum of f on X if and only if the modified variance of f with respect to c^* equals zero, i.e. $V_1(f, c^*) = 0$.*

Definition 3.2 Let X be a metric space, $f: X \to \mathbb{R}^1$, C the set of points of continuity of f. We say f possesses the variance sequential compactness property if for each sequence $\{x_n\} \subset X$,

$$\begin{cases} \{x_n\} \subset C \\ V_1(f, f(x_n)) \to 0 \end{cases} \Rightarrow \begin{array}{l} \text{the sequence } \{x_n\} \text{ possesses} \\ \text{a convergent subsequence } \{x_{n_k}\} \end{array} \tag{3.2}$$

Theorem 3.2 *Let X be a metric space, $f: X \to \mathbb{R}^1$ a bounded below, lower semicontinuous and robust function, and C the set of points of continuity of f. If f possesses the variance sequential compactness property then there exists a robust minimizer x^* such that*
$$x_{n_k} \to x^* \quad \text{and} \quad f(x_{n_k}) \to f(x^*) = \inf_{x \in X} f(x). \tag{3.3}$$

A point $x^* \in X$ is a global minimizer of f with $c^* = f(x^*)$ is the global minimum value if and only if
$$V_1(f, c^*) = 0. \tag{3.4}$$

The reader is refereed to [2,8—10] for more information about integral global optimality conditions.

Proof of Theorem Let c^* be the infimum of f, for each integer n, there is a point $y_n \in X$ such that

$$f(y_n) < c^* + \frac{1}{2n}.$$

With the robustness of the objective function f, we can select $x_n \in C$ (C is the set of points of continuity of f) with the property that

$$f(x_n) < f(y_n) + \frac{1}{2n} < c^* + \frac{1}{n}. \tag{3.5}$$

In this way, we obtain a sequence of point $\{x_n\} \subset C$ satisfied (3.5). Furthermore we can assume that $\{f(x_n)\}$ is a monotone sequence without loss of generality. Therefore, we obtain a sequence of point $\{x_n\} \subset C$ such that

$$f(x_n) \downarrow c^* = \inf_{x \in X} f(x). \tag{3.6}$$

By Theorem 3.1 we have

$$V_1(f, f(x_n)) \to 0. \tag{3.7}$$

Hence, from condition (3.2), there exists a convergent subsequence $\{x_{n_k}\}$ of $\{x_n\}$. Thus, there is a point $x^* \in X$ such that $x_{n_k} \to x^*$. We now prove that x^* is a robust global minimizer of f satisfying (3.3). Since c^* is the global minimum value of f, we have

$$f(x^*) \geq c^*. \tag{3.8}$$

Furthermore, by lower semicontinuity of f, for each $\varepsilon > 0$, there is a neighbourhood $U(x^*)$ of x^* such that

$$f(x) > f(x^*) - \varepsilon, \ \forall x \in U(x^*).$$

Because $x_{n_k} \to x^*$, there exists a positive integer N such that for $n_k > N$, $x_{n_k} \in U(x^*)$ and then

$$f(x_{n_k}) > f(x^*) - \varepsilon \ \forall n_k > N.$$

Letting $n \to \infty$ in the above inequality, we obtain from (3.6) that

$$c^* \geq f(x^*) - \varepsilon.$$

Subsequently, by the arbitrariness of ε, we obtain

$$f(x^*) \leq c^*.$$

It implies

$$f(x^*) = c^* = \min_{x \in X} f(x).$$

Furthermore, since f is assumed to be robust at x^*, x^* is also a robust minimizer of f.

Remarks 3.1 Proposition 2.5 is an easy corollary to Theorem 3.2. Indeed, if f is in $C^1(X)$, then the necessary and sufficient condition $V_1(f, c^*) = 0$ implies that $df(x^*) = \theta$.

Remarks 3.2 The assumption of the variance sequential compactness in Theorem 3.2 is weaker than the Palais-Smale condition. Indeed, simple examples show that for a continuously differentiable function $f \in C^1$, the existence of a sequence $\{x_n\}$, satisfying condition (1.1) ($f(x_n)$ is bounded and $df(x_n) \to \theta$) may not guarantee that $V_1(f, f(x_n)) \to 0$. Hence, Palais-Smale condition requires more sequences having convergent subsequence.

Example 3.1 Let $X = \mathbb{R}^1$, and

$$f(x) = (x^2 - 0.5)\exp(-x^2). \tag{3.9}$$

The function has a unique global minimizer $x^2 = 0$; it has also two maximizers $x =$

$\pm\sqrt{1.5}$, and two asymptotical local minimizers $\pm\infty$. The Palais-Smale condition requires the sequences $\{x_n\}$ converging to 0 and converging to $\sqrt{1.5}$ have convergent subsequence, and they have. The Palais-Smale condition also requires the sequences converging to $\pm\infty$ have convergent subsequence, they do not have. However, the condition of variance sequential compactness (3.2) only requires the sequences converging to 0 have convergent subsequence.

It is proved that the Palais-Smale condition implies the coercivity property [3]. The variance sequential compactness property does not imply the coercivity. Indeed, the function (3.9) satisfies variance sequential compactness property, but it is not coercive. This also shows that the Palais-Smale condition is more stringent than the variance sequential compactness condition.

The most important improvement of Theorem 3.2 is that the theorem can be applied to a minimization problem with a discontinuous objective function.

The following example shows that the conditions of Proposition 2.1 are more restrictive than those of Theorem 3.2

Example 3.2 Let $X=l^2$, and
$$f(x)=(\|x\|^2-0.5)\exp(-\|x\|^2). \tag{3.10}$$
The function has a unique global minimizer $x^2=\theta$. The conditions of Theorem 3.2 hold. However, (3.10) is not inf-compact. Indeed, for each $c>c^*=-0.5$ the level set H_c is a nonempty closed set. Take $0<\varepsilon<c+0.5$ small enough such that
$$B_\varepsilon=\{x: \|x\|<\varepsilon\}\subset H_c.$$
In fact, let $\delta=0.5+c>\varepsilon^2$ and a point $x\in B_\varepsilon$, i.e., $\|x\|\leqslant\varepsilon$, then
$$(\|x\|^2-0.5)\mathrm{enp}\{-\|x\|^2\}\leqslant(\varepsilon^2-0.5)<\delta-0.5=c.$$
Thus, $x\in H_c$. However, the ball B_x is not compact in the space l^2. Hence, the level set H_c is not compact.

Example 3.3 Let $X=\mathbb{R}^1$ and $0<\alpha<1$; let
$$f(x)=|x|^\alpha.$$
The function has a unique global minimizer $x^*=0$ while any reasonable defined derivative of f at x^* cannot exist because $f(x_n)\to\infty$ as $x_n\to x^*$.

For this function the variance is
$$V_1(f,c)=\frac{2\alpha^2}{(1+\alpha)(1+2\alpha)}c^2,$$
and $V(f,f(x_n))\to 0$ implies that $|x_n|^{2\alpha}\to 0$. Therefore, $x_n\to 0$. We see that the condition (3.2) of Theorem 3.2 is satisfied.

4 Applications and Generalizations

4.1 Modifications of Condition (3.2)

The modified variance optimality condition (3.4) has several equivalent forms. The following theorem is established in [2]:

Theorem 4.1 *Let (X,Ω,μ) be a Q-measure space, $f:X\to\mathbb{R}^1$ a measurable realvalued robust function on X. Then the followings are equivalent:*
(1) *$c^*=\inf_{x\in X}f(x)$ is the infimum of f on X.*
(2) *the mean value of f with respect to c^* equals c^**
(3) *the variance of f with respect to c^* equals zero.*
(4) *the modified variance of f with respect to c^* equals zero.*
(5) *the m-th moment of f with respect ot c^* equals zero.*

Here, the mean value, variance and m-th moments of a function f with respect to c are defined as

$$M(f,c)=\frac{1}{\mu(H_c)}\int_{H_c}f(x)d\mu,$$

$$V(f,c)=\frac{1}{\mu(H_c)}\int_{H_c}(f(x)-M(f,c))^2 d\mu,$$

$$M_m(f,c)=\frac{1}{\mu(H_c)}\int_{H_c}(f(x)-c)^m d\mu.$$

Also, see [2,8—10] for the integral global optimality conditions.

Based on this, we can substitute the variance sequential compactness condition by its equivalent conditions:

Theorem 4.2 *Let X be a metric space, $f:X\to\mathbb{R}^1$ a bounded below, lower semicontinuous and robust function, and C the set of points of continuity of f. If f possesses one of the following properties then there exists a robust minimizer x^* such that*

$$x_{n_k}\to x^* \quad \text{and} \quad f(x_{n_k})\to f(x^*)=\inf_{x\in X}f(x). \tag{4.1}$$

(1) *for each sequence $\{x_n\}\subset X$,*

$$\begin{cases}\{x_n\}\subset C\\ M(f,f(x_n))-f(x_n)\to 0\end{cases}\Rightarrow \text{the sequence } \{x_n\} \text{ possesses a convergent subsequence } \{x_{n_k}\} \tag{4.2}$$

(2) *for each sequence $\{x_n\}\subset X$,*

$$\begin{cases}\{x_n\}\subset C\\ V(f,f(x_n))\to 0\end{cases}\Rightarrow \text{the sequence } \{x_n\} \text{ possesses a convergent subsequence } \{x_{n_k}\} \tag{4.3}$$

(3) *for each sequence $\{x_n\}\subset X$ and for some positive integer m,*

$$\begin{cases}\{x_n\}\subset C\\ M_m(f,f(x_n),f(x_n))\to 0\end{cases}\Rightarrow \text{the sequence } \{x_n\} \text{ possesses a convergent subsequence } \{x_{n_k}\} \tag{4.4}$$

(4) *each sequence $\{x_n\}\subset X$ possesses the variance sequential compactness property.*

4.2 Constrained Problems

Let X be a topological space, S a subset of X, and $f:\to\mathbb{R}^1$. Consider a constrained minimization problem: to find infimum of f over S:

$$c^*=\inf_{x\in S}f(x)$$

and the set of global minimizers. Here, the constraint set S may be characterized by a set of equality and inequality constraints. If S is *metrizable*, then Theorem 4.2 is still applicable. Therefore, Theorem 4.2 may be applied to constrained minimization problems.

4.3 Existence of Robust Fixed Points

Let $X=(X,\rho)$ be a metric space, T a robust mapping. Recall that a mapping $T:X\to X$ is said to be robust if for each open set $G\subset X$ the inverse image $T^{-1}(G)$ is a robust set; see [6] and [7]. Finding the set of robust fixed points of a mapping T is equivalent to finding the set of global robust minimizers of $g(x)=\rho(x,Tx)$ with the global minimum value of g being equal to zero. Therefore, we have the following existence theorem of robust fixed points:

Theorem 4.3 *Let (X,ρ) be a metric space, $T:X\to X$ a robust mapping. Suppose that $g(x)=\rho(x,Tx)$ is a lower semicontinuous function and C is the set of points of continuity of g. If*

(i) *there is a sequence $\{y_n\}\subset X$ such that $g(y_n)\to 0$;*

(ii) *for each sequence $\{x_n\}\subset C$, from $V_1(g,g(x_n))\to 0$ implies that there is a convergent subsequence $\{x_{n_k}\}$ of $\{x_n\}$,*

Then There exists a robust fixed point x^* such that
$$x_{n_k}\to x^* \quad \text{and} \quad Tx_{n_k}\to Tx^*=x^*.$$

We have considered approximatability and approximation of fixed points of a robust set-valued mapping in [6] and [11]. We can consider the existence of robust fixed points of a set-valued mapping similarly.

References

[1] Aubin, J. and Ekeland, I. *Applied Nonlinear Analysis*, Wiley-Interscience, New York, 1983.

[2] S. Chew and Q. Zheng. *Integral Global Optimization: Theory, Implementation and Applications*, Lecture Notes in Eoon. & Math. Sys., Springer-Verlag, 1988: 298.

[3] Costa, D. and Silva, E. The Palais-Smale condition versus coercivity, *Nonlinear Analysis, Theory, Methods & Applications*, 1991,16: 371—381.

[4] Ekeland, I. Non-convex minimization problems, *Bull. Amer. Math. Soc. (N.S.)* 1979,1: 443—473.

[5] Palais, R. S. and Smale, S. A generalized Morse theory, *Bull. Amer. Math. Soc.* 1964,70:165—171.

[6] Shi, S., Zheng, Q. and Zhuang, D. Set-valued mappings and approximatable mappings, *Journal of Mathematical Analysis and Applications*, 1994, 183:706—728.

[7] Shi, S.,Zheng, Q. and Zhuang, D. Discontinuous robust mappings are approximatable, *Transaction AMS*, 1995.

[8] Zheng, Q. Robust analysis and global minimization of a class of discontinuous functions (I), *Acta Mathematicae Applicatae Sinica* (English Series), 1990, 6: 205—223.

[9] Zheng, Q. Robust analysis and global minimization of a class of discontinuous functions (II), *Acta Mathematicae Applicatae Sinica* (English Series), 1990, 6: 317—337.

[10] Zheng, Q. Robust analyziz and global optimization, *Computers and Mathematics with Applications*, 1991, 21: 17—24.

[11] Zheng, Q. and Zhuang, D. Equi-robust set-valued mappings and the approximation of fixed points, in *Proceedings of the second International Conference of Fixed point Theory and Applications*, World Scientific, Singapore, 1992: 346—361.

Upper Robust Mappings and Vector Minimization: An Integral Approach*

Abstract: A study of upper robust mapping from a topological space to $\mathbb{R}^n$ and development of optimality conditions for vector minimization of upper robust mappings are presented in the framework of integral based optimization theory. Under some general assumptions, optimality conditions are established for several well developed scalarization techniques such as weighting, ε-constraint and reference point. These optimality conditions are applied to design integral algorithms for finding the set of efficient solutions of a vector optimization problem. A numerical example is presented to illustrate the effectiveness of the algorithm.

1 Introduction

Vector optimization problems originated from decision-making problems appearing in economics, management sciences and other scientific disciplines where it is often required that decision making be based on optimizing several criteria. A vector optimization problem is therefore to find all efficient, i. e. best points in a set with respect to some partial order. In this paper, we consider the vector optimization problems with respect to the partial ordering induced by the nonnegative orthant of $\mathbb{R}^n_+$. However, vector optimization problems with respect to other ordering in $\mathbb{R}^n$ can be treated in a similar fashion. Let X be a topological space and $f=(f^1,f^2,\cdots,f^n):X\to\mathbb{R}^n$ a mapping. A point $\bar{x} \in X$ is said to be a *efficient solution* or *nondominated solution* of a vector minimization problem

$$f(\bar{x})=\min f(x) \tag{1.1}$$

if there exists no other feasible solution x such that $f^i(x)\leqslant f^i(\bar{x})$, for all $i=1,\cdots,n$, with strict inequality for at least one i. If we denote the nonnegative orthant of $\mathbb{R}^n$ by $\mathbb{R}^n_+$, the for $x=(x^1,x^2,\cdots,x^n)$ and $y=(y^1,y^2,\cdots,y^n)$ in $\mathbb{R}^n$, $x\leqslant_{\mathbb{R}^n_+} y$ means that $x^i\leqslant y^i$ for all $i=1,\cdots,n$; $x\lneq_{\mathbb{R}^n_+} y$ means that $x^i\leqslant y^i$ for all $i=1,\cdots,n$ and $x^i\neq y^i$ for at least one i.

Most traditional gradient based scalar optimization techniques usually cannot locate global minimizers but only local minimizers. This shortcoming causes severe difficulties in

---

* In collaboration with Kostreva M M, Zhuang D M. Reprinted from European Journal of Operational Research, 1996, 93:565−581.

numerical vector optimization: when a vector optimization problem is scalarized, the local minimizers of scalarized problem may not lead to efficient solutions of the original vector optimization problem. Integral global optimization offers an alternative. Integral global optimization theory (robust analysis and integral global optimality conditions) and methodology (integral global optimization algorithms) have been developed in the past two decades. The rigorous mathematical foundation of the integral global optimization has been well accepted in mathematics community. The power and flexibility of the integral global optimization algorithms in single objective optimization have been thoroughly demonstrated. In this research, we develop integral global optimization theory and algorithms for vector optimization. We establish the optimality conditions for the well known scalarization methods such as weighting problems and reference point problems. We apply these optimality conditions to design integral algorithms for approximating a set of efficient (nondominated) solutions for a vector minimization problem. Since integral optimization algorithms do deliver global minimizers for scalar problem, it is guaranteed that the solutions generated from the integral algorithms are efficient.

Our integral approach does not attempt to find all efficient solutions of the vector optimization problem (1.1), but only those solutions that could be approximated numerically. The following example illustrates the idea.

Example 1.1 Let
$$f^1(x,y) = \begin{cases} x^2+y^2, & (x,y) \neq (0,0), \\ -1, & (x,y) = (0,0), \end{cases}$$

and
$$f^2(x,y) = \begin{cases} |x|+|y|, & (x,y) \neq (0,0), \\ -1, & (x,y) = (0,0). \end{cases}$$

The mapping $f=(f^1,f^2)^T$ has a unique efficient solution $(0,0)^T$ with the efficient function value $(-1,-1)$. However, there is no reasonable way to numerically approximate such efficient solutions. In other words, such efficient solutions should be excluded when we consider numerical methods of solving vector optimization problems. The concept of *upper robust mapping* is introduced for this purpose.

The following is the organization of the paper. The brief description of integral global optimization theory is presented in Section 2 for the convenience of the reader. Some new results on upper robust mappings and their properties are developed in Section 3. These results are directly related to vector optimization. Optimality conditions for some well known scalarization techniques are established in Section 4. The algorithms and an numerical example are presented in Section 5.

2 Integral Global Minimization

The concept of robustness is an essential component of the theory and methodology of integral global minimization. We highlight some fundamentals here. We also include some basic results of integral approach of global minimization. The reader is referred to [2] and [16—18] for details.

2.1 Robust Sets, Functions and Mappings

Let X be a topological space. A set D in X is said to be *robust* if

$$\text{cl } D = \text{cl int } D, \tag{2.1}$$

where cl D denotes the closure of the set D and int D the interior of D.

A robust set consists of *robust points* of the set. A point $x \in \text{cl } D$ is said to be robust to D (or a robust point of D if $x \in D$), if for each neighbourhood $N(x)$ of x, $N(x) \cap \text{int } D \neq \emptyset$. A set D is robust if and only if each point of D is robust point of D. If x is a robust point of a set D, then D is called a *semineighbourhood* of x. A point x is robust to D if and only if there exists a net $\{x_\lambda\} \subset \text{int } D$ such that $x_\lambda \to x$.

An open set G is robust since $G = \text{int } G$. The empty set is a trivial robust set. A closed set may or may not be robust. A union of robust sets is robust. An intersection of two robust sets may not be robust; but the intersection of an open set and a robust set is robust. If A is robust in X and B is robust in Y, then $A \times B$ is robust in $X \times Y$ with the product topology. A convex set D in a topological vector space is robust if and only if the interior of D is nonempty. An important property of a nonempty robust set is that its interior is not empty. A robust set or its complement can be represented by the union of an open set and a nowhere dense set.

A function $f: X \to \mathbb{R}$ is said to be *upper robust* if the set

$$F_c = \{x: f(x) < c\} \tag{2.2}$$

is robust for each real number c.

An upper semicontinuous (u.s.c.) function f is upper robust since in this case (2.2) is open for each c. A probability function on $\mathbb{R}^n$ is also upper robust. A sum of two upper robust functions may not be upper robust; but the sum of an upper robust function and an u.s.c. function is upper robust.

A function f is upper robust if and only if it is upper robust at each point; f is upper robust at a point x if $x \in F_c$ implies that x is a robust point of F_c. An example of a non upper robust function on $\mathbb{R}^1$ is

$$f(x) = \begin{cases} 0, & x=0, \\ 1, & x \neq 0. \end{cases}$$

f is not upper robust at $x=0$.

2.2 Q-measure Spaces and Integration

In order to investigate a minimization problem with an integral approach, a special class of measure spaces, which are called Q-measure spaces, should be examined.

Let X be a topological space, Ω a σ-field of subsets of X and μ a measure on Ω. A triple (X, Ω, μ) is called a Q-measure space iff

(i) each open set in X is measurable;

(ii) the measure $\mu(G)$ of each nonempty open set G in X is positive: $\mu(G)>0$;

(iii) the measure $\mu(K)$ of a compact set K in X is finite.

The n-dimensional Lebesgue measure space $(\mathbb{R}^n, \Omega, \mu)$ is a Q-measure space; a nondegenerate Gaussian measure μ on a separable Hilbert space H with Borel sets as measurable sets constitutes an infinite dimensional Q-measure space. A specific optimization problem is related to a specific Q-measure space which is suitable for integral global optimization approach.

Once a measure space is given we can define integration in a conventional way.

Since the interior of a nonempty open set is nonempty, the Q-measure of a measurable set containing a nonempty robust set is always positive. This is an essential property we need in the integral approach of minimization. Hence, the following assumptions are usually required:

(A) f is lower semicontinuous and there is a real number b such that $\{x\in S: f(x)\leqslant b\}$ is a nonempty compact set.

(R) f is upper robust on S.

(M) (X,Ω,μ) is a Q-measure space.

The following lemma is useful for the integral approach of global minimization.

Lemma 2.1 *Suppose that the conditions* (M) *and* (R) *hold. If* $c>c^*=\min_{x\in S}f(x)$, *then* $\mu(H_c\cap S)>0$, *where* $H_c=\{x: f(x)\leqslant c\}$ *is the level set of* f.

2.3 Integral Optimality Conditions for Global Minimization

Suppose that the assumptions (A), (M) and (R) hold, and $c>c^*=\min_{x\in S}f(x)$. We define the mean value, modified variance and m-th moment (centered at a), respectively, as follows:

$$M(f,c;S)=\frac{1}{\mu(H_c\cap S)}\int_{H_c\cap S}f(x)\mathrm{d}\mu,$$

and

$$V_1(f,c;S)=\frac{1}{\mu(H_c\cap S)}\int_{H_c\cap S}(f(x)-c)^2\mathrm{d}\mu,$$

$$M_m(f,c;a;S)=\frac{1}{\mu(H_c\cap S)}\int_{H_c\cap S}(f(x)-a)^m\mathrm{d}\mu, m=1,2,\cdots$$

By Lemma 2.1, they are well defined. These definitions can be extended to the case $c\geqslant c^*$ by a limit process. For instance,

$$M_m(f,c;a;S)=\lim_{c_k\downarrow c}\frac{1}{\mu(H_{c_k}\cap S)}\int_{H_{c_k}\cap S}(f(x)-a)^m\mathrm{d}\mu, m=1,2,\cdots$$

The limits exist and are independent of the choice of $\{c_k\}$. The extended concepts are well defined and consistent with the above definitions.

With these concepts we characterize the global optimality as follows:

Theorem 2.1 *Under the assumptions* (A), (M) *and* (R), *the following statements are equivalent*:

(i) $x^*\in S$ *is a global minimizer of* f *over* S *and* $c^*=f(x^*)$ *is the global minimum* *value*.

(ii) $M(f, c^*; S) = c^*$ (the mean value condition).

(iii) $V_1(f, c^*; S) = 0$ (the modified variance condition).

(iv) $M_m(f, c^*; c^*; S) = 0$, *for one of the positive integers* $m = 1, 2, \cdots$ (the higher moment conditions).

3 Upper Robust Mappings

As we pointed out before, the reason to introduce the concept of the robustness of sets and mappings is to exclude from our consideration those points that cannot be approximated numerically. As it turns out, when we design algorithms to solve optimization numerically, the continuity of an objective functions and constraints are not essential, but their approximatability is. In [12] and [13], the approximatability of a mapping is described as follows: let X and Y be topological spaces and $f: X \to Y$. Suppose C is the set of points of continuity of f. f is said to be *approximatable* iff C is dense in X and for each $\bar{x} \in X$, there exists a net $\{x_a\} \subset C$ such that

$$\lim_a x_a = \bar{x} \quad \text{and} \quad \lim_a f(x_a) = f(\bar{x}).$$

We also define a *robust mapping* as follows: Let X and Y be topological spaces. A mapping $f: X \to Y$ is said to be *robust* if for each open set $G \subset Y$, $f^{-1}(G)$ is a robust set in X.

An approximatable mapping is robust. If X is a Baire space and Y satisfies the second axiom of countability, then a mapping is robust if and only if it is approximatable [12,13].

For the purpose of studying vector optimization problems (1.1), we investigate the properties of upper robust mappings from a topological space X to $\mathbb{R}^n$. Among other things, we characterize such mappings by their approximatability at efficient points. The properties of upper robust mappings established here are of significance in other areas of mathematics.

Definition 3.1 Let $f: X \to \mathbb{R}^n$ be a mapping. f is said to be upper robust at x if for each vector c in $\mathbb{R}^n$,

$$x \in F_c = \{x \in X: f(x) <_{\mathbb{R}^n_+} c\} \tag{3.1}$$

implies x is a robust point of F_c. f is upper robust if it is upper robust at each point of $x \in X$, or F_c is a robust set in X.

Proposition 3.1 *Suppose that* $f: X \to \mathbb{R}^n$ *is upper robust. Then for each* j, *the* j-*th component of* f, f^j, *is an upper robust function*.

Proof. For each $c \in \mathbb{R}^1$, the level set F_c of f^j is a union of robust sets:

$$\{x \in X: f^j(x) < c\} = \bigcup_{k=1}^{\infty} \{x \in X: f^j(x) < c, f^i(x) < k, i = 1, \cdots, n; i \neq j\},$$

because f is a upper robust mapping. Thus, f^j is an upper robust real-valued function. □

The following example shows that even if each of $f^i: X \to \mathbb{R}^1$, $i = 1, \cdots, n$, is upper robust, $f=(f^1,\cdots,f^n)$ may not be upper robust.

Example 3.1 Let
$$f^1(x)=\begin{cases}1, & x<0,\\ x, & x\geqslant 0,\end{cases} \text{ and } f^2(x)=\begin{cases}x, & x\leqslant 0,\\ 1, & x>0.\end{cases}$$

Taking $c=(1,1)^T$, we have $\{x: f^1(x)<1\}=[0,1)$ and $\{x: f^2(x)<1\}=(-1,0]$. It is clear that
$$F_c=\{x: f^1(x)<1, f^2(x)<1\}=[0,1)\cap(-1,0]=\{0\}$$
is not a robust set. However, if one of the components of f is upper robust and the remaining ones are upper semi-continuous, then f is an upper robust mapping.

The following proposition describes a convenient way to verify the upper robustness of a mapping.

Proposition 3.2 *Let X be a topological space and $f: X\to\mathbb{R}^n$ a mapping. Then f is upper robust at a point $\bar{x}\in X$ if and only if for any given $\varepsilon=(\varepsilon^1,\cdots,\varepsilon^n)>_{\mathbb{R}^n_+} 0=(0,\cdots,0)$, there is a semineighbourhood $N(\bar{x})$ of $\bar{x}$ such that*
$$f(x)<_{\mathbb{R}^n_+} f(\bar{x})+\varepsilon \quad \forall x\in N(\bar{x}). \tag{3.2}$$

Proof. Suppose that f is upper robust at $\bar{x}$. Then for $\varepsilon=(\varepsilon^1,\cdots,\varepsilon^n)>_{\mathbb{R}^n_+} 0$, letting $c=f(\bar{x})+\varepsilon$, we have
$$\bar{x}\in F_c=\{x: f(x)<_{\mathbb{R}^n_+} f(\bar{x})+\varepsilon\}. \tag{3.3}$$
This implies, by Definition 3.1, that $\bar{x}$ is a robust point of F_c, so $N(\bar{x})=F_c$ is a semineighbourhood of $\bar{x}$. Now for each $x\in N(\bar{x})$, we have by (3.3)
$$f(x)<_{\mathbb{R}^n_+} f(\bar{x})+\varepsilon.$$

Conversely, suppose that (3.2) holds and $c=(c^1,\cdots,c^n)\in\mathbb{R}^n$ is given such that
$$x\in F_c=\{x\in X: f(x)<_{\mathbb{R}^n_+} c\}.$$
Let $\varepsilon=c-f(\bar{x})>_{\mathbb{R}^n_+} 0$. Then there exists a semineighbourhood $N(\bar{x})$ of $\bar{x}$ such that for each point $x\in N(\bar{x})$, we have
$$f(x)<_{\mathbb{R}^n_+} f(\bar{x})+\varepsilon=c.$$
It follows that $\bar{x}\in N(\bar{x})\subset F_c$. Hence $\bar{x}$ is a robust point of F_c and f is upper robust at $\bar{x}$. $\square$

The sum of two upper robust mapping may be non-upper robust. However, the sum of an upper robust mapping and an upper semicontinuous mapping is upper robust. The reader can easily prove this statement by applying Proposition 3.2.

A useful way to study a nonlinear functional is to study its *epigraph*. Here, we use a generalized concept of epigraph to characterize an upper robust mapping geometrically.

Theorem 3.1 *Let X be a topological space. A mapping $f=(f^1,\cdots,f^n): X\to\mathbb{R}^n$ is upper robust if and only if the epigraph*
$$\text{Epi}(f)=\{(x,c)\in X\times\mathbb{R}^n: f(x)\leqslant_{\mathbb{R}^n_+} c, \text{ with } c=(c^1,\cdots,c^n)\} \tag{3.4}$$
is a robust set in the product space $X\times\mathbb{R}^n$.

Proof. Suppose f is upper robust at $\bar{x}$. For each point $(\bar{x},c)\in\text{Epi}(f)$ we must prove that it is a robust point of $\text{Epi}(f)$. Let $\bar{c}=f(\bar{x})$ and $c_1\geqslant_{\mathbb{R}^n_+} \bar{c}$. We have $\bar{x}\in F_{c_1}$. Thus,
$$F_{c_1}\times(c_1,\infty)\subset\text{Epi}(f) \tag{3.5}$$

and
$$\text{int } F_{c_1} \times (c_1, \infty) = \text{int}(F_{c_1} \times (c_1, \infty)) \subset \text{int}(\text{Epi}(F)). \tag{3.6}$$

Since the point $(\bar{x}, c)$ is in $\text{Epi}(f)$, we have $c \geqslant \bar{c} = f(\bar{x})$. For each neighbourhood $N(\bar{x}) \times (c-\varepsilon, c+\varepsilon)$, we have
$$N(\bar{x}) \times (c-\varepsilon, c+\varepsilon) \cap \text{int}(\text{Epi}(f)) \supset N(\bar{x}) \times (c-\varepsilon, c+\varepsilon) \cap (\text{int } F_{c_1} \times (c_1, \infty))$$
$$\supset (N(\bar{x}) \cap \text{int } F_{c_1}) \times (c_1, c+\varepsilon) \neq \emptyset,$$

where we take $\bar{c} \leqslant_{\mathbb{R}^n_+} c_1 \leqslant_{\mathbb{R}^n_+} c + \frac{1}{2}\varepsilon$ in (3.5). The last set is nonempty because $\bar{x}$ is assumed to be robust in the set F_{c_1}.

Conversely, assume that $\text{Epi}(f)$ is a robust set in $X \times \mathbb{R}^n$. If, on the contrary, f is not upper robust at some point, say $\bar{x}$. It means that there exist $\bar{c} \in \mathbb{R}^n$ and a neighbourhood $N(\bar{x})$ of $\bar{x}$ such that
$$f(\bar{x}) <_{\mathbb{R}^n_+} \bar{c} \text{ but } N(\bar{x}) \cap \text{int } F_c = \emptyset, \tag{3.7}$$

where $\text{int } F_c = \text{int}\{x : f(x) <_{\mathbb{R}^n_+} \bar{c}\}$. Let $\varepsilon = \frac{1}{4}(\bar{c} - f(\bar{x})) >_{\mathbb{R}^n_+} 0$ and let $c_0 = \bar{c} - 2\varepsilon$. Then
$$f(\bar{x}) <_{\mathbb{R}^n_+} c_0 - \varepsilon <_{\mathbb{R}^n_+} c_0,$$

i.e., $(\bar{x}, \bar{c}_0) \in \text{Epi}(f)$. Consider the open neighbourhood $G = N(\bar{x}) \times (c_0-\varepsilon, c_0+\varepsilon)$ of $(\bar{x}, \bar{c}_0)$ in $X \times \mathbb{R}^n$. Then, as $(\bar{x}, \bar{c}_0)$ is a robust point of $\text{Epi}(f)$,
$$G \cap \text{int } \text{Epi}(f) \neq \emptyset.$$

Take $(x_1, c_1) \in G \cap \text{int } \text{Epi}(f)$. There is a neighbourhood $N_1(x_1)$ of x_1 and $\varepsilon_1 > 0 (\varepsilon_1 \leqslant \varepsilon)$ such that
$$N_1(x_1) \times (c_1-\varepsilon_1, c_1+\varepsilon_1) \subset N(\bar{x}) \times (c_0-\varepsilon, c_0+\varepsilon) \cap \text{int } \text{Epi}(f).$$

For each point $(y, d) \in N_1(x_1) \times (c_1-\varepsilon_1, c_1+\varepsilon_1)$, we have $(y, d) \in \text{int } \text{Epi}(f) \subset \text{Epi}(f)$, which implies that
$$f(x) \leqslant_{\mathbb{R}^n_+} d \leqslant_{\mathbb{R}^n_+} c_1 + \varepsilon_1 <_{\mathbb{R}^n_+} c_0 + \varepsilon <_{\mathbb{R}^n_+} \bar{c}.$$

In other words, $y \in \{x : f(x) < \bar{c}\}$. We now have
$$N_1(x_1) \subset F_c = \{x : f(x) <_{\mathbb{R}^n_+} \bar{c}\}.$$

Thus, $x_1 \in \text{int } F_c$. But this means that $x_1 \in N(\bar{x}) \cap \text{int } F_c$, or,
$$N(\bar{x}) \cap \text{int } F_c \neq \emptyset.$$

The last statement contradicts (3.7). The contradiction proves that f is upper robust at $\bar{x}$. □

Proposition 3.3 *Let X be a topological space and $f_\lambda : X \to \mathbb{R}^n$, $\lambda \in \Lambda$, be a net of mapping such that each mapping f_λ is upper robust at $\bar{x} \in X$. If $f : X \to \mathbb{R}^n$ is a mapping with the property that*
$$\liminf_\lambda f_\lambda(x) \geqslant f(x), \quad \forall x \in X \tag{3.8}$$

uniformly and, moreover,
$$\lim_\lambda f_\lambda(\bar{x}) = f(\bar{x}), \tag{3.9}$$

then f is also upper robust at $\bar{x}$.

Proof. For give $\varepsilon = (\varepsilon^1, \cdots, \varepsilon^n) >_{\mathbb{R}^n_+} 0$ we have, for sufficiently large $\lambda \in \Lambda$,
$$f(x) <_{\mathbb{R}^n_+} f_\lambda(x) + \frac{1}{3}\varepsilon \quad \forall x \in X \tag{3.10}$$

and
$$f_\lambda(\bar{x}) < f(\bar{x}) + \varepsilon, \quad (3.11)$$
according to (3.8) and (3.9). Since f_λ is upper robust at $\bar{x}$, there is a neighbourhood $N(\bar{x})$ of $\bar{x}$ such that
$$f(x) <_{\mathbb{R}^n_+} f_\lambda(\bar{x}) + \frac{1}{3}\varepsilon \quad \forall x \in N(\bar{x}). \quad (3.12)$$
It follows that for each $x \in N(\bar{x})$,
$$f(x) <_{\mathbb{R}^n_+} f_\lambda(x) + \frac{1}{3}\varepsilon <_{\mathbb{R}^n_+} f_\lambda(\bar{x}) + \frac{2}{3}\varepsilon <_{\mathbb{R}^n_+} f(\bar{x}) + \varepsilon.$$
Therefore, by Proposition 3.2, f is upper robust at $\bar{x}$. □

Next, we study the 'approximatablity' of upper robust mappings. We first consider the sets of points of continuity and discontinuity of an upper robust mapping.

Proposition 3.4 *Suppose that X is a complete metric space and $f: X \to \mathbb{R}^n$ is an upper robust mapping. Then the set D of points of discontinuity is of first category and the set C of points of continuity is of second category.*

Proof. Let $\{r_k^i\}$, $i=1,\cdots,n$, be the set of rational vectors in $\mathbb{R}^n$. Then the set D of points of discontinuity can be represented as (see [10, Chapter I, Section 13])
$$D = \bigcup_{k \neq j} (f^i)^{-1}\Big(\prod_{i=1}^n (r_k^i, r_j^i)\Big) \backslash \text{int}\, (f^i)^{-1}\Big(\prod_{i=1}^n (r_k^i, r_j^i)\Big). \quad (3.13)$$
To prove D is of first category it suffices to show that for any $a^i, b^i \in \mathbb{R}^1$,
$$f^{-1}\Big(\prod_{i=1}^n (a^i, b^i)\Big) \backslash \text{int}\, f^{-1}\Big(\prod_{i=1}^n (a^i, b^i)\Big)$$
is of first category. It is easy to verify the following set equality holds:
$$\prod_{i=1}^n (a^i, b^i) = \prod_{i=1}^n (-\infty, b^i) \cap \Big\{\bigcap_{i=1}^n (a^i, +\infty) \times \prod_{j \neq i}(-\infty, +\infty)\Big\}$$
$$= \prod_{i=1}^n (-\infty, b^i) \cap \Big\{\bigcup_{m=1}^\infty \Big(\bigcap_{i=1}^n \Big[a^i + \frac{1}{m}, +\infty\Big] \times \prod_{j \neq i}(-\infty, +\infty)\Big)\Big\}. \quad (3.14)$$
For an upper robust mapping f, $V = f^{-1}\big(\prod_{i=1}^n (-\infty, b^i)\big)$ is a robust set and
$$f^{-1}\Big([c, +\infty) \times \prod_{i \neq j}(-\infty, \infty)\Big) = X \backslash f^{-1}\Big((-\infty, c) \times \prod_{i \neq j}(-\infty, \infty)\Big)$$
is the complement of a robust set; it is an union of an open set and a nowhere dense set. Thus,
$$f^{-1}\Big(\prod_{i=1}^n (a^i, b^i)\Big) = V \cap \Big\{\bigcup_{m=1}^\infty \Big(\bigcap_{i=1}^n O_m^i \cup T_m^i\Big)\Big\} = V \cap \Big\{\bigcup_{m=1}^\infty G_m \cup \overline{T}_m\Big\}, \quad (3.15)$$
where O_m^i is open and T_m^i is nowhere dense, $m=1,2,\cdots$; $i=1,\cdots,n$, so $G_m = \bigcap O_m^i$ is open and $\overline{T}_m = \bigcap T_m^i$ is nowhere dense. Hence, we have
$$f^{-1}\Big(\prod_{i=1}^n (a^i, b^i)\Big) = \Big\{\bigcup_{m=1}^\infty (V \cap G_m) \cup (V \cap \overline{T}_m)\Big\} = \bigcup_{m=1}^\infty (V_m \cup T_m'), \quad (3.16)$$

where V_m is a robust set (an intersection of a robust set and an open set) and T'_m is a nowhere dense set, $m=1,2,\cdots$; and

$$f^{-1}\left(\prod_{i=1}^{n}(a^i,b^i)\right)\backslash \text{int } f^{-1}\left(\prod_{i=1}^{n}(a^i,b^i)\right)\subset \bigcup_{m=1}^{\infty}(V_m\backslash\text{int } V_m)\cup T'_m. \qquad (3.17)$$

The right hand side of the inclusion (3.17) is obviously of first category, and so is the left hand side.

The set C of points of continuity is of second category because it is the complement of D in the complete metric space X. $\square$

Corollary 3.1 *Suppose that X is a complete metric space and $f: X\to \mathbb{R}^n$ is an upper robust mapping. Then the set C of points of continuity of f is dense in X.*

Theorem 3.2 *Suppose that X is a complete metric space, $f: X\to \mathbb{R}^n$ is a mapping and C is the set of points of continuity. Then f is upper robust if and only if C is dense in X and for each point $x\in X\backslash C$, there exists a sequence $\{x_k\}\subset C$ such that*

$$x_k\to x \quad \text{and} \quad \limsup_{k\to\infty} f(x_k)\leqslant_{\mathbb{R}^n_+} f(x). \qquad (3.18)$$

Proof. Suppose that f is upper robust and $\bar{x}\in X\backslash C$ is a point of discontinuity. For each $k=(k^1,\cdots,k^n)$ and $k^j=1,2,\cdots$, for all $j\in\{1,2,\cdots,n\}$, the set

$$V_k=\{x\in X: f(x)<_{\mathbb{R}^n_+} f(\bar{x})+1/k\}$$

is non-empty robust; $\bar{x}$ is a robust point of this set. Thus, by Proposition 3.4

$$C\cap N_k(\bar{x})\cap \text{int } V_k\neq\varnothing, \quad k=1,2,\cdots, \qquad (3.19)$$

where $N_k(\bar{x})=\{x: d(x,\bar{x})<1/k^j\}$ is the neighbourhood of $\bar{x}$. Taking a point x_k, for each k, from the set (3.19), we obtain a sequence $\{x_k\}\subset C$. We then have

$$x_k\in C, \quad x_k\to\bar{x}, \quad \text{and} \quad f(x_k)<f(\bar{x})+1/k. \qquad (3.20)$$

This implies that

$$x_k\in C, \quad x_k\to\bar{x}, \quad \text{and} \quad \limsup_{k\to\infty} f(x_k)\leqslant_{\mathbb{R}^n_+} f(\bar{x}). \qquad (3.21)$$

Conversely, suppose a point $x\in X$ and there is $c\in \mathbb{R}^n$, $x\in F_c$ such that (3.18) holds. Since $x\in F_c$, we have $f(x)<c$, where $c=(c^1,\cdots,c^n)$. Let $\varepsilon=c-f(x)$. Then by (3.18) there is an integer K such that $x_k\in C$ and

$$f(x_k)<f(x)+\frac{1}{2}\varepsilon<_{\mathbb{R}^n_+} c \quad \forall k\geqslant K.$$

Now, $x_k\in C\cap F_c$. Hence, we also have $x_k\in \text{int } F_c$, for all $k\geqslant K$. It follows that $x_k\in \text{int } F_c$ and $x_k\to\bar{x}$. This proves that $\bar{x}$ is a robust point of f, and the mapping is upper robust. $\square$

Theorem 3.3 *Suppose that X is a complete metric space, $f: X\to \mathbb{R}^n$ is a mapping and C is the set of points of continuity. Then f is upper robust at an efficient solution x^* if and only if there exists a sequence $\{x_k\}\subset C$ such that*

$$x_k\to x^* \quad \text{and} \quad \limsup_{k\to\infty} f(x_k)=f(x^*). \qquad (3.22)$$

Proof. Suppose (3.22) holds. Then by the proof of Theorem 3.2, we have f is upper robust at x^*.

Conversely, if f is upper robust at an efficient point x^*, then there exists a sequence

$\{x_k\} \subset C$ such that

$$x_k \to x^* \quad \text{and} \quad \limsup_{k\to\infty} f(x_k) \leqslant_{\mathbb{R}_+^n} f(x^*). \tag{3.23}$$

If for some $j \in \{1, 2, \cdots, n\}$, $\limsup_{k\to\infty} f^j(x_k) < f^j(x^*)$, Then there exists an integer K such that for all $k \geqslant K$,

$$f^i(x_k) \leqslant f^i(x^*), \ i \neq j, \ \text{and} \ f^j(x_k) < f^j(x^*).$$

We have a contradiction because x^* is assumed to be an efficient solution of f. This verifies (3.22). □

4 Optimality Conditions for Scalarizations

The most common strategy to characterize the efficient solutions of a vector optimization problem is to find a real-valued function representing the decision maker's preference. Once such a function is found, the vector optimization problem is then reduced to a more usual scalar optimization problem. This approach is often referred to as scalarization in the vector optimization literature. There are many papers contributing to the theory of scalarization in vector optimization. Jahn in [5] establishes a series of scalarization results for nonconvex vector optimization problems. Borwein and Zhuang [1] prove several scalarization results for superefficient solutions. In [3, Section 4.3], three common scalarization techniques are presented. The authors call these scalarization techniques *weighting problems*, *k-th-objective Lagrangian problems* and *k-th-objective ε-constraints problems*. They also mention the so-called *weighted norm problem* which are also referred to as *reference point problems*.

The authors of [3] argue that a reference point problem is a generalized version of a weighting problem. In our opinion, there is an intrinsic difference between the two in terms of their applicability: The weighting technique can only handle convex problems while the reference point scalarization technique characterize the efficient solutions of non-convex vector optimization problems under suitable conditions [1, 5, 6]. On the other hand, the weighting problem and the k-th-objective Lagrangian problem are the same technique from a computational point of view, as the authors of [3] noted.

In this section we establish optimality conditions for weighting and reference point methods. Optimality conditions for other scalarization methods can also be derived in a similar fashion. These optimality conditions are novel and important geometrical properties of the scalarization techniques. The optimality conditions not only characterize an efficient solution of vector optimization problems with discontinuous objectives, but also enable us to design integral global optimization algorithms to solve vector optimization problems numerically. Throughout the section we assume the following:

(RV). f is an upper robust mapping.

4.1 Weighting Problems

The weighting problem is one of the most commonly used techniques of scalarization

for solving *convex* vector optimization problems. When the decision space X and the vector objective $f=(f^1,\cdots,f^n)$ are convex, taking each nonnegative weight vector w from $W=\{w\in\mathbb{R}^n: w^i\geq 0; \sum_{i=1}^n w^i=1\}$, one can convert the vector optimization problem
$$\underset{x\in X}{\text{Min}}\ f(x)$$
into a single objective optimization problem:
$$\underset{x\in X}{\text{Min}}\ \sum_{i=1}^n w^i f^i(x). \tag{4.1}$$

We establish a set of optimality conditions to characterize efficient solutions of (4.1). First, we prove that using the weighting method, the scalarized objective $\langle w,f\rangle = \sum_{i=1}^n w^i f^i$ is an upper robust function provided that the vector objective f is an upper robust mapping.

Proposition 4.1 *Suppose X is a topological space, $f: X\to\mathbb{R}^n$ is an upper robust mapping and $w=(w^1,\cdots,w^n)$, where $w^i\geq 0, i=1,\cdots,n$. Then the mapping $(w^1 f^1,\cdots,w^n f^n)$ is upper robust.*

Proof. For each given $c\in\mathbb{R}^n$, we have
$$\{x\in X: w^i f^i(x)<c^i, i=1,\cdots,n\}=\{x\in X: f^i(x)<c^i/w^i\}, \tag{4.2}$$
where $c^j/w^j=\infty$ if $w^j=0$. The set (4.2) is robust, so the mapping $(w^1 f^1,\cdots,w^n f^n)$ is upper robust. □

Theorem 4.1 *Suppose X is a topological space, $f: X\to\mathbb{R}^n$ is an upper robust mapping and $w=(w^1,\cdots,w^n)^\mathrm{T}$, where $w^i\geq 0$, $i=1,\cdots,n$, and $w^1+\cdots+w^n=1$. Then*
$$\langle w,f\rangle = w^1 f^1+\cdots+w^n f^n \tag{4.3}$$
is an upper robust function on X.

Proof. By Proposition 4.1, we need only prove that if f is an upper robust mapping, then $f^1+\cdots+f^n$ is an upper robust function. Consider $n-1$ sets of rational numbers that are ordered as
$$r_1^i, r_2^i, \cdots, r_m^i, \cdots, \quad i=1,\cdots,n-1.$$
For each real number a, we have
$$\text{LHS}=\{x: f^1(x)+\cdots+f^n(x)<a\}$$
$$=\bigcup_{k_1=1}^\infty \cdots \bigcup_{k_{n-1}=1}^\infty \{x: f^1(x)<r_{k_1}^1\}\cap\cdots\cap\{x: f^{n-1}(x)<r_{k_1}^1+\cdots+r_{k_{n-1}}^{n-1}\}$$
$$\cap\{x: f^n(x)<a-(r_{k_1}^1+\cdots+r_{k_{n-1}}^{n-1})\}\}=\text{RHS}. \tag{4.4}$$

Indeed, suppose $x\in\text{RHS}$. Then
$$x\in\{x: f^1(x)<r_{k_1}^1\}\cap\cdots\cap\{x: f^{n-1}(x)<r_{k_1}^1+\cdots+r_{k_{n-1}}^{n-1}\}$$
$$\cap\{x: f^n(x)<a-(r_{k_1}^1+\cdots+r_{k_{n-1}}^{n-1})\}$$
for some $r_{k_1}^i, i=1,\cdots,n$; it follows that
$$f^1(x)+\cdots+f^n(x)<r_{k_1}^1+\cdots+r_{k_{n-1}}^{n-1}+(a-(r_{k_1}^1+\cdots+r_{k_{n-1}}^{n-1}))=a.$$

So $x\in\text{LHS}$. Conversely, for a given a suppose that $x\in\text{LHS}$. Let $a_i=f^i(x), i=1,\cdots,n-1$, define

$$\varepsilon=(a-f^n(x)-(a_1+\cdots+a_{n-1}))/n>0.$$

For each a_i we can find a rational number $r^i_{k_i}$ such that $a_i<r^i_{k_i}$, and $|a_i-r^i_{k_i}|<\varepsilon$, $i=1,\cdots,n-1$, because the rational numbers are dense in $\mathbb{R}^1$. Now the point x satisfies

$$f^i(x)<r^i_{k_i}, \quad i=1,\cdots,n-1 \text{ and } f^n(x)<a-(r^1_{k_1}+\cdots+r^{n-1}_{k_{n-1}}).$$

It follows that $x\in$ RHS.

Thus, under the condition that f is an upper robust mapping, for each given a, RHS is a union of robust sets. Hence LHS is robust. This proves that $f^1+\cdots+f^n$ is an upper robust function. □

Combining Theorem 2.1 with Theorem 4.1, we derive the following theorem.

Theorem 4.2 *Let X be a topological space, $f: X\to\mathbb{R}^n$ an upper robust mapping, and $w\in W=\{w: w^i\geqslant 0; \sum_{i=1}^n w^i=1\}$ be given. Under the assumptions of (A) and (M), the following statements are equivalent:*

(i) $x^*\in X$ *is a solution of the weighting problem* (4.1) *and* $c^*=\langle w,f\rangle$ *is the corresponding value.*

(ii) $M(\langle w,f\rangle, c^*; X)=c^*$ *(the mean value condition).*

(iii) $V_1(\langle w,f\rangle, c^*; X)=0$ *(the modified variance condition).*

(iv) $M_m(\langle w,f\rangle, c^*; c^*; X)=0$, *for one of the positive integers* $m=1,2,\cdots$ *(the higher moment conditions).*

The following example shows how the optimality conditions apply to discontinuous objectives.

Example 4.1 Let $X=\mathbb{R}^1$, $0<\alpha_1\leqslant\alpha_2<\beta_1\leqslant\beta_2<1$, and

$$f_i(x)=\begin{cases}|x|^{\alpha_i}, & \text{if } |x|<1,\\ |x|^{\beta_i}+2, & \text{if } |x|\geqslant 1,\end{cases} \quad i=1,2.$$

The mapping $f=\{f_1,f_2\}^T$ is discontinuous upper robust. We solve the vector optimization problem

$$\min_{x\in\mathbb{R}^2} f(x).$$

This vector minimization problem has a unique solution $x^*=(0,0)^T$. The minimum value is $f^*=(0,0)^T$. For given weight $w=(w_1,w_2)^T$,

$$\langle w,f\rangle=\begin{cases}w_1|x|^{\alpha_1}+w_2|x|^{\alpha_2}, & \text{if } |x|<1,\\ w_1|x|^{\beta_1}+w_2|x|^{\beta_2}+2, & \text{if } |x|\geqslant 1.\end{cases}$$

For simplicity, let $\alpha_1=\alpha_2=\alpha$. Then, by the strictly decreasing property of the mean value for continuous function [2], $M(\langle w,f\rangle, c; X)<c$ if $c>1$. When $c\leqslant 1$, we calculate directly that

$$M(\langle w,f\rangle, c; X)=c/(2+\alpha).$$

The mean value condition implies $c^*=0$ for any given (nonnegative) weight. We can obtain the same result from the variance condition or the higher moment condition.

4.2 Reference Point Method

Nonconvex vector optimization problems arise in a broad range of application. The weighting scalarization technique is not suitable for nonconvex problems. Moreover, it is not uncommon in practice that verifying the convexity of an optimization problem is a nontrivial task. Therefore, the reference point technique [9, 14, 15] is often adopted in practice.

Definition 4.1 Let $f: X \to \mathbb{R}^n$ be a mapping. A point $\hat{y} \in \mathbb{R}^n$ is called a reference point of f if $\hat{y}^j \leqslant f^j(x)$, $\forall x \in X$, and $j = 1, \cdots, n$.

For instance, let $\hat{y}^j = \min_{x \in X} f^j(x)$, $j = 1, \cdots, n$, and $\hat{y}(\hat{y}^1, \cdots, \hat{y}^n)^T$. Then $\hat{y}$ is a reference point.

With a referece point $\hat{y}$, let

$$g_d(x) = \sum_{j=1}^n w^j d^j(\hat{y}^j, f^j(x)), \qquad (4.5)$$

where $w^j \geqslant 0$, $j = 1, \cdots, n$, are weights and $d^j(\cdot, \cdot)$, $j = 1, \cdots, n$, are increasing upper semicontinuous functions with $d^j(y^j, y^j) = 0$, $j = 1, \cdots, n$.

Definition 4.2 A solution $\hat{x}$ of the minimization problem $\text{Min}_{x \in X} g_d(x)$ is called a reference point solution corresponding to a reference point $\hat{y}$, metrics $d^1, \cdots, d^n$ and the set of weights $w^1, \cdots, w^n$.

It is often convenient to take the weighted metrics as weighted norms in $\mathbb{R}^n$, the weighted Euclidean norm or the weighted Chebyshev norm. For example, if we take the weighted Euclidean norm, the reference point problem becomes

$$\underset{x \in X}{\text{Min}} \sqrt{\sum_{j=1}^n w_j (|f^j(x) - \hat{y}^j|)^2}. \qquad (4.6)$$

If we take the weighted Chebyshev norm, the reference point problem becomes

$$\underset{x \in X}{\text{Min}} \max_{i=1, \cdots, n} \{w_j | f^j(x) - \hat{y}^j|\}.$$

For the reference point problem, we have the following results:

Proposition 4.2 *Let X be a topological space, $f: X \to \mathbb{R}^n$ an upper robust mapping, $w^j \geqslant 0$, $j = 1, \cdots, n$, given weights and $\hat{y}$ a given reference point. Suppose that for each j, $d^j(\hat{y}^j, \cdot)$ is a non negative increasing upper semicontinuous function of $y^j \geqslant \hat{y}^j$, $j = 1, \cdots, n$. Then*

$$g_d(x) = \sum_{j=1}^n w^j d^j(\hat{y}^j, f^j(x))$$

is an upper robust function.

Proof. For each given $c \in \mathbb{R}^n$ and for each j, the set

$$\{x : d^j(\hat{y}^j, f^j(x)) < c^j\} = \begin{cases} \varnothing, & \text{if } c^j \leqslant 0, \\ \{x : f^j(x) < b^j\}, & \text{if } c^j > 0, \end{cases}$$

where $b^j = \sup\{y^j : d^j(\hat{y}^j, y^j) < c^j\}$. Thus, for each given $c \in \mathbb{R}^n$, the set $\{x : d^j(\hat{y}^j, f^j(x)) < c^j, j = 1, \cdots, n\}$ is a robust set. This implies that $g_d(x)$ is upper robust by Theorem 4.1. □

Combining Theorem 2.1 with Proposition 4.4, we have the following theorem:

Theorem 4.3 *For a given $\bar{c} = (\bar{c}^1, \cdots, \bar{c}^n)^T$, under the assumptions (A), (M), (RV) and of Proposition 4.4, the following statements are equivalent:*

(i) A point $\bar{x} \in X$ is a reference point solution with $c^* = \sum_{j=1}^{n} w^j d^j(y^j, f^j(\bar{x}))$ as the corresponding value.

(ii) $M(g_d, c^*; X) = c^*$ (the mean value condition).

(iii) $V_1(g_d, c^*; X) = 0$ (the modified variance condition).

(iv) $M_m(g_d, c^*; c^*; X) = 0$, for one of the positive integers $m = 1, 2, \cdots$ (the higher moment conditions).

5 An Integral Algorithm and Numerical Examples

As we pointed out before, the integral global minimization algorithm delivers *global* minimizers for single objective minimization problems. This feature is extremely valuable in solving vector optimization problems. In this section, the optimality conditions established in the previous section are applied to design integral minimization algorithms to approximate the efficient solution set of a vector minimization problem.

For simplicity, we describe an algorithm using a reference point method under the assumption that the objective function of problem (5.1) is bounded below and the set of efficient solutions of the problem is nonempty. The algorithms based on other scalarization methods can also be designed.

Step 1: Find a reference point. Let
$$a^i := \min_{x \in S} f^i(x), \quad i = 1, \cdots, n. \tag{5.1}$$
Take a point $(\hat{y}^1, \cdots, \hat{y}^n)$ as a reference point such that
$$\hat{y}^i < a^i, \quad i = 1, \cdots, n. \tag{5.2}$$

Step 2: Take L sets of positive weights $(w_k^1, \cdots, w_k^n), k = 1, \cdots, L$, and minimize the following L scalar problems:
$$\min_{x \in S} g_k(x), \quad k = 1, \cdots, L, \tag{5.3}$$
where we may take g_k as Euclidean norm or Chebyshev norm or let
$$g_k(x) = \sum_{1}^{n} \{w_k^i(f^i(x) - \hat{y}^i)\}. \tag{5.4}$$
We obtain a sequence of solutions:
$$x_1, \cdots, x_L \text{ and } f(x_1), \cdots, f(x_L). \tag{5.5}$$

Step 3: Use simplices produced by these points as an approximation of the solution set $f(M)$.

Remark 5.1 We assume that the objective functions of the vector minimization problem are bounded below so that the minimum values $a^1, \cdots, a^n$ of (5.1) are finite. The point $(a^1, \cdots, a^n)$ can be found by using the integral minimization method. The reference point $(\hat{y}^1, \cdots, \hat{y}^n)$ satisfying (5.2) can be chosen by the decision maker or can be chosen arbitrarily. From computational point of view, choosing $\hat{y}$ as a reference point is better than choosing a in (5.1).

Remark 5.2 The scalar minimization problems (5.3), as well as (5.1), are nonlinear constrained optimization problems. The objective functions might be discontinuous and the constraint set might be disconnected. We can use the discontinuous penalty function technique to reduce a constrained minimization problem to an unconstrained (or box constrained) ones. For a constrained minimization problem

$$\operatorname*{Min}_{x \in S} \; g(x), \qquad (5.6)$$

let

$$p(x) = \begin{cases} \delta + d(x), & x \notin S, \\ 0, & x \in S, \end{cases} \qquad (5.7)$$

where $\delta > 0$ is a constant, and $d(x)$ is penalty-like function such that $d(x) = 0$ if and only if $x \in S$. The penalized problem is of the following form:

$$\operatorname{Min}[g(x) + \alpha p(x)], \qquad (5.8)$$

where $\alpha > 0$ is the penalty parameter. The most important advantage of using discontinuous penalty function (5.7) is that it such penalized problem is exact without any constraint qualification requirement. See [18] for more details.

The algorithm has been implemented by a properly designed Monte Carlo technique. For a given reference point and a set of weights, the algorithm converges to an efficient solution with pre-specified accuracy. We give a numerical example to illustrate the power of our approach.

Example 5.1 Consider a vector optimization problem (*'Optimal design of a sandwich beam'*) taken from [7] and [8]. This is a bicriterial nonlinear optimization problem of seven variables with seven box constraints and a nonlinear inequality constraint. We will not restate the actual problem in detail. The reader is referred to the original references.

Applying the above algorithm, we obtain efficient elements of the image set of (f_1, f_2) listed in Table 1. In Table 2, we give four compromise solutions. A part of the approximation of the set of efficient solutions is illustrated in Fig. 1.

Table 1 Iterated minimal elements

f^1	f^2	f^1	f^2
8.17994331	591.31296876	23.70762509	0.18756257
8.18313330	486.02233937	26.89154701	0.11288390
8.89529322	223.52841014	29.41982501	0.08078902
9.15373034	178.49739085	30.03870987	0.07715545
9.99660688	63.28892780	33.06210990	0.05492974
10.05567952	22.11224264	36.23951089	0.04281627
10.64656909	12.67675951	39.22120208	0.03570512
11.32437797	7.84447413	40.86787715	0.03273413

续表

f^1	f^2	f^1	f^2
12.19073925	4.79381215	42.08200982	0.03081917
13.60446417	2.57588857	46.89294124	0.02492974
14.44433869	1.74495616	49.30072240	0.02273858
15.64738715	1.25807617	57.14563630	0.01766231
16.10404488	1.09122550	64.61565507	0.01461693
16.50446294	0.96764436	70.64245411	0.01287817
16.85863036	0.87296645	75.91565830	0.01169748
17.18385903	0.79528927	80.70360751	0.01082299
18.00553359	0.63785089	107.09748249	0.00923308
18.53993725	0.55625679	114.50617193	0.00869432
18.89533816	0.50938644	118.37710917	0.00720372
19.12593454	0.48171163	123.11886770	0.00699876
19.60034299	0.43067015	151.35145221	0.00645405

Table 2 Compromise solutions

Estimate as best approximation from the set of minimal elements	Pre-image of the estimate
(18.00553359, 0.63785098)	(0.32647148, 14.65414324, 0.00000009, 233.89503120, 10.00000304, 10.00000226, 10.00000030)
(30.03870987, 0.07507935)	(0.58376922, 26.08598686, 0.00000092, 687.39042936, 10.00000002, 10.00000265, 10.00000602)
(42.08288982, 0.03081971)	(0.79907522, 35.44132713, 0.00000638, 979.14364790, 11.60774125, 12.89346387, 15.16751641)
(49.30072240, 0.02273858)	(0.88538548, 39.18946234, 0.00001474, 961.15533657, 16.90878365, 19.01396637, 21.48119806)

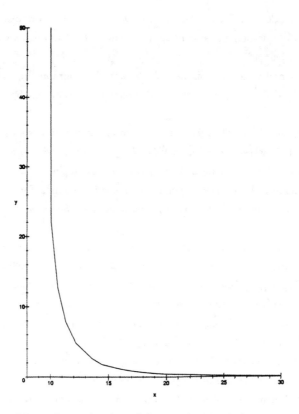

Fig. 1. Approximation of the set of minimal elements.

6 Conclusions

The theory of vector minimization has not successfully handled discontinuous functions, since it has been grounded in differential calculus, starting with Kuhn and Tucker. A powerful and widely applicable alternative has recently been developed in the integral approach. According to the integral approach, and under the assumption that the objective mapping is upper robust, all of the well developed scalarization techniques may be interpreted in a more general context. Such an interpretation has implications for the theory of vector minimization, for characterizing efficient for solutions and for algorithms with numerically compute these solutions.

References
[1] Borwein, J. M., and Zhuang, D. Super efficiency in vector optimization [J]. *Transactions of the AMS* 338(1993)105—122.
[2] Chew, S. H., and Zheng, Q. Integral Global Optimization [J]. *Lecture Notes in Economics and Mathematical Systems* 298, Springer-Verlag, New York, 1988.
[3] Chankong, V. and Haimes, Y. Y. *Multiobjective Decision Making*, North-Holland, Amsterdam, 1983.

[4] Haimes, Y. Y., Lasdon, L., and Wismer, D. On a bicriterion formulation of the problems of integrated system identification and system optimization, *IEEE Transactions on Systems, Man, and Cybernctics* 1(1971)296—297.

[5] Jahn, J. Scalarization of vector optimization, *Mathematical Programming* 29(1984)203—218.

[6] Jahn, J. *Mathematical Vector Optimization in Partially Ordered Linear Spaces*, Verlag Peter Lang, 1986.

[7] Jahn, J. Vector optimization: Theory, methods, and application to design problems in engineering, in: W. Krabs and J. Zowe(eds.), *Modern Methods of Optimization-Proceedings*, Lecture Notes in Economics and Mathematical Systems 378, Springer-Verlag, Berlin, 1992.

[8] Jahn, J., and Merkel, A. Reference point approximation method for the solution of bicriterial nonlinear optimization problems, *Journal of Optimization Theory and Applications* 74 (1992) 87—103.

[9] Jahn, J. A method of reference point approximation in vector optimization, in: H. Schellhaas et al. (eds.), *Operations Research Proceedings 1987*, Springer-Verlag, Berlin, 1988, 576—587.

[10] Kuratowski, K. *Topology, Volume I*, Academic Press, New York, 1966.

[11] Rockafellar, R. T. *Convex Analysis*, Princeton University Press, Princeton, NJ, 1970.

[12] Shi, S., Zheng, Q., and Zhuang, D. Discontinuous robust mappings are approximatable, *Transactions of the AMS* 347(1995)4943—4957.

[13] Shi, S., Zheng, Q., and Zhuang, D. Set-valued mappings and approximatable mappings, *Journal of Mathematical Analysis and Applications* 183(1994)706—726.

[14] Wierzbicki, A. P. A mathematical basis for satisficing decision making, *Mathematical Modelling* 3 (1982)391—405.

[15] Wierzbicki, A. P. On the completeness and constructiveness of parametric characterizations to vector optimization problems, *OR Spektrum* 8(1986)73—87.

[16] Zheng, Q. Robust analysis and global minimization of a class of discontinuous functions(Ⅰ), *Acta Mathematicae Applicatiae Sinica*, English Series 6/3(1990)205—223.

[17] Zheng, Q. Robust analysis and global optimization of a class of discontinuous functions(Ⅱ), *Acta Mathematicae Applicatae Sinica*, English Series 6/4(1990)317—337.

[18] Zheng, Q. Integral global optimization of robust discontinuous functions, Ph. D. Dissertation, Clemson University, 1992.

Integral Global Minimization: Algorithms, Implementations and Numerical Tests*

Abstract: The theoretical foundation of integral global optimization has become widely known and well accepted [4,24,25]. However, more effort is needed to demonstrate the effectiveness of the integral global optimization algorithms. In this work we detail the implementation of the integral global minimization algorithms. We describe how the integral global optimization method handles nonconvex unconstrained or box constrained, constrained or discrete minimization problems. We illustrate the flexibility and the efficiency of integral global optimization method by presenting the performance of algorithms on a collection of well known test problems in global optimization literature. We provide the software which solves these test problems and other minimization problems. The performance of the computations demonstrates that the integral global algorithms are not only extremely flexible and reliable but also very efficient.

1 Introduction

Let X be a topological space, $f: X \to \mathbb{R}^1$ a function and S a subset of X. The problem considered here is to find the infimum of f over S

$$c^* = \inf_{x \in S} f(x) \tag{1.1}$$

and the set of global minimizers

$$H^* = \{x \in S: f(x) = c^*\}, \tag{1.2}$$

if H^* is nonempty.

Most of the conventional optimization theory and methods are gradient-based. They can only be applied to characterize and to find a local minimizer of an objective function. The gradient based iterative algorithms, which are easy to implement, usually have higher convergence rates. The gradient-based theory and methods are the main stream of the research in optimization. However, in many applications, it is often more desirable to find a global minimizer than to find a local one, especially when we deal with a nonconvex optimization problem.

An integral approach of global optimization has been developed to deal with

---

* In collaboration with Zhuang D M. Reprinted from Journal of Global Optimization, 1995, 7:421−454.

nonconvex minimization problems of a class of discontinuous objective functions (see [4], [30],[31]). Integral global optimization algorithms are implemented by properly designed Monte-Carlo techniques. In this work we describe the techniques of the implementations of the algorithms. We also present the performance of the algorithms on a collection of well known test problems. A companion diskette containing all the software necessary for solving unconstrained or constrained minimization problems presented in this paper on an MS-DOS environment is available upon the request to the authors.

The following is the organization of the paper. In Section 2, we describe briefly the main ideas of the integral global optimization theory. Section 3 is devoted to the detailed explanation of the implementation of integral global minimization algorithms for simple unconstrained models. Some statistical analysis of the implementation is also presented in Section 3. More implementation techniques are discussed in Section 4. In Section 5, we consider constrained and discrete or mixed problems. A collection of test problems from global optimization literature are solved by the integral global minimization algorithm in Ssection 6.

2 Integral Global Optimization

We summarize the main ideas of the integral global minimization theory. The reader is referred to [4],[30],[31] for details.

2.1 Optimality Conditions

Recall that a set D in a topological space X is *robust* iff
$$\text{cl } D = \text{cl int } D. \tag{2.1}$$
A function $f: X \to \mathbb{R}^1$ is *upper robust* over S iff the set
$$F_e = \{x \in S: f(x) < c\} \tag{2.2}$$
is robust for each real number c. Upper robustness of a function generalizes the concepte of continuity of a function. Based on such a generalization, a unified approach to continuous, discrete and mixed minimization problems, integral global optimization, is established.

For the problem (1.1) under the assumptions that f is lower semicontinuous and upper robust; (X, Ω, μ) is a Q-measure space (the measure μ have a property that the measure of a nonempty open set is positive); $S \subset X$ is robust and there is a real number b such that $\{x \in S: f(x) \leq b\}$ is compact, the following statements are equivalent:

1. A point $x^* \in S$ is a global minimizer and $c^* = f(x^*)$ is the corresponding global minimum value;
2. $M(f, c^*; S) = c^*$ (mean value condition);
3. $V_1(f, c^*; S) = 0$ (modified variance condition),

where

$$M(f,c;S)=\frac{1}{\mu(H_c\cap S)}\int_{H_c\cap S}f(x)\mathrm{d}\mu \tag{2.3}$$

and

$$V_1(f,c;S)=\frac{1}{\mu(H_c\cap S)}\int_{H_c}(f(x)-c)^2\mathrm{d}\mu \tag{2.4}$$

are the *mean value* and *modified variance*, respectively, of f over its level set

$$H_c=\{x:f(x)\leqslant c\}. \tag{2.5}$$

2.2 The Algorithm

Step 1: Take $c_0 > \varepsilon^*$ and $\varepsilon > 0$; $k:=0$;

Step 2: $c_{k+1}:=M(f,c_k;S); v_{k+1}:=V_1(f,c_k;S); H_{k+1}\cap S:=\{x\in S: f(x)\leqslant c_{k+1}\}$;

Step 3: If $v_{k+1}\geqslant\varepsilon$ then $k:=k+1$; go to Step 2;

Step 4: $c^* \Leftarrow c_{k+1}$; $H^*\Leftarrow H_{c_{k+1}}\cap S$; Stop.

If we take $\varepsilon=0$, then we obtain two monotone sequences:

$$c_0\geqslant c_1\geqslant\cdots\geqslant c_k\geqslant c_{k+1}\geqslant\cdots \tag{2.6}$$

and

$$H_{c_0}\cap S\supset H_{c_1}\cap S\supset\cdots\supset H_{c_k}\cap S\supset H_{c_{k+1}}\cap S\supset\cdots \tag{2.1}$$

Let

$$c^*=\lim_{k\to\infty}c_k \quad\text{and}\quad H^*=\bigcap_{k=1}^{\infty}H_{c_k}\cap S_1, \tag{2.8}$$

then c^* is the global minimum value of f over S and H^* is the set of global minimizers.

From the above algorithm, we realize that the integral method for finding global minimizers requires the computation of a sequence of mean value and modified variances, and a sequence of level sets. Finding a mean value and modified variance are equivalent to computing integrals of a function of several variables; the determination of a level set is, in general, more involved. This suggests that a Monte-Carlo based technique for finding global minimizers is appropriate. The error of integration by the Monte Carlo method is proportional to $\sigma/\sqrt{t}$, where t is the number of samples and σ^2 is the variance of sample distribution. Note that the accuracy at early steps of the algorithm is not generally required. Since σ^2 will tend to zero as the mean value goes to the global minimum value (the modified variance condition), the Monte Carlo approximation will become more accurate near the global minimum value even though the number t of random samples is not very large.

In next section, we will discuss the Monte Carlo implementation of the algorithme.

3 Monte-Carlo Implementation of a Simple Model

Let us first consider a simple model of a global minimization problem. Suppose that the constraint set D is a cuboid in $\mathbb{R}^n$,

$$D=\{x:a^i\leqslant x^i\leqslant b^i, i=1,\cdots,n\} \tag{3.1}$$

and the objective function f is a lower semicontinuous and upper robust function with a

unique global minimizer $x^* \in D$. In other words, for a decreasing sequence $\{c_k\}$ which converges to the global minimum value c^*, the size of the level sets satisfies:
$$\rho_k = \rho(H_{c_k}) = \max_{x,y \in H_{c_k}} \|x-y\| \to 0 \text{ as } k \to \infty. \tag{3.2}$$

We then have
$$c^* = \min_{x \in D} f(x) = \min_{x \in H_{c_k} \cap D} f(x) = \min_{x \in D_k} f(x), \tag{3.3}$$
where D_k is the smallest cuboid containing the level set $H_{c_k} \cap D$.

Instead of computing $M(f, c_k; D)$ and $V_1(f, c_k; D)$ in the algorithm in the previous section, we compute $M(f, c_k; D_k)$ and $V_1(f, c_k; D_k)$ at each iteration. The following is an algorithm for this model:

Step 1: Take $c_0 > \min_{x \in D} f(x)$. Let $D_0 = D$ be an initial cuboid. Set $k=0$.

Step 2: Compute the mean value
$$c_{k+1} = M(f, c_k; D_k) = \frac{1}{\mu(H_{c_k} \cap D_k)} \int_{H_{c_k} \cap D_k} f(x) d\mu,$$
where D_k be the smallest closed cuboid containing the level set $H_{c_k} = \{x: f(x) \leq c_k\}$.

Step 3: Compute the modified variance
$$v_f = V_1(f, c_k; D_k) = \frac{1}{\mu(H_{c_k} \cap D_k)} \int_{H_{c_k} \cap D_k} (f(x) - c_k)^2 d\mu,$$

Step 4: If $v_f \geq \varepsilon$, set, $k := k+1$, and go to Step 2; otherwise, go to Step 5.

Step 5: Let $c^* \Leftarrow c_{k+1}$ and $H^* \Leftarrow H_{c_{k+1}}$, Stop.

At each iteration, we try to find D_k instead of level set H_{c_k}, where
$D_k = \{x: a_k^i \leq x^i \leq b_k^i, i=1, \cdots, n\}$,
$a_k^i = \min\{x_i: (x^1, \cdots, x^i, \cdots, x^n) \in H_{c_k}\}$,
$b_k^i = \max\{x_i: (x^1, \cdots, x^i, \cdots, x^n) \in H_{c_k}\}$.

Let $\varepsilon = 0$. The above algorithm produces a sequence of level constants $\{c_k\}$ and a sequence of cuboid $\{D_k\}$.

Lemma 3.1 *For the foregoing simple model,*
$$\{x^*\} = \bigcap_{k=1}^{\infty} D_k, \tag{3.4}$$
where x^* is the unique global minimizer of the minimization problem.

Proof. By the definition of the level set H_{c_k} and D_k, $x^* \in H_{c_k} \cap D_k$, for each k. We have
$$x^* \in \bigcap_{k=1}^{\infty} (H_{c_k} \cap D_k) \subset \bigcap_{k=1}^{\infty} D_k.$$

It follows form (3.2) and the construction of D_k, the diameter of D_k approaches to 0. The Cantor theorem [2] applies. □

Monte Carlo Implementation

The implementation of the simple model can be desctibed as follows:

1. Approximation of H_{c_0} and $M(f, c_0; D)$:

Let $\xi = (\xi^1, \cdots, \xi^n)$ be an independent n-multiple random number which is uniformly distributed on $[0,1]^n$. Let

$$x^i = a^i + (b^i - a^i) \cdot \xi^i, i = 1, \cdots, n. \tag{3.5}$$

Then $x = (x^1, \cdots, x^n)$ is uniformly distributed on D.

Take km samples and evaluate function values $f(x_j), j = 1, 2, \cdots, km$, at these sample points. Comparing the values of the function f at these points, we obtain a set W of sample points corresponding to the t smallest function values: $FV[j], j = 1, 2, \cdots, t$, ordered by their valuse, i. e.,

$$FV[1] \geqslant FV[2] \geqslant \cdots \geqslant FV[t]. \tag{3.6}$$

The set W is called an *acceptance set* which can be regarded as an approximation to the level set H_{c_0} where $c_0 = FV[1]$ is the largest value of $\{FC[j]\}$. The positive integer t is called the *statistical inder*. It is clear that $f(x) \leqslant c_0$ for all $x \in W$. Also, the mean value of f over the level set H_{c_0} can be approximated by the mean value of $\{FV[j]\}$:

$$c_1 = M(f, c_0; D) \approx (FV[1] + \cdots + FV[t])/t. \tag{3.7}$$

2. Generating a new cuboid by W:

The new cuboid domain of dimension n

$$D_1 = \{x = (x^1, \cdots, x^n) : a_1^i \leqslant x^i \leqslant b_1^i, i = 1, \cdots, n\} \tag{3.8}$$

can be generated by the following procedure. Suppoe that the random samples in W are $\tau_1, \cdots, \tau_n$, Let

$$\sigma_0^i = \min(\tau_1^i, \cdots, \tau_n^i) \quad \text{and} \quad \sigma_1^i = \max(\tau_1^i, \tau_n^i), i = 1, \cdots, n, \tag{3.9}$$

where $\tau_j = (\tau_j^1, \cdots, \tau_j^n), j = 1, \cdots, t$. We use

$$a^i = \sigma_0^i - \frac{\sigma_1^i - \sigma_0^i}{t-1} \quad \text{and} \quad b^i = \sigma_1^i + \frac{\sigma_1^i - \sigma_0^i}{t-1} \tag{3.10}$$

as estimators to generate a_1^i and $b_1^i, i = 1, \cdots, n$.

3. Continuing the iterative process:

The samples are now taken in the new domain D_1. Take a random sample point $x = (x^1, \cdots, x^n)$ in D_1, where

$$x^i = a_1^i + (b_1^i - a_1^i) \cdot \xi^i, i = 1, \cdots, n. \tag{3.11}$$

Evaluate $f(x)$. If $f(x) \geqslant FV[1]$, then drop this sample point; otherwise, update the sets $\{FV[j]\}$ and W such that the new $\{FV[j]\}$ is made up of the t best function valuse obtained so far. The acceptance set W is updated accordingly. Repeating this procedure until $FV[1] \leqslant c_1$, we obtain, new FV and W.

4. Iterative solution:

At each iteration, the smallest value $FV[t]$ in the set $\{FV[j]\}$ and the corresponding point in W can be regarded as an iterative solution.

5. Convergence criterion:

The modified variance v_f of $\{FV[j]\}$, which is given by

$$v_f = \frac{1}{t-1} \sum_{j=2}^{t} (FV[j] - FV[1])^2, \tag{3.12}$$

can be regarded as an approximation of $V_1(f, c_k; D_k)$ at each iteration. If v_f is less than the given precision ε, then the iterative process terminates, and the current iteration in Step 4 would serve as and estimate of the global minimum value and the global minimizer.

4 More Techniques on Implementation

4.1 Adaptive Change of Search Sets

Consider a minimization problem
$$\min_{x \in S} f(x).$$
The adaptive change of search sets technique allows an initial choice of a computationally manageable set S_0 and then during the iteration process moves on to better performing sets S_k while still holding down their "size". The idea of this technique is to make a more perceptive use of the information generated from previous iterations to reduce the size of search sets.

Let c_0 be a real number and S_0 be an initial compact robust search set where $\mu(H_{c_0} \cap S) > 0$. Let
$$c_1 = M(f, c_0; S_0) = \frac{1}{\mu(H_{c_0} \cap S)} \int_{H_{c_0} \cap S} f(x) d\mu.$$
Then $c_0 \geqslant c_1 \geqslant c^* = \min_{x \in S} f(x)$. Take a robust set $S_1 \subset S$ such that $S_0 \cap H_{c_1} \subset S_1$, which implies that $S_0 \cap H_{c_1} \subset S_1 \cap H_{c_1}$.

Furthermore, we have
$$\mu(S_1 \cap H_{c_1}) \geqslant \mu(S_0 \cap H_{c_1}) > 0, \tag{4.1}$$
where $\mu(S_0 \cap H_{c_1}) > 0$ because $\mu(S_0 \cap H_{c_0}) > 0$. Let $c_2 = M(f, c_1; S_1)$.

In general, we require a set S_{k+1} be such that
$$S_{k-1} \cap H_{c_k} \subset S_k, \quad k = 1, 2, \cdots, \tag{4.2}$$
and let $c_{k+1} = M(f, c_k; S_k)$, $k = 0, 1, 2, \cdots$. In this manner we have constructed a sequence of robust search sets and obtain the following two sequences:
$$c_0 \geqslant c_1 \geqslant \cdots \geqslant c_k \geqslant c_{k+1} \geqslant \cdots \tag{4.3}$$
and
$$H_{c_0} \supset H_{c_1} \supset \cdots \supset H_{c_k} \supset H_{c_{k+1}} \supset \cdots \tag{4.4}$$
Denote
$$S_L = \bigcap_{k=1}^{\infty} S_k \text{ and } G_L = \text{cl } S_L. \tag{4.5}$$
Sometimes the structures of sets S_k, $k = 0, 1, 2, \cdots$, are complicated, and a further assumption is required:

(SM): $\quad \mu(S_L) = \mu(\text{cl } S_L).$

Let $c^* = \lim_{k \to \infty} c_k$ and $H^* = \lim_{k \to \infty} H_{c_k} = \bigcap_{k=1}^{\infty} H_{c_k}$.

Theorem 4.1 *Under the assumptions* (A), (M), *and* (SM), *the limit* c^* *is the global minimum value and* $H^* \cap G_L$ *is the set of corresponding global minimizers of* f *over* G_L.

Optimality conditions of our change-of-set model can also be given. Since the search sets are changed step by stey, the optimality conditions are described in limit forms.

Suppose that $\{c_k\}$ is a decreasing sequence which tends to c^*, and $\{S_k\}$ is a sequence of robust sets such that

$$S_k \subset S \quad \text{and} \quad S_k \cap H_{c_{k+1}} \subset S_{k+1}, \quad k=0,1,2,\cdots \tag{4.6}$$

Theorem 4.2 *The following statements are equivalent:*

(i) c^* *is the global minimum value of f over G_L;*

(ii) $\lim\limits_{k\to\infty} \dfrac{1}{\mu(S_k \cap H_{c_k})} \int_{S_k \cap H_{c_k}} f(x) \mathrm{d}\mu = c^*$;

(iii) $\lim\limits_{k\to\infty} \dfrac{1}{\mu(S_k \cap H_{c_k})} \int_{S_k \cap H_{c_k}} (f(x) - c^*)^2 \mathrm{d}\mu = 0.$

A technique of reduction of the skew rate

$$\delta = \frac{2x^* - (a+b)}{b-a} \tag{4.7}$$

was proposed to reduce the amount of computation. Thus, we can adopt the following change-of-set strategy: *to move the search set in such directions so as to reduce the skew rate.*

Take three constant $\delta_0 \geqslant 0$, $\delta_1 > \delta_2 \geqslant 0$. The skew rate δ is considered not too large if $|\delta| \leqslant \delta_0$. In this case, the search domain need not be changed. If $\delta > \delta_0$, then, we use

$$\zeta'_1y = \zeta_1 + \delta_1\delta(\zeta_1 - \zeta_0) \quad \text{and} \quad \zeta'_0 = \zeta_0 + \delta_2\delta(\zeta_1 - \zeta_0) \tag{4.8}$$

as the estimators of the endpoint of the new search domain. Otherwise, if $\delta < -\delta_0$, the following will be used instead:

$$\zeta'_1 = \zeta_1 + \delta_2\delta(\zeta_1 - \zeta_0) \quad \text{and} \quad \zeta'_0 = \zeta_0 + \delta_1\delta(\zeta_1 - \zeta_0). \tag{4.9}$$

The fact remains that the skew rate is unknown because we would otherwise need to know the global minimizers x^* in advance. Suppose that ξ is a random variable with probability density $p(x) > 0$ on $[a,b]$ and $\xi_1, \cdots, \xi_N$, are samples of ξ. Let $\eta_N = \min\limits_{1\leqslant i\leqslant N} f(\xi_i)$. It is not difficult to see that η_N will tend to $f(x^*) = \min\limits_{a\leqslant x\leqslant b} f(x)$ as $N \to \infty$. Moreover, if $f(x)$ has a unique global minimizer x^* on $[a,b]$, then $\xi_N^* \to x^*$ as $N \to \infty$, where ξ_N^* is given by $f(\xi_N^*) = \eta_N$. The above discussion suggests taking

$$\delta = \frac{2\xi_N^* - (\zeta_1 + \zeta_0)}{\zeta_1 - \zeta_0} \tag{4.10}$$

as an estimator for the skew rate δ.

4.2 Multi-Solutions

The Monte Carlo implementation technique in the last section can be extended to the case when the objective function f has multiple global minimizers. The search domain D_k at the k-th iteration can be decomposed into a union of several cuboids of dimension n:

$$D_k = \bigcup_{j=1}^{r_k} D_j^k, \tag{4.11}$$

so that each smaller cuboid D_j^k can be treated individually as in the above subsection. Usually we assume that for each iteration k, the number r_k is less than an integer m which is given in advance.

5 Constrained and Discreat Minimization

Constrained nonconvex minimization problems arise from broad range of applications. General speaking, solving a constrained minimization problem is much harder than solving an unconstrained problem. Integral global minimization technique using a discontinuous penalty method to convert a constrained minimization problem to an unconstrained one without any constrained qualification requirements. We outline the main ideas of the discontinuous penalty method.

5.1 Discontinuous Penalty Method

We use the discontinuous penalty method to solve a constrained problem:
$$c^* = \min_{x \in S} f(x), \tag{5.1}$$
where $S \subset X$ is the constrained set.

The discontinuous penalty function associated with S is defined as follows.

Definition 5.1 A function $p(x)$ on a metric space (X, d) is a penalty function associated with a constraint set $S \subset X$ if

1. p is lower semicontinuous;
2. $p(x) = 0$ if $x \in S$;
3. $\inf_{x \notin S_\beta} p(x) > 0$,

where $S_\beta = \{u : d(u, S) \leqslant \beta\}, \beta > 0$, and $d(x, S)$ is the distance from x to the feasible set S defined by
$$d(x, S) = \inf\{d(x, s) : s \in S\}.$$

Remark 5.1 In the above definition we do not require the continuity of p, unlike the traditional definition [20], [7].

Remark 5.2 It is expected that the renalty increases when the distance from a point x to the constraint set S increases. We replace the traditional property
$$p(x) > 0, \text{ if } x \notin S$$
by condition 3.

With a penalty function p, we examine a penalized unconstrained minimization problem associated with (5.1):
$$\min_{x \in X}\{f(x) + \alpha p(x)\}, \tag{5.2}$$
where $\alpha (> 0)$ is a penalty parameter.

Definition 5.2 A penalty function p for the constraint set S is *exact* for (5.1) if there is a real number $\alpha_0 > 0$ such that for each $\alpha \geqslant \alpha_0$ we have
$$\min_{x \in X}\{f(x) + \alpha p(x)\} = \min_{x \in S} f(x) = c^* \tag{5.3}$$
and
$$\{x \in X : f(x) + \alpha p(x) = c^*\} = \{x \in S : f(x) = c^*\} = H^*. \tag{5.4}$$

We now construct a class of discontinuous penalty functions for the constrained problem

(5.1). Let
$$ps(x,\delta)=\begin{cases}0, & x\in S,\\ \delta+d(x), & x\notin S,\end{cases} \quad (5.5)$$
where δ is a positive number and $d(x)$ is a penalty-like function.

For example, for the inequality-constraint set
$$S=\{x:g_i(x)\leqslant 0, i=1,\cdots,r\},$$
we can take
$$d(x)=\sum_{i=1}^{r}\|\max(g_i(x),0)\|^p \text{ or } d(x)=\max_{i}\|\max(g_i(x),0)\|^p,$$
where $p>0$. If $g_i, i=1,\cdots,r$, are continuous, then d is continuous.

Proposition 5.1 *If f is continuous, and d is upper robust on S, or f is upper robust and d is continuous on S, then $f+\alpha p$ is upper robust on S for every $\alpha>0$.*

Theorem 5.1[32] *The discontinuous penalty function (5.5) is exact.*

Remark 5.3 No constraint qualification is required for the penalty function (5.5).

Remark 5.4 If f is robust piecewise continuous with a robust partition $\{S,S^c\}$, then for each $\alpha>0$ and $\delta>0$ the penalized function $f(x)+\alpha ps(x,\delta)$ is a piecewise robust continouous function.

A penalty algorithm is proposed as follows:

Step 1: Take $c_0>\min_{u\in S}f(x);\varepsilon>0;n:=0;\beta>1.0;$
$$H_0=\{x:f(x)+\alpha_0 p(x)\leqslant c_0\};$$

Step 2: Calculate the mean value
$$c_{n+1}=\frac{1}{\mu(H_n)}\int_{H_n}[f(x)+\alpha_n p(x)]\mathrm{d}\mu; \quad (5.6)$$

Step 3: Calculate the nodified variance
$$v_{n+1}=\frac{1}{\mu(H_n)}\int_{H_n}(f(x)+\alpha_n p(x)-c_n)^2\mathrm{d}\mu.$$

If $v_{n+1}\geqslant \varepsilon$, then $n:=n+1$ and $\alpha_{n+1}=\alpha_n\cdot\beta$, and go to Step 2; otherwise, go to Step 4;

Step 4: $c^*\Leftarrow c_{n+1};H^*\Leftarrow H_{c_{n+1}}$; Stop.

The algorithm may stop in a finite numbers of iteration, in which case we let $c_{n+k}=c_n$ and $H_{n+k}=H_n$, $k=1,2,\cdots$

Applying the above algorithm with $\varepsilon=0$, we obtain a decreasing sequence
$$c_1\geqslant c_2\geqslant\cdots\geqslant c_n\geqslant c_{n+1}\geqslant\cdots \quad (5.7)$$
and a sequence of sets
$$H_1\supset H_2\supset\cdots\supset H_n\supset H_{n+1}\supset\cdots. \quad (5.8)$$

Theorem 5.2[32] *With this algorithm, we have*
$$\lim_{n\to\infty}c_n=c^*=\min_{u\in S}f(x) \quad (5.9)$$
and
$$\lim_{n\to\infty}H_n=\bigcap_{k=1}^{\infty}H_n=H^*. \quad (5.10)$$

5.2 RobustiFication of Integen and Mixed Programming

A discrete or mixed minimization problem can be robustified to be a problem with a robust piecewise continuous function over a robust set. The following example demonstrates the process.

Example 5.1 Consider the following combinatorial optimization problem. Let
$$Z_+^n = \{z = (z^1, \cdots, z^n) : z^i \text{ is a nonnegative integer}, i = 1, \cdots, n\},$$
S be a finite subset of Z_+^n and $f : S \to \mathbb{R}^1$ a function defined on S. Let $f(z) = f(z^1, \cdots, z^n)$. The problem is to find the minimum value of f over S:
$$c^* = \min_{z \in S} f(z)$$
and the set of minima
$$H^* = \{z \in S : f(z) = c^*\}.$$
In this case, H^* is nonempty.

We now consider this problem in the space $\mathbb{R}^n$. The set S is not robust in this space. We define
$$D = \{x = (x^1, \cdots, x^n) \in \mathbb{R}^n : ([x^1 + 0.5], \cdots, [x^n + 0.5]) \in S\}$$
and
$$F(x) = f([x^1 + 0.5], \cdots, [x^n + 0.5]),$$
where $[a]$ denotes the integer part of the real number a. The set D defined above is a union of n-dimensional cubes, which are robust in $\mathbb{R}^n$. For each real number c, the set $\{x : F(x) < c\}$ is also a union of cubes (or the empty set). Thus, D is a robust set and F is an upper robust function in $\mathbb{R}^n$. Let x^* be a global minimizer of F over D, i.e.,
$$F(x^*) = \min_{x \in D} F(x).$$
Then $x^* \in \text{int } D$ (or one can find a point x_1 in the same cube with x^* such that $x_1 \in \text{int } D$). Therefore, we obtain a robustification of this combinatorial optimization problem.

6 Numerical Tests

The performance of a global minimization algorithm can only be ascertained by numerical computations on a variety of test problems. There are a lot of test problems for global minimization available in the literature. We select some here and classify them as follows:

(A) Unconstrained or box-constrained minimization.

(C) Constrained minimization.

(D) Discrete minimization, including integer and mixed programming.

The problems selected here represent some well known test problems in global optimization community. The selection range from problems with two variables to problems with a hundred variables, from problems of differentiable objective functions to the problems of a objective functinon with infinite number of discontinuities; from problems with box constraints to problems with equality and inequality constraints. We also select several discrete or mixed minimization problems. We hope that the selection is general enough to warrant our claim that the integral global optimization technique is powerful, flexible and efficient, and it is competitive with any other existing global optimization algorithms.

All the test problems selected here are solved by packages INTGLOU and INTGLOC, which are the implementations of the algorithms of integral global minimization. The softwares are compiled by MS-FORTRAN 5.1 and are running on MS-DOS environment. These test problems can be solved within a few seconds to a few minutes on an IBM 386/25 personal computer with a math coprocessor.

6.1 Unconstrained or Box Constrained Problems

A set of unconstrained or box constrained test problems are presented in this subsection. We describe each test problem by the following.
1. Objective function.
2. Search domain (boxed constraints).
3. Solution, including the minimum objective function value computed by the integral global minimization algorithm, the corresponding minimizers.
4. Statistics: we list the number iterations, the number of function evaluations and current value of V_1.

The sources of the problems are also provided. Note that the integral global minimization algorithms do not use any start points.

The stopping criterion employed for all the unconstrained problems selected here is the modified variance $V_1 = 1 \times 10^{-20}$.

Problem A.1[6]

Objective Function:
$$f(x) = [1 + (x_1 + x_2 + 1)^2 \cdot (19 - 14x_1 + 3x_1^2 - 14x_2 + 6x_1x_2 + 3x_2^2)]$$
$$\times [30 + (2x_1 - 3x_2)^2 (18 - 32x_1 + 12x_1^2 + 48x_2 - 36x_1x_2 + 27x_2^2)].$$

Search Domain:
$$D = \{(x_1, x_2) \in \mathbb{R}^2 : -2.0 \leqslant x_i \leqslant 2.0, i = 1, 2\}.$$

Solution:
$$x^* = (0.0, -1.0) \quad f^* = 3.0.$$

Statistics:
1. number of iterations: 19,
2. number of function evaluations: 1051,
3. current value of modified variance V_1: 9.233×10^{-21}.

Problem A.2[6]

Objective Function:
$$f(x) = 12x_1^2 - 6.3x_1^4 + x_1^6 + 6x_2(x_2 - x_1).$$

Search Domain:
$$D = \{(x_1, x_2) \in \mathbb{R}^2 : -10.0 \leqslant x_i \leqslant 10.0, i = 1, 2\}.$$

Solution:
$$x^* = (0.0, 0.0) \quad f^* = 2.2497375 \times 10^{-13}.$$

Statistics:

1. number of iterations: 17,
2. number of function evaluations: 951,
3. current value of modified variance V_1: $1.1543449 \times 10^{-21}$.

Remark 6.1 The objective function is so-called *three-hump camel back function*.

Problem A.3[6]

Objective Function:
$$f(x) = 4x_1^2 - 2.1x_1^4 + \frac{1}{3}x_1^6 + x_1 x_2 = 4x_2^2 + 4x_2^4.$$

Search Domain:
$$D = \{(x_1, x_2) \in \mathbb{R}^2 : -2.5 \leqslant x_i \leqslant 2.5, i = 1, 2\}.$$

Solution:
$$x^* = (0.08984133, -0.71267531) \text{ and } (-0.08993914, 0.7126753), \quad f^* = -1.031628.$$

Statistics:

1. number of iterations: 18,
2. number of function evaluations: 931,
3. current value of modified variance V_1: 8.216884×10^{-21}.

Remark 6.2 The objective function is so-called the *six hump camle back function*. It has six minimizers, two maximizers and seven saddle points.

Problem A.4[8]

Objective Function:
$$f(x) = (1 - 2x_2 + c\sin(4\pi x_2) - x_1)^2 + (x_2 - 0.5\sin(2\pi x_1))^2,$$

where c is a parameter which can be varied to modify the number of extraneous sigularities in the function. Here, we take $c = 0.05$, 0.2, and 0.5.

Search Domain:
$$D = \{(x_1, x_2) \in \mathbb{R}^2 : 0.0 < x_1 < 10.0, -10.0 < x_2 < 0.0\}.$$

Solution: The global minimum value of this problem is 0.0 for each c. The following table presents the numerical approximation of the global minimum value and the minimizers.

	$c = 0.05$	$c = 0.2$	$c = 0.5$
x_1	1.85130447	0.98250584	1.89738692
x_2	-0.40208593	-0.05484892	-0.30049412
f	$1.2122348 \times 10^{-22} \cdot 10^{-32}$	$1.7292806 \cdot 10^{-33}$	$7.7683103 \cdot 10^{-32}$

Statistics:

1. number of iterations: 22,
2. number of function evaluations: 1660,

3. current value of modified variance V_1: $1.0411676 \times 10^{-21}$.

Problem A.5[6]

Objective Function:
$$f(x) = \left(x_2 - \frac{5.1}{4\pi^2}x_1^2 + \frac{5}{\pi}x_1 - 6\right)^2 + 10\left(1 - \frac{1}{8\pi}\right)\cos x_1 + 10.$$

Search Donain:
$$D = \{(x_1, x_2) \in \mathbb{R}^2 : -5.0 \leqslant x_1 \leqslant 10.0,\ 0.0 \leqslant x_2 \leqslant 15.0\}.$$

Solution: The integral global algorithm find three global minimizers in this region:
$(-3.14159291, 12.275030), (3.141579, 2.274958), (9.42798, 2.474921)$
with the global minimum value
$$f^* = 0.39788736.$$

Statistics:

1. number of iterations: 23,

2. number of function evaluations: 1267,

3. current value of modified variance V_1: 1.0×10^{-21}.

Problem A.6[6]

Objective Function: Shekel's family (SQRIN)
$$f(x) = \sum_{i=1}^{m} \frac{1}{(x - a_i)^{\mathrm{T}}(x - a_i) + c_n},$$

where the parameters a_i and c_i are given by the following table:

i	a_i				c_i
1	4.0	4.0	4.0	4.0	0.1
2	1.0	1.0	1.0	1.0	0.2
3	8.0	8.0	8.0	8.0	0.2
4	6.0	6.0	6.0	6.0	0.4
5	3.0	7.0	3.0	7.02	0.4
6	2.0	9.0	2.0	9.0	0.6
7	5.0	5.0	3.0	3.0	0.3
8	8.0	1.0	8.0	1.0	0.7
9	6.0	2.0	6.0	2.0	0.5
10	7.0	3.6	7.0	3.6	0.5

Search Domain:
$$D = \{(x_1, \cdots, x_4) \in \mathbb{R}^4 : 0.0 \leqslant x_i \leqslant 10.0,\ i = 1, \cdots, 4\}.$$

Solutions:

Shekel 5:
$$x^* = (4.00003727, 4.00013375, 4.00003730, 4.00013346),\ f^* = -10.153200.$$

Shekel 7:

$x^* = (4.00057280, 4.00069020, 3.99948997, 3.99960620)$, $f^* = -10.402941$.

Shekel 10:

$x^* = (4.00074671, 4.00059326, 3.99966290, 3.99950981)$, $f^* = -10.536410$.

Statistics: Shekel 5

1. number of iterations: 41,
2. number of function evaluations: 2453,
3. current value of modified variance V_1: $1.7979744 \times 10^{-21}$.

Shekel 7

1. number of iterations: 42,
2. number of function evaluations: 3028,
3. current value of modified variance V_1: 1.0×10^{-21}.

Shekel 10

1. number of iterations: 41,
2. number of function evaluations: 2735,
3. current value of modified variance V_1: 1.0×10^{-21}.

Problem A. 7[6]

Objective Function:

$$f(x) = -\sum_{i=1}^{m} c_i \exp\left(-\sum_{j=1}^{n} a_{ij}(x_j - p_{ij})^2\right),$$

where $x = (x_1, \cdots, x_n)$, and the parameters are given in the following tables:

Hartm 3: $m=4$, $n=3$

i	a_{ij}			c_i	p_{ij}		
1	3.0	10.0	30.0	1.0	0.3689	0.1170	0.2673
2	0.1	10.0	35.0	1.2	0.4699	0.4387	0.7470
3	3.0	10.0	30.0	3.0	0.1091	0.8732	0.5547
4	0.1	10.0	35.0	3.2	0.03815	0.5743	0.8828

Hartm 6: $m=4$, $n=6$

i	a_{ij}						c_i
1	10.0	3.0	17.0	3.5	1.7	8.0	1.0
2	0.05	10.0	17.0	0.1	8.0	14.0	1.2
3	3.0	3.5	1.7	10.0	17.0	8.0	3.0
4	17.0	8.0	0.05	10.0	0.1	14.0	3.2

i	p_{ij}					
1	0.1312	0.1696	0.5569	0.0124	0.8283	0.5886
2	0.2329	0.4135	0.8307	0.3736	0.1004	0.9991
3	0.2348	0.1415	0.3522	0.2883	0.3047	0.6650
4	0.4047	0.8828	0.8732	0.5743	0.1091	0.0381

Solutions:

Hartm 3

$x^* = (0.11461478, 0.55564892, 0.85254688)$, $f^* = -3.8627821$.

Hartm 6

$x^* = (0.20169, 0.15001, 0.47687, 0.27533, 0.31165, 0.65703)$, $f^* = -3.322368$.

Statistics:

Hartm 3

1. number of iterations: 23,
2. number of function evaluations: 1150,
3. current value of modified variance V_1: 1.0×10^{-21}.

Hartm 6

1. number of iterations: 49,
2. number of function evaluations: 3345,
3. current value of modified variance V_1: 1.0×10^{-21}.

Problem A.8[9]

Objective Function:

$$f(x) = \sum_{i=1}^{11} \left(a_i - x_1 \frac{b_i^2 + b_i x_2}{b_i^2 + b_i x_3 + x_4} \right)^2,$$

where a_i and b_i, $i = 1, \cdots, 11$ are given as follows:

i	a_i	$1/b_i$
1	0.1957	0.25
2	0.1947	0.5
3	0.1735	1
4	0.1600	2
5	0.0844	4
6	0.0627	6
7	0.0456	8
8	0.0342	10
9	0.0323	12
10	0.0235	14
11	0.0246	16

Search Domain:
$$D=\{(x_1,\cdots,x_4)\in \mathbb{R}^4: -0.3\leqslant x_i\leqslant 0.3, i=1,\cdots,4\}$$

Solution:
$$x^*=(0.19282941, 0.19095407, 0.12315108, 0.13581648), f^*=3.0748802\times 10^{-4}.$$

Statistics:

1. number of iterations: 54,
2. number of function evaluations: 7592,
3. current value of modified variance V_1: 1.0×10^{-21}.

Problem A. 9[17]

Objective Function:
$$f(x)=\sum_{i=1}^{81} R_i^2$$

where
$$R_i=x_1\exp\left\{-\left[\frac{z_i-x_3}{x_5}\right]^2\right\}+x_2\exp\left\{-\left[\frac{z_i-x_4}{x_6}\right]^2\right\}-y_i$$

and
$$z_i=4.0+0.1(i+1), i=1,2,\cdots,81,$$
$$y_i=130.89\exp\left\{-\left[\frac{z_i-6.73}{1.2}\right]^2\right\}+52.6\exp\left\{-\left[\frac{z_i-9.342}{0.97}\right]^2\right\}, i=1,2,\cdots,81.$$

Search Domain:
$$D=\begin{cases}120\leqslant x_1\leqslant 150, 30\leqslant x_2\leqslant 70, 4\leqslant x_3\leqslant 10,\\ 5\leqslant x_4\leqslant 15, 0.5\leqslant x_5\leqslant 4, 0.2\leqslant x_6\leqslant 2.\end{cases}$$

Solution:
$$x_1=130.89, x_2=52.59, x_3=6.73, x_4=9.342, x_5=1.2, x_6=0.97,$$
$$f^*=1.6383836\times 10^{-10}.$$

Statistics:

1. number of iterations: 77;
2. number of function evaluations: 5187;
3. current value of modified variance V_1: 1.0×10^{-21}.

We can consider a minimization of a function
$$f(x)=\sum_{i=1}^{81}|R_i|$$

or
$$f(x)=\max_{i=1,\cdots,81}|R_i|$$

with the same search domain

Problem A. 10[14]

$$f(x)=-\left(\sum_{i=1}^{8}x_i^2\right)\times\left(\sum_{i=1}^{8}x_i^4\right)+\left(\sum_{i=1}^{8}x_i^3\right)^2.$$

Search Domain:

$$D=\{(x_1,\cdots,x_8)\in \mathbb{R}^8: 0.0\leqslant x_i\leqslant 1.0, i=1,\cdots,8\}.$$

Problem A. 11[14]

Objective Function:
$$f(x)=\frac{\pi}{n}\{\sin^2(\pi x_1)+\sum_{i=1}^{n-1}(x_i-1.0)^2[1+10.0\sin^2(\pi x_i^{+1})]+(x_n-1.0)^2\}.$$

Search Domain:
$$D=\{(x_1,\cdots,x_n)\in \mathbb{R}^n: -10.0\leqslant x_i\leqslant 10.0, i=1,\cdots,n\}.$$

Solution:
$$x^*=(1,\cdots,1)\ f^*=0.$$

The following tableau gives the number of iterations N_i, the amount of function evaluation N_f, the function value f^* and the current value of modified variance V_1 corresponding the cases of number of variables $n=5,10,20,50$, respectively.

The stopping criterion for this problem is $V_1 < 10^{-25}$.

n	5	10	20	50	100
N_i	52	93	172	380	863
N_f	2765	5276	12376	49359	128483
f^*	$1.076 \cdot 10^{-13}$	$6.43 \cdot 10^{-13}$	$1.65 \cdot 10^{-12}$	$3.41 \cdot 10^{-12}$	$2.90 \cdot 10^{-12}$
V_1	$4.12 \cdot 10^{-26}$	$8.77 \cdot 10^{-26}$	$7.07 \cdot 10^{-26}$	$8.18 \cdot 10^{-26}$	$9.71 \cdot 10^{-26}$

Problem A. 12[14]

Objective Function:
$$g(x)=\sin^2(3\pi x_1)+\sum_{i=1}^{n-1}(x_i-1.0)^2[1.0+\sin^2(3\pi x_{i+1})]$$
$$+(x_n-1.0)^2[1.0+\sin^2(2\pi x_n)],$$
$$f(x)=g(x)+\frac{[g(x)]}{n},$$

where $[y]$ denote the integer part of y. Thus, the objective function f is discontinuous.

Search Domain:
$$D=\{(x_1,\cdots,x_n)\in \mathbb{R}^n: -10.0\leqslant x_i\leqslant 10.0, i=1,\cdots,n\}.$$

Solution:
$$x^*=(1.0,\cdots,1.0),\ f^*=0.$$

The following tableau gives the number of iterations N_i, the amount of function evaluation N_f, the minimum function value f^* and the current value of the modified variance V_1 corresponding cases of number of variables $n=5,10,20,50$, respectively. The stopping criterion for this problem is $V_1 < 10^{-25}$.

n	5	10	20	50
N_i	56	101	186	412
N_f	3208	5996	12549	54734
f^*	$5.838578 \cdot 10^{-14}$	$6.414436 \cdot 10^{-13}$	$1.180750 \cdot 10^{-12}$	$2.285634 \cdot 10^{-12}$
V_1	$4.986358 \cdot 10^{-26}$	$5.83548 \cdot 10^{-26}$	$5.241681 \cdot 10^{-26}$	$8.942764 \cdot 10^{-26}$

Problem A. 13[4]

Objective Function:
$$f(x)=\begin{cases} 1.0+\dfrac{\sum_{i=1}^{n}|x_i|}{n}+\text{sgn}\left[\sin\left|\sum_{i=1}^{n}|x_i|\right|-0.5\right], & x\neq 0, \\ 0, & x=0. \end{cases}$$

Search Domain:
$$D=\{(x_1,\cdots,x_n): -10.0\leqslant x_i\leqslant 1.0,\ i=1,\cdots,n\}.$$

Solution:
$x^*=(0,\cdots,0)$, $f^*=0$.

Remark 6.3 The function has an infinite number of discontinuous hypersurfaces. Its unique global minimizer is at the origin where the objective function has a discontinuity of "the second kind". Since the restriction of the variable value that sine function can take, the function f takes the value zero when $\sum_{i=1}^{n}|x_i|/n<10^{-9}$. The following tableau gives the data of this text problem.

n	5	10	20	50
N_i	77	128	226	711
N_f	5203	10223	25527	105747

6.2 Constrained Minimization Problems

We present a set constrained problems in this subsection. We describe each test problem by the following format:

1. Objective function.
2. Constraints, including constrain functions and boxed constraints.
3. Solution, the minimum objective function value computed by the integral global minimization algorithm, the corresponding minimizers.
4. Statistics, including the number of iterations, the number of function evaluations and the current value of modified variance V_1.

The discontinuous penalty method presented in Section 5 is used to solve all the constrained problems in this subsection.

Unless otherwise stated explicitly, the stopping criterion used in the programs for solving all numerical tests in this subsection is 1.0×10^{-15}.

Problem C. 1[4]

Objective Function:
$$f(x)=100(x_2-x_1)^2+(1-x_1)^2.$$

Constraints:
$$h(x)=x_1^2-x_1+x_2-0.9=0,\ -1.0\leqslant x_1,\ x_2\leqslant 1.0.$$

Solution:
$$x^*=(0.965932,\ 0.932907)\ \text{and}\ f^*=0.001162$$

with
$$h(x^*) = 2.109617 \cdot 10^{-13}.$$
The penalty function
$$p(x) = \alpha |h(x)|^{1.8}, \quad \alpha = 1000$$
is used to solve this minimization problem.

Statistics:
1. number of iterations: 31;
2. number of function evaluations: 2829;
3. current value of modified variance V_1: 4.05785×10^{-16}.

Problem C. 2[8]

Objective Function:
$$f(x) = -x_1 - x_2 + x_3.$$
Constraints:
$$\sin(4\pi x_1) - 2\sin^2(2\pi x_2) - 2\sin^2(2\pi x_3) \geq 0, \quad -5 \leq x_1, x_2 \leq 5.$$
Solution:
$$x^* = (4.75, 5.0, -5.0), \text{ and } f^* = -14.75.$$

Statistics:
1. number of iterations: 49;
2. number of function evaluations: 4440;
3. current value of modified variance V_1: 0.

Problem C. 3[38]

Objective Function:
$$f(x) = -2x_1^2 - x_1 x_2 - 2x_2.$$
Constraints:
$$x_1 + x_2 \leq 1, \quad 1.5x_1 + x_2 \leq 1.4,$$
$$0.0 \leq x_1 \leq 10.0, \quad -10.0 \leq x_2 \leq 0.0.$$
Solution:
$$x^* = (7.6, -10), \quad f^* = -19.52.$$

Statistics:
1. number of iterations: 43;
2. number of function evalustions: 3914;
3. current value of modified variance V_1: 4.94434×10^{-16}.

Remark 6.4 This is a counterexample to Ritter's method [22]. The global minimizer will not be found by Ritter's method unless one happens to begin with $(7.6, -10)$ as the first local optimum.

Problem C. 4[38]

Objective Functilon:
$$f(x) = -x_1^2 - x_2^2 - (x_3 - 1)^2.$$
Constraints:

$$x_1+x_2-x_3\leqslant 0,\ -x_1+x_2-x_3\leqslant 0,\ 12x_1+5x_2+12x_3\leqslant 22.8,$$
$$12x_1+12x_2+7x_3\leqslant 17.1,\ -6x_1+x_2+x_3\leqslant 1.9,$$
$$-10.0\leqslant x_1\leqslant 10.0,\ 0.0\leqslant x_2\leqslant 10.0,\ 10.0\leqslant x_3\leqslant 10.0.$$

Solution:
$$x^*=(3.42,\ 0,\ -3.42),\ f^*=-31.2328.$$

Statistics:

1. number of iterations: 74;
2. number of function evaluations 8876;
3. current value of modified variance V_1: 4.48476×10^{-16}.

Remark 6.5 This is a counterexample to Tuy's method [26]. Alocal optimum occurs at the vertex $x^0=(0,0,0)$ with $f(x^0)=-1$; Tuy's method will produces an infinite cycling and the process does not terminate.

Problem C. 5[38]

Objective Function:
$$f(x)=-(x_1-1)^2-x_2^2-(x_3-1)^2.$$

Constraints:
$$x_1+x_2-x_3\leqslant 1,\ -x_1+x_2-x_3\leqslant -1,$$
$$12x_1+5x_2+12x_3\leqslant 34.8,\ 12x_1+12x_2+7x_3\leqslant 17.1,$$
$$-6x_1+x_2+x_3\leqslant -4.1,\ 0.0\leqslant x_1,x_2,x_3\leqslant 5.0.$$

Solution:
$$x^*=(1,\ 0,\ 0),\ f^*=-1.$$

Statistics:

1. number of iterations: 37;
2. number of function evaluations: 2043;
3. current value of modified variance V_1: 7.66012×10^{-16}.

Problem C. 6[12]

Objective Function:
$$f(x)=(x_1^4-x_2+x_3)-(x_1+x_2^2-x_3)^2.$$

Constraints:
$$(x_1-x_2-1.2)^2+x_2\leqslant 4.4,\ x_1+x_2+x_3\leqslant 6.5,$$
$$1.4\leqslant x_1\leqslant 5.0,\ 1.6\leqslant x_2\leqslant 5.0,\ 1.8\leqslant x_3\leqslant 5.0.$$

Solution:
$$x^*=(1.4,\ 1.809502,\ 1.8),\quad f^*=4.576804.$$

Statistics:

1. number of iterations: 39;
2. number of function evaluations: 2111;
3. current value of modified variance V_1: 8.17440×10^{-16}.

Problem C. 7[10]

Objective Function:

$$f(x) = f_1(x_1) + f_2(x_2),$$

where

$$f_1(x_1) = \begin{cases} 30x_1, & 0 \leq x_1 < 300, \\ 31x_1, & 300 \leq x_1 < 400, \end{cases} \quad f_2(x_2) = \begin{cases} 28x_2, & 0 \leq x_2 < 100, \\ 29x_2, & 100 \leq x_2 < 200, \\ 30x_2, & 200 \leq x_2 < 1000. \end{cases}$$

Constraints:

$$x_1 = 300 - \frac{x_3 x_4}{131.078}\cos(1.48577 - x_6) + \frac{0.90798 x_3^2}{131.078}\cos(1.47588),$$

$$x_2 = -\frac{x_3 x_4}{131.078}\cos(1.48477 + x_6) + \frac{0.90798 x_4^2}{131.078}\cos(1.47588),$$

$$x_5 = -\frac{x_3 x_4}{131.078}\sin(1.48477 + x_6) + \frac{0.90798 x_4^2}{131.078}\sin(1.47588),$$

$$200 - \frac{x_3 x_4}{131.078}\sin(1.48477 - x_6) + \frac{0.90798}{131.078}x_3^2\sin(1.47588) = 0,$$

$$0 \leq x_1 \leq 400, \ 0 \leq x_2 \leq 1000, \ 340 \leq x_3 \leq 420,$$
$$340 \leq x_4 \leq 420, \ -1000 \leq x_5 \leq 1000, \ 0 \leq x_6 \leq 0.5236.$$

Solution:

$$x^* = (202.99666, 100.0, 383.07092, 419.99999, -10.90767, 0.073148),$$
$$f^* = 8889.8999.$$

Statistics:

1. number of iterations: 56;
2. number of function evaluations: 5893;
3. current value of modified variance V_1: 6.18995×10^{-16}.

Remark 6.6 The objective of this test problem is a discontinuous robust function with four nonlinear equality constraints. We take x_3 and x_6 as independent variables. Then x_1, x_2, x_4 and x_5 are functions of x_3 and x_6. Thus, in addition to the box constraints on these independent variables, there are 8 more nonlinear inequality constraints. The discontinuous penalty function is applied to these inequality constraints.

Problem C.8[21]

Objective Function:

$$f(x) = 0.0204 x_1 x_4 (x_1 + x_2 + x_3) + 0.0187 x_2 x_3 (x_1 + 1.57 x_2 + x_4)$$
$$+ 0.0607 x_1 x_4 x_5^2 (x_1 + x_2 + x_3) + 0.0437 x_2 x_3 x_6^2 (x_1 + 1.57 x_2 + x_4),$$

subject to the inequality constraints:

$$x_i \geq 0, \ i = 1, \cdots, 6,$$
$$g_1(x) = x_1 x_2 x_3 x_4 x_5 x_6 - 2070 \geq 0,$$
$$g_2(x) = 1 - 0.00062 x_1 x_4 x_5^2 (x_1 + x_2 + x_3)$$
$$- 0.0058 x_2 x_3 x_6^2 (x_1 + 1.57 x_2 + x_4) \geq 0$$

The problem was solved by Ballard, Jelink and Schinzinger [3]. The minimization process starts with a feasible point:

$$x_1 = 5.54, \ x_2 = 4.4, \ x_3 = 12.02, \ x_4 = 11.82, \ x_5 = 0.702, \ x_6 = 0.852$$

and leads to a solution

$x_1 = 5.3336$, $x_2 = 4.6585$, $x_3 = 10.4365$, $x_4 = 12.0840$, $x_5 = 0.7525$, $x_6 = 0.8781$.

The objective function value at the solution is $f^* = 135.1155$. Price [21] resolved the problem with the controlled random search method and suggested that it be used as a test problem of constrained global minimization.

The following solution is obtained by the integral global minimization with the discontinuous penalty technique in a large search region D:

$D = \{x \in \mathbb{R}^6 : 0.0 \leq x_i \leq 20.0, i = 1, \cdots, 6\}$.

$x_1 = 5.41411876$, $x_2 = 4.71604587$, $x_3 = 10.34384982$,

$x_4 = 11.88555219$, $x_5 = 0.74910661$, $x_6 = 0.88027699$,

and

$f^* = 135.09767268$.

Statistics:

1. number of iterations: 599;
2. number of function evaluations: 87475;
3. current value of modified variance V_1: 3.0333×10^{-16}.

Remark 6.7 The solution x^* is very closed to the boundary of constraints:

$g_1(x^*) = 9.9685 \cdot 10^{-8}$, and $y_2(x^*) = 1.5982 \cdot 10^{-10}$.

Problem C. 9[13]

Objective Function:

$$f(x) = 0.7854 x_1 x_2^2 (3.3333 x_3^2 + 14.9334 x_3 - 43.0934) - 1.5080 x_1 (x_6^2 + x_7^2)$$
$$+ 7.4770 (x_6^3 + x_7^3) + 0.7854 (x_4 x_6^2 + x_5 x_7^2).$$

Constraints:

$$x_1 x_2^2 x_3 \geq 27, \quad x_1 x_2^2 x_3^2 \geq 397.5,$$

$$x_2 x_3 x_6^4 / x_4^3 \geq 1.93, \quad x_2 x_3 x_7^4 / x_5^3 \geq 1.93,$$

$$\frac{10 \sqrt{\left[\frac{745 x_4}{x_2 x_3}\right]^2 + 16.91 \cdot 10^6}}{x_6^3} \leq 1100, \quad \frac{10 \sqrt{\left[\frac{745 x_5}{x_2 x_3}\right]^2 + 157.5 \cdot 10^6}}{x_7^3} \leq 850,$$

$$x_2 x_3 \leq 40, \quad 5 < x_1/x_2 \leq 12, \quad 1.5 x_6 + 1.9 \leq x_4,$$

$$1.1 x_7 + 1.9 \leq x_5, \quad 2.6 \leq x_1 \leq 3.6, \quad 0.7 \leq x_2 \leq 0.7,$$

$$17 \leq x_3 \leq 28, \quad 7.3 \leq x_4 \leq 8.3, \quad 7.3 \leq x_5 \leq 8.3,$$

$$2.9 \leq x_6 \leq 3.9, \quad 5.0 \leq x_7 \leq 5.5.$$

Solution:

$x^* = (3.5, 0.7, 17.0, 7.30, 7.72, 3.35, 5.29)$, $f^* = 2994.42$.

Statistics

1. number of iterations: 128;
2. number of function evaluations: 8839;
3. current value of modified variance V_1: 2.22273×10^{-16}.

Problem C. 10[23]

Objective Function:
$$f(x) = 1.10471 x_1^2 x_2 + 0.04811 x_3 x_4 (14 + x_2).$$

Constraints:
$$g_2(x) = \frac{13600}{10^6} \sqrt{t_1^2 + \frac{2 t_1 t_2 x_2}{\sqrt{x_2^2 + (x_1 + x_3)^2}} + t_2^2 / 10^6} \geq 0,$$

$$g_3(x) = 3 - \frac{5.04}{x_4 x_3^2} \geq 0,$$

$$g_4(x) = \frac{4.013}{1.96 \times 10^5} \sqrt{EG} \left(1 - \frac{x_3}{28} \sqrt{\frac{E}{G}}\right) \geq 0.006,$$

$$g_5 = 0.25 - \frac{2.1952}{x_4 x_3^3} \geq 0,$$

$$t_1 = 6000 / (1.414 x_1 x_2), \quad E = x_3 x_4^3 10^7 / 4, \quad G = 4 x_3 x_4^3 10^6,$$

$$t_2 = 3000 (14 + x_2 / 2) \sqrt{x_2^2 + (x_1 + x_3)^2} / J,$$

$$J = 0.707 x_1 x_2 \left(\frac{x_2^2}{6} + \frac{(x_1 + x_3)^2}{2}\right),$$

$$0.125 \leq x_1 \leq 20.0, \ 0.0 \leq x_2 \leq 20.0, \ 0.0 \leq x_3 \leq 20.0, \ 0.0 \leq x_4 \leq 20.0.$$

Solution:
$$x^* = (0.15321, 16.93611, 3.00768, 0.32293), \text{ and } f^* = 1.88446227.$$

Statistics:

1. number of iterations: 159;
2. number of function evaluations: 23202;
3. current value of modified variance V_1: 5.81420×10^{-11}.

Remark 6.8 A solution was reported in [23] with $f^* = 2.38116$. Here, we find a different feasible solution with significantly better objective function value.

6.3 Discrete and Mixed Minimization Problems

Robustification technique enables us to treat discrete and mixed programming problems as continuous ones. In this subsection, we present several discrete or mixed test problems. The integral global approach with discontinuous penalty method is applied to solve these problems. The format of the descriptions of the problems is the same as the previous subsection.

Problem D. 1[4]

Objective Function: Source: [6] with discrete constraints.
$$f(x) = [1 + (x_1 + x_2 + 1)^2 \cdot (19 - 14 x_1 + 3 x_1^2 - 14 x_2 + 6 x_1 x_2 + 3 x_2^2)] \times$$
$$[30 + (2 x_1 - 3 x_2)^2 (18 - 32 x_1 + 12 x_1^2 + 48 x_2 - 36 x_1 x_2 + 27 x_2^2)].$$

Constraints:
$$D = \{(x_1, x_2) : x_1, x_2 = 0.001 i, \ i = -2000, -1999, \cdots, 1999, 2000\}.$$

Solution:
$$x^* = (0.000, -1.000), \quad f^* = 3.0.$$

Statistics:

1. number of iterations: 9;
2. number of function evaluations: 291;
3. current value of modified variance V_1: 0.

Problem D. 2[1,27]

Objective Function:
$$\sum_{i=1}^{n} \frac{a_i}{x_i},$$
where $n=3$, $a_1=33.7539$, $a_2=1.4430$ and $a_3=1.3885$.

Constraint:
$$\sum_{i=1}^{n} x_i = M, \ 1 \leqslant x_1 \leqslant N_i, \ x_n \text{ is integer}, \ i = 1, \cdots, n,$$
where $N_1=16$, $N_2=20$, $N_3=28$, and $M=24$.

Solution:
$$x^* = (16, 4, 4) \text{ and } f^* = 2.8150.$$

Statistics:

1. number of iterations: 5;
2. number of function evaluations: 171;
3. current value of modified variance V_1: 0.

Problem D. 3[16]

Objective Function:
$$f(x) = (x_1-3)^2 + (x_2-2)^2 + (x_3+4)^2.$$

Constraints:
$$g_1 = x_1 + x_2^2 + x_3^{0.5} - 10 \geqslant 0.0, \ g_2 = \frac{x_1^2}{4.166} - x_2 + \frac{x_3}{3.921} + 3 \geqslant 0.0,$$
$$g_3 = -4x + x_2^2 + x_3^{-3.5} + 12 \geqslant 0.0, \ x_3 \geqslant 0, \ x_1 \text{ and } x_2 \text{ are integers.}$$

Solution:
$$x^* = (3,3,0.0) \quad \text{and} \quad f^* = 17.0.$$

Statistics:

1. number of iterations: 23;
2. number of function evaluations: 1228;
3. current value of modified variance V_1: 2.48615×10^{-16}.

Remark 6.9 It was reported in [16] that the problem has minimizer $x^* = (4,3,0.598)$ with the function value $f^* = 23.141604$. In Loh's dissertation [15], the constraints have been changed to: $\bar{g}_i \geqslant 0.1$, $i=1,2,3$, where $\bar{g}_1 = x_1 + 2x_2 + x_3^{0.5} - 1.0$ and $\bar{g}_i = g_i$, $i=2,3$. Let us name this new problem as D3A. A solution of D3A given in [15] was $x^* = (4,3,0.631)$ with the function value $f^* = 23.45$.

The solution of D3A obtained by the integral global minimization algorithm is $x^* = (4,3,0.1)$ with the function value $f^* = 18.81$. The following is the related statistics:

Statistics of D3A:

1. number of iterations: 29;
2. number of function evaluations: 1891;
3. current value of modified variance V_1: 5.95563×10^{-16}.

Problem D. 4[5]

Objective Function:
$$f(x) = -x_3 - x_4 - x_5.$$
Constraints:
$$20x_1 + 30x_2 + x_3 + 2x_4 + 2x_5 \leqslant 180, \ 30x_1 + 20x_2 + 2x_3 + x_4 + 2x_5 \leqslant 150,$$
$$-60x_1 + x_3 \leqslant 0, \ -75x_2 + x_4 \leqslant 0, \ 0 \leqslant x_i \leqslant 1, \ i=1,2,$$
$$0 \leqslant x_i \leqslant 75, \ i=3,4,5, \ x_i \text{ integer } i=1,\cdots,5.$$
Solution:
$$x^* = (1,1,24,52,0), \quad f^* = -76.$$
Statistics:

1. number of iterations: 14;
2. number of function evaluations: 1486;
3. current value of modified variance V_1: 0.

Remark 6.10 There are at least six alternative global minimizers. After 1131 function evaluations, the global minimizer is found. The variance does not equal zero until 1486 function evaluations.

Problem D. 5[5]

Objective Function:
$$f(x) = x_1 x_2 x_3 + x_1 x_4 x_5 + x_2 x_4 x_6 + x_6 x_7 x_8 + x_2 x_5 x_7.$$
Constraints:
$$2x_1 + 2x_4 + 8x_8 \geqslant 12, \ 11x_1 + 7x_4 + 13x_6 \geqslant 41, \ 6x_2 + 9x_4 x_6 + 5x_7 \geqslant 60,$$
$$3x_2 + 5x_5 + 7x_8 \geqslant 42, \ 6x_2 x_7 + 9x_3 + 5x_5 \geqslant 53,$$
$$4x_3 x_7 + x_5 \geqslant 13, \ 2x_1 + 4x_2 + 7x_4 + 3x_5 + x_7 \leqslant 69,$$
$$9x_1 x_8 + 6x_3 x_5 + 4x_3 x_7 \leqslant 47, \ 12x_2 + 8x_2 x_8 + 2x_3 x_6 \leqslant 73,$$
$$x_3 + 4x_5 + 2x_6 + 9x_9 \leqslant 31, \ x_i \leqslant 7, \ i=1,3,4,6,8,$$
$$x_i \leqslant 15, \ i=2,5,7, \ x_i \text{ integer } i=1,\cdots,8.$$
Solution:
$$x^* = (5,4,1,1,6,3,2,0), \quad f^* = 110.$$

Remark 6.11 This is the most difficult one among the five test problems presented in [5]. After 919 function evaluations, the global minimizer is found. The variance does not equal to zero until 1370 function evaluations.

Statistics:

1. number of iterations: 15;
2. number of function evaluations: 1370;
3. current value of modified variance V_1: 0.

Problem D. 6[10]

Objective Function:
$$f(x) = 5.3578547x_3^2 + 0.835689x_1x_5 + 37.293239x_1 - 40792.141.$$

Constraints:
$$0 \leqslant 85.334407 + 0.0056858x_2x_5 + 0.0006262x_1x_4 - 0.0022053x_3x_5 \leqslant 92,$$
$$90 \leqslant 80.51249 + 0.0071317x_2x_5 + 0.0029955x_1x_2 + 0.0021813x_3^2 \leqslant 110,$$
$$20 \leqslant 9.300961 + 0.0047026x_3x_5 + 0.0012547x_1x_3 + 0.0019085x_3x_4 \leqslant 25,$$
$$78 \leqslant x_1 \leqslant 102, \ 23 \leqslant x_2 \leqslant 45, \ x_1, x_2 \text{ are integers}, \ 27 \leqslant x_i \leqslant 45, \ i=3,4,5.$$

Solution:
$$x^* = (78, 33, 29.99525603, 45.0, 36.77581291), \quad f^* = -30665.53867176.$$

Statistics:

1. number of iterations: 98;
2. number of function evaluations: 11849;
3. current value of modified variance V_1: 5.55430×10^{-16}.

Remark 6.12 In [5], the problem was restated as a mixed programming problem.

7 Conclusions

The fundamental theory of integral global optimization is based on robust analysis and Q-measure theory. The theory provides a set of necessary and sufficient conditions to characterize global minimizers and suggests an intuitive approach to locate the global minimizers. The theory is mathematically sound and is well received in mathematics community.

The detailed accounts of the implementation of integral global approach for solving unconstrained minimization problems is presented. The discontinuous penalty method and robustification technique provide an unified approach to solve unconstrained problems, constrained problems, continuous, discrete or mixed problems. Most remarkably, the discontinuous penalty method is exact, and there is no constrained qualification requirements for the method. The collection of numerical tests presented here illustrate the effectiveness of this unified approach.

There are many different algorithms available to solve unconstrained, constrained or discrete, mixed optimization problems. Some of them, based on gradient methods or others, may have better performance than the integral approach for some problems with special structures. However, to the best of our knowledge, there is no method which is both flexible enough to handle discontinuous problems or discrete problems in a unified fashion, and very efficient. We are confident that the integral global optimization is a valuable addition to over growing global optimization techniques.

References

[1] Arthanrt, T. S. and Dodge, Y. *Mathematical Programming in Statistics*, John Wiley and Sons, New York, (1981).

[2] Aubin, J. P. and Ekeland, I. *Applied Nonlinear Analysis*, Wiley-Interscience, New York 1983.

[3] Ballard, D. H., Jelinek, C. O. and Schinzinger, R. An algorithm for the solution of constrained generalized polynomial programming problem, *Conmputer Journal*, 17(1974), 261—266.

[4] Chew, S. H. and Zheng, Q. *Integral Global Optimization*, Lecture Notes in Economics and Mathematical Systems, No. 298, Springer-Verlag, 1988.

[5] Dickman, H. B. and Gilman, M. J. Monte Carlo optimization, *Journal of Optimization Theory and its Applications*, 60(1989), 149—157.

[6] Dixon, L. and Szegö, G. *Towards Global Optimization*, North Holland, Amsterdam, 1975.

[7] Fiacco, A. V. and McCormick, G. P. *Nonlinear Programming: Sequential Unconstrained Minimization Techniques*, John Wiley and Sons, New Tork, 1968.

[8] Gomez, S. and Levy, A. V. The tunneling method for solving the constrained global optimization problem with several non-connected feasible regions, in *Numerical Analysis*, J. P. Hennart ed., Lecture Notes in Mathematics, Springer-Verlag, 909, 1982, 34—47.

[9] Hansen, E. *Global Optimization Using Interval Analysis*, Marcel Dekker, New York, 1992.

[10] Himmelblau, D. M. *Applied Nonlinear Programming*, McGraw-Hill, New York, 1972.

[11] Hock, W. and Schittkowski, K. *Test Examples for Nonlinear Programming Code*, Lecture Notes in Economics and Mathematical Systems, No. 187, Springer-Verlag, 1981.

[12] Horst, R. and Tuy, H. *Global Optimization*, Springer-Verlay, Berlin, 1990.

[13] Lee, L. E. Weight minimization of a spped reducer, an ASME publication, 77—DET—163, 1977.

[14] Levy, A. V. and Montalvo, A. The tunneling algorithm for the global minimization of functions, *SIAM J. Sci. Sta. Comput.*, 6 (1985), 15—29.

[15] Loh, H. T. *A Sequential Linearization Approach for Mixed-Discrete Nonlinesr Design Optimization*, Doctoral Dissertation, Department of Mechanical Engineering and Applied Mechanics, The University of Michigan, Ann Arbor, 1989.

[16] Loh, H. T. and Papalambros, P. Y. Sequential linearization approach for solving mixeddiscrete nonlinear design optimization, *Journal of Mechanical Design*, 113 (1991), 325—334.

[17] Morr, R., Hansen, E. and Leclere, A. Rigorous methods for global optimization, in *Recent Advances in Global Optimization*, C. A. Floudas and P. M. Pardalos eds., Princeton University Press, 1992, 321—342.

[18] Muu, L. D. and Oettli, W. Method for minimizing a convex-concave function over a convex set, *Journal of Optimization, Theorem and Applications*, 70 (1991), 377—384.

[19] Pardalos, P. M. and Rosen, J. B. *Constrained Global Optimization: Algorithms and Applications*, Lecture Notes in Computer Science, 268, Springer-Verlag, 1987.

[20] Pillo, G. Di. and Grippo, L. Exact penalty functions in constrained optimization, *SIAM Journal Control and Optimization*, 28 (1989), 1333—1360.

[21] Price, W. L. Global optimization by controlled random search, *Journal of Optimization Theory and Applications*, 40 (1983), 333—348.

[22] Ritter, K. A method for solving maximum-problems with a nonconcave quadratic objective function, *Z. Wahrscheinlichkeitstheorie very. Geb.* 4 (1966), 340—351.

[23] Schittkowski, K. *More Test Examples for Nonlinear Programming Code*, Lecture Note in

Economics and Mathematical Systems, No. 282, Springer-Verlag, New York, 1987.

[24] Shi, S., Zheng, Q. and Zhuang, D. Discontinuous robust mappings are approximatable, *Transaction AMS*, 1995.

[25] Shi, S., Zheng, Q. and Zhuang, D. Set-valued mappings and approximatable mappings, *Journal of Mathematical Analysis and Applications*, 183 (1994), 706—726.

[26] Tui, H. Concave programming under linear constraints, *Dokl. Akad. Naul, SSSR* 159 (1964), 32—35, (English).

[27] Tu, R. and Zheng, Q. Integral global optimization method in statistical applications, to appear in *Computers and Mathematics with Applications*.

[28] Zheng, Q. Strategies of changed domain for searching global extrema, *Numerical Computation and Applications of Computer* 3:4 (1981), 257—261. (In Chinese).

[29] Zheng, Q. Robust Analysis and global optimization, *Annals of Operations Research*, 24 (1990), 273—286.

[30] Zheng, Q. Robust analysis and global minimization of a chass of discontinuous functions (I), *Acta Mathematicae Applicatae Sinica* (English Series), 6:3(1990), 205—223.

[31] Zheng, Q. Robust Analysis and global optimization of a class of discontinuous functions (II), *Acta Mathematicae Applicatae Sinica* (English Series), 6:4 (1990), 317—337.

[32] Zheng, Q. Global minimization of constrained problems with discontinuous penalty functions, to appear.

[33] Zheng, Q. Jiang, B. C. and Zhuang, S. L. A method for finding global extrema, *Acta Mathematicae Applicatae Sinica*, 2:1 (1978), 161—174. (In Chinese).

[34] Zheng, Q. and Zhuang, D. Integral global optimization of constrained problems in function space with discontinuous penalty functions, in *Recent Advances in Global Optimization*, C. A. Floudas and P. M. Pardalos eds., 298—320, Princeton University Press, 1992.

[35] Zheng, Q. and Zhuang, D. Equi-robust set-valued mappings and the approximation of fixed points, in *Proceedings of The Second International Conference on Fixed Point Theory and Applications*, K. K. Tan ed., World Scientific Publishing, 1992, 346—361.

[36] Zheng, Q. and Zhuang, D. Finite dimensional approximation to solutions of minimization problems in function spaces, *Optimization*, 26 (1992), 33—50.

[37] Zheng, Q. and Zhuang, D. Integral global optimization and its Monte Carlo implementation, in *Proceedings of Conference on Scientific and Engineering Computing*, National Defence Industry Press, Beijing, 1993, 262—266.

[38] P. B. Zwart. Nonlinear programming: Counterexamples to global optimization algorithms by Ritter and Tui, *Operations Research*, 21 (1973), 1260—1266.

Robust Analysis and Global Optimization *

Abstract: In this paper, the properties of robust sets and robust functions are studied. Also, we study minimization of a robust function over a robust set and extend the optimality conditions of [3] and the algorithm of [4,5] to our case. The algorithm is shown to be effective.

1 Introduction

Let X be a Hausdorff toplogical space, S be a compact subset of X, and f be a lower semi-continuous (l.s.c.) function defined on S. Then, the minimum of f over S exists:

$$\overline{c} = \min_{x \in S} f(x) \tag{1.1}$$

and the set of minima

$$\overline{H} = \{x \mid f(x) = \overline{c}, x \in S\} \tag{1.2}$$

is nonempty.

Until now, the problem of finding a solution of (1.1) under such loose conditions has rarely been considered, although such a solution is not without value. The objective function may be discontinuous, the constrained set may be disconnected, but many problems from natural and social sciences, as well as from industrial applications, do require minimizing a discontinuous function. On the other hand, problems in application may require the constrained set S to be disconnected by physical forbiddance. If we only consider the problem of finding a local minimum, it would not concern us whether S is connected or not.

However, we still have to place certain restrictions on the set S and the function f. This is the topic that robust analysis studies.

This work is an extension of earlier work[1,2]. We first study the properties of robust sets and robust functions. Then, the minimization problem of a robust function over a robust compact set is considered using the integral approach. Optimality conditions in [3] and the algorithm in [4] and [5] are extended to this case. Numerical tests and industrial applications[6] show that the algorithm is effective.

---

* Reprinted from Annals of Operations Research, 1990, 24:273—286.

2 Robust Sets and Robust Points

We begin with definitions of a robust set and a robust point. Let X be a topological space and D be a subset of X.

Definition 2.1 A set D is said to be robust iff
$$\text{cl } D = \text{cl (int } D) \tag{2.1}$$

Definition 2.2 A point $x \in \text{cl } D$ is said to be robust to set D iff for each neighborhood $N(x)$ of x
$$N(x) \cap \text{int } D \neq \varnothing. \tag{2.2}$$

An open set is robust. The concept of robustness is a generalization of that of openness. A closed set may be nonrobust. For instance, a point x is closed in $\mathbb{R}^1$ but it is nonrobust. Note that the concept of robustness is closely related to the given topology. A subset of integers is nonrobust on $\mathbb{R}^1$, but is robust with respect to discrete topology on the set of integers.

Remark 2.1 We define only the robustness of the points in cl D because if $x \notin \text{cl } D$, then there is a neighborhood $N(x)$ of x such that $N(x) \cap \text{cl } D \neq \varnothing$, i.e. (2.2) does not hold. Thus, the points which are not contained in cl D are always nonrobust.

The following theorem shows that each point of a robust set is robust to this set and vice versa.

Theorem 2.1 *A set D is robust if and only if each point of D is robust to D.*

Proof. Suppose there is a point $x \in D$ which is nonrobust to D, then there exists a neighborhood $N(x)$ of x such that $N(x) \cap \text{int } D = \varnothing$. This implies $x \notin \text{cl (int } D)$. Thus, $x \in \text{cl } D \setminus \text{cl (int } D) \neq \varnothing$. D is then nonrobust.

Conversely, suppose each point of D is robust to D but, by contraries, D is nonrobust. That is, $A = \text{cl } D \setminus \text{cl (int } D) \neq \varnothing$. Take a point $x \in A$. Since $x \in \text{cl (int } D)$, we can find a neighborhood $N(x)$ of x such that $N(x) \cap \text{int } D = \varnothing$. Since $x \in \text{cl } D$, $N(x) \cap D \neq \varnothing$. Take a point $x_1 \in N(x) \cap D$ and take a neighborhood $N_1(x_1)$ of x_1 such that $N_1(x_1) \subset N(x)$. Then, $N_1(x_1) \cap \text{int } D = \varnothing$. This means that x_1 is nonrobust to D. We have a contradiction.

Suppose a point x is robust to both D and G, then point x may be nonrobust to their intersection $D \cap G$. For instance, let $D = [0,1]$ and $G = [0,1/2] \cup [1,2]$. They are robust on $\mathbb{R}^1$. The point $x = 1 \in D \cap G = [0,1/2] \cup \{1\}$ is nonrobust to $D \cap G$.

Theorem 2.2 *Suppose x is robust to D and $x \in \text{int } D$, then x is robust to $D \cap \text{int } G$. Point x is then robust to $D \cap G$.*

Proof. For each neighborhood $N_1(x) \subset N(x) \cap \text{int } G$, we have $N_1(x) \cap \text{int } D \neq \varnothing$ because x is robust to D. Now we have
$$N(x) \cap \text{int } (D \cap \text{int } G) = N(x) \cap \text{int } G \cap \text{int } D \supset N_1(x) \cap \text{int } D \neq \varnothing.$$
Therefore, x is robust to $D \cap \text{int } G$.

With the help of Theorem 2.1 and Theorem 2.2, we can easily prove the following theorems.

Theorem 2.3 *The union of robust sets is robust.*

Theorem 2.4 *The intersection of a robust set and an open set is robust.*

The following statements hold. One can prove them by using the above theorems:
(1) if D is robust, then cl D is also robust;
(2) a point x is robust to D if and only if $x \in \text{cl}(\text{int } D)$;
(3) if D is robust and F is closed, then $D \backslash F$ is robust;
(4) a set D is robust if and only if $\text{bd}(D) = \text{bd}(\text{int } D)$, where $\text{bd}(D) = \text{cl } D \backslash \text{int } D$, the boundary of D.

3 Robust Functions

Let $f: X \to \mathbb{R}$ be a real valued function defined on a topoligical space X. In this section, we will consider a class of discontinuous functions related to the concepts of robust sets and points. A function f is said to be upper remi-continuous (u.s.c.) iff the set
$$F_c = \{x \mid f(x) < c\} \tag{3.1}$$
is open for each real number. f is said to be u.s.c. at a point x_0 iff $x_0 \in F_c$ implies $x_0 \in \text{int}(F_c)$. We generalize these concepts to robust functions.

Definition 3.1 A function f is said to be robust iff the set $F_c = \{x \mid f(x) < c\}$ is robust for each real number c.

Definition 3.2 A function f is said to be robust at a point x_0 iff $x_0 \in F_c$ implies x_0 is robust to F_c.

An u.s.c. function is robust, so it is a continuous function. A monotone function f on $\mathbb{R}^1$ is robust. Indeed, suppose f is increasing, then $F_c = (-\infty, \alpha)$, where $\alpha = f(c)$; the point α may or may not be contained in F_c. In both cases, F_c is robust. If f is u.s.c. at a point x_0, then f is also robust at point x_0.

The following theorem is expected.

Theorem 3.1 *A function f is robust if and only if it is robust at each point.*

The sum of two robust functions may be nonrobust. For example, let
$$f_1(x) = \begin{cases} 1, & x \leqslant 0, \\ 0, & x > 0, \end{cases} \text{ and } f_2(x) = \begin{cases} 0, & x < 0, \\ 1, & x \geqslant 0, \end{cases} \tag{3.2}$$
then f_1 and f_2 are robust. However, their sum
$$f(x) = f_1(x) + f_2(x) = \begin{cases} 1, & x \neq 0, \\ 2, & x = 0, \end{cases} \tag{3.3}$$
is nonrobust at $x = 0$.

Theorem 3.2 *Suppose that f is robust at x_0 and g is u.s.c. at x_0 (for division, g is supposed to be l.s.c. at x_0). Then, the following functions are robust at x_0:*
(1) $\alpha f \quad (\alpha \geqslant 0)$;

(2) $f+g$;

(3) $f \cdot g$ $(g(x_0)>0)$;

(4) f/g $(g(x)>0)$.

It is easy to prove the following proposition using theorem 3.1:

Proposition 3.1 *Suppose that f is robust and g is u.s.c. (for division, g is supposed to be l.s.c.), then the following functions are robust:*

(1) αf $(\alpha \geq 0)$;

(2) $f+g$;

(3) $f \cdot g$ $(g(x)>0)$;

(4) f/g $(g(x)>0)$.

If $f_\alpha(x)$ is robust at a point x_0 for each $\alpha \in \Lambda$, then the function $f(x)=\inf_{\alpha \in \Lambda} f_\alpha(x)$ is also robust at point x_0. The limit of a decreasing sequence of robust functions preserves the robustness, and so on. We will not discuss the properties and structure of robust functions in detail, which is beyond the scope of this paper. Before transferring to global optimization, we would like to mention a proberty related to the epigraph of a function. Recall an epigraph of a function f is defined as (see [7]):

$$\text{epi}(f)=\{(x,c) \mid f(x) \leq c\}. \tag{3.4}$$

The epigraph is a subset of the product space $X \times /\mathbb{R}$.

Theorem 3.3 *A function f is robust at x_0 if and only if each point $(x_0,c) \in \text{epi}(f)$ is robust to the set epi (f) in the product space $X \times \mathbb{R}$ with the product topology. Therefore, a function f is robust if and only if its epigraph epi (f) is robust in the product space $X \times \mathbb{R}$.*

4 Relative Robustness

Return to consider the following minimization problem:

$$\bar{c}=\min_{x \in S} f(x), \tag{4.1}$$

where we assume that

(A1) S is a compact set in X;

(A2) $f: S \to \mathbb{R}$ is an l.s.c. function.

To study such constrained problems, the concept of relative robustness has to be investigated.

Definition 4.1 An objective function f is said to be relatively robust to S at a point $x_0(\in cl\ S)$ if $x_0 \in F_c = \{x \mid f(x) < c\}$ implies x_0 is robust to $F_c \cap S$.

The following proposition gives us sufficient conditions for the relative robustness of a function.

Proposition 4.1 *If (1) f is robust at $x_0 \in \text{int } S$; or (2) x_0 is robust to S and f is u.s.c. at x_0, then f is relatively robust to S and x_0.*

These conditions are sufficient. For instance, let $S=[-A,0] \cup [1,A]$, where $A>1$,

$$f_1(x) = \begin{cases} 1-x, & x \in [-A, 0], \\ x, & x \in [0, A], \end{cases} \tag{4.2}$$

and

$$f_2(x) = \begin{cases} x, & x \in [-A, 0], \\ 1-x, & x \in [0, A], \end{cases} \tag{4.3}$$

In both cases, $x=0$ is not in int S, nor is f continuous at $x=0$. f_1 is relatively robust to S at $x=0$, and f_2 is not.

The concept of inf-robustness is introduced in [8] for minimization problems.

Definition 4.2 A ste S is said to be inf-robust with the minimization problem (4.1) iff for each $c_0 > \bar{c}$ there is $c(\leqslant c_0)$ such that $F_c \cap S$ is a nonempty robust set.

In [8], we consider only the case of continuous objective functions; the definition of inf-robust is simplified as: a set S is inf-robust iff there is a real number c such that $F_c \cap S$ is nonempty and robust.

If S is inf-robust, then f is relatively robust to S at each (global) minimum point. However, for some problems the set of global minima may be empty. In this case, we can utilize the inf-robust concept to construct an algorithm to find the infimum of f over S. For example, let $S = (0, 1]$, $A = \bigcup_{k=1}^{\infty} (1/(2k+1), 1/2k]$, $B = S \setminus A = \bigcup_{k=1}^{\infty} (1/(2k, 1/(2k-1)]$ and

$$f(x) = \begin{cases} x, & x \in A, \\ x, & x \in B \cap (\text{irrational numbers}), \\ 1, & x \in B \cap (\text{rational numbers}). \end{cases} \tag{4.4}$$

f is inf-robust, but the set of minimum points is empty; f is relatively robust to S at $x=0$, which is in the closure of S.

In the following consideratiom, we assume:

(R) f is relatively robust to S at a global minimum point of (4.1).

As an example, consider the following combinatorial optimization problem.

Let $Z_+^n = \{z = (z_1, \cdots, z_n) \mid \text{where } z_i \text{ is a positive integer } i = 1, \cdots, n\}$, S be a finite subset of Z_+^n, $f: S \to \mathbb{R}$ be a function defined on S, $f(z) = f(z_1, \cdots, z_n)$. The problem is to find the minimum value

$$\bar{c} = \min_{x \in S} f(z) \tag{4.5}$$

and the set of miniam,

$$\overline{H} = \{z \in S \mid f(z) = \bar{c}\}. \tag{4.6}$$

For this case, $\overline{H}$ is nonempty.

We define

$$D = \{x = (x_1, \cdots, x_n) \in \mathbb{R}^n \mid ([x_1 + 1/2], \cdots, [x_n + 1/2]) \in S\} \tag{4.7}$$

and

$$F(x) = f([x_1 + 1/2], \cdots, [x_n + 1/2]), \tag{4.8}$$

where $[\alpha]$ denotes the integer part of the real number α. D is a union of cubes and they are robust in $\mathbb{R}^n$. For each real number c, the set $\{x \mid F(x) < c\}$ is also a union of cubes (or empty). Thus, D is a robust set in $\mathbb{R}^n$ and F is a robust function. Let $\bar{x}$ be a global minimum point of F over D, i. e.

$$F(\bar{x}) = \min_{x \in D} F(x), \tag{4.9}$$

then $\bar{x} \in \text{int } D$ (or one can find a point x_1, in the same cube as x, such that $x_1 \in \text{int } D$). Therefore, assumption (R) is satisfied.

5 Optimality Conditions

In order to find global minima with the integral approach, a special class of measure spaces is required. Let X be a normal topological space, Ω be a σ-field of subsets of X. A measure space (x, Ω, μ) is said to be a Q-measure space if:
(M1) each open set is in Ω;
(M2) the measure of each nonempty open set is positive;
(M3) the measure of each compact set is bounded.

The Lebesgue measure in $\mathbb{R}^n$ is a Q-measure; a nondegenerate Gaussian measure on a separable Hilbert space is also a Q-measure. A specific measure space can be utilized to solve a specific minimization problem.

The following lemma is a sufficient condition for global optimality.

Lemma 5.1 *Suppose assumption (A1), (A2), (R), (M1) and (M2) hold, and $S \cap H_c \neq \emptyset$, where $H_c = \{x \mid f(x) \leqslant c\}$ is a level set of f. If*

$$\mu(S \cap H_c) = 0, \tag{5.1}$$

then c is the global minimum value of f over S and $S \cap H_c$ is the set of global minima.

Proof. Suppose, by contraries, that c is not the global minimum value and that $\bar{c} < c$ is. Let $2\eta = c - \bar{c} > 0$. There is a global minimum x such that $\bar{c} = f(x)$ and f is relatively robust to S at x because of assumption (R). $x \in F_{c-\eta}$. Thus, $N(x) \cap \text{int } (S \cap F_{c-\eta}) \neq \emptyset$, where $N(x)$ is a neighborhood of x. We now have int $(S \cap F_{c-\eta})$ and

$$\text{int } (S \cap F_{c-\eta}) \subset S \cap H_c, \tag{5.2}$$

which implies, with the assumption (M2), that

$$\mu(S \cap H_c) \geqslant \mu(\text{int}(S \cap F_{c-\eta})). \tag{5.3}$$

This is a contradiction.

Condition (5.1) is a suffictient one. If c is the global minimum value of f over S, it may happen that $\mu(S \cap H_c) > 0$. From the proof of lemma 5.1, if $c > \bar{c} = \min_{x \in S} f(x)$, then $\mu(S \cap H_c) > 0$.

We now proceed to define the concept of mean value, variance and higher moments of f over its level set and constrained set S as in [3]. These concepts are closely related to optimality conditions and the algorithm for finding global minima.

Definition 5.1 Let $c > \bar{c} = \min_{x \in S} f(x)$ and suppose assumptions (A1), (A2), (R), (M1), (M2) and (M3) hold. We define the mean value, variance, modified variance and the mth moment (centered at a) of a function f over its level set and the constrained set S, respectively, as follows:

$$M(f,c;S) = \frac{1}{\mu(S \cap H_c)} \int_{S \cap H_c} f(x) d\mu, \tag{5.4}$$

$$V(f,c;S) = \frac{1}{\mu(S \cap H_c)} \int_{S \cap H_c} (f(x) - M(f,c;S))^2 d\mu, \tag{5.5}$$

and

$$M_m(f,c;S) = \frac{1}{\mu(S \cap H_c)} \int_{S \cap H_c} (f(x) - a)^m d\mu, \quad m = 1, 2, \cdots. \tag{5.6}$$

The function f is measurable, $H_c \cap S$ is compact, and $\mu(S \cap H_c) > 0$; they are well defined. When $c = \bar{c}$, $\mu(S \cap H_c)$ may be equal to zero. Definition 5.1 has to be extended by a limit process.

Definition 5.2 Under the assumptions of definition 5.1, we can extend it to $c \geqslant \bar{c}$ as follows:

$$M(f,c;S) = \lim_{c_k \downarrow c} \frac{1}{\mu(S \cap H_{c_k})} \int_{S \cap H_{c_k}} f(x) d\mu, \tag{5.7}$$

$$V(f,c;S) = \lim_{c_k \downarrow c} \frac{1}{\mu(S \cap H_{c_k})} \int_{S \cap H_{c_k}} (f(x) - M(f,c;S))^2 d\mu, \tag{5.8}$$

$$V_1(f,c;S) = \lim_{c_k \downarrow c} \frac{1}{\mu(S \cap H_{c_k})} \int_{S \cap H_{c_k}} (f(x) - c)^2 d\mu, \tag{5.9}$$

and

$$M_m(f,c;S) = \lim_{c_k \downarrow c} \frac{1}{\mu(S \cap H_{c_k})} \int_{S \cap H_{c_k}} (f(x) - a)^m d\mu, \quad m = 1, 2, \cdots. \tag{5.10}$$

The limits exist and they are independent of choices of c_k. The extended concepts are well defined and consistent with those of definition 5.1. The proofs are similar to those in [3]. With these concepts, we characterize the global optimality as follows.

Theorem 5.1 *Under assumptions* (A1), (A2), (R), (M1), (M2) *and* (M3), *the following statements are equivalent*:
(1) $\bar{x} \in S$ *is the global minimum of* (4.1) *and* $\bar{c} = f(\bar{x})$ *is the global minimum value*;
(2) $M(f, \bar{c}; S) = \bar{c}$;
(3) $V(f, \bar{c}; S) = 0$;
(4) $V_1(f, \bar{c}; S) = 0$;
(5) $M_m(f, \bar{c}; S) = 0$, *for* $m = 1, 2, \cdots$.

6 An Algorithm

In this section, an algorithm is proposed for finding the global minimum of a discontinuous function under assumptions (A1), (A2), (R), (M1), (M2) and (M3). Take a point $x_0 \in S$. If $c_0 = f(x_0) = \bar{c} = \min_{x \in S} f(x)$, then x_0 is a global minimum point and c_0 is the global minimum value. The algorithm stops. In general, $c_0 > \bar{c}$, and $\mu(S \cap H_{c_0}) > 0$ by

lemma 5.1. Let
$$c_1 = M(f, c_0; S). \tag{6.1}$$
Then
$$\bar{c} \leqslant c_1 \leqslant c_0. \tag{6.2}$$

In general, let
$$c_{k+1} = M(f, c_k; S), \quad k = 0, 1, 2, \cdots. \tag{6.3}$$
If there is a positive integer k_0 such that
$$c_{k_0} = M(f, c_{k_0}; S), \tag{6.4}$$
then the algorithm terminates. Otherwise, let $\bar{c} = c_{k_0}$ and $\bar{H} = S \cap H_{ck_0}$; we obtain a decreasing sequence
$$c_0 \geqslant c_1 \geqslant \cdots \geqslant c_k \geqslant c_{k+1} \cdots \geqslant \bar{c} \tag{6.5}$$
and a monotone sequence of sets
$$S \cap H_{c_0} \supset S \cap H_{c_1} \supset \cdots \supset S \cap H_{c_k} \supset S \cap H_{c_{k+1}} \supset \cdots. \tag{6.6}$$
The limits exist. Let
$$\bar{c} = \lim_{k \to \infty} c_k \quad \text{and} \quad \bar{H} = \lim_{k \to \infty} H_{c_k}.$$

Theorem 6.1 *Under assumptions* (A1), (A2), (R), (M1), (M2) *and* (M3), $\bar{c}$ *is the global minimum value and $\bar{H}$ is the set of global minima of f over S.*

Proof. If the algorithm terminates at a finite step $\bar{c} = c_{k_0}$, then we have $\bar{c} = M(f, \bar{c}; S)$ in (6.4). When the algorithm does not stop in a finite step, we also, from (6.3), by letting $k \to \infty$, obtain
$$\bar{c} = M(f, \bar{c}; S). \tag{6.7}$$
Hence, with theorem 5.1, $\bar{c}$ is the global minimum value. Let $x \in \bar{H} \cap S$; then for each k (or $k > k_0$) we have $f(x) \leqslant c_k$. Letting $k \to \infty$ (or setting $k = k_0$), we obtain
$$f(x) \geqslant \bar{c}. \tag{6.8}$$
However, $f(x) \geqslant \bar{c}$ for all $x \in S$. Hence, $\bar{H} = \{x \mid f(x) = \bar{c}; x \in S\}$, i.e. $\bar{H}$ is the set of global minima.

In applications, we can use a modified variance condition to verify if $V_1 = V_1(f, c_k, S) \leqslant \varepsilon$, where $\varepsilon > 0$ is the precision given in advance. If $V_1 \geqslant \varepsilon$, then the procedure is not terminated.

Note that the errors at each step in the algorithm will not be accumulated. Suppose we calculate $c_1 = M(f, c_0; S)$ with an error Δ_1 and obtain $d_1 = c_1 + \Delta_1$, then calculate $c_2 = M(f, d_1; S)$ with an error Δ_2 and obtain $d_2 = c_2 + \Delta_2$, and so on. In general, we have
$$c_k = M(f, d_{k-1}; S) \quad \text{and} \quad \Delta_k = d_k - c_k, \ k = 1, 2, \cdots, \tag{6.9}$$
and obtain a decreasing sequence $\{d_k\}$. Let
$$\bar{d} = \lim_{k \to \infty} d_k. \tag{6.10}$$

Theorem 6.2 *Under the assumptions of theorem 6.1, $\bar{d}$ is the global minimum value if and only if*
$$\lim_{k \to \infty} \Delta_k = 0. \tag{6.11}$$

The following theorem shows that the algorithm has a descent property.

Theorem 6.3 *Under the assumptions of theorem 6.1, if there is a positive integer k_0 such that*
$$c_{k_0+1}=M(f_1,c_{k_0};S) \text{ or } S\cap H_{c_{k_0}},$$
then the function f is constant on $S\cap H_{c_{k_0}}$.

The algorithm can be implemented by the Monte Carlo technique, as in [4] and [5].

Numerical tests show that the discontinuity of the objective function dose not influence the computation procedure essentially. An industrial application (see [6]) shows that the algorithm is effective.

7 Numerical tests

Two examples show that the algorithm is effective. The numerical tests were performed on an IBM-PC with BASIC implementation.

Example 7.1
$$\underset{x\in D}{\text{minimize}} f(x), \tag{7.1}$$
where
$$f(x)=g(x)-[g(x)]/n, \tag{7.2}$$
$$g(x)=\frac{\pi}{n}\left[\sin(\pi x_1)+\sum_{i=1}^{n-1}(x_i-10)^2(1+\sin(\pi x_{i+1}))+(x_n-10)^2\right], \tag{7.3}$$
$$D=\{x=(x_1,\cdots,x_n)\mid -10\leqslant x_i\leqslant 10,\ i=1,\cdots,n\}, \tag{7.4}$$

$[y]$ denotes the integer part of y. The function f is discontinuous, with many jumps and local minima. It has a unique global minimum at $x=(1,\cdots,1)$. Table 1 gives the number of iterations N_i, the amounts of function computation N_f, $\log V_0-\log V_\varepsilon$ corresponding to variables $n=5,10,20,50$, where V_0 and V_ε are the volumes of the initial and final search domain, respectively.

Table 1 Results for example 1

n	5	10	20	50
N_i	43	85	155	395
N_f	1917	4251	9565	46.623
$\log V_0-\log V_\varepsilon$	74.66405	146.3872	295.586	731.648

Example 7.2
$$\underset{x\in D}{\text{minimize}} f(x), \tag{7.5}$$
where
$$f(x)=\begin{cases}1+n\left\{\sum_{i=1}^{n}|x_i|+\text{sgn}\left(\sin\frac{1}{\sum_{i=1}^{n}|x_i|}-0.5\right)\right\}, & x\neq 0 \\ 0, & x=0,\end{cases} \tag{7.6}$$

and D is the same as (7.4). The function has infinite discontinuous hypersurfaces. Its unique global minimum is at the oright, which has a discontinuity of the second kind. Table 2 gives the data of this example.

Table 2 Results for example 2

n	5	10	20	50
N_i	68	144	261	609
N_f	3027	7375	22,481	71,423
$\log V_0 - \log V_\epsilon$	105.4427	224.0189	459.386	1211.395

References

[1] Q. Zheng. A class of discontinuous functions and local optimization problems, Num. Math., J. Chinese Univ. 1(1985)31—43, in Chinese.

[2] Q. Zheng. Global optimization of a class of discontinuous functions, J. Appl. Sci. 1(1986)93—94, in Chinese.

[3] Q. Zheng. Optimal conditions for global optimization (I) and (II), Acta Atath. Appl. Sinica 1(1985) 46—61; 62—76.

[4] Q. Zheng, B. Jing and S. Zhuang. A method for searching a global extremum, Acta Math. Appl. Sinica 2(1978), in Chinese.

[5] Q. Zheng. Theory and methods for global optimization—an integral approach, *Proc. Optimization Days* (1986).

[6] X. Pan, S. Wang, H. Liu, and Q. Zheng. The optimum design of the arrangement of needles on the neediling board of a preneeding machine, J. China Textile University 6(1986)79—84, in Chinese.

[7] R. T. Rockafeller. *Convex Analysis* (Princeton University Press, Princeton, NJ, 1970).

[8] E. A. Galperin and Q. Zheng. Integral global optimization in functional spaces with application to optimal control, Preprint.

Global Minimization of Constrained Problems with Discontinuous Penalty Functions*

Abstract: With the integral approach to global optimization, a class of discontinuous penalty functions is proposed to solve constrained minimization problems. Optimality conditions of a penalized minimization problem are generalized to a discontinuous case; necessary and sufficient conditions for an exact penalty function are examined; a nonsequential algorithm is proposed. Numerical examples are given to illustrate the effectiveness of the algorithm.

1 Introduction

Let X be a topological space, S a nonempty subset of X, and $f: X \to \mathbb{R}$ a real-valued function. Consider the following constrained optimization problem:
$$c^* = \inf_{x \in S} f(x). \tag{1.1}$$
In general, minimizers of (1.1) may not exist. We will not examine particularly the existence problem of global minimizers here.

Assume that (A): f is lower semicontinuous, S is inf-compact.

Under (A) minimizers of (1.1) exist. Here, inf-compactness means that there is a real number $b > c^*$ such that the level set
$$H_b = \{x: f(x) \leqslant b\}$$
is a nonempty compact set.

The problem of minimizing a function over a constrained set has been investigated since the 17th century with the concepts of derivative and Lagrangian multiplier. The gradient-based approach to optimization is the mainstream of that research. However, the requirement of differentiability restricts its application to many practical problems. Moreover, it can only be utilized to characterize and find a local solution of a general optimization problem. In this work, we will investigate a constrained minimization problem with discontinuous objective function by using the integral approach.

The penalty function method, representing a constrained minimization problem in terms of unconstrained ones, is one of the propular numerical methods of nonlinear

---

* In collaboration with Zhang L S. Reprinted from Computers and Mathematics with Applications, 1999, 37:41−58.

programming because the idea is simple and quite universal. The penalty approach to constrained optimization is attributed to Courant[1], and was developed and popularized by Fiacco and McCormick[2] and others. In recent years, a considerable amount of investigation has been devoted to methods that attempt to solve a constrained problem by means of a single unconstrained minimization. It is termed *exact penalty method*[3–10].

A major disadvantage of the penalty approach is the choice of penalty parameters. The use of large values of the penalty coefficient leads to a minmization problem where the Hessian is ill-conditioned, if one uses a gradient-based method. Moreover, for an exact penalty function, a constraint qualification is required.

Taking advantage of the integral approach of global optimization, a class of discontinuous penalty functions is proposed in this work. Using the theory and algorithms of the intergal global minimization, one can solve a constrained problem by unconstrained minimization technique without requirement of a constraint qualification.

In this paper, we first recall basic concepts of robust sets, functions, and the integral approach to global minimization (Section 2).

In Section 3, we consider general penalty functions which may be discontinuous. We derive conditions for a penalty function to be exact and propose several discontinuous exact penalty functions in Section 4. We study optimality conditions for the penalized problem with the integral approach in Section 5 and propose an algorithm for approximating solutions of constrained optimization problems in Section 6; these problems may have *discontinuous objective function with disconnected constraint set*. Numerical examples are given in Section 7 to illustrate the effectiveness of the algorithm.

2 Robust Sets and Functions. Integral Global Minimization

In this section, we will summarize several concepts and properties of the integral global minimization of robust discontinuous functions, which will be utilized in the following sections. For more details, see [11,12].

2.1 Robust Sets and Functions

Let X be a topological space, a subset D of X is said to be *robust* if

$$\text{cl } D = \text{cl int } D, \tag{2.1}$$

where cl D denotes the closure of the set D and int D denotes the interior of D.

A robust set consists of *robust points* of the set. A point $x \in D$ is said to be a robust point of D, if for each neighborhood $N(x)$ of x, $N(x) \cap \text{int } D \neq \emptyset$. A set D is robust if and only if each point of D is a robust one. A point $x \in D$ is a robust point of D if and only if there exists a net $\{x_\lambda\} \subset \text{int } D$ such that $x_\lambda \to x$.

The interior of a nonempty robust set is nonempty. A union of robust sets is robust. An intersection of two robust sets may be nonrobust; but the intersection of an open set and a robust set is robust. A set D is robust if and only if $\partial D = \partial \text{int} D$, where $\partial D = \text{cl} D \backslash \text{int } D$

denotes the boundary of the set D.

A function $f:X\to\mathbb{R}$ is said to be *upper robust* if the set
$$F_c=\{x:f(x)<c\} \tag{2.2}$$
is robust for each real number c. A sum or a product of two upper robust finctions may be nonupper robust; but the sum of an upper robust function and an upper semicontinuous (u.s.c., for the product case nonnegativity is required) function is upper robust. A function f is upper robust if and only if it is upper robust at each point; f is upper robust at a point x if $x\in F_c$ implies x is a robust point of F_c. An example of a nonupper robust function on $\mathbb{R}^1$ is
$$f(x)=\begin{cases} x^2, & x\neq 0, \\ -1, & x=0. \end{cases}$$
f is not upper robust at $x=0$.

Let S be a robust set in a topological space (X,τ), where τ is the topology of X. We can introduce a relative topology τ_S and obtain a new topological space (S,τ_S). In this new topological space, we also have concepts of robust set and upper robust function with this relative topology. Then, we have concepts of relative robust set and relative upper robust function.

2.2 Q—Measure Spaces and Integration

In order to investigate a minimization problem with an integral approach, a special class of measure spaces, which are called Q-measure spaces, should be examined.

Let X be a topological space, Ω a σ-field of subsets of X, and μ a measure on Ω. A triplet (X,Ω,μ) is called a Q-measure space iff

(1) each open set in X is measurable;

(2) the measure $\mu(G)$ of a nonempty onen set G in X is positive: $\mu(G)>0$;

(3) the measure $\mu(K)$ of a compact set K in X is finite.

The n-dimensional Lebesgue measure space $(\mathbb{R}^n,\Omega,\mu)$ is a Q-measure space; a nondegenerate Gaussian measure μ on a separable Hilbert space H with Borel sets as measurable sets constitutes an infinite dimensional Q-measure space. A specific optimization problem is related to a specific Q-measure space which is suitable for consideration in this approach. Once a measure space is given, we can define intergration in a conventional way.

Since the interior of a nonempty open set is nonempty, the Q-measure of a measurable set containing a nonempty robust set is always positive. This is an essential property we need in the integral approach of minimization. Hence, the following assumptions are usually required.

(A) f is lower semicontinuous (l.s.c.) and S is inf-compact.

(R) f is upper robust on S.

(M) (X,Ω,μ) is a Q-measure space.

2.3 Integral Optimality Conditions for Global Minimization

We now proceed to define the concepts of mean value and modified variance of f over its level set. These concepts are closely related to optimality conditions and algorithms for global minimization.

Suppose that Assumptions (A), (M), and (R) hold, and $c > c^* = \min_{x \in S} f(x)$. We define the mean value and modified variance, respectively, as follows:

$$M(f,c;S) = \frac{1}{\mu(H_c \cap S)} \int_{H_c \cap S} f(x) \mathrm{d}\mu,$$

$$V_1(f,c;S) = \frac{1}{\mu(H_c \cap S)} \int_{H_c \cap S} (f(x) - c)^2 \mathrm{d}\mu.$$

They are well defined. These definitions can be extended to the case $c \geqslant c^*$ by a limit process. For instance,

$$V_1(f,c;S) = \lim_{c_k \downarrow c} \frac{1}{\mu(H_{c_k} \cap S)} \int_{H_{c_k} \cap S} (f(x) - c)^2 \mathrm{d}\mu.$$

The limits exist and are independent of the choice of $\{c_k\}$. The extended concepts are well defined and consistent with the above definitions.

With these concepts, we characterize the global optimality as follows.

Theorem 2.1 *Under Assumptions (A), (M), and (R), the following statements are equivalent:*

(1) $x^* \in S$ *is a global minimizer of f over S and $c^* = f(x^*)$ is the global minimum value,*

(2) $M(f,c^*;S) = c^*$ *(the mean value condition),*

(3) $V_1(f,c^*;S) = 0$ *(the modified variance condition).*

2.4 An Integral Algorithm

An integral global minimization algorithm for finding the global minimum value and the set of global minimizers of an upper robust function over a robust constraint set is given as follows [13].

Step 1. Take $c_0 > c^*$ and $\varepsilon > 0, k := 0$.
Step 2. $c_{k+1} := M(f,c_k;S)$, $v_{k+1} = V_1(f,c_k;S), H_{c_{k+1}} \cap S := \{x \in S: f(x) \leqslant c_{k+1}\}$.
Step 3. If $v_{k+1} \geqslant \varepsilon$, then $k := k+1$, go to Step 2.
Step 4. $c^* \Leftarrow c_{k+1}$, $H^* \Leftarrow H_{c_{k+1}}$; Stop.

If we take $\varepsilon = 0$, the algorithm may stop in a finite number of iteration, and we obtain the global minimum value with the set of global minimizers. Or, we obtain two monotone sequences

$$c_0 \geqslant c_1 \geqslant \cdots \geqslant c_k \geqslant c_{k+1} \geqslant \cdots$$

and

$$H_{c_0} \cap S \supset H_{c_1} \cap S \supset \cdots \supset H_{c_k} \cap S \supset H_{c_{k+1}} \cap S \supset \cdots.$$

Let

$$\bar{c} = \lim_{k \to \infty} c_k \quad \text{and} \quad H^* = \bigcap_{k=1}^{\infty} H_{c_k} \cap S.$$

Theorem 2.2 *Under Assumptions* (A), (M), *and* (R), $\bar{c}$ *is the global minimum value of* f *over* S, *and* H^* *is the set of global minimizers.*

Note, that errors at each iteration in the algorithm are not accumulated. The algorithm has been implemented by a properly designed Monte-Carlo method. The numerical tests show that the algorithm is competitive with other algorithms.

3 Discontinuous Penalty Functions

Let X be a metric space, S a subset of X, and f a real-valued function. Consider the constrained problem
$$c^* = \inf_{x \in S} f(x), \tag{3.1}$$
with the penalty approach. Recall, that a continuous and nonnegative function $p: X \to \mathbb{R}^1$ is said to be a penalty function associated with the constraint set S if
$$p(x) = 0, \quad \text{if and only if } x \in S.$$
With such a penalty function, we can find the set of global minimizers of a constrained problem by an integral algorithm[14]. In this section, we will generalize this definition to the discontinuous case.

Now, suppose S is a closed robust subset of a metric space X and f a real-valued function on X. Under Assumption (A), the set of global minimizers of the constrained problem (3.1) is nonempty. Moreover, (A) also implies that f is bounded below on X, i.e., there is a constant L such that
$$f(x) \geqslant L, \quad \text{for all } x \in X.$$
The minimizers of the constrained problem (3.1) can be approximated by a sequence of solutions of associated penalized unconstrained problems.

The discontinuous penalty function associated with the constraint set S is defined as follows.

Definition 3.1 A function $p(x)$ on a metric space (X, d) is a penalty function associated with a constraint set S if:

(1) p is lower semicontinuous;

(2) $p(x) = 0$ if $x \in S$;

(3) $\inf_{x \notin S_\beta} p(x) > 0$, where $S_\beta = \{u : d(u, v) \leqslant \beta, \forall v \in S\}$ and $\beta > 0$.

Remark 3.1 In the above definition, we relax the requirement of continuity from the traditional definition[2,5] as we wish to utilize discontinuous penalty functions.

Remark 3.2 It is expected that the penalty increases when the distance from a point $x \notin S$ to the constraint set S increases. We replace the traditional property
$$p(x) > 0, \quad \text{if } x \notin S,$$
by assumption (2.2)

With a penalty function p, we examine a penalized unconstrained minimization problem associated with (3.1)

$$\min_{x \in X} \{f(x) + \alpha p(x)\}, \qquad (3.2)$$

where $\alpha(>0)$ is a penalty parameter. Under Assumption (A), the penalized level set
$$H_b^\alpha = \{x : f(x) + \alpha p(x) \leqslant b\}$$
is a nonempty closed subset of H_b. Thus, H_b^α is compact in X. It follows that the minimizers of (3.2) also exist. Furthermore,
$$\min_{x \in X} \{f(x) + \alpha p(x)\} \leqslant \min_{x \in S} \{f(x) + \alpha p(x)\} = \min_{x \in S} f(x) = c^*.$$

We will construct two sequences $\{\alpha_n\}$ and $\{c_n\}$ so that $\alpha_n \uparrow \infty$ and $c_n \downarrow c (\geqslant c^*$, assuming $b > c)$, as $n \to \infty$ with the property that
$$\min_{x \in H_n} \{f(x) + \alpha_n p(x)\} \to c^*, \quad \text{as } n \to \infty, \qquad (3.3)$$
where, in order to simplify the notation, we denote
$$H_n = \{x : f(x) + \alpha_n p(x) \leqslant c_n\}. \qquad (3.4)$$

Proposition 3.1 *If $c_n \downarrow c \geqslant c^*$, then*
$$\min_{n \to \infty} H_n = \bigcap_{n=1}^\infty H_n = H_c \cap S. \qquad (3.5)$$

Proof. We first show that $\{H_n\}$ is a monotone sequence. It follows that the limit in (3.5) exists and equals the intersection. Suppose $x \in H_{n+1}$. Since $\alpha_{n+1} \geqslant \alpha_n$ and $c_{n+1} \leqslant c_n$,
$$f(x) + \alpha_n p(x) \leqslant f(x) + \alpha_{n+1} p(x) \leqslant c_{n+1} \leqslant c_n.$$
Therefore, $x \in H_n$. This proves $H_{n+1} \subset H_n$. Now, we show that
$$\bigcap_{n=1}^\infty H_n = H_c \cap S.$$
If $x \in H_c \cap S$, then $p(x) = 0$ and $f(x) + \alpha_n p(x) = f(x) \leqslant c \leqslant c_n$, $\forall n = 1, 2, \cdots$. Hence, $x \in H_n$, for $n = 1, 2, \cdots$. This proves
$$H_c \cap S \subset \bigcap_{n=1}^\infty H_n.$$
On the other hand, suppose $x \in \bigcap_{n=1}^\infty H_n$. Then, $f(x) \leqslant f(x) + \alpha_n p(x) \leqslant c_n$, for $n = 1, 2, \cdots$.

Letting $n \to \infty$, we have $f(x) \leqslant c$, i.e., $x \in H_c$. If $x \notin S$, the $p(x) > 0$ and $f(x) + \alpha_n p(x) \to \infty$ as $n \to \infty$. This contradicts that $f(x) + \alpha_n p(x) \leqslant c_n \leqslant c_1$, for $n = 1, 2, \cdots$. Hence, $x \in H_c \cap S$. This proves
$$\bigcap_{n=1}^\infty H_n \subset H_c \cap S.$$
The proof of Proposition 3.1 is completed.

Remark 3.3 We will use the concepts of mean value and modified variance to study a global minimization problem. If $c < c^* = \min_{x \in S} f(x)$, then $H_c \cap S = \emptyset$. From the above proposition, there is an integer N such that $H_n = \emptyset$ for $n \geqslant N$. In this case, we cannot even define mean values and variances on X. Thus, this situation should not be allowed to happen in the integral algorithm.

The following proposition shows that in the above framework, the global minimum value of a constrained problem is the limit of the global minimum values of penalized problems.

Proposition 3.2 *Suppose that $\{\alpha_n\}$ is a positive increasing sequence which tends to infinity as $n \to \infty$ and $\{c_n\}$ is a decreasing sequence which tends to $c \geq c^*$ as $n \to \infty$. Under Assumption (A), we have*

$$\min_{x \in x}\{f(x)+\alpha_n p(x)\} = \min_{x \in H_n}\{f(x)+\alpha_n p(x)\} = a_n \to c^* = \min_{x \in S} f(x). \quad (3.6)$$

Proof. Since f and p are l.s.c., H_n is closed, and thus, compact. Therefore,

$$\min_{x \in H_n}\{f(x)+\alpha_n p(x)\}$$

exists for each n. Since $H_c \cap S \subset H_n$, we have

$$\min_{x \in H_n}\{f(x)+\alpha_n p(x)\} \leq \min_{x \in H_n \cap S}\{f(x)+\alpha_n p(x)\} = \min_{x \in H_n \cap S} f(x) = \min_{x \in S} f(x) = c^*.$$

Hence,

$$\limsup_{n \to \infty} \min_{x \in H_n}\{f(x)+\alpha_n p(x)\} \leq c^*. \quad (3.7)$$

We now prove

$$\liminf_{n \to \infty} \min_{x \in H_n} a_n = \{f(x)+\alpha_n p(x)\} = \hat{c} \geq c^*. \quad (3.8)$$

Suppose, on the contrary, $\hat{c} < c^*$. Let $c^* - \hat{c} = 2\eta > 0$; then, there is a subsequence of $\{a_n\}$ (we denote it with the same notation) and an integer N such that $a_n \to \hat{c}$ and $a_n < c - \eta$, $\forall n \geq N$. Let $\hat{x}_n \in H_n$ be a global minimizer of $\min_{x \in H_n}\{f(x)+\alpha_n p(x)\}$, then

$$f(\hat{x}_n) \leq f(\hat{x}_n) + \alpha_n p(\hat{x}_n) \leq c^* - \eta, \quad n = 1, 2, \cdots.$$

We now have $\hat{x}_n \in H_{c^* - \eta} \cap H_n$, $n = N+1, N+2, \cdots$. Because of the monotonicity of $\{H_n\}$, $H_{c^* - \eta} \cap H_n \neq \emptyset$, implies that $H_{c^* - \eta} \cap H_k \neq \emptyset$, $k = 1, \cdots, n-1, n$. Hence, the intersection of these nested closed (compact) sets is also nonempty:

$$\bigcap_{n=1}^{\infty}(H_{c^* - \eta} \cap H_n) = H_{c^* - \eta} \bigcap_{n=1}^{\infty} H_n = H_{c^* - \eta} \cap H_c \cap S \neq \emptyset. \quad (3.9)$$

Therefore, we have a point $\hat{x}$ which is in bost S and $H_{c^* - \eta}$. This contradicts the fact that c^* is the global minimum value of f over S.

Combining (3.7) and (3.8), we obtain (3.6).

4 Discontinuous Exact Penalty Functions

In this section, we will derive conditions for a penalty function to be exact. With these conditions, several discontinuous exact penalty functions are proposed.

Definition 4.1 *A penalty function p for the constraint set S is exact for (3.1), if there is a real number $\alpha_0 > 0$ such that for each $\alpha \geq \alpha_0$, we have*

$$\min_{x \in x}\{f(x)+\alpha p(x)\} = \min_{x \in S} f(x) = c^* \quad (4.1)$$

and

$$\{x: f(x)+\alpha p(x) = c^*\} = \{x \in S: f(x) = c^*\} = H^*. \quad (4.2)$$

Lemma 4.1 *A necessary condition for a penalty function $p(x)$ to be exact is as follows.*
Condition (E1) There are $\alpha_0 > 0$ and $\beta = \beta(\alpha_0) > 0$ such that

$$p(x) \geq \frac{c^* - f(x)}{\alpha_0}, \quad \text{for all } x \in S_\beta. \quad (4.3)$$

Proof. Suppose that $p(x)$ is an exact penalty function, but (E1) does not hold. Then, there are sequences $\alpha_k \uparrow \infty$, $\beta_k > 0$ and $x_k \in S_{\beta_k}$ such that

$$p(x_k) < \frac{c^* - f(x_k)}{\alpha_k} \qquad (4.4)$$

or

$$f(x_k) + \alpha_k p(x_k) < c^*. \qquad (4.5)$$

Let $\tilde{x}_k$ be a solution to the penalized minimization problem

$$\min_{x \in X}[f(x) + \alpha_k p(x)], \qquad (4.6)$$

then

$$f(\tilde{x}_k + \alpha_k p(\tilde{x}_k) \leqslant f(x_k) + \alpha_k p(x_k) < c^*, \quad \text{for } k = 1, 2, \cdots \qquad (4.7)$$

It implies

$$\min_{x \in X}[f(x) + \alpha_k p(x)] < c^*, \quad \text{for } k = 1, 2, \cdots \qquad (4.8)$$

This contradicts the definition of the exact penalty function.

Remark 4.1 Condition (E1) states the following properties.

(i) If $x \in S$, then $p(x) = 0$ and (4.3) becomes $f(x) \geqslant c^*$; this is just the definition of c^*.

(ii) There is a nonnegative function $b(x)$ such that if $x \notin S$, then we have

$$p(x) \geqslant \alpha_0 b(x) \quad \text{and} \quad f(x) \geqslant c^* - b(x). \qquad (4.9)$$

These mean that for points outside of the constraint set S, the objective function $f(x)$ cannot dectease too quickly and the penalty function $p(x)$ cannot increase too slowly.

Example 4.1 Consider the problem $\min_{x \geqslant 0} x$. The penalty function

$$p(x) = \begin{cases} x^2, & x < 0, \\ 0, & x \geqslant 0 \end{cases}$$

is not exact because Condition (E1) or (4.9) does not hold.

Condition (E1) cannot ensure the feasibility of solution of the associated penalized problem. Thus, one more trivial necessary condition is stated.

Condition (E2) There is $\alpha_0 > 0$ such that if $\alpha > \alpha_0$ and x_α is a solution of

$$\min_{x \in X}[f(x) + \alpha p(x)] = c^*, \qquad (4.10)$$

then x_α is feasible.

In their paper, Di Pillo and Grippo[6] state a feasibility assumption (a_4) (see [6, Theorem 1, p. 1339]). It is easy to verify that (a_4) implies (E2). Condition (E2) is easy to verify when we study discontinuous penalty functions.

We are now ready to prove that (E1) and (E2) are necessary and sufficient for an exact penalty funtion.

Theorem 4.1 *A penalty function $p(x)$ is exact for the minimization problem (3.1) if and only if (E1) and (E2) hold.*

Proof. We have shown that conditions (E1) and (E2) are necessary. For the sufficienty, we first prove that there is $\alpha_p > 0$ such that

$$\min_{x \in X}[f(x) + \alpha p(x)] = c^*, \quad \text{for all } \alpha > \alpha_p. \qquad (4.11)$$

Condition (E1) implies that there are $\alpha_0 > 0$ and $\beta > 0$ such that
$$f(x) + \alpha p(x) \geq f(x) + \alpha_0 p(x) \geq c^*, \quad \text{for all } x \in S_\beta, \alpha > \alpha_0. \tag{4.12}$$
Thus,
$$c^* \leq \min_{x \in S_\beta}[f(x) + \alpha p(x)] \leq \min_{x \in S}[f(x) + \alpha p(x)] = \min_{x \in S} f(x) = c^*. \tag{4.13}$$
Since $\min_{x \notin S} p(x) = \eta > 0$ and f is bounded below, $f(x) > L$, there is α_L such that $\alpha_L \eta > |L| + c^*$. It follows,
$$f(x) + \alpha_L p(x) \geq c^*, \quad \text{for all } x \notin S_\beta. \tag{4.14}$$
Thus, if we take $\alpha \geq \alpha_p = \max(\alpha_0, \alpha_L)$, then
$$c^* \leq \min_{x \in X}[f(x) + \alpha p(x)] \leq \min_{x \in S_\beta}[f(x) + \alpha p(x)] \leq c^*. \tag{4.15}$$
This implies (4.11).

If $\hat{x} \in \{x \in S : f(x) = c^*\}$, then $p(\hat{x}) = 0$ and $f(\hat{x}) + \alpha p(\hat{x}) = f(\hat{x}) = c^*$, i.e., $\hat{x} \in \{x : f(x) + \alpha p(x) = c^*\}$, for all α. If $\hat{x} \in \{x : f(x) + \alpha p(x) = c^*\}$ for $\alpha \geq \alpha_p$, then from (E2), $\hat{x}$ should be feasible, i.e., $\hat{x} \in S$. Thus, $\hat{x} \in \{x \in S : f(x) = c^*\}$.

We now construct a class of discontinuous penalty functions for the constrained problem
$$\min_{x \in S} f(x), \tag{4.16}$$
where S is a robust set and f is upper robust on S. Let
$$p(x) = \begin{cases} 0, & x \in S, \\ \delta + d(x), & x \notin S, \end{cases} \tag{4.17}$$
where δ is a positive number and $d(x)$ is a penalty-like function.

Theorem 4.2 *The discontinuous penalty function (4.17) is exact.*

Proof. Take $\alpha_0 \geq (c^* - m_\eta)/\delta$, where $m_\eta = \min_{x \in S_\eta} f(x)$. Then, if $x \in S_\eta$, we have
$$p(x) \geq \delta \geq \frac{c^* - m_\eta}{\alpha_0} \geq \frac{c^* - f(x)}{\alpha_0} \tag{4.18}$$
This is (E1). Suppose, for $\alpha \geq \alpha_0$, we have
$$\min_{x \in X}[f(x) + \alpha p(x)] = c^*. \tag{4.19}$$
If a solution $\hat{x}$ of (4.19) is not feasible, then $p(\hat{x}) \geq \delta$ and
$$\alpha p(\hat{x}) > \alpha_0 p(\hat{x}) \geq \alpha_0 \delta \geq (c^* - m_\eta) \geq c^* - f(\hat{x}).$$
This implies a contradiction
$$f(\hat{x}) + \alpha p(\hat{x}) > c^*, \quad \text{for } \alpha > \alpha_0.$$

Remark 4.2 No constraint qualification is required for this kind of penalty functions. For example, for the inequality-constraint set
$$S = \{x : g_i(x) \leq 0, i = 1, \cdots, r\},$$
we can take
$$d(x) = \sum_{i=1}^r \|\max(g_i(x), 0)\|^\rho \quad \text{or} \quad d(x) = \max_i \|\max(g_i(x), 0)\|^\rho,$$
where $\rho > 0$. If $g_i, i = 1, \cdots, r$, are upper semicontinuous so is d.

In order to apply an integral global algorithm, we still need robustness of $f + \alpha p$.

Proposition 4.1 *If d is upper robust on S, then $p(x)$ is also upper robust on S.*

Proof. For each c, we have

$$\{x \in S: p(x) < c\} = \begin{cases} \varnothing, & \text{if } c < 0, \\ S, & \text{if } 0 \leqslant c \leqslant \delta, \\ \{x \in S: \delta + d(x) < c\}, & \text{if } c > \delta. \end{cases} \quad (4.20)$$

We know that $\varnothing$ and S are robust. The set $\{x \in S: \delta + d(x) < c\}$ is also robust because $d(x)$ is assumed to be upper robust on S. It follows that $\{x \in S: p(x) \leqslant c\}$ is robust for every real number c. Hence, $p(x)$ is upper robust on S.

Proposition 4.2 *If f is u.s.c., and d is upper robust on S, or f is upper robust and d is u.s.c. on S, then $f + \alpha p$ is upper robust on S for every $\alpha > 0$.*

Proof. If d is upper robust on S, then αp, $\alpha > 0$, is also upper robust on S. If f is u.s.c., then as the sum of an u.s.c. function and a upper robust function, $f + \alpha p$ is upper robust.

If f is upper robust on S, we cannot directly apply this result to prove $f + \alpha p$ is upper robust on S. We enumerate all rational numbers $r_1, r_2, \cdots$. For each real number c, we have

$$\{x \in S: f(x) + \alpha p(x) < c\} = \bigcup_{k=1}^{\infty} (\{x \in S: f(x) < r_k\} \cap \{x \in S: \alpha p(x) < c - r_k\}). \quad (4.21)$$

We know that

$$\{x \in S: \alpha p(x) < c - r_k\} = \{x \in S: p(x) < g_k\} = \begin{cases} \varnothing, & \text{if } g_k < 0, \\ S, & \text{if } 0 \leqslant g_k \leqslant \delta, \\ G \cap S, & \text{if } g_k > \delta, \end{cases} \quad (4.22)$$

where

$$g_k = \frac{c - r_k}{\alpha} \quad \text{and} \quad G = \{x: \delta + d(x) < g_k\} = \{x: d(x) < g_k - \delta\}. \quad (4.23)$$

G is open since d is u.s.c. and then $G \cap S$ is robust. Thus, each term in the union of (4.21) is $\varnothing$ which is robust; or $\{x: f(x) < r_k\} \cap S$ which is also robust since f is upper robust on S; or $\{x \in S: f(x) < r_k\} \cap G \cap S$ which is an intersection of robust set and an open set, so it is robust, too. As a union of robust sets, the set $\{x \in S: f(x) + \alpha p(x) < c\}$ is robust for each c. Hence, the function $f + \alpha p$ is upper robust on S.

5 Penalty Optimality conditions

We now generalize the penalty optimality conditions[15,16] for continuous functions to those for upper robust functions. In this section, we will examine the concepts of penalized mean value, modified variance, and higher moments conditions.

Let S be a subset of a metric space X, f a real-valued function on X, and p a penalty function for the constraint set S.

Definition 5.1 Let $c_n < c^* = \inf_{x \in S} f(x)$. We define the penalty mean value, modified variance and m^{th} moment (centered at a), respectively, of $f + \alpha_n p$ over the penalized lever

set
$$H_n = \{x: f(x) + \alpha_n p(x) \leqslant c_n\},$$
with a Q-measure μ on X as follows:
$$M(f, c_n; p) = \frac{1}{\mu(H_n)} \int_{H_n} [f(x) + \alpha_n p(x)] d\mu,$$
$$V_1(f, c_n; p) = \frac{1}{\mu(H_n)} \int_{H_n} [f(x) + \alpha_n p(x) - c_n]^2 d\mu,$$
$$M_m(f, c; a; p) = \frac{1}{\mu(H_n)} \int_{H_n} [f(x) + \alpha_n p(x) - a]^m d\mu, \quad m = 1, 2, \cdots$$

Under Assumptions (A), (R), and (M), they are well defined.

Now, we consider the convergence properties of the penalized mean value, modified variance, and higher moments as $n \to \infty$. As usual, we assume that
$$c_n \downarrow c \geqslant c^* = \min_{x \in S} f(x). \tag{5.1}$$

Theorem 5.1 *Suppose S is robust and $f + \alpha p (\alpha > 0)$ is robust on S. Under Assumptions (A) and (M), we have, for $c \geqslant c^*$,*
$$\lim_{n \to \infty} M(f, c_n; p) = M(f, c; S) \tag{5.2}$$

Proof. We first prove that when $c > c^*$, (5.2) holds. Since $\mu(H_c \cap S) > 0$, we have $\mu(H_n) > 0$ because $S \cap H_c \subset H_n$, $n = 1, 2, \cdots$. Thus,
$$|M(f, c_n; p) - M(f, c; S)| \leqslant I_1 + I_2,$$
where
$$I_1 = \left| \frac{1}{\mu(H_n)} - \frac{1}{\mu(H_c \cap S)} \right| \cdot \left| \int_{H_n} [f(x) + \alpha_n p(x)] d\mu \right|$$
and
$$I_2 = \frac{1}{\mu(H_c \cap S)} \left| \int_{H_n} [f(x) + \alpha_n p(x)] d\mu - \int_{H_c \cap S} [f(x) + \alpha_n p(x)] d\mu \right|.$$
We have, $L \leqslant f(x) \leqslant f(x) + \alpha_n p(x) \leqslant c_n \leqslant c_1$, for all $n = 1, 2, \cdots$. Thus,
$$|I_1| \leqslant \left| \frac{1}{\mu(H_n)} - \frac{1}{\mu(H_c \cap S)} \right| \cdot A \cdot \mu(H_1),$$
where $A = \max(c_1, |L|)$. It follows, by Proposition 3.1, $I_1 \to 0$ as $n \to \infty$. Next, we have
$$|I_2| \leqslant \frac{2A}{\mu(H_c \cap S)} \cdot |\mu(H_n) - \mu(H_c \cap S)|,$$
which tends to zero as $n \to \infty$.

When $c = c^*$, since $f(x) + \alpha_n p(x) \leqslant c_n$ on H_n, $\forall n$, we have
$$M(f, c_n; p) = \frac{1}{\mu(H_n)} \int_{H_n} [f(x) + \alpha_n p(x)] d\mu \leqslant c_n, \quad n = 1, 2, \cdots.$$
It follows that
$$\limsup_{n \to \infty} M(f, c_n; p) \leqslant \min_{n \to \infty} c_n = c = c^*. \tag{5.3}$$
We now prove
$$\liminf_{n \to \infty} \frac{1}{\mu(H_n)} \int_{H_n} [f(x) + \alpha_n p(x)] d\mu \geqslant c^*. \tag{5.4}$$
Suppose, on the contrary, that (5.4) does not hold. Then, there is a subsequence of

$$\frac{1}{\mu(H_n)}\int_{H_n}[f(x)+a_np(x)]d\mu,$$

which we denote with the same notation, such that

$$\lim_{n\to\infty}\frac{1}{\mu(H_n)}\int_{H_n}[f(x)+a_np(x)]d\mu=\hat{c}<c^*.$$

Let $2\eta=c^*-\hat{c}>0$. Thus, there is a positive integer N such that for $n\geqslant N$,

$$\frac{1}{\mu(H_n)}\int_{H_n}f(x)d\mu\leqslant\frac{1}{\mu(H_n)}\int_{H_n}[f(x)+a_np(x)]d\mu\leqslant c^*-\eta.$$

This implies that

$$H_{c^*-\eta}\cap H_n\neq\emptyset,\quad\text{for } n\geqslant N,$$

and hence,

$$H_{c^*-\eta}\cap H_{c^*}\cap S\neq\emptyset.$$

That is to say, we have points both in $H_{c^*-\eta}$ and S. This contradicts the assumption that c^* is the global minimum value of f over S.

Theorem 5.2 *Suppose S is a robust set and $f+ap$ $(a>0)$ is robust on S. Under Assumption (A) and (M), we have, for $c\geqslant c^*$,*

$$\lim_{k\to\infty}V_1(f_1,c_n;p)=V_1(f,c;S). \tag{5.5}$$

Proof. When $c>c^*$, the proof is similar to that of the mean value case. Suppose $c=c^*$. Since

$$V_1(f,c_n;p)\geqslant 0,\quad n=1,2,\cdots,$$

it follows that

$$\liminf_{n\to\infty}V_1(f,c_n;p)\geqslant 0. \tag{5.6}$$

We prove that $\limsup_{n\to\infty}V_1(f,c_n;p)\geqslant 0$. Suppose, on the contrary, it does not hold. Then, there is a subsequence (for which we keep the same notation) such that

$$V_1(f,c_n;p)\to 2\eta>0.$$

Thus, there is an integer N such that

$$V_1(f,c_n;p)>\eta,\quad\text{when } n\geqslant N.$$

Since f is bounded below on $H_1\cap S$, there exists a real number $g\geqslant 0$ such that

$$f(x)+a_np(x)+g\geqslant 0,\quad\forall x\in H_1. \tag{5.7}$$

Therefore,

$$V_1(f,c_n;p)=\frac{1}{\mu(H_n)}\int_{H_n}[f(x)+a_np(x)-c_n]^2d\mu$$

$$=\frac{1}{\mu(H_n)}\Big\{\int_{H_n}[f(x)+a_np(x)+g]^2d\mu+\int_{H_n}(g+c_n)^2d\mu$$

$$-2(g+c_n)\int_{H_n}[f(x)+a_np(x)+g]d\mu\Big\}>\eta.$$

It follows that

$$(c_n+g)^2+(g+c_n)^2>2(g+c_n)\cdot(g+c^*)+\eta.$$

Letting $n\to\infty$ in the above inequality, we obtain

$$(c^*+g)^2+(g+c^*)^2\geqslant 2(g+c^*)\cdot(g+c^*)+\eta,$$

and have a contradiction: $0 \geqslant \eta > 0$. Therefore, whce $c = c^*$, the limit of (5.5) exists and is equal to 0. But, accrding to the modified variance condition, c^* is the global minimum value if and only if $V_1(f, c^*; S) = 0$. Hence, when $c = c^*$, we have
$$\lim_{n \to \infty} V_1(f, c_n; p) = 0 = V_1(f, c^*; S).$$

Theorem 5.3 *Under the assumption of Theorem 5.1, we have, for $c \geqslant c^*$,*
$$\lim_{n \to \infty} M_m(f, c_n; c_n; S) = M_m(f, c; c; S). \tag{5.8}$$

Proof. When $c > c^*$ or when $c = c^*$ and m is odd, the proof is similar to that of the mean value case. Suppose $m = 2r$ and $r > 1$, then $M_m(f, c_n; c_n; p) \geqslant 0$. Thus,
$$\liminf_{n \to \infty} M_m(f, c_n; c_n; p) \geqslant 0. \tag{5.9}$$

On the other hand,
$$M_m(f, c_n; c_n; p) = \frac{1}{\mu(H_n)} \int_{H_n} [f(x) + \alpha_n p(x) - c_n]^m d\mu$$
$$\leqslant A^{2(r-1)} \frac{1}{\mu(H_n)} \int_{H_n} [f(x) + \alpha_n p(x) - c_n]^2 d\mu$$
$$= A^{2(r-1)} V_1(f, c_n; p) \to 0, \quad \text{as } n \to \infty, \tag{5.10}$$
where $|f(x) + \alpha_n p(x) - c_n| \leqslant A, \forall x \in H_1 \cap S$.

Therefore, we have proven that
$$\lim_{n \to \infty} M_m(f, c_n; c_n; p) = 0 = M_m(f, c^*; c^*; S). \tag{5.11}$$

The last equality holds because of the higher moment conditions for global minimization.

The above theorem, in fact, also gives us necessary and sufficient conditions for global minimization with a penalty function.

Theorem 5.4 *Under the assumptions of Theorem 5.1, c^* ($c_n \downarrow c = c^*$) is the global minimum value of f over S if and only if one of the following conditions holds:*

(1) $\lim_{n \to \infty} M(f, c_n; p) = c^*$,

(2) $\lim_{n \to \infty} V_1(f, c_n; p) = 0$,

(3) $\lim_{n \to \infty} M_m(f, c_n; c_n; p) = 0$, for some positive interger $m = 1, 2, \cdots$

6 A Penalty Algorithm

In this section, we propose a penalty algorithm in terms of a penalty mean value and modfied variance. We then prove that the algorithm produces a sequence which converges to the global minimum.

Take a real number
$$c_1 > \min_{x \in S} f(x),$$
an exact penalty function $p(x)$ and a penalty parameter α_1. Let
$$c_2 = M(f, c_1; p) = \frac{1}{\mu(H_1)} \int_{H_1} [f(x) + \alpha_1 p(x)] d\mu.$$

Replace c_1 by c_2 and α, by $\alpha_2 = \alpha_1 \cdot \beta$ (where $\beta \geqslant 1.0$ is a prespecified constant) and go to the next iteration.

Lemma 6.1 *If $\mu(H_1)>0$, then $\mu(H_2)>0$.*

Proof. By the definition of H_1, we see that $c_2 \leqslant c_1$. If $c_2 = c_1$, then $\mu(H_2)>0$. Indeed, suppose, on the contrary, that $\mu(H_2)=0$; then c_2 is the global minimum value of $f+\alpha_2 p$. But,
$$c_1 > \min_{x \in S} f(x) \geqslant \min_{x \in S} f(x) = \min_{x \in X} [f(x)+\alpha_2 p(x)] = c_2.$$
The last equality holds because we have an exact penalty function. This contradicts that $c_1 = c_2$.

Now, suppose $c_2 < c_1$ and suppose, on the contrary, that $\mu(H_2)=0$; then c_2 is the global minimum of $f+\alpha_2 p$ in X, i.e.,
$$f(x)+\alpha_2 p(x) \geqslant c_2, \quad \forall x \in X.$$
Since $\mu(H_1)>0$, there exists $\varepsilon>0$ such that $0<\varepsilon<c_1-c_2$ and
$$\mu(G_\varepsilon \cap S)>0,$$
where
$$G_\varepsilon = \{x: c_2+\varepsilon < f(x) \leqslant c_1\},$$
otherwise, c_1 would be the global minimum of f over S. Hence,
$$c_2 = M(f,c_1;p) = \frac{1}{\mu(H_1)} \int_{H_1} [f(x)+\alpha_1 p(x)] d\mu$$
$$= \frac{1}{\mu(H_1)} \left(\int_{H_1 \backslash G_\varepsilon \cap S} [f(x)+\alpha_1 p(x)] d\mu + \int_{G_\varepsilon \cap S} f(x) d\mu \right)$$
$$\geqslant \frac{c_2}{\mu(H_1)} (\mu_1(H) - \mu(G_\varepsilon \cap S)) + (c_2+\varepsilon) \frac{\mu(G_\varepsilon \cap S)}{\mu(H_1)}$$
$$= c_2 + \varepsilon \cdot \frac{\mu(G_\varepsilon \cap S)}{\mu(H_1)} > c_2.$$
This is a contradiction. The poof is now complete.

Continuing the process described above, we obtain a sequence of real numbers c_n which converges to the global minimum of $f(x)$ on $S \cap X$.

A penalty algorithm is proposed as follows.

Stet 1. Take $c_0 > \min_{x \in S} f(x)$, $\varepsilon > 0$, $n:=0$, $\beta>1.0$, $H_0 = \{x: f(x)+\alpha_0 p(x) \leqslant c_0\}$.

Stet 2. Calculate the mean value
$$c_{n+1} = \frac{1}{\mu(H_n)} \int_{H_n} [f(x)+\alpha_n p(x)] d\mu. \tag{6.1}$$

Stet 3. Calculate the modified variance
$$v_{n+1} = \frac{1}{\mu(H_n)} \int_{H_n} (f(x)+\alpha_n p(x) - c_n)^2 d\mu.$$
If $v_{n+1} \geqslant \varepsilon$, then $n:=n+1$ and $\alpha_{n+1}=\alpha_n \cdot \beta$, and go to Step 2; otherwise, go to Step 4.

Step 4. $c^* \Leftarrow c_{n+1}$, $H^* \Leftarrow H_{c_{n+1}}$. Stop.

Applying this algorithm with $\varepsilon = 0$, we obtain a decreasing sequence
$$c_1 \geqslant c_2 \geqslant \cdots \geqslant c_n \geqslant c_{n+1} \geqslant \cdots, \tag{6.2}$$
and a sequence of sets
$$H_1 \supset H_2 \supset \cdots \supset H_n \supset H_{n+1} \supset \cdots. \tag{6.3}$$

Theorem 6.1 *Suppose that S is robust and $f+\alpha p(\alpha>0)$ is upper robust on S, and Assumptions (A) and (M) hold. With this algorithm, we have*

$$\lim_{k\to\infty} c_n = c^* = \min_{x\in S} f(x) \qquad (6.4)$$

and

$$\lim_{k\to\infty} H_n = \bigcap_{k=1}^{\infty} H_k = H^*. \qquad (6.5)$$

Proof. According to the algorithm, we know that $c_n \geqslant c^*$ for $n=1,2,\cdots$, and the sequence $\{c_n\}$ is decreasing. Thus, the limit

$$\lim_{k\to\infty} c_n = \hat{c} \geqslant c^* \qquad (6.6)$$

exists. Letting $n\to\infty$ in (6.1), we obtain

$$\hat{c} = \lim_{n\to\infty} c_{n+1} = \lim_{n\to\infty} M(f,c_n;p) = M(f,\hat{c};S) \qquad (6.7)$$

It follows from Therem 5.4 that $\hat{c}$ is the global minimum value of f over S, i.e., $\hat{c}=c^*$.

The equality (6.5) is valid by Proposition 3.1.

7 Numerical Tests

An important way to ascertain the performance of a global minimization algorithm is to see if it can pass numerical tests successfully.

There are a lot of test problems for constrained minimization available in the literature. We select four problems, testing as follows.

Example 7.1[17] The objective function is

$$f(x) = f_1(x_1) + f_2(x_2),$$

where

$$f_1(x_1) = \begin{cases} 3x_1, & 0 \leqslant x_1 < 300, \\ 31x_1, & 300 \leqslant x_1 < 400, \end{cases} \qquad f_2(x_2) = \begin{cases} 28x_2, & 0 \leqslant x_2 < 100, \\ 29x_2, & 100 \leqslant x_2 < 200, \\ 30x_2, & 200 \leqslant x_2 < 1000, \end{cases}$$

With constraints

$$x_1 = 300 - \frac{x_3 x_4}{131.078}\cos(1.48577-x_6) + \frac{0.90798 x_3^2}{131.078}\cos(1.47588),$$

$$x_2 = -\frac{x_3 x_4}{131.078}\cos(1.48477+x_6) + \frac{0.90798 x_4^2}{131.078}\cos(1.47588),$$

$$x_5 = -\frac{x_3 x_4}{131.078}\sin(1.48477+x_6) + \frac{0.90798 x_4^2}{131.078}\sin(1.47588),$$

$$200 - \frac{x_3 x_4}{131.078}\sin(1.48477-x_6) + \frac{0.90798}{131.078}x_3^2 \sin(1.47588) = 0,$$

$$0 \leqslant x_1 \leqslant 400,$$
$$0 \leqslant x_2 \leqslant 1000,$$
$$340 \leqslant x_3 \leqslant 420,$$
$$340 \leqslant x_4 \leqslant 420,$$
$$-1000 \leqslant x_5 \leqslant 1000,$$

$$0 \leqslant x_6 \leqslant 0.5236.$$

The objective of this problem is a discontinuous robust function with four nonlinear equality constraints. We take x_3 and x_6 as independent variables. Then, x_1, x_2, x_4 and x_5 are functions of x_3 and x_6. Thus, except box constraints on these independent variables, we have eight more nonlinear inequality constraints. The discontinuous penalty function is applied to these inequality constraints.

With the penalty algorithm, we obtain the solution
$$x^* = (202.9967, 99.99992, 383.071, 420.000, -10.90771, 0.007314806),$$
$$f^* = 8889.899.$$

Example 7.2[13,18] Let
$$f(x) = 0.7854 x_1 x_2^2 (3.3333 x_3^2 + 14.9334 x_3 - 43.0934) - 1.5080 x_1 (x_6^2 + x_7^2)$$
$$+ 7.4770 (x_6^3 + x_7^3) + 0.7854 (x_4 x_6^2 + x_5 x_7^2),$$

with constraints
$$x_1 x_2^2 x_3 \geqslant 27,$$
$$x_1 x_2^2 x_3^2 \geqslant 397.5,$$
$$\frac{x_2 x_3 x_6^4}{x_4^3} \geqslant 1.93,$$
$$\frac{x_2 x_3 x_7^4}{x_5^3} \geqslant 1.93,$$
$$\frac{1}{0.1 x_6^3} \sqrt{\left[\frac{745 x_4}{x_2 x_3}\right]^2 + 16.91 \times 10^6} \leqslant 1100,$$
$$\frac{1}{0.1 x_7^3} \sqrt{\left[\frac{745 x_6}{x_2 x_3}\right]^2 + 157.5 \times 10^6} \leqslant 850,$$
$$x_2 x_3 \leqslant 40,$$
$$5 < \frac{x_1}{x_2} \leqslant 12,$$
$$1.5 x_6 + 1.9 \leqslant x_4,$$
$$1.1 x_7 + 1.9 \leqslant x_5,$$
$$2.6 \leqslant x_1 \leqslant 3.6,$$
$$0.7 \leqslant x_2 \leqslant 0.8,$$
$$17 \leqslant x_3 \leqslant 28,$$
$$7.3 \leqslant x_4 \leqslant 8.3,$$
$$7.3 \leqslant x_5 \leqslant 8.3,$$
$$2.9 \leqslant x_6 \leqslant 3.9,$$
$$5.0 \leqslant x_7 \leqslant 5.5.$$

We recalculate this problem with the discontinuous penalty method, which is more efficient, and obtain the following solution:
$$x^* = (3.5, 0.7, 17.0, 7.30, 7.71531991, 3.35054095, 5.28665446)$$
and

$$f^* = 2994.425.$$

Example 7.3 Consider a nonlinear integer programming problem from [19, 20]. The objective function is

$$f(x) = x_1 x_2 x_3 + x_1 x_4 x_5 + x_2 x_4 x_6 + x_6 x_7 x_8 + x_2 x_5 x_7,$$

with constraints,

$$2x_1 + 2x_4 + 8x_8 \geqslant 12,$$
$$11x_1 + 7x_4 + 13x_6 \geqslant 41,$$
$$6x_2 + 9x_4 x_6 + 5x_7 \geqslant 60,$$
$$3x_2 + 5x_5 + 7x_8 \geqslant 42,$$
$$6x_2 x_7 + 9x_3 + 5x_5 \geqslant 53,$$
$$4x_3 x_7 + x_5 \geqslant 13,$$
$$2x_1 + 4x_2 + 7x_4 + 3x_5 + x_7 \leqslant 69,$$
$$9x_1 x_8 + 6x_3 x_5 + 4x_3 x_7 \leqslant 47,$$
$$12x_2 + 8x_2 x_8 + 2x_3 x_6 \leqslant 73,$$
$$x_3 + 4x_5 + 2x_6 + 9x_8 \leqslant 31,$$
$$x_i \leqslant 7, \quad i = 1, 3, 4, 6, 8,$$
$$x_i \leqslant 15, \quad i = 2, 5, 7,$$
$$x, \text{ integer}, \quad i = 1, \cdots, 8.$$

Solution:

$$x^* = (5, 4, 1, 1, 6, 3, 2, 0), \quad f^* = 110.$$

Remark 7.1 The discontinuous penalty function is applied to handle the constraints. After 919 function evaluations, the global minimizer is found. The modified variance does not equal zero until 1370 function evaluations. The acceptance-rejection technique could not be applied here because the acceptance-rate is extremely low.

Example 7.4 Consider a mixed programming problem from [17, 19]. The objective function is

$$f(x) = 5.3578547 x_3^2 + 0.835689 x_1 x_5 + 37.293239 x_1 - 40792.141,$$

with constraints

$$0 \leqslant 85.334407 + 0.0056858 x_2 x_5 + 0.0006262 x_1 x_4 - 0.0022053 x_3 x_5 \leqslant 92,$$
$$90 \leqslant 80.51249 + 0.0071317 x_2 x_5 + 0.0029955 x_1 x_2 + 0.0021813 x_3^2 \leqslant 110,$$
$$20 \leqslant 9.300961 + 0.0047026 x_3 x_4 + 0.0012547 x_1 x_3 + 0.0019085 x_3 x_4 \leqslant 25,$$
$$78 \leqslant x_1 \leqslant 102, \quad 23 \leqslant x_2 \leqslant 45, \quad x_1, x_2 \text{ are integers},$$
$$27 \leqslant x_i \leqslant 45, \quad i = 3, 4, 5.$$

Solution:

$$x^* = (78, 33, 29.995256, 45.0, 36.77581), \quad f^* = -30665.54.$$

8 Conclusions

In this paper, the methodology of integral global optimization is applied to constrained minimization problems by discontinuous penalty technique. Under very weak assumptions, the discontinuous function is exact without any constraint qualification requirement.

The examples presented in this paper are illustrative of several noteworthy ideas. Example 7.1 has discontinuous objective function. We recalculate Example 7.2 in [13,21] with a discontinuous penalty function. Example 7.3 is a nonlinear integer programming problem for which one cannot use the acceptance-rejection technique because the rate of acceptance is very low, as mentioned in [19]. Example 7.4 is a mixed programming problem. For these examples, the new solution methodology works remarkably well, making computation seem like an almost routine task. It is our claim that there is no existing methodology which can match that performance.

References

[1] R. Courant, *Calculus of Variations and Supplementary Notes and Exercises*, Supplementay notes by M. Kruskal and R. Rubin, revised and amended by J. Moser, New York University, New York, (1962).

[2] A. V. Fiacco and G. P. McCormick, *Nonlinear Programming: Sequential Unconstrained Minimization Techniques*, John Wiley and Sons, New York, (1968).

[3] D. P. Bertsekas, Necessary and sufficient conditions for a penalty method to be exact, *Mathematical Programming* 9, 87—99(1975).

[4] A. R. Conn, Constrained ptimization using a nondifferentiable penalty function, *SIAM J. Numer. Anal.* 10, 760—784(1973).

[5] G. Di Pillo and L. Grippo, On the exactness of a class of nondifferentiable penaty functions, *Journal of Optimization Theory and Applications* 57, 399—410(1988).

[6] G. Di Pillo and L. Grippo, Exact penalty functions in constrained optimization, *SIAM Journal Control and Optimization* 28, 1333—1360(1989).

[7] J. P. Evans, F. J. Gould and J. W. Tolle, Exact penalty function in nonlinear programming, *Mathematical Programming* 4, 72—97(1973).

[8] R. E. Fletcher, An exact penalty function for nonlinear programming with inequalities, *Mathematical Programming* 5, 129—150(1973).

[9] T. Pietrykowski, An exact potential method for constrained maxima, *SIAM J. Numer. Anal.* 6, 294—304(1969).

[10] W. I. Zangwill, Nonlinear programming via penalty function, *Management Science* 13, 344—358 (1967)

[11] Q. Zheng, Robust analysis and global minimization of a class of discontinuous funtions (I), (English Series), *Acta Mathematicae Applicatae Sinica* 6:3, 205—223(1990).

[12] Q. Zheng, Robust analysis and global minimization of a class of discontinuous functions (II), (English Series), *Acta Mathematicae Applicatae Sinica* 6:4, 317—337(1990).

[13] S. H. Chew and Q. Zheng, *Integral Global Optimization*, Lecture Notes in Economics and Mathematical Systems, Springer-Verlag, Vol. 298, New York, (1988).

[14] Q. Zheng and L. S. Zhang, Penalty function and global optimization with inequality constraints (in Chinese), *Computational Mathematics* 3:3, 146—153(1980).

[15] Q. Zheng, Optimality conditions for global optimization (I), (English Series), *Acta Mathematicae Applicatae Sinica* 1:2, 66—78(1985).

[16] Q. Zheng, Optimality conditions for global optimization (II), (English Series), *Acta Machematicae Applicatae Sinica* 1:3, 118—132(1985).

[17] D. M. Himmelblau, *Applied Nonlinear Programming*, McGraw-Hill, New York, (1972).

[18] L. F. Lee, Weight minimization of a speed reducer, an ASME publication, 77—DET—163,(1977).

[19] H. B. Dickman and M. J. Gilman, Monte Carlo optimization, *Journal of Optimization Theory and Applications* 60, 149—157(1989).

[20] E. L. Lawler and M. D. Bell, A method for solving discrete optimization problems, *Operations Research* 14, 1098—1112(1966).

[21] O. Zheng, Strategies of changing domains for searching global extrems, (in Chinese), *Numerical Computation and Applications of Computers* 2, 257—261(1981).

[22] S. P. Han and O. L. Mangasarian, Exact penalty function in nonlinear programming, *Mathematical Programming* 17, 140—155(1979).

Finite Dimensional Approximation to Solutions of Minimization Problems in Functional Spaces[*]

Abstract: In this paper we consider minimization problems whose objectives are defined on functional spaces. The integral global optimization technique is applied to characterize a global minimum as the limit of a sequence of approximating solutions on finite dimensional subspaces. Necessary and sufficient optimality conditions are presented. A variable measure algorithm is proposed to find such approximating solutions. Examples are presented to illustrate the variable measure method.

1 Introduction

Let U be a topological space, S a subset of U and J a real-valued function on U. The problem we consider here is to find.

$$c^* = \inf_{u \in S} J(u) \tag{1.1}$$

and the set of global minima:

$$H^* = \{u \in S | J(u) = c^*\}. \tag{1.2}$$

Under the assumption

(A): J is lower semi-continuous, S is closed and there is a real number b such that the set $H_b = \{u \in S | J(u) \leqslant b\}$ is a nonempty compact set, the set H^* is nonempty. It is clear that under this condition the function J is bounded below, i.e., there is a real number M, such that

$$J(u) \geqslant M, \quad \forall u \in U. \tag{1.3}$$

Problems from calculus of variations, optimal control and differential games require one to consider the case when the underlying space U is infinitedimensional. But, in general, it is difficult to find the global minimum value c^* and the set of global minima H^* when U is an infinite dimensional space. We usually can only find approximation solutions to them:

$$c_n^* = \inf_{u \in S^n} J(u) \quad \text{and} \quad H_n^* = \{u \in S^n | J(u) = c_n^*\}, \tag{1.4}$$

where S^n is a subset of S, the set of such approximation solutions is usually a subset of a subspace U_n of U. It is therefore natural to ask how to construct the sequence $\{S^n\}$ such

---

[*] In Collaboration with Zhuang D. M. Repainted from Optimization, 1992, 26:33—50.

that the sequence $\{c_n^*\}$ converges to the global minimum value c^* and $\{H_n^*\}$ "converges" to the set of global minima H^*. We will use the integral global optimization approach. To do so, it is necessary to define so-called Q-measures μ_n and μ on each space U_n and U, respectively. Furthermore, we need a concept of convergence of the sequence of measures $\{\mu_n\}$ to a measure μ. In this work, we generalize the variable measure method developed in [1] and [7] to the case that the variable measures μ_n are defined on the subspaces U_n which are also variable. In Section 2, several concepts and results in the integral global minimization are summarized, which is useful for later investigation. Concepts and properties of Q-convergence of a sequence of Q-measures are discussed in Section 3. Integral global optimality conditions are provided in Section 4. With these results a variable measure algorithm is proposed in Section 5; a convergence theorem is also demonstrated in this section. Examples from optimal control and differential games are presented in Section 6.

2 Integral Global Optimization in Infinite Dimensional Spaces

In this section we will summarize several concepts and properties of the integral global minimization developed in [10,11], which will be utilized in the following sections.

2.1 Robust Sets and Robust Functions

A set D in a topological space U is *robust* if
$$\text{cl } D = \text{ch int } D. \tag{2.1}$$

An open set G is robust since $G = \text{int } G$. The empty set is a trivial robust set. A closed set may be robust or nonrobust. The concept of the robustness of a set is closely related to a topologicel structure of the set. For instance, the set $D = \{1, 2\}$ is nonrobust on $\mathbb{R}^1$ but it is robust in Z (= set of all integers) with the discrete topology.

The interior of a nonempty robust set is nonempty. A union of robust sets is robust. An intersection of two robust sets may be nonrobust; but the intersection of an open set and a robust set is robust. If A is robust in U and B is robust in V, then $A \times B$ is robust in $U \times V$ with the product topology. A convex set D in a topological vector space is robust if and only if the interior of D is nonempty.

A robust set consist of robust points of the set. A point $u \in \text{cl } D$ is robust to D (or a robust point of D) if for each neighbourhood $N(u)$ of u, $N(u) \cap \text{int } D \neq \varnothing$. A set D is robust if and only if each point of D is robust to D.

A Function J defined on a topological space U is *robust* if the set
$$F_c = \{u \mid J(u) < c\} \tag{2.2}$$
is robust for each real number c.

An upper semicontinuous (u.s.c.) function is robust since (2.2) is open for each c; so is a probability function on $\mathbb{R}^n$. The infimum of a family of robust functions is robut. A sum or a product of two robust functions may be nonrobust; but the sum of a robust function and an u.s.c. (for the product case nonnegativity is required) function is robust.

A function J is robust if and only if it is robust at each point or by each point. Here, J is robust at a point u if $u \in F_c$ implies u is robust to F_c; J is robust by a point u if there is a neighbourhood $N(u)$ of u such that $N(u) \cap F_c$ is robust for each c. An example of a nonrobust function on $\mathbb{R}^1$ is

$$J(u) = \begin{cases} 0, & u=0 \\ 1, & u \neq 0. \end{cases}$$

We see that J is nonrobust at $u=0$.

We can investigate a robust function by its epigraph. A function J is robust if and only if its epigraph

$$\text{epi}(J) = \{(u,c) \mid J(u) \leqslant c\} \tag{2.3}$$

is robust in the product space $U \times \mathbb{R}^1$.

When we consider a constrained minimization problem, the concept of relative robustness is needed. Let S be a given set in a topological space U and $u_0 \in \text{cl } S$. A function J is said to be *relatively robust* to S at u_0 if for each c, $u_0 \in F_c$ implies u_0 is robust to $F_c \cap S$. A function J is relatively robust at $u \in S$ if and only if J is robust at u with the relative topology on S. If J is relatively robust to S at each point u in S, then J is called a relatively robust function on S; or we simply say that J is robust on S.

In the following consideration we always suppose that there is a global minimum point $u^* \in S$ such that J is relatively robust to S at this point x^*. Or we simply make the following assumption:

(R): J is robut on S.

2.2 Q-Measure Spaces and Integrations

In order to investigate a minimization problem with an integral approach, a special class of measure spaces, which are called Q-measure spaces, should be examined.

Let U be a Hausdorff space, Ω a σ-field of subsets of U and μ a measure on Ω. A triple (U, Ω, μ) is called a Q-measure space iff

i) Each open set in U is measurable.

ii) The measure $\mu(G)$ of each nonempty open set G in U is positive: $\mu(G) > 0$.

iii) The measure $\mu(K)$ of a compact set K in U is finite.

The n-dimensional Lebesgue measure space (R^n, Ω, μ) is a Q-measure space; a nondegenerate Gaussian measure μ on a sparable Hilbert space H with Borel sets as measurable sets constitute an infinite dimensional Q-measure space. A specific optimization problem is related to a specific Q-measure space which is suitable for consideration in this approach. The construction of a Q-measure space in an infinite dimensional space is in general nontrivial. For instance, it has been shown that for each $r > 0$ there exists on the space l_∞ a nondegenerate Gaussian measure μ such that the measure of an arbitrary ball with radius r is zero. This measure is not a Q-measure. We will examine several Q-measure spaces later in Section 6.

Since the interior of a nonempty open set is nonempty, the Q-measure of a Q-measurable set containing a nonempty robust set is always positive. This is an essential property we need in the integral approach of minimization. Hence, the following assumption is usually required:

(M): (U, Ω, μ) is a Q-measure space.

The following lemma gives us a sufficient condition for the global minimum.

Lemma 2.1 *Suppose that the conditions* (A), (M) *and* (R) *hold, and* $H_c \cap S \neq \emptyset$, *where* $H_c = \{u | J(u) \leq c\}$ *is the level set of* J. *If*
$$\mu(H_c \cap S) = 0, \tag{2.4}$$
then c is the global minimum value of J and $H_c \cap S$ is the set of global minima.

In the following, we need other form of the above lemma.

Lemma 2.2 *Suppose that the conditions* (A), (M) *and* (R) *hold. If* $c > c^* = \min_{u \in S} J(u)$, *then*
$$\mu(H_c \cap S) > 0. \tag{2.5}$$

2.3 Integral Optimality Conditions for Global Minimization

We now proceed to define the concepts of mean value, variance and higher moments of J over its level set. These concepts are closely related to optimality conditions and algorithms for global minimization.

Suppose that the assumptions (A), (M) and (R) hold, and $c > c^* = \min_{u \in S} J(u)$. We define the mean value, variance, modified variance and mth moment (centred at a), respectively, as follows:

$$M(J, c; S) = \frac{1}{\mu(H_c \cap S)} \int_{H_c \cap S} J(u) d\mu$$

$$V(J, c; S) = \frac{1}{\mu(H_c \cap S)} \int_{H_c \cap S} (J(u) - M(J, c; S))^2 d\mu$$

$$V_1(J, c; S) = \frac{1}{\mu(H_c \cap S)} \int_{H_c \cap S} (J(u) - c)^2 d\mu$$

$$M_m(J, c; a; S) = \frac{1}{\mu(H_c \cap S)} \int_{H_c \cap S} (J(u) - a)^m d\mu.$$

By Lemma 2.2, they are well defined. These definitions can be extended to the case $c \geq c^*$ by limit process. For instance,

$$M_m(J, c; a; S) = \lim_{c_k \downarrow c} \frac{1}{\mu(H_{c_k} \cap S)} \int_{H_{c_k} \cap S} (J(u) - a)^m d\mu, \quad m = 1, 2, \cdots \tag{2.6}$$

The limits exist and are independent of choice of $\{c_k\}$. The extended concepts are well defined and are consistent with the above definitions.

With these introduced concepts, we characterize the global optimality as follows:

Theorem 2.1 *Under the assumption* (A), (M) *and* (R), *the following statements are equivalent:*

i) $u^* \in S$ *is a global minimizer of J over S and $c^* = J(u^*)$ is the global minimum value;*

ii) $M(J, c^*; S) = c^*$ (*the mean value condition*);

iii) $V(J, c^*; S) = 0$ (*the variance condition*);

iv) $V_1(J, c^*; S) = 0$ (*the modified variance condition*);

v) $M_m(J, c^*; c^*; S) = 0$, for one of positive integers $m = 1, 2, \cdots$ (*the higher moment condition*).

3 Q-Convergence of Measures

As we wish to investigate the approximation to an optimal solution in an infinite-dimensional space by a sequence of certain optimal solutions in finitedimensional subspaces, it is instructive to consider a sequence of measure spaces and examine its convergence. We have known several concepts of convergence of measures in the theory of probability and stochastic processes, such as *weak convergence*, etc. But, these concepts of convergence cannot work with Q-measure spaces. Thus, the concept of Q-convergence is introduced as follows.

Let $(\Omega_1, U_1, \mu_1), \cdots, (\Omega_n, U_n, \mu_n)$ be measure spaces and (Ω, U, μ) a Q-measure space, where U_n is a subspace of U and $\Omega_n = \{A \cap U_n | A \in \Omega\}$.

Definition 3.1 A sequence of measures $\{\mu_n\}$ defined on measurable spaces $\{(U_n, \Omega_n)\}$ is said to be Q-convergent to a Q-measure μ defined on (U, Ω) if for each open set $G \subset U$

$$\mu_n(G \cap U_n) \to \mu(G) \quad \text{as} \quad n \to \infty, \tag{3.1}$$

and denoted by $\mu_n \xrightarrow{Q} \mu$.

Remark 3.1 1. In [1] and [7] we introduced the concept of Q-convergent sequence of measures which are defined on a common *compact* space U. Here, we generalize this concept to the case that these Q-measures $\{\mu_n\}$ defined on different spaces.

2. In this work, we concentrate our attention to minimization problems in infinite-dimensional spaces. Thus, we generally assume a finite measure μ defined on a measurable space (U, Ω), i.e., $\mu(U) < +\infty$.

3. Since U is open itself, and $\mu(U) < +\infty$, thus,

$$\mu_n(U \cap U_n) = \mu_n(U_n) \to \mu(U), \quad \text{as} \quad n \to \infty. \tag{3.2}$$

4. Suppose G is a nonempty open set. It follows from (3.1) that there is and integer n_0 such that $\mu_n(G \cap U_n) > 0$ for all $n \geq n_0$ (n_0 may depend on G). Thus, in the following consideration we will simply assume that $\{\mu_n\}$ is a sequence of Q-measures.

The following theorem gives us several equivalent conditions for Q-convergence which are useful in the sequle.

Theorem 3.1 *Suppose* $(U_1, \Omega_1, \mu_1), \cdots, (U_n, \Omega_n, \mu_n), \cdots,$ *and* (U, Ω, μ) *are Q-measure spaces, where U_n is a subspace of U, $n = 1, 2, \cdots$. Then the following statements are equivalent*:

i) *For each bounded lower-semi continuous function J defined on U,*

$$\int_{U_n} J \, d\mu_n \to \int_U J \, d\mu;$$

ii) *For each bounded upper-semi continuous function J defined on U,*

$$\int_{U_n} J \, d\mu_n \to \int_U J \, d\mu;$$

iii) *For each open set G in U,*

$$\mu_n(G \cap U_n) \to \mu(G);$$

iv) *For each closed set F in U,*

$$\mu_n(F \cap U_n) \to \mu(F).$$

Proof. If J is u.s.c., then $-J$ is l.s.c., and vice versa. Thus,

$$\int_{U_n} J \, d\mu_n \to \int_U J \, d\mu \Leftrightarrow -\int_{U_n} J \, d\mu_n \to -\int_U J \, d\mu. \tag{3.3}$$

Hence, i) and ii) are equivalent.

If F is closed, then $U \backslash F$ is open; if G is open, then $U \backslash G$ is closed. For each closed F, if $\mu_n \xrightarrow{Q} \mu$, then by iii), we have,

$$\mu_n(U_n \cap F) = \mu_n(U_n \cap (U \backslash G)) = \mu_n(U_n \backslash U_n \cap G) = \mu_n(U_n) - \mu_n(U_n \cap G)$$
$$\to \mu(U) - \mu(G) = \mu(U \backslash G) = \mu(F), \tag{3.4}$$

i.e., iii) $\Rightarrow$ iv). We can prove iv) $\Rightarrow$ iii) similarly.

We now prove i) and iv) are equivalent.

i) $\Rightarrow$ iv): If F is closed then the indicator $-I_F$ of F is bounded and l.s.c. Thus, we have

$$\mu_n(F \cap U_n) \int_{U_n} I_F \, d\mu_n \to \int_U I_F \, d\mu = \mu(F). \tag{3.5}$$

iv) $\Rightarrow$ i): Denote $c_{i+1} > c_i$,

$$D_i = \{u \in U \mid c_i < J(u) \leqslant c_{i+1}\} = H_{c_{i+1}} \backslash H_{c_i}, \tag{3.6}$$

where $H_{c_i} = \{u \mid J(u) \leqslant c_i\}$ is a level set, which is closed because J is l.s.c. We have for each $c_{i+1} > c_i$,

$$\mu_n(D_i \cap U_n) = \mu_n((H_{c_{i+1}} \backslash H_{c_i}) \cap U_n) = \mu_n(H_{c_{i+1}} \cap U_n) - \mu_n(H_{c_i} \cap U_n)$$
$$\to \mu(H_{c_{i+1}}) - \mu(H_{c_i}) = \mu(H_{c_{i+1}} \backslash H_{c_i}) = \mu(D_i). \tag{3.7}$$

Suppose $M(>0)$ is the bound of J: $|J(u)| \leqslant M$ for all $u \in U$. Construct a partition of $[-M, M]$:

$$-M = c_0 < c_1 < \cdots c_m = M. \tag{3.8}$$

Then we have

$$\left| \int_{U_n} J \, d\mu_n - \int_U J \, d\mu \right| \leqslant \left| \int_{U_n} J \, d\mu_n - \sum_{i=0}^{m-1} c_i \mu_n(D_i \cap U_n) \right|$$
$$+ \left| \sum_{i=0}^{m-1} c_i \mu_n(D_i \cap U_n) - \sum_{i=0}^{m-1} c_i \mu(D_i) \right|$$
$$+ \left| \sum_{i=0}^{m-1} c_i \mu(D_i) - \int_{U_n} J \, d\mu \right| = I_1 + I_2 + I_3. \tag{3.9}$$

The first term on the right can be estimated, for any $\varepsilon > 0$,

$$I_1 = \left| \sum_{i=0}^{m-1} \left[c_i \mu_n (D_i \cap U_n) - \int_{D_i \cap U_n} J \, d\mu_n \right] \right|$$

$$= \left| \sum_{i=0}^{m-1} \int_{D_i \cap U_n} (c_i - J) \, d\mu_n \right|$$

$$\leqslant \max_{0 \leqslant i \leqslant m-1} (c_{i+1} - c_i) \cdot \mu_n(U_n) < \varepsilon/3, \tag{3.10}$$

if we choose the partition (3.8) such that $\max_{0 \leqslant i \leqslant m-1}(c_{i+1}-c_i)$ is sufficiently small. Note also that $\mu_n(U_n)$ is bounded because $\mu_n(U_n) \to \mu(U) < \infty$. Similarly, for such a partition, we can obtain $I_3 < \varepsilon/3$. By (3.7) the second term I_2 approaches 0 as $n \to \infty$. This implies i).

Remark 3.2 We are familiar with the concept of weak convergence of measures in the theories of measures and stochastin processes. Recall that a sequence of measures $\{\mu_n\}$ on Borel sets of a metric space U is said to be weakly convergent to a measure μ if for each bounded *continuous* function $J: U \to \mathbb{R}$, $\int_U J \, d\mu_n \to \int_U J \, d\mu$. The requirement for a Q-convergence is more than that of a weak convergence.

Proposition 3.1 *Under the assumption of Theorem 3.1, $\mu_n \xrightarrow{Q} \mu$ if and only if for each closed set F in U and for each bounded l.s.c. function J on U one has*

$$\int_{U_n \cap F} J \, d\mu_n \to \int_F J \, d\mu. \tag{3.11}$$

Proof. By the equivalence of (i) and (iv) of Theorem 3.1 and by letting $F = U$ in (3.11), we see that the condition (3.11) is sufficient for $\mu_n \xrightarrow{Q} \mu$ because U is closed. Conversely, for each given closed set F and a given bounded l.s.c. function J, we can prove (3.11) similarly to what we did in proving iv)$\Rightarrow$i) of Theorem 3.1. Here, (3.7) becomes

$$\mu_n(D_i \cap F \cap U_n) \to \mu(D_i \cap F). \tag{3.12}$$

I_1 becomes

$$I_1 = \left| \int_{U_n \cap F} J \, d\mu_n - \sum_{i=0}^{m-1} c_i \mu_n(D_i \cap F \cap U_n) \right|$$

$$\leqslant \max_{0 \leqslant i \leqslant m-1} (c_{i+1} - c_i) \cdot \mu_n(F \cap U_n) < \varepsilon/3, \tag{3.13}$$

and I_2 approaches 0 following from (3.12). This completes the proof.

4 Optmality Conditions with Variable Measures

In this section, we will generalize the variable measure models developed in [1] and [7] to consider approximating the constraint set in the space U by a sequence of sets that are contained in the intersections of the constraint set and subspaces U_n of U.

Let S be a closed subset of U, J a real-valued function on U. Suppose that U_n is a closed subspace of U, and S^n is defined as a subset of $S \cap U_N$. (Often, we may choose $S^n = S \cap U_n$.) The functon J restricted on U_n can be regarded as a function on U_n. Later on, we will consider construction of U_n and the measure μ_n on U_n. In this section, under the assumptions (A), (R) and (M), we examine convergent properties of the *mean values*, variances and *higher moments* in this setting.

Definition 4.1 Let $c > \min_{u \in S^n} J(u)$. We define

$$M(J, c; S^n; \mu_n) := \frac{1}{\mu_n(H_c \cap S^n)} \int_{H_c \cap S^n} J(u) \, d\mu,$$

$$V(J, c; S^n; \mu_n) := \frac{1}{\mu_n(H_c \cap S^n)} \int_{H_c \cap S^n} (J(u) - M(J, c; S^n; \mu_n))^2 \, d\mu,$$

$$V_1(J, c; S^n; \mu_n) := \frac{1}{\mu_n(H_c \cap S^n)} \int_{H_c \cap S^n} (J(u) - c)^2 \, d\mu_n,$$

$$M_m(J, c; S^n; a; \mu_n) := \frac{1}{\mu_n(H_c \cap S^n)} \int_{H_c \cap S^n} (J(u) - a)^m \, d\mu_n, \quad M = 1, \cdots,$$

the mean value, variance, modified variance and mth moment (centred at a), respectively, of J over the intersection of the level set $H_c = \{u \mid J(u) \leqslant c\}$ and the constraint set S_n. Under the assumptions (A), (R) and (M), they are well defined.

Now we examine the convergence properties of the mean value, variance and higher moments just defined. As usual, we consider that

$$c_n \geqslant c_n^* = \min_{u \in S^n} J(u), \quad n = 1, \cdots, \quad \text{and} \quad c_n \downarrow c \geqslant \min_{u \in S} J(u) = c^*.$$

Lemma 4.1 *Suppose that* $c \geqslant c^*$, $c_n \geqslant c_n^*$ *and* $c_n \downarrow c$. *If* $\mu_n \xrightarrow{Q} \mu$, *and*

$$\mu_n(S^n) \to \mu(S). \tag{4.1}$$

Then,

$$\lim_{n \to \infty} \mu_n(H_{c_n} \cap S^n) = \mu(H_c \cap S). \tag{4.2}$$

Proof. Note that,

$$0 \leqslant \mu_n(S \cap U_n) - \mu_n(S^n) = (\mu_n(S \cap U_n) - \mu(S)) + (\mu(S) - \mu_n(S^n)).$$

Since S is closed, from $\mu_n \xrightarrow{Q} \mu$ we see that,

$$\mu_n(S \cap U_n) - \mu(S) \to 0;$$

Now, with condition (4.1), we have

$$\mu_n(S \cap U_n) - \mu_n(S^n) \to 0. \tag{4.3}$$

We now prove

$$\lim_{n \to \infty} \mu_n(H_{c_n} \cap S \cap U_n) = \mu(H_c \cap S). \tag{4.4}$$

Since $H_c \subset H_{c_n}$ and $\mu_n \xrightarrow{Q} \mu$, we have,

$$\mu_n(H_{c_n} \cap S \cap U_n) \geqslant \mu_n(H_c \cap S \cap U_n) \to \mu(H_c \cap S).$$

It follows that

$$\liminf_{n \to \infty} \mu_n(H_{c_n} \cap S \cap U_n) \geqslant \mu(H_c \cap S).$$

Fix j. If $n \geqslant j$, then $H_{c_n} \subset H_{c_j}$, and $\mu_n(H_{c_n} \cap S \cap U_n) \leqslant \mu_n(H_{c_j} \cap S \cap U_n)$, thus,

$$\limsup_{n \to \infty} \mu_n(H_{c_n} \cap S \cap U_n) \leqslant \lim_{n \to \infty} \mu_n(H_{c_j} \cap S \cap U_n) = \mu(H_{c_j} \cap S).$$

Letting $j \to \infty$, we then obtain, from the continuity of the measure μ,

$$\limsup_{n \to \infty} \mu_n(H_{c_n} \cap S \cap U_n) \leqslant \lim_{j \to \infty} \mu(H_{c_j} \cap S) = \mu(H_c \cap S).$$

It follows that the limit in (4.4) exists and (4.4) is valid. Finally, letting $n \to \infty$, we obtain

$$|\mu_n(H_{c_n}\cap S^n)-\mu(H_c\cap S)|\leqslant |\mu_n(H_{c_n}\cap S^n)-\mu_n(H_{c_n}\cap S\cap U_n)|$$
$$+|\mu_n(H_{c_n}\cap S\cap U_n)-\mu(H_c\cap S)|\to 0,$$

where the first term tends to zero because of (4.3). To see the second trem tends to zero, note that the followings follows from (4.3) again:

$$0\leqslant \mu_n(H_{c_n}\cap S\cap U_n)-\mu_n(H_{c_n}\cap S^n)$$
$$=\mu_n(H_{c_n}\cap(S\cap U_n\setminus S^n))$$
$$\leqslant \mu_n(S\cap U_n\setminus S^n)\to 0.$$

Theorem 4.1 *Suppose that for the minimization problems* $c^*=\min_{u\in S}J(u)$ *and* $c_n^*=\min_{u\in S^n}J(u)$, $n=1,\cdots,$ *the assumptions* (A), (R) *and* (M) *are satisfied. Under the conditions of Lemma 4.1, we have, for* $c\geqslant c^*$,

(i) $\lim_{n\to\infty}M(J,c_n;S^n;\mu_n)=M(J,c;S;\mu)$;

(ii) $\lim_{n\to\infty}V(J,c_n;S^n;\mu_n)=V(J,c;S;\mu)$;

(iii) $\lim_{n\to\infty}V_1(J,c_n;S^n;\mu_n)=V_1(J,c;S;\mu)$;

(iv) $\lim_{n\to\infty}M_m(J,c_n;S^n;c_n;\mu_n)=M_m(J,c;S;c;\mu)$.

Proof. We first prove that whce $c>c^*$ the first equation (i) holds. Since $\mu(H_c\cap S)>0$, we can assume, by Lemma 4.1, that $\mu_n(H_{c_n}\cap S^n)>0$ for n sufficiently large. Thus, we have

$$M(J,c_n;S^n;\mu_n)-M(J,c;S;\mu)$$
$$=\frac{1}{\mu_n(H_{c_n}\cap S^n)}\int_{H_{c_n}\cap S^n}J(u)\mathrm{d}\mu_n-\frac{1}{\mu(H_c\cap S)}\int_{H_c\cap S}J(u)\mathrm{d}\mu$$
$$=\left(\frac{1}{\mu_n(H_{c_n}\cap S^n)}-\frac{1}{\mu(H_c\cap S)}\right)\int_{H_{c_n}\cap S^n}J(u)\mathrm{d}\mu_n$$
$$+\frac{1}{\mu(H_c\cap S)}\left(\int_{H_{c_n}\cap S^n}J(u)\mathrm{d}\mu_n-\int_{H_c\cap S\cap U_n}J(u)\mathrm{d}\mu_n\right)$$
$$+\frac{1}{\mu(H_c\cap S)}\left(\int_{H_c\cap S\cap U_n}J(u)\mathrm{d}\mu_n-\int_{H_c\cap S}J(u)\mathrm{d}\mu\right)$$
$$=I_1+I_2+I_3.$$

Since

$$|I_1|\leqslant\left|\frac{1}{\mu_n(H_{c_n}\cap S^n)}-\frac{1}{\mu(H_c\cap S)}\right|\cdot A\cdot\mu(H_{c_n}\cap S^n),$$

where A is the bound of $|J(u)|$ on $S^n\cap H_{c_n}$, and $\mu_n(H_{c_n}\cap S^n)\leqslant\mu_n(U_n)$, it follows from Lemma 4.1 that $I_1\to 0$ as $n\to\infty$.

Next, we have

$$|I_2|\leqslant\frac{1}{\mu(H_c\cap S)}\cdot 2A\cdot|\mu_n(H_{c_n}\cap S^n)-\mu_n(H_c\cap S\cap U_n)|$$
$$\leqslant\frac{2A}{\mu(H_c\cap S)}(|\mu_n(H_{c_n}\cap S^n)-\mu(H_c\cap S)|$$
$$+|\mu(H_c\cap S)-\mu_n(H_c\cap S\cap U_n)|),$$

which tends to zero as $n\to\infty$ because of Lemma 4.1 and because $\mu_n\xrightarrow{Q}\mu$. $I_3\to 0$ follows from Proposition 3.2.

When $c=c^*$, since $J(u)\leqslant c_n$ on $H_{c_n}\,\forall n$, we have,

$$M(J, c_n; S^n; n) = \frac{1}{\mu_n(H_{c_n} \cap S^n)} \int_{H_{c_n} \cap S^n} J(u) d\mu_n \leqslant c_n.$$

It follows,
$$\limsup_{n \to \infty} M(J, c_n; S_n; \mu_n) \leqslant \lim_{n \to \infty} c_n = c = c^*.$$

On the other hand, $M(J, c_n; S^n; \mu_n) \geqslant c_n^* \geqslant c^*$, thus,
$$\liminf_{n \to \infty} M(J, c_n; S^n; \mu_n) \geqslant c^*.$$

Therefore, the limit in (i) exists, and
$$\lim_{n \to \infty} M(J, c_n; S^n; \mu_n) = c^* = M(J, c^*; S; \mu).$$

The last equality is valid because of the global optimality conditions for constrained minimization, see [2] and [7]. We now prove that (iv) holds. (Equation (ii) and (iii) follow from (iv).) When $c > c^*$ or when $c = c^*$ and m is odd, the proof is similar to that of the mean value case. Now we suppose $m = 2r$ is even and $c = c^*$. We consider the case $r = 1$ first. Since
$$V_1(J, c_n; S^n; \mu_n) \geqslant 0, \quad k = 1, 2, \cdots$$

we have,
$$\liminf_{n \to \infty} V_1(J, c_n; S^n; \mu_n) \geqslant 0.$$

We now prove that $\limsup_{n \to \infty} V_1(J, c_n; S^n; \mu_n) = 0$. Suppose, on the contrary, it does not hold. Then there is a subsequence, we keep the same notation, $V_1(J, c_n; S^n; \mu_n) \to 2\eta > 0$. Thus, there is an integer N such that
$$V_1(J, c_n; S^n; \mu_n) > \eta, \quad \text{when } n \geqslant N.$$

Since J is bounded below on $H_c \cap S$, so there exists a real number $g \geqslant 0$, such that
$$J(u) + g \geqslant 0, \quad \forall u \in H_{C_1} \cap S.$$

Thus,
$$\begin{aligned}
V_1(J, c_n; S^n; \mu_n) &= \frac{1}{\mu_n(H_{c_n} \cap S^n)} \int_{H_{c_n} \cap S^n} (J(u) - c_n)^2 d\mu_n \\
&= \frac{1}{\mu_n(H_{c_n} \cap S^n)} \Big[\int_{H_{c_n} \cap S^n} (J(u) + g)^2 d\mu_n \\
&+ \int_{H_{c_n} \cap S^n} (g + c_n)^2 d\mu_n - 2(g + c_n) \int_{H_{c_n} \cap S^n} (J(u) + g) d\mu_n \Big] > \eta.
\end{aligned}$$

It follows that
$$(c_n + g)^2 + (g + c_n)^2 > 2(g + c_n) \cdot (g + c_n^*) + \eta \geqslant 2(g + c_n) \cdot (g + c^*) + \eta.$$

Letting $n \to \infty$ in the above inequality, we obtain
$$(c^* + g)^2 + (g + c^*)^2 \geqslant 2(g + c^*) \cdot (g + c^*) + \eta,$$

which is a contradiction: because $0 \geqslant \eta > 0$. Therefore, whce $c = c^*$ the limit of (iv) exists and is equal to 0. But, according to the variance condition, c^* is the global minimum value if and only if $V_1(J, c^*; S; \mu) = 0$. Hence, when $c = c^*$, we have
$$\lim_{n \to \infty} V_1(J, c_n; S^n; \mu_n) = 0 = V_1(J, c^*; s: \mu).$$

When $m = 2r$ and $r > 1$, $M_m(J, c_n; S^n; C_n; \mu_n) \geqslant 0$. Thus,

$$\liminf_{n\to\infty} M_m(J, c_n; S^n; c_n; \mu_n) \geq 0.$$

On the other hand,

$$M_m(J, c_n; S^n; c_n; \mu_n) = \frac{1}{\mu_n(H_{c_n} \cap S^n)} \int_{H_{c_n} \cap S^n} (J(u) - c_n)^m d\mu_n$$

$$\leq A^{2(r-1)} \frac{1}{\mu_n(H_{c_n} \cap S^n)} \int_{H_{c_n} \cap S^n} (J(u) - c_n)^2 d\mu_n$$

$$= A^{2(r-1)} V_1(J, c_n; S^n; \mu_n) \to 0, \quad \text{as} \quad k \to \infty,$$

where $|J(u) - c_n| \leq A$, $\forall u \in H_{c_1} \cap S$.

These prove that

$$\lim_{n\to\infty} M_m(J, c_n; S^n; c_n; \mu_n) = 0 = M_m(J, c^*; S; c^*; \mu).$$

The last equality hold because of the higher moment conditions for global minimization. The ablve theorem in fact gives us necessary and sufficient conditions for global minimization with variable measure.

Theorem 4.2 *Under the assumptions of Theorem 4.1, c^* ($c_n \downarrow c = c^*$) is the global minimum value of J over S if and only if one of the following conditions holds:*

(i) $\lim_{n\to\infty} M(J, c_n; S^n; \mu_n) = c^*$;

(ii) $\lim_{n\to\infty} V(J, c_n; S^n; \mu_n) = 0$;

(iii) $\lim_{n\to\infty} V_1(J, c_n; S^n; \mu_n) = 0$;

(iv) $\lim_{n\to\infty} M_m(J, c_n; S^n; c_n; \mu_n) = 0$, $m = 1, 2, \cdots$

5 A Variable Measure Method

In the previous section we have discussed the optimality conditions with variable measures. There, the condition (4.1) is required. In this section we first give a sufficient condition for (4.1) to be valid. With this condition an algorithm with variable measures is proposed. We then prove that the algorithm produces a sequence of reals which converges to the global minimum.

Theorem 5.1 *Suppose $S^n \supset S$ and $\mu_n \xrightarrow{Q} \mu$. If*

$$\mu_n(S^n) \geq \mu(S), \quad n = 1, 2, \cdots \tag{5.1}$$

then

$$\mu_n(S^n) \to \mu(S).$$

Proof. We have, from (5.1)

$$\liminf_{n\to\infty} \mu_n(S^n) \geq \mu(S). \tag{5.2}$$

On the other hand, since $S^n \subset S \cap U_n$, so

$$\mu_n(S^n) \leq \mu_n(S \cap U_n), \quad n = 1, 2, \cdots$$

It follows from $\mu_n \xrightarrow{Q} \mu$ that

$$\limsup_{n\to\infty} \mu_n(S^n) \leq \limsup_{n\to\infty} \mu_n(S \cap U_n) = \lim_{n\to\infty} \mu_n(S \cap U_n) = \mu(S). \tag{5.3}$$

Combining (5.2) and (5.3), we have proved that

$$\lim_{n \to \infty} \mu_n(S^n) = \mu(S).$$

Remark 5.1 At first glance, it seems that the condition (5.1) is unrealistic, because $S^n \subset S \cap U_n \subset S$. However, quite often one can construct a measure in an infinite dimensional space which satisfies this condition. See examples in Section 6.

We now proceed to describe the proposed algorithm. Let $U_1, U_2, \cdots$, be a sequence of subspaces of U such that
$$U_1 \subset U_2 \subset U_3 \cdots \subset U$$
and
$$\mathrm{cl}\left\{\bigcup_{n=1}^{\infty} U_n\right\} = U.$$

Let $S^1 = S \cap U_1$, then S^1 is robust in the subspace U_1. Take a real number $c_1 > \min_{u \in S_1} J(u)$. Construct a Q-measure μ_1 satisfying (5.1). We then have $\mu_1(H_{c_1} \cap S^1) > 0$. Let
$$c_2 = M(J, c_1; S^1; \mu_1).$$
Let
$$S^2 = S \cap U_2,$$
then S^2 is robust on the subspace U_2. Construct a Q-measure μ_2 such that the condition (5.1) is satisfied. In order to continue this process we need to prove the following lemma.

Lemma 5.1 *If $\mu_1(H_{c_1} \cap S^1) > 0$ then $\mu_2(H_{c_2} \cap S^2) > 0$.*

Proof. If $c_2 = c_1$, then $\mu_2(H_{c_2} \cap S^2) > 0$. Indeed, suppose, on the contrary, $\mu_2(H_{c_2} \cap S^2) = 0$, then c_2 is the global minimum of J over S^2, but $c_1 > \min_{u \in S^1} J(u) \geqslant \min_{u \in S^2} J(u) = c_2$, this is a contradiction.

Now suppose $c_2 < c_1$. If $\mu_2(H_{c_2} \cap S^2) = 0$, then c_2 is the global minimum value of J over S^2, i.e.,
$$J(u) \geqslant c_2, \quad \forall u \in S^2.$$
Since $S^1 \subset S^2$, thus
$$J(u) \geqslant c_2, \quad \forall u \in S^2.$$
Because $\mu_1(H_{c_1} \cap S^1) > 0$, so there exists $\varepsilon > 0$ such that $0 < \varepsilon < c_1 - c_2$, and
$$\mu_1(G_\varepsilon \cap S^1) > 0,$$
where
$$G_\varepsilon = \{u \mid c_2 + \varepsilon < J(u) \leqslant c_1\}$$
Hence,
$$c_2 = M(J, c_1; S^1; \mu_1) = \frac{1}{\mu_1(H_{c_1} \cap S^1)} \int_{H_{c_1} \cap S^1} J(u) \, d\mu_1$$
$$= \frac{1}{\mu_1(H_{c_1} \cap S^1)} \left(\int_{H_{c_1} \cap S^1 \setminus G_\varepsilon \cap S^1} J(u) \, d\mu_1 + \int_{G_\varepsilon \cap S^1} J(u) \, d\mu_1 \right)$$
$$\geqslant \frac{c_2}{\mu_1(H_{c_1} \cap S^1)} (\mu_1(H_{c_1} \cap S^1) - (\mu_1(G_\varepsilon \cap S^1))) + (c_2 + \varepsilon) \frac{\mu_1(G_\varepsilon \cap S^1)}{\mu_1(H_{c_1} \cap S^1)}$$
$$= c_2 + \varepsilon \frac{\mu_1(G_\varepsilon \cap S^1)}{\mu_1(H_{c_1} \cap S^1)} > c_2.$$

It deduces a contradiction. These complete the proof.

Replacing c_1 by c_1, we can construct S^3 and μ_3 in a similar way, so that $\mu_3(H_{c_3} \cap S^3) > 0$. In general, for each positive integer n, from c_{n-1} we construct S^n such that
$$S^{n-1} \subset S^n \subset S$$
and construct a Q-measure μ_n such that
$$\mu_n(S^n) \geq \mu(S)$$
and let
$$c_{n+1} = M(J, c_n; S^n; \mu_n). \tag{5.4}$$
Applying this algorithm, we obtain a decreasing sequence
$$c_1 \geq c_2 \geq \cdots \geq c_n \geq c_{n+1} \geq \cdots$$
and a sequence of sets
$$H_{c_n} \cap S^n = \{u \in S^n \mid J(u) \leq c_n\}, \quad n=1, 2, \cdots \tag{5.5}$$

Remark 5.2 Since $\mu_n(H_{c_n} \cap S^n) > 0$, $n=1, 2, \cdots$,
$$c_n > c_n^* = \min_{u \in S^n} J(u).$$

Theorem 5.2 *With this algorithm, we have*
$$\lim_{n \to \infty} c_n = c^* = \lim_{u \in S} J(u),$$
and
$$\emptyset \neq \bigcup_{k=1}^{\infty} \text{cl} \bigcup_{n=k}^{\infty} (H_{c_n} \cap S^n) \subset H^*. \tag{5.7}$$

Proof. According to the algorithm, we know that $c_n \geq c_n^* \geq c^*$, for $n=1, 2, \cdots$, and the sequence $\{c_n\}$ is decreasing. Thus, the limit
$$\lim_{n \to \infty} c_n = \hat{c} \geq c^* \tag{5.8}$$
exists. Letting $n \to \infty$ in (5.4), we obtain
$$\hat{c} = \lim_{n \to \infty} c_{n+1} = \lim_{n \to \infty} M(J, c_n; S^n; \mu_n) = M(J, \hat{c}; S; \mu).$$
It follows from Theorem 4.2 that $\hat{c}$ is the global minimum value of J over S, i.e., $\hat{c} = c^*$.

Furthermore, since $H_{c_n} \cap S^n \subset S$, $n=1,2,\cdots$, so we have $\bigcup_{n=k}^{\infty}(H_{c_n} \cap S^n) \subset S$, $k=1, 2, \cdots$. By the assumption (A), S is closed, thus, we also have, $\text{cl}\bigcup_{n=k}^{\infty}(H_{c_n} \cap S^n) \subset S$, $k=1, 2, \cdots$. Hence,
$$\bigcap_{k=1}^{\infty} \text{cl} \bigcup_{n=k}^{\infty} (H_{c_n} \cap S^n) \subset S. \tag{5.9}$$
Moreover, suppose u is a point of the set $\bigcap_{k=1}^{\infty} \text{cl} \bigcup_{n=k}^{\infty}(H_{c_n} \cap S^n)$, then it is a limit point of a subsequence u_{n_i} which consists of elements in $H_{c_n} \cap S^n$: $\lim_{n_i \to \infty} u_{n_i} = u$. But $J(u_{n_i}) \leq c_{n_i}$, it follows from lower semi-continuity of J that
$$J(u) \leq \lim_{n_i \to \infty} c_{n_i} = c^*,$$
i.e., $u \in H^*$. Finally, from the assumption (A), the set H_{c_1} is compact, the sets $\text{cl}\bigcup_{n=k}^{\infty}(H_{c_n} \cap S^n)$, $k=1, 2, \cdots$, are compact as they are closed and contained in the compact set H_{c_1}. Note also that these sets are decreasing (nested). This implies that
$$\bigcap_{k=1}^{\infty} \text{cl} \bigcup_{n=k}^{\infty} (H_{c_n} \cap S^n) \neq \emptyset. \tag{5.10}$$

The proof of the theorem is now complete.

Corollary 5.1 Let $c_n^* = \min_{u \in S^n} J(u)$ and $H_n^* = \{u \in S^n \mid J(u) = c_n^*\}$, $n=1,2,\cdots$. Then

$$\lim_{n \to \infty} c_n^* = c^*;$$

$$\emptyset \neq \bigcap_{k=1}^{\infty} \text{cl}(\bigcup_{n=k}^{\infty} H_n^*) \subset H^*.$$

Remark 5.3 In this corollary the value c_n^* and the set H_n^* is independent of the choice of the measure μ_n. It is only required the existence of a sequence of Q-measures μ_n on U_n, $n=1,2,\cdots$. In practice, we usually take a fixed integer n and find c_n^* and H_n^* as the approximations of c^* and H^*, respectively. Moreovevr, if J is continuous, then the last set inclusion above becomes equality.

6 Examples

In the previous discussion, we construct a sequence of subspaces $\{U_n\}$ of U with the property that $\text{cl}\{\bigcup_{n=1}^{\infty} U_n\} = U$ and a sequence of Q-measures $\{\mu_n\}$ defined on subsets $S^n = U_n \cap S$ of subspaces $\{U_n\}$, where S^n is robust on U_n, $n=1,2,\cdots$. In order to prove the convergence theorem we require that $\{\mu_n\}$ Q-converge to μ and that the condition (5.1) be satisfied. At present stage, we are unable to provied sufficient conditions to guarantee the existence of the constructios of $\{U_n\}$ and $\{\mu_n\}$. However, with specific structures of certaing given problems, one oftem can realize the required constructions of $\{U_n\}$ and $\{\mu_n\}$ in order to employ our variable measure algorithm. In this section we give two examples to show the constructions $\{S^n\}$ and $\{\mu_n\}$ for a given constraint set S. One of them is from an optimal control model, and the other one is from the theory of differential games.

Example 6.1 Let $U = l^2$ and

$$S = \{u \in l^2 \mid \|u\| \leq M\},$$

where M is a given constant. In optimal control the constant M means the bound of energy of the control u. See [5]. Let

$$U_n = \{u \in l^2 \mid u = (a_1, a_2, \cdots, a_n, 0, 0\cdots)\} \tag{6.1}$$

and

$$S^n = U_n \cap S$$

i.e., the $n+1$st, $n+2$nd, $\cdots$, components of each element of S^n are zeros. Obviously

$$S^n \subset S^{n+1} \subset \cdots \subset S, \quad n=1,2,\cdots.$$

Suppose μ is a nondegenerate Gaussian measure on l^2 (see [9]). It is a Q-measure. For each measurable set D in l^2, let

$$\hat{D}^n = \{u = (a_1, \cdots, a_n, b_{n+1}, \cdots) \in l^2 \mid (a_1, \cdots, a_n, a_{n+1}, \cdots) \in D\}, \tag{6.2}$$

i.e., $\hat{D}^n$ and D have the same projection on U_n. $\hat{D}^n$ is a measurable set in l^2. Now we define the measure of D as

$$\mu(\hat{D}^n) = \mu_n(D \cap U_n). \tag{6.3}$$

We remark that, according to the construction (6.2), we have
$$S \subset \hat{S}^n, \quad n=1,2,\cdots.$$
Indeed, suppose $u=(a_1,\cdots,a_n,a_{n+1},\cdots) \in S$, and $\|u\| \leqslant M$, i.e., $\sum_{i=1}^{\infty} a_i^2 \leqslant M^2$. It follows that,
$$\sum_{i=1}^{n} a_i^2 \leqslant M^2, \text{ i.e., } (a_1,\cdots,0,\cdots) \in S^n, \quad \forall n=1,2,\cdots$$
Thus, $u \in \{u \in l^2 \mid u \in S\} = \hat{S}^n$, $n=1,2,\cdots$. Hence,
$$\mu_n(S \cap U_n) = \mu_n(S^n) = \mu(\hat{S}^n) \geqslant \mu(S), \quad \forall n=1,2,\cdots.$$

Finally, we have to prove that the sequence of measures $\{\mu_n\}$ Q-converges to μ. Suppose F is a given closed set in $U=l^2$, then
$$F \subset \hat{F}^n, \quad \forall n=1,2,\cdots, \quad F \subset \bigcap_{n=1}^{\infty} \hat{F}^n.$$
Conversely, suppose that there exists an element $u \in \bigcap_{n=1}^{\infty} \hat{F}^n$ and $u=(a_1,\cdots,a_n,\cdots)$. Then for $n=1,2,\cdots$,
$$u_n := (a_1,\cdots,a_n,0,\cdots) \in F.$$
Note that
$$\|u_n - u\|^2 = \sum_{k=n+1}^{\infty} a_k^2 \to 0 \quad as \quad n \to \infty.$$
Thus $u = \lim_{n \to \infty} u_n$. As F is closed, $u \in F$. Therefore,
$$F = \lim_{n \to \infty} \hat{F}^n = \bigcap_{n=1}^{\infty} \hat{F}^n.$$
It follows from the continuity of the measure u,
$$\mu_n(F \cap U_n) = \mu(\hat{F}^n) \to \mu(F), \quad n \to \infty,$$
i.e., $\{\mu_n\}$ is Q-convergent to μ.

Example 2 Let $\{b_n\}$ be given sequence satisfying the following conditions:
$$b_n > 0, \quad \forall n=1,2,\cdots, \quad \sum_{n=1}^{\infty} b_n = M.$$
For instance, we can take, $b_n = M/2^n$, $n=1,2,\cdots$. Let
$$S = \{\{a_n\} \mid |a_n| \leqslant b_n, n=1,2,\cdots\}.$$
It is a convex compact set of the Frechet space $U = \prod_{n=1}^{\infty} \mathbb{R}_n$, where $\mathbb{R}_n$ is a one-dimensional space consisting of real numbers, $n=1,2,\cdots$ Since S has nonempty interior, S is a robust set in U.

Let
$$\rho_n(t) = \begin{cases} \dfrac{1}{2b_n}, & -b_n \leqslant t \leqslant b_n, \\ 0, & \text{otherwise.} \end{cases}$$

Let B^n be a Borel set in $\mathbb{R}^n$, B_n a cylindrical set with a base B^n. Let Ω be the smallset σ-field generated by this kind of cylindrical sets. Then we have a measurable space (U, Ω). Define

$$\mu_n(B^n) = \int_{B_n} \rho_1(t_1)\cdots\rho_n(t_n)\,\mathrm{d}t_1\cdots\mathrm{d}t_n, \tag{6.4}$$

then we have a family of consistent measures. By the Kolmogorov Extension Theorem [8], we obtain a measure μ, and (U, Ω, μ) becomes a Q-measure space. See [4].

Suppose D is a measurable set of U. Let.

$$U_n = \{u \in l^2 \mid u = (a_1, a_2, \cdots, a_n, 0, 0, \cdots)\} = \prod_{i=1}^n \mathbb{R}_i \times \vec{0} \tag{6.5}$$

where $\vec{0} = (0, 0, \cdots)$, and

$$\hat{D}^n = \{u = (a_1, \cdots, a_n, b_{n+1}, \cdots) \mid (a_1, \cdots, a_n, a_{n+1}, \cdots) \in D\}$$

i. e., $\hat{D}^n$ is a cylindrical set with the base which is the projection of D on $\prod_{i=1}^n \mathbb{R}_i$. Define

$$\mu_n(D \cap U_n)\mu = (\hat{D}^n)$$

and

$$S^n = \{u \in S \mid u = (a_1, a_2, \cdots, a_n, 0, \cdots)\}.$$

Obviously, $S^n \subset S^{n+1} \subset S$. Moreover, S^n is a robust set in $\mathbb{R}^n = \prod_{i=1}^n \mathbb{R}_i$. And, it follows from the definition,

$$S \subset \hat{S}^n, \quad n = 1, 2, \cdots \tag{6.6}$$

and

$$\mu(S) \leqslant \mu(\hat{S}^n) = \mu_n(S^n), \quad n = 1, 2, \cdots \tag{6.7}$$

We can prove that $\mu_n \xrightarrow{Q} \mu$ similarly, and obtain $\{S^n\}$ and $\{\mu_n\}$ with the required properties.

7 Conclusion

Approximating global optimalities of objectives on functional spaces by finite dimensional solutions is of fundamental significance because numerically one can only find finite dimensional approximations to the global minima on functional spaces. The variable measure method developed above is not only of theoretical interests but also of practical value. In our recent work [12], the method is utilized to derive a discontinue penalty function method which enables us to numerically solve optimal control problems with nonconvex state constraints with great efficiency.

References

[1] Quan Zueng. A variable measure method of integral global optimization [J]. *Applied Mathematics, A Journal of Chinese Universities*, (1988) 2, pp 281—288 (in Chinese)

[2] Quan Zheng. Optimality conditions for global optimization (I) [J]. *Acta Mathematicae Applicatae Sinica* (1985) 2, pp 63—78

[3] Quan Zheng Optimality conditions for global optimization (II) [J]. *Acta Mathematicae Applicatae Sinica*, (1985) 3, pp 118—134.

[4] E. G alperin and Zheng, Q. Integral global optimization method for differential games with application

to pursuit-evasion games [J]. *Computer Mathematics with Applications*, (1989) 18, 209—234.
[5] Galperin, E. and Zheng, Q. Variation-free iterative method for global optimal Control [J]. *International Journal of Control*, (1989) 50, 1731—1743.
[6] Quan, Zheng. Robust analysis and global minimization (Ⅰ) [J]. *Acta Mathematicae Applicatae Sinica*.
[7] Quan Zheng. Robust analysis and global minimization (Ⅱ) [J]. *Acta Mathematicae Applicatae Sinica*.
[8] Ash, R. B. *Real Analysis and Probability* [M]. Academic Press, New York (1972).
[9] Vakhania, N. N. *Probability Distrbutions on Linear Spaces* [M]. North Holland, New York (1981).
[10] Chew, S. H. and Zheng, Q. *Integral Global Optimizations* [M]. Lecture Notes in Economics and Mathematics Systems, No. 298, Springer-Verlag (1988).
[11] Zheng, Q., Jiang, B. C. and Zhuang, S. L. A method for finding global extrema [J]. *Acta Mathematicae Applicatae Sinica*, (1978) 2, 161—174 (in Chinese).
[12] Zheng, Q. and Zhuang, D. Integral global optimization of constrained problems in functional spaces with discontinuous penalty functions [J]. to appear.

Solution and Control of PDE VIA Global Optimization Methods*

Abstract: Based on the concept of η-equivalent solutions (not to be confused with approximations to the exact solution), a new consideration is given to ill-posed[1,2] and overdetermined PDE problems and to problems with nonexistent solutions[3]. Then a new method based on full global optimization techniques is developed for solution and control of processes described by partial differential equations. The ideas are illustrated by examples, and a case study is proesented in comparison with the quasireversibility method[4].

1 Introduction

For solution of ordinary differential equations, effective numerical methods (e. g., the Runge-Kutta schemes, etc.) are available, so that system of ODEs, for which a control problem is formulated, is integrated independently and without the use of a global optimization method. Unfortunately, this is not the case for PDEs where the solution, even its existence is a problem in itself. That is why, in nontrivial cases, the problems of solving and control of PDE should be approached together in one synthetic algorithm.

The very popular method of finite differences delivers an η-equivalent (see below) direct solution presented as a set of points on a finite grid. To determine an intermediate point on such discrete representation of a surface, one has to interpolate or to refine the grid and make another iteration. Due to the fixed structure of finite difference schemes, they are generally not appropriate for solution of optimal control problems for distributed parameter systems (PDE), except for problems that admit (or can be perturbed to admit) reverse-time integration; see [4] for details.

The finite element methods, see, e. g.,[7,8] and some recent results in [9,10], are applied usually under the assumption of global Lipschitz condition[8−10]. The basis functions $\phi_i^{(n)}(x)$ are fixed and the solution is represented in the form: $w = \sum_{i=1}^{n} q_i^{(n)} \phi_i^{(n)}(x)$; the time coordinate is usually singled out, and simply $q_i^{(n)} = q_i^{(n)}(t)$, cf. [9, p. 60, Formula (2.13)]. This usually leads to more iterations in comparison with a scheme

---

* In collaboration with Efim A. Galperin. Reprinted from Computer Math. Applic., 1993,25(10):103−118.

where basis functions are not fixed. Of course, this method also finds an η-solution (as probably any iterative method, excepting special cases where an exact solution might be found in a finite number of iterations).

In the framework of global optimization, any method involving undetermined parameters can be used for solution and control of PDE systems. Here we outline a possible procedure for a recent very promising grid free scheme, with floating hyperbolic interpolants as basis functions. The method, initially developed to represent topographic profiles[11], has been tested and proved to be an efficient tool for accurate spatial approximations and partial derivative estimates in $\mathbb{R}^n$; see [11,12] and bibliography therein.

Consider an rth order system of m partial differential equations in q unknown real-valued C^r-functions $w_1, \cdots, w_q$, defined on an open set $X \subset \mathbb{R}^n, n \geq 1$:

$$F_i(\mathbf{x}, D^\beta w_j(\mathbf{x})) = 0, \quad i=1,\cdots,m; \quad 1 \leq j \leq q; \quad \mathbf{x} \in X \subset \mathbb{R}^n. \tag{1.1}$$

Here, D^β runs over all local differential operators on C^r-functions and has the form:

$$D^\beta = \frac{\partial^\beta}{\partial x_1^{\alpha_1} \cdots \partial x_{n-1}^{\alpha_{n-1}} \partial t^{\alpha_n}}; \quad \beta = \alpha_1 + \cdots + \alpha_n \leq r, \tag{1.2}$$

where we set $x_n \equiv t$, the time variable. The numbers m, q, r are unrelated, and we use x_n instead of t for symmetry where appropriate, so that $\mathbf{x} = (x_1, \cdots, x_{n-1}, t) = (x_1, \cdots, x_n) \in X \subset \mathbb{R}^n$. We assume that $F_i, i=1,\cdots,m$, are continuous functions of their arguments and we use vector notations $\mathbf{F} = (F_1, \cdots, F_m), \mathbf{w} = (w_1, \cdots, w_q)$, to write (1.1) in a shorter form:

$$\mathbf{F}(x, D^\beta \mathbf{w}(\mathbf{x})) = 0, \quad \mathbf{x} \in X \subset \mathbb{R}^n, \quad \mathbf{F} \in \mathbb{R}^m, \quad \mathbf{w} \in \mathbb{R}^q. \tag{1.3}$$

2 Exact and η-Equivalent Solutions of PDE

Let $\mathbf{w}(\mathbf{x}) \in C^r$, then we have from (1.1), (1.3):

$$F_i(\mathbf{x}, D^\beta w_j(\mathbf{x})) \equiv f_i(\mathbf{x}), \quad i=1,\cdots,m \quad \text{or} \tag{2.1}$$

$$\mathbf{F}(\mathbf{x}, D^\beta \mathbf{w}(\mathbf{x})) \equiv \mathbf{f}(\mathbf{x}), \quad \mathbf{x} \in X \subset \mathbb{R}^n \tag{2.2}$$

where $\mathbf{f}(\mathbf{x}) = \{f_1(\mathbf{x}), \cdots, f_m(\mathbf{x})\}$ is a continuous vector-function corresponding to $\mathbf{F}$ and $\mathbf{w}$. If $\mathbf{w}(\mathbf{x})$ is a solution of (1.3), then $\mathbf{f}(\mathbf{x}) \equiv 0$, otherwise $\mathbf{f}(\mathbf{x}) \not\equiv 0$ in (2.2).

Assume that X is bounded, then the closure $\overline{X} = \operatorname{cl} X \subset \mathbb{R}^n$ is compact, thus, from any cover of $\overline{X}$ by open sets Ω_s one can extract a *finite* cover $\{\Omega_s\}$, $\overline{X} \subset \bigcup \Omega_s$. Consider all possible finite covers $\{\Omega_s\}$ and assume that the equations (1.1), (1.3) and $w \in C^r$ are defined over the union $\bigcup \Omega_s$.

Lemma 2.1 *A C^r-function $w(x)$ is a solution of (1.1) if and only if for any finite cover $\{\Omega_s\}$, we have*

$$\int_{\Omega_s} F_i(\mathbf{x}, D^\beta \mathbf{w}(\mathbf{x})) d\mathbf{x} \equiv \int_{\Omega_s} f_i(\mathbf{x}) d\mathbf{x} = 0 \quad i=1\cdots,m; \quad \forall \Omega_s, \forall \{\Omega_s\}, \bigcup \Omega_s \supseteq X. \tag{2.3}$$

Proof. Necessity is obvious since if $\mathbf{w}(\mathbf{x})$ is a solution of (1.1), then $f_i(\mathbf{x}) \equiv 0, i=1,\cdots,m$.

Sufficiency. Suppose, on the contrary, that (2.3) holds but $\mathbf{w}(\mathbf{x})$ is not a solution of (1.1). Then there is an index i_0, $1 \leq i_0 \leq m$, and a point $\mathbf{x}_0 \in X$ such that $f_{i_0}(\mathbf{x}_0) \neq 0$, say, $f_{i_0}(\mathbf{x}_0) < 0$. By continuity of f_{i_0}, there is a neighborhood $N_\delta(\mathbf{x}_0) \subset X$ such that $f_{i_0}(\mathbf{x}_0) < 0$ for all $\mathbf{x} \in N_\delta(\mathbf{x}_0)$. Since the measure $\mu(N_\delta(\mathbf{x}_0)) > 0$, so we get

$$\int_{N_\delta(\mathbf{x}_0)} f_{i_0}(\mathbf{x}) d\mathbf{x} < 0,$$

contradicting (2.3) if we take $N_\delta(\mathbf{x}_0)$ as one of Ω_s in a finite $\{\Omega_s\}$.

Lemma 2.2 *A C^r-function $w(x)$ is a solution of (1.3) if and only if*

$$\int_X \| \mathbf{F}(\mathbf{x}, D^\beta \mathbf{w}(\mathbf{x})) \| d\mathbf{x} \equiv \int_X \| \mathbf{f}(\mathbf{x}) \| d\mathbf{x} = 0. \tag{2.4}$$

Here $\| \cdot \|$ is a norm in $\mathbb{R}^m$.

Proof. *Necessity.* If $\mathbf{w}(\mathbf{x})$ is a solution of (1.3), then $\mathbf{f}(\mathbf{x}) \equiv 0$ and (2.4) follows.

Sufficiency. Suppose, on the contrary, that (2.4) holds but $\mathbf{w}(\mathbf{x})$ is not a solution of (1.3). Then there is an index i_0, $1 \leq i_0 \leq m$, and a point $\mathbf{x}_0 \in X$ such that $f_{i_0}(\mathbf{x}_0) \neq 0$, hence, $\| f(\mathbf{x}_0) \| > 0$. By continuity of $\| f(\mathbf{x}) \|$, there is a neighborhood $N_\delta(\mathbf{x}_0) \subset X$ such that $\| f(\mathbf{x}) \| > 0$ for all $\mathbf{x} \in N_\delta(\mathbf{x}_0)$, contradicting (2.4) since $\mu(N_\delta(\mathbf{x}_0)) > 0$.

Definition 2.1 For a function $\mathbf{w} \in C^r$ and an equation $F_i = 0, 1 \leq i \leq m$, of (1.1) we difine the divergence Δ_i as follows:

$$\Delta_i = \Delta(F_i, \mathbf{w}(\cdot)) = \max[\sup_{x \in X} f_i(\mathbf{x}), |\inf_{x \in X} f_i(\mathbf{x})|] \geq 0. \tag{2.5}$$

If F_i, $\mathbf{w}(\mathbf{x})$ are defined over the union $\cup \Omega_s \supset \overline{X}$, then in the bracket one can replace X by the closure $\overline{X}$ and sup, inf by max, min, which do exist since $f_i(\mathbf{x})$ is continuous over a compact $\overline{X}$.

Definition of a devergence for the whole system (1.1), cf. (1.3) with a vector-function $\mathbf{F}$ (obvious possibilities: $\Delta = \max \Delta_i$ or $\Delta = \sum \Delta_i$), depends on a physical sense of the problem and may involve multi-objective global optimization, see [13, Chapter 8]. We do not consider this question here.

Clearly, $\mathbf{w}(\mathbf{x})$ is a solution of (1.1), (1.3) if and only if all $\Delta_i = 0, i = 1, \cdots, m$. Otherwise, a $\Delta_{i_0} > 0$ signals either a large discrepancy of a candidate $\mathbf{w}(\mathbf{x})$ (which, thus, has to be discarded) or an imprecision that could be attributed to inaccuracy of the model (1.1). In the latter case, $\mathbf{w}(\mathbf{x})$ is acceptable as a description of the process (not as an exact mathematical solution of the system (1.1), (1.3)). This justifies the following definition.

Definition 2.2 Given $\eta > 0$, a function $\mathbf{w}_\eta(\mathbf{x}) \in C^r$ is called an η-equivalent solution (η-solution) of (1.1) iff

$$\Delta_i = \Delta(F_i, \mathbf{w}_\eta(\cdot)) < \eta, \quad i = 1, \cdots, m. \tag{2.6}$$

The η-equivalent solutions form a class $\mathcal{F}_\eta \subset C^r$ of functions that are "equally good" (i.e., proesent the same goodness of fit quality) with respect to equations (1.1), (1.3). This concept can be naturally extended onto problems with initial and boundary conditions, i.e., requirement (2.6) can be extended to include boundary, initial, intermediate and other conditions, see Section 3 below. Obviously, two η solutions do not have to be close themselves (in any sense, see Examples 3.1, 3.2 in Section 3). They are "close" with respect to the conditions that are included in a particular concept of η equivalence similar to Definition 2.2.

The class $\mathfrak{I}_\eta \subset C^r$ of η-equivalent solutions contains all exact solutions; a particular η solution may approximate one, several or none of exact solutions. Moreover, η-equivalent solutions may exist when no exact solution exists, see Section 4 below. To emphasize the difference between an η solution (i.e., η-equivalent solution) and an *approximation* of a solution (i.e., "approximate" solution, an ambiguous term we try to avoid), the following definition is introduced.

Definition 2.3 Given $\gamma > 0$ and a solution $\mathbf{w}(\mathbf{x}) \in C^r$ (*no matter, exact or η-equivalent*), a *function* $\widetilde{\mathbf{w}}(\mathbf{x})$ defined on X is said to be a *γ-approximation to* $\mathbf{w}(\mathbf{x})$ iff

$$\| \mathbf{w}(\mathbf{x}) - \widetilde{\mathbf{w}}(\mathbf{x}) \| \leqslant \gamma \quad \text{for all } \mathbf{x} \in X. \tag{2.7}$$

Here $\| \cdot \|$ is a norm in $\mathbb{R}^q$.

It is clear, that $\widetilde{\mathbf{w}}(\mathbf{x})$ may *not* satisfy any of the equations in a PDE problem; $\widetilde{\mathbf{w}}(\mathbf{x})$ may be non-differentiable and even discontinuous. At first glance, the consideration of such $\widetilde{\mathbf{w}}(\mathbf{x})$ may seem irrelevant to PDE problems; however, pointwise surfaces delivered by the finite difference method, see, e.g., [5,6], represent a discrete γ-approximation $\widetilde{\mathbf{w}}(\mathbf{x})$ to an exact $\mathbf{w}(\mathbf{x})$ or η-equivalent $\mathbf{w}_\eta(\mathbf{x})$ solutions, which approximation tends to $\mathbf{w}(\mathbf{x})$ or $\mathbf{w}_\eta(\mathbf{x})$ with infinite refinement of the grid. This convergence follows from (2.7) as $\gamma \to 0$, and it will be convergent to the exact solution, if a finite difference scheme starts from an exact initial or boundary condition.

3 Ill-Posed Problems Revisited

To provide further motivation for the consideration of η-equivalent solutions and to extend this consideration onto boundary and initial conditions, let us examine two examples.

Example 3.1 (J. Hadamard, [1]). Consider the initial value problem

$$\frac{\partial^2 w}{\partial x^2} + \frac{\partial^2 w}{\partial y^2} = 0 \tag{3.1}$$

$$w(x,0) = 0, \quad w_y(x,0) = \frac{1}{n} \sin n x. \tag{3.2}$$

Here $w_y = \frac{\partial w}{\partial y}$. The exact solution is

$$w(x,y) = \frac{1}{n^2} \sin n x \, \sinh n y. \tag{3.3}$$

The Cauchy data (3.2) tend to zero uniformly as $n \to \infty$ whereas the solution (3.3), if $y \neq 0$, oscillates between increasing limits and is unbounded as $n \to \infty$. Since $w(w,y) \equiv 0$ is the solution of (3.1) with zero data $w(x,0) = w_y(x,0) = 0$, we see that for large n in (3.2) a small change in the data, cf. (3.2), produces a large change in the solution, cf. (3.3), for $y\neq 0$ and large n. Thus, the dependence of the solution on the data is not continuous. Such problems are called *ill-posed*. In contrast, problems for which small perturbations in the data result in correspondingly small perturbations in the solution are called *well-posed*.

Now, consider the family of η-equivalent solutions

$$w_\eta(x,y) = \begin{cases} \dfrac{1}{n^2}\sin nx \sinh ny, & n \leqslant \dfrac{1}{\eta}, \\ 0, & n > \dfrac{1}{\eta}. \end{cases} \tag{3.4}$$

Here, we see that (3.4) satisfies (3.1), the condition $w_\eta(x,0)=0$ holds, and

$$\left|\frac{\partial w_\eta}{\partial y} - \frac{\partial w}{\partial y}\right| \leqslant \frac{1}{n}\sin nx < \eta, \quad \text{at the point } (x,0), \quad \forall n \tag{3.5}$$

so that (3.4) is η-equivalent to (3.3) and to the solution $w(x,y)\equiv 0$ in the sense of Definition 2.2, with possible non zero divergence only in the condition on $w_y(x,0)$. We see also that with a small change in data (3.2), as $n>1/\eta$, one can simply take $w_\eta \equiv 0$ as universal η-equivalent solution which remains the same for any such small changes in (3.2). Hence, the problem is not ill-posed if we agree to accept $w_\eta \equiv 0$ as η-equivalent solution.

Example 3.2 (E. T. Copson, [2, p. 53]). Consider the same equation (3.1) and two Cauchy initial value problems:

$$\text{(a)} \quad w_1(x,0)=x^2, \quad \frac{\partial w_1(x,0)}{\partial y}=0, \tag{3.6}$$

$$\text{(b)} \quad w_2(x,0)=x^2, \quad \frac{\partial w_2(x,0)}{\partial y}=\frac{1}{n}\sin nx. \tag{3.7}$$

The solutions are

$$\text{(a)} \quad w_1 = x^2 - y^2, \tag{3.8}$$

$$\text{(b)} \quad w_2 = x^2 - y^2 + \frac{1}{n^2}\sin nx \sinh ny. \tag{3.9}$$

Although the data for w_2 tend to the data for w_1 as $n\to\infty$, the solution w_2 does dot tend to w_1. Thus, there is no continuity with respect to initial data and the problems are ill-posed.

However, if we consider η-equivalent solutions and take

$$w_\eta = \begin{cases} w_2, & n \leqslant \dfrac{1}{\eta}, \\ w_1, & n > \dfrac{1}{\eta}, \end{cases} \tag{3.10}$$

then we see that it solves both problems (a) and (b) in the sense of Definition 2.2, since

$$\left|\frac{\partial w_\eta}{\partial y} - \frac{\partial w_i}{\partial y}\right| \leqslant \frac{1}{n}\sin nx < \eta, \quad \text{at the point } (x,0), \quad \forall n, (i=1,2).$$

Moreover, if $n\to\infty$, then (3.7) tend to (3.6) and $w_\eta \to w_1$, which means continuity with respect to initial data.

Remark 3.1 It should be noted that the term *continuity* is improper with respect to η

solutions meant as a *class* of η-equivalent solutions; however, a particular η-solution may include exact solutions like (3.4), (3.10) with respect to which the limit operation and the term continuity can be applied.

We see that the notion of well-posedness [2, pp. 51–53; pp. 108, 109, 450–455] concerns only exact solutions. It is dissolved when applied to η-equivalent solutions. However, η-equivalent solutions are natural due to the imprecision of model equations and to impurity of environment in which physical problems are considered. Moreover, it is η-equivalent solutions (or their γ-approximation $\tilde{w}(x)$, see Definition 2.3) that are obtained in computations. We have, therefore, to consider sets (classes) of η-equivalent solutions pertaining to particular problems. Here, the notion of well-posedness reappears again in the *global structure* of the set of η-equivalent solutions and *not* in the behavior of η-equivalent solutions in the neighborhood of the initial data.

4 Overdetermined PDE and Problems with Nonexistent Exact Solution

If $m < q$ in (1.1), then system (1.1) is said to be under-determined; such systems are studied, e. g., in [14] via the convex integration method introduced in [15]. If $m > q$, then system (1.1) is overdetermined and, in general, does not have a solution (exact) especially with initial and/or boundary conditions added. If $m = q$, then such a system normally has a solution which is unique under certain initial and/or boundary conditions; though, even in this case, there are examples to the contrary.

Systems or equations with nonexistent solutions are usually discarded as badly formulated. However, such systems can be viewed as approximate physical models with appended supplementary conditions intended to provide certain desirable features to the process. In this respect, one could mention overdetermined or degenerate linear algebraic systems $\mathbf{Ax} = \mathbf{b}$ with rank $(\mathbf{A}, \mathbf{b}) >$ rank $\mathbf{A}$ which do not have a solution in the usual sense but do have many least-squares solutions that deliver min $\|\mathbf{Ax} - \mathbf{b}\|$ and represent, in fact, η-equivalent solutions to the system. One of those η-solutions is the Penrose [16, 17] solution which renders min $\|\mathbf{x}\|$ and, thus, provides accommodation of conflicting requirements in $\mathbf{Ax} = \mathbf{b}$ with the minimum resource alloction. This solution is given by the so-called Moore-Penrose pseudo-inverse matrix, $\mathbf{x} = \mathbf{A}^{\#}\mathbf{b}$, which in the usual case coincides with the inverse matrix, $\mathbf{A}^{\#} = \mathbf{A}^{-1}$ if det $\mathbf{A} \neq 0$; for an extensive account on overdetermined linear systems and corresponding generalized inverses, see [18].

It is clear that overdetermined PDEs and problems with nonexistent solution may have η-equivalent solutions, and in this case may represent a physical reality despite mathematical nonexistence of an exact solution. Let us see that a problem may have η-equivalent solutions for any $\eta > 0$ but not for $\eta = 0$.

Example 4.1 (P. R. Garabedian, [3, p. 451]). Consider the Cauchy initial value problem of determining a solution $w = w(x, y)$ of the Laplace equation

$$w_{xx}+w_{yy}=0, \quad x\in(0,\varepsilon), \quad y\in(-\varepsilon,\varepsilon), \tag{4.1}$$

which fulfills initial conditions of the form

$$w(0,y)=0, \quad w_x(0,y)=f(y), \quad y\in(-\varepsilon,\varepsilon), \tag{4.2}$$

where $w_x=\dfrac{\partial w}{\partial x}, w_{xx}=\dfrac{\partial^2 w}{\partial x^2}, w_{yy}=\dfrac{\partial^2 w}{\partial y^2}$.

It is shown [3, pp. 451—452] that, if $f(y)$ is not analytic at $y=0$, for example, if

$$f(y)=|y|, \tag{4.3}$$

then no solution of (4.1)—(4.2) can exist in the neighborhood indicated.

However, the function (4.3) can be uniformly approximated up to any precision $\eta>0$ by polynomials (which are analytic functions) and by the Cauchy-Kowalewski theorem, there is a unique analytical solution of (4.1)—(4.2) for each of those approximations of $f(y)$. Hence, there are η-equivalent solutions of (4.1)—(4.3) for any $\eta>0$, but not for $\eta=0$ (the exact solution). In a physical reality, one cannot expect that conditions (4.1)—(4.3) can be realized exactly, thus, it is the η-solutions that really count. In this sense, the problem (4.1)—(4.3) is correct and perfectly solvable and the series method with the Cauchy-Kowalewski theorem presents a powerful tool for solution of problems that admit analytic approximations.

We see that, if one considers η-equivalent solutions, the situation with ill-posed and well-posed problems and problems with nonexistent (exact) solutions is quite different. Here we have to study the *set* of η-equivalent solutions and the structure of this set may provide an insight into the question of which problem is correct and well-posed and which is not.

We see also that with the notion of η-equivalent solutions overdetermined PDEs and problems with nonexistent exact solution can be considered and solved (in a new sense). Moreover, the solution of those problems can be obtained through an iterative method in the same way as the solution of a "normal" problem with an existing exact well-posed solution.

To devise such a method, we use full global optimization techniques [13,19,20] with the special multiquadric [11,12] representation for an η-equivalent solution.

5 Solution and Control of PDEs Preliminary Lemmas

For most partial differential equations currently used, the functions F_i in (1.1) are Lipschitz continuous. If we consider C^r-functions $w_j(\mathbf{x})$ that have piecewise continuous $(r+1)^{\text{th}}$ derivatives in $\overline{X}$ or in $\cup\Omega_s\supset \overline{X}$, then $w_j(\mathbf{x})$ and the functions $f_i(\mathbf{x})$ in (2.1) will be Lipschitzian over $\overline{X}$, that is,

$$|f_i(\mathbf{x})-f_i(\mathbf{x}')|\leqslant L_i\|\mathbf{x}-\mathbf{x}'\|, \quad i=1,\cdots,m; \quad \mathbf{x},\mathbf{x}'\in\overline{X}, \tag{5.1}$$

for some constants $L_i>0$ that can be calculated if Lipschitzian constants for F_i and $\sup|w_j^{(k)}|$, $k=1,\cdots,r+1$, are known. We assume, henceforth, that F_i and w_j are such that (5.1) holds and we call this case Lipschitzian PDE (Lip PDE) problem.

Given $\varepsilon>0$, there is a finite ε-net $\mathbf{x}_s=\{\mathbf{x}_1,\cdots,\mathbf{x}_{N(\varepsilon)}\}\in\overline{X}$ for a compact $\overline{X}\subset\mathbb{R}^n$. Denote by
$$\overline{\Omega}_s=\{\mathbf{x}|\ \|\mathbf{x}-\mathbf{x}_s\|\leqslant\varepsilon,\mathbf{x}\in\overline{X}\},\quad s=1,\cdots,N(\varepsilon), \tag{5.2}$$
where $\|\cdot\|$ is the Euclidian norm in $\mathbb{R}^n$, the compact subsets associated with this ε-net. A family of such subsets, obviously, represents a compact ε-cover for $\overline{X}$ and, in view of (5.2), we have
$$\overline{X}=\bigcup_{s=1}^{N(\varepsilon)}\overline{\Omega}_s. \tag{5.3}$$

Lemma 5.1 *If for a Lip PDE problem $\mathbf{w}(\mathbf{x})$ is such that*
$$F_i(\mathbf{x},D^\beta\mathbf{w}(\mathbf{x}))|_{x=x_s}=f_i(\mathbf{x}_s)=0,\quad s=1,\cdots,N(\varepsilon),\quad i=1,\cdots,m, \tag{5.4}$$
then
$$\Delta_i\leqslant L_i\varepsilon\quad i=1,\cdots,m. \tag{5.5}$$

Proof. Let $\mathbf{x}_i^*$ be the arguments (different for different i) at which the values of Δ_i in (2.5) with X, max, min instead of X, sup, inf are achieved, i.e., $\Delta_i=|f_i(\mathbf{x}_i^*)|$. For every fixed i, there is a subset $\overline{\Omega}_{s_i}$ of (5.2) such that $\mathbf{x}_i^*\in\overline{\Omega}_{s_i}$, $1\leqslant s_i\leqslant N(\varepsilon)$. Taking $\mathbf{x}_{s_i}\in\overline{\Omega}_{s_i}$, we obtain from (5.1), (5.2), (5.4):
$$\Delta_i=|f_i(\mathbf{x}_i^*)|=|f_i(\mathbf{x}_i^*)-f_i(\mathbf{x}_{s_i})|\leqslant L_i\|\mathbf{x}_i^*-\mathbf{x}_{s_i}\|\leqslant L_i\varepsilon.$$

Remark 5.1 It is clear that condition (5.4) in Lemma 5.1 can be relaxed. In fact, we need only $f_i(\mathbf{x}_{s_i})=0$ for those s_i that indicate $\overline{\Omega}_{s_i}$ to which x_i^* belong. This reduces the number of required roots in (5.4).

Lemma 5.2 *Suppose there exist $w_j(\mathbf{x})\in C^r$ satisfying (5.4) and let $\widetilde{w}_s^j(\mathbf{x})$ be a collection of functions defined over $\overline{\Omega}_s$, $s=1,\cdots,N(\varepsilon)$, and such that*

1. *$\widetilde{w}_s^j(\mathbf{x})$ is Lipschitzian over $\overline{\Omega}_s$, with a constant L_s^j;*
2. *there are points $x_s^j\in\overline{\Omega}_s$ such that $\widetilde{w}_s^j(\mathbf{x}_s^j)=w_j(\mathbf{x}_s^j),s=1,\cdots,N(\varepsilon)$.*

Then within each $\overline{\Omega}_s$ we have
$$|w_j(\mathbf{x})-\widetilde{w}_s^j(\mathbf{x})|\leqslant 2(L_j+L_s^j)\varepsilon. \tag{5.6}$$

Proof.
$$|w_j(\mathbf{x})-\widetilde{w}_s^j(\mathbf{x})|=|w_j(\mathbf{x})-w_j(\mathbf{x}_s^j)+\widetilde{w}_s^j(\mathbf{x}_s^j)-\widetilde{w}_s^j(\mathbf{x})|$$
$$\leqslant|w_j(\mathbf{x})-w_j(\mathbf{x}_s^j)|+|\widetilde{w}_s^j(\mathbf{x}_s^j)-\widetilde{w}_s^j(\mathbf{x})|\leqslant L_j\|\mathbf{x}-\mathbf{x}_s^j\|+L_s^j\|\mathbf{x}-\mathbf{x}_s^j\|$$
$$=(L_j+L_s^j)\|\mathbf{x}-\mathbf{x}_s+\mathbf{x}_s-\mathbf{x}_s^j\|\leqslant(L_j+L_s^j)(\|\mathbf{x}-\mathbf{x}_s\|+\|\mathbf{x}_s-\mathbf{x}_s^j\|)$$
$$\leqslant 2(L_j+L_s^j)\varepsilon,$$
where L_j is the Lipschitzian constant for $w_j(\mathbf{x})$ existing since $w_j(\mathbf{x})$ are C^r and defined over $\cup\overline{\Omega}_s=\overline{X}$.

This almost obvious Lemma is important since $\widetilde{w}_s^j(\mathbf{x})$ may be nondifferentiable over $\overline{\Omega}_s$. Of course, $\widetilde{w}_s^j(\mathbf{x})$ do *not* satisfy a given PDE (1.1) and do *not* represent an η equivalent solution for (1.1). The functions $\widetilde{w}_s^j(\mathbf{x})$ are γ-approximations, cf. (5.6) and (2.7), with $\gamma=2\varepsilon\max_{j,s}(L_j+L_s^j)$, of an existing η-equivalent solution $w_j(\mathbf{x})$ with $\eta\leqslant\varepsilon$

$\max_{1 \leqslant i \leqslant m} L_i$, see Lemma 5.1; *computationally*, $\widetilde{w}_s^j(\mathbf{x})$ can be used to calculate $2(L_j + L_s^j)$ ε-precise values of an *unknown* $w_j(\mathbf{x})$.

Of course, it is difficult to guess a candidate $w(\mathbf{x})$ satisfying (5.4) for an ε-net chosen in advance. However, we can always take a convenient family of C^r-functions $\mathbf{w}(\mathbf{w}, \mathbf{q})$ where $\mathbf{q} \in \mathbb{R}^N$ is a vector of undetermined parameters, fix basic points (nodes) $\mathbf{x}_s \in \mathbb{R}^n$, $s = 1, \cdots, N^*$, $N^* \leqslant N$, and make a convenient partition (or a covering) of $\overline{X}$ into $\{\overline{\Omega}_s\}$, $\overline{X} \subseteq \bigcup \overline{\Omega}_s$, *without fixing* $\varepsilon > 0$ as in (5.2). Then, we substitute $\mathbf{w}(\mathbf{w}, \mathbf{q})$ for $\mathbf{w}(\mathbf{x})$ in (5.4) and solve the system for q:

$$\mathbf{f}(\mathbf{x}, \mathbf{q}) = 0, \quad \mathbf{f} = (f_1, \cdots, f_m), \quad s = 1, \cdots, N^*, \quad (5.7)$$

which can be converted to a simple global optimization problem and solved, e.g., by the cubic algorithm, see [13, Section 11.1].

Let $\mathbf{q}^0$ be a solution of (5.7). Then $\mathbf{w}^0(\mathbf{x}) = \mathbf{w}(\mathbf{x}, \mathbf{q}^0)$ satisfies (5.4) and we are only lacking ε which corresponds to our partition (or covering).

Consider the closed sets $\overline{\Omega}_s$ of our partition in place of X in (2.5); this will define partial divergencies δ_{si} which can be readily computed by (2.5) with max, min instead of sup, inf. Now, we have

$$\Delta_i = \max_{1 \leqslant s \leqslant N^*} \delta_{si}, \quad i = 1, \cdots, m, \quad (5.8)$$

which can be used as a quality test for $\mathbf{w}^*(\mathbf{x})$. In this procedure we do not need ε nor the Lipschitz constants L_i in (5.5).

Vice versa, if we know all L_i and can calculate

$$\varepsilon = \max_{1 \leqslant s \leqslant N^*} \max_{x \in \overline{\Omega}_s} \| \mathbf{x} - \mathbf{x}_s \|, \quad (5.9)$$

which is easy for convenient coverings by cubes or spheres, then we use the estimate (5.5) and we need not solve optimization problems (2.5) for δ_{si}.

6 Iterative Method Based on MQ-Functions

Following R. L. Hardy [11, pp. 164–166], consider a finite sum of straightline segments in $\mathbb{R}^2$:

$$H(x) = \sum_{k=1}^{N} \alpha_k |x - x_k|, \quad x \in [a, b], \quad x_k \in \mathbb{R}. \quad (6.1)$$

A plane Lipschitzian curve $w(x)$ of finite support (i.e., defined over a finite interval) can be represented by (6.1) with any desired accuracy. This means that, given $\gamma > 0$, there are $N(\gamma)$, x_k, α_k (some points x_k may be fixed, then $N = N(\gamma, \{x_k\})$), such that

$$|H(x) - w(x)| < \gamma, \quad \text{for all } x \in [a, b].$$

If $w(x)$ is given by a differential equation and we want to approximate also its slopes, then we have to provide for the existence of derivatives of $H(x)$. This is done by considering hyperbolas in (6.1) instead of straightline segments. If we want to accommodate surfaces in $\mathbb{R}^3$, then we have to convert hyperbolas to hyperboloids (circular for simplicity), this yielding the equation:

$$H(x,y) = \sum_{k=1}^{N} a_k [(x-x_k)^2 + (y-y_k)^2 + c_k^2]^{1/2}. \tag{6.2}$$

Extension to $\mathbb{R}^n$ is straightforward. Let $\mathbf{x} \in \mathbb{R}^n$, $\mathbf{x}^k \in \mathbb{R}^n$, then we can write [12, p. 129]:

$$H(\mathbf{x}) = \sum_{k=1}^{N} a_k [\|\mathbf{x} - \mathbf{x}^k\|^2 + c_k^2]^{1/2} = \sum_{k=1}^{N} a_k \left[\sum_{i=1}^{n} (x_i - x_i^k)^2 + c_k^2\right]^{1/2}, \tag{6.3}$$

where x_i, x_i^k are coordinates of $\mathbf{x}, \mathbf{x}^k \in \mathbb{R}^n$. Of course, the construction (6.3) can be modified by introducing other interpolants or by adding certain terms (e.g., see [12, pp. 130, 133, 148, 150]) according to particular problems, which may improve the approximation or speed up the computations. Here we consider the original quadric surface (6.3) and describe how to use it in the general global optimization framework for solution and control of partial differential equations.

Consider again equation (1.1) or (1.3) and assume for simplicity that $m = q = 1$. Substituting $H(\mathbf{x})$, (6.3), for $\mathbf{w}(\mathbf{x})$ yields the relation

$$F(\mathbf{x}, D^{\beta} H(\mathbf{x})) = f(\mathbf{x}, \{a_k\}, \{\mathbf{x}^k\}, \{c_k\}) = 0, \quad \forall \mathbf{x} \in X \subset \mathbb{R}^n. \tag{6.4}$$

Since H has the standard form (6.3) and F is given, so $f(\cdot)$ can be easily computed as a function (by a special subroutine) or as a number (for fixed $\mathbf{x}$, a_k, $\mathbf{x}^k$, c_k). If $m > 1, q > 1$, then f in (6.4) will be an m-vector $\mathbf{f}$, and a_k, $\mathbf{x}^k$, c_k will carry second index $j = 1, \cdots, q$. In the sequel, we include this case in the general framework and introduce simplified notations as follows. All undetermined parameters are considered as components of a vector $\mathbf{q}$ of variable dimension (not to be confused with q in (1.1) as a bound on index j), whereby nodes $\mathbf{x}^k \in \mathbb{R}^n$ are sometimes removed from $\mathbf{q}$ and considered separately. When convenient, certain entries may be included or excluded in a function notation, for example, f in (6.4) may be written as $\mathbf{f}(\mathbf{x}, \mathbf{q})$, $\mathbf{f}(\mathbf{x}, \mathbf{q}, \mathbf{x}^k)$, $\mathbf{f}(\cdot)$ depending on the accent on certain entries. Throughout this section, we use the Euclidian norm $\|\cdot\|$.

Procedure 6.1

Consider the functional

$$J(\mathbf{q}) = \int_X \|\mathbf{f}(\mathbf{x}, \mathbf{q})\| \, d\mathbf{x}, \tag{6.5}$$

and apply a full global optimization technique [13, 19, 20], to find the global minimum value

$$p^0 = \min_{\mathbf{q} \in \overline{Q}} J(\mathbf{q}) \geq 0 \tag{6.6}$$

and the set of all global minimizers

$$\overline{Q}^0 = \{\mathbf{q} \in \overline{Q} \mid J(\mathbf{q}) = p^0\}. \tag{6.7}$$

Here, $\overline{Q} = \overline{E} \times \overline{K}$ where $\mathbf{x}^k \in \overline{E} \subset \mathbb{R}^n$ (the sets X and $\overline{E}$ are unrelated) and $\overline{K}$ is a known rectangular set (box) of parameters $\{a_{k_j}\}, \{c_{k_j}\}$.

If $p^0 = 0$, then by virtue of Lemma 2.2, exact solutions are provided by $H(\mathbf{x}, \mathbf{q})$, (6.3), with $\mathbf{q} = \{a_k, x_i^k, c_k\} \in \overline{Q}^0$. If $p^0 > 0$, then we can either accept an η-equivalent solution, $\eta = \max_i \Delta_i$, (2.6), corresponding to actually employed parameters from the set

$\overline{Q}^0$ of (6.7), or increase N in (6.3) adding a number of new parameters and continue the process. If the box $\overline{K}$ contains zero, then necessarily the new global minimum value $p_1^0 \leqslant p^0$, and the process will be monotonic.

Procedure 6.2 *Finite Cover Scheme for η-equivalent Solutions*

For a compact $\overline{X} = \text{cl } X \subset \mathbb{R}^n$, there is a finite cover $\{\Omega_s\}$, $\overline{X} \subset \cup \Omega_s$. If we use Ω_s instead of X in (6.5), we obtain partial surfaces over Ω_s, $s=1,\cdots,v$, that represent respective exact, if $p_s^0 = 0$, or η-equivalent if $p_s^0 > 0$, solutions. It is clear that over small sets Ω_s one can take fewer terms in (6.3) and get greater precisionl; η-solutions over separate Ω_s are to be adjusted in order to represent a γ-approximation (2.7) of a physical process $\mathbf{w}(\mathbf{x}) \in C^r$ (for computational purposes there is no need to stick them together).

In both procedures points $\mathbf{x}^k \in \overline{E} \subset \mathbb{R}^n$ can be fixed or free. For illustration, see Section 7 below.

Procedure 6.3 *Spherical Fixed Node Schemes for η-equivalent Solutions*

Take $\gamma > 0$ and make a 2γ uniform grid within X (mesh size 2γ). Then spheres of radius $\gamma\sqrt{n}$ centered at grid points (nodes) $\mathbf{x}_s$, render a spherical finite cover $\{\Omega_s\}$. For every $\mathbf{x}_s \in \Omega_s$ consider a function of q:

$$\mathbf{F}(\mathbf{x}, D^\beta H(\mathbf{x},\mathbf{q}))|_{\mathbf{x}=\mathbf{x}_s} \equiv \mathbf{f}(\mathbf{x}_s, \mathbf{q}). \tag{6.8}$$

Here $\mathbf{q}$ stands for the parameters α_k, x_i^k, c_k in $H(\mathbf{x})$ of (6.3).

Apply a full global optimization method to find the global minimum value

$$p_s^* = \min_{\mathbf{q} \in \overline{Q}_s} \|\mathbf{f}(\mathbf{x}_s,\mathbf{q})\| \geqslant 0 \tag{6.9}$$

and the set of all global minimizers

$$\overline{Q}_s^* = \{\mathbf{q} \in \overline{Q}_s \|\mathbf{f}(\mathbf{x}_s,\mathbf{q})\| = p_s^*\}. \tag{6.10}$$

If $p_s^* = 0$, then by Lemma 5.1, we have $\Delta_i \leqslant L_i \gamma \sqrt{n}$, $i = 1, \cdots, m$, for equations of (1.1), meaning that $H(\mathbf{x})$ in (6.8) represents a $\gamma \sqrt{n} \times \max L_i$-equivalent solution over Ω_s.

In another version of the procedure, we can set $N=1$, $\mathbf{x}^1 = \mathbf{x}_s$ in (6.3) and find the global minimum value:

$$\widetilde{p}_s = \min_{\substack{x \in \overline{Q}_s \\ (\alpha_1, c_1) \in \overline{K}_1}} \|\mathbf{f}(\mathbf{x}, \alpha_1, c_1)\| \geqslant 0. \tag{6.11}$$

If $\widetilde{p}_s = 0$, then by Lemma 5.1 the surface $H(\mathbf{x}) = \alpha_1^0 (\|\mathbf{x} - \mathbf{x}_s\|^2 + c_1^{02})^{1/2}$ represents a $2\gamma\sqrt{n} \times \max L_i$-equivalent solution over Ω_s. Here, the coefficient 2 appears because, in general, the point $\mathbf{x}^0$ yielding $\mathbf{f}(\mathbf{x}^0, \alpha_1^0, c_1^0) = 0$ is *not* at the center of Ω_s.

If for every $s=1,\cdots,v$ in a finite cover $\{\Omega_s\}$ we have either $p_s^* = 0$ or $\widetilde{p}_s = 0$, then we have an η-equivalent solution over the whole $X \subset \cup \Omega_s$ represented by a collection of v partial surfaces (overlapping pieces of surfaces) that are to be adjusted in order to represent a γ-approsimation (2.7) of a physical process $\mathbf{w}(\mathbf{x}) \in C^r$ (no need of joining them together).

Remarks 6.1

1. It is clear that initial and boundary conditions can be included in the above considerations. They can be taken into account either separately and specifically as restrictions on **q**, thus, on the set $\overline{K}$, see Case Study, Section 7, or in combination with the equations (1.1), (1.3) by their inclusion in the norms in (6.5), (6.9), (6.11). The latter pepresents a scalarization of a multi-objective (with respect to each equation of (1.1) and each boundary and initial condition) global optimization problem. Another alternative is to consider initial and boundary conditions as successive criteria for optimization over the set $\overline{Q}^0$, (6.7), or those $\overline{Q}_s^*$, (6.10), for wich Ω_s has a nonempty intersection with the boundary ∂X. If a PDE problem has an exact solution within the class of interpolants employed, then the corresponding multicriteria problem is balanced (in the sense of [13, Chapter 8]) and the solution can be obtained by successive optimization or by scalarization of any kind. Otherwise, there exists a positive balance number [13, p. 139] which corresponds to a set of η-equivalent solutions of the problem.

2. It is also clear that optimal control problems for PDE can be considered in the same framework as above. This important and difficult topic needs much research. An example of a direct way of solving an optimal control PDE problem is presented below.

3. Obviously, inclusion of the multiquadrics (MQ) into a full global optimization scheme can only enhance the MQ method providing it with deterministic guarantee of obtaining (in a monotonic global set-to-set descent process) the best (in the limit) or an acceptable (in a finite number of iterations) η-equivalent solution within the class of MQ interpolants employed.

7 Case Study

Consider an optimal control problem formulated for one-dimensional heat equation in [4], see [4, Section 7.1, equstions (7.1)−(7.4), with $\alpha(x) \equiv 1$, $\chi(x) = x(1-x)$ as in Section 8.2].

$$\frac{\partial w}{\partial t} - \frac{\partial^2 w}{\partial x^2} = 0, \quad t \in (0, T), \quad x \in (0, 1), \tag{7.1}$$

$$w(0, t) = w(1, t) = 0, \quad t \in [0, T], \tag{7.2}$$

$$w(w, 0) = \xi(x), \quad x \in [0, 1], \tag{7.3}$$

$$\inf_{\xi} J(\xi) = \left\{ \int_0^1 [w(x, T) = \chi(x)]^2 \, dx \right\}^{1/2} \leqslant \theta. \tag{7.4}$$

Here, $w(x, t)$ is the temperature in a unit rod at position x at time t. The ends of the rod are kept at zero temperature, see (7.2). For a given $\theta > 0$ and a function $\chi(x)$, it is required to find the initial temperature in the rod $w(x, 0) = \xi(x)$, (7.3), such that the final temperature distribution $w(x, T)$ be as close as possible (in the L_2-metric (7.4)) to the function $\chi(x)$, and at least θ-close, see (7.4). By (7.2) and by continuity of $w(x, t)$, we should have $\xi(0)=\xi(1)=0$; in contrast, $\chi(0)=\chi(1)=0$ are not necessary in the L_2-metric (7.4). This problem has been numerically solved in [4] by the quasi-reversibility method for $T=0.1$. We present here a solution by the global optimization method with multiquadrics for the same $\chi(x)=x(1-x)$ as in [4, Section 8.2.2].

1. Let us evaluate the magnitude of θ in (7.4) for which a nontrivial solution would arise. The function $w(x,t)\equiv 0$ is the solution of (7.1)—(7.3) for $\xi(x)\equiv 0$, and for this solution we have

$$J(0) = \left[\int_0^1 \chi^2(x)\mathrm{d}x\right]^{1/2} = \left[\int_0^1 x^2(1-x)^2\mathrm{d}x\right]^{1/2} = \frac{1}{\sqrt{30}} = 0.1826. \qquad (7.5)$$

If we take another norm, sometimes simpler in computations, then we have

$$J^0(0) = \int_0^1 |\chi(x)|\,\mathrm{d}x = \int_0^1 |x(1-x)|\,\mathrm{d}x = \int_0^1 x(1-x)\mathrm{d}x = \frac{1}{6} = 0.17. \qquad (7.6)$$

It means that for $\theta \geqslant 0.1826$ in L_2-metric and for $\theta \geqslant 0.17$ in the metric (7.6), the trivial solution $\xi(x)\equiv 0$ and $w(x,t)\equiv 0$ is the solution of the problem. Hence, a case of interest is when $\theta < 0.17$ in (7.5) or (7.6), for $\chi(x)=x(1-x)$.

2. Given $\theta > 0$ in (7.4), let $\chi(x)=\theta\sqrt{\delta}$ for $x\in[0,\delta]$ and $x(x)\equiv 0$ for $x\in(\delta,1)$. Then in the metric (7.4) we have

$$J(0) = \left[\int_0^\delta \frac{\theta^2}{\delta}\mathrm{d}x\right]^{1/2} = \theta$$

for any $\delta \in (0,1]$ including $\delta \to 0$ for which $\chi(x)\to\infty$ as $x\in[0,\delta]$.

Similarly, for $\chi(x)=\theta/\delta$, $x\in[0,\delta]$ and $\chi(x)\equiv 0$, $x\in(\delta,1]$, we have in the metric (7.6):

$$J^*(0) = \int_0^\delta \frac{\theta}{\delta}\mathrm{d}x = \theta, \quad \text{for any } \delta \in (0,1].$$

Of course, one can change the function $\chi(x)$ on $[0,\delta]$ keeping the same value of the integrals.

It means that metrics (7.4), (7.6) are good only for $\theta=0$ (*exact concidence* solution, cf. [4, Section 1.2, Formula (1.5)], otherwise the metrics (7.4), (7.6) are inadequate providing same optimal solutions for a bunch of different functions, whatever small $\theta>0$ may be. Vice versa, for a fixed $\chi(x)$ the metrics in (7.4), (7.6) allow quite different initial functions $\xi(x)$ to produce different exact solution $w(x, t)$ that render the same "proximity" to $\chi(x)$, causing rampant instability in the solution of the problem; this instability can be seen in many graphs in [4].

The question of an adequate metric in (7.4) or other devices which may be required to stabilize the problem by exclusion of physically unreasonable $\chi(x)$ (or, vice versa, wildly oscillation $\xi(x)$ and $w(x,t)$ for a fixed $\chi(x)$) in the case when

$$0 < \inf_\xi J(\xi) \leqslant \theta, \quad \forall \theta > 0 \qquad (7.7)$$

is beyond the scope of this research.

Remark 7.1 We note that deficiency of the metrics (7.4), (7.6) is most visible when a solution for $\xi(x)$ is sought within the entire functional space. If a direct method on a class of functions is used, then the instability caused by the metrics (7.4), (7.6) is tempered; for example, a direct method with the use of multiquadrics excludes automatically delta-functions and functions with too steep slopes and high peaks. That is why we can use the integral (6.5) in Procedures 6.1, 6.2 to obtain tempered solutions if $p^0 > 0$, $p_s^0 > 0$. In contrast, Procedure 6.3 does not use integrals and is free of that flaw. In the case of positive global minimum valuse, all three procedures deliver multiple solutions if $\overline{Q}^0, \overline{Q}_s^*$ are not singletons. This is natural for the problem and presents an advantage allowing us to select a convenient solution among the available η-solutions (equi-optimal for an optimal control PDE problem).

With the intention of illustrating the application of global optimization methods and multiquadrics for direct control and solution of PDEs, we accept here the metrics (7.4) and (7.6) for numerical solution of the problem (7.1)—(7.4) as a tutorial example.

3. In accordance with (6.2), (6.3) and considering t as a special variable, we set

$$w(x,t) = \sum_{k=1}^{N} \alpha_k(t)[(x-x_k)^2 + c_k^2]^{1/2}, \quad x \in [0,1], \quad t \in [0,0.1], \quad (7.8)$$

where $\alpha_k(t)$, x_k, c_k are to be determined to yield an η-equivalent solution to the problem (7.1)—(7.4) in the sense of Definition 2.2. With $w(x,t)$ of (7.8), we have, for the derivatives in (7.1), the following expressions:

$$w_t = \frac{\partial w}{\partial t} = \sum_{k=1}^{N} \frac{d\alpha_k(t)}{dt}[(x-x_k)^2 + c_k^2]^{1/2},$$

$$w_{xx} = \frac{\partial^2 w}{\partial x^2} = \sum_{k=1}^{N} \alpha_k(t)c_k^2[(x-x_k)^2 + c_k^2]^{-3/2}. \quad (7.9)$$

For the general term in (7.9), we should have, due to (7.1):

$$w_t - w_{xx} = \frac{d\alpha_k(t)}{dt}[(x-x_k)^2 + c_k^2]^{1/2} - \alpha_k(t)c_k^2[(x-x_k)^2 + c_k^2]^{-3/2} = 0, \quad (7.10)$$

whence, fixing $x = \tilde{x} \in [0,1]$, we get

$$\frac{d\alpha_k(t)}{\alpha_k(t)} = \frac{c_k^2 dt}{[(\tilde{x}-x_k)^2 + c_k^2]^2},$$

$$\alpha_k(t) = r_k \exp \frac{c_k^2 t}{[(\tilde{x}-x_k)^2 + c_k^2]^2}, \quad r_k \neq 0, \quad (7.11)$$

yielding one parameter family of MQ-functions (7.8) with $\alpha_k(t)$ of (7.11) that satisfy the heat equation (7.1) exactly at $x = \tilde{x}$. By varying $\tilde{x}$, one can choose a surface with arbitrarily precise fit to (7.1) in a particular neighborhood $N_\delta(\tilde{x})$, uniformly with respect to r_k, x_k, c_k. This opens the way of constructing a cover based on a choice of $\{\tilde{x}_i\}$ with automatic precise fit to (7.1), (7.2). This approach needs further research. Here, we construct an η-equivalent solution in the form of a one piece surface for the entire region $X \times [0, T]$. To satisfy (7.2), it is reuired that

$$w(0,t) = \sum_{k=1}^{N} r_k(x_k^2 + c_k^2)^{1/2} \exp \frac{c_k^2 t}{[(\tilde{x} - x_k)^2 + c_k^2]^2} \equiv 0, \quad (7.13)$$

$$w(1,t) = \sum_{k=1}^{N} r_k[(1-x_k)^2 + c_k^2]^{1/2} \exp \frac{c_k^2 t}{[(\tilde{x} - x_k)^2 + c_k^2]^2} \equiv 0. \quad (7.12)$$

Due to (7.3), the function $\xi(x)$ is given by the relation:

$$w(x,0) = \sum_{k=1}^{N} r_k[(x-x_k)^2 + c_k^2]^{1/2} = \xi(x), \quad (7.14)$$

which is independent of the choice of $\tilde{x} \in [0,1]$.

Now, to solve the problem (7.1)–(7.4), we have to determine r_k, $\tilde{x}$, x_k, c_k yielding the best fit to (7.1), (7.12) and (7.13) and such that the integral (7.4) be less than a given $\theta > 0$ for $\chi(x) = x(1-x)$, some $\tilde{x} \in [0,1]$ and

$$w(x,T) = w(x,0.1) = \sum_{k=1}^{N} r_k[(x-x_k)^2 + c_k^2]^{1/2} \exp \frac{0.1 c_k^2}{[(\tilde{x} - x_k)^2 + c_k^2]^2}. \quad (7.15)$$

Once $J(\xi) \leqslant \theta$, the initial temperature distribution $\xi(x)$ is given by (7.14) with known r_k, x_k, c_k. For $3N$ parameters, we have two identities (7.12), (7.13) and one minimization (7.4). Since exponents $e^{c_i t}$, $i = 1, 2, \cdots$, are linearly independent if $c_i \neq c_j$ for $i \neq j$, we see that (7.12), (7.13) cannot be satisfied exactly unless we have pairwise equal exponents in (7.12), (7.13) that cancel out if

$$x_k = x_{k+1}, \quad c_k = c_{k+1}, \quad r_k = -r_{k+1}, \quad k = 1, 3, 5, \cdots \quad (7.16)$$

However, in this case we return to the trivial solution $w(x,t) \equiv 0$ by virtue of (7.8), (7.11), (7.16). This means that the boundary conditions (7.2) cannot be fulfilled exactly within the class of functions (7.8), (7.11). Thus, if we are going to use multiquadrics (7.8), we have to accept η-equivalent solutions *vis-a-vis* (7.1), (7.2).

Remark 7.2 Equations (7.1), (7.2) can be satisfied exactly by some other functions. For example, we can take

$$w(x,t) = \sum_{k=1}^{N} \frac{r_k}{\pi k} e^{-\pi^2 k^2 t} \sin \pi k x \quad (7.17)$$

and try to meet (7.4) by an appropriate choice of r_k. The possibility of using a Fourier series is mentioned in [4, Section 8.2.1] for the case when $\chi(x)$ can be represented by a Fourier sine series, with the indication that computations via the quasi-reversibility method become unstable for $T > 0.2$ (see [4, Section 9] about stability of numerical integration of parabolic systems induced by quasi-reversibility method). Using a global optimization method, we do not need Fourier coefficients for $\chi(x)$; computations are stable and we get $J(\xi) < 0.007$ for $N = 1$, $r_1 = 2.175$, with $\xi(x) = 0.6920 \sin \pi x$. However, such specific expansions (in one or two dimensions) can be used only for specific PDE problems whereas the multiquadric expansions are more universal, multidimensional and can serve many different PDE problems, if we accept η-equivalent solutions.

Returning to our example, we shall demonstrate that an acceptable η-solution can be obtained within the class of MQ-functions. We observe that $(x-x_k)^2 \leqslant 1$, if $x \in [0,1]$ and $x_k \in [0,1]$. Let $N=1$, $\tilde{x}=0$, $x_1=0.5$, $c_1=5$, $r_1=0.033$, then the fit in (7.10) is $\eta_1 < 0.000132$ and in (7.12)−(7.14) we have

$$w(0,t)=w(1,t)=0.033(0.25+25)^{1/2} \exp \frac{25t}{25 \cdot 25^2}=0.166 e^{0.04t} < 0.167, \quad \text{for all } t \in [0,0.1];$$

$$w(x,0)=0.033[(x-0.5)^2+25]^{1/2}=\xi(x), \quad \xi(0)=\xi(1)=0.166,$$

and since $(x-0.5)^2 \leqslant 1/4$, so $0.165 \leqslant w(x,0) \leqslant 0.166$ for all $x \in [0,1]$.

For $t=T=0.1$, we have

$$w(x,0.1) \cong 0.03313[(x-0.5)^2+25]^{1/2}, \quad \text{for all } \tilde{x} \in [0,1],$$

so that $0.1656 \leqslant w(x,0.1) \leqslant 0.1665$, and with $w(x,0.1) \cong 0.17$, we get

$$J(\xi) = \left[\int_0^1 [0.17 - x(1-x)]^2 \, dx \right]^{1/2} = 0.075,$$

which is more than two times better fit compared to (7.5), however, at the expense of η-equivalent solutions with $\eta_0 = 0.167$ regarding boundary conditions, and $\eta_1 < 0.000132$ regarding the equation (7.1), for all $\tilde{x} \in [0,1]$. If $\theta \geqslant 0.075$, this is a θ-optimal η-equivalent solution of the problem.

Following [12, pp. 133, 148], we can add to (7.8) polynomial terms or other interpolants. In our case, adding a constant to (7.8) does not disturb the fit to PDE (7.1) and may improve the fit to the boundary conditions (7.2). So, keeping $N=1$, $x_1=0.5$, we take $c_1=2.5$ and

$$w=(x,t)=r_0+r_1[(x-0.5)^2+c_1^2]^{1/2} \exp \frac{c_1^2 t}{[(\tilde{x}-0.5)^2+c_1^2]^2}. \tag{7.18}$$

This yields the requirement (for $\tilde{x}=0.5$):

$$w(0,t)=w(1,t)=r_0+2.55 r_1 e^{0.16t}=0, \quad t \in [0, 0.1]. \tag{7.19}$$

Since for $t \in [0, 0.1]$ we have $1 \leqslant e^{0.16t} \leqslant 1.016$, so we replace the exponent in (7.19) by its average value 1.008 and get

$$r_0+2.57 r_1=0, \quad r_1=-0.39 r_0, \quad \text{same for all } \tilde{x} \in [0,1]. \tag{7.20}$$

With these r_0, r_1 we have from (7.19):

$$w(0,t)=w(1,t)=r_0(1-0.99 e^{0.16t}),$$

$$-0.006 r_0 < w(0,t)=w(1,t) < 0.01 r_0, \quad \text{if } r_0 > 0, \tag{7.21}$$

yielding a guaranteed estimate: $|w(0,t)|=|w(1,t)| < 0.01|r_0|$. Now, to have an η-equivalent solution, that is, $|w(0,t)|=|w(1,t)| < \eta_0$, we require that

$$0.01|r_0| \leqslant \eta_0, \quad \text{i.e., } |r_0| \leqslant 100 \eta_0, \quad \eta_0 > 0. \tag{7.22}$$

For example, to have $\eta_0=0.06$, as above, we require that $|r_0| \leqslant 6.00$. Substituting (7.20) into (7.18), we have for $t=0.1$ and all $\tilde{x} \in [0,1]$:

$$w=r_0\{1-0.396[(x-0.5)^2+6.25]^{1/2}\}=r_0 \varnothing(x). \tag{7.23}$$

It remains to solve one parameter minimization problem:

$$\min_{|r_0|\leqslant 6} J = \min_{|r_0|\leqslant 6}\left\{\int_0^1 [r_0\phi(x)-x(1-x)]^2 dx\right\}^{1/2} \leqslant \theta. \tag{7.24}$$

We calculate the optimal value $r_0=6.00$. Taking $r_0=6.00$, we obtain the value $J(\xi)=0.05$ in (7.24), the actual value of $\eta_0 = 0.01|r_0| = 0.06$, and the required initial temperature distribution

$$\xi(x)=w(x,0)=6\{1-0.39[(x-0.5)^2+6.25]^{1/2}\}. \tag{7.25}$$

The boundary conditions fit (7.21): $-0.04 < w(0,t)=w(1,t) < 0.06$. Howver, fit to the equation (7.1) is poorer: $\eta_1=0.19$, due to the smaller $c_1=2.5$.

It is clear that with $N>1$ and without simplifying adjustments, the MQ-solution can be improved, yielding smaller η_0, η_1 and θ (at the expense of a larger volume of computations).

According to Procedures 6.1~6.3 above, there may be several solution schemes, equivalent in the limit if an exact solution can be obtained but different vis-a-vis η solutions and involving different amount of computations. A general scheme can be described as follows. One takes an MQ-expansion (7.8) and forms a functional

$$\min_{q\in\overline{Q}}\psi(\mathbf{q}) = \min_{q\in\overline{Q}}\Big[\beta_0\int_x |w_t - w_{xx}| du + \beta_1\int_0^T |w(0,t)| dt + \beta_2\int_0^T |w(1,t)| dt$$

$$+\beta_3\int_0^1 |w(\mathbf{x},T)-\chi(\mathbf{x})| d\mathbf{x}\Big], \quad \mathbf{q}=\{\mathbf{r}_k,\mathbf{x}_k,c_k\}\in\overline{Q}, \tag{7.26}$$

where $\beta_i\geqslant 0$, $i=0,1,2,\cdots$, are weighting coefficients for different components. In our example, with $c_1=5$, we have almost exact fit ($\eta_1<0.0001$) to PDE (7.1) and the scheme is simplified ($\beta_0=0$). If one needs differentiability of integrands in (7.26), then absolute values in (7.26) can be squared and the L_2-norm (7.4) applied instead. However, the norms in (7.26) are less sensitive around zero and simpler in computations with derivative-free and variation-free full global optimization methods. The solution for $\mathbf{q}$ in (7.26) is generally not a singleton but a set $\overline{Q}^0$ which corresponds to a set of η-equivalent θ-optimal solutions; see Section 8.

It is quite possible that within the class of MQ-functions (7.8) we may have

$$\inf_{\xi\in MQ} J(\xi) > 0, \tag{7.27}$$

despite the fact that over the entire functional space we have, under certain conditions, see [4]:

$$\inf_{\xi} J(\xi) = 0. \tag{7.28}$$

In practice, however, we do not need (7.28). For a given $\theta>0$, we need only an η solution for which

$$\inf_{\xi\in MQ} J(\xi) \leqslant \theta. \tag{7.29}$$

For many PDE problems this can be achieved within the class of multiquadrics. The use of MQ-functions with a full global optimization method excludes delta-functions and provides for stability of computations, otherwise not guaranteed under the metrics (7.4), (7.6) usually employed in functional spaces.

8 Further Numerical Investigation

To illustrate how to use functionals of the type (7.26) and improve the solution (7.25), we return to the representation (7.18) and use a two parameter global optimization procedure.

Take an MQ-function (7.18) with $c_1^2=25$. Consider the average value $e^{0.04t}\cong 1.002$ on $[0,0.1]$, yielding in (7.18):

$$w(0, t)=w(1, t)=r_0+5.035 r_1. \tag{8.1}$$

Then the functional (7.26) becomes ($\beta_1 T=\beta_2 T=\frac{1}{2}\beta$, $\beta_3=1$, $\beta_0=0$ due to $\eta_1<0.0012$ for $|r_1^0|<0.3$; see Table 1):

$$\min_{r_0, r_1} \psi(r_0, r_1)=\beta(r_0+5.035 r_1)^2+\int_0^1 [r_0+r_1\phi(x)-x(1-x)^2]dx, \tag{8.2}$$

where we squared the absolute values to allow for the use of gradient methods and denoted, cf. (7.18), for $c_1^2=25$, $t=0.1$:

$$\phi(x)=1.004[(x-0.5)^2+25]^{1/2}. \tag{8.3}$$

Solving problem (8.2) for different β, we find the dependence of the solution on β and see that a set of η solutions is not a singleton.

For $\beta=1$, the results are summarized in the followong table (obtained with SHARP EL-586 pocket calculator and five point trapezoidal integration on $[0,1]$) $a_1<w(0, t)=w(1, t)<a_2$.

Table 1

β	r_0^0	r_1^0	$J(\xi)$	a_1	a_2	η_0
1	1.591	−0.298	0.1035	0.087	0.094	0.094

Note that determinant of the gradient equation $\nabla \psi=0$ for r_0 and r_1 is of the order 0.01 (for $\beta=0$, it is ~ 0.000006), so that the system of gradient equations is extremely ill-conditioned. It is *always* the case if there is a *set* of optimal solutions. That is why we have to refrain from using gradient equations and apply instead a set-to-set full global optimization methods [13, 19, 20]. If a point-to-point limited global optimization method is applied, then, due to the existence of a *set* of θ-optimal η equivalent solutions, the answers may be different depending on the method employed, on its numerical realization and on the precision of computations. Such deviations are normal for a point-to-point global method applied to a problem with multiple solutions. Clearly, if a method is local, it may fail altogether, indicating the absence of a solution for a problem that has a solution obtainable by a global method.

References

[1] J. Hadamard, *Lectures on Cauchy's Problem in Linear Partial Differential Equations*, Yale, (1923), reprinted by Dover, New York, (1952).

[2] E. T. Copson, *Partial Differential Equations*, Cambridge University, Cambridge, (1975).

[3] P. R. Garabedian, *Partial Differential Equations*, John Wiley & Sons, New York, (1964).

[4] R. Lattes and J. -L. Lions, *Méthode de Quasi-Reversibilité et Applications*, Dunod, Paris, (1967).

[5] R. Courant, K. O. Friedrichs and H. Lewy, Uber die partiellen Differenzengleichungen der Mathematischen Physik, *Math. Annalen* 100, 32—74(1928).

[6] B. Epstein, *Partial Differential Equations*, R. E. Krieger Publ., New York, (1975).

[7] G. A. Baker, V. A. Dougalis and O. Karakasian, On multistep Galerkin discretizations of semilinear hyperbolic and parabolic equations, *Nonlinear Analysis* 4, 579—597(1980).

[8] J. Douglas and T. Dupont, Galerkin methods for parabolic equations, *SIAM J. Num. Anal.* 7, 575—626(1970).

[9] I. Farago, Finite element method for solving nonlinear parabolic equations, *International J. Computers and Mathematics with Applications* 21(1), 59—69(1991).

[10] I. Farage, Finite element method for solving nonlinear parabolic systems, *International J. Computers and Mathematics with Applications* 21(1), 49—57(1991).

[11] R. L. Hardy, Theory and applications of the multiquadric-biharmonic method (20 years of discovery, 1968—1988), *International J. Computers and Mathematics with Applications* 19(8/9), 163—208 (1990).

[12] E. J. Kansa, Multiquadrics—A scattered data approximation scheme with applications to computational fluid dynamics, *International J. Computers and Mathematics with Applications* 19 (8/9), I—Surface approximations and partial derivative estimates, 127—145, II—Solution to parabolic, hyperbolic and elliptic partial differential equations, 147—161(1990).

[13] E. A. Galperin, *The Cubic Algorithm for Optimization and Control*, NP Research Publ., Montréal, (1990).

[14] D. Spring, Convex integration of nonlinear systems of partial differential equations, *Ann. Inst. Fourier. de l'Univ. de Grenoble* 33 (3), 121—177(1983).

[15] M. L. Gromov, Convex integration of differential relations, *Math. USSR Izvestia* 7, 329—343 (1973).

[16] R. Penrose, A generalized inverse for matrices, *Proc. Cambridge Philos. Soc.* 51, 406—413(1955).

[17] R. Penrose, On best approximate solution of linear matrix equations, *Proc. Cambridge Philos. Soc.* 52, 17—19(1956).

[18] A. Ben-Israel and T. N. E. Greville, *Generalized Inverses: Theory and Applications*, J. Wiley & Sons, (1974).

[19] S. H. Chew and Q. Zheng, Integral global optimization, *Lecture Notes in Economics and Mathematical Systems*, Vol. 298, Springer-Verlag, (1988).

[20] E. A. Galperin and Q. Zheng, *New Theory of Continuous Games*, NP Research Publ., Montreal, (1990).

Automatic Design of Optical Thin-Film Systems-Merit Function and Numerical Optimization Method*

Abstract: A combination of analytical synthesis methods and automatic numerical design is currently used for the synthesis of optical thin-film systems. The validity of this combination strongly depends not only on the optimization technique chosen but also on the construction of the merit function used in the automatic design. The present paper introduces a statistical testing method by which global extrema of a merit function can be found with a certain probalility. Some examples of the construction of the merit function based on analytical synthesis are gien.

1 Introduction

Optical interference coatings are widely used for optics, spectroscopy, laser optics, solar energy, and space technology. For these various applications not only are different transmittances and reflectances of optical thin-film systems specified but so too are the spectral absorption, phase change, and state of polarization. Dielectric multilayer coatings have been used frequently. However, in recent years much attention has been paid to the design and manufacture of absorbing film systems. For an interference film system of average complexity, a satisfactory design can be obtained with analytical synthesis methods.[1] However, for some cases in which a system with a specific spectral behavior is required,[2,3] the analytical synthesis methods are too complicated or even impossible to apply. For such cases, gradient, dampedleast-squares, or orthogonal methods, etc. for automatic design of optical thin-film systems have been developed. However, these traditional methods can reach only local extrema, which often are far from the desired goal because any merit function in the design of optical thin-film systems is usually complicated and multimodal. It is, therefore, most important to select a refinement method that can escape from local minima and find the overall minimum. Dobrowolski[4,5] has done excellent work on the subject. We have found that the global extrema can be approached with a certain probability by using a statistical testing method.

---

* In collaboration with Tang J F. Reprinted from J. Ope. Soe. Am. , 1982, 72(11):1522—1528.

2 Method for Finding Global Extrema

2.1 Grid Method and Random Search Approach

The originl methods for finding global extrema are the grid method and random searching. Let a merit function $Y=F(x)$ be an n-dimensional function at domain D in n-dimensional space. Domain D, an n-dimensional rectangle, is defined as
$$D=\{x|a_i \leqslant x_i \leqslant b_i, i=1,2,\cdots,n\}.$$
The so-called grid method checks the variation ranges of all components in n-dimensional rectangular space, calculates the functional values at check points, and compares their magnitude to determine the best points corresponding to the lowest values among all points. Let range (a_i, b_i) be divided into r_i equal parts,
$$e_i=(b_i-a_i)/r_i, i=1,2,\cdots,n,$$
where the components of the check points are
$$x_i=a_i+j \cdot e_i, j=0,1,2,\cdots,r_i, i=1,2,\cdots,n.$$
The global extrema at domain D can be found by using the grid method to a certain precision that depends on how finely domain D is divided. Let the n-dimensional volume of the rectangular domain D be unity and the volume of each divided element be ε. Then the total amount of calculation of the functional value at each check point is
$$N \cong 1/\varepsilon.$$
Random searching for global extrema has also been suggested. Let the volume of D be unity again. The probability that at least one point falls into a small domain of volume ε by random and uniform sampling over D is $P=1-(1-\varepsilon)^N$. To find an optimization domain of volume ε in a unit volume of n-dimensional rectangular space, the total amount of sampling is
$$N=[\ln(1-p)\ln(1-\varepsilon)] \cong c_1/\varepsilon,$$
where $c_1=\ln[1/(1-p)]$. To have a probability of 0.9, then $c_1=2.3$.

The main difficulty in using the grid method and random search approach is the large number of calculations needed. For instance, if the variables are ten-dimensional, then even though only four different values are taken for each component, the total number of calculations of the function value is so great ($N \cong 4^{10}$) that it is not practical.

2.2 Model of a Method for Finding Global Extrema

The total amount of sampling will be manageable if ε is not too small. However, if only the lowest points are accepted after a large amount of sampling, other useful information provided by the sampling will be lost. Therefore it would be advantageous to reduce the search region by selecting useful information provided after a limited amount of sampling. Also, the process of reducing the search volume can be continued to from an iterative procedure. According to this idea, we suggested a method for finding global extrems[6].

Let $F(x)$ be a continuous function at domain D in n-dimensional space $\mathbb{R}^n$. Cutting the function $Y=F(x)$ with $Y=c_0$, a level set H_0 is obtained:

$$H_0 = \{x \mid F(x) \leqslant c_0, \ x \in D\}. \tag{2.1}$$

The term H_0 contains points whose function values are not greater than c_0 (see Fig. 1). If c_0 is so small that it is below the global extrema, then H_0 will be empty. Therefore we assume that H_0 is not empty. Then the mean value c_1 of $F(x)$ is calculated in H_0. The mean value c_1 must be less than c_0, i. e., $c_0 \leqslant c_1$. In a new level set obtained by cutting the function $Y = F(x)$ with $Y = c_1$, we have

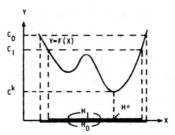

Fig. 1 Series of level sets and mean values

$$H_1 = \{x \mid F(x) \leqslant c_1, \ x \varepsilon D\}. \tag{2.2}$$

Similarly, the mean value c_2 of $F(x)$ in H_1 can be found, and $c_1 \geqslant c_2$, and so on. Eventually we get a series of mean values, $c_0 \geqslant c_1 \geqslant c_2 \geqslant \cdots \geqslant c_k \geqslant \cdots$, and a series of monotonically descending level sets, $H_0, H_1, \cdots, H_k, \cdots$. Let $\lim\limits_{k \to \infty} c_k = c^*$ and $\lim\limits_{k \to \infty} H_k = H^*$. Then it can be proved that c^* is just the global extremum of $F(x)$ in D, and $H^* = [x \mid F(x) = c^*, \ x \in D]$ is the assembly of such variables x, at which $F(x)$ is the overall minimum in D. In the above procedure, c_k will not be the mean value exactly because of computational errors and for other reasons. If we have a series of arbitrary monotonically descending sets $c_0 \geqslant c_1 \geqslant c_2 \geqslant \cdots c_k \geqslant \cdots$, then $\lim\limits_{k \to \infty} c_k = c$. Let

$$H_k = \{x \mid F(x) \leqslant c_k, \ x \in D\}; \tag{2.3}$$

then the sufficient and necessary condition for c being the global extrema in D is c_k and $m_k \to 0 \ (k \to \infty)$, where m_k is the mean value of $F(x)$ at H_{k-1}. In addition, if σ_k^2 is the variance of the function $F(x)$ at H_{k-1}, i. e., if σ_k^2 is the mean value of $[F(x) - C_{k-1}]^2$ at H_{k-1}, then the sufficient and necessary condition can also be expressed as

$$\sigma_k^2 \to 0 \quad (k \to \infty). \tag{2.4}$$

In both cases, $\lim\limits_{k \to \infty} H_k = H_c$ is just the assembly of variables x, at which $F(x) = c$ is the global extremum at D.

2.3 Statistical Testing

It can be seen that the above algorithm model is reduced to finding a series of mean values $\{c_k\}$ and a series of level sets $\{H_k\}$. However, a series of mean values is equivalent to computing a series of n-dimensional integrals, and it is even more complicated to find the level sets. But the algorithm model can be realized by using a statistical testing approach.

Consider a continuous function $F(x)$ in n-dimensional rectangular space

$$D = \{x \mid a_i \leqslant x_i \leqslant b_i, \ i = 1, 2, \cdots, n\}, \tag{2.5}$$

which is an initial domain. The aim is to find the global minimum and the corresponding variable set. Let two integral numbers m and t be chosen, where m is the number of first-round sampling points and t is the statistical index. Then the following five-step iteration procedure is performed.

Step 1: Producing H_0 and C_0.

Let $\xi=(\xi_1,\xi_2,\cdots,\xi_n)$ be n independent computer-generated random numbers. [ξ_i is a random number, $i=1,2,\cdots,n$, which is uniformly distributed in $(0,1)$ and is available in the form of a standard computer function.]

Setting $x_i=a_i+(b_i-a_i)\xi_i$, $i=1,2,\cdots,n$ to get random sampling $x^{(k)}$, $k=1,2,\cdots,m$, calculate the value of $F[X^{(k)}]$, $k=1,2,\cdots,m$. Compare their function values after sampling and accept the lowest function values F_i, $i=1,2,\cdots,t$, which are arranged in descending order of magnitude, i.e., $F_1 \geqslant F_2 \geqslant F_3 \cdots \geqslant F_t$. At the same time a set W is obtained that contains t sampling points of x corresponding to the accepted t values of F. With increasing sampling, t functional values in F are to be continuously replaced by smaller ones, and t corresponding points of x in W, too.

The set W is considered to be an approximate H_0, and the largest functional value F_1 in F is taken as C_0. As for all the points in W, $F(x) \leqslant C_0$. Besides, the mean value in F, $(1/t)(F_1+F_2+\cdots+F_t)$, can be taken as an approximate mean value C_1 at H_0.

Step 2: Creating a New Search Region.

To keep computation continuous and to form an iterative procedure, we create a new n-dimensional rectangular space D_1 containing W by using statistical methods in the set W. Let η_i and ξ_i be the minimum and maximum of the i th component in set W, respectively,

$$\eta_i=\min\{x_i^{(1)}, x_i^{(2)}, \cdots, x_i^{(t)}\}, \tag{2.6}$$

$$\xi_i=\max\{x_i^{(1)}, x_i^{(2)}, \cdots, x_i^{(t)}\}, \quad i=1,2,\cdots,n. \tag{2.7}$$

Then the expressions

$$a_{1i}=\eta_i-(\xi_i-\eta_i)/(t-1), \tag{2.8}$$

$$b_{1i}=\xi_i+(\xi_i-\eta_i)/(t-1), \quad i=1,2,\cdots,n \tag{2.9}$$

can form a new search region

$$D_1=(x\,|\,a_{1i} \leqslant x_i \leqslant b_{1i}, \quad i=1,2,\cdots,n). \tag{2.10}$$

Since we know that

$$W \subset D,$$

then

$$D_1 \subset D.$$

Step 3: Continuing the Iterative Procedure.

Make random sampling at D_1 such that

$$x_i=a_{1i}+(b_{1i}-a_{1i}) \cdot \xi_i, \quad i=1,2,\cdots,n. \tag{2.11}$$

Calculating the function values F, obtain a new set W containing t points and a new set F of functional values arranged in descending order of magnitude, just as in Step 1. With increasing sampling, t functional values in F and points in W are continuously to be renewed, until the largest one in present F is less than C_1, i.e., $F_1 \leqslant C_1$. W will be considered to be an approximate H_1 and the mean value in F an approximate C_2. An n-dimensional rectangular D_2 containing W can be obtained from the present set W. Repeating the procedure, we will have a series of monotonically reducing mean values $\{C_k\}$ and an n-dimensional rectangular set $\{D_k\}$.

Step 4: Iteration Solution.

The least function F_t at the end of each iteration can be taken as an approximate solution to judge how well the performance fits the desired goal.

Step 5: Criterion of Convergence.

Variance

$$D_f = \frac{1}{t-1} \sum_{i=1}^{t} (F_i - \overline{F})^2, \quad \overline{F} = \left(\frac{1}{t}\right) \sum_{i=1}^{t} F_i \qquad (2.12)$$

or the volume (or length) of search region can be used as a criterion to judge whether to stop the computation at the present iteration. Figure 2 is a block diagram of the algorithm.

In the final part of this section, we demonstrate the use of the statistical testing

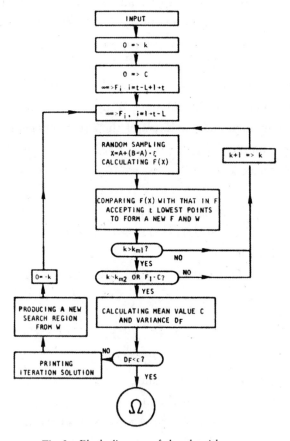

Fig. 2 Block diagram of the algorithm

Input: (1) Statistical index t, (2) minimum and maximum sampling number k_{m1}, k_{m2}, (3) original search region A, B, (4) remaining number L, (5) precision ε.

technique in the design of several different thin-film coatings. To facilitate easy comparison of the results with those of other well-known techniques, these design problems are taken from the survey by Bloom[7]. There are three different problems:

Table 1 High Reflector Using Gradient Method and Statistical Testing[a]

Layer	Gradient			Statistical Testing			
	Starting Design	Steps		Initial Search Region	Steps		
		10	20		10	18	46
1H	0.6000	1.0207	1.0000	0.0—2.000	0.9743	1.0010	1.0005
2L	0.4000	0.9653	1.0000	0.0—2.000	1.0174	1.0032	1.0005
3H	0.6000	0.9803	1.0000	0.0—2.000	0.9845	0.9971	1.0005
4L	1.2000	0.9932	1.0001	0.0—2.000	1.0182	1.0066	1.0005
5H	0.8000	1.0319	1.0000	0.0—2.000	0.9331	0.9905	1.0005
6L	1.6000	1.0380	1.0000	0.0—2.000	1.0490	1.0096	1.0005
7H	1.6000	1.0445	1.0000	0.0—2.000	1.0207	1.0091	1.0005

[a] Target: $R=1.0$; one point only at $\lambda=1\mu m$. The refractive indices are $n(H)=2.3$, $n(L)=1.45$, $n(S)=1.52$, air medium. Thicknesses are in units of quarter-waves centered at 1 μm.

Table 2 Same Optimization Problem as in Table 1 Except that the Target is $R=0.93$, 11 Equally Spaced Points from $\lambda=0.9-1.1\mu m$

Layer	Gradient			Statistical Testing		
	Starting Design	Steps		Initial Search Region	Steps	
		10	20		10	18
1H	0.6000	0.7859	0.9696	0.0—2.000	0.9688	0.9915
2L	0.4000	1.1024	0.9920	0.0—2.000	0.9668	0.9869
3H	0.6000	1.2543	0.9941	0.0—2.000	1.0035	0.9931
4L	1.2000	0.9142	0.9918	0.0—2.000	0.9995	0.9927
5H	0.8000	0.9162	1.0014	0.0—2.000	1.0046	0.9854
6L	1.6000	0.9523	0.9865	0.0—2.000	0.9754	0.9919
7H	1.6000	0.8642	0.9828	0.0—2.000	1.0014	0.9885
Q.M.S. $\times 10^3 =$			9.0785	—	4.1953	4.1150

Table 3 Broadband Antireflection Coatings for the Visible[a]

Design	1 Original	2 Damped Least Squares (20 steps)	3 Grad. (20 steps)	4[b] From Q.W.S. (95 steps)	Initial Search Region	Statistical Testing Steps	
						20	32[c]
1L	0.1960	0.1960	0.1960	0.7008	0.0—1.000	0.8468	0.8312
2H	0.0980	0.1291	0.1408	0.0905	0.0—1.000	0.1055	0.0989
3L	0.2695	0.2652	0.2248	0.2646	0.0—1.000	0.1904	0.1964
4H	0.3330	0.4064	0.4856	0.4001	0.0—1.000	0.6077	0.5953
5L	0.1470	0.1230	0.0707	0.0993	0.0—1.000	0.0299	0.0128
6H	0.3350	0.3686	0.4077	0.3900	0.0—1.000	0.3428	0.4041
7L	0.5735	0.5730	0.5480	0.5535	0.0—1.000	0.5200	0.5103
Q.M.S. $\times 10^3 =$	2.48	1.73	1.32	1.30	(Q.M.S. consists of 31 equally spaced points at $\lambda=400-700$nm)	2.073	0.1103

[a] Thicknesses are in units of quarter-waves centered at 1 μm. $n(S)=1.52$, $n(L)=1.45$, $n(H)=$dispersive about 2.4 or fixed at 2.4.
[b] The reflectance of this desingn is $<0.2\%$ over the range $\lambda=420-620$nm and is 0.25% at $\lambda=660$nm.
[c] The reflectance is $<0.2\%$ over the range $\lambda=410-675$nm.

(1) Designing a high reflector consisting of seven alternate high-and low-index layers whose indices are fixed at $n(H)=2.3$, $n(L)=1.45$. The thicknesses are the only desing parameters. Target: $R=1.0$, one point only at $\lambda=1\mu m$.

(2) Same optimization poroblem as in (2.1) except that the target is $R=0.93$ at 11 equally spaced points from $\lambda=0.9$ to $\lambda=1.1\mu m$.

(3) Broadband antireflection coatings in the visible using only two materials.

The results are summarized in Tables 1—4. The results from the gradient and damped least-squares methods are quoted from Ref. 7. In problem (2.1), for the statistical testing method, the quadratic merit function consists of two points at $\lambda=1.000\mu m$ and $\lambda=1.001\mu m$ rather than one single point because of the easy arrangement of the program. The initial search region for each layer thickness is from 0 to 2 quarter-waves centered at $\lambda=1\mu m$. In this case the optimum solution should be a quarter-wave stack centered at $\lambda=1.005\mu m$. After 46 steps of iteration, this exact solution was reached (see Table 1). The theoretical solution of the second problem is a quarter-wave stack at $\lambda=0.99\mu m$ rather than at $\lambda=1\mu m$. Table 2 shows that, after 20 steps, the statistical testing technique approached a desing that is closer to the expected solution. Table 3 shows some results in the design of a broadband antireflection coating for the entine visible spectrum using only two materials—SiO_2 and TiO_2. Column 1 of Table 3, as an original desingn, was obtained initially by using Herpin equivalent indices and a great deal of trial and error on the computer. Columns 2 and 3 of Table 3 show the solutions obtained by the damped-least-squares and gradient methods. Column 4 of Talbe 4 shows the conversion by the gradient method of a quarter-wave stack, which is a highreflection coating, to an almost perfect antireflection coating on the 95th iteration. In these processes, the refractive index of TiO_2 is taken from a disperson table centered about $n=2.4$. Instead of using a starting design, we take an original search region from zero to a quarter-wave at $\lambda=1\mu m$ for each layer thickness. The solutions on the 20th and 32nd iterations are shown in Table 3. In these designs the TiO_2 films have a fixed index of 2.4, and no dispersion is taken into account. Their performance is shown in Fig. 3. Finally, we tried to desing a beam splitter that would give a reflectance of around 0.5 at normal incidence between $\lambda=0.9$ and $\lambda=1.1\mu m$. This is the optimization problem in which the gradient method failed to get any solution by starting from a design G, HLH, A centered at $0.1\mu m$. The result obtained by the statistical testing method is shown in Table 4.

Table 4 Beam Splitter for 0.9—1.1μm[a]

Layer	Initial Search Region	Steps (11)
1H	0.0—1.000	0.5076
2L	0.0—1.000	0.9127
3H	0.0—1.000	1.1930

[a] Thicknesses are in units of quarter-waves centered at 1 μm designed by the statistical testing program. $n(s)=1.52$, $n(H)=2.3$, $n(L)=1.45$, air medium. Q. M. S. $=6.734\times10^{-3}$, reflectances$=0.47-0.53$ in wavelengths 0.9—1.1μm.

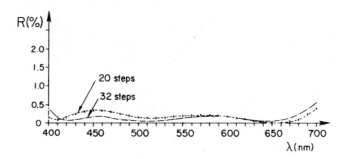

Fig. 3 Broadband antireflection coating designed by the statistical testing program as shown in Table 3

3 Some Examples of the Constructilon of Merit Fungtions

A critical step in using automatic programs for the design of thin-film systems is the construction of an appropriate merit function and the selection of the parameters that are involved in the merit function. This is even more important in the design of some special thin-film systems. Consider, for example, the design of a nonpolarizing beam splitter with zero R and T polarization at a designated wavelength and having a specified R/T ration at oblique incidence. We have tried to define the merit function directly in terms of the reflectances R_P and R_S for p- and s-polarized radiation,

$$F(x) = \sum_{i=1}^{M}(|R_{pi}-R_i^D|^2+|R_{si}-R_i^D|^2). \qquad (3.1)$$

No satisfactory solution can be obtained, even after long computations, because no suitable initial desing is known, nor can any be found by examinimg a range of designs. But we know from optical thin-film theory that, for a quarter-wave stack,

$$n_S|n_{2k+1}, n_{2k}, \cdots, n_3, n_2, n_1|n_0,$$

the reduced admittance N at the center wavelength is given by

$$N=\frac{Y}{\eta_0}=\frac{\eta_1^2\eta_3^2\cdots\eta_{2k+1}^2}{\eta_2^2\eta_4^2\cdots\eta_{2k}^2\eta_S\eta_0} \qquad (3.2)$$

The reflectance and the transmittance of the system are given, respectively, by

$$R=\left(\frac{1-N}{1+N}\right)^2 \qquad (3.3)$$

and

$$T=1-R=\frac{4N}{(1+N)^2} \qquad (3.4)$$

In the ablve expressions $\eta_0, \eta_1, \cdots \eta_{2k+1}$, and η_s are the modified admittances of the incident medium, of each layer of thin films, and of the substrate, respectively. Y is the assemble admittance. Obviously, to eliminate polarization, the reduced admittances for both p and s polarizations must equal each other and the polarization separation ΔN must equal unity, i. e.,

$$\Delta N=\frac{N_p}{N_s}=1. \qquad (3.5)$$

To achieve this in practice, quarter-wave stacks composed of three materials were devised by Thelen.[8] Various combinations of three materials are possible. Let

$$n_2 = n_4 = n_6 = \cdots = n_{2k}, \quad n_1 = n_5 = n_9 = \cdots = n_{2k-1},$$

and

$$n_3 = n_7 = n_{11} = \cdots n_{2k+1},$$

where k is and odd number. Because the reduced admittance at the center wavelength is:

$$N = \frac{\eta_1^{(k+1)} \eta_3^{(k+1)}}{\eta_2^{2k} \cdot \eta_0 \cdot \eta_s}, \tag{3.6}$$

the following two equations must hold if the polarization effect is to be eliminated and the required T/R raton satisfied:

$$\Delta N = \frac{N_P}{N_S} = 1, \tag{3.7}$$

$$\frac{4N}{(1+N)^2} = T. \tag{3.8}$$

A direct solution of the above transcendental equations is impossible. A trial-and-error approach was adopted by Thelen[8]. We chose his physical model to construct a merit function and used the method mentioned above for finding global extrems to solve the equations. A satisfactory result was obtained in this way. The merit function was

$$F(x) = W_1 (1 - \Delta N)^2 + W_2 \left[T^D - \frac{4N}{(1+N)^2} \right], \tag{3.9}$$

where W_1 and W_2 are the weight factors assigned to the polarization effect and to the desired values of (T/R), respectively. The desired values of the polarization separation and of the transmittance are 1 and T^D, respectively. Thus we used the polarization separation and the transmission to construct the merit function and used the statistical testing approach to obtain a satisfactory result. For a nonpolarizing beam splitter, it took only 1 min on the minicomputer TW-16 to get a good solution[9]. For nonpolarizing beam splitters composed of a metal layer and dielectric layers, it is doubtful whether one can find a setisfactory solution by using either a square sum or any other version of the merit function, if it is defined in terms of T and R only. According to the potential transmittance concept of absorbing thin-films systems, the absorption of a metal film not only is determined by its optical constants but also is closely dependent on the admittances of the neighboring media. As long as the admittance of the multilayer on the exit side is correctly matched, the potential transmittance of the system will be a maximum. However, there are many structures of the multilayer stack that give a matched admittance. Therefore there are other factors that will affect the choice of one structure, such as simplicity of design and ease of manufacture. In our particular design, equal potential transmittances for p and s polarizations are required instead of simplicity of desing or ease of manufacture. Now, if the thin-film structure on the incident side is also designed in such a way that it satisfies $R_p = R_s$ and yields the desired T/R ratio, then the requirements for the design of a nonpolarizing beam splitter will be fulfilled.

According to this analysis, one can independently design the multilayer for the incident and exit sides of the metal film. The merit function for the multilayer on the exit side is

$$F(x) = \sum_{i=1}^{M} \left[(\psi_{pi} - \psi_i^D)^2 + (\psi_{si} - \psi_i^D)^2 \right], \tag{3.10}$$

where ψ_{pi} and ψ_{si} are the potential transmittances for p and s polarizations, respectively, and ψ^D is the desired value.

The merit function for the multilayer on the incident side is

$$f(x) = \sum_{i=1}^{M}[(R_{pi}-R_i^D)^2+(R_{si}-R_i^D)^2]. \qquad (3.11)$$

In the desing of the nonpolarizing beam splitter, a merit function based on the above physical model led successfully to the refinement to the lowest minimum in the given search region[10]. It is possible that there are other more-complicated absorbing multilayer systems in which a merit function of this type may not give rise to a satisfactory solution.

We could use ellipsometry of thin films as an example in the identification of a thin film. It is well known that an elliptical function

$$\hat{\rho}=\frac{\hat{r}_p}{\hat{r}_s}=\frac{|\hat{r}_p|}{|\hat{r}_s|}\exp[i(\phi_p-\phi_s)] \qquad (3.12)$$

is a function of the parameters (n, d) of a dielectric film, where r_p and r_s are complex amplitude reflectances and ϕ_p and ϕ_s are phase changes on reflection for p and s polarizations, respectively. It can also be expressed as

$$\hat{\rho}=\tan\psi\exp(i\Delta), \qquad (3.13)$$

where

$$\tan\psi=\frac{|\hat{r}_p|}{|\hat{r}_s|} \qquad (3.14)$$

and

$$\Delta=\phi_p-\phi_s. \qquad (3.15)$$

The terms Δ and ψ, called the elliptical parameters, are usually those that are obtained in ellipsometery and definitely correspond to the unknown parameters of a thin film. In this case the following from of merit function can be constructed:

$$F(x)=(\Delta-\Delta^D)^2+(\psi-\psi^D)^2, \qquad (3.16)$$

where Δ and ψ are currently computed values and Δ^D and ψ^D are actual measured ones. The desired parameters that give the lowest functional value that is close to zero can be obtained simply by using the statistical testing approach. As for an absorbing thin film, there are three parameters (n,k,d) to be determined. Obviously, two equations are not enough for finding three parameters. It is desirable to measure the elliptical parameters twice light incident upon each side of a sample so that two sets of elliptical parameters are obtained. Then the merit function can be

$$F(x) = \sum_{i=1}^{2}[(\Delta_i-\Delta_i^D)^2+(\psi_i-\psi_i^D)^2]. \qquad (3.17)$$

A technique that involes surface plasma waves on a metal film excited by attenuated total reflection in likely to be useful for measuring optical constants of thin films[11]. In one arrangement, a thin metal layer of the correct thickness on the base of a prism is illuminated in p-polarized light from within the prism beyond the critical angle. The coupling of the incident light to a surface plasmon on the outer surface of the metal layer is marked by a sharp rise in absorption in the metal film and by a sharp drop in internal reflectance. The reflectance resonance with angles of incidence is a sensitive function of the optical constants of the metal film and the conditions at the outer surface, so the reflectance resonance can be used to construct a merit function. To simplify the measuring procedure and to reduce computation time, we take only three reflectances in the merit function. These are the minimum reflectance at the coupling angle and two other reflectances at around the half-width. Some computation results are shown in Tables 5 and

6. Table 5 is for a metal film with a thickness of 75nm. Table 6 is for the same kind of metal layer covered with a dielectric layer, which leads to a displacement of the reflectance resonance.

Table 5 Determination of Optical Constants of a Metal Layer

	Example 1	Example 2
Expected paramters		
n	0.033	0.033
k	3.35	3.35
Assumed reflectance readings		
$R_{0(\theta_0)}$	0.0126	0.0126
$R_{1(\theta_1)}$	0.5659	0.5659
$R_{2(\theta_2)}$	0.3969	0.3969
Search region		
n	0—0.1	0—0.3
k	3.0—4.0	2.0—5.0
Final solution		
n	0.033	0.033
k	3.35	3.35
Computed reflectances		
$R_{0(\theta_0)}$	0.0124	0.0127
$R_{1(\theta_1)}$	0.5637	0.5664
$R_{2(\theta_2)}$	0.3978	0.3968

Table 6 Determination of Optical Constants of a Dielectric Layer

Expected parameters	
n	2.0
d	10.0
Assumed reflectance readings	
$R_{0(\theta_0)}$	0.0037
$R_{1(\theta_1)}$	0.4757
$R_{2(\theta_2)}$	0.3791
Search region	
n	1.7—2.3
d	5.0—15.0
Final solution	
n	1.977
d	10.157
Computed reflectances	
$R_{0(\theta_0)}$	0.0037
$R_{1(\theta_1)}$	0.4762
$R_{2(\theta_2)}$	0.3816

4 Conclusions

In this paper we have discussed a method for finding global extrema realized by the statistical testing approach and the construction of some of the merit functions used in the design of optical thin-film systems. The purpose of using a merit function in automatic numerical design is to guide the refinement procedure to a minimum of the function. Therefore the property and structure of the merit function will affect the efficiency of the refinement. In selecting the refinement method, the shape and the property of the merit function in the parameter space should be considered. Furthermore, the merit function must have a significant physical meaning in order to reflect the desired requirements. We can now see that, to succeed in automatic thin-film design, one must not only find the best mathematical method but also construct a proper merit function based on the relevant conditions.

We begin to understand the relation between automatic numerical synthesis and analytical synthesis. The analytical synthesis method is based on the optical theory of thin films, and it still cannot be replaced or ignored, despite the widespread use of computer technology and refinement methods. It has many advantages. It is highly appropriate for the solution of some problems, and the calculations are easy. Multilayer systems obtained by this method have an unambigious physical significance, and the effect of the layer parameters on the performance of the whole layer system are readily understood. For most systems the layer thicknesses are regular, and the refractive indices are available, which facilitates their manufacture. Up to now, most of the available optical interference multilayer systems have been designed by analytical methods. Of course, as we mentioned at the beginning of this paper, analytical methods have their limitations. This is exactly the problem that automatic numerical methods have been designed to overcome. Hence these two types of methods complement each other. The development of thin-film automatic numerical desing methods does not negate the validity and usefulness of the optical theory of thin films or of analytical methods.

Furthermore, on developing thin-film automatic numerical desing methods one should make full use of analytical synthesis methods. We feel strongly that it is not necessary to separate and contrast analytical and automatic design methods. The proper concept in thin-film desing is to combine them intimately. The two methods have been combined in various examples presented in this paper for the construction of merit functions and for the selection of the thin-film performances that should enter into the merit function. It should be pointed out that, in a way, the combination of the two approaches is also determined by the choice of the initial design used for the automatic design. The normal refinement method can converge only to the closest minimum of the starting point. The initial design will therefore have a significant influence on the behavior of the final system. Usually it is difficult to select an initial design that is close to the best solution. In this connection, for example, the equivalent index concept for a symmetrical system, the effective interfaces concept, or the expansion in terms of a series are significant in setting up an initial design. A beginning in this new direction has been made[12], and there is a bright future in this field for the cooperation of thin-film workers and mathematicians.

References

[1] H. A. Macleod, *Thin-Film Optical Filters* (Adam Hilger, London, 1969).
[2] J. A. Dobrowolski, "Interference filters with irregular spectral transmittance characteristics," Proc. Soc, Photo-Opt. Instrum. Eng. 50, 171—181(1974).
[3] J. E. Rogers, "Optical coating needs of the aerospoace industry," Proc. Soc. Photo-Opt. Instrum. Eng. 50, 209—213(1974).
[4] J. A. Dobrowolski, "Completely automatic synthesis of optical thin film systems," Appl. Opt. 4, 937—946(1965).
[5] J. A. Dobrowolski, "Subtractive method of optical thin-film interference filter design," Appl. Opt. 12, 1885—1893(1973).
[6] Q. Zheng, "Method for finding global extrema," Nature (China) 1, 1—2(1978).
[7] A. L. Bloom, "Refining and optimization in multilayers," Appl. Opt. 20, 66—73(1981).
[8] A. J. Thelen, "Nonpolarizing interference films inside a glass cube," Appl. Opt. 15, 2983—2985 (1976).
[9] J. F. Tang, "Theory and desing of non-polarizing beam splitters," J. Zhejiang Univ. 1, 6—14(1978).
[10] J. F. Tang and P. F. Gu, "Theory and desing of absorbing thin film systems," J. Zhejian Univ. 1, 1—9(1979).
[11] J. F. Tang and H. A. Macleod, "Measurement of small changes in thin films by surface electromagnetic waves," J. Opt. Soc. Am. 71, 1575(1981).
[12] J. A. Dobrowolski and D. Lowe, "Optical thin film synthesis program based on the use of Fourier transforms," App. Opt. 17, 3039—3050(1978).

Vector Minimization of Upper Robust Mappings*

Abstract: In this research, we study upper robust mappings from a topological space to $\mathbb{R}^N$ and vector minimization of those mapping. Under some general assumptions, optimality conditons are established for several scalarization techniques. These optimality conditions are applied to desing integral algorithms for finding the solution set of a vector optimization problem.

1 Introduction

Let X be a topological space and $f=(f^1, f^2, \cdots): X \to \mathbb{R}^N$ a mapping. In this paper, we consider the vector optimization problems with respect to the partical ordering induced by the nonnegative orthant of the product space $\mathbb{R}^N$. A point $\bar{x} \in X$ is said to be a *efficient solution* or *nondominated solution* of a vector minimization problem

$$\min f(x), \quad x \in X \tag{1.1}$$

if there exists no other $x \in X$ such that $f^i(x) \leqslant f^i(\bar{x})$ for all $i=1,2,\cdots$, with strict inequality for at least one i. Vector optimization problems originated from decision-making problems appearing in economics, management sciences and other scientific disciplines where it is often required that decision making be based on optimizaing several criteria. A vector optimization problem is therefore to find all efficient points, i. e. best points in a set with respect to some partial order.

Most traditional gradient based scalar optimization techniques usually cannot locate global minimizers but only local minimizers. This shortcoming causes severer difficulties in numerical vector optimization: when a vector optimization problem is scalarized, the local minimizers of scalarized problem may not lead to efficient solutions of the original vector optimization problem. For instance, an optimal desing problem (two objectives) of a sandwich bean was studied in [2] and [3]([3], Example 3.2). The authors use tunneling technique ([3], section 2.2) and obtain minimal elements ([3], Table 4). Thanks to Professor Jahn who provides the source file of the objective functions, we use integral global optimization method and obtain the minimal elements which are different from those by tunneling technique. The deviations are significant. Thus, a powerful global optimization theory and method are essential for vector minimization.

---

* In collaboration with Shi Shuzhong. Reprinted from Operations Research Transactions, 1997, 1(2): 20−33.

In this research, we apply the integral global optimization theory and algorithms to vector optimization of upper robust mappings generalizing the results in [5]. A brief description of concepts of robust sets and functions are presented in Section 2 for the convenience of the reader. Some results on upper robust mappings and their properties are developed in Section 3. These results are directly related to vector optimization. Optimality conditions for some scalarization techniques are established in Section 4. These optimality conditions are applied to design integral algorithm for approximating the solution set.

2 Robust Sets and Functions

The concept of robustness is an essential component of theory and methodology of integral global minimization. We highlight some fundamentals here. The reader is referred to [1, 10, 11] for details.

Lex X be a topological space. A set D in X is said to be *robust* if
$$\operatorname{cl} D = \operatorname{cl} \operatorname{int} D, \tag{2.1}$$
where cl D denotes the closure of the set D and int D the interior of D.

A robust set consists of *robust points* of the set. A point $x \in \operatorname{cl} D$ is said to be robust to D (or a robust point of D if $x \in D$), if for each neighborhood $N(x)$ of x, $N(x) \cap \operatorname{int} D \neq \varnothing$. A set D is robust if and only if each point of D is a robust point of D. If x is a robust point of a set D, then D is called a *semineighborhood* of x. A point x is robust to D if and only if there exists a net $\{x_\lambda\} \subset \operatorname{int} D$ such that $x_\lambda \to x$.

Every open set G is robust since $G = \operatorname{int} G$. The empty set is a trivial robust set. A closed set may or may not be robust. A union of robust sets is robust. An intersection of two robust sets may not be robust; but the intersection of an open set and a robust set is robust. If A is robust in X and B is robust in Y, then $A \times B$ is robust in $X \times Y$ with the product topology. A convex set D in a topological vector space is robust if and only if the interior of D is nonempty. An important property of a nonempty robust set is that its interior is not empty. A robust set or its complement can be represented by the union of an open set and a nowhere dense set.

A function $f: X \to \mathbb{R}^1$ is said to be *upper robust* if the set
$$F_c = \{x : f(x) < c\} \tag{2.2}$$
is robust for each real number c.

An upper semicontinuous (u.s.c.) function f is upper robust since in this case (2.2) is open for each c. A sum of two upper robust functions may not be upper robust; but the sum of an upper robust function and an u.s.c. function is upper robust.

A function f is upper robust if and only if it is upper robust at each point; f is upper robust at a point x if $x \in F_c$ implies that x is a robust point of F_c. An example of a non upper robust function on $\mathbb{R}^1$ is

$$f(x)=\begin{cases}0, & x=0,\\ 1, & x\neq 0,\end{cases}$$

where f is not upper robust at $x=0$.

3 Upper Robust and Upper Approximatable Mappings

For the purpose of studying vector optimization problems (1.1), we investigate the properties of upper robust mappings from a topological space X to $\mathbb{R}^N$. Recall that N is the set of all natural numbers and the space $\mathbb{R}^N$ is the product space $\prod_{i=1}^{\infty} Y^i$ with product topology, where $Y^i = \mathbb{R}^1$—the one-dimensional Euclidean space (real line). The space has a countable base and is then separable. It is a locally convex, complete and metrizable space (Fréchet space). Convergence in $\mathbb{R}^N$ is equivalent to coordinate convergence. The metric between two vector $y=(y^1, \cdots y^k, \cdots)$ and $z=(z^1, \cdots, z^k, \cdots)$ is defined as

$$d(y, z) = \sum_{k=1}^{\infty} \alpha_k \frac{|y^k - z^k|}{1+|y^k - z^k|}, \tag{3.1}$$

where α_k, $k=1, 2, \cdots$, are positive and $\sum_{k=1}^{\infty} \alpha_k < \infty$. The product space has as basis all sets of the form $\prod_\alpha U_\alpha$, where U_α is open in Y^α for each α and U_α equals to Y^α except for finitely many α.

3.1 Upper Robust Mappings

Let $\sigma \subset N$ be a finite index set. We denote $\mathbb{R}^\sigma = \prod_{i \in \sigma} Y^i$, where $Y^i = \mathbb{R}^1$.

Definition 3.1 A mapping $f: X \to \mathbb{R}^N$ is said to be upper robust at x if for each finite index set $\sigma = \{i_1, \cdots, i_m\}$ and each $c^\sigma \in \mathbb{R}^\sigma$,

$$x \in F_{c^\sigma} = \{x \in X: f^i(x) < c^i, i \in \sigma\} \tag{3.2}$$

implies that x is a robust point of F_{c^σ}. A mapping f is upper robust if it is upper robust at each point $x \in X$, or for any finite index set σ and $c^\sigma \in \mathbb{R}^\sigma$, the set F_{c^σ} is robust in X.

It is clear that by definition, if $f: X \to \mathbb{R}^N$ is upper robust, then for each i, the i-th component of f, f^i, is an upper robust function. However, the converse statement is incorrect.

The following proposition describes a convenient way to verify the upper robustness of a mapping.

Proposition 3.1 *Let x be a topological space and $f: X \to \mathbb{R}^N$ be a mapping. Then f is upper robust at a point $\bar{x} \in X$ if and only if for any given finite index set σ and $\varepsilon > 0$ there is a semineighborhood $U(\bar{x})$ of $\bar{x}$ such that*

$$\forall x \in U(\bar{x}), \quad f^i(x) < f^i(\bar{x}) + \varepsilon, \quad i \in \sigma. \tag{3.3}$$

Proof. Suppose that f is upper robust at $\bar{x}$. For a given finite index set σ and $\varepsilon > 0$, letting $c^i = f^i(\bar{x}) + \varepsilon$, $i \in \sigma$, we have

$$\bar{x} \in F_{c^\sigma} = \{x: f^i(x) < f^i(\bar{x}) + \varepsilon\}. \tag{3.4}$$

This implies, by Definition 3.1, that $\bar{x}$ is a robust point of F_{c^σ}, so $U(\bar{x}) = F_{c^\sigma}$ is a semineighborhood of $\bar{x}$. Now for each $x \in U(\bar{x})$, by (3.4), we have that
$$f^i(x) < f^i(\bar{x}) + \varepsilon, \ i \in \sigma.$$

Conversely, suppose that for any given finite index set σ, (3.3) holds and $c^\sigma = (c^{i_1}, \cdots, c^{i_m}) \in \mathbb{R}^\sigma$ is given such that
$$x \in F_{c^\sigma} = \{x \in X: f^i(x) < c^i, \ i \in \sigma\}.$$
Let $\varepsilon = \min_{i \in \sigma}[c^i - f^i(\bar{x})] > 0$. Then there exists a semineighborhood $U(\bar{x})$ of $\bar{x}$ such that for each point $x \in U(\bar{x})$, we have
$$f^i(x) < f^i(\bar{x}) + \varepsilon \leqslant c^i, \ i \in \sigma.$$
It follows that
$$\bar{x} \in U(\bar{x}) \subset F_{c^\sigma}.$$
Hence, $\bar{x}$ is a robust point of F_{c^σ} and f is upper robust at $\bar{x}$.

The sum of two upper robust mapping may be non upper robust. However, the sum of an upper robust mapping and an upper semicontinuous mapping is upper robust. The reader can easily prove this statement by applying Proposition 1.

Proposition 3.2 *Let X be a topological space, $f_m: X \to \mathbb{R}^N$, $m = 1, 2, \cdots$, be a sequence of mappings such that each mapping f_m is upper robust at $\bar{x} \in X$. If $f: X \to \mathbb{R}^N$ is a mapping with the property that*
$$\forall x \in X, \ \liminf_m f_m(x) \geqslant f(x) \tag{3.5}$$
uniformly and
$$\lim_m f_m(\bar{x}) = f(\bar{x}), \tag{3.6}$$
then f is also upper robust at $\bar{x}$.

Proof. For a given $\varepsilon > 0$ and a given finite index set σ we have, for sufficiently large $m > M$
$$\forall x \in X, \ f^i(x) < f^i_m(x) + \varepsilon/3, \ i \in \sigma, \tag{3.7}$$
and
$$f^i_m(\bar{x}) < f^i(\bar{x}) + \varepsilon/3, \ i \in \sigma, \tag{3.8}$$
according to (3.5) and (3.6). Since f_m is upper robust at $\bar{x}$, there is a semineighborhood $U(\bar{x})$ of $\bar{x}$ such that
$$\forall x \in U(\bar{x}), \ f^i_m(x) < f^i_m(\bar{x}) + \varepsilon/3, \ i \in \sigma.. \tag{3.9}$$
It follows that for each $x \in U(\bar{x})$,
$$f^i(x) < f^i_m(x) + \varepsilon/3 < f^i_m(\bar{x}) + 2\varepsilon/3 < f^i(\bar{x}) + \varepsilon, \ i \in \sigma.$$
Therefore, by Proposition 3.1, f is upper robust at $\bar{x}$.

3.2 Robustness of Epigraphs

A useful way to study a nonlinear function is to study its *epigraph*. Here, we use a generalized concept of epigraph to characterize an upper robust mapping geometrically. Let $f: X \to \mathbb{R}^N$ be a mapping. For a given finite index set $\sigma \subset N$ we define an epigraph of f^σ, a subset of the product space $X \times R^\sigma$, as follows:
$$\text{Epi}(f^\sigma) = \{x, c^\sigma\} \in X \times \mathbb{R}^\sigma : f^i(x) \leqslant c^i, \ i \in \sigma\}. \tag{3.10}$$

Proposition 3.3 Let X be a topological space. A mapping $f: X \to \mathbb{R}^N$ is upper robust at a point $\bar{x}$ if and only if for any finite index set $\sigma \subset N$, each point $(x, c^\sigma) \in Epi(f^\sigma)$ is its robust point with the product topology on $X \times \mathbb{R}^\sigma$.

Proof. Suppose f is upper robust at $\bar{x}$. Then for any finite $\sigma \subset N$ and $c_1^\sigma > \bar{c}^\sigma = f^\sigma(\bar{x})$, $\bar{x}$ is a robust point of $F_{c_1^\sigma} = \{x: f^i(x) < c_1^i, i \in \sigma\}$. Thus,

$$(\bar{x}, c_1^\sigma) \in F_{c_1^\sigma} \times \prod_{i \in \sigma} [c_1^i, \infty] \subset \text{Epi}(f^\sigma).$$

It implies that

$$(\bar{x}, c_1^\sigma) \in \text{cl int } F_{c_1^\sigma} \times \prod_{i \in \sigma} \text{cl int } [c_1^i, \infty] = \text{cl int } [F_{c_1^\sigma} \times \prod_{i \in \sigma} [c_1^i, \infty)] \subset \text{cl int Epi }(f^\sigma),$$

i.e., $(\bar{x}, c_1^\sigma)$ is a robust point of Epi (f^σ), so is $(\bar{x}, c^\sigma)$ such that $f^\sigma(\bar{x}) \leqslant c^\sigma$.

Conversely, suppose that $(\bar{x}, c^\sigma) \in$ Epi (f^σ) implies that $(\bar{x}, c^\sigma)$ is its robust point. Suppose that $f^\sigma(\bar{x}) < c^\sigma$, we will prove that $\bar{x}$ is a robust point of F_{c^σ}, i.e.,

$$\bar{x} \in \text{cl int } F_{c^\sigma} \quad \text{or} \quad U(\bar{x}) \cap \text{int } F_{c^\sigma} \neq \emptyset$$

where $U(\bar{x})$ is any given neighborhood of $\bar{x}$. Let $\bar{c}^\sigma = f^\sigma(\bar{x})$. Since $(\bar{x}, \bar{c}^\sigma) \in$ Epi (f^σ), we have that

$$G = [U(\bar{x}) \times V(\bar{c}^\sigma)] \cap \text{int Epi }(f^\sigma),$$

is a nonempty open set, where $V(\bar{c}^\sigma)$ is a neighborhood of $\bar{c}^\sigma$ in the space $\mathbb{R}^\sigma$. Take a point $(x_1, c^\sigma) \in G$. There are neighborhoods $U_1(x_1)$ and $V_1(c_1^\sigma)$ such that $U_1(x_1) \times V_1(c_1^\sigma) \subset G$. We now prove $U_1(x_1) \subset F_{c^\sigma}$. Indeed, let $(x, d^\sigma) \in U_1(x_1) \times V_1(c_1^\sigma) \subset \text{Epi }(f^\sigma)$. We have $f^\sigma(x) \leqslant d^\sigma < c^\sigma$. Now we have $U_1(x_1) \subset \text{int } F_{c^\sigma}$ and $U_1(x_1) \subset U(\bar{x})$, hence $U(\bar{x}) \cap \text{int } F_{c^\sigma} \neq \emptyset$.

We now have the following theorem.

Theorem 3.1 Let X be a topological space. A mapping $f: X \to \mathbb{R}^N$ is upper robust if and only if for each finite index set $\sigma \subset N$, the epigraph Epi (f^σ) is a robust set of the product space $X \times \mathbb{R}^\sigma$.

3.3 Approximatable Mappings

We now generalize the concept of approximatability of robust mappings[7] and study the "approximatability" of upper robust mappings.

Definition 3.2 Let X be a metric space. A mapping $f: X \to \mathbb{R}^N$ is said to be upper approximatable if and only if

1. The set of points of continuity C of f is dense in X;

2. For each point $x \in X$, there is a sequence $\{x_k\} \subset C$ such that

$$x_k \to x \quad \text{and} \quad \limsup_{k \to \infty} f^i(x_k) \leqslant f^i(x); \quad i \in N.$$

Obviously, by using the diagonal method, 2. may be replace by

2'. For each point $x \in X$, there is a sequence $\{x_k\} \subset C$ such that

$$x_k \to x \quad \text{and} \quad \lim_{k \to \infty} f^i(x_k) \leqslant f^i(x); \quad i \in N.$$

We first consider the sets of points of continuity and of discontinuity for an upper robust mapping.

Proposition 3.4 *Suppose the X is a complete metric space, $f: X \to \mathbb{R}^N$ is an upper robust mapping. Then the set D of points of discontinuity is of first category and the set C of points of continuity is of second category.*

Proof. The set of points discontinuity D can be represented as (see [6, Chapter I, Section 13]):

$$D = \bigcup_{G \in S} (f^{-1}(G) \setminus \mathrm{int}\, f^{-1}(G)), \tag{3.11}$$

where S is a subbase of $\mathbb{R}^N$. Let Q be the set of all rational numbers of $\mathbb{R}^1$. We can take

$$\left\{ (a^i, b^i) \times \prod_{j \neq i} (-\infty, \infty)_j \right\}$$

as the subbase of $\mathbb{R}^N$, where $a^i < b^i$ and $a^i, b^i \in Q$. The subbase is countable. Thus, to prove D is of first category, it suffices to show that for any $a^i, b^i \in Q$,

$$D_0 = f^{-1}\left((a^i, b^i) \times \prod_{j \neq i}(-\infty, \infty)_j\right) \setminus \mathrm{int}\, f^{-1}\left((a^i, b^i) \times \prod_{j \neq i}(-\infty, \infty)_j\right)$$

is of first category. It is easy to see that the following set equality holds:

$$(a^i, b^i) \times \prod_{j \neq i}(-\infty, \infty)_j = (-\infty, b^i) \times \prod_{j \neq i}(-\infty, \infty)_j \cap$$
$$\left\{ \bigcup_{m=1}^{\infty} [a^i + \frac{1}{m}, \infty) \times \prod_{j \neq i}(-\infty, \infty)_j \right\}. \tag{3.12}$$

For an upper robust mapping f,

$$V = f^{-1}\left((-\infty, b^i) \times \prod_{j \neq i}(-\infty, \infty)_j\right)$$

is a robust set and

$$f^{-1}\left([a^i + \frac{1}{m}, \infty] \times \prod_{j \neq i}(-\infty, \infty)_j\right) = X \setminus f^{-1}\left((-\infty, a + \frac{1}{m}) \times \prod_{j \neq i}(-\infty, \infty)_j\right)$$
$$= Q_m^i \cup T_m^i$$

is the complement of a robust set; it is an union of an open set and a nowhere dense set. Thus,

$$f^{-1}\left((a^i, b^i) \times \prod_{j \neq i}(-\infty, \infty)_j\right) = V \cap \left\{ \bigcup_{m=1}^{\infty} (O_m^i \cup T_m^i \times \prod_{j \neq i}(-\infty, \infty)_j) \right\}$$
$$= V \cap \left\{ \bigcup_{m=1}^{\infty} G_m \cup T_m \right\},$$

where

$$G_m = Q_m^i \times \prod_{j \neq i}(-\infty, \infty)_j \quad \text{and} \quad T_m = T_m^i \times \prod_{j \neq i}(-\infty, \infty)_j.$$

It is easy to see that G_m is open and T_m is nowhere dense $m = 1, 2 \cdots$. Hence, we have

$$f^{-1}\left((a^i, b^i) \times \prod_{j \neq i}(-\infty, \infty)_j\right) = \left\{ \bigcup_{m=1}^{\infty} (V \cap G_m) \cup (V \cap T_m) \right\} = \bigcup_{m=1}^{\infty} (V_m \cup T'_m), \tag{3.13}$$

where V_m is a robust set (an intersection of a robust set and an open set) and T'_m is a nowhere dense set, $m = 1, 2, \cdots$; and

$$f^{-1}\left((a^i, b^i) \times \prod_{j \neq i}(-\infty, \infty)_j\right) \setminus \mathrm{int}\, f^{-1}\left((a^i, b^i) \times \prod_{j \neq i}(-\infty, \infty)_j\right)$$
$$\subset \bigcup_{m=1}^{\infty} (V_m \setminus \mathrm{int}\, V_m) \cup T'_m. \tag{3.14}$$

The right hand side of the inclusion (3.14) is obviously of first category, and so is the left hand side. Thus, the set C of points of continuity is of second category, because it is the complement of D in the complete metric space X.

Corollary 3.1 *Suppose that X is a complete metric space and $f: X \to \mathbb{R}^N$ is an upper robust mapping. Then the set C of points of continuity of f is dense in X.*

Theorem 3.1 *Suppose that X is a complete metric space, $f: X \to \mathbb{R}^N$ is a mapping and C is the set of points of continuity. Then f is upper robust if and only if f is upper approximatable, i.e., C is dense in X and for each point $\bar{x} \in X \backslash C$, there exists a sequence $\{x_k\} \subset C$ such that*

$$x_k \to \bar{x} \quad \text{and} \quad \limsup_{k \to \infty} f^i(x_k) \leqslant f^i(\bar{x}), \ i \in N. \tag{3.15}$$

Proof. Suppose that f is upper robust, and $\bar{x} \in X \backslash C$ is a point of discontinuity. For each given k and the index set $\sigma_k = \{1, \cdots, k\}$, the set

$$R_k = \{x \in X: f^i(x) < f^i(\bar{x}) + 1/k, \ i \in \sigma_k\}$$

is a nonempty robust set; $\bar{x}$ is a robust point of this set. Thus, by Proposition 3.4

$$C \cap U_k(\bar{x}) \cap \text{int } R_k \neq \varnothing, \ k=1, 2, \cdots, \tag{3.16}$$

where

$$U_k(\bar{x}) = \{x \in X: d(x, \bar{x}) < 1/k\}$$

is a neighborhood of $\bar{x}$ and d is the metrioc on X. Taking a point x_k, for each k, from the set (3.16), we obtain a sequence $\{x_k\} \subset C$. We then have

$$x_k \in C, \ d(x_k, \bar{x}) < 1/k, \ \text{and} \ f^i(x_k) < f^i(\bar{x}) + 1/k, \ i \in \sigma_k. \tag{3.17}$$

It implies that for a fixed i,

$$x_k \in C, \ x_k \to \bar{x}, \ \text{and} \ \limsup_{k \to \infty} f^i(x_k) \leqslant f^i(\bar{x}). \tag{3.18}$$

Conversely, suppose that for a given point $\bar{x} \in X$ and a finite index set σ, $c^\sigma \in \mathbb{R}^\sigma$, $\bar{x} \in F_{c^\sigma}$ such that (3.15) holds for all $i \in \sigma$. Since $\bar{x} \in F_{c^\sigma}$, we have $f^i(\bar{x}) < c^i$, $i \in \sigma$. Let $\varepsilon = \min_{i \in \sigma}[c^i - f^i(\bar{x})]$. Then by (3.15) there is an integer K such that $x_k \in C$ and

$$\forall k \geqslant K, \quad f^i(x_k) < f^i(\bar{x}) + \varepsilon/2 < c^i, \ i \in \sigma.$$

Now, $x_k \in C \cap F_{c^\sigma}$. Hence, we have also that for all $k \geqslant K$, $x_k \in \text{int } F_{c^\sigma}$. It follows that

$$x_k \in \text{int } F_{c^\sigma} \quad \text{and} \quad x_k \to \bar{x}.$$

This proves that $\bar{x}$ is a robust point of f^σ for any given finite index set σ, and thus the mapping is upper robust.

4 Scalarizations and Optimality Conditions

4.1 Scalarization of an Upper Robust Mapping

The most common strategy to characterize the efficient solutions of a vector optimization problem is to find a real-valued function representing the decision maker's preference. Once such a function is found, the vector optimization problem is then reduced to a more usual scalar optimization problem. This approach is often referred as scalarization in vector optimization literature.

Definition 4.1 Let $E: \mathbb{R}^N \to \mathbb{R}^1$ and $y, z \in \mathbb{R}^N$. E is said to be monotonic if
$$\forall i \in N, \ y^i \leqslant z^i \text{ and } y \neq z \Rightarrow E(y) < E(z). \tag{4.1}$$

The following proposition is obvious.

Proposition 4.1 *Suppose $f: X \to \mathbb{R}^N$ is a mapping defined on a topological space X and $E: \mathbb{R}^N \to \mathbb{R}^1$ is a monotonic real-valued function. If*
$$\forall x \in X, \quad E(f(x^*)) \leqslant E(f(x)), \tag{4.2}$$
then x^* is an efficient solution of (1.1)

The composite function $E(f(x))$ in Proposition 4.1 may be not upper robust even for a well behaved mapping f.

Proposition 4.2 *Let X be a complete metric space and $f: X \to \mathbb{R}^N$ be an upper robust mapping on X. Suppose $E: \mathbb{R}^N \to \mathbb{R}^1$ is a real-valued function satisfying the following conditions:*

1. *$E(y^1, \cdots, y^n, \cdots)$ is an increasing function with respect to each variable;*
2. *E is continuous.*

Then the composite real-valued function $E(f(x))$ is an upper robust function on X.

Proof. From Proposition 3.2 the set C of points of continuity of f is dense in X. The composite function $E(f(x))$ is also continuous on C. Furthermore, let D be the set of points of discontinuity of the composite function $E(f)$ and $\bar{x} \in D$ be any given points, we now prove that it is upper approximatable by points in C. Let $\{x_k\} \subset C$ be a sequence such that $x_k \to \bar{x}$ and $\lim_{k \to \infty} f^i(x_k) \leqslant f^i(\bar{x})$, for any $i \in N$. We have, by continuity of E, that
$$\lim_{k \to \infty} E(f^1(x_k), \cdots, f^i(x_k), \cdots) = E(\lim_{k \to \infty} f^1(x_k), \cdots, \lim_{k \to \infty} f^i(x_k), \cdots).$$
By monotonicity of E with respect to each variable and $\lim_{k \to \infty} f^i(x_k) \leqslant f^i(\bar{x})$, $i \in N$, we have that
$$x_k \to \bar{x} \quad \text{and} \quad \lim_{k \to \infty} E(f(x_k)) \leqslant E(f(\bar{x})).$$
It implies that $E(f)$ is upper approximatable at each point of X. Hence, $E(f(x))$ is an upper robust function.

4.2 Weighting Problems

The weighting problem is one of the most commonly used technique of scalarization for solving convex vector optimization problems. Let $d^i(y^i)$ be an increasing and continuous function of variable y^i, $i = 1, 2, \cdots$, and the sum $\sum_{i=1}^{\infty} d^i(y^i)$ is uniformly convergent. Let
$$E(y^1, \cdots, y^n, \cdots) = \sum_{i=1}^{\infty} d^i(y^i). \tag{4.3}$$
The function E defined by (4.3) is continuous and increasing with respect to each variable. Thus, this function satisfies conditions of Proposition 4.2. Especially, let $d^i(y^i) = w^i y^i$, $i = 1, \cdots$, with given nonnegative weights $w^1, \cdots, w^n, \cdots$, such that $\sum_{i=1}^{\infty} w^i <$

∞, we have

$$E(y^1, \cdots, y^n, \cdots) = \sum_{i=1}^{\infty} w^i y^i. \qquad (4.4)$$

With function (4.4), we have the weighting problem

$$\min_{x \in X} \sum_{i=1}^{\infty} w^i f^i(x). \qquad (4.5)$$

By Proposition 4.2, we have the following corollary:

Corollary 4.1 *Suppose X is a complete metric space, $f: X \to \mathbb{R}^N$ is an upper robust mapping and $w^1, \cdots, w^n, \cdots$, with $w^i \geqslant 0$, $i=1, 2, \cdots$, are weights such that $\sum_{i=1}^{\infty} w^i < \infty$. Then*

$$g(x) = w^1 f^1(x) + \cdots + w^n f^n(x) + \cdots \qquad (4.6)$$

is an upper robust function on X.

4.3 Reference Point Method

Nonconvex vector optimization problems arise in broad range of appliction. The weighting scalarization technique is not suitable for nonconvex problems. Moreover, it is not uncommon in practive that verifying the convexity of an optimization problem is a nontrivial task. Therefore, the reference point technique [3,8,9] is often adopted in practice.

Definition 4.2 Let $f: X \to \mathbb{R}^N$ be a mapping. A point $\hat{y} = (\hat{y}^1, \cdots, \hat{y}^n, \cdots) \in \mathbb{R}^N$ is called a reference point of f if for any $x \in X$, $\hat{y}^i < f^i(x)$, $i=1,2,\cdots$

Suppose that the function f is bounded below. Let

$$\hat{y}^i = \inf_{x \in X} f^i(x) - \varepsilon, \quad i=1,2,\cdots,$$

where $\varepsilon > 0$ and $\hat{y} = (\hat{y}^1, \cdots, \hat{y}^n, \cdots)$, then $\hat{y}$ is a reference point.

With a reference point $\hat{y}$, let

$$g(x) = \sum_{i=1}^{\infty} w^i d^i(\hat{y}^i, f^i(x)), \qquad (4.7)$$

where $w^i \geqslant 0$, $i=1, \cdots, n$, are weights and $d^i(\cdot, \cdot)$, $i=1,2,\cdots$, are positive continuous functions with $d^i(y^i, y^i) = 0$, $i=1,2,\cdots$

It is often convenient to take a weighted metric as weighted norm in $\mathbb{R}^N$. The weighted Eucliden norm or the weighted Chebyshev norm are defined as follows.

$$g(x) = \sqrt{\sum_{i=1}^{\infty} w_i (f^i(x) - \hat{y}^i)^2}. \qquad (4.8)$$

$$g(x) = \max_i \{w_i | f^i(x) - \hat{y}^i | \}. \qquad (4.9)$$

Definition 4.3 A solution $\hat{x}$ of the minimization problem

$$\min_{x \in X} g(x) \qquad (4.10)$$

is called a *reference-point solution* of (1.1) corresponding to a reference point $\hat{y}$, metrics $d^1, \cdots, d^n, \cdots$ and the set of weights $w^1, \cdots, w^n, \cdots$

Proposition 4.3 Let X be a complete metric space, $f: X \to \mathbb{R}^N$ an upper robust mapping, $w^i \geqslant 0$, $i=1, 2, \cdots$ be given weights and $\hat{y}$ a given reference point. Suppose that for each

i, $d^i(\hat{y}^i, \cdot)$ is a nonnegative increasing continuous function of $y^i \geqslant \hat{y}^i$, $i=1, \cdots$. Then the function (4.7)(including (4.8) and (4.9)) is upper robust.

4.4 Integral Optimality Conditions

We are now ready to use integral optimization theory and methods to the scalarization of a vector minimization problem. The optimal solutions can be characterized by the integral optimality conditions as follows:

Theorem 4.1 *Suppose that* (1) *the solution set of the vector minimization is nonempty,* (2) *there is a Q-measure space* (X, Ω, μ) *and* (3) *the scalarization g is upper robust and measuralb, then the following statements are equivalent*:

(i) *A point* $\bar{x} \in X$ *is a solution of* (4.10) *with* $c^* = g(\bar{x})$ *as the corresponding value*;

(ii) $M(g, c^*; X) = c^*$ (*the mean value condition*);

(iii) $V_1(g, c^*; X) = 0$ (*the modified variance condition*).

We omit the definitions of Q-measure space, mean value and modified variance here. For more about integral global minimization and related theory and methods, see [1], [10] and [11].

5 An Integral Algorithm for Finding Solution Set

The integral global minimization algorithm delivers *global* minimizers for single objective minimization problems. This feature is extremely valuable in solving vector optimization problems. In this section, the optimality conditions established in the previous section are applied to desing integral minimization algorithms to approximate the efficient solution set of a vector minimization problem. We first consider approximating the solution set with its finite-dimensional counterpart. We then propose an algorithm for finding this finite-dimensional approximation.

5.1 Finite-Dimensional Approximation of Solution Set

Let $f: X \to \mathbb{R}^N$ be a mapping and $S^* \subset X$ be the solution set of (1.1). We now consider a problem of finding a set $S \subset X$ approximating S^*. Suppose σ is a finite index set: $\sigma = \{i_1, i_2, \cdots, i_m\}$ and f^σ is a mapping $f^\sigma: X \to \mathbb{R}^\sigma$ such that f^{i_k} if the i_k-th component of f. Let S^σ be the solution set of the mapping f^σ. Each point $x \in S^*$ should also be in S^σ by the definition of optimal solution. Thus we have

$$S^* \subset S^\sigma \quad \text{and} \quad S^* = \bigcap_\sigma S^\sigma. \tag{5.1}$$

Definition 5.1 Let $f: X \to \mathbb{R}^N$. A set $S \subset X$ is said to be an ε-approximation to the solution set of (1.1) $S^* \subset X$ if and only if for each $x \in S$, there is a pont $x^* \in S^*$ such that

$$d(f(x^*), f(x)) \leqslant \varepsilon. \tag{5.2}$$

Since the solution set S^* is smaller than its finite-dimensional approximation, we intend obtain a set S that for each point in S, there is an associated point in S^* with small deviation in the above sense.

When we consider multicriterion problem, we can rearrange the criteria in a way such

that the important ones put in the first. For a given $\varepsilon>0$, there is an integer m such that
$$\sum_{k=m+1}^{\infty} \alpha_k < \varepsilon.$$
Let $\sigma=\{1, 2, \cdots, m\}$ and $\mathbb{R}^\sigma=\mathbb{R}^m$. Suppose the solution set of the mapping $f^\sigma:X\to\mathbb{R}^\sigma$ is S^σ. Then S^σ is an ε-approximation to the solution set S.

5.2 An Algorithm

For simplicity, we describe an algorithm using a reference point method under the assumption that the objective function of problem (5.3) is bounded below and the set of efficient solutions of the problem is nonempty. The algorithms based on other scalarization methods can also be designed.

Step 1: Find a reference point. Let
$$a^i := \min_{x \in X} f^i(x), \quad i=1, \cdots, m. \tag{5.3}$$
Take a point $(\hat{y}^1, \cdots, \hat{y}^m)$ as a reference point such that
$$\hat{y}^i < a^i, \quad i=1, \cdots, m. \tag{5.4}$$

Step 2: Take L sets of positive weights $(w_k^1, \cdots, w_k^m)$, $k=1, \cdots, L$, and minimize the fowwlwing L scalar problems by the integral global minimization algorithm:
$$\min_{x \in X} g_k(x), \quad k=1, \cdots, L, \tag{5.5}$$
where we may take g_k as Chebyshev norm
$$g_k(x) = \min_{i=1,\cdots,m} \{w_k^i (f^i(x) - \hat{y}^i)\}. \tag{5.6}$$
We obtain a sequence of solutions:
$$x_1, \cdots, x_L \text{ and } f(x_1), \cdots, f(x_L). \tag{5.7}$$

Step 3: Use simplexes produced by these points as an approximation of the solution set.

5.3 Solution Set of a Vector Minimization Problem

The algorithm proposed above can be used to find the solution set of a vector minimization problem. Indeed, we have known that each minimizer of $g(x)$ is a solution to the vector minimization problem. Conversely, for each solution $\bar{x}$ to the vector minimization problem, there are weights such that $\bar{x}$ is a minimizer of $g(x)$. Thus, we can find each solution to a vector minimization problem by selecting weights.

Proposition 5.1 *A point $\bar{x}$ is a solution to the vector minimization problem (1.1) if and only if there is a weight vector w such that $\bar{x}$ is a minimizer of the corresponding scalarization $g(x)$.*

Proof. We need only prove the "only if" part. Indeed, we can take
$$w^i = \frac{1}{f^i(\bar{x}) - \hat{y}^i} > 0, \quad i=1, \cdots, m$$
as the weights, and then $g(\bar{x}) = \min_{x \in X} g(x) (g(\bar{x})=1)$. Suppose, on the contrary, there is an $\tilde{x} \in X$ such that $g(\tilde{x}) < g(\bar{x})$, then we have
$$\max_{i=1,\cdots,m} \frac{f^i(\tilde{x}) - (\hat{y}^i)}{f^i(\bar{x}) - \hat{y}^i} < 1.$$
It implies that

$$f^i(\tilde{x})-\hat{y}^i < f^i(\overline{x})-\hat{y}^i \quad \text{or} \quad f^i(\tilde{x}) < f^i(\overline{x}), \quad i=1, \cdots, m$$

and $\overline{x}$ is not a solution to the vector minimization problem.

5.4 A Remark

The scalar minimization problems (5.5), as well as (5.3), are unconstrained optimization problems. We can use the discontinuous penalty function technique to reduce a constrained minimization problem to an unconstrained ones. For a constrained minimization problem

$$\min_{x \in S} g(x), \qquad (5.8)$$

where $S \subset X$, let

$$p(x) = \begin{cases} \delta + q(x), & x \notin S, \\ 0, & x \in S, \end{cases} \qquad (5.9)$$

where $\delta > 0$ is a constant, and $q(x)$ is penalty-like function defined on S. The penalized problem is of the following form:

$$\min [g(x) + \alpha p(x)], \qquad (5.10)$$

where $\alpha > 0$ is the penalty parameter. The most important advantage of using discontinuous penalty function (5.9) is that such a penalized problem is exact without any constraint qualification requirement. See [12] for more details.

The algorithm has been implemented by proper designed Monte Carlo techniue. For a given reference point and a set of weights, the algorithm converges to an efficient solution with pre-specified accuracy, see [4] and [5].

References

[1] S. H. Chew and Q. Zheng. *Integral Global Optimization* [R]. Lecture Notes in Economics and Mathematical Systems, No. 298, Springer-Verlag, New York, 1988.

[2] J. Jahn. Vector optimization: theory, methods, and application to design problems in engineering [R]. in *Modern Methods of Optimization-Proceedings*, W. Krabs and J. Zowe eds., Lecture Notes in Economics and Mathematical Systems, No. 378, Berlin, 1992.

[3] J. Jahn and A. Merkel. Reference point approximation method for the solution of bicriterial nonlinear optimization problems [J]. *Journal of Optimization Theory and Applications*, 74 (1994), 87—103.

[4] M. M. Kostreva, Q. Zheng and D. Zhuang, A method for approximating solutions of multicriterial nonlinear optimization problems [J]. *Optimization Nethods and Software*, 5 (1995), 209—226.

[5] M. M. Kostreva, Q. Zheng and D. Zhuang. Upper robust mapping and vector minimization: and integral approach [J]. *European Journal of Operations Research*, 93(1996), 565—581.

[6] K. Kuratowski. *Topology*, Volume, I. Academic Press, 1966.

[7] S. Shi, Q. Zheng and D. Zhuang. Discontinuous robust mappings are approximatable [J]. *Trans. Amer. Math. Soc.*, 347(1995), 4943—4957.

[8] A. P. Wierzbicki. A mathematical basis for satisficing decision making [J]. *Mathematical Modelling* 3 (1982), 391—405.

[9] A. P. Wierzbicki, On the completeness and constructiveness of parametric characterizations to vector

optimization problems [J]. *OR Spektrum*, 8 (1986), 73—87.
[10] Q. Zheng. Robust analysis and global minimization of a class of discontinuous functions (I) [J]. *Acta Mathematicae Applicatae Sinica* (English Series), 6:3 (1990), 205—223.
[11] Q. Zheng. Robust Analysis and global optimization of a class of discontinuous functions (II) [J]. *Acta Mathematicas Applicatae Sinica* (English Series), 6:4 (1990), 317—337.
[12] Q. Zheng and L. Zhang. Global minimization of constrained problems with discontinuous penalty function. to appear on *Computers and Mathematics with Applications*.

Optimality Conditions for Global Optimization (I) *

Abstract: With the help of the theory of measure and integration several global optimality conditions, which are sufficient and necessary, are given for minimizing a continuous function over a topological space.

1 Introduction

Let X be a Hausdorff topological space, $f: X \to \mathbb{R}$ a real-valued function and S a closed subset of X. The problem considered here is to find the infimum of f over S

$$\bar{c} = \inf_{x \in S} f(x), \tag{1.1}$$

and the set of global minima

$$\overline{H} = \{x \mid f(x) = \bar{c}, x \in S\} \tag{1.2}$$

if the solution set of (1.1) is nonempty.

In what follows we assume that

(A_1) $f: X \to \mathbb{R}$ is continuous;

(A_2) There is a real c such that the level set

$$H_c = \{x \mid f(x) \leqslant c\} \tag{1.3}$$

is compact, and $S \cap H_c \neq \emptyset$.

Thus we have

$$\bar{c} = \min_{x \in H_n \cap S} f(x), \tag{1.4}$$

and the set of global minima $\overline{H}$ is nonempty and compact.

In this paper we will discuss the global optimality conditions.

The study of optimality conditions, conditions by which one can determine if a point x is in the set of minima or its candidate, forms one of the vital topics in the theory of optimization. Many optimality conditions have been obtained by various researchers in optimization theory. Nevertheless, most of these conditions (if not all) are local in nature and even then require several of differentiability (cf., e.g. [1]—[3]). Therefore, to find global optimality criteria for nonconvex problem is an intriguing area of research.

Here we will take an approach to study the problem of global optimality conditions, which is different form the traditional ones. Our method is based upon the theory of

---

* Reprinted from Acta Mathematicae Applicate Sinica, 1985 2(1):66—78.

measure and integration.

In Section 2 we will discuss the measure space. Afterwards, in Sections 3—5 the concepts and conditions of mean value, variance and higher moments will be introduced. The penalty method is mentioned in Section 6. All of these are sufficient and necessary conditions. They remain valid in the (more restrictive) convex or differentiable cases and reduce to the optimality conditions which are well known. As can be seen in Section 7, a specific measure space corresponds to a specific optimality condition.

2 An Appropriate Concept of Measure

Let X be a Hausdorff topological space, Ω a σ-field of subset of X and μ a measure on Ω. The triple (X, Ω, μ) is called a measure space. We require a set of further requirements which are compatible with the topological properties of X.

(i) Ω is a Boral field, i.e., each open set of X is in Ω.

(ii) Any nonempty open set has positive measure.

(iii) The measure of a compact set in X is bounded.

A measure space which has all thess properties (properties (i) and (ii) is said to be a Q-measure space (Q_1-measure space). A measure space (X, Ω, μ_0) is said to be a Q_0-measure space if $\mu_0 = \lim_{n \to \infty} \mu_n$ and $\{(X, \Omega, \mu_n)\}$ is a sequence of Q-measures.

Example 2.1 The Lebesque measure space in the Euclidean space of dimension n, ($\mathbb{R}^n$, $\mathscr{B}$, μ), is a Q-measure space.

Example 2.2 The Lebesque measure space on a manifold L of dimension m in $\mathbb{R}^n$, (L, $\mathscr{B}_L$, μ_L), is a Q-measure space too.

Example 2.3 The Gaussian measure on a separable Hilbert space H, (H, Ω, μ), is also a Q-measure space.

Example 2.4 (X, Ω, μ), where $\mu(A)=1$ if $x_0 \in A$ or 0 if $x_0 \bar{\in} A$, is, not a Q-measure space but a Q_0-measure space for $X=\mathbb{R}^n$.

In our framework, we will deal with a variety of Q-measure space tailored to the specific contexts of the optimization problems. How can we establish the connection between measure theory and global optimization? The following lemma yield a sufficient global optimality condition which plays an important role in the subsequent development.

Definition 2.1 A subset G of a topological space X is said to be robust if cl (int G)=cl G.

Lemma 2.1 *Let (X, Ω, μ) be a Q_1-measure space and G be a robust subset of X. Suppose the intersection of level set $H_c = \{x \mid f(x) \leqslant c\}$ and G is nonempty. If $\mu(H_c \cap G) = 0$, then c is the global minimum value of f over G and $H_c \cap G$ is the set of global minima.*

Proof. Let us first establish the following intermediate result. Suppose E is an open set and G is a robust set. If $E \cap G \neq \varnothing$, then there exists an open set B contained in $E \cap G$. Let $x \in E \cap G$.

Since E is an open set, there is an open set B_1 such that $x \in B_1 \subset E$. On the other hand $x \in G \subset$ cl G = cl int G. Therefore, $B_1 \cap$ int $G \neq \emptyset$. So there is an open set $B \subset B \cap$ int G, $B \subset E \cap G$.

Suppose c is not the global minimum value of f over G whereas $\hat{c}$ is. Then
$$c - \hat{c} = 2\eta > 0.$$
Let $E = \{x \mid f(x) < c - \eta\}$ which is nonempty and open since f is continuous and $c - \eta > \hat{c}$. We have
$$E \cap G \subset H_c \cap G.$$
Therefore, there is an open set B such that
$$\emptyset \neq B \subset E \cap G \subset H_c \cap G.$$
However,
$$0 < \mu(B) \leq \mu(H_c \cap G),$$
because μ is a Q_1-measure. We have a contradiction with respect to the condition $\mu(H_c \cap G) = 0$.

Note that the condition $\mu(H_c \cap G) = 0$ is not necessary (see the following counter example).

Example 2.5 Let $f(x) = 0$ for $0 < x < 1$. Here $X = \mathbb{R}^1$ and the Lebesque measure space on $\mathbb{R}^1$ is used as a Q-measure space. $G = [0, 1] \subset \mathbb{R}^1$ and $c = 0$ is the global minimum value of f over G. But $\mu(H_c \cap G) = 1 \neq \emptyset$.

In the following discussion we always assume that the measure space (X, Ω, μ) is a Q-measure space.

We restate Lemma 2.1 below in the opposite way.

Lemma 2.2 Let (X, Ω, μ) be a Q-measure space and G a robust set. If $c > \bar{c}$ ($\bar{c}$ is the global minimum value of f over G). Then
$$\mu(H_c \cap G) > 0.$$

3 Mean Value Conditions

In this section, the concept of mean value of a function over its level sets will be introduced. This concept is useful to consider the global optimality conditions and global algorithm. In section 3.3, we prove the mean value condition theory, which gives us two sufficient and necessary conditions for global optimality.

3.1 Mean Value Over Level Sets

Let X be a Hausdorff topplogical space, f be a real-valued function on X and (X, Ω, μ) be a Q-measure space. Suppose assumptions (A_1) and (A_2) in Section 1 hold.

Definition 3.1 Suppose $c > \bar{c} = \min f(x)$. We define
$$M(f, c) = \frac{1}{\mu(H_c)} \int_{H_c} f(x) \mathrm{d}\mu \tag{3.1}$$
to be the mean value of the function f over its level set
$$H_c = \{x \mid f(x) \leq c\}. \tag{3.2}$$

According to Lemm 2.2, $\mu(H_c)>0$, for $c>\bar{c}$. Consequently, given the continuity of f the mean value (3.1) is then well defined.

The following are properties of our mean value which are easy to be verified.

Proposition 3.1 For $c>\bar{c}$,
$$M(f, c) \leqslant c.$$

Proposition 3.2 If $c_2 \geqslant c_1 > \bar{c}$, then
$$M(f, c_2) \geqslant M(f, c_1).$$

Proposition 3.3 *The mean value of a function over its level sets has the following properties*:

(1) Constancy. $M(\lambda, c) = \lambda$, for a constant $\lambda \geqslant c$.

(2) Homogeneity. $M(\lambda f, \lambda c) = \lambda M(f, c)$, for constant $\lambda > 0$ and $c > \bar{c}$.

(3) Translation. $M(f+\lambda, c+\lambda) = M(f, c) + \lambda$, for constant λ and $c > \bar{c}$.

Proposition 3.4 *Suppose $\{c_k\}$ is a decreasing sequence whose limit is $c > \bar{c}$. Then*
$$M(f, c) = \lim_{c_k \downarrow c} M(f, c_k) \tag{3.3}$$

Proof. According to Proposition 3.2, the sequence $\{M(f, c_k)\}$ is decreasing and $M(f, c_k) \geqslant M(f, c)$, for $k=1,2,\cdots$, so that the limit (3.3) exists. Moreover,

$$0 \leqslant \frac{1}{\mu(H_{c_k})} \int_{H_{c_k}} f(x) d\mu - \frac{1}{\mu(H_c)} \int_{H_c} f(x) d\mu$$

$$\leqslant \left| \frac{1}{\mu(H_{c_k})} \int_{H_{c_k}} f(x) d\mu - \frac{1}{\mu(H_c)} \int_{H_{c_k}} f(x) d\mu \right|$$

$$+ \left| \frac{1}{\mu(H_c)} \int_{H_{c_k}} f(x) d\mu - \frac{1}{\mu(H_c)} \int_{H_c} f(x) d\mu \right|$$

$$\leqslant \left| \left(\frac{1}{\mu(H_{c_k})} - \frac{1}{\mu(H_c)} \right) \int_{H_{c_k}} f(x) d\mu \right| + \frac{1}{\mu(H_c)} \left| \int_{H_{c_k} \setminus H_c} f(x) d\mu \right|.$$

The last two terms will tend to zero as c_k goes to c because of that $\left\{ \int_{H_{c_k}} f(x) d\mu \right\}$ is bounded and the continuity of μ and the absolute continuity of the integral of a bounded measurable function f.

3.2 A limit-based definition

We have defined the concept of mean value for $c > \bar{c}$. What happens at $\bar{c}$? When $c = \bar{c}$, the measure $\mu(H_c)$ may vanish and in this case definition (3.1) would not make sense. The following definitions circumvent the above difficulty.

Definition 3.2 Let $c \geqslant \bar{c}$ and $\{c_k\}$ be a decreasing sequence whose limit is c. The mean value $M(f,c)$ is defined to be:
$$M(f, c) = \lim_{c_k \downarrow c} \frac{1}{\mu(H_{c_k})} \int_{H_{c_k}} f(x) d\mu. \tag{3.4}$$

The above limit is well defined since $\{M(f, c_k)\}$ is a decreasing bounded sequence. Moreover, this limit is independent of the choice of the decreasing sequence. Suppose we take another decreasing sequence $\{b_k\}$, which tends to c as $k \to \infty$. Combining the two sequences $\{c_k\}$ and $\{b_k\}$ and reordering them, we obtain a new decreasing sequence $\{d_k\}$ which still tends to c. Now, we have a new bounded decreasing sequence $\left\{\dfrac{1}{\mu(H_{d_m})}\displaystyle\int_{H_{d_m}} f(x)\mathrm{d}\mu\right\}$, the limit of which exists. Therefore, being those of two subsequences of the same sequence, the following limits exist and are equal:

$$\lim_{k\to\infty}\frac{1}{\mu(H_{c_k})}\int_{H_{c_k}} f(x)\mathrm{d}\mu = \lim_{k\to\infty}\frac{1}{\mu(H_{b_k})}\int_{H_{b_k}} f(x)\mathrm{d}\mu.$$

By Proposition 3.4, it is clear that Definition 3.2 extends Definition 3.1 to the case of $c\geqslant\bar{c}$. By the same token, Propositions 3.1~3.4 remain valid for $c\geqslant\bar{c}$.

An alternative equivalent definition of mean value in terms of a right-hand limit process is given by:

Definition 3.3 Let $c\geqslant\bar{c}$, the mean value $M(f, c)$ is defined to be the limit

$$M(f, c) = \lim_{\substack{d\to c \\ d>c}} \frac{1}{\mu(H_d)}\int_{H_d} f(x)\mathrm{d}\mu. \tag{3.5}$$

The equivalence between the (3.4) and (3.5) is obvious.

3.3 Mean Value Conditions

We are now ready to prove our mean value characterization of global optimality.

Theorem 3.1(*Mean value conditions*). *For the problem* (1.1) *under assumptions* (A_1) *and* (A_2), *a point* $\bar{x}$ *is a global minimum with* $\bar{c}=f(\bar{x})$ *as the corresponding global minimum value of* f *if and only if*

$$M(f, c)\geqslant\bar{c}, \text{ for } c>\bar{c} \tag{3.6}$$

or

$$M(f, \bar{c})=\bar{c}. \tag{3.7}$$

Proof. Suppose $\bar{c}$ is not the global minimum value of f and $\hat{c}$ is. Then $\bar{c}-\hat{c}=2\eta>0$. According to Lemma 2.2, $\mu(H_{\hat{c}+\eta})>0$ and $\mu(H_{\bar{c}})>0$. We have

$$M(f, \bar{c}) = \frac{1}{\mu(H_{\bar{c}})}\int_{H_{\bar{c}}} f(x)\mathrm{d}\mu = \frac{1}{\mu(H_{\bar{c}})}\left(\int_{H_{\bar{c}}\setminus H_{\hat{c}+\eta}} f(x)\mathrm{d}\mu + \int_{H_{\hat{c}+\eta}} f(x)\mathrm{d}\mu\right)$$

$$\leqslant \frac{\bar{c}}{\mu(H_{\bar{c}})}(\mu(H_{\bar{c}})-\mu(H_{\hat{c}+\eta})) + \frac{\hat{c}+\eta}{\mu(H_{\bar{c}})}\mu(H_{\hat{c}+\eta}) = \bar{c}-\beta,$$

where

$$\beta = \eta\frac{\mu(H_{\hat{c}+\eta})}{\mu(H_{\bar{c}})}>0. \tag{3.8}$$

This establishes the sufficiency of (3.7).

To demonstrate the necessity of (3.6) and (3.7), suppose $\bar{c}$ is the global minimum value of f. Then $f(x)\geqslant\bar{c}$ for all x. So, for $c>\bar{c}$, we have

$$M(f, c) = \frac{1}{\mu(H_c)}\int_{H_c} f(x)\mathrm{d}\mu \geqslant \frac{1}{\mu(H_c)}\int_{H_c} \bar{c}\,\mathrm{d}\mu = \bar{c},$$

which is (3.6). Take a decreasing sequence $\{c_k\}$ such that $\lim\limits_{k\to\infty} c_k=\bar{c}$. From (3.6) we have

$$\lim_{c_k\downarrow \bar{c}} M(f, c_k)\geqslant \bar{c},$$

i.e.,

$$M(f, \bar{c})\geqslant\bar{c}.$$

But $M(f, c) \leqslant c$ for $c > \bar{c}$, so that $M(f, \bar{c}) \leqslant \bar{c}$. Therefore
$$M(f, \bar{c}) = \bar{c}.$$

4 Variance and Higher Moment Conditions

In this section we will go a step further introducing the concepts of variance and higher moments to prove the corresponding global optimality conditions. In doing so, we shall retain all the relevant assumptions in the proceeding sections.

4.1 Variance

Definition 4.1 Suppose $c > \bar{c} = \min f(x)$. We define
$$V(f,c) = \frac{1}{\mu(H_c)} \int_{H_c} (f(x) - M(f, c))^2 \mathrm{d}\mu \tag{4.1}$$
and
$$V_1(f,c) = \frac{1}{\mu(H_c)} \int_{H_c} (f(x) - c)^2 \mathrm{d}\mu \tag{4.2}$$
to be the variance and the modified variance, respectively, of the function f over its level set H_C.

Obviously, both variance (4.1) and modified variance (4.2) are well defined. They have the following properties:

Proposition 4.1 *For $c > \bar{c}$, we have*
$$V(f, c) = M_2(f, c; 0) - (M(f, c))^2, \tag{4.3}$$
where
$$M_2(f, c; 0) = \frac{1}{\mu(H_c)} \int_{H_c} (f(x))^2 \mathrm{d}\mu.$$

Proposition 4.2 *The variance of a function over its level set has the following properties:*

(1) *Positivity* $V(f, c) \geqslant 0$; $\qquad(4.4)$
(2) $V(\lambda, c) = 0$, *for a constant* $\lambda \geqslant c$; $\qquad(4.5)$
(3) *Second-degree homogeneity* $V(\lambda f, \lambda c) = \lambda^2 V(f, c)$, *for $\lambda > 0$ and $c > \bar{c}$*; $\qquad(4.6)$
(4) *Cancellation* $V(f + \lambda, c + \lambda) = V(f, c)$, *for $c > \bar{c}$*. $\qquad(4.7)$

The following lemma is needed in the proof of Proposition 4.3

Lemma 4.1 $\dfrac{1}{\mu(H_c)} \displaystyle\int_{H_c} (f(x) + \lambda)^2 \mathrm{d}\mu$ *is nondecreasing in c for $c > \bar{c}$ if $f + \lambda \geqslant 0$.*

Proof. Suppose $c_1 \geqslant c_2 > \bar{c}$, then
$$\frac{1}{\mu(H_{c_1})} \int_{H_{c_1}} (f(x) + \lambda)^2 \mathrm{d}\lambda$$
$$= \frac{1}{\mu(H_{c_1})} \int_{H_{c_1} \setminus H_{c_2}} (f(x) + \lambda)^2 \mathrm{d}\mu + \frac{1}{\mu(H_{c_1})} \int_{H_{c_2}} (f(x) + \lambda)^2 \mathrm{d}\mu$$
$$\geqslant (c_2 + \lambda)^2 \frac{\mu(H_{c_1}) - \mu(H_{c_2})}{\mu(H_{c_1})} + \frac{1}{\mu(H_{c_1})} \int_{H_{c_2}} (f(x) + \lambda)^2 \mathrm{d}\mu$$

$$\geq \frac{\mu(H_{c_1})-\mu(H_{c_2})}{\mu(H_{c_1})}\frac{1}{\mu(H_{c_2})}\int_{H_{c_2}}(f(x)+\lambda)^2 d\mu+\frac{1}{\mu(H_{c_1})}\int_{H_{c_2}}(f(x)+\lambda)^2 d\mu$$

$$=\frac{1}{\mu(H_{c_2})}\int_{H_{c_2}}(f(x)+\lambda)^2 d\mu.$$

Hence, $\frac{1}{\mu(H_c)}\int_{H_c}(f(x)+\lambda)^2 d\mu$ is nondecreasing in c for $c>\bar{c}$.

Proposition 4.3 *Suppose $\{c_k\}$ is a decreasing sequence which tends to $c>\bar{c}$. Then*
$$V(f, c) = \lim_{c_k \downarrow c} V(f, c_k). \tag{4.8}$$

Proof. Since the sequence $\left\{\frac{1}{\mu(H_{c_k})}\int_{H_{c_k}}(f(x)+\lambda)^2 d\mu\right\}$ is decreasing (Lemma 4.1) bounded from below by $\frac{1}{\mu(H_c)}\int_{H_c}(f(x)+\lambda)^2 d\mu$, limit

$$\lim_{c_k \downarrow c}\frac{1}{\mu(H_{c_k})}\int_{H_{c_k}}(f(x)+\lambda)^2 d\mu \tag{4.9}$$

exits. Moreover

$$0\leq \frac{1}{\mu(H_{c_k})}\int_{H_{c_k}}(f(x)+\lambda)^2 d\mu - \frac{1}{\mu(H_c)}\int_{H_c}(f(x)+\lambda)^2 d\mu$$

$$\leq \left|\frac{1}{\mu(H_{c_k})}\int_{H_{c_k}}(f(x)+\lambda)^2 d\mu - \frac{1}{\mu(H_c)}\int_{H_{c_k}}(f(x)+\lambda)^2 d\mu\right|$$

$$+\left|\frac{1}{\mu(H_c)}\int_{H_{c_k}}(f(x)+\lambda)^2 d\mu - \frac{1}{\mu(H_c)}\int_{H_c}(f(x)+\lambda)^2 d\mu\right|$$

$$\leq \left|\left(\frac{1}{\mu(H_{c_k})}-\frac{1}{\mu(H_c)}\right)\int_{H_{c_k}}(f(x)+\lambda)^2 d\mu\right|+\frac{1}{\mu(H_c)}\left|\int_{H_{c_k}\setminus H_c}(f(x)+\lambda)^2 d\mu\right|.$$

The continuity of measure and absolute continuity of the integral of a bounded continuous function $(f(x)+\lambda)^2$ imply that each of the terms on the right-hand side tends to zero. Furthermors, according to Propositions 3.3 and 3.4, we have

$$(M(f+\lambda, c+\lambda))^2 = (M(f, c+\lambda))^2 = \lim_{c_k \downarrow c}(M(f, c_k+\lambda))^2 = \lim_{c_k \downarrow c}(M(f+\lambda, c_k+\lambda))^2.$$

Hence, since $\{x \mid f(x)+\lambda \leq c_k+\lambda\} = H_{c_k}$, we obtain

$$\lim_{c_k \downarrow c} V(f, c_k) = \lim_{c_k \downarrow c} V(f+\lambda, c_k+\lambda)$$

$$= \lim_{c_k \downarrow c}\left(\frac{1}{\mu(H_{c_k})}\int_{H_{c_k}}(f(x)+\lambda)^2 d\mu - (M(f+\lambda, c_k+\lambda))^2\right)$$

$$= V(f+\lambda, c+\lambda) = V(f, c).$$

The following proposition is useful in deriving properties for the modified variance from those of variance.

Proposition 4.4 *For $c>\bar{c}$, we have*
$$V_1(f, c) = V(f, c) + (M(f, c)-c)^2. \tag{4.10}$$

Proposition 4.5 *The modified variance of a function over its level sets has the following properties:*

(1) $V_1(f, c) \geq V(f, c)$, *for $c>\bar{c}$;*

(2) *Suppose $\{c_k\}$ is a decreasing sequence which tends to $c>\bar{c}$. Then*

$$\lim_{c_k \to c} V_1(f, c_k) = V_1(f, c). \tag{4.12}$$

4.2 A Limit-Based Definition

We can also define the variance $V(f, c)$ and modified variance $V_1(f, c)$ over its level sets for all $c \geq \bar{c}$ by a limiting process.

Definition 4.2 Let $c \geq \bar{c} = \min f(x)$ and $\{c_k\}$ be a. decreasing sequence which tened to c as $k \to \infty$. The limits

$$V(f, c) = \lim_{c_k \to c} \frac{1}{\mu(H_{c_k})} \int_{H_{c_k}} (f(x) - M(f, c))^2 d\mu \tag{4.13}$$

and

$$V_1(f, c) = \lim_{c_k \to c} \frac{1}{\mu(H_{c_k})} \int_{H_{c_k}} (f(x) - c)^2 d\mu \tag{4.14}$$

are called the variance and modified variance, respectively, of f over its level set H_c.

Both limits (4.13) and (4.14) exist by the proof of Proposition 4.4 and Proposition 4.6. Like the mean value case, these limits are independent of the choice of the decreasing sequences. Note that, Definitions (4.13) and (4.14) are consistent with (4.1) and (4.2) by Propositions 4.4 and 4.6. Moreover, Propositions 4.1, 4.2, and 4.4—4.6 remain valid for $c \geq \bar{c}$ after applying a similar limit-based argument.

That Definitions (4.13) and (4.14) are equivalent to the following alternative definition.

Definition 4.3 Let $c \geq \bar{c}$. The limits

$$V(f, c) = \lim_{\substack{d \to c \\ d > c}} \frac{1}{\mu(H_d)} \int_{H_d} f(x) - M(f, c))^2 d\mu, \tag{4.15}$$

and

$$V_1(f, c) = \lim_{\substack{d \to c \\ d > c}} \frac{1}{\mu(H_d)} \int_{H_d} f(x) - c)^2 d\mu \tag{4.16}$$

are called the variance and the modified variance of f over its level set H_0, respectively.

4.3 Variance Conditions

In this subsection, variance condition and modified variance conditions will be stated and proved.

Theorem 4.1(*Variance Conditions*) *For the problem* (1.1) *under assumptions* (A_1) *and* (A_2), *a point $\bar{x}$ is a global minimum with $\bar{c} = f(\bar{x})$ as the corresponding minimum value of f if and only if*

$$V(f, \bar{c}) = 0 \tag{4.17}$$

or

$$V_1(f, \bar{c}) = 0 \tag{4.18}$$

Proof. Sufficiency of condition (4.17). To prove by contradiction, suppose $\bar{x}$ is not a global minimum so that $\bar{c} = f(\bar{x})$ is not the global minimum value of f. Using Lemma 2.2, we have that $\mu(H_{\bar{c}}) > 0$. We shall show that $V(f, \bar{c}) > 0$. Suppose the contrary that

$$V(f, \bar{c}) = \frac{1}{\mu(H_{\bar{c}})} \int_{H_{\bar{c}}} f(x) - M(f, \bar{c}))^2 d\mu = 0.$$

Then $f(x)=M(f, \bar{c})$ for all $x \in H_{\bar{c}}$ since f is a continuous function. But $\bar{x} \in H_{\bar{c}}=\{x | f(x) \leqslant \bar{c}\}$. Therefore $\bar{c}=f(\bar{x})=M(f, \bar{c})$; i.e., $\bar{x}$ is a gloabl minimum of $f(x)$ by Theorem 3.5. This is a contradiction.

To prove the necessity of condition (4.17), suppose $\bar{x}$ is a global minimum point while $V(f, \bar{c})=2\eta>0$ with $\bar{c}=f(\bar{x})$. Let $\{c_k\}$ be a decreasing sequence which tends to c as $k \to \infty$. Therefore there is a positive integer N such that
$$V(f, c_k) > \eta, \text{ for } k > N. \tag{4.19}$$
This means (applying Propositions 4.1 and 4.2) that
$$\frac{1}{\mu(H_{c_k})}\int_{H_{c_k}} (f(x)+\lambda)^2 d\mu > \frac{1}{\mu(H_{c_k})}\int_{H_{c_k}} (f(x)+\lambda) d\mu)^2 + \eta, \tag{4.20}$$
where λ is a real number such that $f(x)+\lambda \geqslant 0$. Since $\bar{c} \leqslant f(x) \leqslant c_k$ for $x \in H_{c_k}$, we have, from (4.20),
$$(c_k+\lambda)^2 > (\bar{c}+\lambda)^2 + \eta. \tag{4.21}$$
As k tends to ∞, (4.21) implies that
$$(c+\lambda)^2 \geqslant (\bar{c}+\lambda)^2 + \eta,$$
which is a contradiction.

We now turn our attention to the modified variance condition. If $V_1(f, \bar{c})=0$, then since $0 \leqslant V(f, \bar{c}) \leqslant V_1(f, \bar{c})$, $V(f, \bar{c})=0$; so that $\bar{x}$ is a global minimum and $\bar{c}$ is the global minimum value of f.

Conversely, if $\bar{x}$ is a global minimum of f, then $M(f, \bar{c})=\bar{c}=f(x)$. This means that $V_1(f, \bar{c})=V(f, \bar{c})$. Therefore, $V_1(f, \bar{c})=V(f, \bar{c})=0$.

4.4 Higher Moments

Suppose $c > \bar{c} = \min f(x)$. Then $\mu(H_c) > 0$.

Definition 4.4 Suppose m is a positive integer and $c > \bar{c}$, we define
$$M_m(f, c; a) = \frac{1}{\mu(H_c)} \int_{H_c} (f(x)-a)^m d\mu \tag{4.22}$$
to be the m-th moment of f over its level set H_c centered at a.

This concept extends those of mean value, variance and modified variance. Specifically,
$$M(f, c) = M_1(f, c; 0); \tag{4.23}$$
$$V(f, c) = M_2(f, c; M(f, c)) \tag{4.24}$$
and
$$V_1(f, c) = M_2(f, c; c). \tag{4.25}$$

Proposition 4.6 *The m-th moment of f over its level set has the following properties:*

(1) *m-th degree positive homogeneity*,
$$M_m(\lambda f, \lambda c; \lambda a) = \lambda^m M_m(f, c; a), \text{ for } c > \bar{c} \text{ and } \lambda \geqslant 0; \tag{4.26}$$

(2) *Cancellation*
$$M_m(f+\lambda, c+\lambda; a+\lambda) = M_m(f, c; a)$$
$$= \sum_{i=0}^{m} (-1)^{m-i} \binom{m}{i} M((f+\lambda)^i, (c+\lambda)^i)(a+\lambda)^{m-i},$$

$$\text{for } c > \bar{c} \text{ and real } \lambda \quad (f(x)+\lambda \geqslant 0), \qquad (4.27)$$

where
$$\binom{m}{i} = \frac{i!(m-i)!}{m!}.$$

Proof. (1) Since $\{x \mid \lambda f(x) \leqslant \lambda c\} = \{x \mid f(x) \leqslant c\} = H_c$ for $\lambda > 0$, so

$$M_m(\lambda f, \lambda c; \lambda a) = \frac{1}{\mu(H_c)} \int_{H_c} (\lambda f(x) - \lambda a)^m \mathrm{d}\mu$$

$$= \frac{\lambda^m}{\mu(H_c)} \int_{H_c} (f(x)-a)^m \mathrm{d}\mu = \lambda^m M_m(f, c; a).$$

(2) Since $\{x \mid f(x)+\lambda \leqslant c+\lambda\} = H_c$ for real number λ, we have

$$M_m(f+\lambda, c+\lambda; a+\lambda) = \frac{1}{\mu(H_c)} \int_{H_c} (f(x)+\lambda-(a+\lambda))^m \mathrm{d}\mu$$

$$= M_m(f, c; a)$$

$$= \sum_{i=0}^m (-1)^{m-i} \binom{m}{i} \left(\frac{1}{\mu(H_c)} \int_{H_c} (f(x)+\lambda)^i \mathrm{d}\mu\right) (a+\lambda)^{m-i}$$

$$= \sum_{i=0}^m (-1)^{m-i} \binom{m}{i} M((f+\lambda)^i, (c+\lambda)^i)(a+\lambda)^{m-i}.$$

Like the mean value and the variance cases, $M_m(f, c; a)$ is right-hand continuous in c.

Proposition 4.7 *Suppose $\{c_k\}$ is a decreasing sequence which tends to c as $k \to \infty$ and $c > \bar{c}$. Then*

$$M_m(f, c; a) = \lim_{c_k \downarrow c} M_m(f, c_k; a), \text{ for } m \in \{1, 2, \cdots\}. \qquad (4.28)$$

Proof. Take a real number λ such that $f(x)+\lambda \geqslant 0$ for $x \in H_{c_1}$. Now $\{(c_k+\lambda)^i\}$ is a decreasing sequence which tends to $(c+\lambda)^i$. By Proposition 4.6

$$\lim_{c_k \downarrow c} M_m(f, c_k; a) = \lim_{c_k \downarrow c} \sum_{i=0}^m (-1)^{m-i} \binom{m}{i} M((f+\lambda)^i, (c_k+\lambda)^i)(a+\lambda)^{m-i}$$

$$= \sum_{i=0}^m (-1)^{m-i} \binom{m}{i} M((f+\lambda)^i, (c+\lambda)^i)(a+\lambda)^{m-i}$$

$$= M_m(f, c; a),$$

since

$$\lim_{c_k \downarrow c} M((f+\lambda)^i, (c_k+\lambda)^i) = M((f+\lambda)^i, (c+\lambda)^i), \qquad (4.29)$$

applying Proposition 3.4.

The following extends Definition 4.4 to include for possibility of $c = \bar{c}$.

Definition 4.5 Suppose $c \geqslant \bar{c}$ and m is a positive interger. Then the m-th moment of f over its level set H_c centered at a is defined to be

$$M_m(f, c; a) = \lim_{c_k \downarrow c} \frac{1}{\mu(H_{c_k})} \int_{H_{c_k}} (f(x)-(a))^m \mathrm{d}\mu. \qquad (4.30)$$

The limit (4.29) exists for each i, so the definition (4.30), which does not depend on the choice of the decreasing sequence $\{c_k\}$, is well defined. Note that Definition 4.5 is consistent with Definition 4.4, and Propositions 4.6 and 4.7 are also valid for $c \geqslant \bar{c}$.

Applying Proposition 4.7, the following offers an aquivalent alternative definition of

$M_m(f, c; a)$.

Definition 4.6 Suppose $c \geqslant \bar{c}$ and m is a positive integer. Then the m-th moment of f over its level set H_c centered at a is defined to be

$$M_m(f, c; a) = \lim_{\substack{d \to c \\ d > c}} \frac{1}{\mu(H_d)} \int_{H_d} (f(x) - (a))^m d\mu. \qquad (4.31)$$

4.5 Higher Moment Conditions

We shall demonstrate that the mean value and variance conditions of the earlier subsections are special cases of the higher moment conditions developed in this subsection. In particular, they correspond to the odd and the even higher moments respectively.

We first provide the odd moment conditions below.

Theorem 4.2 *For the problem* (1.1) *under assumptions* (A_1) *and* (A_2), *a point $\bar{x}$ is a global minimum and $\bar{c} = f(\bar{x})$ is the corresponding minimum value of f if and only if*

$$M_{2m-1}(f, c; 0) \geqslant \bar{c}^{2m-1}, \text{ for } c > \bar{c} \qquad (4.32)$$

or

$$M_{2m-1}(f, \bar{c}; 0) = \bar{c}^{2m-1}, \qquad (4.33)$$

for some integer m.

Proof. Note that $\bar{c}$ is the global minimum value of f if and only if $\bar{c}^{2m-1}$ is the global minimum value of f^{2m-1}. Also, the level set H_c induced by f is identical to the level set $H_{c^{2m-1}}$ induced by f^{2m-1} over its level sets $H_{c^{2m-1}}$ induced by f^{2m-1}. Expressions of (4.32) and (4.33) are the simply restatement of the mean value conditions in Theorem 1.8 for f^{2m-1} over its level sets $H_{c^{2m-1}}$ parameterized by c^{2m-1}.

Theorem 4.3 *With respect to the above problem, a point $\bar{x}$ is a global minimum point and $\bar{c} = f(\bar{x})$ is the corresponding global minimum value if and only if*

$$M_{2m}(f, \bar{c}; M(f, \bar{c})) = 0, \qquad (4.34)$$

for some positive integer m.

Proof. Suppose condition (4.34) holds but $\bar{c} = f(\bar{x})$ is not the global minimum value of f, then $\mu(H_{\bar{c}}) > 0$. We have

$$\frac{1}{\mu(H_{\bar{c}})} \int_{H_{\bar{c}}} (f(x) - M(f, \bar{c}))^{2m} d\mu = 0, \qquad (4.35)$$

which implies that $f(x) = M(f, \bar{c})$ for all $x \in H_{\bar{c}}$ since f is continuous. It follows that

$$M(f, \bar{c}) = f(\bar{x}),$$

so that $\bar{x}$ is a global minimum point of f which yields a contradiction.

Observe that $|f(x)| \leqslant L$ for $x \in H_{c_0}$, where $c_0 > \bar{c}$ and $L = \max\{c_0, |\bar{c}|\}$. We have, for $x \in H_{c_0}$,

$$0 \leqslant (f(x) - M(f, c))^{2m} \leqslant (2L)^{2m-2} (f(x) - M(f, c))^2,$$

so that

$$0 \leqslant M_{2m}(f, c; M(f, c)) \leqslant (2L)^{2m-2} V(f, c), \quad m = 1, 2, \cdots.$$

If $\bar{c} = f(\bar{x})$ is the global minimum value, then $V(f, \bar{c}) = 0$ which implies that

$$M_{2m}(f, \bar{c}; M)(f, \bar{c})) = 0.$$

This proves the necessity of (4.33).

Conditions (4.32) and (4.33) are not extendable to the even case neither can condition (4.34) be extended to the odd case. A more general form of higher moment condition which applies to odd as well as even moments is given bolow.

Theorem 4.4 *A point $\bar{x}$ is a global minimum point, for the problem in Theorem 4.2, and $\bar{c}=f(\bar{x})$ is the corresponding global minimum value if and only if*

$$M_m(f, \bar{c}; \bar{c})=0 \tag{4.36}$$

for some positive integer m.

Proof (Necessity). Suppose $\bar{c}=f(\bar{x})$ is the global minimum value and m is odd, then

$$M_m(f, c; c) \leqslant 0, \text{ for } c > \bar{c},$$

since $f(x)-c \leqslant 0$ for $x \in H_c$. But, for any decreasing sequence $\{c_k\}$ which tends to $\bar{c}$, we have

$$\lim_{c_k \downarrow \bar{c}} M_m(f, c_k; c_k)$$

$$= \lim_{c_k \downarrow \bar{c}} \sum_{i=0}^{m} (-1)^{m-i} \binom{m}{i} \frac{1}{\mu(H_{c_k})} \left(\int_{H_{c_k}} (f(x)-\bar{c})^i d\mu \right) (\bar{c}-c_k)^{m-i}$$

$$+ \lim_{c_k \downarrow \bar{c}} \frac{1}{\mu(H_{c_k})} \int_{H_{c_k}} (f(x)-\bar{c})^m d\mu = M_m(f, \bar{c}; \bar{c}). \tag{4.37}$$

Thus,

$$M_m(f, \bar{c}; \bar{c}) \leqslant 0. \tag{4.38}$$

On the other hand, since $f(x)-\bar{c} \geqslant 0$ for all x,

$$M_m(f, \bar{c}; \bar{c}) = \lim_{c_k \downarrow \bar{c}} M_m(f, c_k; \bar{c}) = \lim_{c_k \downarrow \bar{c}} \frac{1}{\mu(H_{c_k})} \int_{H_{c_k}} (f(x)-\bar{c})^m d\mu \geqslant 0. \tag{4.39}$$

Hence, from (4.38) and (4.39), we have

$$M_m(f, \bar{c}; \bar{c})=0.$$

If m is even and $\bar{c}=f(\bar{x})$ is the global minimum value, then $M(f, \bar{c})=\bar{c}$, so that (4.35) is equivalent to

$$M_m(f, \bar{c}; \bar{c})=0.$$

(Sufficiency). If m is even and $M_m(f, \bar{c}; \bar{c})=0$ but $\bar{c}=f(\bar{x})$ is not the global minimum value of f, then $\mu(H_{\bar{c}}) > 0$. We have

$$\frac{1}{\mu(H_{\bar{c}})} \int_{H_{\bar{c}}} (f(x)-\bar{c})^m d\mu = 0,$$

which implies that $f(x)=\bar{c}$ for all $x \in H_{\bar{c}}$ since $f(x)$ is continuous. It follows that

$$M(f, \bar{c})=\bar{c}.$$

Therefore, $\bar{c}$ is the global minimum value.

Suppose m is odd, $\bar{x}$ is not the global minimum point and $\bar{c}=f(\bar{x})$ is not the global minimum value of f, while $\hat{c}$ is. Let $2\eta=\bar{c}-\hat{c}>0$. We have that $\mu(H_{\bar{c}})$ and $\mu(H_{\bar{c}-\eta})$ are both positive. Meanwhile,

$$f(x) \leqslant \bar{c}-\eta, \text{ for } x \in H_{\bar{c}-\eta}.$$

For m odd, we have that

$$(f(x)-\bar{c})^m \leqslant -\eta^m, \text{ for } x \in H_{\bar{c}-\eta}$$

and

$$(f(x)-\bar{c})^m \leqslant 0, \text{ for } x \in H_{\bar{c}}.$$

We now have

$$\begin{aligned}
M_m(f, \bar{c}; \bar{c}) &= \frac{1}{\mu(H_{\bar{c}})} \int_{H_{\bar{c}}} (f(x)-\bar{c})^m d\mu \\
&= \frac{1}{\mu(H_{\bar{c}})} \int_{H_{\bar{c}} \setminus H_{\bar{c}-\eta}} (f(x)-\bar{c})^m d\mu + \frac{1}{\mu(H_{\bar{c}})} \int_{H_{\bar{c}-\eta}} (f(x)-\bar{c})^m d\mu \\
&\leqslant -\eta^m \frac{\mu(H_{\bar{c}-\eta})}{\mu(H_{\bar{c}})} < 0.
\end{aligned}$$

This is a contradiction to condition (4.36).

References

[1] I. V. Girsanov. Lecture on Mathematical Theory of Extremum Problems [R]. Lecture Notes in Economics and Mathematical Systems, No. 67, Springer-Verlag, New York, 1972.

[2] O. L. Mangasarian. Nonlinear Programming [M]. McGraw-Hill, New York, 1969.

[3] R. T. Rockafellar. Convex Analysis [M]. Princeton University Press, Princeton, N. J., 1970.

[4] Zheng Quan. On optimality conditions for global extremum problems [J]. *Numerical Mathematics, A Journal of Chinese Universities*, 3(1981), 273—275.

[5] Zheng Quan. Higher moment and optimality conditions for global extremum problems [J]. *Chinese Journal of Operations Research*, 1(1982), 73—74.

[6] Zheng Quan. Optimality conditions for global optimization (II). *Acta Math. Appl. Sinica* (in preparation).

Optimality Conditions for Global Optimization (II) *

Abstract: In this paper we continue to investigate the global optimality conditions for constrained problems by the theory of measure and integration.

Let X be a Hausdorff topological space, $f: X \to \mathbb{R}$ a real-valued function and S a closed subset of X. The problem considered here is to find the infimum of f over S,
$$\bar{c} = \inf_{x \in S} f(x)$$
and the set of global minima.

Here, as in [12], we also asumme that the following two conditions are satisfied:
(A_1) $f: X \to \mathbb{R}$ is continuous;
(A_2) There is a real c such that the level set
$$H_c = \{x \mid f(x) \leqslant c\}$$
is compact and $S \cap H_c \neq \varnothing$.

For a knowledge about Q-measure, refer to [12].

5 The Constrained Case

This section parallels, the development in the previous sections of the mean value, variance and higher-moment characterizations of global optimality for some constrained cases. Specifically, we treat the case of a robust feasible set, the case where the feasible set is a manifold and the case of the intersection of these two sets. An exposition in terms of a linear manifold in $\mathbb{R}^n$ corresponding to a set of linear equality constraints has been discussed in detail in [10].

5.1 Rejection Conditions

Suppose the set $S \subset X$ is robust. Consider the problem of finding the global minimum value of a real-valued function f on X over S. As before, we assume that assumptions (A_1) and (A_2) are satisfied.

Let (X, Ω, μ) be a Q-measure space. We can construct a derived Q-measure space $(X \cap S, \Omega_s, \mu_s)$ in the following manner. The set $O \cap S$ is regarded as an open set if set O is an open set in X. The family of sets $\Omega_s = \{S \cap B \mid B \in \Omega\}$ is a σ-field.

The measure μ_s is defined by

---

* Reprinted from Acta Mathematicsae Applicatae Sinica, 1985, 2(2):118—132.

$$\mu_s(A) = \mu(A \cap S), \text{ for } A \in \Omega. \tag{5.1}$$

A nonempty open set in $X \cap S$ is written as $O \cap S (\neq \emptyset)$. By the proof of Lemma 2.2, we have

$$\mu_s(O) = \mu(O \cap S) > 0.$$

Hence, $(X \cap S, \Omega_s, \mu_s)$ is a Q-measure space.

Definiton 5.1 Suppose $S \subset X$ is a robust set. The measure space $(X \cap S, \Omega_s, \mu_s)$ is called a rejection measure space.

The rejection versions of mean value, variance and higher moments of a function over its level sets are defined below.

Definition 5.2 Suppose $\{c_k\}$ is a decreasing sequence which tends to $c \geq \bar{c} = \min_{x \in S} f(x)$. The limits

$$M(f, c; S) = \lim_{c_k \downarrow c} \frac{1}{\mu(H_{c_k} \cap S)} \int_{H_{c_k} \cap S} f(x) d\mu, \tag{5.2}$$

$$V(f, c; S) = \lim_{c_k \downarrow c} \frac{1}{\mu(H_{c_k} \cap S)} \int_{H_{c_k} \cap S} (f(x) - M(f, c; S))^2 d\mu, \tag{5.3}$$

$$V_1(f, c; S) = \lim_{c_k \downarrow c} \frac{1}{\mu(H_{c_k} \cap S)} \int_{H_{c_k} \cap S} (f(x) - c)^2 d\mu \tag{5.4}$$

and

$$M_m(f, c; a; S) = \lim_{c_k \downarrow c} \frac{1}{\mu(H_{c_k} \cap S)} \int_{H_{c_k} \cap S} (f(x) - a)^m d\mu, m = 1, 2, \cdots \tag{5.5}$$

arc called, respectively, rejection mean value, rejection variance, rejection modified variance and rejection m-th moment of f over $H_c \cap S$.

Since a rejection measure derived from a Q-measure is also a Q-measure, the above definitions are well dfined. Consequently, we inherit for the rejection moments all the properties of the moment of f over its level sets H_c developed in Sections 4 and 5. The corresponding rejection global optimality conditions are collected in Theorem 5.1 below.

Theorem 5.1 *With respect to the constrained minimization problem* (1.1) (*under assumptions* (A_1) *and* (A_2)) *with a robust constrained set* S, *the following are equivalent*:

    a. $\bar{x} \in S$ is a global minimum and $\bar{c} = f(\bar{x})$ is the corresponding global minimum value;

    b. $M(f, c; S) \geq \bar{c}$, for $c > \bar{c}$;   (5.6)

    c. $M(f, \bar{c}; S) = \bar{c}$;   (5.7)

    d. $V(f, \bar{c}; S) = 0$;   (5.8)

    e. $V_1(f, \bar{c}; S) = 0$;   (5.9)

    f. $M_{2m-1}(f, c; 0; s) \geq (\bar{c})^{2m-1}$, for $c > \bar{c}$ and some positive integer m;   (5.10)

    g. $M_{2m-1}(f, \bar{c}; 0; S) = (\bar{c})^{2m-1}$, for some positive integer m;   (5.11)

    h. $M_{2m}(f, \bar{c}; M(f, \bar{c}; S); S) = 0$, for some positive integer m;   (5.12)

    i. $M_m(f, \bar{c}; \bar{c}; S) = 0$, for some positive integer m.   (5.13)

Example 5.1 Consider the problem of finding the minimum of $f(x)=X$ over the robust set $S=[1,2]$. For any c, the level set $H_c=\{x\mid x\leqslant c\}=(-\infty,c]$ so that

$$M(f,c;S)=\frac{1}{\mu(H_c\cap S)}\int_{H_c\cap S}f(x)\mathrm{d}\mu=\frac{1}{c-1}\int_1^c x\mathrm{d}x=\frac{1}{2(c-1)}(c^2-1)=\frac{c+1}{2}$$

for $c\geqslant 1$. Applying the mean value condition, we have

$$M(f,\bar{c};S)=\bar{c}=\frac{\bar{c}+1}{2}.$$

Hence, $\bar{c}=1$ and $\overline{H}=\{1\}$.

5.2 Reduction Conditions

A manifold L in a Hausdorff space X is a Hausdorff topological subspace of X in which each point has an open neighborhood homeomorphic to a topological space Y. Sometimes the topological space Y is endowed with a special structure. For instance, $Y=\mathbb{R}^m$; in this case the manifold L is called a topological m-manifold. In this subsection we only consider a general case of manifold. In [10], we consider linear m-manifold in $X=\mathbb{R}^m$ in detail.

Suppose the constrained set L is a manifold in X. Then the minimization problem is restricted to the manifold L. In L, the open set has the form $L\cap O$, where O is an open set in X. Let $\Omega_L=\{L\cap B\mid B\in\Omega\}$, where Ω is a Borel field of subsets of X. We further suppose that there is a Q-measure μ_L on Ω_L. Thus we have a reduction Q-measure space (L,Ω_L,μ_L).

Definition 5.3 Suppose $L\subset X$ is a manifold. The Q-measure space (L,Ω_L,μ_L) is called a reduction measure space.

We can also provide the reduction version of the moments of a function over its truncated level sets.

Definition 5.4 Suppose $\{c_k\}$ is a decreasing sequence which tends to $c\geqslant\bar{c}=\min_{X\in L}f(x)$ as $k\to\infty$. The limits

$$M(f,c;L)=\lim_{c_k\downarrow c}\frac{1}{\mu_L(H_{c_k}\cap L)}\int_{H_{c_k}\cap L}f(x)\mathrm{d}\mu_L, \tag{5.14}$$

$$V(f,c;L)=\lim_{c_k\downarrow c}\frac{1}{\mu_L(H_{c_k}\cap L)}\int_{H_{c_k}\cap L}(f(x)-M(f,c;L))^2\mathrm{d}\mu_L, \tag{5.15}$$

$$V_1(f,c;L)=\lim_{c_k\downarrow c}\frac{1}{\mu_L(H_{c_k}\cap L)}\int_{H_{c_k}\cap L}(f(x)-c)^2\mathrm{d}\mu_L \tag{5.16}$$

and

$$M_m(f,c;a;L)=\lim_{c_k\downarrow c}\frac{1}{\mu_L(H_{c_k}\cap L)}\int_{H_{c_k}\cap L}(f(x)-a)^m\mathrm{d}\mu_L, m=1,2,\cdots \tag{5.17}$$

are called, respectively, reduction mean value, reduction variance, reduction modified variance and reduction m-th moment of f over $H_c\cap L$.

As in the rejection case, these limits are well defined and the useful properties of various moments of f over its level sets H_c treated in Sections 3 and 4 remain valid. The optimality conditions in terms of the reduction moments are given below.

Theorem 5.2 *With respect to the constrained minimization problem* (1.1) *over a manifold* $S = L \cap X$ *(under the assumptions* (A_1) *and* (A_2)*), the following are equivalent:*

a. $\bar{x} \in L$ *is a global minimum and* $\bar{c} = f(\bar{x})$ *is the corresponding global minimum value;*

b. $M(f,c;L) \geqslant \bar{c}$, *for* $c > \bar{c}$;   (5.18)

c. $M(f,\bar{c};L) = \bar{c}$;   (5.19)

d. $V(f,\bar{c};L) = 0$;   (5.20)

e. $V_1(f,\bar{c};L) = 0$;   (5.21)

f. $M_{2m-1}(f,c;0;L) \geqslant (\bar{c})^{2m-1}$, *for* $c > \bar{c}$ *and some positive integer* m;   (5.22)

g. $M_{2m-1}(f,\bar{c};0;L) = \bar{c}$, *for some positive integer* m;   (5.23)

h. $M_{2m}(f,\bar{c};M(f,\bar{c};L);L) = 0$, *for some positive integer* m;   (5.24)

i. $M_m(f,\bar{c};\bar{c};L) = 0$, *for some positive integer* m.   (5.25)

Suppose (L, Ω_L, μ_L) is a Q-measure space, G is a robust set in X and $L \cap \text{int } G \neq \emptyset$. Then a rejection-reduction measure $\mu_{L \cap G}$ can also be introduced

$$\mu_{L \cap G}(A) = \mu_L(A \cap G), \quad \text{for } A \in \Omega_L. \tag{5.26}$$

The following definitions and theorem are similar to those of the rejection and the reduction cases:

Definition 5.5 Suppose $\{c_k\}$ is a decreasing sequence which tends to $c \geqslant \bar{c} = \min_{x \in L \cap G} f(x)$ as $k \to \infty$. The limits

$$M(f,c;L \cap G) = \lim_{c_k \downarrow c} \frac{1}{\mu_L(H_{c_k} \cap L \cap G)} \int_{H_{c_k} \cap L \cap G} f(x) \, d\mu_L, \tag{5.27}$$

$$V(f,c;L \cap G) = \lim_{c_k \downarrow c} \frac{1}{\mu_L(H_{c_k} \cap L \cap G)} \int_{H_{c_k} \cap L \cap G} (f(x) - M(f,c;L \cap G))^2 \, d\mu_L, \tag{5.28}$$

$$V_1(f,c;L \cap G) = \lim_{c_k \downarrow c} \frac{1}{\mu_L(H_{c_k} \cap L \cap G)} \int_{H_{c_k} \cap L \cap G} (f(x) - c)^2 \, d\mu_L, \tag{5.29}$$

$$M_m(f,c;L \cap G) = \lim_{c_k \downarrow c} \frac{1}{\mu_L(H_{c_k} \cap L \cap G)} \int_{H_{c_k} \cap L \cap G} (f(x) - a)^m \, d\mu_L, m = 1, 2, \cdots \tag{5.30}$$

are the rejection-reduction mean value variance, modified variance and m-th moment of f over $H_c \cap L \cap G$, respectively.

Theorem 5.3 *With respect to the constrained minimization problem* I. (1.1) *over* $S = L \cap G$ *(under assumptions* (A_1) *and* (A_2)*), the following are equivalent:*

a. $\bar{x} \in L \cap G$ *is a global minimum and* $\bar{c} = f(\bar{x})$ *is the corresponding global minimum value;*

b. $M(f,c;L \cap G) \geqslant \bar{c}$, *for* $c > \bar{c}$;   (5.31)

c. $M(f,\bar{c};L \cap G) = \bar{c}$;   (5.32)

d. $V(f,\bar{c};L \cap G) = 0$;   (5.33)

e. $V_1(f,\bar{c};L \cap G) = 0$;   (5.34)

f. $M_{2m-1}(f,c;0;L \cap G) \geqslant (\bar{c})^{2m-1}$, *for* $c > \bar{c}$ *and some positive integer* m;   (5.35)

g. $M_{2m-1}(f,\bar{c};0;L\cap G)=\bar{c}$, *for some positive integer m*; (5.36)

h. $M_{2m-1}(f,\bar{c};M(f,\bar{c};L\cap G);L\cap G)=0$, *for some positive integer m*; (5.37)

i. $M_m(f,\bar{c};\bar{c};L\cap G)=0$, *for some positive integer m*. (5.38)

We observe that our constrained global optimality conditions share a unified form with those of the unconstrained case. The difference between them arises mainly from the definition of different Q-measure space for the same problem. In the working paper[10], we treat the case of linear equality constraints in $\mathbb{R}^n$ as an example of the application of the reduction conditions.

6 Penalty Global Optimality Conditions

In this section, the concepts of mean value, variance, modified variance and higher moments over level sets will be extended to the case of penalty functions. The corresponding global optimality conditions turn out to be particularly implementable when we discuss theoretical algorithms of penalty[11]. We will assume that the topological space X is a metric space in addition to the assumptions (A_1) and (A_2) maintained so far.

6.1 Penalty Mean Value

Let S be a closed subset of X. Consider the constrained minimization problem:
$$\bar{c}=\min_{x\in S}f(x). \tag{6.1}$$

Definition 6.1 A function p on X is a penalty function for the constrained set S if

(i) p is continuous;

(ii) $p(x)\geqslant 0$ for all $x\in X$

and

(iii) $p(x)=0$ if and only if $x\in S$.

In this section we will consider the case where S is a robust set in X. We introduce now a sequence of penalty level sets which is useful in our definitions of a penalty mean value. Suppose $\{c_k\}$ is a decreasing sequence which tends to $c>\bar{c}$ as $k\to\infty$ and $\{a_k\}$ is a positive increasing sequence which tends to infinity as $k\to\infty$. Let
$$H_k=\{x\mid f(x)+a_kp(x)\leqslant c\}, k=1,2,\cdots. \tag{6.2}$$

Lemma 6.1 *The sequence $\{H_k\}$ given by (6.2) is decreasing by inclusion. Moreover,*
$$\lim_{k\to\infty}H_k=\bigcap_{k=1}^{\infty}H_k=H_c\cap S. \tag{6.3}$$

Proof. Suppose $x\in H_{k+1}$, then
$$f(x)+a_{k+1}p(x)\leqslant c_{k+1}.$$
Since $a_{k+1}\leqslant a_k$ and $c_{k+1}\geqslant c_k$, so
$$f(x)+a_kp(x)\leqslant f(x)+a_{k+1}p(x)\leqslant c_{k+1}\leqslant c_k.$$
Therefore, $x\in H_k$, i.e., $H_{k+1}\subset H_k$.

Suppose $x\in \bigcap_{k=1}^{\infty}H_k$, then $x\in H_k$ and
$$f(x)+a_kp(x)\leqslant c_k\leqslant c_1, \text{ for all } k. \tag{6.4}$$

If $x \in S$ then $p(x) > 0$. Hence, $a_k p(x) \to \infty$ as $k \to \infty$ which contradicts (6.4). Therefore, $x \in S$ and
$$f(x) + a_k p(x) = f(x) \leqslant c_k, \text{ for all } k.$$
This implies that $x \in H_c$. Thus, we have proved
$$\bigcap_{k=1}^{\infty} H_k \subset H_c \cap S.$$
On the other hand, if $x \in H_c \cap S$, then
$$f(x) + a_k p(x) = f(x) \leqslant c \leqslant c_k, \text{ for all } k.$$
Hence, $x \in H_k$ for all k, i.e.,
$$H_c \cap S \subset \bigcap_{k=1}^{\infty} H_k.$$

By using Lemma 6.1, we now proceed to prove:

Lemma 6.2 *Suppose $c > \bar{c}$, $\{c_k\}$ is a decreasing sequence which tends to c as $k \to \infty$ and $\{c_k\}$ is a positive increasing sequence which tends to infinity as $k \to \infty$. Then*
$$\lim_{k \to \infty} \frac{1}{\mu(H_k)} \int_{H_k} f(x) d\mu = \frac{1}{\mu(H_c \cap S)} \int_{H_c \cap S} f(x) d\mu. \tag{6.5}$$

We defined in Section 5 the rejection mean value of f over its level set with robust constrained set S to be
$$M(f, c; S) = \frac{1}{\mu(H_c \cap S)} \int_{H_c \cap S} f(x) d\mu$$
if $c > \bar{c}$. Therefore,
$$\lim_{k \to \infty} \frac{1}{\mu(H_k)} \int_{H_k} f(x) d\mu = M(f, c; S) \tag{6.6}$$
and the limit does not depend on the choice of sequence $\{c_k\}$ and $\{a_k\}$.

Definition 6.2 Suppose $c > \bar{c}$. The limit
$$M(f, c; p) = \lim_{k \to \infty} \frac{1}{\mu(H_k)} \int_{H_k} f(x) d\mu \tag{6.7}$$
is called the penalty mean value of f over its level set with respect to the penalty function p defined on the feasible set S.

Note that the penalty mean value $M(f, c; p)$ does not depend on the choice of $\{c_k\}$ and $\{a_k\}$ when $c > \bar{c}$. What about the case $c = \bar{c}$?

Lemma 6.3 *Suppose $\bar{c} = f(\bar{x})$ is the global minimum value of f over S, then*
$$\bar{c} = M(f, \bar{c}; S) = M(f, \bar{c}; p). \tag{6.8}$$

Proof. If $\bar{c} = f(\bar{x})$ is the global minimum value of f over S then $\bar{c} = M(f, \bar{c}; S)$. Suppose $\{c_k\}$ is a decreasing sequence which tends to $\bar{c}$ as $k \to \infty$ and $\{a_k\}$ is a positive increasing sequence which tends to infinity, then
$$\frac{1}{\mu(H_k)} \int_{H_k} f(x) d\mu \leqslant \frac{1}{\mu(H_k)} \int_{H_k} (f(x) + a_k p(x)) d\mu \leqslant c_k, \text{ for } k = 1, 2, \cdots.$$
Hence
$$\limsup_{k \to \infty} \frac{1}{\mu(H_k)} \int_{H_k} f(x) d\mu \leqslant \bar{c}. \tag{6.9}$$

We will prove that
$$\liminf_{k\to\infty} \frac{1}{\mu(H_k)} \int_{H_k} f(x) d\mu \geq \bar{c}. \tag{6.10}$$

Otherwise, there is a subsequence of $\left\{\frac{1}{\mu(H_k)}\int_{H_k} f(x)d\mu\right\}$ such that
$$\lim_{k_i\to\infty} \frac{1}{\mu(H_{k_i})} \int_{H_{k_i}} f(x) d\mu = \hat{c} < c.$$

Let $2\eta = \bar{c} - \hat{c} > 0$. Then there is an integer N such that
$$\frac{1}{\mu(H_{k_i})} \int_{H_{k_i}} f(x) d\mu < \bar{c} - \eta, \text{ for all } k_i > N. \tag{6.11}$$

It follows that there is at least a point $x_{k_i} \in H_{k_i}$ such that
$$f(x_{k_i}) < \bar{c} - \eta, \quad k_i > N. \tag{6.12}$$

Therefore, we have constructed a sequence $\{x_{k_i}\}_{k_i=N}^{\infty}$ which has a convergent subsequence because of the assumption of compactness (A_2). Without loss of generality, suppose $\{x_{k_i}\}$ is a convergent sequence $x_{k_i} \to \hat{x}$ as $k_i \to \infty$. It is clear that $\hat{x}$ is contained in $\bigcap_{k=1}^{\infty} H_k$ which is closed. Hence,
$$f(\hat{x}) = \lim_{k_i\to\infty} f(x_{k_i}) \leq \bar{c} - \eta. \tag{6.13}$$

According to Lemma 6.1, $\hat{x} \in H_{\bar{c}} \cap S$. This implies that $f(\hat{x}) \geq \bar{c}$, which contradicts (6.13).

The result follows from by observing that
$$\bar{c} \leq \liminf_{k\to\infty} \frac{1}{\mu(H_k)} \int_{H_k} f(x) d\mu \leq \limsup_{k\to\infty} \frac{1}{\mu(H_k)} \int_{H_k} f(x) d\mu \leq \bar{c}. \tag{6.14}$$

6.2 Penalty Mean Value Conditions

Since penalty mean value coincides with rejection one, by Theorem 5.1 we have

Theorem 6.1 *The following are equivalent:*

  a. *A point $\bar{x} \in S$ is a global minimum with $\bar{c} = f(\bar{x})$ as the corresponding global minimum value of f over S;*
  b. $M(f, c; p) \geq \bar{c}$, *for* $c > \bar{c}$; \hfill (6.15)
  c. $M(f, \bar{c}; p) = \bar{c}$. \hfill (6.16)

It is natural to think that one can use
$$M'(f, c; p) = \lim_{k\to\infty} \frac{1}{\mu(H_k)} \int_{H_k} (f(x) + a_k p(x)) d\mu \tag{6.17}$$

as an alternative definition of penalty mean value. The following two lemmas tell us that they are equivalent.

Lemma 6.4 *Suppose* $c > \bar{c}$, $\{c_k\}$ *is a decreasing sequence which tends to c as $k \to \infty$ and $\{a_k\}$ is a positive increasing sequence which tends to infinity. Then*
$$\lim_{k\to\infty} \frac{1}{\mu(H_k)} \int_{H_k} (f(x) + a_k p(x)) d\mu = \frac{1}{\mu(H_c \cap S)} \int_{H_c \cap S} f(x) d\mu. \tag{6.18}$$

Proof. Since $c > \bar{c}$, we have $\mu(H_c \cap S) > 0$ and after applying Lemma 2.2. We have

$$\left|\frac{1}{\mu(H_k)}\int_{H_k}(f(x)+a_kp(x))\mathrm{d}\mu-\frac{1}{\mu(H_c\cap S)}\int_{H_c\cap B}f(x)\mathrm{d}\mu\right|$$

$$\leqslant\left|\frac{1}{\mu(H_k)}-\frac{1}{\mu(H_c\cap S)}\right|\left|\int_{H_k}(f(x)+a_kp(x))\mathrm{d}\mu\right|$$

$$+\frac{1}{\mu(H_c\cap S)}\left|\int_{H_k}(f(x)+a_kp(x))\mathrm{d}\mu-\int_{H_c\cap S}(f(x)+a_kp(x))\mathrm{d}\mu\right|.$$

Now, by Lemma 6.1, we have

$$\left|\frac{1}{\mu(H_k)}-\frac{1}{\mu(H_c\cap S)}\right|\left|\int_{H_k}(f(x)+a_kp(x))\mathrm{d}\mu\right|\leqslant L\frac{|\mu(H_c\cap S)-\mu(H_k)|}{\mu(H_c\cap S)}\to 0,$$

as $k\to\infty$,

and

$$\frac{1}{\mu(H_c\cap S)}\left|\int_{H_k}(f(x)+a_kp(x))\mathrm{d}\mu-\int_{H_c\cap S}(f(x)+a_kp(x))\mathrm{d}\mu\right|$$

$$\leqslant\frac{2L|\mu(H_k)-\mu(H_c\cap S)|}{\mu(H_c\cap S)}\to 0,\text{ as }k\to\infty.$$

Lemma 6.5 *Suppose $\bar{c}$ is the global minimum value of f over S. Then*

$$\lim_{k\to\infty}\frac{1}{\mu(H_k)}\int_{H_k}(f(x)+a_kp(x))\mathrm{d}\mu=M(f,\bar{c};S)=\bar{c}. \tag{6.19}$$

Proof. Let $\{c_k\}$ be a decreasing sequence which tends to $\bar{c}$ as $k\to\infty$ and $a_k>0$, $a_k\uparrow\infty$. We have

$$\frac{1}{\mu(H_k)}\int_{H_k}f(x)\mathrm{d}\mu\leqslant\frac{1}{\mu(H_k)}\int_{H_k}(f(x)+a_kp(x))\mathrm{d}\mu\leqslant c_k.$$

As $k\to\infty$, we have

$$\bar{c}=M(f,\bar{c};p)\leqslant\liminf_{k\to\infty}\frac{1}{\mu(H_k)}\int_{H_k}(f(x)+a_kp(x))\mathrm{d}\mu$$

$$\leqslant\limsup_{k\to\infty}\frac{1}{\mu(H_k)}\int_{H_k}(f(x)+a_kp(x))\mathrm{d}\mu\leqslant\bar{c}.$$

Hence, we have the following theorem.

Theorem 6.2 *The following are equivalent*

    a. *A point $\bar{x}\in S$ is a global minimum with $\bar{c}=f(\bar{x})$ as the corresponding global minimum value of f over S;*

    b. $M'(f,c;p)\geqslant\bar{c}$, *for* $c>\bar{c}$;

    c. $M'(f,\bar{c};p)=\bar{c}$. (6.20)

Remark Although $M'(f,c;p)=M(f,c;p)$ for $c\geqslant\bar{c}$, we adopt the latter as the definition of penalty mean value for computational case. In practice, it is more convenient to compute $f(x)$ rather than $f(x)+a_kp(x)$ especially when a_k becomes very large.

6.3 Penalty Variance and Higher Moment Conditions

As in the preceding subsection, the corresponding concepts of penalty variance, modified variance and higher moments are introduced.

Definition 6.3 Suppose $c\geqslant\bar{c}$, where $\bar{c}$ is the global minimum value of f over S, $\{c_k\}$ is a decreasing sequence which tends to c as $k\to\infty$, and $\{a_k\}$ is a positive, increasing and unbounded sequence. The limits

$$V(f,c;p) = \lim_{k\to\infty} \frac{1}{\mu(H_k)} \int_{H_k} (f(x)-M(f,c;p))^2 d\mu, \tag{6.21}$$

$$V_1(f,c;p) = \lim_{k\to\infty} \frac{1}{\mu(H_k)} \int_{H_k} (f(x)-c)^2 d\mu \tag{6.22}$$

and

$$M_m(f,c;a;p) = \lim_{k\to\infty} \frac{1}{\mu(H_k)} \int_{H_k} (f(x)-a)^m d\mu, m=1,2,\cdots \tag{6.23}$$

are called the penalty variance, penalty modified variance and penalty m-th moment of f over its level set H_c with respect to penalty function $p(x)$ depending on the constrained set S, where

$$H_k = \{x | f(x)+a_k p(x) \leqslant c_k\}, k=1,2,\cdots.$$

Of course, we should prove that (6.21), (6.22) and (6.23) are well defined, i.e., the limits exist and do not depend on the choice of sequences $\{c_k\}$ and $\{a_k\}$. This is the content of the following lemma.

Lemma 6.6 *Suppose* $c \geqslant \bar{c}$, *then*

$$V(f,c;p) = V(f,c;S), \tag{6.24}$$
$$V_1(f,c;p) = V_1(f,c;S) \tag{6.25}$$

and

$$M_m(f,c;a;p) = M_m(f,c;a;S), m=1,2,\cdots. \tag{6.26}$$

Proof. The results of Lemma 6.6 for the case of $c > \bar{c}$ follow by applying method of the proof of Lemma 6.2 For the case $c = \bar{c}$ we will only prove (6.26).

Since

$$\frac{1}{\mu(H_k)} \int_{H_k} (f(x)-a)^m d\mu = \sum_{i=0}^{m} (-1)^{m-i} \binom{m}{i} \frac{1}{\mu(H_k)} \int_{H_k} (f(x)-\bar{c})^i d\mu (a-\bar{c})^{m-i} \tag{6.27}$$

and

$$M_m(f,c;a;S) = \sum_{i=0}^{m} (-1)^{m-i} \binom{m}{i} M_i(f,c;\bar{c};S)(a-\bar{c})^{m-i} \tag{6.28}$$

for $c \geqslant \bar{c}$, it is sufficient to prove that

$$\lim_{k\to\infty} \frac{1}{\mu(H_k)} \int_{H_k} (f(x))^i d\mu = M_i(f,\bar{c};\bar{c};S), \text{ for } i=1,2,\cdots. \tag{6.29}$$

For the Case 1 is odd the proof is similar to that of Lemma 6.3. Suppose $i=2r$ is even. Then

$$0 \leqslant \frac{1}{\mu(H_k)} \int_{H_k} (f(x)-\bar{c})^{2r} d\mu.$$

It follows that

$$0 \leqslant \liminf_{k\to\infty} \frac{1}{\mu(H_k)} \int_{H_k} (f(x)-\bar{c})^{2r} d\mu. \tag{6.30}$$

Suppose

$$\limsup_{k\to\infty}\frac{1}{\mu(H_k)}\int_{H_k}(f(x)-\bar{c})^{2r}\,d\mu\geq\eta>0. \qquad (6.31)$$

Then we can also find a subsequence $\{x_{k_i}\}$ such that $x_{k_i}\in H_{k_i}$, $x_{k_i}\to\hat{x}$ as $k_i\to\infty$, so that
$$(f(\hat{x})-\bar{c})^{2r}\geq\eta.$$

Hence, we have either
$$(f(\hat{x})-\bar{c})\geq\eta^{\frac{1}{2r}} \qquad (6.32)$$

or
$$(f(\hat{x})-\bar{c})\leq-\eta^{\frac{1}{2r}}. \qquad (6.33)$$

Suppose (6.32) holds, i.e., $f(\hat{x})\geq\bar{c}+\eta^{\frac{1}{2r}}$. Note that, $f(\hat{x})\leq c_k$, and $x_k\in H_k$, $k=1,2,\cdots$, so $\hat{x}\in H_{\bar{c}}\cap S$. Therefore, $f(\hat{x})\leq\bar{c}$ which is a contradiction. Condition (6.33), i.e., $f(\hat{x})\leq\bar{c}-\eta^{\frac{1}{2r}}$ contradicts the assumption that $\bar{c}$ is the global minimum value of f over S since $\bar{x}\in S$. This completes our proof for the even case since $M_{gr}(f,\bar{c};\bar{c};S)=0$.

Hence, we have the following theorem.

Theorem 6.3 *The following are equivalent:*

    a. *A point $\bar{x}\in S$ is a global minimum with $\bar{c}=f(\bar{x})$ as the corresponding global minimum value of f over S;*

    b. $V(f,\bar{c};p)=0$; $\qquad\qquad(6.34)$

    c. $V_1(f,\bar{c};p)=0$; $\qquad\qquad(6.35)$

    d. $M_{2m-1}(f,c;0;p)\geq(\bar{c})^{2m-1}$, *for $c>\bar{c}$, for some positive integer m;* $\qquad(6.36)$

    e. $M_{2m-1}(f,\bar{c};0;p)=(\bar{c})^{2m-1}$, *for some positive integer m;* $\qquad(6.37)$

    f. $M_{2m}(f,\bar{c};M(f,\bar{c};p);p)=0$, *for some positive integer m;* $\qquad(6.38)$

    g. $M_m(f,\bar{c};\bar{c};p)=0$, *for some positive integer m.* $\qquad(6.39)$

We can also define penalty variance, modified variance and m-th moments, respectively, of f over its level sets with respect to penalty function as follows:

$$V'(f,c;p)=\lim_{k\to\infty}\frac{1}{\mu(H_k)}\int_{H_k}(f(x)+a_k p(x)-M'(f,c;p))^2\,d\mu, \qquad (6.40)$$

$$V'_1(f,c;p)=\lim_{k\to\infty}\frac{1}{\mu(H_k)}\int_{H_k}(f(x)+a_k p(x)-\bar{c})^2\,d\mu \qquad (6.41)$$

and

$$M'_m(f,c;p)=\lim_{k\to\infty}\frac{1}{\mu(H_k)}\int_{H_k}(f(x)+a_k p(x)-a)^m\,d\mu, m=1,2,\cdots, \qquad (6.42)$$

and prove that
$$V'(f,c;p)=V(f,c;p)=V(f,c;S), \qquad (6.43)$$
$$V'_1(f,c;p)=V_1(f,c;p)=V(f,c;S) \qquad (6.44)$$

and

$$M'_m(f,c;a;p)=M_m(f,c;a;p)=M_m(f,c;a;S), m=1,2,\cdots. \qquad (6.45)$$

Theorem 6.3 would also be valid for these alternative penalty variance, modified variance and higher moments.

Since penalty mean value, variance, modified variance and higher moments of f

coincide with the constrained ones, they share the same properties. For instance, the penalty mean value $M(f,c;p)$ is an increasing function of $c(c \geq \bar{c})$. In our discussion of theoretical algorithms and implementations, the penalty optimality condition (in an appropriate form) turns out to be more useful than the constrained ones.

7 Examples

All of the previously mentioned optimality criteria are sufficient and necessary under non-stringent assumptions. They can be reduced to other known optimality conditions. A specific measure corresponds to a specific criterion. Here we list a few examples.

Example 7.1 In the Nelder-Mead simplex method for nonlinear minimization problem ([4]) the following requirements have been suggested in the criteria:

$$\frac{1}{n} \sum_{i=1}^{n+1} (f(x_i) - f(x_c))^2 < \varepsilon \tag{7.1}$$

and

$$\frac{1}{n} \sum_{i=1}^{n+1} (f(x_i) - f_{\max})^2 < \varepsilon, \tag{7.2}$$

where $x_c = (x_1 + x_2 + \cdots + x_{n+1})/(n+1)$ and $f_{\max} = \max(f(x_1), f(x_2), \cdots, f(x_{n+1}))$. In our setting, they can be regarded as approximation forms for variance conditions $V(f,\bar{c}) = 0$ and $V_1(f,\bar{c}) = 0$, respectively.

Example 7.2 (Convex Case) Suppose X is a locally convex linear topological space, S is a closed convex set of X and f is a continuous convex function. Let

$$f_{\xi}(x) = \bar{c} + \langle \xi, x - \bar{x} \rangle, \tag{7.3}$$

where ξ is a vector in the dual space X' and $\bar{c} = f(\bar{x})$.

The following lemma can be proved.

Lemma 7.1 *A point $\bar{x} \in S$ is a global minimal point of f over S if and only if there is a vector $\xi \in \partial f(\bar{x})$ such that*

$$M(f_{\xi}, c; S) \geq \bar{c}, \text{ for } c > \bar{c} \tag{7.4}$$

holds, where $\partial f(\bar{x})$ is the subdifferential of f at point $\bar{x}$.

From Lemma 7.1, one can prove the following lemma.

Lemma 7.2 *A point $\bar{x} \in S$ is a global minimal point of f over S if and only if*

$$\partial f(\bar{x}) \cap P \neq \emptyset, \tag{7.5}$$

where P is the set of the support functionals.

We know that the set of support functionals P coincides with the dual cone of the tangent directions of set S. It also coincides with the dual cone of the feasible directions when S is a robust set. Hence one can establish the optimality conditions in the convex case by Lemma 7.2.

Example 7.3 (Generalized Gradient)

Here, we will establish the link between our integral characterization of global optimality and Clarke's[1,2] generalized derivative approach to obtain necessary conditions for nonconvex programming.

Let X be a Banach space and f a real valued function on X. The function f is said to be locally Lipschitz if for any point $x \in X$, there is a neighborhood $O(x)$ such that for some K and any y and z in $O(x)$, we have

$$|f(y)-f(z)| \leqslant K\|y-z\|. \tag{7.6}$$

For each v in X, the generalized directional derivative $f^\circ(x;v)$ in the direction y is defined by

$$f^\circ(x;v) = \limsup_{\substack{h \to 0 \\ \lambda \downarrow 0}} [f(x+h+\lambda v) - f(x+h)]/\lambda.$$

The generalized directional derivative $f^\circ(x;v)$ can be taken to be convex in direction v.

Definition 7.1 The generalized gradient of f at x, denoted by $\partial_c f(x)$, is defined to be the subdifferential of the convex generalized directional derivative $f^\circ(x; \cdot)$ at 0.

Lemma 7.3 If $\bar{x}$ is a local minimum for f, then 0 is a global minimum of $f^\circ(\bar{x}; \cdot)$.

Applying the global optimality conditions of Theorems 3.6, 4.7 and 4.10, to the generalized directional derivative $f^\circ(\bar{x};v)$ at a local minimum $\bar{x}$ in the above lemma, we obtain the following conditions:

Corollary 7.1 If $\bar{x}$ is a local minimum of f, then

$$M(f^\circ(\bar{x}; \cdot), c) \geqslant 0, \text{ for } c > 0; \tag{7.7}$$

$$M(f^\circ(\bar{x}; \cdot), 0) = 0; \tag{7.8}$$

$$V(f^\circ(\bar{x}; \cdot), 0) = 0; \tag{7.9}$$

$$V_1(f^\circ(\bar{x}; \cdot), 0) = 0, \tag{7.10}$$

where M, V and V_1 are defind with respect to any Q-measure μ on a Borel field of X.

By Lemma 7.1, we have

Corollary 7.2 If $\bar{x}$ is a local minimum for f, then there exists $\xi \in \partial_c f(\bar{x})$ such that

$$M(\langle \xi, \cdot \rangle, c) \geqslant 0, \text{ for } c > 0. \tag{7.11}$$

We are now going to consider the constrained case:

$$\min_{x \in S} f(x). \tag{7.12}$$

Recall that the cone of tangents of S at $\hat{x}$, denoted by $T = T(\hat{x}, S)$, consists of all directions d such that $d = \lim_{k \to 0} \lambda_k (x_k - \hat{x})$, where $\lambda_k > 0, x_k \in S$ for each k and some $\{x_k\}$ which converges to x. Note that T is a closed cone.

Theorem 7.1 If the point $\bar{x} \in S$ is a local minmum of f over S, then 0 is a global minimum of $f^\circ(\bar{x}; \cdot)$ over $T(\bar{x}, S)$.

Suppose T_1 is a non-empty closed convex cone included in $T(\bar{x}, S)$, then

$$\min_{d \in T_1} f^\circ(\bar{x}; d) \geqslant \min_{d \in T} f^\circ(\bar{x}; d) \geqslant f^\circ(\bar{x}; 0).$$

Therefore, we have

Corollary 7.3 If $\bar{x}$ is a local minimum of f over S, then 0 is a global minimum of $f^\circ(\bar{x}; \cdot)$ over T_1.

We consider reduced problem of minimizing the convex function $f^\circ(\bar{x}; \cdot)$ over T_1. By

Lemma 7.1 and Corollary 7.3, we have

Theorem 7.2 *If $\bar{x}$ is a local minimum of f over S, then for any non-empty closed convex cone T_1 included in $T(\bar{x}, S)$, there exists $\xi \in \partial_c f(\bar{x})$ such that*
$$M(\langle \xi, \cdot \rangle, c; T_1) \geq 0, \text{ for } c > 0. \tag{7.13}$$

Lemma 7.1 tells us that if $\bar{x} \in S$ is a global minimum of f over S, then there is $\xi \in \partial_c f(\bar{x})$ such that
$$\langle \xi, d \rangle \geq 0, \text{ for all } d \in T_1.$$
That is, ξ is a vector in the dual of T_1. Hence

Corollary 7.4 *If $\bar{x}$ is a local minimum of f over S, then for any non-empty closed convex cone T_1 included in $T(\bar{x}, S)$,*
$$\partial_c f(\bar{x}) \cap (T_1)^* \neq \emptyset. \tag{7.14}$$

Note that, the tangent cone $J(x, S)$ is closed and convex. The following lemma shows that $J(x, S)$ is included in the cone of tangents $T(x, S)$.

Lemma 7.4 *Suppose S is a closed subset of X and $\bar{x} \in S$. Then*
$$J(\bar{x}, S) \subset T(\bar{x}, S).$$

The following results of Clarke[2] and Hiriart-Urruty[3] are stated as an proof for the sake of completeness.

Theorem 7.3 *If $\bar{x}$ is a local minimum of f over S, then*
$$\partial_c f(\bar{x}) \cap (-N(\bar{x}, S))^* \neq \emptyset \tag{7.15}$$
and
$$\partial_c f(\bar{x}) \cap J(\bar{x}, S)^* \neq \emptyset, \tag{7.16}$$
where $N(\bar{x}, S)$ is a normal cone.

Example 7.4 (Integer Minimization Problems) Let $X = \{x_1, \cdots, x_n, \cdots\}$ and $\tau = 2^X$ be the power set of X. Under the discrete topology (X, τ) is a topological space.

Let S be a subset of X and $f: X \to \mathbb{R}$ be a real-valued function. We are interested in finding the minimum value $\bar{c}$ of f over the constrained set S
$$\bar{c} = \min_{x \in S} f(x), \tag{7.17}$$
and the set $\bar{H}$ of global minima
$$\bar{H} = \{x \mid f(x) = \bar{c}\}, \tag{7.18}$$
if there are solutions to (7.17).

For each real c, the level set
$$H_c = \{x \mid f(x) \leq c\}$$
and the set
$$H_c^\circ = \{x \mid f(x) < c\}$$
are subsets of X. Since any subset of X is open as well as closed, each real-valued function on X is continuous.

We replace assumption (A_2) by

(A_2') There is a real number α such that the level set
$$H_\alpha = \{x \mid f(x) \leq \alpha\}$$

is finite and the intersection $H_a \cap S$ is non-empty. Let $a_i > 0$, $i = 1, 2, \cdots$. Take
$$\Omega = \{A | A \subset X\} \tag{7.19}$$
and define the measure μ on Ω by:
$$\mu(A) = \sum_{x_i \in A} a_i. \tag{7.20}$$

Proposition 7.1 (X, Ω, μ) *is a Q-measure space.*

We define the concepts of mean value, variance, modified variance and higher moments as follows:

Definition 7.2 Suppose $a \geq c \geq \bar{c} = \min f(x)$. We label
$$M(f, c) = \frac{1}{\sum_{x_i \in H_c} a_i} \sum_{x_i \in H_c} a_i f(x_i), \tag{7.21}$$

$$V(f, c) = \frac{1}{\sum_{x_i \in H_c} a_i} \sum_{x_i \in H_c} a_i (f(x_i) - M(f, c))^2, \tag{7.22}$$

$$V_1(f, c) = \frac{1}{\sum_{x_i \in H_c} a_i} \sum_{x_i \in H_c} a_i (f(x_i) - c)^2 \tag{7.23}$$

and
$$M_m(f, c; d) = \frac{1}{\sum_{x_i \in H_c} a_i} \sum_{x_i \in H_c} a_i (f(x_i) - d)^m, m = 1, 2, \cdots \tag{7.24}$$

respectively, as the mean value, variance, modified variance and m-th moment centered at d of f over level set H_c.

Since $\mu(H_c) = \sum_{x_i \in H_c} a_i > 0$ and $|f(x_i)|$ is bounded on H_c, (7.21)—(7.24) are well defined, so that there is no need for a limit-based definition as in the general case.

We can also define the constrained version of the above concepts as follows:

Definition 7.3 Suppose $a \geq c \geq \bar{c} = \min_{x \in S} f(x)$. We label
$$M(f, c; S) = \frac{1}{\sum_{x_i \in H_c \cap S} a_i} \sum_{x_i \in H_c \cap S} a_i f(x_i), \tag{7.25}$$

$$V(f, c; S) = \frac{1}{\sum_{x_i \in H_c \cap S} a_i} \sum_{x_i \in H_c \cap S} a_i (f(x_i) - M(f, c))^2, \tag{7.26}$$

$$V_1(f, c; S) = \frac{1}{\sum_{x_i \in H_c \cap S} a_i} \sum_{x_i \in H_c \cap S} a_i (f(x_i) - c)^2 \tag{7.27}$$

and
$$M_m(f, c; d; S) = \frac{1}{\sum_{x_i \in H_c \cap S} a_i} \sum_{x_i \in H_c \cap S} a_j (f(x_i) - d), m = 1, 2, \cdots \tag{7.28}$$

respectively, as the constrained mean value, variance, modified variance and m-th moment centered at d of f over $H_c \cap S$.

Now, the optimality conditions for integer minimization problem can be stated as follows:

Theorem 7.4 *The following are equivalent*:

a. *A point $\bar{x} \in S$ is a global minimum and $\bar{c} = f(\bar{x})$ is the corresponding global minimum value of f over S*;

b. $M(f,c;S) \geqslant \bar{c}$, *for* $c > \bar{c}$; (7.29)

c. $M(f,\bar{c};S) = \bar{c}$; (7.30)

d. $V(f,\bar{c};S) = 0$; (7.31)

e. $V_1(f,\bar{c};S) = 0$; (7.32)

f. $M_{2m-1}(f,\bar{c};0;S) \geqslant (\bar{c})^{2m-1}$, *for* $c > \bar{c}$ *and some positive integer* m; (7.33)

g. $M_{2m-1}(f,\bar{c};0;S) = (\bar{c})^{2m-1}$, *for some positive integer* m; (7.34)

h. $M_{2m}(f,\bar{c};M(f,\bar{c};S);S) = 0$, *for some positive integer* m; (7.35)

i. $M_m(f,\bar{c};\bar{c};S) = 0$, *for some poitive integer* m. (7.36)

Remark The theory can be also generalized to minimize a class of discontinuous functions. For more details see [8].

References

[1] F. H. Clarke. Generalized Gradients and Applications [J]. *Trams. Amer. Math. Soc.*, 205(1975), 247—262.

[2] F. H. Clarke. A New Approach to Lagrange Multipliers [J]. *Math. Oper. Res.*, 2(1976),165—174.

[3] J. B. Hiriart-Urruty. Tangent Cones, Generalized Gradients and Mathematical Programming in Banach Spaces [J]. *Math. Oper. Res.*, 2(1979),79—97.

[4] J. A. Nelder and R. Mead. A Simplex Method for Function Minimization [J]. *Computer J.*, 7(1965), 308—313.

[5] R. T. Rockafellar. Convex Analysis [M]. Princeton University Press, Princeton, N. J., 1970.

[6] Zheng Quan. Penalty Global Optimality Conditions [J]. *Chinese Journal of Operations Research*, 1 (1983), 56—58.

[7] Zheng Quan. Global Optimization in Integer and Mixed Programming [J]. *Numerical Mathematics, A Journal of Chinese Universities*, 1(1984),91—94.

[8] Zheng Quan. Global Optimization of a Class of Discontinuous Functions [J]. *Numerical Mathematics, A Journal of Chinese Universities*, 1(1985), 31—43.

[9] Zheng Quan, Jiang Baichuan and Zhuang Songlin. A Method for Finding Global Extrema [J]. *Acta Mathematicae Applicatae Sinica*, 2(1978),161—174.

[10] Zheng Quan and Z. Tao. Reduction Method and Optimality Conditions for Global Extremum Problem with Linear Equality Constraints [M]. Math. Dept. PSU, University Park, PA 16802, 1981.

[11] Zheng Quan and L. Zhang. Penalty Function and Global Optimization Problem with Inequality Constraints [J]. *Math. Numer. Sinica*, 2(1980),146—153.

[12] Zheng Quan. Optimality Conditions for Global Optimization (I) [J]. *Acta Mathematicae Applicatae Sinica* (English Series), 2:1(1985), 66—78.

Integral Global Optimization Method for Solution of Nonlinear Complementarity Problems*

Abstract: The mapping in a nonlinear complementarity problem may be discontinuous. The integral global optimization algorithm is proposed to solve a nonlinear complementarity problem with a robust piecewise continuous mapping. Numerical examples are given to illustrate the effectiveness of the algorithm.

1 Introduction

Historically, the use of optimization methods to solve nonlinear complementarity problems has been obstructed by the fact that the solution of global optimization problems was required. In general, these global optimization problems involved constraint sets which were not convex, and did not always satisfy constraint qualifications. Sometimes the defining functions were not differentiable. The objective functions for such optimization approaches to complementarity were also difficult to handle and were neither concave nor convex. The depth of the technical difficulties resulting from all these factors has discouraged the research community from this line of thinking. However, recent progress in global optimization, now causes a re-examination of the problem. A new method of global optimization which is based on integration of functions has been developed [6—12]. From this fresh point of view, it is possible to handle the technical difficulties mentioned above and to resolve them in a systematic way. In this research we will investigate the solution of nonlimear complementarity problems via integral global minimization methods.

Some related work has been recently completed by Mangasarian and Solodov[4]. In their paper, the nonlinear complementarity problem is reformulated as an unconstrained minimization problem and then solved by local methods. Applying these methods from many starting points, they are often able to solve the nonlinear complementarity problem. However, with their approach it is quite possible that a suitable starting point will not be chosen and hence they will miss the solution to the nonlinear complementarity problem. They also assume the functions are differentiable in order to apply existing local methods of optimization. In the approach followed here, such assumptions are not necessary.

Let $f: \mathbb{R}^n \to \mathbb{R}^n$ be a given mapping, O an orthant in $\mathbb{R}^n$. The complementarity

---

* In collaboration with Kostreva M M. Reprinted from Journal of Global Optimization, 1994, 5:181—193.

problem associated with f is:

$$\text{Find } x \in \mathbb{R}^n \text{ such that } x \in O, \quad f(x) \in O^* = O, \quad \langle x, f(x) \rangle = 0, \quad (1.1)$$

where

$$\langle x, f(x) \rangle = x_1 f_1(x) + \cdots + x_n f_n(x).$$

The mapping f is not necessarily assumed to be continuous. For instance, Habetler and Kostreva [2] consider problem (1.1) when f is a P-mapping. Recall that in [5] a mapping $f: \mathbb{R}^n \to \mathbb{R}^n$ is said to be a P-mapping on a set S if for all $x, y \in S$ with $x \neq y$, there exists an index $i = i(x, y)$ such that $(x_i - y_i)(f_i(x) - f_i(y)) > 0$. A P-mapping must be one-to-one, but need not be continuous.

Let $N = \{1, 2, \cdots, n\}$ and $I^k, k = 1, 2, \cdots, 2^n$ be subsets of N. Let $f: \mathbb{R}^n \to \mathbb{R}^n$ be a P-mapping on $\mathbb{R}^n$. If for each $k = 1, \cdots, 2^n$ the mapping

$$f_i^k(x) = \begin{cases} f_i(x), & i \in I^{(k)}, \\ x_i, & i \in N \setminus I^{(k)} \end{cases}$$

is a mapping from $\mathbb{R}^n$ onto $\mathbb{R}^n$, then f is called a *nondegenerate P-mapping*.

The following theorem represents a quite general result for nonlinear complementarity problems, since the functions are not required to be differentiable or even continuous and the orthant of definition is left general. However, this level of generality is nevertheless compatible with an approach through the integral global optimization.

Theorem 1.1[2] *Let: $\mathbb{R}^n \to \mathbb{R}^n$ be a nondegenerate P-mapping. Then for each $O \subset \mathbb{R}^n$, (1.1) has a unique solution.*

The complementarity problem (1.1) can be formulated as the following minimization problem:

$$\min_{x \in S} g(x), \quad (1.2)$$

where

$$g(x) = \langle x, f(x) \rangle \text{ and } S = \{x \in \mathbb{R}^n : x \in O, f \in O\}. \quad (1.3)$$

The problem (1.1) has solutions if and only if the global minimum value of (1.2) is equal to 0 and the set of global minimizers is the solution set of (1.1).

To solve (1.2), a nonsequential unconstrained minimization algorithm for finding the set of global minimizers of a constrained problem is proposed as follows:

Algorithm

Step 1: Take $c_0 > \min_{x \in S} g(x)$ and $\varepsilon > 0$; take $\alpha_0 > 0$ sufficiently large and $\beta > 1.0$;

$$H_0 := \{x : g(x) + \alpha_0 p_S(x, \delta) \leq c_0\}; k := 0;$$

Step 2: Calculate the penalized mean value

$$c_{k+1} := \frac{1}{\mu(H_k)} \int_{H_k} [g(x) + \alpha_k p_S(x, \delta)] d\mu;$$

with

$$H_k = \{x : g(x) + \alpha_k p_S(x, \delta) \leq c_k\};$$

Step 3: Calculate the penalized variance

$$v := \frac{1}{\mu(H_k)} \int_{H_k} [g(x) + \alpha_k p_S(x,\delta) - c_k]^2 d\mu;$$

if $v > \varepsilon$ then $\alpha_{k+1} = \alpha_k \cdot \beta; k := k+1$; go to Step 2; otherwise, go to Step 4;

Step 4: $c^* \Leftarrow c_{k+1}; H^* \Leftarrow H_{k+1}$; Stop.

Here $\varepsilon > 0$ is the accuracy requirement given in advance and $p_S(x,\delta)$ is a penalty function defined by (3.4) and (3.5).

As was discussed in [6,7], a problem formulated with a nonrobust mapping may be numerically unapproximatable and unstable. Thus, we restrict ourselves to study the problem of a *robust piecewise continuous mapping* f. In the next section, we will review a few basic concepts of robust sets, mappings and the integral approach of minimization which we will use for further consideration. We will examine robust piecewise continuous mappings in Section 3. In Section 4, we will give numerical examples to illustrate the effectiveness of the algorithm.

2 Integral Global Minimization

In this section we will summarize several concepts and properties of the integral global minimization of robust discontinuous functions, which will be utilized in the following sections. For more details, see [8,9,12].

Let X be a topological space, a set D in X is said to be *robust* if

$$\text{cl } D = \text{cl int } D, \qquad (2.1)$$

where cl D denotes the closure of D and int D the interior of D.

A robust set consists of *robust points* of the set. A point $x \in D$ is said to be a robust point of D, if for each neighbourhood $N(x)$ of x, $N(x) \cap \text{int } D \neq \emptyset$. A set D is robust if and only if each point of D is a robust point of D. A point $x \in D$ is a robust point of D if and only if there exists a net $\{x_\lambda\} \subset \text{int } D$ such that $x_\lambda \to x$.

The interior of a nonempty robust set is nonempty. A union of robust sets is robust. An intersection of two robust sets may be nonrobust; but the intersection of an open set and a robust set is robust. A set D is robust if and only if $\partial D = \partial \text{int } D$, where $\partial D = \text{cl } D \setminus \text{int } D$ denotes the boundary of D. A robust set can be represented as a union of an open set and a *nowhere dense* set.

A function $f: X \to \mathbb{R}^n$ is said to be *upper robust* if the set

$$F_c = \{x : f(x) < c\} \qquad (2.2)$$

is robust for each real number c.

An upper semicontinuous function is upper robust since (2.2) is open for each c. If X is a complete metric space, then the set of points of discontinuity (continuity) of an upper robust function is of first (second) category.

A function f is upper robust if and only if it is upper robust at each point; f is upper robust at a point x if $x \in F_c$ implies x is robust to F_c.

Example 2.1 An example of a non upper robust function on $\mathbb{R}^1$ is
$$f(x)=\begin{cases} 0, & x=0, \\ 1, & x\neq 0. \end{cases}$$
f is nonrobust at $x=0$.

In [6], robust and approximatable mappings are studies. Let X and Y be topological spaces. A mapping $f: X \to Y$ is said to be *robust* if for each open set $G \subset Y$, $f^{-1}(G)$ is a robust set in X.

The following example shows that a P-mapping may be nonrobust.

Example 2.2 Let $f=(f_1, f_2): \mathbb{R}^2 \to \mathbb{R}^2$ be defined as follows:
$$f_1(x_1, x_2)=\begin{cases} x_1+1, & x_1>0 \text{ and } \forall x_2, \\ 0.1, & x_1=0 \text{ and } \forall x_2, \\ x_1-1, & x_1<0 \text{ and } \forall x_2, \end{cases}$$
and
$$f_2(x_1, x_2)=x_2+0.5, \quad \forall x_1 \text{ and } x_2.$$

It is easy to verify that the mapping f is a P-mapping. For this mapping the complementarity problem (1.1) has a solution $x=(0,0)^T$ and $y=(0.1, 0.5)^T$. However, f is nonrobust. Take $G=(-0.5, 0.5)\times(0, 1)$, then $f^{-1}(G)=\{0.1\}\times(-0.5, 0.5)$. $f^{-1}(G)$ is a nonrobust set in $\mathbb{R}^2$.

Suppose C is the set of points of continuity of f. f is said to be *approximatable* iff C is dense in X and for each $\bar{x}\in X$, there exists a net $\{x_a\}\subset C$ such that
$$\min_a x_a=\bar{x} \quad \text{and} \quad \min_a f(x_a)=f(\bar{x}).$$

An approximatable mapping is robust. If X is a Baire space and Y satisfies the second axiom of countability, then a mapping is robust if and only if is approximatable.

In order to investigate a minimization problem with an integral approach, a special class of measure spaces, which are called Q-measure spaces, should be examined.

Let X be a topological space, Ω a σ-field of subsets of X and μ a measure on Ω. A triple (X, Ω, μ) is called a Q-measure space iff

(i) Each open set in X is measurable;

(ii) The measure $\mu(G)$ of each nonempty open set G in X is positive: $\mu(G)>0$;

(iii) The measure $\mu(K)$ of a compact set K in X is finite.

The n-dimensional Lebesgue measure space $(\mathbb{R}^n, \Omega, \mu)$ is a Q-measure space; a nondegenerate Gaussian measure μ on a separable Hilbert space H with Borel sets as measurable sets constitutes an infinite dimensional Q-measure space. A specific optimization problem is related to a specific Q-measure space which is suitable for consideration in this approach.

Once a measure space is given we can define integration in a conventional way.

Since the interior of a nonempty open set is nonempty, *the Q-measure of a measurable set containing a nonempty robust set is always positive*. This is an essential property we need in the integral approach of minimization. Hence, the following assumptions are usually required:

Assumption (A′) f is Q-measurable.

Assumption (R) f is upper robust and bounded below on S.

Assumption (M) (X, Ω, μ) is a Q-measure space.

In the following application, we need a lemma.

Lemma 2.1 Suppose that the conditions (A′), (M) and (R) hold. If $c > c^* = \min_{x \in S} f(x)$, then
$$\mu(H_c \cap S) > 0.$$

Suppose that the assumptions (A′), (M) and (R) hold, and $c > c^* = \inf_{x \in S} f(x)$. We define the mean value, variance, modified variance and m-th moment (centered at a), respectively, as follows:

$$M(f, c; S) = \frac{1}{\mu(H_c \cap S)} \int_{H_c \cap S} f(x) \, d\mu,$$

$$V(f, c; S) = \frac{1}{\mu(H_c \cap S)} \int_{H_c \cap S} f(x) - M(f, c; S))^2 \, d\mu,$$

$$V_1(f, c; S) = \frac{1}{\mu(H_c \cap S)} \int_{H_c \cap S} (f(x) - c)^2 \, d\mu,$$

$$M_m(f, c; a; S) = \frac{1}{\mu(H_c \cap S)} \int_{H_c \cap S} (f(x) - a)^m \, d\mu, \quad m = 1, 2, \cdots$$

By Lemma 2.1, they are well defined. These definitions can be extended to the case $c \geqslant c^*$ by a limit process. For instance,

$$M_m(f, c; a; S) = \lim_{c_k \downarrow c} \frac{1}{\mu(H_{c_k} \cap S)} \int_{H_{c_k} \cap S} (f(x) - a)^m \, d\mu, \quad m = 1, 2, \cdots$$

The limits exist and are independent of the choice of $\{c_k\}$. The extended concepts are well defined and consistent with the above definitions.

With these concepts we characterize the global optimality as follows:

Theorem 2.1 Under the assumptions (A′), (M) and (R), the following statements are equivalent:

(i) $x^* \in S$ is a global minimizer of f over S and $c^* = f(x^*)$ is the global minimum value;

(ii) $M(f, c^*; S) = c^*$ (the mean value condition);

(iii) $V(f, c^*; S) = 0$ (the variance condition);

(iv) $V_1(f, c^*; S) = 0$ (the modified variance condition);

(v) $M_m(f, c^*; c^*; S) = 0$, for one of positive integers $m = 1, 2, \cdots$ (the higher moment conditions).

3 Robust Piecewise Continuous Mappings

In this section we will examine basic properties of robust piecewise continuous maping and formulate a nonlinear complementarity problem as an unconstrained minimization by using a discontinuous penalty function.

Definition 3.1 Suppose S is a robust set of a topological space X. If there is a family of robust sets $\{V_\lambda\}$, $\lambda \in \Lambda$ such that
$$S = \bigcup_{\lambda \in \Lambda} V_\lambda \quad \text{and} \quad \forall_\alpha \neq \lambda, \ V_\alpha \cap V_\lambda = \neq \varnothing, \tag{3.1}$$
then $\{V_\lambda\}$ is called a robust partition of S. Suppose $\{U_\alpha\}$, $\alpha \in A$ is another robust partition of S. If for each V_λ there is U_α such that $U_\alpha \subset V_\lambda$, then $\{U_\alpha\}$, $\alpha \in A$ is called a robust subpartition of $\{V_\lambda\}$.

Definition 3.1 Let X and Y be two topological spaces, S a robust set in X. A mapping $f:S \subset X \to Y$ is said to be robust piecewise continuous iff there exists a robust partition $\{V_\lambda\}$ of S, such that for any $\lambda \in \Lambda$, the restriction of f to V_λ is continuous.

Proposition 3.1 *Let X and Y be topological spaces, and $f:X \to Y$ a mapping. If f is robust piecewise contionuous with a robust partition $\{V_\lambda\}$ of a robust set S, then it is robust.*

Proof. Suppose $G \subset Y$ is an open set, we will prove that $f^{-1}(G) \cap S$ is a robust set. Indeed,
$$f^{-1}(G) \cap S = f^{-1}(G) \cap \bigcup_\lambda V_\lambda = \bigcup_\lambda (f^{-1}(G) \cap V_\lambda).$$
The intersection of the open set $f^{-1}(G)$ and the robust set V_λ is robust, and the union of robust sets is robust.

Remark 3.1 Note that if in the above definition the partition of S is not required to be *robust*, a piecewise continuous mapping may be non robust.

The class of robust piecewise continuous mappings with the *same* robust partition has some desirable properties.

Proposition 3.2 *Let X be a topological spaces, Y a linear topological space, and f, $g:X \to Y$ mappings. If f and g are robust piecewise mappings with the same robust partition, then for real numbers α and β, $\alpha \cdot f + \beta \cdot g$ is also a robust piecewise continuous mapping.*

Proof. Suppose f and g are robust piecewise continuous with a robust partition $\{V_\lambda\}$. For each give robust set V_λ in the partition, f and g are continuous on it; so is the function $\alpha \cdot f + \beta \cdot g$. Hence, $\alpha \cdot f + \beta \cdot g$ is robust piecewise continuous with the partition $\{V_\lambda\}$.

The following two propositions can be proved similarly.

Proposition 3.3 *Let X be a topological space and f, $g:X \to \mathbb{R}^1$ functions. If f and g are robust piecewise continuous with the same robust partition, then $f \cdot g$, $f/g \ (g \neq 0)$, $\max(f, g)$, $\min(f, g)$ and $|f|$ are also robust piecewise continuous.*

Proposition 3.4 *Let X be a topological space, then $f = (f_1, \cdots, f_n)^T: X \to \mathbb{R}^n$ is a robust piecewise continuous mapping if and only if each of the component functions f_i, $i=1, \cdots, n$ is robust piecewise continuous with the same robust partition.*

For the complementarity problem (1.1), the feasible set is
$$S = \{x \in \mathbb{R}^n : x \in O, \ f \in O\}. \tag{3.2}$$
We assume S and S^c are robust and $X = \{S, S^c\}$ has a robust subpartition, and assume that

f is robust piecewise continuous with respect to this robust subprtition.

We can use a discontinuous penalty function to formulate the constrained minimization problem (1.2) as an unconstrained one, where we assume that $X=\mathbb{R}^n$ and $O=\{x=(x_1, \cdots, x_n)^T : x_i \geqslant, i=1, \cdots, n\}$:
$$\min[\langle x, f(x)\rangle + \alpha p_s(x,\delta)], \tag{3.3}$$
where $p_s(x, \delta)$ is defined as follows:
$$p_s(x,\delta) = \begin{cases} 0, & x \in S, \\ \delta + d(x), & x \in S^c, \end{cases} \tag{3.4}$$
where $\delta > 0$ is given and
$$d(x) = \sum_{i=1}^n [|\min(x_i, 0)| + |\min(f_i(x), 0)|]. \tag{3.5}$$

Note that in the above definition we relax the requirement of continuity from the traditional definition [1,3] as we wish to utilize discontinuous penalty functions.

Definition 3.3 A function $p(x)$ on X is a penalty function for a constraint set S it
(i) $p(x)=0$ if $x \in S$;
(ii) $\inf_{x \notin S_\beta} p(x) > 0$, where $S_\beta = \{u : \|u-v\| \leqslant \beta, \forall_v \in S\}$ and $\beta > 0$.

Remark 3.2 It is expected that the penalty will be increasing when the distance of a pint X to the constraint set S is getting larger. We replace the traditional property
$$p(x) > 0, \text{ if } u \notin S$$
by (ii).

Definition 3.4 A penalty function p for the constraint set S is exact for a minimization problem
$$\min_{x \in S} g(x) \tag{3.6}$$
if there is a real number $\alpha_0 > 0$ such that for each $\alpha \geqslant \alpha_0$ we have
$$\min_{x \in X} \{g(x) + \alpha p(x)\} = \min_{x \in S} g(x) = c^* \tag{3.7}$$
and
$$\{x : g(x) + \alpha p(x) = c^*\} = \{x \in S : g(x) = c^*\} = H^*. \tag{3.8}$$

Proposition 3.5 *Suppose $X = \mathbb{R}^n$ and f is robust piecewise continuous with a robust subpartition of $\{S, S^c\}$, then for each $\alpha > 0$ and $\delta > 0$ the penalized function*
$$\langle x, f(x)\rangle + \alpha p_s(x,\delta) \tag{3.9}$$
is a piecewise robust continuous function.

Proof. Suppose $\{V_\lambda\}$ is the robust partition with which f is robust piecewise continuous. Then the component functions f_i, $i=1, \cdots, n$ are robust piecewise with it. Thus,
$$\langle x, f(x)\rangle = x_1 f_1(x) + \cdots + x_n f_n(x)$$
is robust piecewise continuous. (The functions $|\min(x_i, 0)|$) and $|\min(f_i, 0)|$, $i=1, \cdots, n$ are robust piecewise continuous, so is the function $\delta + d(x)$.) Since, $\{V_\lambda\}$ is a subpartition of $\{S, S^c\}$, thus, the penalty function $p_s(x, \delta)$ is robust piecewise continuous with $\{V_\lambda\}$. As the sum of $\langle x, f(x)\rangle$ and $\alpha p_s(x, \delta)$, the penalized function (3.9) is robust piecewise with $\{V_\lambda\}$.

When we use the integral approach to deal with minimization problems, a Q-measure space is used. Then we require that each set V_λ in the robust partition is measurable in the given Q-measure space. A robust partition $\{V_\lambda\}$ is called a *measurable robust partition* if each set in the partition is measurable. If $\{V_\lambda\}$ is a measurable robust partition, then a robust piecewise continuous function with this partition is measurable.

Observe that the conditions (A'), (M) and (R) hold for problem (3.3). The penalty function (3.4) with (3.5) is exact (see, [10, 11]). We can use integral minimization algorithms to solve the unconstrained problem (3.3).

Return to the *algorithm* in Section 1. Let $\varepsilon = 0$ in the algorithm. It may stop in a finite number of steps or we obtain a decreasing sequence

$$c_0 > c_1 > \cdots > c_k > c_{k+1} > \cdots \geq c^* \tag{3.10}$$

and a monotone sequence of sets

$$H_0 \supset H_1 \supset \cdots \supset H_k \supset H_{k+1} \supset \cdots. \tag{3.11}$$

The limits of these sequences exist. Let

$$c^* = \lim_{n \to \infty} c_k \tag{3.12}$$

and

$$H^* = \lim_{k \to \infty} H_k = \bigcap_{k=1}^{\infty} H_k. \tag{3.13}$$

The following theorems can be proved by applying Theorem 2.1 (see [12], Theorem 5.3.3).

Theorem 3.1 *Under the assumptions (A'), (M) and (R), the limit c^* of (3.12) is the global minimum value and the limit H^* of (3.13) is the set of global minimizers of g over S.*

Corollary 3.1 *Under the assumptions of Theorem 3.1, if f is a nondegenerate P-mapping, then complementarity problem (1.1) is solvable by the integral optimization method.*

Note that the errors at each iteration in the algorithm are not accumulated. Suppose we calculate $c_1 = M(g, c_0; S)$ with an error Δ_1 and obtain $d_1 = c_1 + \Delta_1$; then calculate $c'_2 = M(f, d_1; S)$ with an error Δ_2, and obtain $d_2 = c'_2 + \Delta_2$, and so on. In general, we have

$$c'_k = M(g, d_{k-1}; S) \quad \text{and} \quad \Delta_k = d_k - c'_k, \quad k = 1, 2, \cdots \tag{3.14}$$

and obtain a decreasing sequence $\{d_k\}$. Let

$$d = \lim_{k \to \infty} d_k. \tag{3.15}$$

Theorem 3.2 *Under the assumptions of Theorem 3.1, d is the global minimum value of g over S if and only if*

$$\lim_{k \to \infty} \Delta_k = 0. \tag{3.16}$$

The algorithm has been implemented by a properly designed Monte-Carlo method. At each iteration we need to find: (1) A level set; (2) a mean value and (3) a modified variance (multi-dimensional integrations). Monte-Carlo technique can handle higher dimensional integration with lower accuracy:

$$\delta \approx \frac{C_p}{\sqrt{N}} \sigma,$$

where N is the number of sample points and σ^2 is the variance. $\delta \to 0$ as $\sigma \to 0$ by the modified variance condition.

The numerical tests show that the algorithm is competitive with other algorithms.

4 Numerical Examples

The examples of this section are quite challenging. One example was proposed by Habetler and Kostreva [2] to illustrate the concept of discontinuous nondegenerate P-mapping. A solution was not provided there. Indeed, the existence of mathematical methods to handle nonlinear equation systems with discontinuous functions was unknown at that time.

The second example is even more elaborate and complex, involving polynomial and trigonometric functions as well as the greatest integer function. It is solved here as a demonstration of the capabilities of the integral global optimization method on nonliear complementarity problems with a high level of complexity.

Example 4.1 Let $f(x_1, x_2) = (-1, -2)^T + h(x_1, x_2)$, where

$$h(x_1, x_2) = \begin{cases} \frac{\sqrt{2}}{2} \begin{pmatrix} 1 & -1 \\ 1 & 1 \end{pmatrix} \begin{pmatrix} x_1 \\ x_2 \end{pmatrix}, & \text{if } x_1^2 + x_2^2 < 1, \\ \begin{pmatrix} x_1 \\ x_2 \end{pmatrix}, & \text{if } x_1^2 + x_1^2 \geq 1. \end{cases}$$

For this example the constraint set is
$$S = \{x = (x_1, x_2)^T : x_1 \geq 0, x_2 \geq 0; f_1(x_1, x_2) \geq 0, f_2(x_1, x_2) \geq 0\}.$$
It has a robust partition:
$$S = S_1 \cup S_2,$$
where
$$S_1 = S \cap \{x = (x_1, x_2)^T : x_1^2 + x_2^2 < 1\}$$
and
$$S_2 = S \cap \{x = (x_1, x_2)^T : x_1^2 + x_2^2 \geq 1\}.$$
f_1 and f_2 are relatively robust piecewise continuous. Then we can use discontinuous penalty function to solve the following minimization problem:
$$\min_{x \in S} [x_1 \cdot f_1(x_1, x_2) + x_2 \cdot f_2(x_1, x_2)]. \tag{4.1}$$
As we have expected (4.1) has a unique minimizer $x^* = (1.0, 2.0)^T$ with the global minimum value 0.

Example 4.2 Let
$$X = \{(x_1, x_2)^T : x_1, x_2 = 0.001 \cdot j, j = 0, 1, 2, \cdots, 10000\},$$
$$g_1(x) = [1 + (x_1 - x_2 - 1)^2 (59 - 26x_1 - 3x_1^2 - 26x_2 + 6x_1 x_2 + 3x_2^2]$$
$$\times [30 + (2x_1 + 3x_2)^2 (5 - 20x_1 + 12x_1^2 - 30x_2 + 36x_1 x_2 + 27x_2^2)],$$
$$g_2(x) = 10.0 \sin^2(\pi x_1) + (x_1 - 1.0)^2 [1.0 + 10.0 \sin^2(\pi x_2)] + x_2^2$$

and
$$f_1(x) = g_1(x) - [g_1(x)/10], \quad f_2(x) = g_2(x) - [g_2(x)/5],$$
where $[y]$ denoted the integer part of y. The mapping $f = (f_1, f_2)^T : X \to \mathbb{R}^2$ is discontinuous and the admissible set is discrete. Let
$$D = \{(z_1, z_2)^T : ([1000 \cdot Z_1]/1000, [1000 \cdot z_2])/1000)^T \in X\}.$$
It is easy to verify that $D = [0, 10.001) \times [0, 10.001)$ which is robust.

We define a new mapping $F = (F_1, F_2)^T : D \to \mathbb{R}^2$, where
$$F_i(z) = f_i([1000 \cdot z_1]/1000, [1000 \cdot z_2]/1000), \quad i = 1, 2.$$
For this example the feasible set is
$$S = \{z = (z_1, z_2)^T \in D : z_1 \geqslant 0, z_2 \geqslant 0, F_1(z) \geqslant 0, F_2(z) \geqslant 0\}.$$
F_1 and F_2 are robust piecewise continuous. Then we can use a discontinuous penalty function to solve the following minimization problem:
$$\min_{z \in S} [z_1 \cdot F_1(z_1, z_2) + z_2 \cdot F_2(z_1, z_2)]. \tag{4.2}$$
The constrained minimization problem (4.2) has a solution corresponding to a unique minimizer $x^* = (1.0, 0.0)^T \in X$ with the global minimum value 0. After 13 iterations with 670 function evaluations, we obtain
$$x_1 = 1.0, \quad x_2 = 0.0, \quad F_1 = 0.0, \quad F_2 = 3.0, \quad v_1 = 0.0,$$
where v_1 is the modified variance.

5 Conclusions

In this paper the methodology of integral global optimization is applied to nonlinear complementarity problems under the assumption that the mapping is robust, piecewise continuous, and a nondegenerate P-mapping. Under such weak assumptions, the analysis which arises is the first which can handle these problems. Difficult nonlinear complementarity problems arise in a number of contexts in economics, engineering and management and also may arise as subproblems in system models such as those of constrained parameter estimation and optimal control. Therefore, the contribution of this paper has wide raning application and, potentially, it may open new avenue of research uniting the subjects of complementarity theory and global optimization.

The examples presented in this paper are illustrative of several noteworthy ideas. Examples 2.1 and 2.2 show that there are solvable nonlinear complementarity problems which are not within the theoretical framework covered here. Examples 4.1 and 4.2, however, are covered by this paper. For these examples, the new solution methodology works remarkably well, making computation seem like an almost routine task. It is our claim that there is no existing methodology which can match that performance.

References

[1] G. Di Pillo and L. Grippo. Exact penalty functions in constrained optimization [J]. *SIAM Journal*

Control and Optimization, 1989, 28, 1333—1360.

[2] G. J. Habetler and M. M. Kostreva. On a direct algorithm for nonlnear complementarity problems [J], *SIAM J. Control and Optimization*, 1978, 16, 504—511.

[3] A. V. Fiacco and G. P. McCormick. *Nonlinear Programming: Sequential Unconstrained Minimization Techniques* [M]. John Wiley and Sons, New York, 1968.

[4] O. L. Mangasarian and M. V. Solodov. Nonlinear complementarity as unconstrained and constrained minimization [R]. Computer Sciences Technical Report No. 1074, Computer Sciences Department, University of Wisconsin-Madison, 1992.

[5] J. Moréand W. Rheinboldt. On P-and S-functions and related classes of n-dimensional nonlinear mappings [J]. *Linear Algebar Appl*, 1973, 6, 45—68.

[6] S. Shi, Q. Zheng and D. Zhuang. Discontinuous robust mappings are approximatable [J]. preprint.

[7] S. Shi, Q. Zheng and D. Zhuang. Set-valued mappings and approximatable mappings [J]. preprint.

[8] Q. Zheng. Robust analysis and global minimization of a class of discontinuous functions (I)[J]. *Acta Mathematicae Applicatae Sincia (English Series)*, 1990, 6(3), 205—223.

[9] Q. Zheng. Robust analysis and global optimization of a class of discontinuous functions (II)[J]. *Acta Mathematicae Applicatae Sinica (English Series)*, 1990, 6(4), 317—337.

[10] Q. Zheng. Global minimization of constrained problems with discontinuous penalty functions [J]. preprint.

[11] Q. Zheng and D. Zhuang. Integrl global optimization of constrained problems in functional space with discontinuous penalty functions [M]// C. A. Floudas and P. M. Pardalos (eds.), *Recent Advances in Global Optimization*, 1992, 298—320, Princeton University Press.

[12] Q. Zheng. Integral global optimization of robust discontinuous functions [D], Clemson University, 1992.

Robust Analysis and Global Minimization of A Class of Discontinuous Functions (I) *

Abstract: In this paper we define and investigate robust points, sets and functions which will be utilized to study a global minimization problem of a discontinuous function over a disconnected set by an integral approach.

1 Introduction

Let X be a Hausdorff topological space, $S \subset X$ a closed set and f a real-valued function. The problem considered here is to find the infimum of f over S,

$$\bar{c} = \inf_{x \in S} f(x). \tag{1.1}$$

Under the assumption that

(A) S is compact and f is lower semi-continuous (l.s.c.), the set of global minima

$$\overline{H} = \{x \mid f(x) = c, \ x \in S\} \tag{1.2}$$

is nonempty. In this case we want also to find the set $\overline{H}$.

The problem of maximizing or minimizing a function over a constrained set has been investigated since the seventeenth century with the concepts of derivative and Lagrangian multiplier. These concepts have been enhanced progressively, owing their motivation to practice, such as gradient, variation, subgradient and generalized gradient and so on. The theory of optimization was founded. Convex analysis and nonsmooth analysis are accepted and become popular. One can easily notice, however, that the core of these concepts is not changed substantially; they have only been generalized.

The gradient-based approach of optimization has its distinct advantages. It is intuitive geometrically; the calculation of a gradient is quite convenient. Because this approch is well developed many mathematical areas such as linear algebra, differential equation etc. are infiltrated with it. From the numerical point of view, the grdient-based methods usually have a higher rate of convergence. There are quite a lot of available sophisticated softwares to be chosen. Thus, it is the main strain of the research of optimization so far. But its straits are also clear. The requirement of differentiability restricts it to be applied to many practical problems. Moreover, it can only be utilized to characterize and find a local solution of an optimization problem.

---

* Reprinted from Acta Mathematicsae Applicatae Sinica, 1990, 6(3):205−223.

Up to now people rarely consider the problem of finding the solution (1.1) under such a loose condition (A) not because it is useless. The objective function may be discontinuous, the constrained set may be disconnected. But many problems in natural and social sciences, as well as in industrial applications do require minimizing a discontinuous function. On the other hand, problems in applications may require the constraint set S to be disconnected for physical reasons, if we are concerned only with the problem of finding a local minimum, it would not bother us whether S is conected or not.

We know that as a function of price and quantity of a commodity the cost may be discontinuous since the price depends on how much to purchase. This implies that the objective function appearing in economical and management sciences may be discontinuous. An optimization problem involving probability distribution functions may require minimizing a discontinuous function. Every combinatorial optimization problem can be converted into a minimization problem of a discontinuous function, so can a mixed programming. We can easily get an exact penalty function without any constrained qualification if we can solve an unconstrained minimization problem of a discontinuous functions. Thus, it is very flexible to investigate problems of optimal design, inventory, optimal control etc., if we can use discontinuous objective functions. We believe that it will become popular in the next decade to consider problems of minimizing discontinuous functions over a disconnected set.

Several works consider a minimization problem of a discontinuous function [4, 5, 6] by combining smoothing technique with tranditional minimization methods to obtain a solution. They are complicated, especially when the number of variables of the objective function is large.

We will utilize an integral approach. In this paper and in [1], with a title of "Robust Analysis and Global Optimization of a Class of Discontinuous Functions", we extend earilor works [9] and [10]. We first consider a class of sets, robust sets, and a class of discontinuous functions, robust functions, in a toplogical space in Section 2 and Section 3. In Section 4 we investigate the structure of robust sets and discontinuities of robust functions on the real line in detail. We study the relative robustness and robustization of a function in Section 5 and Section 6. In [1] optimality conditions are examined; algorithms are proposed, and their convergence properties are studied. Numerical tests show that these methods are effective.

2 Robust Sets and Points

2.1 Definitions

We begin with defining the concepts of robust sets and points. Let X be a topological space, D be a subset of X.

Definition 2.1 A set $D \subset X$ is said to be robust iff

$$\operatorname{cl} D = \operatorname{cl} \operatorname{int} D, \tag{2.1}$$

An open set G is robust since $G = \operatorname{int} G$. The empty set is a trivial robust set. A closed set may be robust or nonrobust.

Remark 2.1 A robust set may be disconnected.

Remark 2.2 The concept of robustness defined here is closely related with the topological structure. For instance, the set $D = \{1, 2\}$ is nonrobust if we consider it in $X = \mathbb{R}^1$, it is robust if $X = Z = \{\text{the set of the interers with discrete topology}\}$.

A set G is open if and only if each point on G is an interior point of G. Similarly, a robust set consists of robust points of the set.

Definition 2.2 A point $x \in \operatorname{cl} D$ is said to be robust to D (or a robust point of D) iff it is a cluster point of $\operatorname{int} D$, i.e., for each neighborhood $N(x)$ of x,
$$N(x) \cap \operatorname{int} D \neq \emptyset. \tag{2.2}$$

An interior point x in D is always robust to D; $x \in \operatorname{int} D$ implies $\operatorname{int} D \neq \emptyset$ and $\{x\} \subset N(X) \cap \operatorname{int} D$ for each neighborhood $N(x)$ of x.

In Definition 2.2 we only consider the robustness of the points which are in $\operatorname{cl} D$ because if x is not in $\operatorname{cl} D$, then there is a neighborhood $N(x)$ of x such that $N(x) \cap \operatorname{cl} D = \emptyset$. Thus, the point which is not contained in $\operatorname{cl} D$ is always nonrubust to D.

The following theorem connects the concept of robust sets and that of robust points.

Theorem 2.1 *A set D is robust if and only if each point x of D is robust to D.*

2.2 Robust Points

From Theorem 2.1, the properties of a robust set is closely associated with those of robust points of the set. In this subsection we will discuss properties of robust points. We first give several propositions which are easily proved by Definition 2.2.

Proposition 2.1 *If x is robust to D and $\operatorname{int} D \subset A$, then x is robust to A.*

Remark 2.3 If a point x is robust to D, then x is robust to $\operatorname{cl} D$ because $D \subset \operatorname{cl} D$. Conversely, if x is robust to $\operatorname{cl} D$, the point x may be nonrobust to D. For instance, let $D = [0,1] \cup \{\text{rational numbers in } (1,2]\}$. Then $\operatorname{cl} D = [0,2]$, $x = 2$ is robust to $\operatorname{cl} D$ on $\mathbb{R}^1$. But $\operatorname{int} D = (0,1)$; $x = 2$ is nonrobust to D because there is a neighborhood $(1.5, 2.5)$ of $x = 2$, $(1.5, 2.5) \cap (0,1) = \emptyset$.

Proposition 2.2 *A point $x \in D$ is robust if and only if $x \in \operatorname{cl} \operatorname{int} D$.*

If a point x is robust to a set D, as well as to a set G, then x may be nonrobust to $D \cap G$ even if $x \in D \cap G$.

Example 2.1 Let $D = [0,1]$ and $G = [1,2]$. The point $x = 1$ is in $D \cap G$ and is robust to both of D and G. But $D \cap G = \{1\}$, $x = 1$ is nonrobust to $D \cap G$ on $\mathbb{R}^1$.

Theorem 2.2 *Suppose x is robust to D and $x \in \operatorname{int} G$. Then x is robust to $D \cap \operatorname{int} G$. The point is then robust to $D \cap G$.*

Proof. For each neighborhood $N(x)$ of x, we can find a new neighborhood $N_1(x)$ of x such that
$$N_1(x) \subset N(x) \cap \operatorname{int} G, \tag{2.3}$$

because $x \in N(x) \cap \text{int } G$. Since x is robust to D, so we have
$$N_1(x) \cap \text{int } D \neq \emptyset. \tag{2.4}$$
But
$$N_1(x) \cap \text{int } D \subset N(x) \cap \text{int } G \cap \text{int } D = N(x) \cap \text{int}(D \cap \text{int } G). \tag{2.5}$$
From (2.5), $N(x) \cap \text{int}(D \cap \text{int } G) \neq \emptyset$. Therefore, x is robust to $D \cap \text{int } G$.

2.3 Robust Sets

With the help of Theorem 2.1 and Theorem 2.2, we can easily prove the following two theorems on the properties of robust sets.

Theorem 2.3 *The union of robust sets is robust.*

Proof. Suppose that each set D_p, $p \in \Lambda$, is robust, where Λ is a given index set. Let
$$D = \bigcup_{p \in \Lambda} D_p. \tag{2.6}$$
We now prove D is robust. For each fixed point $x \in D$, we have $x \in D_{p_0}$, for some $p_0 \in \Lambda$. The point x is robust to D_{p_0}, so it is also robust to D since $D_{p_0} \subset D$. We have proved that each point of D is robust to D. Hence D is robust by Theorem 2.1.

Theorem 2.4 *The intersection $D \cap G$ of a robust set D and an open set G is robust.*

Proof. For each fixed point $x \in D \cap G$, $x \in G = \text{int } G$. Thus, x is robust to $D \cap G$ by applying Theorem 2.2. Hence, $D \cap G$ is robust by Theorem 2.1.

Corollary 2.1 *If D is robust and F is closed, then $D \setminus F$ is robust.*

Proposition 2.3 *A set D is robust if and only if*
$$\text{bd}(D) = \text{bd}(\text{int } D), \tag{2.7}$$
where $\text{bd}(D) = \text{cl } D \setminus \text{int } D$, *the boundary of D.*

Proposition 2.4 *A set D is robust if and only if each point $x \in \text{bd}(D)$ is robust to D.*

Corollary 2.2 *If D is robust, then $\text{cl } D$ is also robust.*

We now consider the robustness of a convex set in a linear topological space X.

Proposition 2.5 *Suppose X is a linear topological space, C is a nonempty convex set. Then C is robust if and only if $\text{int } C \neq \emptyset$.*

We finally consider the robust set in a product space $X \times Y$. Suppose X and Y are topological spaces; $A \subset X$ and $B \subset Y$ are robust on X and Y, respectively.

Proposition 2.6 *If A is robust on X and B is robust on Y, then $A \times B$ is robust on $X \times Y$ with the product topology.*

3 Robust Functions

3.1 Definitions

Let X be a topological space and $f: X \to \mathbb{R}^1$ a real function on X. In this section we will consider a class of discontinuous functions related with the concepts of robust sets and points. Recall a function f is upper semi-continuous (u.s.c.) if the set
$$F_c = \{x \mid f(x) < c\}$$
is open for each real number c. We generalize this concept to robust functions.

Definition 3.1 A function f is sain to be robust iff the set
$$F_c = \{x \mid f(x) < c\} \tag{3.1}$$
is robust for every real number c.

An u.s.c. function f is robust since each open set is robust.

Example 3.1 A monotone function f on $\mathbb{R}^1$ is robust. Indeed, suppose f is increasing, for each real number, c, $F_c = \{x \mid f(x) < c\} = (\infty, b\rangle$, where $b = f(c)$. The point b may be contained in F_c or not. In both cases F_c is robust. If f is decreasing, then $F_c = \langle b, \infty)$, it is also robust. Similarly, one can prove that a probability distribution function on $\mathbb{R}^n$ is robust.

Definition 3.2 A function f is said to be robust at (or by) a point x_0 if $x_0 \in F_c$ implies x_0 is robust to F_c (or, there is a neighborhood $N(x_0)$ of x_0 such that $N(x_0) \cap F_c$ is robust) for each real number c.

Example 3.2 If a function f is u.s.c. at x then it is also robust at x. Indeed, a function f is u.s..c. at x iff $x \in F_c$ implies $x \in \text{int } F_c$ for each real number c. But every interior point of F_c is always robust to F_c.

The following theorem is expected.

Theorem 3.1 *The following statements are equivalent:*

(1) *f is robust;*

(2) *f is robust by each point;*

(3) *f is robust at each point.*

Proof. It is easy to see by Definition 3.2 that (1) implies (2) and (2) implies (3). We need only prove that (3) implies (1). Suppose f is robust at each point $x \in X$. For each given real number c, every point $x \in F_c$ is robust to F_c. By Theorem 2.1, F_c is robust. Thus, f is a robust function.

3.2 Properties of Robust functions

The sum of two robust functions may be nonrobust.

Example 3.3 Let
$$f_1(x) = \begin{cases} 1, & x < 0, \\ 0, & x \geq 0, \end{cases} \text{ and } f_2(x) = \begin{cases} 0, & x \leq 0, \\ 1, & x > 0. \end{cases} \tag{3.2}$$
Both of f_1 and f_2 are robust. But the sum
$$f(x) = f_1(x) + f_2(x) = \begin{cases} 1, & x \neq 0, \\ 0, & x = 0 \end{cases} \tag{3.3}$$
is nonrobust, f is nonrobust at $x = 0$.

Theorem 3.2 *Suppose that f is robust at x_0 and g is u.s.c. at x_0 (for the division case g is supposed to be l.s.c. at x_0). Then the following functions are robust at x_0:*

(1) $a \cdot f$ ($a \geq 0$ *and constant*);

(2) $f + g$;

(3) $f \cdot g$ ($g(x_0) \geq 0$);

(4) f/g ($g(x_0) > 0$).

Proof. (1) If $a=0$, then $a \cdot f$ is continuous. Suppose $a>0$. Then we have
$$F_{c/a} = \{x | f(x) < c/a\} = \{x | a \cdot f(x) < c\}. \tag{3.4}$$
If $x_0 \in F_{c/a}$ then x_0 is robust to the set $F_{c/a} = \{x | a \cdot f(x) < c\}$. Thus, $a \cdot f$ is robust at x_0.

(2) Let the set of rational numbers be ordered as
$$r_1, r_2, \cdots, r_n, \cdots. \tag{3.5}$$
Then we have, for each real number c,
$$FG_c = \{x | f(x) + g(x) < c\} = \bigcup_{k=1}^{\infty} \{x | f(x) < r_k\} \cap \{x | g(x) < c - r_k\} \tag{3.6}$$
(see [7], p. 56). If $x_0 \in FG_c$ for some c, then x_0 is, at least, contained in one set of the union. Say, $x_0 \in \{x | f(x) < r_1\} \cup \{x | g(x) < c - r_1\} = F_{r_1} \cap G_{c-r_1}$. Then $x_0 \in F_{r_1}$ and $x_0 \in G_{c-r_1}$. We also have $x_0 \in \text{int } G_{c-r_1}$ because g is u.s.c. at x_0. By Theorem 2.2, we have that x_0 is robust to FG_c. This proves that $f+g$ is robust at x_0.

(3) For each real number c, we have
$$\{x | f(x) \cdot g(x) < c\} = \bigcup_{k=1}^{\infty} \{x | f(x) < r_k\} \cap \{x | g(x) < c/r_k\}, \tag{3.7}$$
and (3) can be proved similarly.

(4) If $g(x_0) > 0$ and g is l.s.c. at x_0, then $1/g$ is u.s.c. at x_0. And $f/g = f \cdot 1/g$, we obtain (4) from (3).

Theorem 3.3 *Suppose that for each $p \in \Lambda$, $f_p(x)$ is robust at x_0, where Λ is a given index set. Then $f(x) = \inf_{p \in \Lambda} f_p(x)$ is robust at x_0.*

Proof. For each real number c, if $x_0 \in \{x | f_p(x) < c\}$ then $f(x_0) \leq f_p(x_0) < c$, i.e., $x_0 \in F_c = \{x | f(x) < c\}$. Thus,
$$\{x | f_p(x) < c\} \subset F_c, \quad \forall p \in \Lambda, \tag{3.8}$$
or we have
$$\bigcup_{p \in \Lambda} \{x | f_p(x) < c\} \subset F_c. \tag{3.9}$$
Conversely, for each $x_0 \in F_c$ there is, at least, an index $p_0 \in \Lambda$ such that $f_{p_0}(x_0) < c$. Suppose, on the contrary that $f_p(x_0) \geq c$, for each $p \in \Lambda$. Then we would obtain that
$$f(x_0) = \inf_{p \in \Lambda} f_p(x_0) \geq c,$$
which contrdicts $x_0 \in F_c$. This proves that
$$x_0 \in \bigcup_{p \in \Lambda} \{x | f_p(x) < c\}.$$
Hence, we have the equality:
$$F_c = \bigcup_{p \in \Lambda} \{x | f_p(x) < c\}. \tag{3.10}$$
Now if $x_0 \in F_c$, then $x_0 \in \{x | f_{p_0}(x) < c\}$, for some $p_0 \in \Lambda$. Since f_{p_0} is supposed to be robust at x_0, so x_0 is robust to the set $\{x | f_{p_0}(x) < c\}$. Therefore, x_0 is robust to F_c itself, i.e., f is robust at the point x_0.

Proposition 3.1 *Suppose f_n, $n = 1, 2, \cdots$ are robust at a point x_0, amd $\{f_n\}$ is a decreasing sequence. Then the limit f of $\{f_n\}$ is also robust at x_0.*

It is easy to prove the following propositions by Theorem 3.2, Theorem 3.3 and Proposition 3.1.

Proposition 3.2 *Suppose that f is robust and g is u.s.c. (for division, g is supposed to be l.s.c.). Then the following functions are robust:* (1) $a \cdot f$ $(a \geqslant 0)$; (2) $f+g$; (3) $f \cdot g$; (4) f/g.

Proposition 3.3 *Suppose that $f_p(x)$, $p \in \Lambda$ are robust, where Λ is given index set. Then $f(x) = \inf_{p \in \Lambda} f_p(x)$ is also robust.*

Proposition 3.4 *Suppose thet f_m, $n = 1, 2, \cdots$ are robust on X, and $\{f_n\}$ is a decreasing sequence. Then the limit*

$$f(x) = \lim_{n \to \infty} f_n(x). \tag{3.11}$$

is also robust.

3.3 Examples

In this subsection we will examine several examples of robust functions which are useful for the application of robust analysis.

Example 3.4 Consider a minimization problem of f with constraints $g_i(x) \leqslant 0$, $i = 1, \cdots, r$. Let $g(x) = \max\{g_1(x), \cdots, g_r(x)\}$ and $G = \{x \mid g_i(x) \leqslant 0, i = 1, \cdots, r\}$. In fact, we have $G = \{x \mid g(x) \leqslant 0\}$. Suppose that f, $g_1, \cdots, g_r$ are continuous and G is a robust set. We define, with a real number $\delta > 0$,

$$g(\delta, x) = \begin{cases} \delta + g(x), & \text{if } g(x) > 0, \\ 0, & \text{if } g(x) \leqslant 0, \end{cases} \tag{3.12}$$

and

$$f_1(x) = f(x) + M \cdot g(\delta, x), \quad x \in X, \tag{3.13}$$

where M is a positive number. It is easy to prove that there is a number M such that the solution of constrained minimization problem

$$\min_{x \in G} f(x) \tag{3.14}$$

is equivalent to that of an unconstrained one:

$$\min f_1(x), \tag{3.15}$$

if f is bounded. Now f is discontinuous, but f_1 is robust. In order to prove the robustness we need only to prove that $g(\delta, x)$ is robust. Indeed, if $c \leqslant \delta$, then we have

$$\{x \mid g(\delta, x) \leqslant c\} = G \text{ or } \varnothing; \tag{3.16}$$

if $c > \delta$, then

$$\{x \mid g(\delta, x) < c\} = \{x \mid g(x) < c - \delta\} \tag{3.17}$$

is open. These prove that $g(\delta, x)$ is robust.

Example 3.5 Consider a function $h(a_i, x)$ defined on $I \times X$, where $I = \{a_0, \cdots, a_m\}$, and X is a topological space. We want to minimize h. This is an example of mixed programming problem. Consider a new function f defined on $[0, m+1] \times X$ with the product topology of $\mathbb{R}^1 \times X$ as follows: $x = (r, x)$, where $r \in [0, m+1]$, and

$$f(z) = h(a_{[r]}, x), \tag{3.18}$$

where $a_{[r]}$ means that if the integer part of r equals k, then $a_{[r]} = a_k$, except for the cases $a_{[r]} = a_1$, for $0 \leqslant r \leqslant 1$ and $a_{[r]} = a_m$, for $m \leqslant r \leqslant m+1$. The function f is well defined. We now prove that if $h(a_i, x)$ is robust on X for each given i, then $f(z)$ is robust on $\mathbb{R}^1 \times X$.

For each c, the set
$$\{x | h(a_i, x) < c\} \tag{3.19}$$
is robust on X, for $i = 0, 1, \cdots, m$. Then, by the set
$$\{(r, x) | h(a_{[r]}, x) < c\} \tag{3.20}$$
is also robust on $\mathbb{R}^1 \times X$ and the set
$$\{r | a_{[r]} = a_i\} = \{r | [r] = i\} \tag{3.21}$$
is robust on $\mathbb{R}^1$, $i = 0, 1, \cdots, m$. Now, for each c, the set
$$F_c = \{z | f(z) < c\} \tag{3.22}$$
is just a union of robust sets, which is robust by Theorem 2.3:
$$\bigcup_{i=0}^{m} \{(r, x) | h(a_i, x) < c, i = [r]\}. \tag{3.23}$$

3.4 Robustness of Epigraphs

In this subsection we consider the robustness of an epigraph of a function where an epigraph of a function is defined as
$$\mathrm{epi}(f) = \{(x, c) | f(x) \leqslant c\}. \tag{3.24}$$
An epigraph is a subset of the product space $X \times \mathbb{R}^1$, which has been well in vestigated in convex analysis (see [8]).

Theorem 3.4 *A function f on X is robust at point x_0 if and only if each point $(x_0, c) \in \mathrm{epi}(f)$ is robust, with the product topology on $X \times \mathbb{R}^1$, to the set $\mathrm{epi}(f)$.*

Proof. Suppose f is robust at x_0 and $c_0 = f(x_0)$. For each $c_1 > c_0$, we have $x_0 \in F_{c_1}$,
$$F_{c_1} \times (c_1, \infty) \subset \mathrm{epi}(f) \tag{3.25}$$
and
$$\mathrm{int}(F_{c_1} \times (c_1, \infty)) = \mathrm{int}\, F_{c_1} \times (c_1, \infty) \subset \mathrm{int}\,(\mathrm{epi}\,(f)). \tag{3.26}$$

For each point $(x_0, c) \in \mathrm{epi}\,(f)$, we now prove the point is robust to $\mathrm{epi}\,(f)$. Since the point (x_0, c) is in $\mathrm{epi}\,(f)$, we have $c \geqslant c_0 = f(x_0)$. For each neighborhood $N(x_0) \times N(c, \varepsilon)$ of (x_0, c), where $N(c, \varepsilon) = (c - \varepsilon, c + \varepsilon)$, we have
$$N(x_0) \times N(c, \varepsilon) \cap \mathrm{int}(\mathrm{epi}(f)) \supset N(x_0) \times N(c, \varepsilon) \cap \mathrm{int}\, F_{c_1} \times (c_1, \infty)$$
$$\supset (N(x_0) \cap \mathrm{int}\, F_{c_1}) \times (c_1, c + \varepsilon) \neq \varnothing, \tag{3.27}$$
where we take $c_0 \leqslant c_1 \leqslant c + \varepsilon/2$ in (3.26). The nonemptiness of the last set is from the assumption that x_0 is robust to F_{c_1}.

Conversely, suppose that each point $(x_0, c) \in \mathrm{epi}(f)$ is robust to $\mathrm{epi}(f)$. We now prove that f is robust at x_0. Suppose, on the contrary, f is nonrobust at x_0. Then there is a real number c and a neighborhood $N(x_0)$ of x_0 such that
$$x_0 \in F_c \tag{3.28}$$
and
$$N(x_0) \cap \mathrm{int}\, F_c \neq \varnothing. \tag{3.29}$$
(3.28) implies $f(x_0) < c$. Take $\varepsilon = (c - f(x_0))/4 > 0$ and $c_0 = c - 2\varepsilon$. Then
$$f(x_0) < c_0 - \varepsilon < c_0 < c_0 + \varepsilon < c, \tag{3.30}$$

i. e., $(x_0, c_0) \in \text{epi}(f)$. We now prove that (x_0, c_0) would be nonrobust to epi(f). Suppose it is. Then
$$G = N(x_0) \times N(c_0, \varepsilon) \cap \text{int epi}(f) \neq \emptyset. \tag{3.31}$$
Say, $(x_1, c_1) \in G$, and it is an interior point of G since G is open. Thus, there is a neighborhood $N_1(x_1)$ of x_1 and $\varepsilon_1 > 0 (\varepsilon_1 \leqslant \varepsilon)$ such that
$$N_1(x_1) \times N(c_1, \varepsilon) \subset N(x_0) \times N(c_0, \varepsilon) \cap \text{int epi}(f). \tag{3.32}$$
For each point $(x, d) \in N_1(x_1) \times N(c_1, \varepsilon)$, we have $(x, d) \in \text{int epi}(f) \subset \text{epi}(f)$, which implies that
$$f(x) \leqslant d < c_0 + \varepsilon < c, \tag{3.33}$$
i. e., $x \in F_c$. We now have
$$N_1(x_1) \subset F_c \text{ and } x_1 \in \text{int } F_c. \tag{3.34}$$
But this means that
$$x_1 \in N(x_0) \cap \text{int } F_c \neq \emptyset, \tag{3.35}$$
which contradicts (3.29). This proves that f is robust at x_0.

Corollary 3.1 *A function f is robust if and only if its epigraph epi(f) is robust in the produt space $X \times \mathbb{R}^1$.*

4 Robust Sets and Functions on the Real Line

In this section we will investigate the structure of robust sets and discontinuities of robust functions defined on the real line.

4.1 Singular Robust Points and Structure of Robust Sets

Intervals $[a, b]$, (a, b), $[a, b)$ and $(a, b]$ with $a < b$ (we denote each of them by) $\langle a, b \rangle$) on $\mathbb{R}^1$ are robust sets, so is the union of intervals. The following example shows that the structure of a robust set on $\mathbb{R}^1$ is more complicated than that of open sets.

Example 4.1 Let
$$B_0(a, b) = \bigcup_{k=1}^{\infty} (a + (b-a)/(2k+1), a + (b-a)/(2k-1))$$
and
$$B_1(a, b) = \bigcup_{k=1}^{\infty} (b - (b-a)/(2k-1), b - (b-a)/(2k+1)).$$
Denote $D_0 = B_0(a, b) \cup \{a\}$ and $D_1 = B_1(a, b) \cup \{b\}$. Then int $D_0 = B_0(a, b)$ and int $D_1 = B_1(a, b)$. Moreover, for each neighborhood $N(a, \delta) = (a-\delta, a+\delta)$, $N(a, \delta) \cap \text{int } D_0 \neq \emptyset$, i. e., the point a is robust to D_0. Similarly, b is robust to D_1. Both of D_0 and D_1 are robust.

Definition 4.1 A robust point x of a set D is said to be singular if x is neither in any interval nor an end point of any interval within D.

The points a and b in Example 4.1 are singularly robust to D_0 and D_1, respectively.

Lemma 4.1 *Suppose that x is singularly robust to a set D. Then there is a sequence $\{I_n = \langle a_n, b_n \rangle\}$ of disjoint intervals within D with $b_n < a_{n+1}$ or $b_{n+1} < a_n$, $n = 1, 2, \cdots$. Such*

that x is the common limit of the end points of I_n, $n=1, 2, \cdots$. Moreover $[b_n, a_{n+1}] \cap D^c \neq \varnothing$ for the cases $b_n < a_{n+1}$, $n=1, 2, \cdots$, or $[b_{n+1}, a_n] \cap D^c \neq \varnothing$ for the cases $b_{n+1} < a_n$, $n=1, 2, \cdots$.

Proof. Take $\delta_1 > 0$. Then $N(x, \delta_1) \cap \text{int } D \neq \varnothing$. Let $y_1 \in N(x, \delta_1) \cap \text{int } D$ and look for the largest interval $I_1 = \langle a_1, b_1 \rangle \subset D$ containing y_1. The point is neither in I_1 nor an end point of I_1; the distance $d_1 = \rho(x, I_1)$ from x to I_1 is positive. Let $\delta_2 = \min(d_1, \delta_1/2)$ and $y_2 \in N(x, \delta_2) \cap \text{int } D$. Again, find the largest interval $I_2 = \langle a_2, b_2 \rangle \subset D$ containing y_2. By construction $I_1 \cap I_2 \neq \varnothing$. Suppose we have constructed k disjoint intervals $I_1, \cdots, I_k$ within D; $I_i = \langle a_i, b_i \rangle$ and $x \neq a_i, b_i$, $i=1, \cdots, k$. Let $d_k = \rho(x, I_k)$ amd $\delta_{k+1} = \min(d_k, \delta_k/2)$. Then $N(x, \delta_{k+1}) \cap I_i \neq \varnothing$, $i=1, 2, \cdots, k$ and $N(x, \delta_{k+2}) \cap \text{int } D \neq \varnothing$ since x is robust to D. Take $y_{k+1} \in N(x, \delta_{k+1}) \cap \text{int } D$ and look for the largest interval $I_{k+1} = \langle a_{k+1}, b_{k+1} \rangle \subset D$ containing y_{k+1}, and so on. We obtain a sequence $\{I_n\}$ of disjoint intervals. There is, at least, an infinite subsequence of $\{I_n\}$ on one side of x, say, on the left hand side, and then we have $b_n < a_{n+1}$, $n=1, 2, \cdots$ case. We still denote the subsequence by $\{I_n\}$. By construction, we have $I_n \subset N(x, \delta_{n-1})$. Indeed, if there is $z \in I_n$ and $z \in N(x, \delta_{n-1})$, then we have $z < x - \delta_{n-1} < y_{n-1} y_n$ and $[z, y_n] \subset I_n$. It implies that $y_{n-1} \in I_{n-1} \cap I_n \neq \varnothing$. This is a contradiction. Now, $\{\delta_n\}$ is a decreasing sequence and $\lim \delta_n = 0$. Both of the points a_n, b_n of the interval I_n, $n=1, 2, \cdots$ converge to x. The last assertion of the lemma is clear by construction.

Theorem 4.1 *A robust set D on the real line is a countable union of disjoint intervals including possibly a set of singular robust points to D.*

Proof. Suppose $D = D_1 \cup E_1$, where D_1 is a countable union of intervals, and each point in E is singularly robust to D. Each interval on the real line is robust, so is their union D_1. Each point of D_1 is robust to D_1, as well as to D itself. Adding singularly robust points to D, we have proved each point of D is robust to D. Hence D is robust.

Conversely, suppose D is a nonempty robust set. For each point $x \in \text{int } D$, let $I(x)$ be the largest interval within D containing x. Let

$$D_0 = \bigcup_{x \in \text{int } D} I(x).$$

Then D_0 is a union of at most countable many disjoint intervals because the number (power) of disjoint interval on the real line is, at most, countable. Moreover, int $\langle D \setminus D_0 \rangle \neq \varnothing$. The remaining points in $D \setminus D_0$ are singular; each of the them is neither in any interval contained in D_0 nor its end point.

The following example shows that the power of the set of singularly robust points of a robust set may be uncountable.

Example 4.2 From the interval $[0, 1]$ remove the open interval $(1/3, 2/3)$ and add sets $B_0(1/3, 1/2)$ and $B_1(1/2, 2/3)$, where the notations are the same as those of Example 4.1. Next, remove the open intervals $(1/9, 2/9)$ and $(7/9, 8/9)$ from $[0, 1/3]$ and $[2/3, 1]$; add $B_0(1/9, 1/6)$, $B_1(1/6, 2/9)$, $B_0(7/9, 5/6)$ and $B_1(5/6, 8/9)$, and so on. At each succeeding stage remove the open middle third (a, b) of each remaining closed interval like the construction of the Cantor ternary set (see [6]), and add two $B_0 - B_1$-type robust sets with a and b as their singularly robust points, respectively. If the process is carried out denumerably many times, the result is the union $D = G \cup E$, where G is the union of countable open intervals and E is the Cantor set.

By construction, int $D = G$ and $N(x) \cap G \neq \emptyset$ for each point $x \in E$ and each neighborhood $N(x)$ of x. Thus, D is robust. Moreover, each point x of G is contained in $[0, 1] \setminus E$ and can have 1 as its ternary decimal, so does any end point of each interval contained in G. But each point in E can only have 0 and/or 2 as its ternary decimals. But any point in E is neither in any interval within D nor its end point, i.e., it is singularly robust to D. We now have an example with noncountable singular robust points.

Remark 4.1 In a similar way one can construct an example of a robust set on $\mathbb{R}^1$ with the property that its set of singularly robust points has a positive Lebesgue measure.

A robust point x in a set D may be the left (or right) end point of an interval within D but it is the limit of sequence $\{I_n\}$ of disjoint intervals with the property as in Lemma 4.1. Even though the point x is not eingular to D, it has also some singularity.

Definition 4.2 A point x is said to be left (or right) singularly robust to D if x is a singularly robust point to $D \cap (-\infty, x]$ (or to $D \cap [x, \infty)$).

In the next subsection we will consider the relation of left or right singularity with the discontinuity of a robust function.

4.2 Discontinuities of Robust Functions

A robust function may be discontinuous. Moreover, the singularity of robustness can be utilized to characterize a discontinuity of the second kind.

Theorem 4.2 *Suppose f is robust at x_0. If there is a real number c such that $x_0 \in F_c$ and x_0 is left (or right) singularly robust to F_c, then x_0 has a discontinuity of the second kind of f.*

Proof. We only prove the case where x_0 is left singularly robust to F_c for some c such that $x_0 \in F_c$. Let $\{I_n = \langle a_n, b_n \rangle, n = 1, 2, \cdots\}$ be a sequence of disjoint intervals within F_c such that $a_n \to x_0$ and $b_n \to x_0$ as $n \to \infty$, and $[b_n, a_{n+1}] \cap (F_c)^c \neq \emptyset$ (see Lemma 4.1). Take a point $z_n \in [b_n, a_{n+1}]$ such that $z_n \in (F_c)^c$, $n = 1, 2, \cdots$. We have $z_n \to x_0$ and $f(z_n) \geq c$, $n = 1, 2, \cdots$. Hence, $\limsup_{x \to x_0 - 0} f(x) \geq c$.

On the other hand, $x_0 \in F_c$ implies $f(x_0) c$. Let $c - f(x_0) = 2e > 0$. We still have $x_0 \in F_{c-e}$, and x_0 is robust to F_{c-e} either. Thus, for $\delta_n \downarrow 0$, $(x_0 - \delta_n, x_0] \cap \text{int } F_{c-e} \neq \emptyset$. Taking $y_n \in (x_0 - \delta_n, x_0]$, we have $f(y_n) < c - e$ and $y_n \to x_0$. Thus
$$\liminf_{x \to x_0 - 0} f(x) \leq c - e.$$

We have proved
$$\liminf_{x \to x_0 - 0} f(x) \leq c - e < c \leq \limsup_{x \to x_0 - 0} f(x). \qquad (4.1)$$

The left limit of f at x_0 does not exist. Therefore, f has a discontinuity of the seeond kind at x_0.

Theorem 4.3 *Suppose f is robust by x_0. If f has a discontinuity of the second kind at x_0, then there is a real number c such that x_0 is left (or right) singularly robust to F_c.*

Proof. Since f has a discontinuity of the second kind at x_0, one of the following inequalities holds:
$$\liminf_{x \to x_0-0} f(x) < \limsup_{x \to x_0-0} f(x) \quad \text{or} \quad \liminf_{x \to x_0+0} f(x) < \limsup_{x \to x_0+0} f(x). \tag{4.2}$$

Say, $\liminf_{x \to x_0-0} f(x) = \alpha < \beta = \limsup_{x \to x_0-0} f(x)$. Take a real number c such that $\alpha < c < \beta$, and let $\varepsilon = \min((\beta-c)/2, (c-\alpha)/2) > 0$. We now prove $x_0 \in \text{cl } F_c$ and x_0 is robust to F_c. Indeed, since $\liminf_{x \to x_0-0} f(x) = \alpha$, for each $\delta_n > 0 (\delta_n \downarrow 0)$ there is, at least, a point x_n such that $x_0 - \delta_n < x_n < x_0$ and $f(x_n) < \alpha + \varepsilon < c$, i.e., $x_n \in F_c$. But $x_n \to x_0$ as $x \to \infty$, thus, $x_0 \in \text{cl } F_c$. Since f is robust by x_0, there is a neighborhood $N(x_0)$ of x_0 such that $N(x_0) \cap F_c$ is nonempty and robust. x_0 is robust to $N(x_0) \cap F_c$, so it is also robust to F_c.

To prove x_0 is a left singularly robust point of F_c we need only prove that (1) for each $\eta > 0$, $(x_0 - \eta, x_0] \cap \text{int } F_c \neq \varnothing$, and (2) x_0 is not the right end point of an interval within $(-\infty, x_0] \cap F_c$. Since $N(x_0) \cap F_c$ in nonempty and robust, there is a small positive number $\delta(<\eta)$ such that $(x_0 - \delta, x_0 + \delta) \cap F_c$ is robust. The above sequence $\{x_n\}$ is contained in F_c, so $x_m \in (x_0 - \delta, x_0) \cap F_c$ when m is large enough. The point x_m is robust to $(x_0 - \delta, x_0) \cap F_c$, so there is a neighborhood $N_1(x_m) (\subset (x_0 - \delta, x_0))$ such that $N_1(x_m) \cap \text{int } (x_0 - \delta, x_0) \cap \text{int } F_c = N_1(x_m) \cap \text{int } F_c \neq \varnothing$. Hence, $x_m \in (x_0 - \eta, x_0] \cap \text{int } F_c \neq \varnothing$. To prove (2), suppose, on the contrary, x_0 is the right end point of some interval $(x_0 - a, x_0) \subset F_c$. Since $\limsup_{x \to x_0-0} f(x) = \beta > c$, there exists a sequence $\{y_n\}$ such that $y_n < x_0$, $y_n \to x_0$ and $f(y_k) \geq c + \varepsilon$, for $k \geq n_n$, where n_1 is a large positive integer. Now $y_k \in (x_0 - a, x_0)$, so $y_k \in F_c$ when k large enough. This contradicts $f(y_k) < c$. Therefore, x_0 is left singularly robust to F_c.

Corollary 4.1 *Suppose f is robust at x_0. If x_0 is nonsingular to F_c for any real number c such that $x_0 \in \text{cl } F_c$, then f is continuous at x_0 or has a discontinuity of the first kind.*

5 Relative Robustness

5.1 Relatively Robust Functions

The concept of robust function utilized in considering an unconstrained minimization problem is not enough in a constrained one since the constrained set may produce some nonrobust behaviors.

Example 5.1 Let $S = (-\infty, 0] \cup [1, \infty)$ and
$$f_1(x) = \begin{cases} 1-x, & x \in (-\infty, 0), \\ x, & x \in [0, \infty). \end{cases} \tag{5.1}$$

Even though f is robust on $X = R^1$, but if we consider a constrained problem with the feasible set S, we have a restricted one:

$$f_s(x) = \begin{cases} 1-x, & x \in (-\infty, 0), \\ 0, & x = 0, \\ x, & x \in [1, \infty), \end{cases} \tag{5.2}$$

and the function f_s is nonrobust at $x=0$.

Thus, a concept of robustness related to a constrained problem has to be introduced. This is that of rolative robustness.

Definition 5.1 Let S be a given set in a topological space X, f be a real-valued function and $x_0 \in \text{cl } S$. The function f is said to be relatively robust at x_0 if for each real number c, $x_0 \in F_c = \{x \mid f(x) < c\}$ implies x_0 is robust to $F_c \cap S$. If f is relatively robust to S at each point x in S, then f is called a relatively robust function on S.

The following theorem gives us two sufficient conditions of relative robustness of a function.

Theorem 5.1 *If (1) f is robust at x_0 and $x_0 \in \text{int } S$; or (2) x_0 is robust to S and f is upper semi-continuous (u.s.c.) at x_0, then f is relatively robust to S at x_0.*

Proof. (1) Suppose that for some real c, $x_0 \in F_c = \{x \mid f(x) < c\}$. Then x_0 is robust to F_c since f is supposed to be robust. We also have $x_0 \in \text{int } S$; thus, by Theorem 2.2 of [1], x_0 is a robust point of $F_c \cap S$. This proves that f is relatively robust to S at x_0.

(2) Suppose $x_0 \in F_c$ for some real c. Then $x_0 \in \text{int } F_c$ since f is supposed to be u.s.c. at x_0. But x_0 is a robust point of S, which implies that x_0 is also robust to $F_c \cap S$. Thus, f is relatively robust to S at x_0.

Note that these conditions are sufficient.

Example 5.2 Let

$$S = (-\infty, 0] \cup [1, \infty], \tag{5.3}$$

and

$$f_2(x) = \begin{cases} x, & x \in (-\infty, 0), \\ x+1, & x \in (0, \infty). \end{cases} \tag{5.4}$$

f_2 is robust at each point of S.

5.2 Inf-Robust Function

A concept of inf-robustness is introduced in [2] for minimization problems in functional spaces.

Definition 5.2 A function f defined on a set S is said to be inf-robust iff for each real $c_0 (> \bar{c} = \inf\limits_{x \in S} f(x))$, there is a real $c(\bar{c} < c \leq c_0)$ such that $F_c \cap S$ is a robust set.

In [2] we only consider the case of continuous objective functions, and the definition of the inf-robustness is simplified as: A function f defined on a set S is inf-robust iff there is a real number c such that $F_c \cap S$ is nonempty and robust.

The following assumption is needed when we consider the optimality conditions or algorithms:

(R) f is relatively robust to S at a global minimum point.

Theorem 5.2 shows that the condition of inf-robustness is stronger than that of (R).

Theorem 5.2 *If the function f defined on S is inf-robust, then f is relatively robust to S at each global minimum of f over S.*

Proof. Let $\bar{c} = \min_{x \in S} f(x)$ and $\bar{x} \in S$ be a global minimum of f over S. For each real number c, $\bar{x} \in F_c$ implies $c < \bar{c}$. Since f is supposed to be inf-robust, there is $c_1 \leqslant c$ and $c_1 > \bar{c}$ such that $S \cap F_{c_1}$, is nonempty and robust. But $\bar{x} \in S \cap F_{c_1}$, thus, $\bar{x}$ is a robust point of $S \cap F_{c_1}$. Therefore, $\bar{x}$ is also a robust point of $S \cap F_c$. This proves that f is relatively robust to S at $\bar{x}$.

The following example shows that a function which is relatively robust at a global minimum, is general, is not inf-robust.

Example 5.3 Let $X = \mathbb{R}^1$ and $S = [-1, 1]$. The objective function f is defined as follows:
$$f(x) = \begin{cases} -x, & \text{if } x \text{ is a rational number in } [-1, 0), \\ -2x, & \text{if } x \text{ is an irrational number in } [-1, 0), \\ x, & \text{if } x \in [0, 1]. \end{cases} \quad (5.5)$$

We have $c = 0$ and $x = 0$. f is relatively robust to S at $x = 0$. Indeed, $0 \in F_c$ if $c > 0$, and $0 \in \text{int } S$. Thus, 0 is a robust point of F_c because the intersection of each neighborhood of the origin and int F_c is nonempty for $c > 0$. But for any $c > 0$, F_c is nonrobust.

However, for some problems the set of global minima may be empty. In this case we can utilize inf-robust condition to characteriza and find the infimum of f over S. See the following example.

5.3 Robust Sets and Functions with Relative Topology

Let S be a robust set in a topological space (X, τ), where τ is the topology of X. We can introduce a relative topology τ_s and obtain a new topological space (S, τ_s), where τ_s consists of the following neighborhoods:
$$\tau_s = \{N_s(x) \mid N_s(x) = N(x) \cap S, \ x \in S, \ N(x) \in \tau\}. \quad (5.6)$$
In this new topological space, we also have concepts of robust sets and functions. Theorem 5.3 below establishes the relation between the robustness with the relative topology and relative robustness. Before proving this theorem, we prove a lemma first.

Lemma 5.1 *Let S be a robust set in a topological space X, G be an open set in X. Suppose*
$$G \cap S \neq \emptyset. \quad (5.7)$$
Then we have
$$G \cap \text{int } S \neq \emptyset. \quad (5.8)$$

Proof. Since $G \cap S \neq \emptyset$, we can take a point $x \in G \cap S$. The intersection $G \cap S$ is also a robust set, so x is a robust point of $G \cap S$. Thus, for each neighborhood $N(x)$ of x,
$$N(x) \cap \text{int } (G \cap S) \neq \emptyset. \quad (5.9)$$
or
$$N(x) \cap G \cap \text{int } S \neq \emptyset. \quad (5.10)$$
This proves (5.8).

Theorem 5.3 *Suppose f is a real-valued function defined on a robust set. The function f is relatively robust to S at $x \in S$ if and only if f is robust at x with relative topology on S.*

Proof. Suppose f is relatively robust to S at x. If for some real number c, $x \in F_c = \{x \mid f(x) < c\}$, then x is a robust point of $F_c \cap S$, i.e., for each neighborhood $N(x)$ of x, we have

$$N(x) \cap \text{int } (F_c \cap S) \neq \varnothing, \tag{5.11}$$

or $N(x) \cap \text{int } S \cap \text{int } F_c \neq \varnothing$ and $N(x) \cap S \cap \text{int } S \neq \varnothing$. Since $N(x)$ is an arbitrary neighborhood of x, thus, for each neighborhood $N_s(x) \in \tau_s$,

$$N_S(x) \cap \text{int } F_c \neq \varnothing. \tag{5.12}$$

This proves that x is a robust point of F_c and f is robust at x with the relative topology on S.

Conversely, if f is robust at x with relative topology on S, then $x \in F_c$ for some real c implies that for each neighborhood $N_S(x)$ of x we have

$$N_S(x) \cap \text{int } F_c \neq \varnothing. \tag{5.13}$$

or

$$N(x) \cap S \cap \text{int } F_c \neq \varnothing. \tag{5.14}$$

$N(x) \cap \text{int } F_c$ is a nonempty open set and S is a robust set, their intersection is nonempty. Thus, by the lemma 5.1, we have

$$N(x) \cap \text{int } F_c \cap \text{int} S \neq \varnothing, \tag{5.15}$$

or for each neighborhood $N(x)$ in τ,

$$N(x) \cap \text{int } (F_c \cap S) \neq \varnothing. \tag{5.16}$$

This implies x is robust to $F_c \cap S$ and proves that f is relatively robust to S at x.

5.4 Robustness of Combinatorial Minimization Problems

As an example we consider the following combinatorial optimization problem. Let

$$Z_+^n = \{z = (z^1, \cdots, z^n) \mid z^i \text{ is a nonnegative integer}, i = 1, \cdots, n\}, \tag{5.17}$$

S be finite set Z_+^n and $f: S \to \mathbb{R}^1$ be a function on S. Let $f(z) = f(z^1, \cdots, z^n)$. The problem is to find the minimum value of f over S:

$$\bar{c} = \min_{z \in S} f(z) \tag{5.18}$$

and the set of minima:

$$\bar{H} = \{x \in S \mid f(x) = \bar{c}\}. \tag{5.19}$$

In this case $\bar{H}$ is nonempty.

We define

$$D = \{x = (x^1, \cdots, x^n) \in \mathbb{R}^n \mid ([x^1 + 0.5], \cdots, [x^n + 0.5]) \in S\} \tag{5.20}$$

and

$$F(x) = f([x^1 + 0.5], \cdots, [x^2 + 0.5]) \tag{5.21}$$

where $[a]$ denotes the integer part of the real number a. D is a union of cubes, they are robust in $\mathbb{R}^n$. For each real number c, the set $\{x \mid F(x) < c\}$ is also a union of cubes (or empty). Thus, D is a robust set and F is a robust function in $\mathbb{R}^n$. Let x be a global minimum point of F over D, i.e.,

$$F(\bar{x}) = \min_{x \in D} F(x). \tag{5.22}$$

Then $\bar{x} \in \text{int } D$ (or one can find a point x_1 in the same cube with $\bar{x}$ such that $x_1 \in \text{int } D$).

Therefore, the assumption (R) is satisfied.

6 Robustiztion

6.1 Robustized Function

We are considering a minimization problem whose objective function is supposed to be robust and l.s.c.. A function without such properties can be robustized to be one with such properties. The process to obtain such a function is called a robustization procedure.

Suppose we have a function f defined on a topological space X with its epigraph epi(f). Let
$$R_f = \mathrm{cl}(\mathrm{int}\ \mathrm{epi}(f)), \tag{6.1}$$
where closure and interior operations are taken in the product space $X \times \mathbb{R}^1$. Even though epi(f) may be nonclosed and nonrobust, R_f is closed and robust, i.e.,

Proposition 6.1 R_f is closed and robust in the product space $X \times \mathbb{R}^1$.

The set R_f is generated from the epigraph of f. As an epigraph epi(f) of a function f it has a property that $(x_0, c_0) \in \mathrm{epi}(f)$ implies $(x_0, c_1) \in \mathrm{epi}(f)$, for each $c_1 \geq c_0$. The set R_f in (6.1) preserves this property.

Proposition 6.2 If $(x_0, c_0) \in R_f$, then $(x_0, c') \in R_f$ for all $c' > c_0$.

Proof. Suppose $(x_0, c_0) \in R_f$. For each neighborhood $N_0(x_0)$, let $N(x_0, c_0) = N_0(x_0) \times (c_0 - \varepsilon, c_0 - \varepsilon)$ (we take $0 < \varepsilon < c' - c_0$). By (6.1), we have
$$N(x_0, c_0) \cap \mathrm{int}(\mathrm{epi}\ (f)) \neq \varnothing. \tag{6.2}$$
Since $N(x_0, c_0)$ and int(epi(f)) are open, there is at least a point (x_1, c_1) with neighborhood $N_1(x_1) \times (c_1 - \varepsilon_1, c_1 + \varepsilon_1)$ such that
$$N_1(x_1) \times (c_1 - \varepsilon_1, c_1 + \varepsilon_1) \subset \mathrm{int}(\mathrm{epi}(f)) \subset \mathrm{epi}(f), \tag{6.3}$$
where $N_1(x_1) \subset N_0(x_0)$ and $(c_1 - \varepsilon_1, c_1 + \varepsilon_1) \subset (c_0 - \varepsilon, c_0 + \varepsilon)$. From (6.3) and by the property of an epigraph, we have
$$f(x) \leq c_1 + \varepsilon_1 \leq c_0 + \varepsilon < c', \quad \forall x \in N_1(x_1), \tag{6.4}$$
which implies that
$$N_1(x_1) \times (c' - \delta, c' + \delta) \subset \mathrm{epi}(f) \tag{6.5}$$
with small $\delta > 0$. Thus,
$$N_1(x_1) \times (c' - \delta, c' + \delta) = \mathrm{int}(N_1(x_1) \times (c' - \delta, c' + \delta)) \subset \mathrm{int}(\mathrm{epi}(f)). \tag{6.6}$$
Since $N_1(x_1) \subset N_0(x_0)$, we have
$$N_0(x_0) \times (c' - \delta, c' + \delta) \cap \mathrm{int}(\mathrm{epi}(f)) \neq \varnothing. \tag{6.7}$$
We then conclude that $(x_0, c') \in \mathrm{cl}\ \mathrm{int}(\mathrm{epi}(f)) = R_f$.

We are now ready to define a robustization of a function.

Definition 6.1 A function f_r defined on X is said to be the robustization of f iff
$$f_r(x) = \inf\{c \mid (x, c) \in R_f\}. \tag{6.8}$$

From Definition 6.1 and the closedness of R_f, we can easily prove

Proposition 6.3 $(x_0, f_r(x_0)) \in R_f$.

Proof. We first prove that, for each $c > f_r(x_0)$, $(x_0, c) \in R_f$. Suppose the statement is not true, there is a real number $c_1 (> f_r(x_0))$ such that (x_0, c_1) is not in R_f. Then, by Proposition 6.2, for all $c \leqslant c_1$, (x_0, c) is not in R_f. This implies $f_r(x_0) \geqslant c_1$. Now we have a contradiction:

$$f_r(x_0) \geqslant c_1 < f_r(x_0). \tag{6.9}$$

Thus $(x_0, c) \in R_f$, for all $c > f_r(x_0)$. which implies, by the closefness of R_f, that $(x_0, f_r(x_0)) \in R_f$.

We now prove that $R_f = \text{epi}(f_r)$, which is expected.

Theorem 6.1 *With the Definitions 6.1 and (6.8), we have*

$$R_f = \text{epi}(f_r). \tag{6.10}$$

Proof. For each point $(x_0, c_0) \in R_f$

$$f_r(x_0) = \inf\{c \mid (x_0, c) \in R_f\} \leqslant c_0. \tag{6.11}$$

This implies $(x_0, c_0) \in \text{epi}(f_r)$, i.e., we have proved that

$$R_f \subset \text{epi}(f_r). \tag{6.12}$$

Conversely, for each point $(x_0, c_0) \in \text{epi}(f_r)$, we have $f_r(x_0) \leqslant c_0$. By Proposition 6.3, $(x_0, f_r(x_0)) \in R_f$, and then $(x_0, c_0) \in R_r$ by Proposition 6.2. Therefore,

$$\text{epi}(f_r) \subset R_f. \tag{6.13}$$

From (6.12) and (6.13) we conclude $R_f = \text{epi}(f_r)$.

Since R_f is robust, so f_r is robust (see Corollary 3.1). The lower semi-continuity of f_r is from the closedness of R_f. Indeed, from

$$\text{epi}(f_r) = \{(x, c) \mid f_r(x) \leqslant c\}, \tag{6.14}$$

we have

$$H_c = \{x \mid f_r(x) \leqslant c\} \tag{6.15}$$

is closed for each c. This implies f_r is l.s.c.. Hence, we have proved

Theorem 6.2 *The robustization f_r of a function f is robust and l.s.c..*

6.2 A Function and Its Robustization

In this subsection we will prove that if a function f is robust and l.s.c. at a point then the function value of f and that of its robustization f_r is equal. We first prove

Proposition 6.4 *If f is robust at x_0, then $(x_0, f(x_0)) \in R_f$.*

Proof. Tke a neighborhhod $N(x_0, f(x_0)) = N_0(x_0) \times (f(x_0) - d, f(x_0) + d)$ of $(x_0, f(x_0))$ and let $c = f(x_0) + d/2$. We have (x_0, c) is robust to epi (f) because if f is robust at x_0 then for each $c > f(x_0)$, (x_0, c) is robust to epi(f). Thus,

$$N_0(x_0) \times (c - d/2, c + d/2) \cap \text{int epi}(f) \neq \varnothing. \tag{6.16}$$

But $(c - d/2, c + d/2) \subset (f(x_0) - d, f(x_0) + d)$. Hence,

$$N(x_0, f(x_0)) \cap \text{int epi}(f) \neq \varnothing, \tag{6.17}$$

which means that

$$(x_0, f(x_0)) \in \text{cl int }(\text{epi}(f)) = R_f.$$

Applying Proposition 6.4, we can easily prove

Proposition 6.5 *If f is robust at x_0, then*

$$f_r(x_0) \leqslant f(x_0). \tag{6.18}$$

Proof. If f is robust at x_0, then $(x_0, f(x_0)) \in R_f$. Thus, $(x_0, c) \in R_f$, for each $c \geqslant f(x_0)$. Hence,
$$f(x_0) \geqslant \inf\{c \mid (x_0, c) \in R_f\} = f_r(x_0).$$

Proposition 6.6 *If f is l.s.c. at x_0, then*
$$f_r(x_0) \geqslant f(x_0). \tag{6.19}$$

Proof. Suppose, on the contrary, $f_r(x_0) < f(x_0)$. Then there are a_0 and a_1 such that
$$f_r(x_0) < a_0 < a_1 < f(x_0). \tag{6.20}$$
$f(x_0) > a_1$ and the lower semi-continuity of f at x_0 imply that there is a neighborhood $N(x_0)$ of x_0 such that
$$f(x) > a_1 \quad \forall x \in N_0(x_0). \tag{6.21}$$
And thus for each point of $N_0(x_0) \times (a_0 - d, a_0 + d)$ $(0 < d < a_1 - a_0)$ which could not be in $\text{epi}(f)$, i.e.,
$$N_0(x_0) \times (a_0 - d, a_0 + d) \cap \text{epi}(f) = \varnothing, \tag{6.22}$$
we then have
$$N_0(x_0) \times (a_0 - d, a_0 + d) \cap \text{int}(\text{epi}(f)) = \varnothing, \tag{6.23}$$
or
$$(x_0, a_0) \overline{\in} R_f. \tag{6.24}$$
But $(x_0, f_r(x_0)) \in R_f$ which implies $(x_0, a_0) \in R_f$. This contradiction shows that (6.12) is valid.

Combining Proposition 6.5 and Proposition 6.6, we have

Theorem 6.3 *If f is robust and l.s.c. at x_0 then*
$$f(x_0) = f_r(x_0).$$

The following example shows a robustization process.

Example 6.1 Let
$$f(x) = \begin{cases} 0, & c \leqslant 0, \\ 1, & 0 < x \leqslant 1, \\ 0, & 1 < x < 2, \\ -1, & x = 2, \\ 0, & x > 2. \end{cases}$$

We then have
(1) $\text{epi}(f) = (-\infty, 0] \times [0, \infty) \cup (0, 1] \times [1, \infty] \cup (1, 2)$
$\times [0, \infty] \cup \{2\} \times [-1, \infty] \cup (2, \infty) \times [0, \infty]$.
(2) $\text{int epi}(f) = (-\infty, 0) \times (0, \infty) \cup (0, 1) \times (1, \infty) \cup (1, \infty) \times (0, \infty)$.
(3) $\text{cl int}(\text{epi}(f)) = (-\infty, 0] \times [0, \infty) \cup (0, 1) \times [1, \infty) \cup [1, \infty) \times (1, \infty)$.

We finally obtain the robustization f_r of the function f:
$$f_r(x) = \begin{cases} 0, & x \leqslant 0, \\ 1, & 0 < x < 1, \\ 0, & x \geqslant 1. \end{cases}$$

6.3 Reltive Robustization

We are now considering a constrained minimization problem:
$$\bar{c} = \inf_{x \subset S} f(x). \quad (6.25)$$

The constrained set S may be nonrobust. We first make the set S to be robust and closed:
$$S_r = \mathrm{cl\ int} S, \quad (6.26)$$
and then construct a relative robustization of f over S.

Example 6.2 Consider an inequality constrained minimization problem in $\mathbb{R}^n$:
$$\min f(x) \quad (6.27)$$
$$\text{s. t. } g_i(x) \leqslant 0, \quad i=1, \cdots, l.$$

The constrained set $G = \{x \mid g_i(x) \leqslant 0, i=1, \cdots, l\}$ may be nonrobust even though $g_i(x)$, $i=1, \cdots, l$ are continuous. Let
$$G_r = \mathrm{cl\ int\ } G \quad (6.28)$$
or let
$$G_r = \mathrm{cl\ } G_0 \quad (6.29)$$
where $G_0 = \{x \mid g_i(x) < 0, i=1, \cdots, l\}$. Since g_i, $i=1, \cdots, l$ are continuous, so the set G_0 is open.

Note that if the problem (6.27) is such that the minimum is not attained at points in G_r, then there would be no access to the minima. Therefore, we assume that S is a closed and robust set, i. e., $S = S_r$.

We now consider a minimization problem in the topological space (S, τ_S) with the relative topology τ_S, and make the objective function to be robustized with respect to the relative topology in the space (S, τ_S). All of the propositions and theorems in subsections 6.1 and 6.2 are valid, i. e., we obtain a relative robustization.

References

[1] Zheng Quan. Robust Analysis and Global Minimiztion of a Class of Discontinuous Functions (II). preprint.

[2] E. Galperin, Q. Zheng. Integral Global Optimization Methods for Differential Games with Application to Pursuit-evasion Games [J]. *Computers Math. Applic.*, 18:1−3(1989), 209−243.

[3] X. Pan, S. Wang, H. Lui, Q. Zheng. The Optimum Design for the Arrangement of Needles on the Needle Board of Pre-needling Machine [J]. *Journal of China Textile University*, 12:6(1986), 79−84.

[4] I. Zang. Discontinuous Optimization by Smoothing [J]. *Mathematics of Operations Research*, 6:1 (1981), 140−152.

[5] I. V. Mayurova, R. G. Strongin. Minimization of Multi-extremum Function with a Discontinuity [J]. *USSR Computational Mathematics and Mathematical Physics*, 24:6(1984), 21−126.

[6] V. D. Batuchtin, L. A. Mauboroda, Optimization of Discontinuous Functions [J], Nauka, Moskow, 1984.

[7] J. J. Benedetto. Real Variable and Integration. B. G. Teubner Stuttgart, 1976.

[8] R. T. Rockafellar. Convex Analysis [M]. Princeton University Press, 1970.

[9] Zheng Quan. A Class of Discontinuous Functions and Its Global Optimization Problems, Numericc Mathematics [J], *A Journal of Chinese Universities*, 7:1(1985),31—43.

[10] Zheng Quen. Global Optimization of a Class of Discontinuous Functions [J]. *Journal of Applied Sciences*, 4:1(1986),93—94.

Robust Analysis and Global Minimization of A Class of Discontinuous Functions (II) *

Abstract: In this paper we continue to investigate global minimization problems. An integral approach is applied to treat a global minimization problem of a discontinuous function. With the help of the theory of measure (Q-measure) and integration, optimality conditions of a robust function over a robust set are derived. Algorithms and their implementations for finding global minima are proposed. Numerical tests and applications show that the algorithms are effective.

7 Q-measure Spaces and Q-convergence of Measures

7.1 Q-measure Spaces

In order to consider minimization problems with an integral approach, a special class of measure spaces should be investigated. These are the so-called Q-measure spaces.

Let X be a Hausdorff space, Ω a σ-field of subsets of X, and μ a measure on Ω.

Definition 7.1 A measure space (X, Ω, μ) is called a Q-measure space iff

(M1) Each open set is measurable;

(M2) The measure of each nonempty open set is positive;

(M3) The measure of each compact set is finite.

Since the interior of each robust set D is nonempty this implies the following theorem:

Theorem 7.1 *If D is a measurable nonempty robust set and μ satisfies* (M2), *then* $\mu(D) > 0$.

The Lebesgue measure space $(\mathbb{R}^n, \Omega, \mu)$ is a Q-measure space; a nondegenerate Gaussian measure μ on a separable Hilbert space H with Borel sets as measurable sets consists a Q-measure space (H, Ω, μ), see [6]. A specific optimization problem is related to a specific Q-measure space which is suitable for consideration. For instance, an optimal control problem was considered in [3]. The control $u(t)$ is taken in the space $L^2[t_0, T]$ with the restriction $|u(t)| \leq M$, for $f \in [t_0, T]$, where $M > 0$ is a given bound of the control. With the topology in $L^2[t_0, T]$, the interior of the set

$$U_M = \{u(.) \in L^2[t_0, T] \mid |u(t)| \leq M, t \in [t_0, T]\} \tag{7.1}$$

---

* Reprinted from Acta Mathematics Applicatae Sinica, 1990, 6((4):317—337.

is empty. To circumvent this difficulty, a special metric and measure were constructed with the properties (M1), (M2) and (M3). The process of constructing this Q-measure is quite involved. This happens especially in infinite-dimensional spaces. In the next subsection we will consider the problem for constructing a Q-measure on a compact convex set in an infinite-dimensional space.

7.2 Construction of Q-measure on Compact Convex Sets

Definition 7.2 A convex subset K of a linear topological space is said to be a Keller space iff K is affinely homeomorphic to an infinite-dimensional compact convex set in the Hilbert space l_2.

The following propositions are known [4]:

Proposition 7.1 *Every infinite-dimensional compact convex subset of an arbitrary Frechet space is a Keller space. Every Keller space K is homeomorphic to the Hilbert cube HQ.*

Recall that the Hilbert cube $HQ=I$, which can be regarded as a subset of the Frechet space $\mathbb{R}$, where $I=[-1, 1]$.

In [2] we have constructed a Q-measure on the Hilbert cube HQ with the properties (M1)~(M3).

7.3 Q-convergence of Measures

We are familiar with the concept of weak convergence of measures in the theory of probability and stochastic process. Recall that a sequence of measures $\{\mu_n\}$ on the Borel sets of a metric space X is said to be weakly convegent to a measure μ iff

$$\int_X f \, d\mu_n \to \int_X f \, d\mu, \text{ for all bounded continuous function } f:X \to \mathbb{R} \quad (7.2)$$

(see [7]). This convergence concept does not fit the usage in the following consideration; a new concept of convergence of measures is required.

Suppose that X is a compact Hausdorff space and μ_n, $n=1,2,\cdots$ and μ are measures on the Borel sets of X.

Definition 7.3 A sequence $\{\mu_n\}$ of measures is said to be Q-convergent to a Q-measure μ iff for each open set G in X,

$$\mu_n(G) \to \mu(G). \quad (7.3)$$

Remark 7.1 Since the space X itself is open, we have, automatically,

$$\mu_n(X) \to \mu(X). \quad (7.4)$$

Remark 7.2 Since μ is a Q-measure and X is compact, thus $\mu(X)<+\infty$ and so $\mu_n(X)<\infty$, for $n \geq n_0$. Moreover, for each nonempty open set G, $\mu(G)>0$, so $\mu_n(G)>0$ for $n \geq n_1$ (n_1 may depend on G). Therefore, even though we only assume that μ is a Q-measure, in the following consideration we will suppose that the measures μ_n, $n=1, 2, \cdots$ in the sequence are Q-measures.

The concept of Q-convergence is stronger than that of weak convergence. The following theorem gives us several equivalent conditions of Q-convergence.

Theorem 7.2 *Let $\mu_1, \cdots, \mu_n, \cdots$ and μ be Q-measures on the Borel sets of a compact Hausdorff space* X. *Then the following conditions are equivalent*:

(1) $\int_X f d\mu_n \to \int_X f d\mu$, *for all bounded l.s.c. function* $f: X \to \mathbb{R}$;

(2) $\int_X f d\mu_n \to \int_X f d\mu$, *for all bounded u.s.c. functions* $f: X \to \mathbb{R}$;

(3) $\lim_{n\to\infty} \mu_n(G) \to \mu(G)$, *for all open sets G in X i.e.*, $\{\mu_n\}$ *is Q-convergent to* μ;

(4) $\lim_{n\to\infty} \mu_n(F) \to \mu(F)$, *for all closed sets F in X*.

Proof. If $-f$ is l.s.c. then f is u.s.c. and vice versa, so

$$\int_X f d\mu_n \to \int_X f d\mu \Leftrightarrow -\int_X f d\mu_n \to -\int_X f d\mu. \qquad (7.5)$$

Thus, (1) and (2) are equivalent.

If F is closed then $X\backslash F$ is open; if G is open then $X\backslash G$ is closed. We have, for each closed set F,

$$\mu_n(F) = \mu_n(X\backslash G) = \mu_n(X) - \mu_n(G) \to \mu(X) - \mu(G) = \mu(X\backslash G) = \mu(F), \qquad (7.6)$$

i.e., (3)$\Rightarrow$(4). We can prove (4)$\Rightarrow$(3) similarly.

(1)$\Rightarrow$(3). If G is open, then the indicator I_G of G is bounded and l.s.c., and we now have

$$\mu_n(G) = \int_X I_G d\mu_n \to \int_X I_G d\mu = \mu(G). \qquad (7.7)$$

(4)$\Rightarrow$(1). Denote

$$D_i = \{x \mid c_i < f(x) \leq c_{i+1}\} = H_{c_{i+1}} - H_{c_i}, \quad c_{i+1} > c_i, \qquad (7.8)$$

where $H_{c_i} = \{X \mid f(x) \leq c_i\}$ is a level set, which is closed because f is l.s.c. We have, for each $c_{i+1} > c_i$,

$$\begin{aligned}
\mu_n(D_i) &= \mu_n(H_{c_{i+1}} - H_{c_i}) \\
&= \mu_n(H_{c_{i+1}}) - \mu(H_{c_i}) \to \mu(H_{c_{i+1}}) - \mu(H_{c_i}) \\
&= \mu(H_{c_{i+1}} - H_{c_i}) = \mu(D_i).
\end{aligned} \qquad (7.9)$$

Construct a partition of $[-M, M]$, where $M > 0$ is the bound of f: $-M = c_0 < c_1 < \cdots < c_m = M$. Then we have

$$\begin{aligned}
\left| \int_X f d\mu_n - \int_X f d\mu \right| &\leq \left| \int_X f d\mu - \sum_{i=0}^{m-1} c_i \cdot \mu_n(D_i) \right| + \left| \sum_{i=0}^{m-1} c_i \cdot \mu_n(D_i) - \sum_{i=0}^{m-1} c_i \cdot \mu(D_i) \right| \\
&\quad + \left| \sum_{i=0}^{m-1} c_i \cdot \mu(D_i) - \int_X f d\mu \right| = I_1 + I_2 + I_3.
\end{aligned} \qquad (7.10)$$

The first term on the right can be estimated, for small $\varepsilon > 0$, as

$$\begin{aligned}
I_1 &= \left| \sum_{i=0}^{m-1} c_i \cdot \mu(D_i) - \int_{D_i} f d\mu \right| \\
&= \left| \sum_{i=0}^{m-1} \int_{D_i} (c - f(x)) d\mu_n \right| \\
&\leq \max_{0 \leq i \leq m-1} (c_{i+1} - c_i) \mu_n(X) < \varepsilon/3,
\end{aligned} \qquad (7.11)$$

if we choose the partition such that $\max_{0\leq i\leq m-1}(c_{i+1}-c_i)$ is small enough and $\mu_n(X)$ is bounded becuse $\mu_n(X)\to\mu(X)<\infty$. Similarly, we can obtain

$$I_3<\varepsilon/3, \quad \text{for such a partition.} \tag{7.12}$$

The second term I_2 approaches 0 as $n\to\infty$ from (7.10). These prove (1).

8 Optimality Conditions for Global Minimization

8.1 Sufficient conditions for Global Minima

We are now in a position to investigate the optimality conditions for global minimization. Let X be a topological space, S be a subset of X, $f:S\to\mathbb{R}$ be a real-valued function and

$$\bar{c}=\inf_{x\in S}f(x). \tag{8.1}$$

To investigate the optimality condition by an integral-measure approach, some of the following assumptions are required:

(A) S is compact and f is l.s.c.;

(M) (X,Ω,μ) is a Q-measure space;

(R) There is a global minimum point $\bar{x}\in S$ such that f is relatively robust to S at x;

(A′) S is a measurable robust set and f is a measurable function;

(M′) (X,Ω,μ) is a Q_1-measure space, i.e., (M1) and (M2) hold;

(R′) f is inf-robust to S.

The following theorem gives us sufficient conditions for global minimality.

Theorem 8.1 *Suppose that the conditions* (A), (M′) *and* (R) *hold, and* $S\cap H_c\neq\emptyset$, *where* $H_c=\{x|f(x)\leq c\}$ *is the level set of* f. *If*

$$\mu(H_c\cap S)=0, \tag{8.2}$$

then c is the global minimum value and $H_c\cap S$ is the set of all global minima.

Proof. Suppose, on the contrary, that c is not the globsl minimum value of f over S, and it is $\hat{c}<c$. Let $2a=c-\hat{c}>0$, and $\hat{x}\in S$ be the global minimum at which f is relatively robust to S. So $F_{\hat{c}-a}=\{x|f(x)<\hat{c}-a\}$ is nonempty, $\hat{x}\in F_{\hat{c}-a}$ and $\hat{x}$ is a robust point of $S\cap F_{\hat{c}-a}$. Thus, for each neighborhood $N(\hat{x})$ of $\hat{x}$,

$$N(\hat{x})\cap\text{int}(S\cap F_{\hat{c}-a})\neq\emptyset. \tag{8.3}$$

Now we have

$$N(\hat{x})\cap\text{int}(S\cap F_{\hat{c}-a})\subset\text{int}(S\cap F_{\hat{c}-a})\subset S\cap H_c. \tag{8.4}$$

which implies by the assumption (M′) that

$$\mu(S\cap H_c)\geq\mu(\text{int}(S\cap F_{\hat{c}-a}))>0. \tag{8.5}$$

This contradicts (8.2).

When (A) does not hold, the set of global minima may be empty, but, we have a similar result.

Theorem 8.2 *Suppose that the conditions* (M′), (A′) *and* (R′) *hold, and* $S\cap H_{c_1}\neq\emptyset$

for $c_1 > c$. If
$$\mu(H_c \cap S) = 0, \tag{8.6}$$
then c is the infimum of f over S.

Proof. Suppose $\hat{c}(<c)$ is the infimum of f over S. By inf-robustness assumption (R′), there exists a c_1, $\hat{c} < c_1 \leqslant c$ such that $S \cap F_{c_1}$ is robust and nonempty. Now we have
$$\varnothing \neq S \cap H_{c_1} \subset S \cap H_c \tag{8.7}$$
which implies by assumptions (M′) and (A′) that
$$\mu(S \cap H_c) \geqslant \mu(S \cap H_{c_1}) > 0. \tag{8.8}$$
This contradicts (8.6).

Remarks 8.1 (1) The condition $\mu(H_c \cap S) = 0$ is a sufficient condition. For instance, suppose $f = c$ on S and $\mu(S) > 0$. Then $\mu(H_c \cap S) > 0$. But, c is the global minimum value of f over S.

(2) From Theorem 8.1 or Theorem 8.2, under the assumptions of one of them, if $c > \bar{c} = \inf\limits_{x \in S} f(x)$ then $\mu(H_c \cap S) > 0$.

(3) For simplicity, in the following discussion we will only observe the theorem and algorithms under the assumptions (A), (M) and (R). We have a similar result under the assumptions (A′), (M′) and (R′).

8.2 Mean Value, Variance and Higher Moments

We now proceed to define concepts of mean value, variance and higher moments of f over its level set S as in [8,9]. These concepts are closely related to optimal conditions and algorithms for finding global minima.

Definition 8.1 Suppose that the assumptions (A), (M) and (R) hold, and
$$c > \bar{c} = \min_{x \in S} f(x).$$
We define the mean value, variance, modified variance and the m-th moment (centered at a) of the function f ovewr its level set H_c and constrained set S, respectively, as follows:

$$M(f, c; S) = \frac{1}{\mu(S \cap H_c)} \int_{S \cap H_c} f(x) d\mu, \tag{8.9}$$

$$V(f, c; S) = \frac{1}{\mu(S \cap H_c)} \int_{S \cap H_c} (f(x) - M(f, c; S))^2 d\mu, \tag{8.10}$$

$$V_1(f, c; S) = \frac{1}{\mu(S \cap H_c)} \int_{S \cap H_c} (f(x) - c)^2 d\mu, \tag{8.11}$$

and

$$M_m(f, c; a; S) = \frac{1}{\mu(S \cap H_c)} \int_{S \cap H_c} (f(x) - a)^m d\mu, \quad m = 1, 2, \cdots. \tag{8.12}$$

The function f is measurable, $S \cap H_c$ is a subset of the compact set S and $\mu(S \cap H_c) > 0$, by Remark 8.1(2). They are well defined. It is easy to prove the properties of mean value:

(1) $\bar{c} \leqslant M(f, c; S) \leqslant c$, for $c > \bar{c} = \min\limits_{x \in S} f(x)$;

(2) $M(f, c_1; S) \leqslant M(f, c_2; S)$, for $c_2 \geqslant c_1 \geqslant \bar{c}$;

(3) $\lim_{c_k \downarrow c} M(f, c_k; S) = M(f, c; S)$, if $c > \bar{c}$.

When $c = \bar{c}$, $\mu(S \cap H_{\bar{c}})$ may be equal to zero, Definition 8.1 has to be extended by a limit process.

Definition 8.2 Under the assumptions of Definition 8.1, we extend the definitions of mean value, variance, modified variance and the m-th moment of f over $S \cap H_c$ for $c \geqslant \bar{c}$, respectively, as follows:

$$M(f, c; S) = \lim_{c_k \downarrow c} \frac{1}{\mu(S \cap H_{c_k})} \int_{S \cap H_{c_k}} f(x) \, d\mu, \tag{8.13}$$

$$V(f, c; S) = \lim_{c_k \downarrow c} \frac{1}{\mu(S \cap H_{c_k})} \int_{S \cap H_{c_k}} (f(x) - M(f, c; S))^2 \, d\mu, \tag{8.14}$$

$$V_1(f, c; S) = \lim_{c_k \downarrow c} \frac{1}{\mu(S \cap H_{c_k})} \int_{S \cap H_{c_k}} (f(x) - c)^2 \, d\mu \tag{8.15}$$

and

$$M_m(f, c; a; S) = \lim_{c_k \downarrow c} \frac{1}{\mu(S \cap H_c)} \int_{S \cap H_c} (f(x) - a)^m \, d\mu, \ m = 1, 2, \cdots. \tag{8.16}$$

Since $\{M(f, c_k; S)\}$ is a decreasing sequence and bounded below by $\bar{c}$, the limit of (8.13) exists and is independent of the choice of $\{c_k\}$. The extended concept of mean value is well defined and consistent with (8.9) (see the property (3) of mean value). Moreover, these properties are still valid for the extended mean value. Similar to those in [8,9], we can prove that (8.14), (8.15) and (8.16) are well defined and consistent.

8.3 Optimality Conditions

With the concepts introduced in the last subsection, we characterize the global optimality as follows.

Theorem 8.3 *Under the assumptions (A), (M) and (R), the following statements are equivalent:*

(1) $\bar{x} \in S$ *is a global minimum point of f over S and $\bar{c} = f(\bar{x})$ is the global minimum value;*

(2) $M(f, \bar{c}; S) = \bar{c}$;

(3) $V(f, \bar{c}; S) = 0$;

(4) $V_1(f, \bar{c}; S) = 0$;

(5) $M_m(f, \bar{c}, \bar{c}; S) = 0$, for some positive integer $m = 1, 2, \cdots$.

Proof. We only prove the equivalence between (1) and (5).

Suppose $\bar{c}$ is the global minimum value of f over S. Then $(f(x) - \bar{c})^m \geqslant 0$ for all $x \in S$. Thus for $c > \bar{c}$, we have

$$M_m(f, c; \bar{c}; S) = \frac{1}{\mu(S \cap H_c)} \int_{S \cap H_c} (f(x) - \bar{c})^m \, d\mu \geqslant 0. \tag{8.17}$$

Therefore, we have

$$M_m(f, \bar{c}; \bar{c}; S) \geqslant 0. \tag{8.18}$$

Whe now prove that (5) holds. Suppose, on the contrary, $M_m(f, \bar{c}; \bar{c}; S) = 2e > 0$, strictly. By Definition 8.2, for a given decreasing sequence $\{c_k\}$ having a limit $\bar{c}$, there exists a positive integer k such that

$$\frac{1}{\mu(S \cap H_{c_k})} \int_{S \cap H_{c_k}} (f(x) - \bar{c})^m d\mu > e > 0. \tag{8.19}$$

However we have $\bar{c} \leqslant f(x) \leqslant c_k$ on $S \cap H_{c_k}$, and thus $(f(x) - \bar{c})^m \leqslant (c_k - \bar{c})^m$. Hence, we obtain

$$(c_k - \bar{c})^m \geqslant \frac{1}{\mu(S \cap H_{c_k})} \int_{S \cap H_{c_k}} (f(x) - \bar{c})^m d\mu > e > 0. \tag{8.20}$$

Letting $k \to \infty$ in the above inequalities, we obtain a contradiction

$$0 \geqslant e > 0. \tag{8.21}$$

Conversely, suppose $M_m((f, \bar{c}; \bar{c}; S)) = 0$, but $\bar{c}$ is not the global minmum value of f over S and $\hat{c} = f(\hat{x}) < \bar{c}$, where $\hat{x}$ is the global minimum at which f is relatively robust to S. Let $2e = \bar{c} - \hat{c} > 0$. Now both $\mu(S \cap H_{\bar{c}-e}) \mu(S \cap H_{\bar{c}})$ are positive by Theorem 8.1. Moreover, $f(x) \leqslant \bar{c} - e$ for all $x \in S \cap H_{\bar{c}-e}$. So when m is odd we have

$$(f(x) - \bar{c})^m \leqslant -e^m, \text{ for } x \in S \cap H_{\bar{c}-e} \tag{8.22}$$

and

$$(f(x) - \bar{c})^m \leqslant 0, \text{ for } x \in S \cap H_{\bar{c}}. \tag{8.23}$$

Therefore,

$$\begin{aligned} 0 = M(f, c; c; S) &= \frac{1}{\mu(S \cap H_c)} \int_{S \cap H_c \setminus S \cap H_{\bar{c}-e}} (f(x) - c)^m d\mu \\ &+ \frac{1}{\mu(S \cap H_{\bar{c}})} \int_{S \cap H_{\bar{c}-e}} (f(x) - c)^m d\mu \\ &\leqslant -e^m \frac{\mu(S \cap H_{\bar{c}-e})}{\mu(S \cap H_c)} < 0, \end{aligned} \tag{8.24}$$

which is a contradiction. When m is even, we have

$$0 = M(f, \bar{c}; \bar{c}; S) \geqslant e^m \cdot \frac{\mu(S \cap H_{\bar{c}-e})}{\mu(S \cap H_{\bar{c}})} > 0, \tag{8.25}$$

which is also a contradiction.

Remark 8.2 Instead of assumptions (A), (M) and (R) in Theorem 8.3, we suppose that (A'), (M) and (R') hold. In this case the set of global minma may be empty. Then the following statement is equivalent to one of (2), (3), (4) and (5) in the theorem:

(1') c is the infimum of f over S.

9 An Integral Minimization Algorithm

9.1 Description of the Algorithm

An integral algorithm is proposed in this section for finding the global minimum value and the set of global minima of a robust function f over a robust set S under the assumptions (A), (M) and (R) in Section 8.

We now describe $M - L$ Algorithm (mean value-level set algorithm) with some propositions useful for understanding the algorithm.

Take a point $x_0 \in S$. If $c_0 = f(x_0) = \bar{c} = \min_{x \in S} f(x)$, then c_0 is the global minimum value and $S \cap H_{c_0}$ is the set of global minima. The algorithm terminates. We usually have
$$c_0 > \bar{c} \tag{9.1}$$
and by Theorem 8.1,
$$\mu(S \cap H_{c_0}) > 0.$$
Let
$$c_1 = M(f, c_0; S). \tag{9.2}$$
Then
$$\bar{c} < c_1 < c_0. \tag{9.3}$$

In general, let
$$c_{k+1} = M(f, c_k; S), \quad k = 0, 1, 2, \cdots. \tag{9.4}$$
The following lemma and proposition insure that the iterative process (9.4) is well defined.

Lemma 9.1 *Under the assumptions* (A), (M) *and* (R), *if* $\mu(S \cap H_{c_0}) > 0$, *then* $\mu(S \cap H_{c_1}) > 0$.

Proof. If $c_1 = c_0$ then $S \cap H_{c_1} = S \cap H_{c_0}$ and $\mu(S \cap H_{c_1}) = \mu(S \cap H_{c_0}) > 0$. So we need only consider the case where $c_1 < c_0$. Suppose, on the contrary, that
$$\mu(S \cap H_{c_1}) = 0.$$
Then c_1 is the global minimum value and $S \cap H_{c_1}$ is the set of global minima, i.e.,
$$f(x) \geq c_1, \quad \text{for all } x \in S. \tag{9.5}$$
Let
$$G_n = \{x \mid c_i + (c_0 - c_1)/(n+1) < f(x) \leq c_0\}, \quad n = 1, 2, \cdots. \tag{9.6}$$
$\{G_n\}$ is an increasing sequence of sets and
$$\lim_{n \to \infty} G_n = \bigcup_{n=1}^{\infty} G_n = H_{c_1} \setminus H_{c_0}. \tag{9.7}$$
We have
$$\mu(S \cap (\bigcup_{n=1}^{\infty} G_n)) = \mu(S \cap H_{c_1}) - \mu(S \cap H_{c_0}) = \mu(S \cap H_{c_0}) > 0, \tag{9.8}$$
and it implies, by the continuity of the measure μ, that
$$\lim_{n \to \infty} \mu(S \cap G_n) = \mu(S \cap H_{c_0}) > 0. \tag{9.9}$$
Thus, there is a positive number n_0 such that
$$\mu(S \cap G_n) > 0, \quad \text{for } n \geq n_0. \tag{9.10}$$
Let $e = (c_0 - c_1)/(n_0 + 1)$, and denote
$$G_e = \{x \mid c_1 + e < f(x) \leq c_0\}. \tag{9.11}$$
We then have $\mu(S \cap G_e) > 0$. From (9.5) and (9.10), we obtain
$$c_1 = M(f, c_0; S) = \frac{1}{\mu(S \cap H_{c_0})} \int_{S \cap H_{c_0}} f(x) d\mu$$
$$= \frac{1}{\mu(S \cap H_{c_0})} \left[\int_{S \cap H_{c_0} \setminus S \cap G_e} f(x) d\mu + \int_{S \cap G_e} f(x) d\mu \right]$$
$$\geq c_1 (\mu(S \cap H_{c_0}) - \mu(S \cap G_e))/\mu(S \cap H_{c_0})$$
$$+ (c_1 + e)\mu(S \cap G_e)/\mu(S \cap H_{c_0})$$

$$= c_1 + e \cdot \mu(S \cap G_e)/\mu(S \cap H_{c_0}) > c_1. \tag{9.12}$$

This is a contradiction.

c_2 is taken to replace c_0. Then we obtain $\mu(S \cap H_{c_2}) > 0$, and so on. That is, we have proved the following proposition.

Proposition 9.1 *Under the assumptions (A), (M) and (R), if $\mu(S \cap H_{c_0}) > 0$, then $\mu(S \cap H_{c_k}) > 0$, for $k=1, 2, \cdots$.*

If the objective function f is not constant on $S \cap H_{c_k}$ for some k, then the mean value c_{k+1} is always strictly less then c_k, we then obtain a strictly decreasing sequence $\{c_k\}$, which will be shown with a limit $\bar{c}$ as the global minimum value.

Proposition 9.2 *Under the assumptions (A), (M) and (R), if there is an integer k in the iterative process such that the mean value of f over $S \cap H_{c_k}$ is equal to c_k itself, i.e.,*

$$M(f, c_k; S) = c_k, \tag{9.13}$$

then $c_k = \bar{c}$ is the global minimum value and f is constant on the set $S \cap H_{c_k}$.

Proof. By the mean value condition in Theorem 8.3, (9.13) implies that c_k is the global minimum value and $H = S \cap H_{c_k}$ is obviously the set of global minima. f is constant on H.

If (9.13) happens the algorithm will be terminated and the minimization problem has been sloved in a finite number of iterations. In [10] we mentioned that the iterative process will not be terminated in a finite steps for the case where $X = \mathbb{R}^n$, f is continuous and S is a (conected) domain in $\mathbb{R}^n$, unless f is constant on S. This result can be generalized if f is continuous and S is a robust and connecled set in a Hausdorff space X (see Proposition 9.3). The finitely terminated case does happen when we consider a minimization problem of a robust function over a robust set S.

Example 9.1 Let $S = [-1, 1]$ and

$$f(x) = \begin{cases} 0, & -1 \leqslant x < 0, \\ 1, & 0 \leqslant x \leqslant 1. \end{cases} \tag{9.14}$$

Take $c_0 = 2$. Then $c_1 = 1/2$, $c_2 = 0$ and $c_3 = M(f, c_2; S) = 0 = c_2$.

Example 9.2 Let $s = [-1, 0] \cup [1, 2]$ and

$$f(x) = \begin{cases} 0, & -1 \leqslant x < 0, \\ x, & 0 \leqslant x < 1, \\ 1, & 1 \leqslant x \leqslant 2. \end{cases} \tag{9.15}$$

In this example, f is continuous, but S is disconnected. Take $c_0 = 2$. Then $c_1 = 1/2$, $c_2 = 0$, and we also have $c_3 = M(f, c_2; S) = c_2$.

Proposition 9.3 *Suppose f is continuous on a robust and connected constrained set S. With the same assumptions as in Proposition 9.1, we have*

$$c_{k+1} < c_k \quad \text{and} \quad S \cap H_{c_{k+1}} \neq S \cap H_{c_k}, \quad k = 0, 1, 2, \cdots \tag{9.16}$$

in the algorithm unless f is constant on $S \cap H_{c_0}$.

Proof. If $c_{k+1} = c_k$, then c_k is the global minimum value of f and $f(x) = c_k$ on $S \cap H_{c_k}$. This would imply that f is constant on $S \cap H_{c_0}$. Suppose

$$c_{k-1} > c_k = \bar{c} \quad \text{with} \quad k > 1. \tag{9.17}$$

Let $c_{k-1}-c_k=4e>0$. By the continuity of f and connectedness of S, there is a point $x_0\in S$ such that $f(x_0)=c_k+2e$. Thus, the set $G=\{x|\bar{c}+e<f(x)<\bar{c}+3e\}$ is a nonempty open set with a nonempty intersection with S: $G\cap S\neq\varnothing$, i.e., $\mu(S\cap S)>0$. Now, we have

$$\begin{aligned} c_k=\bar{c} &= \frac{1}{\mu(S\cap H_{c_{k-1}})}\int_{S\cap H_{c_{k-1}}} f(x)\mathrm{d}\mu \\ &= \frac{1}{\mu(S\cap H_{c_{k-1}})}\left[\int_{S\cap H_{c_{k-1}}\backslash S\cap G} f(x)\mathrm{d}\mu + \int_{S\cap G} f(x)\mathrm{d}\mu\right] \\ &\geq \frac{1}{\mu(S\cap H_{c_{k-1}})}[\bar{c}(\mu(S\cap H_{c_{k-1}})-\mu(S\cap G))+(\bar{c}+e)\cdot\mu(S\cap G)] \\ &= \bar{c}+e\frac{\mu(S\cap G)}{\mu(S\cap H_{c_{k-1}})}>\bar{c}. \end{aligned} \qquad (9.18)$$

This is a contradiction. Hence, $c_{k-1}=c_k$ and $H_{c_{k-1}}=H_{c_k}$, and $f(x)=c_{k-1}=c_k$ on $H_{c_{k-1}}$. With the same process, we prove that $c_{k+1}=c_k=c_{k-1}=\cdots=c_0$ and $f(x)=c_k=\bar{c}$ for all $x\in H_{c_0}\cap S$.

9.2 The Algorithm and Its Convergence

Combining with the modified variance condition, we propose the algorithm (see [3, 4]) as follows:

Step 0: Take a point $x_0\in S$ and $\varepsilon>0$; $k:=0$; $c_0:=f(x_0)$;
$$S\cap H_{c_0}:=\{x|f(x)\leqslant c_0\}\cap S;$$
Step 1: $c_{k+1}:=M(f,c_k;S)$; $S\cap H_{c_{k+1}}:=\{x|f(x)\leqslant c_{k+1}\}\cap S$;
Step 2: $V:=V_1(f,c_k;S)$; If $V\geqslant\varepsilon$ then $k:=k+1$; and go to Step 1; otherwise, go to Step 3;
Step 3: $c\Leftarrow c_{k+1}$; $H\Leftarrow S\cap H_{c_{k+1}}$; Stop.

Here $\varepsilon>0$ is the accuracy given in advance. Let $\varepsilon=0$ in the above algorithm. It may be stopped in a finits number of steps, as the above examples show, or we obtain a decreasing sequence

$$c_0>c_1>\cdots>c_k>c_{k+1}>\cdots\geqslant c \qquad (9.91)$$

and a monotone sequence of sets

$$S\cap H_{c_0}\supset S\cap H_{c_1}\supset\cdots\supset S\cap H_{c_k}\supset S\cap H_{c_{k+1}}\supset\cdots. \qquad (9.20)$$

The limits exist. Let

$$\bar{c}=\lim_{k\to\infty} c_k \qquad (9.21)$$

and

$$\overline{H}\lim_{k\to\infty} S\cap H_{c_k}=\bigcap_{k=1}^{\infty}(S\cap H_{c_k}). \qquad (9.22)$$

Theorem 9.1 *Under the assumptions (A), (M) and (R), $\bar{c}$ is the global minimum value and $\overline{H}$ is the set of global minima of f over S.*

Proof. If the algorithm is terminated in a finite number of iterations, and $c=c_{k_0}$ for some positive integer k_0, then we have $\bar{c}=M(f,\bar{c};S)$. When the algorithm is not stopped in a finite number of iterations, then from $c_{k+1}=M(f,c_k;S)$, we also obtain, by letting $k\to\infty$,

$$\bar{c} = M(f, \bar{c}; S). \tag{9.23}$$

In both cases, with the mean value condition, $\bar{c}$ is the global minimum value of f over S. Let $x \in \overline{H}$. Then for each k (or $k > k_0$) we have $f(x) \leqslant c_k$. Letting $k \to \infty$ (or setting $k = k_0$), we obtain

$$f(x) \leqslant \bar{c}. \tag{9.24}$$

But $f(x) \geqslant \bar{c}$ for all $x \in S$. Hence $\overline{H} = \{x \mid f(x) = \bar{c}, x \in S\}$, i.e., H is the set of global minima.

Note that the errors at each iteration in the algorithm are not accumulated. Suppose we calculate $c_1 = M(f, c_0; S)$ with an error Δ_1 and obtain $d_1 = c_1' + \Delta_1$; then calculate $c_2' = M(f, d_1; S)$ with an error Δ_2, and obtain $d_2 = c_2' + \Delta_2$, and so on. In general, we have

$$c_k' = M(f, d_{k-1}; S) \quad \text{and} \quad \Delta_k = d_k - c_k', \quad k = 1, 2, \cdots \tag{9.25}$$

and obtain a decreasing sequence $\{d_k\}$. Let

$$d = \lim_{k \to \infty} d_k. \tag{9.26}$$

Theorem 9.2 *Under the assumptions of Theorem 9.1, d is the global minimum value of f if and only if*

$$\lim_{k \to \infty} \Delta_k = 0. \tag{9.27}$$

Proof. The condition (9.27) is equivalent to

$$\lim_{k \to \infty} c_k' = \lim_{k \to \infty} d_k = d. \tag{9.28}$$

Letting $k \to \infty$ in (9.25), we obtain

$$d = M(f, d; S). \tag{9.29}$$

This is also the mean value condition which insures d to be the global minimum value of f over S.

10 A Variable Measure Method

10.1 Mean Value, Variance and Higher Moments Depending on Measure

In order to utilize more information adaptively, a variable measure method is proposed in this section. We begin with introducing concepts of mean value, variance and higher moments depending on measure, which are the generalization of those in [5, 6].

Definition 10.1 Suppose f is a l.s.c. function defined on a robust compact set S, μ is a Q-measure, $c > \bar{c} = \min_{x \in S} f(x)$, and f is relatively robust to S at a minimum point $x \in S$. We call

$$M(f, c; S; \mu) = \frac{1}{\mu(S \cap H_c)} \int_{S \cap H_c} f(x) \, d\mu \tag{10.1}$$

$$V(f, c; S; \mu) = \frac{1}{\mu(S \cap H_c)} \int_{S \cap H_c} (f(x) - M(f, c; S; \mu))^2 \, d\mu, \tag{10.2}$$

$$V_1(f, c; S; \mu) = \frac{1}{\mu(S \cap H_c)} \int_{S \cap H_c} (f(x) - c)^2 \, d\mu \tag{10.3}$$

and

$$M_m(f, c; a; S; \mu) = \frac{1}{\mu(S \cap H_c)} \int_{S \cap H_c} (f(x)-a)^m \mathrm{d}\mu, \quad m=1, 2, \cdots \quad (10.4)$$

to be the mean value, variance, modified variance and the m-th moment centered at a of the function f over the constrained level set $S \cap H_c$ with respect to the measure μ, respectively.

These definitions can be extended with a limit process to $c \geqslant \bar{c}$ as in Section 8. For instance,

$$M(f, c; S; \mu) = \lim_{c_k \downarrow c} \frac{1}{\mu(S \cap H_{c_k})} \int_{S \cap H_{c_k}} f(x) \mathrm{d}\mu. \quad (10.5)$$

Definitions (10.1)~(10.5) are well defined and the extended definitions are consistent with the original ones. All of the proofs are similar to those in Section 8.

Suppose we have a sequence $\{\mu_k\}$ of Q-measures and a Q-measure μ defined on a measurable space (X, Ω), where X is a compact Hausdorff space and Ω is the Borel field on X. We assume:

(VM) $\{\mu_k\}$ is Q-convergent to μ and the function f is bounded.

Remark 10.1 Since we consider the minimization problem over a compact set, the assumption of compactness of X is not a restriction. Furthermore, as we are considering a minimization problem, the minimum is attained and the upper bound of the function is not essential for a minimization problem.

The following theorem is essential to the variable measure method.

Theorem 10.1 *Suppose $c \geqslant \bar{c} = \min_{x \in S} f(x)$, $c_k \downarrow c(k \to \infty)$, and μ_k, $k=1, 2, \cdots$ and μ are Q-measures. Under the assumptions (A), (R), (M) and (VM), we have*

$$\lim_{k \to \infty} M(f, c_k; S; \mu_k) = M(f, c; S; \mu); \quad (10.6)$$

$$\lim_{k \to \infty} V(f, c_k; S; \mu_k) = V(f, c; S; \mu); \quad (10.7)$$

$$\lim_{k \to \infty} V_1(f, c_k; S; \mu_k) = V_1(f, c; S; \mu); \quad (10.8)$$

$$\lim_{k \to \infty} M_m(f, c_k; a; S; \mu_k) = M_m(f, c; a; S; \mu), \quad k=1, 2, \cdots. \quad (10.9)$$

Proof. Suppose $c > \bar{c}$. We first prove that

$$\lim_{k \to \infty} \mu_k(S \cap H_{c_k}) = \mu(S \cap H_c). \quad (10.10)$$

Since $H_c \subset H_{c_k}$, then $\mu_k(S \cap H_{c_k}) \geqslant \mu S \cap H_c)$, $k=1, 2, \cdots$. From Theorem 7.3 and $S \cap H_c$ being a closed set, we have

$$\liminf_{k \to \infty} \mu_k(S \cap H_{c_k}) \geqslant \liminf_{k \to \infty} \mu_k(S \cap H_c) = \lim_{k \to \infty} \mu_k(S \cap H_c) = \mu(S \cap H_c). \quad (10.11)$$

We now fix j and let $k \geqslant j$. Then we have $\mu_k(S \cap H_{c_j}) \geqslant \mu(S \cap H_{c_k})$. We can obtain, similarly,

$$\limsup_{k \to \infty} \mu_k(S \cap H_{c_k}) \leqslant \lim_{k \to \infty} \mu_k(S \cap H_{c_j}) = \mu(S \cap H_{c_j}). \quad (10.12)$$

We then let $j \to \infty$, $\lim_{j \to \infty} \mu(S \cap H_{c_j}) = \mu(S \cap H_c)$; thus,

$$\limsup_{k \to \infty} \mu_k(S \cap H_{c_k}) \leqslant \mu(S \cap H_c). \quad (10.13)$$

Combining (10.11) and (10.13), we have proved that the limit in (10.10) exists and

(10.10) holds.

We now have
$$M(f, c_k; S; \mu_k) - M(f, c; S; \mu)$$
$$= \left(\frac{1}{\mu_k(S \cap H_{c_k})} - \frac{1}{\mu(S \cap H_c)}\right)\int_{S \cap H_{c_k}} f(x)d\mu$$
$$+ \frac{1}{\mu(S \cap H_c)}\left(\int_{S \cap H_{c_k}} f(x)d\mu_k - \int_{S \cap H_c} f(x)d\mu_k\right)$$
$$+ \frac{1}{\mu(S \cap H_c)}\left(\int_{S \cap H_c} f(x)d\mu_k - \int_{S \cap H_c} f(x)d\mu\right)$$
$$= J_1 + J_2 + J_3. \tag{10.14}$$

Since
$$\left[\int_{S \cap H_{c_k}} f(x)d\mu\right] \leqslant A \cdot \mu(S \cap H_{c_k}) \leqslant A \cdot \mu(S \cap H_{c_1}), \tag{10.15}$$
where A is the bound of $|f(x)|$, and also $\mu_k(S \cap H_{c_1}) \to \mu(S \cap H_{c_1})$ by Theorem 7.3, thus, the integral in (10.15) is bounded. Under the assumptions and $c < \bar{c}$ and $\mu(S \cap H_c) > 0$, $1/\mu_k(S \cap H_{c_k}) \to 1/\mu(S \cap H_c)$. These prove that $J_1 \to 0$ as $k \to \infty$. Next, we have
$$|J_2| \leqslant \frac{1}{\mu(S \cap H_c)}\left|\int_{S \cap (H_{c_k} \setminus H_c)} f(x)d\mu_k\right|$$
$$\leqslant \frac{A}{\mu(S \cap H_c)}(\mu_k(S \cap H_{c_k}) - \mu(S \cap H_c)),$$
which tends to zero as $k \to \infty$ because
$$\lim_{k \to \infty}\mu_k(S \cap H_{c_k}) = \mu(S \cap H_c) = \lim_{k \to \infty}\mu_k(S \cap H_c). \tag{10.16}$$

Finally, we have
$$|J_3| \leqslant \frac{1}{\mu(S \cap H_c)}\left|\int_{S \cap H_c} f(x)d\mu_k - \int_{S \cap H_c} f(x)d\mu\right|$$
$$= \frac{1}{\mu(S \cap H_c)}\left|\int_X I_{S \cap H_c} f(x)d\mu - \int_X I_{S \cap H_c} f(x)d\mu\right|,$$
where $I_{S \cap H_c}$ denotes the indicator of the set $S \cap H_c$. The function $I_{S \cap H_c} f(x)$ is l.s.c. on X. From Theorem 7.3, again, $|J_3|$ tends to zero as $k \to \infty$. We complete the proof for the case $c > \bar{c}$ of (10.6).

When $c = \bar{c}$, we have, with the properties of mean value,
$$\bar{c} \leqslant M(f, c_k; S; \mu_k) = \frac{1}{\mu_k(S \cap H_{c_k})}\int_{S \cap H_{c_k}} f(x)d\mu_k \leqslant c_k. \tag{10.17}$$
Letting $k \to \infty$, we obtain
$$\lim_{k \to \infty} M(f, c_k; S; \mu_k) = \bar{c}. \tag{10.18}$$
But when $c = \bar{c}$, from the optimality condition in Section 8, we also have $M(f, \bar{c}; S; \mu) = \bar{c}$, because μ is a Q-measure. These prove that (10.6) holds for all $c \geqslant \bar{c}$.

We can prove (10.7)~(10.9) similarly.

The following theorem is concluded from Theorem 8.3 and Theorem 10.1.

Theorem 10.2 *Under the assumptions* (A), (M), (R) *and* (VM), *the following* statements are equivalent:

(1) $\bar{x} \in S$ is a global minimum point and $\bar{c} = f(\bar{x})$ is the global minimum value of f over S;

(2) $\lim\limits_{c_k \downarrow \bar{c}} M(f, c_k; S; \mu_k) = \bar{c}$;

(3) $\lim\limits_{c_k \downarrow \bar{c}} V(f, c_k; S; \mu_k) = 0$;

(4) $\lim\limits_{c_k \downarrow \bar{c}} V_1(f, c_k; S; \mu_k) = 0$;

(5) $\lim\limits_{c_k \downarrow \bar{c}} M_m(f; c_k; c_k; S; \mu_k) = 0$, for some $m = 1, 2, \cdots$.

Remark 10.2 It is easy to prove that the above statement (5) is equivalent to

(5') $\lim\limits_{c_k \downarrow \bar{c}} M_m(f; c_k; \bar{c}; S; \mu_k) = 0$.

10.2 A Variable Measure Method

A variable measure method for finding global minimum value and the set of global minima is proposed in this subsection under the assumptions (A), (M), (R) and (VM) by utilizing Theorem 10.1 and Theorem 10.2, and the Propositions 9.1.

Step 0: Take a point $x_0 \in S$ and $\varepsilon > 0$ (the accuracy); $k := 0$; $c_0 := f(x_0)$; $S \cap H_{c_0} := \{x \mid f(x) \leqslant c_0\} \cap S$;

Step 1: Calculate $c_{k+1} := M(f, c_k; S; \mu_k)$ and $S \cap H_{c_{k+1}} := S \cap \{x \mid f(x) \leqslant c_{k+1}\}$;

Step 2: Calculate $V := V_1(f, c_k; S; \mu_k)$; If $V \geqslant \varepsilon$ then $k := k+1$; and go to Step 1; otherwise go to Step 3;

Step 3: $\bar{c} \Leftarrow c_{k+1}$; $\overline{H} \Leftarrow \overline{H}_{c_{k+1}}$; Stop.

Let $\varepsilon = 0$ in the algorithm. It may be stopped in a finite number of steps, or we obtain a decreasing sequence

$$c_0 > c_1 > \cdots > c_k > c_{k+1} > \cdots \geqslant \bar{c}, \tag{10.19}$$

and a sequence of monotone sets

$$S \cap H_{c_0} \supset S \cap H_{c_1} \supset \cdots \supset S \cap H_{c_k} \supset S \cap H_{c_{k+1}} \supset \cdots. \tag{10.20}$$

The limits exist because they are all monotone and bounded:

$$\bar{c} = \lim_{k \to \infty} c_k \tag{10.21}$$

and

$$\overline{H} = \lim_{k \to \infty} S \cap H_{c_k} = S \cap \left(\bigcap_{k=1}^{\infty} H_{c_k}\right). \tag{10.22}$$

Theorem 10.3 *Under the assumptions* (A), (R), (M) *and* (VM), $\bar{c}$ *is the global minimum value and* $\overline{H}$ *is the set of global minima of* f *over* S.

Proof. The proof is similar to that of Theorem 9.1. We have

$$c_{k+1} = M(f, c_k; S; \mu_k), \quad k = 1, 2, \cdots. \tag{10.23}$$

When the algorithm is stopped or is not stopped in a finite number of steps, we always have

$$\bar{c} = M(f, \bar{c}; S; \mu), \tag{10.24}$$

where $\bar{c} = c_k = c_{k+1} = \cdots$ or $\bar{c} = \lim c_k$. This proves that $\bar{c}$ is the global minimum value and $\overline{H}$ is the set of global minima.

The argument on the problem of error accumulation is also valid as in subsection 9.2, and the same theorem as Theorem 9.2 holds. We omit them here.

11 Adaptive Change of Search Sets

11.1 A Simple Model

In order to lessen the amount of computation associated with too large an initial search set, in this section we consider a model of adaptive change of search sets. This model was described briefly in [14] for a continuous objective function and with search domains without proof. We now extend it to a robust function and robust sets, and go into detail. The change-of-set techniue allows an initial choice of a computationally manageable set S_0 and then move on to better performing sets while still holding down their "sizes". This achieves, in some sense, a more judicial use of computationally generated information.

Let c_0 be a real number and S_0 be an initial compact robust search set where $\mu(H_{c_0} \cap S) > 0$ (see Lemma 7.1). Let

$$c_1 = M(f, c_0; S_0) = \frac{1}{\mu(H_{c_0} \cap S_0)} \int_{S_0 \cap H_{c_0}} f(x)\,d\mu. \tag{11.1}$$

Then

$$c_0 \geqslant c_1 \geqslant \bar{c} = \min_{x \in S} f(x). \tag{11.2}$$

Take a robust search set $S_1 \subset S$ such that

$$S_0 \cap H_{c_1} \subset S_1, \tag{11.3}$$

which implies that

$$S_0 \cap H_1 \subset S_1 \cap H_{c_1}, \tag{11.4}$$

where S is a given compact set in the Hausdorff space X we considered. Not that (11.3) and (11.4) do not require $S_0 \subset S_1$ but $S_0 \cap H_{c_1} \subset S_1 \cap H_{c_1}$, and we have

$$\mu(S_1 \cap H_{c_1}) \geqslant \mu(S_0 \cap H_{c_1}) > 0, \tag{11.5}$$

where $\mu(S_0 \cap H_{c_1}) > 0$ because of $\mu(S_0 \cap H_{c_0}) > 0$ and Proposition 9.1. Let

$$c_2 = M(f, c_1; S_1). \tag{11.6}$$

In general, we require that

$$S_k \cap H_{c_{k+1}} \subset S_{k+1}, \quad k = 0, 1, 2, \cdots, \tag{11.7}$$

f is relatively robust to S_k at a minimum point of f over S_k and $S_k \subset S$, for $k = 0, 1, 2, \cdots$. Let

$$c_{k+1} = M(f, c_k; S_k), \quad k = 0, 1, 2, \cdots. \tag{11.8}$$

In this manner we have constructed a sequence of robust search sets and obtain the following two sequences:

$$c_0 \geqslant c_1 \geqslant \cdots \geqslant c_k > c_{k+1} \geqslant \cdots \tag{11.9}$$

and

$$H_{c_0} \supset H_{c_1} \supset \cdots \supset H_{c_k} \supset H_{c_{k+1}} \supset \cdots. \tag{11.10}$$

Denote

$$S_L = \bigcup_{k=1}^{\infty} S_k \quad \text{and} \quad G_L = \text{cl } S_L. \tag{11.11}$$

Proposition 11.1 *G_L is a compact and robust set.*

Proof. Since S_L is the union of robust sets S_1, S_2, $\cdots$, it is robust and so is its closure G_L. $S_k \subset S$, $k=0, 1, 2, \cdots$ imply that cl $S_L \subset S$. This proves G_L is compact.

A further assumption is required so that the structure of sets S_k, $k=0, 1, \cdots$ we take may not be too complicated:

(SM) $\qquad\qquad\qquad \mu(S_L) = \mu(\text{cl } S_L),$

i.e., we would not choose such a kind of pathological robust set S_L like that in Example 4.2 of [1].

11.2 Convergence

Let
$$\bar{c} = \lim_{k \to \infty} c_k \tag{11.12}$$

and

$$\overline{H} = \lim_{k \to \infty} H_{c_k} = \bigcap_{k=1}^{\infty} H_{c_k}. \tag{11.13}$$

Theorem 11.1 *Under the assumptions (A), (M) and (SM), suppose that f is relatively robust at a minimum point of f over G_L. Then the limit c is the global minimum value and $\overline{H} \cap G_L$ is the set of corresponding global minima of f over G_L.*

Proof. From (11.7) and the mean value property, we have

$$\min_{x \in S_k} f(x) \leqslant c_{k+1}, \quad k=1, 2, \cdots, \tag{11.14}$$

so that

$$\min_{x \in G_L} f(x) \leqslant c_{k+1}, \quad k=1, 2, \cdots. \tag{11.15}$$

Hence,

$$\min_{x \in G_L} f(x) \leqslant \bar{c}. \tag{11.16}$$

We proceed to prove the opposite inequality. If, on the contrary,

$$\hat{c} = \min_{x \in G_L} f(x) < \bar{c},$$

then from (11.16),

$$G_L \cap H_{\bar{c}} \neq \varnothing; \tag{11.17}$$

f is relatively robust to G_L at a minimum point $\hat{x}$ such that $\hat{c} = f(\hat{x})$. Let $e = (\bar{c} - \hat{c})/2 > 0$ and $F_{\bar{c}-e} = \{x \mid f(x) < \bar{c} - e\}$. Then $\hat{x} \in F_{\bar{c}-e}$ and x is robust to $G_L \cap F_{\bar{c}-e}$. This implies that int $(G_L \cap F_{\bar{c}-e}) \neq \varnothing$ and then $\mu(G_L \cap F_{\bar{c}-e}) > 0$. On the other hand, from the assumption (SM), we also have

$$\mu(S_L \cap F_{\bar{c}-e}) > 0. \tag{11.18}$$

Hence, there is, at least, one set S_j such that

$$\mu(S_j \cap F_{\bar{c}-e}) > 0. \tag{11.19}$$

Otherwise, we would have $\mu(S_L \cap F_{\bar{c}-e}) = 0$ by the countable additivity of the measure μ. From (11.18), we now have

$$\mu(S_j \cap H_{\bar{c}-e}) > 0. \tag{11.20}$$

We now fix j. Moreover, we can prove that

$$\mu(S_n \cap H_{\bar{c}-e}) > 0, \text{ for all } n \geq j. \tag{11.21}$$

Indeed, from the construction of the model (11.6),

$$S_k \cap H_{c_{k+1}} \subset S_{k+1} \cap H_{c_{k+1}}, \quad k = 0, 1, 2, \cdots \tag{11.22}$$

and

$$S_k \cap H_{c_{k+1}} \cap H_{c-e} \subset S_{k+1} \cap H_{c_{k+1}} \cap H_{\bar{c}-e}, k = 0, 1, 2, \cdots, \tag{11.23}$$

i.e.,

$$S_k \cap H_{\bar{c}-e} \subset S_{k+1} \cap H_{\bar{c}-e}, k = 0, 1, 2, \cdots, \tag{11.24}$$

since $H_{\bar{c}-e} \subset H_{\bar{c}} \subset H_{c_{k+1}}$, $k = 0, 1, 2, \cdots$. Hence, if $k \geq j$, we have

$$\mu(S_n \cap H_{\bar{c}-e}) \geq \mu(S_j \cap H_{\bar{c}-e}) > 0. \tag{11.25}$$

Taking $n \geq j$, we have

$$\mu(S_n \cap H_{c_n}) \cdot c_{n+1} = \int_{S \cap H_{c_n}} f(x) \mathrm{d}\mu$$

$$= \int_{(S_n \cap H_{c_n}) \setminus (S_n \cap H_{\bar{c}-e})} f(x) \mathrm{d}\mu + \int_{S_n \cap H_{\bar{c}-e}} f(x) \mathrm{d}\mu$$

$$= c_n \cdot (\mu(S_n \cap H_{c_n}) - \mu(S_n \cap H_{\bar{c}-e})) + (\bar{c}-e) \cdot \mu(S_n \cap H_{\bar{c}-e}).$$

$$\tag{11.26}$$

Rearranging the terms, we obtain

$$c_n - c_{n+1} \geq e \cdot \frac{\mu(S_n \cap H_{\bar{c}-e})}{\mu(S_n \cap H_{c_n})} \geq e \cdot \frac{\mu(S_j \cap H_{\bar{c}-e})}{\mu(G_L \cap H_{c_0})}, \tag{11.27}$$

where $\mu(G_L \cap H_{c_0}) \geq \mu(S_n \cap H_{c_n})$, for all n and $\mu(S_j \cap H_{\bar{c}-e})$ for $n \geq j$. Letting $n \to \infty$ in (11.27), we have

$$0 = \bar{c} - \bar{c} \geq e \cdot \frac{\mu(S_j \cap H_{\bar{c}-e})}{\mu(G_L \cap H_{c_0})} > 0 \tag{11.28}$$

which is a contradiction. Therefore, $\bar{c}$ is the global minmum value of f over G_L. The proof of $G_L \cap H$ being the corresponding set of global minima of f over G_L is similar to that of Theorem 9.1.

11.3 Optimality Conditions

Optimality conditions of our change-of-set model can also be given. Since the search sets are changed step by step, the optimality conditions are described in limit forms.

Suppose $\{c_k\}$ is a decreasing sequence which tends to c, and $\{S_k\}$ is a sequence of robust sets such that

$$S_k \subset S \text{ and } S_k \cap H_{c_{k+1}} \subset S_{k+1}, k = 0, 1, 2, \cdots, \tag{11.29}$$

where S is a given compact set. Let

$$G_L = \mathrm{cl}(\bigcup_{k=1}^{\infty} S_k). \tag{11.30}$$

Theorem 11.2 *Under the assumptions of Theorem* 11.1, *the following statements are equivalent*:

(1) $\bar{c}$ *is the global minimum value of f over* G_L;

(2) $\lim_{k\to\infty}\dfrac{1}{\mu(S_k\cap H_{c_k})}\displaystyle\int_{S_k\cap H_{c_k}} f(x)\,d\mu = \bar{c}$;

(3) $\lim_{k\to\infty}\dfrac{1}{\mu(S_k\cap H_{c_k})}\displaystyle\int_{S_k\cap H_{c_k}} (f(x)-\bar{c})^2\,d\mu = 0$;

(4) $\lim_{k\to\infty}\dfrac{1}{\mu(S_k\cap H_{c_k})}\displaystyle\int_{S_k\cap H_{c_k}} (f(x)-c_k)^m\,d\mu = 0$, for some integer $m = 1, 2, \cdots$.

The proof is left to the reader.

12 Monte Carlo Implementation and Numerical Tests

From Section 9, we realize that the method for finding global minima requires the computation of a sequence of mean values and a sequence of level sets. Finding a mean value is tantamount to computing an integral of a function with several variables; the determination of a level set is, in general, more involved. But accuracy at early steps is not generally required by Theorem 9.2. This suggests that a Monte Carlo based technique for finding global minima is appropriate. The error by Monte Carlo method is proportional to $\sigma/\sqrt{t}$, where t is the number of samples and σ^2 is the variance of sample distribution. Since σ^2 will tend to zero as the mean value goes to the global minimum value (the variance condition), the Monte Carlo approximation will become more accurate near global minimum value even though the number t of random samples is not very large.

12.1 Monte Carlo Implementation of a Simple Model

Consider a box constrained minimization problem in $\mathbb{R}^n$:
$$\min_{x\in D} f(x) \tag{12.1}$$
with a unique global minimum point $\bar{x}$, where
$$D = \{x = (x^1, \cdots, x^n) \mid a^i \leqslant x^i \leqslant b^i,\ i=1, \cdots, n\}. \tag{12.2}$$
Let D_k be the smallest cuboid which contains the level set $D\cap H_c$, for $k=1, 2, \cdots$. Denote
$$D_k = \{x = (x^1, \cdots, x^n) \mid a_k^i \leqslant x^i \leqslant c_k^i,\ i=1, \cdots, n\}. \tag{12.3}$$
Then we have
$$\bar{c} = \min_{x\in D} f(x) = \min_{x\in D_k} f(x) \tag{12.4}$$
and it is easy to see that
$$H = \{\bar{x}\} = \bigcap_{k=1}^{\infty} D_k. \tag{12.5}$$

Instead of $M(f, c_k; D)$ and $V_1(f, c_k; D)$ in the algorithm of subsection 9.2 we take $M(f, c_k; D_k)$ and $V_1(f, c_k; D_k)$ at each iteration.

(1) Approximation H_c and $M(f, c_0; D)$:

Let $\xi = (\xi^1, \cdots, \xi^n)$ be an independent n-multiple random number which is nuiformly distributed on $[0,1]^n$. Let
$$x^i = a^i + (b^i - a^i)\cdot\xi^i,\quad i=1, \cdots, n. \tag{12.6}$$
Then $x = (x^1, \cdots, x^n)$ is uniformly distributed on D.

Take km samples and compute function valuse $f(x_j)$, $j=1, 2, \cdots, km$. Comparing the values of the function f at each point, we obtain a set W of sample points corresponding to the t smallest function values $FV[j]$, $j=1, 2, \cdots, t$ ordered by their values, i. e.,

$$FV[1] \geqslant FV[2] \geqslant \cdots \geqslant FV[t]. \tag{12.7}$$

The set W is called the acceptance set which can be regarded as an approximation to the level set H_{c_0} with $c_0 = FV[1]$, the largest value of $\{FV[j]\}$. Clearly, $f(x) \leqslant c_0$ for all $x \in W$. Also, the mean value of f over H_{c_0} can be approximated by the mean value of $\{FV[j]\}$:

$$c_1 = M(f, c_0) \approx (FV[1] + \cdots + FV[t])/t. \tag{12.8}$$

(2) Generating a new cuboid by W:

The new cuboid domain of dimension n

$$D_1 = \{x = (x^1, \cdots, x^n) \mid a_1^i \leqslant x^i \leqslant b_1^i, i=1, \cdots, n\} \tag{12.9}$$

can be generated statistically. The following procedure is proposed. Suppose that the random samples in W are $\tau_1, \cdots, \tau_t$. Let

$$\sigma_0^i = \min(\tau_1^i, \cdots, \tau_t^i) \text{ and } \sigma_1^i = \max(\tau_1^i, \cdots, \tau_t^i), i=1, \cdots, n, \tag{12.10}$$

where $\tau_j = (\tau_j^1, \cdots, \tau_j^n)$, $j=1, \cdots, t$. We use

$$a^i = \sigma_0^i - (\sigma_1^i - \sigma_0^i)/(t-1) \text{ and } \beta^i = \sigma_1^i + (\sigma_1^i - \sigma_0^i)/(t-1) \tag{12.11}$$

as estimators to generate a_1^i and b_1^i, $i=1, \cdots, n$.

(3) Continuing the iterative process:

The samples are now taken in the new domain D_i. Consider a random point $x = (x^1, \cdots, x^n)$, where

$$x^i = a_1^i + (b_1^i - a_1^i) \cdot \xi^i, \quad i=1, \cdots, n.$$

Compute $f(x)$. If $f(x) \geqslant FV[1]$, then drop it; otherwise, reconstruct $\{FV[j]\}$ and W such that the new $\{FV[j]\}$ is made up of the t best function values obtained so far. The acceptance set W is modified accordingly. Repeating this procedure until $FV[1] \leqslant c_1$, we obtain new FV and W.

(4) Iterative solution:

At each iteration, the smallest value $FV[t]$ in the set $\{FV[j]\}$ and the corresponding point in W can be regarded as an iterative solution.

(5) Convergence criterion:

The modified variance V_1 of $\{FV[j]\}$, which is given by

$$V_1 = \frac{1}{t-1} \sum_{j=2}^{\infty} (FV[j] - FV[1])^2, \tag{12.12}$$

can be regarded as an approximation to $V_1(f, c)$. If V_1 is less than the given precision ε then the iterative process terminates, and the current iteration in (4) would serve as an estimate of the global minimum value and the global minimum point.

Under suitable assumptions we can prove (see [3])

Theorem 12.1 The number N_f of computation of the function f for capturing the global minimum point in a small cuboid of volume δ^n from an initial cuboid of unit volume has the

following asymptotic bound
$$N_f \leqslant c_f \ln(1/\delta^n) \cdot \ln\ln(1/\delta^n) \qquad (12.13)$$
as δ goes to zero, where c_f is a constant independent of δ.

12.2 Numerical Tests and Applications

Two examples show that the algorithm is effective. The numerical tests are performed by IBM-PC with Basic implementation.

Example 12.1 $\underset{x\in D}{\text{Minimize}} f(x)$

where
$$f(x) = g(x) - [g(x)]/n, \qquad (12.14)$$
$$g(x) = \pi/n \cdot \{\sin(\pi x^i) + \sum_{i=1}^{n}(x^i - 1.0)^2 \cdot (1 + \sin(\pi x^{i+1})) + (x^n - 1.0)^2\}$$
$$D = \{x = (x^1, \cdots, x^n) - 10 \leqslant x^i \leqslant 10, i = 1, \cdots, n\}, \qquad (12.15)$$

and $[y]$ denotes the integer part of y. The function is discontinuous with jumps and local minima. It has a unique global minimum point at $x = (1, \cdots, 1)$. Table 1 gives the numbers of iteration N_i, the amounts of function computation N_f and $\ln V_0 - \ln V_e$ corresponding variable $n = 5, 10, 20, 50$, where V_0 and V_e are the volumes of the initial and final search domain, respectively.

Table 1

n	5	5	20	50
N^i	43	85	155	395
N^f	1917	4251	9565	46623
$\ln V_0 - \ln V_e$	74.66405	146.3872	295.5860	731.6480

The function value in each case is about $10^{-11} (\approx 0.0)$.

Example 12.2 $\underset{x\in D}{\text{Minimize}} f(x)$,

where
$$f(x) = \begin{cases} 1 + n \cdot \{\sum_{i=1}^{n}|x^i| + \text{sgn}[\sin(1/(\sum_{i=1}^{n}|x^i|) - 0.5)]\}, & x \neq 0, \\ 0, & x = 0, \end{cases} \qquad (12.16)$$

and D is the same as in (12.14). The function has an infinite number of discontinuous hypersurfaces. Its unique global minimum point is at the origin which has a discontinuity of the second kind. Table 2 gives the data of this example.

Table 2

n	5	10	20	50
N^i	68	144	261	609
N_f	3027	7375	22481	71426
$\ln V_0 - \ln V_e$	105.4427	244.0189	456.3860	1211.395

The algorithm has been successfully applied to industrial problems such as the optimum design in the arrangement of needles on a needle board of a pre-needling machine [15].

References

[1] Zheng Quan. Robust Analysis and Global Minimization of a Class of Discontinuous Functions (I) [J]. *Acta Mathematicae Applicatae Sinina* (English Series), 6:3(1990), 205—223.

[2] E. Galperin, Q. Zheng. Integral Global Optimization Method for Differential Games with Application to Pursuit-evasion Games. To appear.

[3] E. A. Galperin, Q. Zheng. Integral Global Optimization in Functional Spaces with Application to Optimal Control. preprint.

[4] C. Bessaga, A. Pelczynski. Selected Topics in Infinite-dimensional Topology [M]. Warszawa, 1975.

[5] R. B. Ash, Measure. Integration and Functional Analysis [M]. Academic Press [M] New York, 1972.

[6] N. N. Vakchania. Probability Distribution on Linear Spaces [M]. North Holland, New York, 1981.

[7] H. Bergstrm. Weak Convergence of Measure [M]. Academic Press, New York, 1982.

[8] Zheng Quan. Optimality Conditions for Global Optimization (I) [J]. *Acta Mcthematicae Applicatae Sinica* (English Seris), 2:1(1985), 66—78.

[9] Zheng Quan. Optimality Conditions for Global Optimization (II) [J]. *Acta Matnematicae Applicatae Sinica* (English Series), 2:2(1985), 118—132.

[10] Zheng Quan, Jiang Baichuan, Zhuang Songlin. A Method for Finding Global Extrema [J]. *Acta Mathematicae Applicatae Sinica*, 1:2(1978), 161—174.

[11] Zheng Quan. A Class of Discontinuous Functions and Its Global Optimization Problems, Numerical Mathematics [J]. *A Journal of Chinese Universities*, 7:1(1985), 31—43.

[12] Zhen Quan. A Variable Measure Method for Finding Global Minima. preprint.

[13] Zheng Quan. An Integral Variable Measure Method and Some Applications. preprint.

[14] Zhen Quan. On Problems of Global Optimization with Adaptive Change of Search Domain [J]. *Journal of Applied Science*, 1:1(1983), 92—94.

[15] X. Pan, S. Wng, H. Lui, Q. Zheng. The Optimal Desing for the Arrangement of Needles on the Needle Board of Pre-needling Machine [J]. *Journal of China Textile University*, 12:6(1986), 79—84.

Minimax Methods for Open-loop Equilibra in N-person Differential Games
Part III: Duality and Penalty Finite Element Methods*

Abstract: The equilibrium strategy for N-person differential games can be obtained from a min-max problem subject to differential constraints. The differential constraints can be treated by the duality and penalty methods and then an unconstrained problem can be obtained. In this paper we develop methods applying the finite element methods to compuite solutions of linear-quadratic N-person games using duality and penalty formulations.

The calculations are efficient and accurate. When a $(4,1)$-system of Hermite cubic splines are used, our numerical results agree well with the theoretical predicted rate of convergence for the Lagrangian. Graphs and numerical data are included for illustration.

1 Introduction

As in Part I and Part II, we consider an N-person differential game with the following dynamics:

$$(DE) \equiv \dot{x}(t) - A(t)x(t) - \sum_{i=1}^{N} B_i(t)u_i(t) - f(t) = 0, \quad \text{on } [0, T],$$

$$x(0) = x_0 \in \mathbb{R}^n. \tag{1.1}$$

The matrix and vector functions $A(t), f(t), B_i(t), u_i(t), i = 1, \cdots, N$, satisfy the same conditions as in Part I and II ([6] and [7]). Each player wants to minimize his cost

$$J_i(x, u) = J_i(x, u_1, \cdots, u_N), i = 1, \cdots, N. \tag{1.2}$$

Let

$$F(x, u; X, v) = F(x, u_1, \cdots, u_N; x^1, \cdots, x^N, v_1, \cdots, v_N)$$

$$= \sum_{i=1}^{N} [J_i(x, u) - J_i(x^i, v^i)], \tag{1.3}$$

where $X = (x^1, \cdots, x^N), v^i = (u_1, \cdots, u_{i-1}, v_i, u_{i+1}, \cdots, u_N)$ and each x^i is the solution of

$$(DE)_i \equiv \dot{x}^i(t) - A(t)x^i(t) - \sum_{j \neq i} B_j(t)u_j(t) - B_i(t)v_i(t) - f(t) = 0, \quad \text{on } [0, T],$$

$$x^i(0) = x_0, \quad i = 1, \cdots, N. \tag{1.4}$$

---

* In collaboration with Gong Chen, Wendell H. Miies, Wan-Hua Shaw. Reprinted from Journal of Computational Mathematics, 1992, 10(4): 321-338.

Following [6] and [7], we consider the primal and dual problems:

(P) $\inf\limits_{x,u} \sup\limits_{X,v} \{F(x,u;X,v) | (x,u) \in H_n^1 \times U$ subject to (1.1), $(X,v) \in [H_n^1]^N \times U$

subject to (1.4), $i=1,\cdots,N\}$

(D) $\sup\limits_{p_0 \in L^2} \inf\limits_{p \in [L^2]^N} L(p_0,p)$, where $L(p_0,p) = L(p_0,p_1,\cdots,p_N) = \inf\limits_{x,u} \sup\limits_{X,v} L(p_0,p;x,u;$

$X,v)$ with the Lagrangian $L: L^2 \times [L^2]^N \times H_n^1 \times U \times [H_n^1]^N \times U$ defined by

$$L(p_0,p;x,u;X,v) \equiv F(x,u;X,v) + \left\langle p_0, \dot{x} - Ax - \sum_{j=1}^N B_j u_j - f \right\rangle$$

$$+ \sum_{i=1}^N \left\langle p_i, \dot{x}^i - Ax^i - \sum_{j \neq i} B_j U_j - B_i v_i - f \right\rangle \quad (1.5)$$

for x, X satisfying $x(0) = x_0$, $X(0) = X_0 = (x_0,\cdots,x_0)$. We inherit the notations $U = \prod_{i=1}^N U_i$ with $U_i L_m^2(0,T)$ from Part I, and the notations of L^2 and Sobolev spaces H_n^k, $H_{0_n}^1$ and $H_{n_0}^1$ are the same as in [6] and [7]. We sometimes denote $L^2 = L^2(0,T)$ without mention of dimensions.

In this paper, we consider the linear quadratic problem whose cost functionals are given by

$$J_i(x,u) = \frac{1}{2} \int_0^T [|C_i(t)x(t) - z_i(t)|_{R^{k_i}}^2 + \langle M_i(t)u_i(t), u_i(t) \rangle_{R^{m_i}}] dt, \quad (1.6)$$

$i=1,\cdots,N$, (x,u) feasible

just as in [6], [7]; here we assume that $C_i(t)$ and $M_i(t)$ are matrix-valued functions of appropriate sizes and smoothness, and $z_i(t)$ is a vector-valued function. Furthermore, $M_i(t)$ induces a linear operator $M_i: L_{m_i}^2 \to L_{m_i}^2$ which is positive definite:

$$\langle M_i u_i, u_i \rangle_{L_{m_i}^2} \geq \mu \|u_i\|_{L_{m_i}^2}^2, \quad 1 \leq i \leq N, \text{ for some } \mu > 0. \quad (1.7)$$

In Section 2, we formally derive the matrix Riccati equation from the duality point of view. Section 3 is devoted to error estimates and numerical computations. We prove sharp error bounds using the Aubin-Nitche trick. We finally present in Section 4 some numerical results obtained by dualty and penalty scheme briefly. These results agree well with the theoretical estimates.

2 The Dual Max-min Problem for Linear Quadratic Games

In this section, we give a formal derivation of the dual functional $L(p_0,p)$. This formal derivation will be justified later by assumptions (A3), (A4), and the Primal-Dual Equivalence Theorem.

Let the Lagrangian L be defined as in (1.5), using (1.6). We first study

$$\sup \{L(p_0,p;x,u;X,v) | \text{for } (X,v) \text{ such that } X(0) = X_0\}.$$

For given p_0, p, x, u, $L(p_0,p;x,u;X,v)$ is strictly concave in v, and concave in X. Assume that this maximization problem has a solution $(\hat{X}, \hat{v})$, which depends on $(p_0, p; x, u)$. By a simple variational analysis on x^i, we have, necessarily,

$$-\langle C_i^*(C_i\hat{x}^i-z_i),y^i\rangle_{L_n^2}+\langle p_i,y^i-Ay^i\rangle_{L_n^2}=0, C^*=\text{adjoint of } C, \quad (2.1)$$

for all $y^i \in H_{n_0}^1, i=1,\cdots,N$. The above has a solution $\hat{X}$ if and only if p satisfies

$$p \in [H_{0_n}^1]^N. \quad (2.2)$$

Indeed, (2.2) is a necessary and sufficient condition for

$$\sup_{\substack{(X,v)\\X(0)=X_0}} L(p_n,p;x,u;X,v) = L(p_0,p;x,u;X,v). \quad (2.3)$$

(2.1) and (2.2) yield

$$-\langle C_i^*(C_i\hat{x}^i-z_i)+\dot{p}_i+A*p_i,y^i\rangle=0, i=1,\cdots,N.$$

Hence

$$\dot{p}_i = -A*p_i - C_i^*(C_i\hat{x}^i-z). \quad (2.4)$$

Similar variational analysis on v_i gives

$$-\langle M_i\hat{v}_i,w_i\rangle - \langle p_i,B_iw_i\rangle=0, \quad \forall w_i \in L_{m_i}^2,$$

or

$$\hat{v}_i = M_i^{-1}B_i^* p_i, \quad i=1,\cdots,N. \quad (2.5)$$

Note that $(\hat{X},\hat{v})$ is independent of (x,u).

Next, we consider $\inf_{\substack{(x,u)\\x(0)=x_0}} L(p_0,p;x,u;X,v)$. For given $p_0 \in L_n^2$, $p \in [H_{n0}^1]^N$, using the same reasoning as before, we can show that

$$\inf_{\substack{(x,u)\\x(0)=x_0}} L(p_0,p;x,u;\hat{X},\hat{v}) = L(p_0,p;\hat{x},\hat{u};\hat{X},\hat{v})$$

for some (x,u) if and only if

$$p_0 \in H_{0n}^1, \quad (2.6)$$

$$\dot{p}_0 = -A^*p_0 + \sum_{i=1}^N C_i^*(C_i\hat{x}-z_i), \quad (2.7)$$

$$\hat{u}_i = M_i^{-1}B_i^*\left(p_0+\sum_{j\neq 1}p_j\right) = M_i^{-1}B_i^*(p_0+p_s-p_i), p_s = \sum_{j=1}^N p_j. \quad (2.8)$$

Let $L(p_0,p)$ be as defined in Section 1. If the problem $\sup_{p_0}\inf_p L(p_0,p)$ attains its maxmin at $(\hat{p}_0,\hat{p})$, $\hat{p}_0$ and $\hat{p}$ satisfy (2.6), (2.7), (2.3) and (2.4). Therefore, we obtain $\hat{X},\hat{v},\hat{x},\hat{u},\hat{p}_0,\hat{p}$ as the solution to the following two-point boundary problem:

Theorem 2.1 *Assume that* $\max_{p_0 \in L_n^2}\min_{p\in[L_n^2]^N} L(p_0,p)$ *is attained by* $(\hat{p}_0,\hat{p})$. *Then* $(\hat{p}_0,\hat{p})\in H_{0n}^1 \times [H_{0n}^1]^N$,

$$L(\hat{p}_0,\hat{p}) = \max_{p_0\in L_n^2}\min_{p\in[L_n^2]^N} L(p_0,p) = \max_{p_0}\min_p L(p_0,p;x,u;X,v)$$

$$= \max_{p_0}\min_p \min_{\substack{(x,u)\in H_{0n}^1\times U\\x(0)=x_0}} \max_{\substack{(X,v)\in[H_{0n}^1]^N\times U\\X(0)=X_0}} L(p_0,p;x,u;X,v)$$

and $x, X=(x^1,\cdots,x^N), p_0$ *and* $p=(p_1,\cdots,p_N)$ *are coupled through*

$$\frac{\mathrm{d}}{\mathrm{d}t}\begin{bmatrix}\hat{x}\\\hat{x}^1\\\vdots\\\hat{x}^N\\\hat{p}_0\\\hat{p}_1\\\vdots\\\hat{p}_N\end{bmatrix}=\begin{bmatrix}A & 0 & 0 & S & S_1 & \cdots & S_N\\0 & A & 0 & S_1 & S_{11} & \cdots & S_{1N}\\\vdots & \vdots & \ddots & \cdots & \cdots & \cdots & \cdots\\0 & 0 & A & S_N & S_{N1} & \cdots & S_{NN}\\\sum_{i=1}^{N}C_i^*C_i & 0 & 0 & -A^* & 0 & \cdots & 0\\0 & -C_1^*C_1 & 0 & 0 & -A^* & & 0\\\vdots & \vdots & \ddots & \vdots & \vdots & \ddots & \vdots\\0 & 0 & -C_N^*C_N & 0 & 0 & & -A^*\end{bmatrix}$$

$$\times\begin{bmatrix}\hat{x}\\\hat{x}^1\\\vdots\\\hat{x}^N\\\hat{p}_0\\\hat{p}_1\\\vdots\\\hat{p}_N\end{bmatrix}+\begin{bmatrix}f\\f\\\vdots\\f\\\sum_{i=1}^{N}C_i^*z_i\\C_1^*z_1\\\vdots\\C_N^*z_N\end{bmatrix} \tag{2.9}$$

$\hat{x}(0)=\hat{x}^1(0)=\cdots=\hat{x}^N(0)=x_0$, $\hat{p}_0(T)=\hat{p}_1(T)=\cdots=\hat{p}_N(T)=0$,
and $\hat{u}$, $\hat{v}$ *satisfy*

$$\hat{u}_i=M_i^{-1}B_i^*(p_0+p_s-p_i), \quad \hat{v}_i=-M_i^{-1}B_i^*p_i,$$

with

$$S=\sum_{j=1}^{N}B_jM_j^{-1}B_j^*, \quad S_i=\sum_{j\neq i}B_jM_j^{-1}B_j^*,$$

$$S_{ik}=S-(1-\delta_{ik})B_iM_i^{-1}B_i^*-B_kM_k^{-1}B_k^*, \quad \delta_{ik}=\text{Kronecker's }\delta. \tag{2.10}$$

We now study the dual problem. Henceforth, for simplicity, we denote the operators $C_i^*C_i$ and $\sum_{i=1}^{N}C_i^*C_i$ (induced by the matrices $C_i^*(t)C_i(t)$ and $\sum_{i=1}^{N}C_i^*(t)C_i(t)$) in L_n^2 as $\mathbb{C}_i(1\leqslant i\leqslant N)$ and $\mathbb{C}_0$, respectively.

Several assumptions are needed as we proceed. First, we assume

(A3) each operator $\mathbb{C}_i(1\leqslant i\leqslant N)$ is strictly positive definite in L^2.

From (2.4), we get

$$\hat{x}^i=-\mathbb{C}_i^{-1}(\dot{p}_0+A^*p_i-C_i^*z_i). \tag{2.11}$$

By (A3), $\mathbb{C}_0$ is also strictly poitive definite. By (2.7), we get

$$\hat{x}=\mathbb{C}_0^{-1}\left(\dot{p}_0+A^*p_0+\sum_{i=1}^{N}C_i^*z_i\right). \tag{2.12}$$

We now substitute (2.11), (2.12), (2.5) and (2.8) into (1.5). Integrating by parts with respect to p_0 and $p_i(1\leqslant i\leqslant N)$ once, using the end conditions $p_i(T)=0, 0\leqslant i\leqslant N$, and simplifying, we get

$$L(p_0,p)=L(p_0,p;\hat{x};\hat{u};\hat{X},\hat{v})=-\frac{1}{2}\langle \dot{p}+A^* p_0, \mathbb{C}_0^{-1}(\dot{p}+A^* p_0)\rangle$$

$$+\frac{1}{2}\sum_{i=1}^{N}\langle \dot{p}_i+A^* p_i, \mathbb{C}_i^{-1}(\dot{p}+A^* p_i)\rangle - \frac{1}{2}\langle p_0+p_s, S(p_0+p_s)\rangle$$

$$+\langle p_0+p_s, \sum_{i=1}^{N} B_i M_i^{-1} B_i^* p_i\rangle - \langle \dot{p}_0+A^* p_0, \mathbb{C}_0^{-1}\sum_{i=1}^{N} C_i^* z_i\rangle$$

$$-\sum_{i=1}^{N}\langle \dot{p}+A^* p_i, \mathbb{C}_i^{-1} C_i^* z_i\rangle - \langle p_0+p_s, f\rangle - \langle p_0(0)+p_s(0), x_0\rangle$$

$$-\frac{1}{2}\langle \mathbb{C}_0^{-1}(\sum_{j=1}^{N} C_j^* z_j), \sum_{j=1}^{N} C_j^* z_j\rangle + \frac{1}{2}\|z\|^2 \equiv \sum_{i=1}^{10} T_i, \qquad (2.13)$$

where $\|z\|^2 = \sum_{i=1}^{N}\|z_i\|_{L^2}^2$, and p_s is defined as in (2.8).

It is easy to see that $L(p_0, p)$ is strictly concave in p_0 for any given p. However, for any given p_0, $L(p_0, p)$ is not necessarily convex in p because of the negative sign in front of T_3. This causes a severe handicap for the duality approach; see Remark 2.1, below. To circumvent this, we need the following important assumption:

(A4) The positive definite operators $\mathbb{C}_i^{-1} (1 \leqslant i \leqslant N)$ in L_n^2 are large enough so that

$$\frac{1}{2}\sum_{i=1}^{N}\langle \dot{p}_i+A^* p_i, \mathbb{C}_i^{-1}(\dot{p}_i+A^* p_i)\rangle - \frac{1}{2}\langle p_s, Sp_s\rangle$$

$$+\langle p_s, \sum_{i=1}^{N} B_i M_i^{-1} B_i^* p_i\rangle \geqslant v\sum_{i=1}^{N}\|\dot{p}\|^2, \qquad (2.14)$$

for some $v>0$, and for all $p \in [H_{0n}^1]^N$.

We remark that, even if $\mathbb{C}_i^{-1}$, $1 \leqslant i \leqslant N$, are not large enough, the above assumption can still be valid provided that T is chosen sufficiently small, because in this case the first positive definite quadratic form in (2.14) will have a large coercivity coefficient to absorb L^2-norm, when the interval $[0,T]$ is small. This is consistent with the assumption that t_1-t_0 is sufficiently small in [13].

Another special case where (A4) holds without requiring $\mathbb{C}_i^{-1}$, $1 \leqslant i \leqslant N$, be large is when

$$N=2, \quad U_1=U_2, \quad B_1 M_1^{-1} B_1^* = B_2 M_2^{-1} B_2^* \equiv B, \text{ for some } B \geqslant 0.$$

It is easily seen that now

$$(2.14)=\frac{1}{2}\sum_{i=1}^{2}\langle \dot{p}+A^* p_i, \mathbb{C}_i^{-1}(\dot{p}_i+A^* p_i)\rangle - \frac{1}{2}2\langle p_s, Bp_s\rangle + \langle p_s, Bp_s\rangle$$

$$=\frac{1}{2}\sum_{i=1}^{2}\langle \dot{p}_i+A^* p_i, \mathbb{C}_i^{-1}(\dot{p}_i+A^* p_i)\rangle, \qquad (2.15)$$

so (A4) holds.

Remark 2.1 The fact that an assumption like (A2) in [7] is indispensable for the tractahility of the dual problem can be observed as follows: If $\mathbb{C}_i^{-1}$, $i=1,\cdots,N$, are not large enough in comparison with $B_i M_i^{-1} B_i^*$, $i=1,\cdots,N$, so as to cause the existence of some $\tilde{p} \in [H_{0n}^1]^N$ satisfying

$$\frac{1}{2}\sum_{i=1}^{N}\langle \dot{\tilde{p}}_i + A^*\tilde{p}_i, C_i^{-1}(\dot{\tilde{p}}+A^*\tilde{p}_i)\rangle - \frac{1}{2}\langle \tilde{p}_s, S\tilde{p}_s\rangle$$

$$+\left\langle \tilde{p}_s, \sum_{i=1}^{N} B_i M_i^{-1} B_i^* \tilde{p}_i \right\rangle < 0, \tag{2.16}$$

then for any given $p_0 \in H_{0n}^1$, we deduce from (2.15) that

$$\lim_{k\to\infty} L(p_0, k\tilde{p}) = -\infty \text{ and } \inf_{p\in[H_{0n}^1]^N} L(p_0, p) = -\infty$$

for any given $p_0 \in H_{0n}^1$. Therefore, the dual problem is rendered completely worthless. A situation like (2.16) should be avoided to ensure mathematical tractability. For the computational purpose we will need the uniqueness of p. Thus we take a step further to assume coercivity and strict convexity of p in $L(p_0, p)$ in hypothesis (A4) to achieve this goal.

Let us list the above and other usefull properties in the following, which is readily verifiable.

Lemma 2.1 *Assume* (A3) *and* (A4); *then*

(i) *For each given* $p_0 \in H_{0n}^1$, $L(p_0, p)$ *is strictly convex in* p *for all* $p \in [H_{0n}^1]^N$ *and, for each given* $p \in [H_{0n}^1]^N$, $L(p_0, p)$ *is strictly concave in* p_0 *for all* $p_0 \in H_{0n}^1$.

(ii) *The following coercivity conditions are satisfied*:

$$\lim_{\|p\|_{[H_{0n}^1]^N}\to\infty} L(p_0, p) = \infty, \quad \forall p_0 \in H_{0n}^1,$$

$$\lim_{\|p_0\|_{H_{0n}^1}\to\infty} L(p_0, p) = \infty, \quad \forall p \in [H_{0n}^1]^N. \tag{2.17}$$

Using the above lemma and the minimax theorem, we conclude

Proposition 2.1 *Under* (A3) *and* (A4), *the dual problem* $\sup_{p_0} \inf_p L(p_0, p)$ *has a unique solution* $(\hat{p}_0, \hat{p})$ *satisfying*

$$L(\hat{p}_0, \hat{p}) = \sup_{p_0\in H_{0n}^1}\inf_{p\in[H_{0n}^1]^N} L(p_0, p) = \max_{p_0\in H_{0n}^1}\min_{p\in[H_{0n}^1]^N} L(p_0, p) = \min_{p\in[H_{0n}^1]^N}\max_{p_0\in H_{0n}^1} L(p_0, p).$$

Theorem 2.2 (Primal-Dual Equivalence Theorem) *Let* $C_i(t), z_i(t), i=1,\cdots,N$, $f(t)$ *and* $\mathbb{C}_0^{-1}$, $\mathbb{C}_i^{-1}$, $i=1,\cdots,N$, *be sufficiently smooth* (*as functions and operators, respectively*). *Let* $F(x, u; X, v)$ *be defined as in* (1.3). *Assume that there exists* $(x,u) \in H_n^1 \times U > (x,v) \in [H_n^1]^N \times U$ *such that*

$$\inf_{\substack{(x,u)\\ \text{feasible}}} \sup_{\substack{(X,v)\\ \text{feasible}}} F(x,u;X,x) = \min_{\substack{(x,u)\\ \text{feasible}}} \max_{\substack{(X,v)\\ \text{feasible}}} F(x,u;X,v) = f(\hat{x}, \hat{u}; \hat{X}, \hat{v}) < \infty \tag{2.18}$$

and that (A2) *in* [7] *is also satisfied*, *i.e.*,

$$\psi(x,u) = \sup_{\substack{(X,v)\\ \text{feasible}}} F(x,u;X,v) \tag{2.19}$$

is convex in (x,u) *for all* $(x,u) \in H_n^1 \times U, x(0) = x_0$. *Assume that* (A3) *and* (A4) *hold and let* $(\hat{p}_0, \hat{p})$ *be the solution in Proposition 2.4. Then*

(i) $L(\hat{p}_0, \hat{p}) = \max_{p_0\in H_{0n}^1}\min_{p\in[H_{0n}^1]^N} L(p_0, p)$

$$= \max_{p_0\in H_{0n}^1}\min_{p\in[H_{0n}^1]^N}\min_{\substack{(x,u)\in H_n^1\times U\\ x(0)=x_0}}\max_{\substack{(X,v)\in[H_{0n}^1]^N\\ X(0)=X_0}} L(p_0, p; x, u; x, v)$$

$$= \min_{\substack{(x,u)\\ \text{feasible}}} \max_{\substack{(X,v)\\ \text{feasible}}} F(x,u;X,v) = f(\hat{x},\hat{u},\hat{X},\hat{v}); \tag{2.20}$$

(ii) $(\hat{x},\hat{u};\hat{X},\hat{v})$ is related to $(\hat{p}_0,\hat{p})$ through

$$\hat{x} = \mathbb{C}_0^{-1}(\dot{\hat{p}}_0 + A^*\hat{p}_0 + \sum_{i=1}^{N} C_i^* z_i), \tag{2.21}$$

$$\hat{u}_i = M_i^{-1} B_i^*(\hat{p}_0 + \hat{p}_s - \hat{p}_i), \quad i=1,\cdots,N, \tag{2.22}$$

$$\hat{x}^i = -\mathbb{C}_i^{-1}(\dot{\hat{p}}_i + A^*\hat{p}_i - C_i^* z_i), \quad i=1,\cdots,N, \tag{2.23}$$

$$\hat{v}_i = -M_i^{-1} B_i^* \hat{p}_i, \quad i=1,\cdots,N \tag{2.24}$$

and $(\hat{x},\hat{u};\hat{X},\hat{v})$ satisfies differential equations (1.1) and (1.4).

Proof. Because all the assumptions are satisfied, we can apply Theorem 2.1 of [7] (particularly (2.17) in the proof) to conclude (i). Note that all the sup's and inf's can be replaced by max's and min's due to the quadratic nature of the problem.

(2.21)~(2.24) are verified in a straightforward way as in (2.8), (2.5) and as in (2.11) and (2.12), but now every procedure is justified.

To show that $(\hat{x},\hat{u};\hat{X},\hat{v})$ satisfies differential equations (1.1) and (1.4), we can make a variational analysis on $L(p_0,p)$. Because

$$L(p_0,\hat{p}) \leq L(\hat{p}_0,\hat{p}) \leq L(\hat{p}_0,p), \quad \forall (p_0,p) \in H_{0n}^1 \times [H_{0n}^1]^N,$$

we get

$$\frac{\partial}{\partial p} L(p_0,p)\Big|_{p=\hat{p}} = 0. \tag{2.25}$$

This yields the Euler-Lagrange equations

$$\begin{cases} \frac{d}{dt}\mathbb{C}_i^{-1}(\dot{\hat{p}}_i + A^*\hat{p}_i) - A\mathbb{C}_i^{-1}(\dot{\hat{p}}_i + A^*\hat{p}_i) + S(\hat{p}_0 + \hat{p}_s) - \sum_{j=1}^{N} B_j M_j^{-1} B_j^* \hat{p}_j \\ \quad - B_i M_i^{-1} B_i^*(\hat{p}_0 + \hat{p}_s) + A\mathbb{C}_i^{-1} C_i z_i - \frac{d}{dt}(\mathbb{C}_i^{-1} C_i^* z_i) + f = 0, \\ p_i(T) = 0, \\ \mathbb{C}_i^{-1}(0)[\dot{\hat{p}}(0) + A^*(0)\hat{p}_i(0)] = -x_0 + \mathbb{C}_i^{-1}(0) C_i^*(0) z_i(0), \quad \text{for } i=1,\cdots,N. \end{cases} \tag{2.26}$$

From the assumption that $\mathbb{C}_i, C_i, z_i, f$ are sufficiently smooth, and that (2.20)~(2.24) hold, we see that the above equations agree with (1.4). Similarly, from

$$\frac{\partial}{\partial p_0} L(p_0,p)\Big|_{p_0=\hat{p}_0} = 0, \tag{2.27}$$

we can also show that (1.1) is satisfied by (2.21)(2.22).

Note that for a linear-quadratic differential game, $\psi(x,u)$ in (2.19) can be calculated expticitly and is equal to

$$\psi(x,u) = \max_{\substack{(X,v)\\ \text{feasible}}} F(x,u;X,v) = \sum_{i=1}^{N} \frac{1}{2} \Big\{ \|C_i x - z_i\|^2 + \langle M_i u_i, u_i \rangle$$

$$- \|C_i(\mathbb{L}_0 x_0 + \sum_{j \neq i} \mathbb{L}_j u_j + \mathbb{L}_{N+1} f) - z_i\|^2$$

$$+ \langle \mathbb{L}_i^* C_i^* [C_i(\mathbb{L}_0 x_0 + \sum_{j \neq i} \mathbb{L}_j u_j + \mathbb{L}_{N+1} f) - z_i],$$

$$(M_i + L_i^* C_i^* C_i L_i)^{-1} L_i^* C_i^* \Big[C_i \Big(L_0 x_0 + \sum_{j \neq i} L_j u_j + L_{N+1} f \Big) - z_i \Big] \Big\rangle \Big\}. \quad (2.28)$$

The reader should refer to Part I, Section 2, for the notations and derivation of the above.

Corollary 2.1 *Consider the linear-quadratic differential game* (1.1), (1.6). *Assume*

$(A0)'$ $\min\limits_{\substack{(x,u)\\ \text{feasible}}} \max\limits_{\substack{(X,v)\\ \text{feasible}}} F(x,u;X,v)=0$ *holds, so the differential game has a solution* (x,u);

$(A2)'$ $\psi(x,u)$ *given in* (2.28) *is convex in* (x,u) *for* $(x,u) \in H_{0n}^1 \times U$, $x(0)=x_0$; *and assume also* (A3) *and* (A4). *Then there exists a unique* $(p_0, p) \in H_{0n}^1 \times [H_{0n}^1]^N$ *such that* (2.20) *holds and the solution* (x,u) *of the differential game can be obtained from* (p_0, p) *via*

$$x = \mathbb{C}_0^{-1}(\dot{\hat{p}}_0 + A^* \hat{p}_0 + \sum_{i=1}^N C_i^* z_i),$$

$$\hat{u}_i = M_i^{-1} B_i^* (\hat{p}_0 + \hat{p}_s - \hat{p}_i), \quad i=1,2,\cdots,N,$$

as given in (2.12) *and* (2.8).

Remark 2.2 Many evidences seem to suggest that assumption $(A2)'$ in Corollary 2.1 is redundant because of (A4). Nevertheless, we are still unalbe to prove or disprove this.

3 The Dual Variational Problem and Finite Element Approximations

In this section we devote ourselves to the study of the finite element numerical method for differential games. It is fair to say that the methods of solution for N-person differential games are still very incomplete. More efforts are needed to develop good analytic and approximation methods to solve them. The finite etement method is a rigorously established, highly accurate numerical method which is becoming increasing popularly in recent years. Due to the special minimax structure of differential games, we are able to apply and generalize the existing theory of finite element analysis to our own problem to establish rigorous error bounds and to obtain numerical solutions.

The unique solution (p_0, p) of the max-min problem satisfies (2.25) and (2.27). From (2.13), by a simple calculation, we obtain

$$\partial_{p_0} L(\hat{p}_0, \hat{p}).r = -\langle \dot{\hat{p}}_0 + A^* \hat{p}_0, \mathbb{C}_0^{-1}(\dot{r} + A^* r) \rangle - \langle \hat{p}_0 + \hat{p}_s, Sr \rangle + \Big\langle r, \sum_i^N B_i M_i^{-1} B^* p_i \Big\rangle$$

$$- \Big\langle \dot{r} + A^* r, \mathbb{C}_0^{-1} \sum_1^N C_i^* z_i \Big\rangle - \langle r, f \rangle - \langle r(0), x_0 \rangle = 0, \quad \forall r \in H_{0n}^1,$$

(3.1)

$$\partial_p L(\hat{p}_0, \hat{p}).s = \sum_1^N \langle \dot{\hat{p}}_i + A^* \hat{p}_i, \mathbb{C}_i^{-1}(\dot{s} + A^* s_i) \rangle - \Big\langle \hat{p}_0 + \hat{p}_s, S \sum_1^N s_i \Big\rangle$$

$$+ \Big\langle \hat{p}_0 + \hat{p}_s, \sum_1^N B_i M_i^{-1} B_i^* S_i \Big\rangle + \Big\langle \sum_1^N s_i, \sum_1^N B_i M_i^{-1} B_i^* \hat{p}_i \Big\rangle$$

$$- \sum_1^N \langle \dot{s}_i + A^* s_i, \mathbb{C}_i^{-1} C_i^* z_i \rangle - \Big\langle \sum_1^N s_i, f \Big\rangle - \Big\langle \sum_1^N s_i(0), x_0 \Big\rangle = 0,$$

$$\forall\, s=(s_1,\cdots,s_N)\in [H^1_{0n}]^N. \quad (3.2)$$

The above two relations induce a bilinear form on $H^1_{0n}\times [H^1_{0n}]^N$: for $r^1, r^2\in H^1_{0n}$ and $s^1=(s^1_1,s^1_2,\cdots,s^1_N)$, $s^2=(s^2_1,\cdots,s^2_N)\in [H^1_{0n}]^N$,

$$a\left(\begin{bmatrix}r^1\\s^1\end{bmatrix},\begin{bmatrix}r^2\\s^2\end{bmatrix}\right)\equiv -\left\langle \dot{r}^1+A^*r^1, \mathbb{C}_0^{-1}(\dot{r}^2+A^*r^2)\right\rangle -\left\langle r^1+\sum_{j=1}^N s^1_j, Sr^2\right\rangle$$
$$+\left\langle r^2, \sum_1^N B_iM_i^{-1}B_i^*s^1_i\right\rangle +\sum_i^N \left\langle \dot{s}^1_i+A^*s^1_i, \mathbb{C}_i^{-1}(\dot{s}^2_i+A^*s^2_i)\right\rangle -\left\langle r^1+\sum_{j=1}^N s^1_j, S\sum_{j=1}^N s^2_j\right\rangle$$
$$+\left\langle r^1+\sum_1^N s^1_i, \sum_1^N B_iM_i^{-1}B_i^*s^2_i\right\rangle +\left\langle \sum_1^N s^2_i, \sum_1^N B_iM_i^{-1}B_i^*s^1_i\right\rangle, \quad (3.3)$$

and a linear form θ: for $r\in H^1_{0n}$ and $s=(s_1,\cdots,s_N)\in [H^1_{0n}]^N$,

$$\theta\left(\begin{bmatrix}r\\s\end{bmatrix}\right)=\left\langle r+\sum_1^N s_j, f\right\rangle +\left\langle r(0)+\sum_1^N s_j(0), x_0\right\rangle +\left\langle \dot{r}+A^*r, \mathbb{C}_0^{-1}\sum_1^N C_i^*z_i\right\rangle$$
$$=\sum_1^N \langle \dot{s}_i+A^*s_i, \mathbb{C}_i^{-1}C_i^*z_i\rangle. \quad (3.4)$$

Thus, (3.1) and (3.2) are equivalent to

$$a\left(\begin{bmatrix}p_0\\p\end{bmatrix},\begin{bmatrix}r\\s\end{bmatrix}\right)=\theta\left(\begin{bmatrix}r\\s\end{bmatrix}\right), \quad \forall\,(r,s)\in H^1_{0n}\times [H^1_{0n}]^N. \quad (3.5)$$

We are now in a position to compute $(\hat{p}_0,\hat{p})$ be the finite element method. As in [1], we say that $S_h^2\subset H^{t_2}_{r^2}(0,T)$ is a (t_1,t_2)-system (t_1,t_2 are nonnegative integers) if, for all $v\in H^{k_0}_{r^0}(0,T)$, there exists $v_h\in S_h$ such that

$$\|v-v_h\|_{H^k_r}\leq Kh^m\|v\|_{H^{m+k}_r}, \quad \forall\, 0\leq k\leq \min(k_0,t_2),\quad k\in N, \quad (3.6)$$

where $m=\min(t-k, k_0-k)$ and $K>0$ is independent of h and v.

Let $S_h\subset H^1_{0n}$ be a $(t,1)$-system. We consider

$$\max_{p_0\in S_h}\min_{p\in [S_h]^N} L(p_0,p). \quad (3.7)$$

It is easy to see that under (A4), there exists a unique saddle point $(\hat{p}_{0h},\hat{p}_h)\in S_h\times [S_h]^N$ such that

$$L(\hat{p}_{0h},\hat{p}_h)=\max_{p_0\in S_h}\min_{p\in [S_h]^N} L(p_0,p).$$

This point (p_{0h},p_h) is characterized as the solution to the variational equation

$$a\left(\begin{bmatrix}p_{0h}\\p_h\end{bmatrix},\begin{bmatrix}r_h\\s_h\end{bmatrix}\right)=\theta\left(\begin{bmatrix}r_h\\s_h\end{bmatrix}\right), \quad \forall\,(r_h,s_h)\in S_h\times [S_h]^N. \quad (3.8)$$

If $\{\phi^i\}_{k=1}^J, \{\psi^i\}_{i=1}^{N,J}$ are basis for $S_h, [S_h]^N$, respectively, then (3.8) is a matrix equation $\overline{M}_h\overline{y}_h=\overline{\theta}_h$, where the entries of $\overline{M}_h$ and $\overline{\theta}_h$ are

$$[\overline{M}_h]_{ij}=a\left(\begin{bmatrix}\psi^j\\\phi^j\end{bmatrix},\begin{bmatrix}\psi^i\\\phi^i\end{bmatrix}\right), \quad 1\leq i,j\leq (N+1)J,$$

$$(\theta_h)_j=\theta\left(\begin{bmatrix}\psi^j\\\phi^j\end{bmatrix}\right), \quad 1\leq j\leq (N+1)J.$$

Proposition 3.1 *Under (A4), the bilinear form $a(\cdot,\cdot)$ satisfies*

$$\inf_{\left\|\begin{bmatrix}r^2\\s^2\end{bmatrix}\right\|=1} \sup_{\left\|\begin{bmatrix}r^1\\s^1\end{bmatrix}\right\|=1} \left|a\left(\begin{bmatrix}r^1\\s^1\end{bmatrix},\begin{bmatrix}r^2\\s^2\end{bmatrix}\right)\right| > 0, \tag{3.9}$$

and the space $\{S_h\}_h$ satisfies

$$\inf_{\left\|\begin{bmatrix}r_h^2\\s_h^2\end{bmatrix}\right\|=1} \sup_{\left\|\begin{bmatrix}r_h^1\\s_h^1\end{bmatrix}\right\|=1} \left|a\left(\begin{bmatrix}r_h^1\\s_h^1\end{bmatrix},\begin{bmatrix}r_h^2\\s_h^2\end{bmatrix}\right)\right| = \gamma_h > \gamma > 0, \tag{3.10}$$

for some $\gamma > 0$, $\forall h > 0$.

Proof. In (3.3), for any given $(r^2, s^2) \in H_{0n}^1 \times [H_{0n}^1]^N$, with norm 1, let
$$r^1 = -r^2, \quad s^1 = s^2.$$
Then the norm of (r^1, s^1) in $H_{0n}^1 \times [H_{0n}^1]^N$ is also equal to 1, and

$$a\left(\begin{bmatrix}r^1\\s^1\end{bmatrix},\begin{bmatrix}r^2\\s^2\end{bmatrix}\right) = a\left(\begin{bmatrix}-r^2\\s^2\end{bmatrix},\begin{bmatrix}r^2\\s^2\end{bmatrix}\right)$$

$$= \langle r^2 + A^* r^2, \mathbb{C}_0^{-1}(r^2 + A^* r^2)\rangle + \langle r^2, Sr^2\rangle$$

$$+ \left\langle \sum_{i=1}^N s_i^2, \sum_{i=1}^N B_i M_i^{-1} B_i^* s_i^2 \right\rangle + \sum_{i=1}^N \langle s_i^2 + A^* s_i^2, \mathbb{C}_0^{-1}(s_i^2 + A^* s_i^2)\rangle$$

$$- \left\langle \sum_{i=1}^N s_i^2, S \sum_{i=1}^N s_i^2 \right\rangle + 2\left\langle \sum_{i=1}^N s_i^2, \sum_{i=1}^N B_i M_i^{-1} B_i^* s_i^2 \right\rangle$$

$$\geq \langle \dot{r}_2 + A^* r^2, \mathbb{C}_0^{-1}(\dot{r}^2 + A^* r^2)\rangle + \langle r^2, Sr^2\rangle + 2\mu \sum_{i=1}^N \|s_i^2\|_{L^2} \quad \text{(by (A4))}$$

$$\geq \mu' \left\|\begin{bmatrix}r^2\\s^2\end{bmatrix}\right\|_{H_{0n}^1 \times [H_{0n}^1]^N} = \mu'$$

for some $\mu' > 0$. So (3.9) also follows in exactly the same way.

Theorem 3.1 *Let $(\hat{p}_{0h}, \hat{p}_h)$ be the solution of (3.7) and let S_h be a $(t, 1)$-system. Assume that $C_i(t), z_i(t), i=1, \cdots, N$, are sufficiently smooth. Under (A3), (A4), we have*

$$\|\hat{p}_0 - \hat{p}_{0h}\|_{H_{0n}^1} + \|\hat{p} - \hat{p}_h\|_{[H_{0n}^1]^N} \leq Kh^m (\|\hat{p}_0\|_{H_n^r} + \|\hat{p}\|_{[H_n^r]^N}), \tag{3.11}$$

$$\|\hat{p}_0 - \hat{p}_{0h}\|_{L^2} + \|\hat{p} - \hat{p}_h\|_{[L^2]^N} \leq Kh^{m+1} (\|\hat{p}_0\|_{H_n^r} + \|\hat{p}\|_{[H_n^r]^N}) \tag{3.12}$$

provided $(\hat{p}_0, \hat{p}) \in [H_{0n}^1 \cap H_n^r] \times [H_{0n}^1 \cap H_n^r]^N$, where $m = \min(t-i, r-1)$ and $K > 0$ is a constant independent of $(\hat{p}_0, \hat{p})$. Consequently,

$$|L(\hat{p}_0, \hat{p}) - L(\hat{p}_{0n}, \hat{p}_h)| \leq K_2 h^{2m}(\|\hat{p}_0\|_{H_n^r}^2 + \|\hat{p}\|_{[H_n^r]^N}^2) \tag{3.13}$$

holds for some $K_2 > 0$ independent of $(\hat{p}_0, \hat{p})$.

Proof. Because (p_{0h}, p_h) satisfies (3.8) and $(\hat{p}_0, \hat{p})$ satisfies (3.5), we get

$$a\left(\begin{bmatrix}\hat{p}_0 - \hat{p}_{0h}\\ \hat{p} - \hat{p}_h\end{bmatrix}, \begin{bmatrix}r_h\\s_h\end{bmatrix}\right) = 0, \quad \forall (r_h, s_h) \in S_h \times [S_h]^N.$$

Therefore[1], by Proposition 3.1, we get

$$\|(\hat{p}_0 - \hat{p}_{0h}, \hat{p} - \hat{p}_k)\|_{H_{0n}^1 \times [H_{0n}^1]^N}$$

$$\leq \left(1 + \frac{c}{\gamma}\right) \inf_{(r_h, s_h) \in S_h \times [S_h]^N} (\|\hat{p}_0 - r_h\|_{H_{0n}^1} + \|\hat{p} - s_h\|_{[H_{0n}^1]^N})$$

for some $c > 0$ independent of h. Using (3.6), we obtain (3.11).

To prove (3.12) we use Nitsh's trick ([8],[15]). By Proposition 3.1 and [1], for any $g \in L^2 \times [L^2]^N$, we have a unique $w(g) \in H_{0n}^1 \times [H_{0n}^1]^N$ such that
$$a(w(g),y) = \langle g,y \rangle_{L^2 \times [L^2]^N}, \quad \forall y \in H_{0n}^1 \times [H_{0n}^1]^N.$$
Furthermore, we have $w(g) \in [H_{0n}^1 \cap H_n^2] \times [H_{0n}^1 \cap H_n^2]^N$, provided that $C_i(t)$ and $z_i(t)$, $i=1,2,\cdots,N$, are sufficiently smooth (this $w(g)$ can be obtained explicitly from integration by parts). It is not difficult to verify that
$$\|w(g)\|_{H_n^2 \times [H_n^2]^N} \leq K' \|g\|_{L^2 \times [L^2]^N},$$
where K' is independent of g. By the very same proof of the Aubin-Nitsche lemma[7], which remains valid under Proposition 3.1, we get
$$\|\hat{p}_0 - \hat{p}_{0h}\|_{L^2} + \|\hat{p} - \hat{p}_h\|_{[L^2]^N} \leq Ch^m (\|\hat{p}_0\|_{H_n^r} + \|\hat{p}\|_{[H_n^r]^N})$$
$$\cdot \sup_{g \in L^2 \times [L^2]^N} (1/\|g\| \inf_{\zeta_h \in S_n \times [S_h]^N} \|w(g) - \zeta_h\|). \quad (3.14)$$

But, by (3.6),
$$\frac{1}{\|g\|} \inf_{\zeta_h \in S_h \times [S_h]^N} \|w(g) - \zeta_h\| \leq \frac{1}{\|g\|} K''h \|w(g)\|_{H_n^2} \leq \frac{1}{\|g\|} K''hK' \|g\| = K'K''h,$$
for some $K'' > 0$ independent of g and $w(g)$. Using the above in (3.14), we get (3.12).

To show (3.13), we note that
$$L(\hat{p}_{0h},\hat{p}_h) - L(\hat{p}_0,\hat{p}) = 2\left\{a\left(\begin{bmatrix}\hat{p}_0\\\hat{p}\end{bmatrix},\begin{bmatrix}\hat{p}_{0h}-\hat{p}_0\\\hat{p}_h-\hat{p}\end{bmatrix}\right) - \theta\begin{bmatrix}\hat{p}_{0h}-\hat{p}_0\\\hat{p}_h-\hat{p}\end{bmatrix}\right\}$$
$$+ a\left(\begin{bmatrix}\hat{p}_{0h}-\hat{p}_0\\\hat{p}_h-\hat{p}\end{bmatrix},\begin{bmatrix}\hat{p}_{0h}-\hat{p}_0\\\hat{p}_h-\hat{p}\end{bmatrix}\right).$$
The first term on the right above is zero because of (3.5). The second term on the right can be estimated by using (3.11). Hence we get (3.13).

Corollary 3.1 *Let*
$$\hat{x}_h = \mathbb{C}_0^{-1}\left(\dot{\hat{p}}_{0h} + A^* \hat{p}_{0h} + \sum_{i=1}^N C_I^* z_i\right), \quad (3.15)$$
$$\hat{u}_{h,i} = M_i^{-1} B_i^* \left(\hat{p}_{0h} + \sum_{j=1}^N \hat{p}_{h,j} - \hat{p}_{h,i}\right), \quad i=1,\cdots,N, \quad (3.16)$$
$$\hat{x}_h^i = -\mathbb{C}_0^{-1}(\dot{\hat{p}}_{h,i} + A^* \hat{p}_{h,i} - C_i^* z_i), \quad i=1,\cdots,N, \quad (3.17)$$
$$\hat{v}_{h,i} = -M_i^{-1} B_i^* \hat{p}_{h,i}, \quad i=1,\cdots,N \quad (3.18)$$
and
$$\hat{X}_h = (\hat{x}_h^1,\cdots,\hat{x}_h^N), \quad \hat{v}_h = (\hat{v}_{h,1},\cdots,\hat{v}_{h,N}), \quad \hat{u}_h = (\hat{u}_{h,1},\cdots,\hat{u}_{h,N}).$$
Then
$$\|\hat{u} - \hat{u}_h\|_{L^2} + \|\hat{v} - \hat{v}_h\|_{[L^2]^N} \leq K_3 h^{m+i} (\|\hat{p}_0\|_{H_n^r} + \|\hat{p}\|_{[H_n^r]^N}), \quad (3.19)$$
$$\|\hat{x} - \hat{x}_h\|_{L^2} + \|\hat{X} - \hat{X}_h\|_{[L^2]^N} \leq K_3 h^m (\|\hat{p}_0\|_{H_n^r} + \|\hat{p}\|_{[H_n^r]^N}), \quad (3.20)$$
for some $K_3 > 0$ independent of $\hat{x},\hat{u},\hat{X},\hat{v},p_0$ and p.

The convergence rate (3.19) is the sharpest possible[2],[14]. The rate (3.20) is not optimal. To obtain a faster rate of convergence for x and X, we can use $\hat{u}_h$ and $\hat{v}_h$ in $(DE) = 0$ and $(DE)_i = 0, i=1,\cdots,N$, and integrate to solve for more accurate x and X.

4 Examples and Computation Results

In this section, we apply the finite element method and the penalty method to some examples and present our numerical results.

Example 4.1 We consider the following two-person non-zero-sum game:

$$\dot{x}(t) = x(t) + u_1(t) + 2u_2(t) + 1, \quad t \in [0, T], \quad T = \pi/4,$$
$$x(0) = 0,$$
$$J_1(x, u) = \int_0^T [|x(t) + (\cos t + 1/2)|^2 + 1/2|u_1(t)|^2] dt,$$
$$J_2(x, u) = \int_0^T [|x(t) - \sin t|^2 + 2|u_2(t)|^2] dt. \tag{4.1}$$

The Lagrangian $\mathbb{L}$ in (2.13) corresponding to this problem is

$$\begin{aligned} L(p_0, p_1, p_2) = &-1/2\langle \dot{p}_0 + p_0, 1/2(\dot{p}_0 + p_0)\rangle + 1/2[\langle \dot{p}_1 + p_1, \dot{p}_1 + p_1\rangle \\ &+ \langle \dot{p}_2 + p_2, \dot{p}_2 + p_2\rangle] - 1/2\langle p_0 + p_1 + p_2, 4(p_0 + p_1 + p_2)\rangle \\ &+ \langle p_0 + p_1 + p_2, 2p_1 + 2p_2\rangle - \langle \dot{p}_0 + p_0, 1/2[(\cos t + 1/2) + \sin t]\rangle \\ &- [\langle \dot{p}_1 + p_1, \cos t + 1/2\rangle + \langle \dot{p}_2 + p_2, \sin t\rangle] - \langle p_0 + p_1 + p_2, 1\rangle \\ &- 1/2\langle 1/2[-(\cos t + 1/2) + \sin t], -(\cos t + 1/2) + \sin t\rangle \\ &+ 1/2[\langle \cos t + 1/2, \cos t + 1/2\rangle + \langle \sin t, \sin t\rangle]. \end{aligned} \tag{4.2}$$

In order to apply the theory and analysis in Section 3 to this example, we need to verify that assumptions (A2), (A3) and (A4) are satisfied, and

(A0)' $\min\max_{\substack{(x,u) \\ \text{feasible}}} \max_{\substack{(X,v) \\ \text{feasible}}} F(x, u; X, v) = 0$ holds so that the differential game has a solution $(\hat{x}, \hat{u})$.

Instead of checking (A0)' directly, we show that the "decision operator" $\mathbb{D}$ as defined in (2.6) in Part I[6] is invertible so that the differential game has a unique solution, so (A0)' is satisfied. But here

$$\mathbb{D} = \begin{bmatrix} M_1 + L_1^* C_1^* C_1 L_1 & L_1^* C_1^* C_1 L_2 \\ L_2^* C_2^* C_2 L_1 & M_2 + L_2^* C_2^* C_2 L_2 \end{bmatrix} = \begin{bmatrix} 1/2I + L_1^* L_1 & 2L_1^* L_1 \\ 2L_1^* L_1 & 2I + 4L_1^* L_1 \end{bmatrix} \tag{4.3}$$

because $L_2 = 2L_1$ and $L_2^* = 2L_1^*$, and $C_1 = C_2 = 1$, $C_1^* = C_2^* = 1$, where

$$L_1 : U \to H_n^1(0, t), \quad L_1 u = \int_0^t e^{t-s} u(s) ds.$$

We easily see that $\mathbb{D}$ in (4.3) above is symmetric and strictly positive denfinite, so $\mathbb{D}$ is invertible. Hence (A0)' is satisfied.

To check (A2), we write out $\psi(x, u)$ explicitly:

$$\begin{aligned} \psi(x, u) = &1/2\{\|x(t) + (\cos t + 1/2)\|^2 + 1/2\|u_1(t)\|^2 + \|x(t) - \sin t\|^2 + 2\|u_2(t)\|^2 \\ &- \|L_0 x_0 + L_1 u_1 + L_3 f - \sin t\|^2 - \|L_0 x_0 + 2L_1 u_2 + L_3 f + (\cos t + 1/2)\|^2 \\ &+ \langle L_1^* (L_0 x_0 + 2L_1 u_2 + L_3 f + (\cos t + 1/2)), (1/2I + L_1^* L_1)^{-1} L_1^* (L_0 x_0 \\ &+ 2L_1 u_2 + L_3 f + (\cos t + 1/2))\rangle + \langle 2L_1^* (L_0 x_0 + L_1 u_1 + L_3 f - \sin t), \\ &(2I + 4L_1^* L_1)^{-1} 2L_1^* (L_0 x_0 + L_1 u_1 + IL_3 f - \sin t)\rangle, \end{aligned} \tag{4.4}$$

where we have used $L_2 = 2L_1, L_2^* = 2L_1^*, C_1 = C_2 = I, C_1^* = C_2^* = I$ and

$$L_0 x_0 = e^t x_0, \quad L_3 = \int_0^t e^{t-s} f(s) \, ds.$$

In (4.4), it is easy to see that $\psi(x,u)$ is convex with respect to x because $\psi(x,u)$ has $\|x\|^2$ as the only quadratic term involving x. The quadratic terms involving u_1 and u_2 are

$$1/2 \{\langle [1/2I - L_1^* L_1 + 4 L_1^* L_1 (2I + 4 L_1^* L_1)^{-1} L_1^* L_1] u_1, u_1 \rangle$$
$$+ \langle [2I - 4 L_1^* L_1 + 4 L_1^* L_1 (1/2I + L_1^* L_1)^{-1} L_1^* L_1] u_2, u_2 \rangle \}$$
$$= 1/2 \{\langle (2I + 4 L_1^* L_1)^{-1} [1/2I + 4 L_1^* L_1) - (2I + 4 L_1^* L_1) L_1^* L_1$$
$$+ 4(L_1^* L_1)(L_1^* L_1)] u_1, u_1 \rangle + \langle (2I + 4 L_1^* L_1^*)^{-1} [2(2I + 4 L_1^* L_1)$$
$$- 4(2I + 4 L_1^* L_1) L_1^* L_1 + 16(L_1^* L_1)(L_1^* L_1)] u_2, u_2 \rangle \}$$
$$= 1/2 \{\langle (2I + 4 L_1^* L_1)^{-1} u_1, u_1 \rangle + 4 \langle (2I + 4 L_1^* L_1)^{-1} u_2, u_2 \rangle \}.$$

The above is a strictly positive definite quadratic form in u_1 and u_2. Therefore, $\psi(x,u)$ is also convex with respect to $u=(u_1,u_2)$. In fact, in this example, $\psi(x,u)$ is strictly convex with respect to x and u.

It is easy to see that (A3) is satisfied, so only (A4) remains. This can be done straight forwardly from (4.2) with little work. Hence all assumptions have been verified and by Theorem 2.5 $(\hat{x}, \hat{u})$ is the solution.

We choose a (4.1)-system of Hermite cubic splines as in [15]. The interval $[0, T]$ is divided into N equal subintervals, each with mesh length $h = T/N$. The matrix M_h is a $(6N+3) \times (6N+3)$ matrix. We use the IMSL high accuracy subroutine LEQ2S to solve the matrix equation $\overline{M}_h \overline{\gamma}_h = \overline{\theta}_h$ with double precision on an IBM370/model 3033 at Pennsylvania State University.

In Table 1, we list some values of $\hat{u}_1, \hat{u}_2, \hat{x}, \hat{x}^1, \hat{x}^2, \hat{p}_0, \hat{p}_1$ and p_2 at certain selected nodal points. For this example, there is no known closed form exact solutions to compare. Therefore, the only way to show that our numerical scheme works is to check the rate of convergence (3.13) by a different method; see Example 4.1. Using the data, we have plotted the logarithmic error graph. The asymptotic rate of convergence, which is indicated by the slope of line segment is $O(h^{6.2})$ which is extremely close to the predicted rate $O(h^6)$ in (3.13). Note here that $m=4-1=3$, so $2m=6$ in (3.13), provided that $(\hat{p}_0, \hat{p})$ is at least $H_1^3 \times [H_1^3]^2$ regular.

Example 4.2 We consider the following 2-person non-zero-sum game:

$$\dot{x}(t) = x(t) + \cos t u_1(t) + \sin t u_2(t) + 1, \, 0 \leqslant t \leqslant 2\pi,$$
$$x(0) = 0,$$
$$J_1(x,u) = \int_0^T [|x(t) + (\cos t + 1/2)|^2 + 1/3 u_1^2(t)] dt,$$
$$J_2(x,u) = \int_0^T [|x(t) - 0.9 \sin t|^2 + u_2(t)] dt.$$

It is not clear to us as to whether conditions (A0)', (A2), (A3) and (A4) are satisfied. The numerical evidence below suggests that the rate of convergence of L to 0 is not close to $O(h^6)$, thus it is likely that Corollaries 2.1 and 3.1 do not hold for this example. Thus we believe at least one of the conditions (A0)', (A2), (A3), and (A4) is violated.

Using the computational scheme in Section 3, we obtain

$$L=1.493\times 10^{-1}, \quad h=2\pi/4; \quad L=4.646\times 10^{-2}, \quad h=2\pi/8;$$
$$L=1.267\times 10^{-2}, \quad h=2\pi/16; L=1.771\times 10^{-2}, \quad h=2\pi/32;$$
$$L=1.1755\times 10^{-2}, \quad h=2\pi/64.$$

The logarithmic error is also plotted. Here we find that the rate of convergence is $O(h^{1.93})$ at best, which is way off the predicted rate $O(h^6)$.

Table 1. Numerical Values of u_1, u_2, x, x^1, x^2, P_0, P_1 and P_2 at $t=\frac{1}{4}\cdot\frac{\pi}{4}$, $\frac{1}{2}\cdot\frac{\pi}{4}$, $\frac{3}{4}\cdot\frac{\pi}{4}$, and $\frac{\pi}{4}$ for Example 1.

	$t=\frac{1}{4}\cdot\frac{\pi}{4}$			$t=\frac{1}{2}\cdot\frac{\pi}{4}$		
	$h=\frac{\pi}{4}/16$	$h=\frac{\pi}{4}/32$	$h=\frac{\pi}{4}/64$	$h=\frac{\pi}{4}/16$	$h=\frac{\pi}{4}/32$	$h=\frac{\pi}{4}/64$
u_1	-2.020419	-2.078747	-2.078747	-1.239453	-1.239453	-1.239453
u_2	0.441072	0.441072	0.441072	0.285282	0.285282	0.285282
x	-0.125895	-0.125896	-0.125896	-0.136733	-0.136733	-0.136733
x^1	-0.125895	-0.125896	-0.125896	-0.136733	-0.136733	-0.136733
x^2	-0.125895	-0.125896	-0125896	-0.136733	-0.136733	-0.136733
P_0	-0.598302	-0.598302	-0.598302	-0.334444	-0.334444	-0.334444
P_1	1.039374	1.039374	1.039374	0.619726	0.619726	0.619726
P_2	-0.441072	-0.441072	-0.441072	-0.285282	-0.285282	-0.285282

	$t=\frac{3}{4}\cdot\frac{\pi}{4}$			$t=\frac{\pi}{4}=T$		
	$h=\frac{\pi}{4}/16$	$h=\frac{\pi}{4}/32$	$h=\frac{\pi}{4}/64$	$h=\frac{\pi}{4}/16$	$h=\frac{\pi}{4}/32$	$h=\frac{\pi}{4}/64$
u_1	-0.562914	-0.562913	-0.562913	0.0	0.0	0.0
u_2	0.131964	0.131964	0.131964	0.0	0.0	0.0
x	-0.053732	-0.053732	-0.053732	0.118645	0.118645	0.118646
x^1	-0.053731	-0.053732	-0.053732	0.118645	0.118646	0.118646
x^2	-0.053732	-0.053732	-0.053732	0.118644	0.118645	0.118646
P_0	-0.149492	-0.149492	-0.149492	0.0	0.0	0.0
P_1	0.281457	0.281457	0.281457	0.0	0.0	0.0
P_2	-0.131964	-0.131964	-0.131964	0.0	-0.0	-0.0

Remark 4.1 The numerical values of v_1, v_2 are identical, respectively, with u_1, u_2. All entries above are rounded off figures with six decimal place accuracy. "″" entries have the same values as the one immediately above.

The penalty method developed in Section 3 can also be combined with finite elements to do numerical calculations. Analysis of error can be found in [5]. The penalty-finite element scheme seems to be less stable than the duality-finite element as given in Section 3, and its error estimates are hard to verify experimentally. We have successfully computed Example 4.1 by the penalty-finite element scheme, as shown below.

Example 4.3 We consider the very same example as in (4.1). $F_e(x, u; X, v)$ is given as in [7]. We choose for x, x^1 and x^2 approximation spaces S_h^0 which are a $(3,1)$-system of quadratic splines, and use a $(2,0)$-system of piecewise linear elements as approximation spaces S_h^1 for u_1, u_2, v_1 and v_2.

Numerical data for $\hat{u}_1$, $\hat{u}_2$ and $\hat{x}$ at selected points are given in Table 2 below, with
$$h=(\pi/4)/32, \quad \text{uniform meshes for } S_h^0, \quad \text{and } S_h^1, \quad e_0=e_1=e_2.$$
They compare very well with the duality-finite element solutions, which use $(4,1)$-cubics and $h=(\pi/4)/32$.

Note that numerical solutions of $\hat{x}^1, \hat{x}^2, \hat{v}_1$ and $\hat{v}_2$ also satisfy
$$\hat{x}^1=\hat{x}^2=\hat{x}, \quad \hat{v}_1=\hat{u}_1, \quad \hat{v}_2=\hat{u}_2.$$
For more numerical examples and detailed discussions, see [7].

Table 2. P_1: penalty solution with $e_0=e_1=e_2=10^{-3}$.
P_2: penalty solution with $e_0=e_1=e_2=10^{-5}$.
D: duality solution.

	$t=$	$(\pi/4)/4$	$(\pi/4)/2$	$(\pi/4)(3/4)$	$\pi/4=T$
u_1	P_1	-2.077473	-1.238577	-0.562432	0.000086
	P_2	-2.078433	-1.239262	-0.562789	-0.004539
	D	-2.078747	-1.239453	-0.562913	0.0
u_2	P_1	0.440848	0.285103	0.131847	-0.000053
	P_2	0.441103	0.285264	0.131923	-0.002366
	D	0.441072	0.285282	0.131964	0.0
u_x	P_1	-0.125946	-0.136808	-0.053823	0.118535
	P_2	-0.125870	-0.136707	-0.053713	0.118661
	D	-0.125896	-0.136733	-0.053732	-0.118645

References

[1] I. Babuska, A. K. Aziz. The Mathematical Foundations of the Finite Element Method with Applications to Partial Differential Equations [M]. A. K. Aziz, ed., Academic Press, New York, 1972.

[2] W. E. Bosarge, O. G. Johnson. Error bounds of high order accuracy for the state regulator problem via piecewise polynomial approximation [J]. *SIAM J. Control*, 9(1971),15—28.

[3] G. Chen and W. H. Mills. Finite elements and terminal penalization for quadratic cost optimal control problems governed by ordinary differential equations [J]. *SIAM J. Contrl Opt.*, 19(1981), 749—764.

[4] G. Chen, W. H. Mills, S. Sun and D. Yost. Sharp error estimates for a finite elementpenalty approach to a class of regulator problems [J]. *Math, Comp.*, 37(1983), 151—173.

[5] G. Chen, Q. Zheng, G. Chen, W. H. Miles, Q. Zheng and W. Shaw. Minimax methods for open-loop equilibra in differential games [R]. NASA Contractor Report 16110 and 16111, ICASE, Hampton, Virginia, April 1983.

[6] G. Chen, Q. Zheng and J. X. Zhou. Minimax methods for open-loop equilibra in N-person differential games. Part I [C]. Proceedings of Royal Society of Edunburgh, 103A, 1986, 15—24.

[7] G. Chen and Q. Zheng. Minimax methods for open-loop equilibra in N-person differential games. Part II, preprint.

[8] P. G. Ciarlet. The Finite Element Method for Elliptic Problems [M]. North Holland, Amsterdam, 1978.

[9] T. Eisele. Non-existence and non-uniqueness of open-loop equilibra in linear-quadratic differential games [J]. *J. Opt. Theory Appl.*, 37(1982), 443—468.

[10] A. Friedman. Differential Games [M]. Wiley-Interscience, New York, 1971.

[11] W. W. Hager and S. K. Mitter. Lagrange duality theory for convex control problems [J]. *SIAM J. Control Opt.*, 14(1976), 843—856.

[12] R. Issacs. Differential Games [M]. Wiley, New York, 1965.

[13] D. L. Lukes and D. L. Russell. A global theory for linear quadratic differential games [J]. *J. Math. Anal. Appl.*, 33(1971), 96—123.

[14] F. H. Maths and G. W. Rddien. Ritz-Treftz approximation in optimal control [J]. *SIAM J. Control Opt.*, 17(1979), 307—310.

[15] G. Strang and G. Fix. An Analysis of the Finite Element Method [M]. Prentice-Hall, Englewood Cliffs, New Jersey, 1973.

A Method for Approximating Solutions of Multicriterial Nonlinear Optimization Problems*

Abstract: An algorithm for approximating solutions of multicriterial nonlinear optimization problems of a class of discontinuous objective functions with disconnected constraint set is proposed in the framework of integral based optimization theory under some weak general assumptions. Numerical examples are given to illustrate the effectiveness of the algorithm.

1 Introduction

Let X be a topological space, $\mathbf{f}: X \to \mathbb{R}^n$ a mapping and S a nonempty subset of X. Consider the following multicriterial optimization problem:

$$\mathbf{f}(\bar{x}) = \inf_{x \in S} \mathbf{f}(x) \tag{1.1}$$

Let C be a pointed cone of $\mathbb{R}^n$ to define the order of points in this space. Especially, we may take

$$C = O = \{y = (y^1, \cdots, y^n)^T \in \mathbb{R}^n : y^i \geqslant 0, i=1, \cdots, n\}, \tag{1.2}$$

the nonnegative orthant of $\mathbb{R}^n$.

Definition 1.1 An element $\bar{x} \in S$ is called a minimal point of $\mathbf{f}$ over S if

$$(\{\mathbf{f}(\bar{x})\} - C) \cap \mathbf{f}(S) = \{\mathbf{f}(\bar{x})\}.$$

An element $\bar{x} \in S$ is called a weakly minimal element of $\mathbf{f}$ over S if

$$(\{\mathbf{f}(\bar{x})\} - \mathrm{int}\, C) \cap \mathbf{f}(S) = \varnothing.$$

Note that instead of the orthant O of (1.2), we may use another pointed cone C in $\mathbb{R}^n$ to define the order.

In this work we will study the problem of determining the solution set M of (1.1) and the set $\mathbf{f}(M)$. For the case $n=2$, Polak (1976) proposed a spline approximation to $\mathbf{f}(M)$, Jahn and Merker (1992) proposed a piecewise linear approximation to $\mathbf{f}(M)$. They use the following algorithm.

(1) Determine an interval $[a, b]$ on y^1-axis, where

$$\begin{cases} a := \min_{x \in S} f^1(x), \\ b := f^1(\hat{x}), \quad \text{with} \quad f^2(\hat{x}) = \min_{x \in S} f^2(x). \end{cases} \tag{1.3}$$

---

* In collaboration with Kostreva M M, Zhuang D M. Reprinted from Optimization Methods and Software, 1995, 5: 209—226.

(2) Discretize the interval $[a, b]$ by $m+1$ points:
$$y_k^1 := a + k(b-a)/m, \quad \text{for} \quad k = 0, 1, \cdots, m$$
where m is a given positive integer. For each point y_k^1, $k = 0, 1, \cdots, m$ solve the following minimization problem:
$$\min_{x \in S, f^1(x) = y_k^1} f^2(x). \tag{1.4}$$
Then we obtain a minimizer x_k and $y_k = \mathbf{f}(x_k)$.

(3) Select a decreasing sequence
$$y_{k_1}^2 > y_{k_2}^2 > y_{k_3}^2 > \cdots,$$
so that the set $\{x_{k_1}, x_{k_2}, \cdots, x_{k_l}\}$ is an approximation of the set M of minimizers.

(4) If the set $\mathbf{f}(M)$ is connected, Polak uses splines to connect the points $\mathbf{f}(x_{k_j})$ and Jahn and Merker use piecewise straight lines.

To solve a minimization problem (1.4), a global minimization problem with constraints, a tunneling technique (see [5]) is applied.

Note that the above algorithm can only be applied to approximate $\mathbf{f}(M)$ of bicriterial objective function. We also note that the tunneling technique is combining with a local minimization algorithm which is usuall gradient-based. If the objective function in (1.4) is nonsmooth, then this approach is not valid.

Scalarization of multicriterial nonlinear optimization problems is a widely used tool for finding their solutions numerically; see, for instance, [6] and [7]. There are still other approaches without using scalarized objective function, see [1] and [2]. In this research, we popose a method for approximating $\mathbf{f}(M)$ by using scalarization and simplices. The multicriterial problem is turned into a set of constrained scalar global minimization problems. We use the integral global optimization (see [13-15]) to solve these scalar minimization problems.

In this paper, we first review basic concepts of robust sets, functions and mappings in Section 2, which are useful in the remaining consideration. In Section 3, we consider a general scalarization procedure for an upper robust mapping and study optimality conditions of the scalarized problem. We propose an algorithm for approximating solutions of multicriteral optimization problems in Section 4; these problems may have *discontinuous objective functions with disconnected constraint set*. Numerical examples are given in Section 5 to illustrate the algorithm. In Section 6, some concluding remarks are given.

2 Integral Global Minimization

In this section we will summarize several concepts and properties of the integral global minimization of robust discontinuous functions, which will be utilized in the following sections. For more details, see [13-15].

2.1 Robust Sets, Functions and Mappings

Let X be a topological space, a set D in X is said to be *robust* if

$$\text{cl } D = \text{cl int } D, \tag{2.1}$$

where cl D denotes the closure of the set D and int D the interior of D.

A robust set consists of *robust points* of the set. A point $x \in \text{cl } D$ is said to be robust to D (or a robust point of D if $x \in D$), if for each neighbourhood $N(x)$ of x, $N(x) \cap \text{int } D \neq \emptyset$. A set D is robust if and only if each point of D is robust to D. If x is a robust point of a set D, then D is called a *semineighborhood* of x. A point $x \in D$ is a robust point of D if and only if there exists a net $\{x_\lambda\} \supset \text{int } D$ such that $x_\lambda \to x$.

An open set G is robust since $G = \text{int } G$. The empty set is a trivial robust set. A closed set may be robust or nonrobust. The concept of the robustness of a set is closely related to a topological structure of the space X. For instance, the set $D = \{1, 2\}$ is nonrobust in $\mathbb{R}^1$ but it is robust in $Z = \{$set of all integers with the discrete topology$\}$.

The interior of a nonempty robust set is nonempty. A union of robust sets is robust. An intersection of two robust sets may be nonrobust; but the intersection of an open set and a robust set is robust. If A is robust in X and B is robust in Y, then $A \times B$ is robust in $X \times Y$ with the product topology. A convex set D in a topological vector space is robust if and only if the interior of D is nonempty. A set D is robust if and only if $\partial D = \partial \text{ int } D$, where $\partial D = \text{cl } D \backslash \text{int } D$ denotes the boundary of the set D. A robust set can be represented as a union of an open set and a *nowhere dense* set.

A function $f: X \to \mathbb{R}$ is said to be *upper robust* if the set

$$F_c = \{x: f(x) < c\} \tag{2.2}$$

is robust for each real number c.

An upper semicontinuous (u.s.c.) function is upper robust since (2.2) is open for each c; so is a probability function of $\mathbb{R}^n$. The infimum of a family of upper robust functions is upper robust. A sum or a product of two upper robust functions may be non upper robust; but the sum of an upper robust function and an u.s.c. (for the product case nonnegativity is required) function is upper robust. If X is a complete metric space, then the set of points of discontinuity (continuity) of an upper robust function is of first (second) category.

A function f is upper robust if and only if it is upper robust at each point; f is upper robust at a pont x if $x \in F_c$ implies x is a robust point of F_c. An example of a non upper robust function on $\mathbb{R}^1$ is

$$f(x) = \begin{cases} 0, & x = 0, \\ 1, & x \neq 0. \end{cases}$$

f is not upper robust at $x = 0$.

Let S be a robust set in a topological space (X, τ), where τ is the topology of X. We can introduce a relative topology τ_S and obtain a new topological space (S, τ_S). In this new topological space, we also have concepts of robust set and upper robust function with this relative topology. Then we have oncepts of relative robust set and relative upper robust function.

In [9, 10], robust and approximatable mapping and set-valued mapping are studied.

Let X and Y be topological spaces. A mapping $f: X \to Y$ is said to be *robust* if for each open set $G \subset Y$, $f^{-1}(G)$ is a robust set in X.

Suppose C is the set of points of continuity of f. f is said to be *approximatable* iff C is dense in X and for each $\bar{x} \in X$, there exists a net $\{x_a\} \subset C$ such that
$$\lim_a x_a = \bar{x} \quad \text{and} \quad \lim_a f(x_a) = f(\bar{x})$$

An approximatable mapping is robust. If X is a Baire space and satisfies the second axiom of countability, then a mapping is robust if and only if it is approximatable.

2.2 Q-Measure Spaces and Integration

In order to investigate a minimization problem with an integral approach, special class of measure spaces, which are called Q-measure spaces, should be examined.

Let X be a topological space, Ω a σ-field of subsets of X and μ a measure on Ω. A triple (X, Ω, μ) is called a Q-measure space iff

(i) Each open set in X is measurable;

(ii) The measure $\mu(G)$ of each nonempty open set G in X is positive: $\mu(G) > 0$;

(iii) The measure $\mu(K)$ of a compact set K in X is finite.

The n-dimensional Lebesgue measure space $(\mathbb{R}^n, \Omega, \mu)$ is a Q-measure space; a nondegenerate Gaussian measure μ on a separable Hilbert space H with Borel sets as measurable sets constitutes an infinite dimensional Q-measure space. A specific optimization problem is related to a specific Q-measure space which is suitable for consideration in this approach.

Once a measure space is given we can define integration in a conventional way.

Since the interior if a nonempty open set is nonempty, the Q-measure of a measurable set containing a nonempty robust set is always positive. This is an essential property we need in the integral approach of minimization. Hence the following assumptions are usually required:

(A): f is lower semicontinuous and there is a real number b such thet $\{x \in S: f(x) \leqslant b\}$ is a nonempty compact set.

(R): f is upper robust on S.

(M): (X, Ω, μ) is a Q-measure space.

2.3 Integral Optimality Conditions for Global Minimization

We now proceed to defined the concepts of mean value, variance and higher moments of f over its level set. These concepts are closely related to optimality conditions and algorithms for global minimization.

Suppose that the assumptions (A), (M) and (R) hold, and $c > c^* = \min_{x \in S} f(x)$. We define the mean value, variance, modified variance and m-th moment (centered at a), respectively, as follows:

$$M(f, c; S) = \frac{1}{\mu(H_c \cap S)} \int_{H_c \cap S} f(x) \mathrm{d}\mu,$$

$$V(f, c; S) = \frac{1}{\mu(H_c \cap S)} \int_{H_c \cap S} (f(x) - M(f, c; S))^2 \mathrm{d}\mu,$$

$$V_1(f, c; S) = \frac{1}{\mu(H_c \cap S)} \int_{H_c \cap S} (f(x) - c)^2 d\mu,$$

$$M_m(f, c; a; S) = \frac{1}{\mu(H_c \cap S)} \int_{H_c \cap S} (f(x) - a)^m d\mu, \quad m = 1, 2, \cdots$$

They are well defined. These definitions can be extended to the case $c \geqslant c^*$ by a limit process. For instance,

$$M_m(f, c; a; S) = \lim_{c_k \downarrow c} \frac{1}{\mu(H_{c_k} \subset S)} \int_{H_{c_k} \cap S} (f(x) - a)^m d\mu, \quad m = 1, 2, \cdots$$

The limits exist and are independent of the choice of $\{c_k\}$. The extended concepts are well defined and consistent with the above definitions.

With these concepts we characterize the global optimality as follows:

Theorem 2.1 *Under the assumptions (A), (M) and (R), the following statements are equivalent*:

(i) $x^* \in S$ *is a global minimizer of f over S and $c^* = f(x^*)$ is the global minimum value*;

(ii) $M(f, c^*; S) = c^*$ (*the mean value condition*);

(iii) $V(f, c^*; S) = 0$ (*the variance condition*);

(iv) $V_1(f, c^*; S) = 0$ (*the modified variance condition*);

(v) $M_m(f, c^*; c^*; S) = 0$ *for one of the positive integers $m = 1, 2, \cdots$* (*the higher moment conditions*).

2.4 An Integral Algorithm

An integral global minimization algorithm for finding the global minimum value and the set of global minimizers of an upper robust function over a robust constraint set is given as follows:

Step 1: Take $c_0 > c^*$ and $\varepsilon > 0$; $k := 0$;

Step 2: $c_{k+1} := M(f, c_k; S)$; $v_{k+1} = V_1(f, c_k; S)$; $H_{c_{k+1}} := \{x \in S: f(x) \leqslant c_{k+1}\}$;

Step 3: If $v_{k+1} \geqslant \varepsilon$ then $k := k+1$; go to Step 2;

Step 4: $c^* \Leftarrow c_{k+1}$; $H^* \Leftarrow H_{c_{k+1}}$; Stop.

If we take $\varepsilon = 0$, the algorithm may stop in a finite number of iterations; and we obtain the global minimum value with the set of global minimizers. Or, we obtain two monotone sequences:

$$c_0 \geqslant c_1 \geqslant \cdots \geqslant c_k \geqslant c_{k+1} \geqslant \cdots$$

and

$$H_{c_0} \supset H_{c_1} \supset \cdots \supset H_{c_k} \supset H_{c_{k+1}} \supset \cdots.$$

Let

$$c^* = \lim_{k \to \infty} c_k \quad \text{and} \quad H^* = \bigcap_{k=1}^{\infty} H_{c_k},$$

then c^* is the global minimum value of f over S, and H^* is the set of global minimizers.

The algorithm has been implemented by a properly designed Monte-Carlo method. The numerical tests show that the algorithm is competitive with other algorithms.

3 Upper Robust Mappings and Their Scalarization

3.1 Upper Robust Mappings

We will mainly consider a multicriterial optimization problem of an upper robust mapping which is defined as follows. Let X be a topological space and $\mathbf{f}: X \to \mathbb{R}^n$ a mapping.

Definition 3.1 A mapping $\mathbf{f}$ is said to be upper robust at x iff for each vector $\mathbf{c}$ in $\mathbb{R}^n$,
$$x \in \mathbf{F_c} = \{x \in X : f^i(x) < c^i, i=1, \cdots, n\} \tag{3.1}$$
implies x is a robust point of $\mathbf{F_c}$. A mapping $\mathbf{f}$ is upper robust if it is upper robust at each point of $x \in X$, or $\mathbf{F_c}$ is a robust set in X for each $\mathbf{c} \in \mathbb{R}^n$.

If each of $f^i: X \to \mathbb{R}^1$, $i=1, \cdots, n$ is upper robust then $\mathbf{f} = (f^1, \cdots, f^n)^T$ may be not upper robust. If one of its components is upper robust and the remaining ones are upper semicontinuous, then $\mathbf{f}$ is and upper robust mapping. In particular, a robust piecewise continuous mapping $\mathbf{f}: X \to \mathbb{R}^n$ is upper robust.

Definition 3.2 Let X and Y be two topological spaces. A mapping $f: X \to Y$ is said to be robust piecewise continuous iff there exists a robust partition of X, i.e.,
$$X = \bigcup_{\lambda \in \Lambda} V_\lambda \text{ and } \forall \alpha \neq \lambda, V_\alpha \cap V_\lambda = \varnothing, \tag{3.2}$$
where for any λ, V_λ is robust in X, and for any $\lambda \in \Lambda$, the restriction of f to V_λ is continuous.

A robust piecewise continuous mapping is robust. If in the above definition the partition of X is not required to be *robust*, a piecewise continuous mapping may not be robust. Suppose that X is a complete metric space, $\mathbf{f}: X \to \mathbb{R}^n$ is a mapping and C is the set of points of continuity. Then $\mathbf{f}$ is upper robust at a minimal point x^* if and only if there exists a sequence $\{x_k\} \subset C$ such that
$$x_k \to x^* \text{ and } \limsup_{k \to \infty} f^i(x_k) = f^i(x^*), \forall_i = 1, \cdots, n. \tag{3.3}$$

Example 3.1 A multicriterial integer programming problem can be converted as a problem of a robust piecewise continuous mapping (see [4] Example 3.1).

For more details on upper robust mapping, also see [4].

3.2 Scalarization of an Upper Robust Mapping

Definition 3.3 Let D be a nonempty subset of a partially ordered real linear topological space Y with an ordering cone C and $y, z \in D$.
$$y \leq z \Leftrightarrow y \in (\{z\} - C) \cap D.$$
$$y < z \Leftrightarrow y \in (\{z\} - \text{int } C) \cap D.$$

Definition 3.4 Let $G: S \subset \mathbb{R}^n \to \mathbb{R}^1$. G is said to be monotonic if
$$y \leq z \Rightarrow G(y) \leq G(z) \text{ and } y < z \Rightarrow G(y) < G(z).$$

Theorem 3.1 *Suppose $\mathbf{f}: X \to \mathbb{R}^n$ is a mapping defined on a topological space and $G: \mathbb{R}^n \to \mathbb{R}^1$ is a monotonic real-valued function. Then*

(1) A point x^* is an optimal solution if

$$G(f(x^*)) < G(f(x)), \quad \forall x \in S, \ x \neq x^*.$$

(2) A *point x^* is a weakly optimal solution if*
$$G(f(x^*)) < G(f(x)), \quad \forall x \in S.$$

Proof. Suppose $x^* \in S$ is not an minimal solution. Then there is a point $\bar{x} \in S$ such that $f(\bar{x}) \neq f(x^*)$ and
$$f(\bar{x}) \in (\{f(x^*)\} - C) \cap f(S).$$
This implies
$$f(\bar{x}) \leq f(x^*) \quad \text{and} \quad G(f(\bar{x})) \leqslant G(f(x^*)),$$
which is a contradiction.

Suppose $x^* \in S$ is not weakly minimal solution. Then
$$(f(x^*) - \text{int } C) \cap f(S) \neq \emptyset.$$
Thus, there is a point $\bar{x} \in S$, such that
$$f(\bar{x}) \in f(x^*) - \text{int } C) \cap f(S).$$
This implies
$$f(\bar{x}) < f(x^*) \quad \text{and} \quad G(f(\bar{x})) < G(f(x^*)),$$
which is also a contradiction.

The composed function $G(\mathbf{f}(x))$ in Theorem 3.1 may be non robust no matter how well behaved the mapping $\mathbf{f}$ would be.

Example 3.2 Let $G: \mathbb{R}^1 \to \mathbb{R}^1$ be a strict increasing function defined as
$$G(y) = \begin{cases} y - 1, & \text{if } y < 0, \\ 0, & \text{if } y = 0, \\ y + 1, & \text{if } y > 0 \end{cases}$$
and $f: \mathbb{R}^1 \to \mathbb{R}^1$ be defined as
$$f(x) = x^2.$$
Then the composed function is
$$G(f(x)) = \begin{cases} x^2 + 1, & \text{if } x \neq 0, \\ 0, & \text{if } x = 0. \end{cases}$$
The function $G(f(x))$ is non robust.

Theorem 3.2 *Let $f: X \to \mathbb{R}^n$ be an upper robust mapping on a topological space X. Suppose $G: \mathbb{R}^n \to \mathbb{R}^1$ is a real-valued function satisfying the following conditions:*

(1) $G(y^1, \cdots, y^n)$ *is an increasing function with respect to each variable;*

(2) G *is upper semicontionus.*

Then the composite real-valued function $G(\mathbf{f}(\mathbf{x}))$ is an upper robust function on X.

Proof. For each real number d, we first prove the following set equality:
$$A = \{x: G(f^1(x), \cdots, f^n(x)) < d\} = B, \tag{3.4}$$
where
$$B = \bigcup_{G(c^1, \cdots, c^n) < d} \{x: f^1(x) < c^1, \cdots, f^n(x) < c^n\}. \tag{3.5}$$

Indeed, let x is a point in B, then x is in one of the sets in the above union (3.5), i.e., there is a point $(c^{1'}, \cdots, c^n)$ such that

$$G(c^1, \cdots, c^n) < d \quad \text{and} \quad F^1(x) < c^1, \cdots, f^n(x) < c^n.$$

Thus, by monotonicity assumption of G, we have

$$G(f^1(x), \cdots, f^n(x)) \leqslant G(c^1, \cdots, C^n) < d.$$

This proves that $B \subset A$.

Conversely, suppose x is a point in A and let $c^1 = f^1(x), \cdots, c^n = f^n(x)$. Then $G(c^1, \cdots, c^n) < d$. This implies, by the upper semicontinuity of G that there is $\varepsilon > 0$ such that

$$G(c^1 + \varepsilon, \cdots, c^n + \varepsilon) < d \quad \text{and} \quad f^i(x) = c^i < c^i + \varepsilon.$$

This means that $x \in B$, or $A \subset B$. Therefore we obtain the set equality (3.4).

Now for each given real number d, the set $\{x : G(f^1(x), \cdots, f^n(x)) < d\}$ is a union of sets with the form $\{x : f^1(x) < c^1, \cdots f^n(x) < c^n\}$. Since $\mathbf{f}$ is assumed to be an upper robust mapping, the sets in the union (3.5) are all robust. As a union of robust sets, the set A is robust. Hence, $G(\mathbf{f}(x))$ is an upper robust function.

Remark 3.1 For different quantities of sizes, weights, etc., people may have different preferences. For instance, prices of potato are a function $p(x)$ of weights x:

$$p(x) = \begin{cases} 20, & 0 \leqslant x < 5, \\ 15, & 5 \leqslant x < 50, \\ 5, & 50 \leqslant x < 1000, \\ 2, & x \geqslant 1000. \end{cases}$$

Thus, the cost function $c(x)$ is

$$c(x) = \begin{cases} 20, & 0 \leqslant x < 5, \\ 15x, & 5 \leqslant x < 50, \\ 5x, & 50 \leqslant x < 1000, \\ 2x, & x \geqslant 1000. \end{cases}$$

It is a discontinuous increasing function. Hence, applying a discontinuous scalarization, as we are doing here, is reasonable in physical or/and economical sense. People usually avoid using this kind of scalarization because it introduces difficulty, which cannot be handled by gradient-based theory.

Example 3.3 Let $d^i(y^i)$ be an increasing and upper semicontinuous function of variable y^i, $i = 1, \cdots$, and let

$$G(y, \cdots, y^n) = \sum_{i=1}^{i} d^i(y^i). \tag{3.6}$$

The function G defined by (3.6) is upper semicontinuous and increasing with respect to each variable. Thus, this function satisfies conditions of Theorem 3.2. Especially, let $d^i(y^i) = w^i y^i$, $i = 1, \cdots, n$ with a given nonnegative weights $w^1, \cdots, w^n$, we have

$$G(y^1, \cdots, y^n) = \sum_{i=1}^{n} w^i y^i. \tag{3.7}$$

With function (3.7), we have the weighting problem

$$\min_{x \in S} \sum_{i=1}^{n} w^i f^i(x), \tag{3.8}$$

By Theorem 3.2, we have the following corollary:

Corollary 3.1 *Suppose X is a topological space, $\mathbf{f}: X \to \mathbb{R}^n$ is an upper robust mapping and $w = (w^1, \cdots, w^n)^T$, here $w^i \geq 0$, $i=1, \cdots, n$. Then*
$$(\mathbf{w}, \mathbf{f}) = w^1 f^1 + \cdots + w^n f^m \tag{3.9}$$
is an upper robust function on S.

Example 3.4 Let $d^i(y^i)$ be an increasing and upper semicontinuous function of variable y^i, $i=1, \cdots$, and let
$$G(y^1, \cdots, y^n) = \max_{i=1, \cdots, n} d^i(y^i) \tag{3.10}$$

The function G defined by (3.10) is upper semicontinuous and increasing with respect to each variable. Thus, this function satisfies conditions of Theorem 3.2. Especially, let $d^i(y^i) = w^i(y^i - \hat{y}^i)$, $i=1, \cdots, n$ with a given nonnagative weight $w^1, \cdots, w^n$, where $(\hat{y}^1, \cdots, \hat{y}^n)$ is a given reference point, then we have
$$G(y^1, \cdots, y^n) = \max_{i=1, \cdots, n} \{w^i(y^i - \hat{y}^i)\}. \tag{3.11}$$

The function (3.11) is upper robust. With the function (3.11), we have an upper robust objective function
$$g_d(x) = \max_{i=1, \cdots, n} \{w^i(f^i(x) - \hat{y}^i)\}. \tag{3.12}$$

Remark 3.2 Recall the concept of the reference point as follows.

Definition 3.5 Let $\mathbf{f}: X \to \mathbb{R}^n$ be a mapping. A point $\hat{y} \in \mathbb{R}^n$ is called a reference point $\hat{y}^j < f^j(x)$, $\forall x \in X$ and $j=1, \cdots, n$

For instance, let
$$y^{*j} < \inf f^j(x), j=1, \cdots, n$$
and $y^* = (y^{*1}, \cdots, y^{*n})^T$, then y^* is a reference point.

With a reference point $\hat{\mathbf{y}}$, we may also consider a scalarization as follows. Let
$$g_d(x) = \sum_{i=1}^{n} w^i d^i(\hat{y}^i, f^i(x)). \tag{3.13}$$
where $w^i \geq 0$, $j=1, \cdots, n$ are weights and $d^j(.,.)$, $j=1, \cdots, n$ are increasing upper semicontinuous functions with $d^j(y^j, y^j) = 0, j=1, \cdots, n$.
$$d^j(y^j, f^j(x)) = f^j(x) - y^j, \tag{3.14}$$
then
$$g_d(x) = \sum_{j=1}^{n} w^j(f^j(x) - \hat{y}^j) = \sum_{j=1}^{n} w^j f^j(x) - \sum_{j=1}^{n} w^j \hat{y}^j = \langle \mathbf{w}, \mathbf{f} \rangle - \langle \mathbf{w}, \hat{\mathbf{y}} \rangle.$$
With the metrics (3.14), we have a problem which is equivalent to the weighted scalarization.

Definition 3.6 A solution $\hat{x}$ of the minimization problem
$$\min_{x \in S} g_d(x)$$
is called a reference-point solution corresponding to reference point $\hat{\mathbf{y}}$, metrics $d^1, \cdots, d^n$ and weights $w^1, \cdots, w^n$.

Corollary 3.2 *Let X be a topological space, $\mathbf{f}: X \to \mathbb{R}^n$ an upper robust mapping, $w^j \geq 0$, $j=1, \cdots, n$ a given weights and $\hat{\mathbf{y}}$ a given reference point. Suppose that for each j, $d^j(\hat{y}^j, \cdot)$ is a nonnegative increasing upper semicontinuous function of $y^j \geq \hat{y}^j$ $j=1, \cdots, n$. Then*

$$g_d(x) = \sum_{j=1}^{n} w^j d^i(\hat{y}^j, f^j(x))$$

is an upper robust function.

3.3 Optimdlity Conditions of Vector Optimization

In [4], we study the optimality conditions of a scalarization of an upper robust mapping. They are special cases of Theorem 3.3.

Combining Theorem 2.1 with Theorem 3.2, we have the following theorem.

Theorem 3.3 *Let X be a topological space*, $\mathbf{f}:X\to \mathbb{R}^n$ *an upper robust mapping* $G:\mathbb{R}^n\to \mathbb{R}^1$ *be a monotonic upper semicontinuous function. Under the assumptions of (A) and (M) for G(**f**), the following statements are equivalent*:

(i) $x^* \in S$ *is a solution of the problem* (1.1) *and* $c^* = G(f(x^*))$ *is the corresponding value*;

(ii) $M(G(\mathbf{f}), c^*; S) = c^*$ (*the mean value condition*);

(iii) $V(G(\mathbf{f}), c^*; S) = 0$ (*the variance condition*);

(iv) $V_1(G(\mathbf{f}), c^*; S) = 0$ (*the modified variance condition*);

(v) $M_m(G(\mathbf{f}), c^*; c^*; S) = 0$, *for one of the positive integers* $m = 1, 2, \cdots$ (*the higher moment conditions*).

Corollary 3.3 *Let X be a topological space*, $\mathbf{f}:X\to \mathbb{R}^n$ *an upper robust mapping, and* $\mathbf{w} \in W = \{\mathbf{w}: w^i \geq 0\}$ *be given. Under the assumptions of (A) and (M), the following statements are equivalent*:

(i) $x^* \in S$ *is a solution of the weightin problem* (3.8) *and* $c^* = \langle \mathbf{w}, \mathbf{f}(x^*)\rangle$ *is the corresponding value*;

(ii) $M(\langle \mathbf{w}, \mathbf{f}\rangle, c^*; S) = c^*$ (*the mean value condition*);

(iii) $V(\langle \mathbf{w}, \mathbf{f}\rangle, c^*; S) = 0$ (*the variance condition*);

(iv) $V_1(\langle \mathbf{w}, \mathbf{f}\rangle, c^*; S) = 0$ (*the modified variance condition*);

(v) $M_m(\langle \mathbf{w}, \mathbf{f}\rangle, c^*; c^*; S) = 0$, *for one of the positive integres* $m = 1, 2, \cdots$ (*the higher moment conditions*).

Corollary 3.4 *For a given* $\mathbf{c}^* = (c^{*1}, \cdots, c^{*n})^T$, *under the assumptions (A), (M), (RV), the following statements are equivalent*:

(i) *A point* $x^* \in S$ *is a reference point solution with* $c^* = \sum_{j=1}^n w^j d^j(y^j, f^j(x^*))$ *as the corresponding value*;

(ii) $M(g_d, c^*; S) = c^*$ (*the mean value condition*);

(iii) $V(g_d, c^*; S) = 0$ (*the variance condition*);

(iv) $V_1(g_d, c^*; S) = 0$ (*the modified variance condition*).

(v) $M_m(g_d, c^*; c^*; S) = 0$ *for one of the positive integers* $m = 1, 2, \cdots$ (*the higher moment conditions*).

4 An Algorithm

We propose an algorithm for approximating solutions of a multicriterial minimization problem of an upper robust mapping by using a scalarization technique. For simplicity, we describe the algorithm with a reference point method under the assumption that the objective functions of problems (4.1) are bounded below. We may use other scalarization methods to substitute for the reference point method.

Step 1: Find a reference point. Let
$$a^i := \inf_{x \in S} f^i(x), \quad i=1, \cdots, n. \tag{4.1}$$

Take a point $(\hat{y}^1, \cdots, \hat{y}^n)$ as a reference point such that
$$a^i > \hat{y}^i, \quad i=1, \cdots, n. \tag{4.2}$$

Step 2: Take a sequence of positive numbers $(w_k^1, \cdots, w_k^n)$, $k=1, \cdots, L$ and minimize the following scalar problems:
$$\min_{x \in S} g_k(x), \quad k=1, \cdots, L, \tag{4.3}$$

where, say, we may take
$$g_k(x) = \max_{i=1, \cdots, n} \{w_k^i (f^i(x) - \hat{y}^i)\} \tag{4.4}$$

We obtain a sequence of solutions:
$$x_1, \cdots, x_L \quad \text{and} \quad \mathbf{f}(x_1), \cdots, \mathbf{f}(x_L). \tag{4.5}$$

Step 3: After obtaining a set of solutions, we use simplices produced by these points to approximate the solution set $\mathbf{f}(M)$.

Remark 4.1 We assume that the objective functions of the multircriterial minimization problem are bounded below so that the minimum values $a^1, \cdots, a^n$ of (4.1) are finite. The point $(a^1, \cdots, a^n)$ can be found by using the integral minimization method. We take the reference point $(\hat{y}^1, \cdots, \hat{y}^n)$ satisfying (4.2) because it is numerically good for solving scalar minimization problems (4.3) with (4.4).

Remark 4.2 The scalar minimization problems (4.3), well as (4.1), are constrained ones. The objective function might be discontinuous and the constraint set might be disconnected. We can use penalty function technique to reduce a constrained minimization problem to an unconstrained (or box constrained) ones. For a constrained minimization problem
$$\min_{x \in S} g(x), \tag{4.6}$$

let
$$p(x) = \begin{cases} \delta, & x \notin S, \\ 0, & x \in S, \end{cases} \tag{4.7}$$

where $\alpha > 0$ is the penalty parameter, $\delta > 0$ is a constant. and $d(x)$ is penalty-like function such that $d(x)=0$ if and only if $x \in S$ consider the penalized problem
$$\min[g(x) + \alpha p(x)]. \tag{4.8}$$

The advantage of using discontinuous penalty function (4.7) is that it is exact without constraint qualification requirement. See [15] for more details.

Remark 4.3 When $n=2$, a simplex is a linear segment; and the solutions of a bicriterial minimization problem is approximated by piecewise straight lines. When $n \geq 3$, the solution set can be approximated by its "triangularization". Let $x_1, \cdots, x_{n+1}$ be $n+1$

points of the solution set which form an n-dimensional simplex, then the set

$$\{x: x + \sum_{j=1}^{n+1} a_j x_j, \ 0 \leqslant a_j \leqslant 1, \ j=1, \cdots, n+1)$$

is the n-dimensional simplex produced by these points. The solution set is approximated by this kind of simplices.

5　Numerical Examples

Example 5.1　Consider the following multi criteria optimization problem taken from [3]. This example looks easy but its set of solutions is disconnected. For each given weights, minimizaing a scalarized problem is equivalent to find a distance from a point to a nonconvex set.

$$\min \begin{pmatrix} x_1 \\ x_2 \end{pmatrix},$$

$$\text{s. t.} \begin{cases} x_2 - 2.5 \leqslant 0, \\ (x_1 - 0.5)^2 - x^2 - 4.5 \leqslant 0, \\ -x_1 - x_2^2 \leqslant 0, \\ -(x_1+1)^2 - (x_2+3)^2 + 1 \leqslant 0, \\ (x_1, x_2)^T \in \mathbb{R}^2. \end{cases} \quad (5.1)$$

Solution　Take the point $(-10.0, -10.0)$ as the reference point and consider a scalar minimization problem of an objective function

$$g(x) = \max\{w_1(x_1+10.0); w_2(x_2+10.0)\}$$

with the same constraints as (5.1), where w_1 and w_2, are positive weights. We can take w_1 as a constant, say, 1.0 and let w_2 change. We obtain a sequence of solutions by using the integral global minimization technique combining with discontinuous penalty function to convert a constrained problem to a unconstrained one. The following table lists solutions corresponding to given weights. The stopping criterion in the integral algorithm is the modified variance $V_1 < 10^{-10}$. The average number of function exaluation for given weights is 1419.

w_2	$\mathbf{f}(x) \in M$	w_2	$\mathbf{f}(x) \in M$
2.0	(0.4999820, −4.500000)	1.16	(−0.7552708, −2.030403)
1.9	(0.4539958, −4.497883)	1.15	(−1.080112, −2.003214)
1.85	(0.2715485, −4.447810)	1.1	(−1.107507, −1.915925)
1.8	(0.1370919, −4.368291)	1.05	(−1.197915, −1.6717084)
1.75	(0.02306769, −4.272535)	1.0	(−1.291287, −1.291287)
1.7	(−0.07936519, −4.164334)	0.9	(−1.329472, −1.153031)
1.6	(−0.2645885, −3.915404)	0.75	(−1.562502, 1.250007)
1.5	(−0.3568753, −3.765764)	0.7	(−1.949601, 1.500553)
1.2	(−0.5366086, −2.113844)	0.65	(−2.084205, 2.178148)
1.18	(−0.6393894, −2.067280)	0.5	(−2.145741, 2.499954)

Remark 5.1 The advantage of our algorithm is that the decision maker can select reference points and weights to meet his needs.

Example 5.2 Consider the following multi criteria optimization problem.

$$\min = \begin{pmatrix} x_1 \\ x_2 \\ x_3 \end{pmatrix},$$

$$\text{s. t.} \begin{cases} \max\{l_1(x), l_2(x)\} \geqslant 0, \quad \text{where} \\ l_1(x) = 1 - x_1^2 - x_2^2 - x_3^2, \\ l_2(x) = 0.49 - (x_1 + 0.2)^2 - (x^2 + 0.5)^2 - x_3^2, \\ -2.5 \leqslant x_1 \leqslant 1.1, \\ -2.5 \leqslant x_2 \leqslant 1.1, \\ 0 \leqslant x_3 \leqslant 1.1, \\ (x_1, x_2, x_3)^T \in \mathbb{R}^3, \end{cases} \quad (5.2)$$

Solution Take the point $(-10.0, -10.0 - 10.0)$ as the reference point and consider a scalar minimization problem of an objective function

$$g(x) = \max\{w_1 \cdot (x_1 + 10.0), w_2 \cdot (x_2 + 10.0), (w_3) \cdot (x_3 + 10.0)\}$$

with the same constraints as (5.2), where w_1, w_2 and w_3 are positive weights. We can take $w_1 = 1.0$ as a constant, and let w_2 and w_3 change. We obtain a sequence of solutions by using the integral global minimization technique. The stopping criterion is also taken $V_1 < 1^{-10}$.

w_2, w_3	$\mathbf{f}(x) \in M$
1.0, 1.0	$(-0.5813401, -0.5814602, -0.5813238)$
1.1, 1.1	$(-0.0030460, -0.7071097, -0.7070885)$
1.05, 1.05	$(-0.2236959, -0.6891872, -0.6891861)$
0.8, 0.8	$(-0.0000071, -0.0001145, -0.0004878)$
0.95, 0.95	$(-0.8518369, -0.3703590, -0.3703766)$
1.2, 1.0	$(-0.1985384, -1.199995, -0.0016831)$
1.05, 1.0	$(-0.4772033, -0.9306482, -0.4771791)$
0.95, 1.0	$(-0.6924472, -0.2025711, -0.6924456)$
0.9, 1.0	$(-0.7071113, -0.0001619, -0.7070919)$
1.0, 1.2	$(-0.0029247, -0.0018540, -0.9999909)$
1.0, 1.05	$(-0.3828099, -0.3828046, -0.8407777)$
1.0, 0.95	$(-0.7749711, -0.7749708, -0.2894734)$
1.0, 0.9	$(-0.8216952, -0.8216965, -0.0014718)$
1.02, 0.97	$(-0.6696085, -0.8525359, -0.3810176)$
0.97, 0.94	$(-0.8461164, -0.5630351, -0.2618349)$
1.05, 0.95	$(-0.6090661, -1.056258, -0.1150661)$
1.1, 1.05	$(-0.2013773, -0.9590151, -0.5284872)$
0.95, 1.1	$(-0.9504571, -0.0011165, -0.9954716)$
1.05, 1.1	$(-0.0016060, -0.4561081, -0.8899136)$
0.95, 1.02	$(-0.6046262, -0.1101289, -0.788491)$

6 Conclusions

The theory of vector minimization has not succesfully handled discontinuous functions, since it has been grounded in the differential calculus, starting with Kuhn and Tucker. A powerful and widely applicable alternative has recently been developed in the integral approach. According to the integral approach, and under the assumption that the objective mapping is upper robust all of the well developed scalarization techniques may be interpreted in a more general context. Such an interpretation has implications to the theory and methods of vector minimization, to characterizing globally efficient solutions and to algorithms which locate these solutions.

References

[1] Yu. G. Evtushenko. *Numerical Optimization Techniques*, Optimization Software Inc. New York, (1980).

[2] Yu. G. Evtushenko and M. A. Potapov. Methods of Numerical solution of multicriterion problems. *Soviet Math. Dokl.*, (1987) 34, 420−423.

[3] J. Jahn and A. Merkel. Reference point approximation method for the solution of bicriterial nonlinear optimization problems, *Journal of Optimization Theory and Applications*, (1992) 74, 87−103.

[4] M. M. Kostreva and Q. Zheng. Optimality conditions of vector global minimization: an integral approach, Clemson University, Clemson, South Carolina (1993).

[5] A. V. Levy and A. Montalvo. The tunnelling algorithm for global minimization of functions, *SIAM J. Sci. Sta. Comput.*, (1985)6,15−29.

[6] A. Lewandowski and V. Volkovich (eds). *Multiobjective Problems of Mathematical Programming*, Lecture Notes in Economics and Mathematical Systems, 351, Springer-Verlag (1991).

[7] D. L. Markin and R. G. Strongin. Uniform estimates for the set of weakly effective points in multiextremum multicriterion optimization problems, *Comput. Maths. Math. Phys.*, (1993) 33, 171−179.

[8] E. Polak. On the approximation of solutions to multi criteria decision making problems, *Multi Criteria Decision Making*, *Kyoto* 1975, Edited by M. Zeleny, Springer-Verlag Berlin, (1976) 271−281.

[9] S. Shi. Q. Zheng and D. Zhuang. Discontinuous robust mapping are approximatable. Transactions AMS, to appear 1995.

[10] S. Shi, Q. Zheng and D. Zhuang. Set-valued mappings and approximatable mappings, *Journal of Mathematical Analysis and Application*, (1994)183, 706−726.

[11] A. P. Wierzbicki. A mathematical basis for satisficing decision making, *Mathematical Modelling*, (1982) 3, 391−405.

[12] A. P. Wierzbicki. On the completeness and constructiveness of parametric characterizations to vector optimization problems, *OR Spektrum*, (1986)8, 73−87.

[13] Q. Zheng. Robust analysis and global minimization of a class of discontinuous functions (I), *Acta Mathematicae Applicatae Sinica* (English series), (1990)6:3, 205—223.

[14] Q. Zheng. Robust Analysis and global optimization of a class of discontinuous functions (II), *Acta Mathematicae Applicatae Sinica* (English Series), (1990)6:4, 317—337.

[15] Q. Zheng. Integral global optimization of robust discontinuous function, Ph. D. Dissertation, Clemson University, (1992).

下 篇
忆郑权

缅怀郑权教授

陶宗英*

我和郑权同是1955年复旦大学数学系第三班的同学,他长我三岁,是我的老大哥。

我们两家住得很近,我常去他家玩,除了讨论功课外,还聊天,谈天说地。郑权知识面广,兴趣多样,又善于唱歌,我只是一个聆听者,受益匪浅。

在我们三班中,吴立德、郑权和我关系比较好,常一起讨论功课,他们知识面广,博学多才,我知识面较为狭窄,孤陋寡闻,只是津津有味地做个听众。郑权体育活动也很积极,擅长短跑,又是年级男声小合唱的成员,活动能力极强,曾担任过系学生会主席,自1958年工作后我与郑权的联系就减少了。

1977年我调到嘉定中科院原子核所工作,与郑权接触的机会又增加了,每逢寒暑假他常来我家,曾劝我去上海科学技术大学数学系工作,由于我父亲刚病逝,母亲和儿子都在徐汇区而未成,对于他的热忱友好之情我一直铭记于心。

郑权一生勤勉用功,孜孜不倦,努力钻研。不愧为上海市的运筹学带头人,他的音容笑貌历历在目,永远活在我心中。

左一郑权,右三陶宗英,摄于2008年7月3日

---

* 陶宗英,上海交通大学教授.

从一次班级活动的照片说起

邹 悦*

  大约是 1959 年,班级在刚建成的杨浦公园搞了一次活动,大家在一起划船、唱歌……。正好我姐姐已回上海,我向她借了相机,尚汉冀同学带上了他的手风琴,给这次活动增添了意外的乐趣,也留下了难忘的快乐!
  说起大学五年,我们年级的课余活动一直是十分活跃,每每想起这一切,就会想起活动的组织者——老同学郑权。
  郑权同学不仅学习好,还特别热心,一年级时他就是我们年级的班主席,后来成了我们数学系的学生会主席。在体育上,他是一位优秀的短跑运动员,带动大家积极参加劳卫制锻炼,我们年级的同学几乎都通过了劳卫制 1—2 级。在文娱上,他和班上的同学组成的男声小合唱多次登上了学校的大礼堂表演。我当时也是学生干部,我们常常在一起组织活动,因此也很谈得来。
  大学四年级,郑权同学和我分在函数论专门化组,在组内他的学习能力是最强的,在学习上也对我帮助很多,我更佩服他了,我总是觉得他将来一定会做出一些成就来的。大学毕业后,我们分到了不同的工作单位,就很少联系了。后来我又离开了上海,从同学那里得知他确实做出了非常好的成绩。
  郑权同学是我大学时代最佩服、最尊敬的同学之一。

左一郑权,右一邹悦

---

* 邹悦,郑权大学时同班同学。

与郑权共同创作歌曲事宜

尚汉冀[*]

听闻俞丽和同学询问关于与郑权兄共同创作歌曲一事,其实日前上海财经大学的谢志刚教授(郑权兄的学生)也传来消息,说郑权夫人涂老师正在筹备纪念郑权兄的书籍,其中既包括郑权兄的学术著作,也包括其他方面的内容。她还请一位朋友根据我唱过的这首《毕业生之歌》的录音写成歌谱发给我要我校对一下,我已校对并修改一些内容后通过谢志刚寄还给了涂老师。

至于当时创作和演唱这首歌的情况,因为年代久远,我只记得在 1960 年毕业前夕,由我写了歌词(当时共有几段,现在能完整背出的只有第一段了),由郑权兄作曲,班里男声小合唱队(我记得除了我和郑权兄,还有区锐森兄、孙家昌兄等)共同讨论定稿后,在班级聚会中演唱过,地点好像在数学楼(当时叫 600 号),其他细节就说不出多少了。还有一个相关的记录,就是我们年级通讯录第一版前言曾引了这首歌的第一段,现附上供参阅。在此特别想感谢涂老师为出版这一纪念书籍所作的努力,待出版后大家一定会非常高兴地捧读这本书,重温当年的同学情谊。

愿友情长存!

尚汉冀作词、郑权作曲《毕业生之歌》

---

[*] 尚汉冀,复旦大学数学科学学院教授.

前排左一郑权,后排右四尚汉冀

四个复旦毕业生在"上工"

俞丽和[*]

"上工"是上海工学院的简称。1960年,上海决定开办一所完全属于上海自己的大学,命名为上海工学院,目标是服务上海蓬勃发展的工业系统。

"上工"设置了仪表系、电机系、冶金系、自动化系等专业。

现在已经没有"上工"了,上海工学院后来更名为上海工业大学,现在是上海大学。

"上工"初办的时候,想办一个数理力学系。一个工学院想要办数理力学系,应该属于一种难得的高瞻远瞩。数学力学的确是科学的基石,也是工科的基础。

可惜,这只是一个"梦"。害苦了我们四个刚刚从复旦大学毕业的意气风发的年轻人。

复旦大学很认真地为"上工"配搭了一个创办数理力学系新专业的班子,把我们四人分配到了"上工"。

郑权是函数论专业,施惟慧是几何专业,程沅生是力学专业,而我是方程专业。堪称相当完美!

"上工"开始的确真心要办数理力学系的,也招收了第一届数理力学系学生。

但是,数理力学系始终是"上工"的一个烫手山芋,他们老是认为师资力量不足。

第一年,数理力学系的学生就被送到华东师范大学。郑权作为助教随数理力学系也到华东师范大学去了。

施惟慧和我留在"上工"教"高等数学"和"工程数学"。程沅生留在"上工"教"工程力学"。

那个年代,没有"跳槽"一说,我们只能服从国家分配。

我们尽心尽责辛勤地在"上工"努力教书,也得到学校领导的肯定和学生的称赞。

如果当时"上工"把创办数理力学系的担子压在我们四个人身上,我们相信我们一定会团结一心勇敢地撑起来。因为,后面有我们的母校复旦大学,我们有五年扎实基础和各个学科的专业根底,我们有一颗火热的心。我们非常年轻,我们不害怕,我们就是抱着这样的心志,到"上工"来的哦!可惜,这只是"如果"。

"文革"初期,郑权很早就被红卫兵关进了"牛棚",我们三人(郑、施、俞)也莫名其妙地被打成为"上工"的"三家村",一直处于不能参加数学教研组的"靠边"状态。

施和我无事可做,除了背读"毛选"外,开始学习"马克思数学手稿",钻研"0/0究竟是什么"。

"文革"总算结束了。不知什么原因,上海科学技术大学要求"上工"把我调去工作。当时,我丈夫在南京大学工作,我一个人带着两个年幼的孩子,实在很为难。

---

[*] 俞丽和,上海大学自动化系和机械系.

郑权为了帮助我,主动向"上工"领导提出,他要求顶替我去上海科学技术大学。

这件事,知道的人不多,可是,我永远记在心里。为难之处,见真心。五年同学,一辈子亲。

当然,郑权去上海科学技术大学的决定是完全正确的。他回到数学系不久后,在运筹学方面做出了很好的成绩,成为数学系系主任。

后来,程沅生去了美国。再后来,施惟慧去了法国。

我一个人留在"上工"。但是我也离开了数学教研组,去了自动化系和机械系,并改行从事计算机基础教学。但不管做什么工作,我们都是在数学的基础上。

我们还是应该要感谢"上工"。"上工"让郑权遇到了第一届数理力学系学生涂仁进,结为恩爱夫妻。

"上工"为了留住我,千方百计帮助我,把我的丈夫区锐森从南京大学调回上海。两地分开11年,总算一家团圆。

人生不是自己能够完全掌控的。但是,我们不论在什么环境下,都可以扪心自问:我们对得起自己,对得起父母,对得起社会,对得起母校复旦大学。

郑权安息吧!我们有共同的信仰,我们在天上还会再相见!

前排左三俞丽和,第二排右三郑权

忆上海工学院时期的郑权

程沅生*

在复旦大学读书时我与郑权不在同一个小班,最后两年又不在同一专业班,所以来往不多。毕业后郑权分到上海工学院数学教研组。我于1961年10月从复旦大学调到上海工学院机械系力学教研组,从此与郑权接触比较多。

上世纪60年代初上海工学院刚建立,规模很小,总共只有四个系。白天教师阅览室没有什么人光临,晚上当然是不开放的。每天下午教师阅览室关门时就剩下郑权和我两个人,天天如此。教师阅览室的负责人是刚从北京大学图书馆系毕业分配来的张玉藻,我们的同龄人。到底是北京大学的毕业生,对读书人很尊重,很关爱我们,干脆把教师阅览室的钥匙给了我们一把,并说以后晚上你们自己开门来这里看书,到时候你们自己关灯关门就行了。于是我们俩每天晚上都来教师阅览室学习,晚上十点钟关门一起回青年教师宿舍。郑权是上海人,每星期六下午回家,给我印象很深至今没有忘记的一点是,星期天傍晚郑权

自左至右:涂仁进、郑权、程沅生,2014年夏摄于上海亲和源公寓

准时会回教师阅览室,晚上十点钟我们俩一道回宿舍。我想"文化大革命"前这几年郑权的勤奋钻研对他以后业务的成长是有很大帮助的。

以此短文怀念我们的老同学郑权。

---

* 程沅生,明尼苏达大学研究员.

深切缅怀郑权教授

沈海华[*]

我在1958年考入复旦大学数学系时,郑权是数学系四年级的学生,因为都喜爱唱歌,于是,我这个小师弟结识了这位大师兄。从此郑权就成为我亦师亦友的一生知交,是我一生敬重的数学大家!

在我印象中,清晨,郑权就在操场上跑步晨练,冬天也坚持洗冷水浴,所以身体很健壮;穿着十分简朴,背着装满了书籍的大书包,疾步如飞般地穿梭在教室与图书馆。见着他总是生机勃勃、乐乐呵呵、开朗活泼,他很爱歌唱,歌唱时,声音响亮,动作大方,十分放开,他和尚汉冀同学、区锐生同学的男声三重唱还唱得很不错!

我从未看到过他生气发脾气,他待同学们都十分友善!但他在读书和钻研学问时却常常废寝忘食,十分刻苦用功,因此,常可看到他的双眼因熬夜而充满血丝,他是一位充满活力、不怕困难的人!所以,在2013年我从纽约到乔治亚州,在康复医院中看到他时,我心情十分难受,一个从不怕困难的人,今天却是举步维艰、寸步难行的情景,真是英雄只怕病来磨!但,郑权就是郑权,依然十分乐观开朗!

20世纪50年代末、60年代初,我因经常要代表上海大学生去参加各个外国代表团演出男高音独唱(与男低音温可铮,女高音周碧珍、鞠秀芳等一起),许多俄文歌曲如《俄罗斯》、《连斯基咏叹调》都是郑权帮我纠正唱词的。特别是我唱意大利歌曲时的意大利文的发音启蒙也是郑权教我的。如《啊,我的太阳》《负心人》等等,每当我唱起这些歌时,都会念着他!至今,我仍珍藏着他当时送给我的两本歌谱——《苏联独唱歌曲集》《意大利歌曲集》!

我因家境贫寒,虽有助学金,但仅能解决在校生活,其他诸如我每周日需去上海音乐学院上声乐课以及其他生活上的所需费用,郑权也时常像兄长般的给我支持和帮助。他毕业后,知我牙齿掉了,特意还帮我付钱去装了假牙,此情此景,虽然已经相隔半个多世纪了,如今回忆,依然历历在目!

虽然,而今我也已耄耋之年,但时常念及郑权教授的点点滴滴,他的睿智、聪明、刻苦、勤奋、开朗、善良、宽厚的品格,依然是我永远学习的榜样,我对他万分敬重,愿他在天堂安息!

---

[*] 沈海华,上海大学国际商学院计算机系原副主任。

左起：郑权、沈海华和屠世谷（复旦大学物理系61届的合唱团团员），照片拍摄时间约1959年末、1960年初的冬天，地点在襄阳公园和襄阳路的俄国东正教堂前

忆郑权教授

汤生江[*]

我大学毕业分配到上海科学技术大学四系工作,当时四系有多个专业,计算数学、应用数学、自动控制、电视、计算机等专业。郑权教授是学校里的名师,我是刚开始工作的年轻教师,但在工作中我们很快熟悉起来。我在四系工作了四年,后调去学校团委、校长办公室工作。1986年的一天,校长郭本瑜把我叫去,说四系需要一位党总支书记,希望我能回四系工作。当时四系的专业设置有所调整,四系就是数学系,工科专业全部调出。数学系系主任就是郑权教授。去数学系之前,郭校长告诫我:郑权教授是个非常称职的系主任,学术水平很高,工作能力很强,人光明磊落,平易近人,你去后一定要与他互相配合好。又说:党政班子要互相尊重、互相支持;党政领导要多交流、多谅解,工作就会顺利,数学系会有更好发展。

在数学系与郑权教授合作共事多年,校长的期望我们做到了。数学系在郑权教授的主持和带领下,在全系教职工的共同努力下,取得了有目共睹的成绩与发展。那几年,招收的硕士生、博士生、外籍留学生的数量与质量都排在学校的前例;在获得国家自然科学基金项目的经费上,在三大检索发表论文的数量上,都为学校争得了荣誉。特别是在全国同类高校数学系中,有两个博士点,办两份全国性数学期刊的,上海科学技术大学是全国唯一的。与郑权教授一起工作,关系融洽,心情愉快,工作效率高。党政工作虽有分工,但分工不分家。他投身教书育人、科学研究、学科建设、学术交流、期刊管理、国际合作,工作十分繁忙,从早到晚全身心投入到工作中。有段时间他夫人在外地工作,不在身边,他一个人住在居民小区,生活十分简朴。有天傍晚,我专程去他家看看,只见他饭桌上一碗稀饭、一锅汤,里面放着白菜、萝卜、西红柿,我想如果他想吃点荤菜,就是放点肉一起煮。我问他就吃这些?他说营养都有了。实际上他为了节省时间,应付了事。他每天把时间放在教学科研上,唯独不把时间放在生活上,他为自己钟爱的数学事业,为数学系的发展,奉献了自己全部的时间和精力。

我与郑权教授工作上互相支持,通力合作体现在方方面面。由于他工作忙,时间紧,经常由我代他参加学校会议,个别领导会有微词,我有点尴尬。他知道后及时与领导沟通,说明原因,提出解决办法,有效缓解了各方矛盾,而我更感受到他对我工作的支持和关心。上世纪80年代,国门已打开,出国留学成风,但公派出国的名额少之又少,教师出国深造,僧多粥少,一个公派出国了,不少人有各种各样的想法,有怨言,思想工作难度很大。这时,郑权教授会主动出来做工作,利用师生情、朋友同事关系,大家的情绪得到缓解,问题容易解决。在工资晋升、职称评定、住房分配等方面,都关系到教师的切身利益,思想工作无处不在。郑权教授主动承担了大量思想工作,为我减轻了不少压力,我至今难以忘怀。高校是典型的

---

[*] 汤生江,上海大学理学院原党委书记.

"清水衙门",但校系总得为教职员工谋点福利。有一年年底,到了评级发奖的时候,我正好在外地出差,大家认为有系主任在,评级发奖工作按时进行,这当然完全可行的。但郑权教授说,只要时间许可,还是等书记回来共同商量决定为好。后来我还是赶了回来,党政班子一起商量,共同做了方案,工作圆满完成。郑权教授对党总支工作的支持和帮助,对我工作的尊重和认可,我一直铭记于心。

社会上有句话叫"谁人背后无人说,哪有背后不说人"。一个单位、一个集体,常有些矛盾和不和谐的现象。背后议论人的事时有发生,也增加了矛盾的复杂性和解决问题的困难。郑权教授为人真诚、心胸开阔、做事大度。与他一起工作多年,从未听到过他在背后议论人、背后说人家闲话的时候。就这一点,足以受人尊重、让人钦佩,够我学习一辈子。去年5月9日,郑权教授因病在美国仙逝,未能送别郑权教授最后一程,实为遗憾。今天能在编辑出版郑权教授纪念图书的时候,撰写一篇纪念小文,深感欣慰。

汤生江

深切缅怀郑权教授

张荣欣*

郑权在原上海科学技术大学数学系的教学科研建设中,作出了重大贡献。

郑权调来上海科学技术大学后,积极展开总极值理论和方法及其在控制论中的应用与微分对策的研究,取得了很好的成果。这种理论和方法已被应用于非线性观测、系统辨识和最优控制之中。为此,他曾获上海市、国家级科技进步二等奖,获加拿大科技理事会的国际科学交流奖。

郑权在任数学系主任期间,注重教学科研的一体化,注重师资的培养,注重学生的全面发展。他以身作则,担负着繁重的研究生教学和指导任务。他以最快的速度调配人力物力,筹建应用数学教研室。并不失时机地让新专业招收本科生和硕士研究生,直到批准创立"运筹学与控制论"博士点。

这样,数学系在以郭本瑜为核心的计算数学博士点的基础上,又新增了以郑权为核心的另一博士点。形成了全系中青年教师认真教学、抢挑重担,又在科研中攻坚克难,争取丰硕成果的蓬勃发展局面。

一个名气不大、缺少权威的数学系,在不长的时间里,依靠中青年的力量,发展成拥有三个有规模的教研室,拥有两个博士点,拥有两份全国发行的数学刊物。全系发表的论文,无论数量和质量,都得到外界的关注和好评。全系教师获得的学校、上海市、国家级奖励,也是十分突出和难能可贵的。这一切,自然是大家做出来的,但郑权和校系的规划领导,确实发挥了出色的作用。

郑权教授生活简朴,刻苦自强,心胸广阔。无论酷暑严寒,他都坚持锻炼身体。他体格健壮,手劲特强。越是好友,越怕与他握

张荣欣和郑权(右)

手。他患病早期,我们去医院看他,医生说他像运动员,全身都有肌肉。然而,不幸的是,病魔夺去了他的肌肉,最后夺走了他的宝贵生命。他虽然仙逝了,但他的音容笑貌仍历历在目,永存我们心中!

---

* 张荣欣,上海科学技术大学教授、教务处原处长.

运筹先驱　丰碑永存

盛万成[*]

转眼郑权教授离开我们已有一年多,郑先生的音容笑貌时常浮现在我的眼前。我与郑先生的交往虽然不多,但他平易近人,严谨的治学态度,追求真理的科学精神,给人以强烈的震撼。2000年初,我来到上海大学理学院数学系工作,与郑先生有过一段交往。当时郑先生被聘为"上海大学自强教授",每年回国工作两个月。我们时常一起工作、散步、游泳。他虽然年事已高,但仍然坚持科研,指导博士研究生。他深深地热爱着上海大学数学系,为上海大学数学学科的发展建设出谋划策。他德高为师、学高为范,不断地激励数学系新一代年轻人献身科学,为上海大学的建设作贡献。

郑权教授长期在原上海科学技术大学数学系工作,为上海大学数学学科的建设和发展作出了不可磨灭的贡献。他是我国运筹学界著名学者,创立了求总极值的积分型水平集方法等,成就卓著,是上海大学运筹学与控制论博士点的创办人之一。郑权先生终生勤奋治学,诲人不倦,桃李芬芳。其治学精神和学术成就永久嘉惠学林,激励后学。失去郑权先生是上海大学的一大损失,我们将永远怀念郑权先生。

上海大学数学学科经过郑权等老一辈先驱的创建,新一代上大人的辛勤耕耘,目前已成

盛万成

---

[*] 盛万成,上海大学理学院党委书记、数学系教授.

为在国内外具有一定影响力的教学科研、人才培养的重要基地。上海大学1998年设立数学博士后流动站,2006获批数学一级学科博士点,2012年设立一级统计学科硕士点。数学学科先后入选上海市重点学科、一流学科、高原学科。2021年英国QS世界大学学科排名中上海大学数学学科排第251—300位。在上一轮教育部学科评估中为B+学科。最新ESI全球排名名列前5.05‰。

  我们将继续努力,拼搏奋斗,继承先驱的遗志,把上海大学数学系建设成为世界著名的人才培养与科学研究基地,以告慰郑先生的在天之灵。

我们怀念郑权教授

许梦杰 李志良*

尊敬的郑权教授离开我们已经一年多了。回忆过去岁月中与郑权教授在一起的美好时光,历历在目,难以忘怀。

郑权教授是复旦大学数学系60届毕业的高材生,他于1972年由上海工学院调入上海科学技术大学数学系执教,并在1983年至1987年间担任数学系主任。他曾是我们的学长、同事、领导,他留给我们的"专业精、业绩丰、人品好"的高尚印象,永远铭记在我们心中。

郑权教授作为教师,他真正做到了教书育人,培养人才,桃李满天下。他的教学任务很繁重,除了上研究生课外,同时承担本科生课程。他讲课深入浅出,启发思维,深受学生好评。在工作上,认真负责,以身作则,团结同事,创造良好的学术研讨环境。他鼓励青年教师攻读在职研究生;他促成教师编写教材,参加全国学科教材的投标;他组织计算机编程讲座,推动教师使用电脑计算工具;他重视数学理论与国民经济相结合的社会实践,将自己创立的积分型总极值优化理论和算法,编制成计算程序,实现光学优化设计的效果,为数学的应用创造了很好的经济价值。

郑权教授是上海科学技术大学"运筹学与控制论"专业的奠基人。凭借他在运筹学方面的学术研究水平,曾担任全国运筹学会理事。在他的带领下,数学系1979年开始招收运筹学硕士生,1990年获批成为运筹学与控制论博士点,1991年招博士生,上海科学技术大学的"运筹学与控制论"专业被列为全国重点学科。1980年在一次运筹学学术交流会上,他争取到全国《运筹学杂志》在上海科学技术大学出版。为此,他悉心组建编辑部,并担任该杂志的副主编。第一期刊物《运筹学杂志》于1982年正式出版,至今这本刊物一直是运筹学学术交流的重要平台。

尤为可敬的是,郑权教授不仅师德高尚,心胸坦荡,一切以工作为重,而且从不计较名利得失。由于他出色的教学和科研成绩,他曾被评为上海市先进工作者,因此可以享受假期休养,但他却把名额让给了其他同事。又如,他为创建数学系计算机应用实验室,竟然把自己的科研经费也投入于实验室的建设之中。他的所作所为,得到老师们的钦佩和好评。

郑权教授也是一位好男人、好丈夫。在日常生活中,他平易近人,体贴别人。在出差开会的行途中,他十分照顾体弱的教师,总是乘车让座。他对于两地分居的同事也十分关心,为了使从外地来探亲的同事家属在市内办事便利,免于天天往返嘉定,就无偿提供自己的市区住房给他们住。这些行为看似平凡,但体现出郑权教授是位品德高尚的不平凡之人。

郑权教授高贵的品格和深厚的学识,他那淡泊名利、襟怀博大、谦逊儒雅的崇高形象,永远铭刻在我们心里。郑权好友,我们永远怀念你!

---

* 许梦杰、李志良,上海大学数学系教授.

许梦杰、李志良

丰 碑 永 在

朱国勇[*]

朱国勇

我敬爱的老师郑权教授已驾鹤西去,然而他对教学与科研事业的追求与奉献,对学生与同仁的关爱,对生活的热爱与襟怀坦荡的风格,将长留人间。

我有幸作为上海科学技术大学数学系计算数学专业的一名学生,曾经在教室里聆听过郑权教授风趣幽默的授课,更有幸在毕业后留系任教的十多年里,在郑权教授的耳提面命之下学习与工作,亲身感受和见证了郑权教授怀着满腔的热忱和激情,殚精竭虑,孜孜不倦,把自己对教学与科研的理想倾注到了数学系的教书育人和学科建设之中。

1981年间,由于郑权教授及计算数学专业在最优化理论与计算领域中的开创性工作,使得上海科学技术大学数学系争取到了承办中国数学会运筹学会创建全国性运筹学专业学术期刊《运筹学杂志》的机会。郑权教授兼任了期刊的编委及副主编,我被选派去兼任期刊的编辑,在他的直接指导下开展编辑部的工作。经过繁杂的组稿、审稿、定稿,并由上海科学技术出版社设计排版,次年(1982年)10月,每年2期的《运筹学杂志》正式出版发行。郑权教授为此倾注了大量的时间与心血,除了协调组稿,还亲自承担审稿。在1983年郑权教授出任数学系主任后,他始终如一地直接指导着期刊的进展。这本刊物的出版对中国运筹学领域的重要意义毋用置评(注:1997年《运筹学杂志》已经升格并改名为《运筹学学报》,迄今已出版25卷),对数学系来说,更是获得了一个重要的学术交流平台,拓展了青年教师的视野,促进了教学与科研的发展,提高了数学系的知名度,在招生与人才引进方面也起到了一个良性循环的建设性作用。郑权教授当年高瞻远瞩,运筹帷幄,为数学系的发展留下了浓重一笔。

1987年1月,在我国著名数学家、复旦大学苏步青教授与谷超豪教授的关注与支持下,郑权老师与时任上海科学技术大学校长郭本瑜教授一起主持创办的《应用数学与计算数学学报》正式出版,郭本瑜教授为主编,郑权教授兼任副主编。这份学报的问世不仅进一步推动了上海科学技术大学数学系相关学科的发展,并且为我国应用数学与计算数学领域的教

---

[*] 朱国勇,上海科学技术大学数学系原副系主任.

学与科研提供了一个重要的学术交流平台。

郑权教授平易近人,起居简朴,热爱体育运动。他工作繁忙,教学、科研、学科建设占去了他每天的大部分时间。为了教学与科学研究的崇高理想,郑权教授贡献了他毕生的精力。虽然他已驾鹤西去,但他在我们心中的丰碑永在!

于美国旧金山

难以忘却的记忆

邬冬华*

到 2022 年初，我行将回归故里，开始我的退休生活。曾经，我已不准备落笔留下什么文字。除了我喜欢的日常教学及与长辈、小辈们的其乐融融的家庭生活外，几乎对外面生活没有了太多的兴趣。父母和老师们对我的精心培养和教育，使我今天有能力选择我自己想要过的生活。当下自己最大的愿望是自己在教学生涯结束前，尽可能培养学生返璞归真，使他们能够有能力做真正的自己。

郑权先生患病多年，不时看到涂仁进先生在"郑权老师学生"的微信群里推送郑先生的病情进展，对于郑先生的病情，现代医学目前还无能为力，所以也不怎么特别关注。时常倒是一直为涂先生一个弱小女子单独在美国照顾郑先生生活是否能承受下来而特别担心。一个清晨，当得知郑先生逝世的那一刻，我心中产生一种莫名的冲动，想写一段文字表达我对郑权先生的无限思念，同时有机会让我袒露在心中埋藏多年的秘密，以便大家对郑先生有更多了解和认识。

我于 1978 年进入上海科学技术大学数学系学习，入学之后因年龄较小一直承蒙许多老师特别照顾。1982 年，在我班指导员王翼飞老师和我曾经的任课老师张荣欣老师的特别推荐下，我本科毕业后留校任教。教研室安排我与我心里一直崇拜的郑权先生及涂仁进先生在同一办公室，那时的郑先生来去匆匆，平时我们见面的时间不多，也就没有太多的交流。此时，我也正跟随楼老师、姚老师开始不分日夜地学习和研究解析数论，那种学习热情很大程度受到郑权先生和郭本瑜先生的影响。

有一件事令我对郑权先生的印象极其深刻且一直影响并激励着我。在郑先生担任上海科学技术大学数学系系主任期间，1988 年我已不清楚是哪一天，平时不苟言笑的郑先生跟我说，他要跟我聊聊，我一听到郑先生的话，我心里特别紧张。郑先生跟我说：系里有一个升讲师的名额，系里研究决定把这个名额给你。但系里有位 77 届毕业的老师，他家里是农村户口，他升了中级职称就可以马上解决家属子女农转非及其解决子女进城入学问题。其实，平时即便是我外婆在"文革"时被她救助过的人伤害过她，但她仍然教导我们："如果别人遇到困难，你们有能力就应该出手帮助别人，说明你那时还比别人强，你是幸运的。"通过这件事我实际上是最大受益者，没过二个月我也升上了讲师。其次，郑老师在坚守规则的同时，亲自切实帮助职工解决生活问题的举动深深地激励并感动我。从毕业的先后顺序，先给就职在先的老师顺理成章，但郑先生及系里领导没有这么做，他们按照系里制定的规则办事，而不是使用自己手中的权力任性地破坏规则，郑先生的行动深深地影响了我。当我服务大家的时候，我把郑先生的按规则行事始终作为自己行为准则。正因为这样，我经历的有些事

---

* 邬冬华，上海大学数学系教授．

其最终效果着实也令我终身难忘。

经过了近十年在解析数论领域对哥德巴赫猜想和黎曼猜想的学习与研究,我清醒地认识到自己的能力,因此也一度对自己的未来产生了迷茫。有幸的是,1997年9月我考取了在职研究生,跟随张连生先生攻读硕士和博士学位。平时与张先生的交谈中,他经常提起当年杭州大学王兴华教授在上海科学技术大学数学系作报告时提出的计算数学中的若干问题,其中之一是郑先生提出的积分—水平集的方法的理论算法与实现算法问题。在选择研究课题时,我对张先生提出我是否继续研究郑先生的求总极值的积分—水平集方法,此想法马上得到张先生的肯定回应。

在硕士和博士的四年学习生涯中,从起初对郑先生提出的算法仰慕及对王兴华教授所提出的问题的好奇,我逐渐对郑先生的算法有了一些研究心得,顺利地获得了博士学位。主要的结论有两个方面:

(1) 首先利用水平割(即将水平值上面的山峰割去)并利用华罗庚、王元提出的高维一致分布"华—王"法作逼近,得到郑先生提出的理论算法与实现算法相匹配的算法,其结果从理论角度实现了完美,但牺牲了实现算法的计算效率。再次说明二全其美的事是很难得的。

(2) 在郑先生的算法的极限状态下,其与求解均值方程的根是等价的,进一步发现:关于相应的均值方程求根的牛顿迭代法与郑先生的迭代算法完全一致。继而使得我脑洞大开,用牛顿法研究郑先生算法收敛准则所提出的有关水平值方差方程的根。研究得到一类求全局优化的积分—水平集方法的不精确牛顿迭代算法,并给出了该算法收敛性质。

在我的认知中,与牛顿法相联系的算法一定是较有意思的。

由于数学中全局分析工具缺失,使研究全局最优化(或整体最优)变得相当困难,而日常生活中要求的极值又往往都是全局最优值。郑先生与他的合作者最初在解决光学薄膜设计的最优设计时采用蒙特兴洛方法计算,他们从实践中提炼出具有针对性的求总极值的积分—水平集方法及其实现算法,一个有意义的理论一定是对实践的提升和支撑。此一直是几十年来运筹学这个学科发展的生命源泉。

如果仔细阅读并研究郑先生及其合作者的工作,我认为王兴华教授提出的有关郑先生的总极值方法的有关问题是非本质的。因为没有其他全局搜索的工具,郑先生的总极值方法的实现算法只能是通过蒙特卡罗随机投点实现全局搜索。怎么提高搜索效率,我始终认为是一个关键问题。对于算法设计而言,主要是针对某类问题设计尽可能高效的算法。一个朴素的想法就是如何在信息好的区域作尽可能多的搜索,此促使我们产生利用相对熵与重点样本相结合的想法,后来其作为我指导的一个博士研究生的研究课题。经过该博士生自身不断的努力,其在该领域大家公认的不错的国际杂志上发表了近十篇论文,毕业不久申请到了国家自然科学基金,毫无悬念地晋升为正教授。其中一些论文我们与郑先生一起共同发表。

在此,我还得说明一件事,为了使得我另外一位博士研究生能安心研究课题,我、学生与郑先生讨论先完成一篇学生博士毕业要求发表的论文,讨论后由我执笔完成了有关本质下确界的一篇论文,郑先生为该文章作了大量的文字处理并给文章写了总结,文章于2010年发表在《Applied Mathematics Letter》第1期上。其实,该研究生后来在学期间发表了6~7篇SCI论文,根本无须我担心。因为我认为郑先生对文章有重要贡献,就没有经过郑先生同意擅自把他作为作者一起发表,但文章发表后发现第一个定理有关"本质下界"的充分必要条件出现笔误写成"本质下确界",其实看了该文后面内容很容易发现这完全是笔误。但此事我一直没有机会跟郑先生当面解释,成为一个永远的误会。

郑先生虽然已经离开了我们,但他开拓了许多值得我们去研究的领域,为我和我的学生,为大家留下了许许多多可以研究的课题。我指导的本科生进行课外研究,他们的论文每年都有在郑先生等老前辈创刊的《运筹学学报》中、英版杂志上发表,均是有关对郑先生的算法的研究。另外,在博弈论的研究方面,人不可能是完全理性的,人是有限理性的;有限理性当然不能远离完全理性,对有限理性的一个合理表述就是有限理性最终能无限接近于完全理性。许多年前我就有一个想法:通过郑先生提出的算法可以实现有限理性对完全理性的逼近架构,这可能也是对有限理性的一个很好描述,非常值得我们去研究。事实上,对郑先生提出的方法的研究课题非常非常多。

谨以此文聊慰自己,以作为学生、同事对郑先生的怀念。

邬冬华

追思我的挚友郑权教授

陈明仪*

光阴荏苒,花开花落,年复一年,如长江流水奔腾入海不复回……

郑权教授离开我们已一年了。得悉他的夫人涂仁进教授正在整理他发表的遗作,准备结集成册,将他在运筹学与控制论研究中的杰出成果,尤其是他创立的求总体极值点的积分型方法及其相应的理论基础和应用实践等,留给学校。此举令我动容,更勾起我对老郑无尽的思念与悲痛。

记得还在"文革"中,一天,我的好友上海光学仪器研究所的庄松林问我说,你们数学系(原上海科学技术大学)有位郑权教授你熟悉吗?我说,久闻其名,但不熟。他说此人厉害,睿智又诚挚……或许是有缘吧,1978年老郑和我都通过了公费出国留学的考试,于是我们一起进入了学校的英语强化训练班,成了同学、挚友。

还记得,此前他一直与上海光学仪器研究所合作,应用他的总体极值优化方法,克服基于把光学透镜视为线性系统的经典光学透镜自动设计的问题,以满足按傅里叶光学原理,透镜应是一个空间信息变换器——空间带通滤波器,这是经典方法无法满足的要求。最终,郑权教授成功地发明了一种"带迭代序列的蒙特卡洛总极值的求解"方法,取得了突破;又如,浙江大学为解决光学干涉滤波器多层膜系自动设计中的瓶颈问题,也与老郑合作。最终,成功地发展了基于总体极值优化方法的"抗反射宽带光学薄膜的优化设计"方法。当我每每和他谈及此类事情,他总是淡淡一笑,还不时地自谦,戏称自己是"野路子"。其实,这正是他敢于突破、勇于践行的一位科学工作者的高贵品格的显露。

至于在育人上,听说,他更是一丝不苟,严谨又不乏风趣。可惜无缘成为他的学生,去聆听他的讲课与接受他的教诲。这里也有一个小故事:庄松林院士曾对我说,他终生不会忘记,是老郑曾嘱咐他——你一定要学一学泛函分析,学后必能大受其益。他听了,也学了,深深觉得收益匪浅也!由此可见郑权教授诲人不倦、诚挚待人的可贵品格。在这里不得不提的是,老郑是上海大学(原上海科学技术大学)运筹学与控制论博士点和《运筹学杂志》的创办人,是我国和国际运筹学界的著名学者。

总之,我觉得他是一位可爱、可亲、睿智、可敬,又可信赖的学长和挚友。每每思及他的离去,不免黯然伤神、热泪盈眶、悲从心生。他的仙逝实是上海大学的一大损失,也是运筹学界的一大损失。可喜的是,一旦郑权教授的"遗作文集"付梓问世,其治学精神和学术成就将永久惠及学林,激励后生。

---

* 陈明仪,上海大学机械自动化学院教授,新中国成立70周年纪念章获得者.

陈明仪

数学思维比数学运算更重要

汤德祥*

郑权先生是我的老师,也是我的好友。说亦师亦友是很恰当的。我们的同学都亲切地称他为郑先生。他性格开朗,善于钻研,对问题不搞清楚决不罢休。他在数学研究和数学教学方面都有卓著的成绩,令学生们佩服,是一位资深的学者和教育专家。

我跟郑先生的相识是在大学一年级,我是他的开门弟子,他是我大学数学的启蒙老师。当时他刚从复旦大学数学系毕业,就来华东师范大学辅导我们重要的基础课——"数学分析"。他悉心教学,采用多种方法启发学生,既重视数学运算的基本功,更重视数学思维的开发和培养。有一件事始终难忘,那就是在我们学到不定积分的部分,他在习题课上用了一个办法,拿出三十道题要我们三十分钟完成,评判的标准是谁做对的多,谁就领先。我当时得了个第二名,受到了他的关注。另外,他还组织部分学生,经常展开专题的讨论,他也参与讨论。有些问题我们自己提出来,到习题课上又展开更广泛的讨论,侧重于数学的已学和未学的概念和性质,启发大家对数学思维的探索,获得了大多数同学的赞许和认可。现在回忆起来,扎实的基础为我们后继课程的学习带来了极大的好处。在讨论式的教学后,郑先生给我们归纳了一个数学思维的规律:用问题的提出、问题的分析、问题的解决、问题的应用及余下的问题这样一个思维去学习数学的课程是一个最有效的工具,也是搞科研的一个重要手段。让我在毕生的数学教学和数学课题研究中受益匪浅。郑先生的教诲让我们始终不忘。我把他的这种数学思维的教学方法也传授给了我的学生们。

再谈谈我们生活上的接触,他夫人是我们同班同学,毕业后我们分到了同一个省份不同的城市。郑先生在上海工作,有一年暑假他来沈阳探亲。我回上海时去沈阳转车,与郑先生巧遇在同学工作的学校。好久不见面,谈得十分开心,结果在赶火车等候公交车时,眼看着一辆末班车刚开走,我们没有赶上。当时我有点无奈,怕赶不上火车,郑先生马上就说不要着急,我来想办法,当即向邻居借了一辆自行车,把我从沈阳皇姑区的学校,用自行车带到了和平区的火车站,足足用了半小时。郑先生思维敏捷、决策果断、身体健壮,令我难忘!

还有一件险事。一次在上海送他夫人回沈阳时,我们在火车上聊着聊着忘记提前下车,直到听到广播里通知送客的人赶紧下车时,我们马上来到列车的车门口,但列车员已经将上下门的铁板放下了,郑先生毫不犹豫,纵身一跃跳下了火车,我也随即跳到站台上,刚在站台上站稳,列车缓缓启动开行了。我打趣地说了一句:"好险呀,否则我们就要到苏州了!"郑先生笑了笑说:"学数学的人思维就要敏捷,行动就要果断!"这两件事在后来我们见面时或者老同学聚会时,一直被大家传为笑谈。

再谈谈我的工作变动。我和我的夫人在东北也是两地生活,"文革"结束后,工作的调动

---

* 汤德祥,宁波大学数学系、宁波教育学院数学系.

有所松动，我们就想能否从北方调回南方。当时我回上海后第一个征询人就是郑先生。我去南昌路郑先生的寓所，他替我分析说有两种方法，一种可以通过考研到上海，但考研后解决的两地生活不确定性比较大；另一种方法，先直接调回到浙江祖籍，这样解决两地生活更有把握。我经过调查研究，浙江"文革"后恢复高校也确实需要我们这样的教育人才，对解决两地生活把握也会更大。郑先生的数学思维强化了我调动工作的思考，我确实也是这样操作的，事情就这样成功了，真正实现了我的愿望。看来数学的思维对解决实际问题也是大有益处的。

郑先生重视数学思维的观点一直影响着我，尤其当我调回家乡后，在高校数学教学和数学研究的工作中没有忘记件件事情都要从思维出发，所以做成了许多有益的工作。不仅我受益，我的学生们也受益。因为他们不仅在教学岗位上成为优秀的教育工作者，有的在从商或者从政的岗位上做出了许多不平凡的成绩，我在回访他们的时候，问过他们学数学对你们有用吗？他们告诉我："汤老师啊！数学思维无论在哪里都有用。"我感到十分欣慰，心里默默地念道：郑先生啊，您给我的影响我已经传承下去，让我的学生们也受益！太感谢您了！

郑先生，虽然您已经离开了我们，但是您重视数学思维的精神永远留在我们的心中！愿您在天堂如意！

汤德祥

我终生的导师——郑权教授

孙世杰*

1979年,我考入了原上海科学技术大学数学系,攻读运筹学方向的研究生。一年后,郑权教授成为我的论文指导老师。多年以后,当我自己也开始指导研究生时,才慢慢体会到,要当一个好的研究生导师,需要做到以下几点:

(1) 自己要搞科研并走在前列;
(2) 要上课并上好课;
(3) 外语要好;
(4) 作为运筹学方向的导师,计算机要熟练并能解决实际问题。

现在回想起来,郑老师正是这样的一位好导师。

郑老师是国内运筹学研究方向上的一个享有盛名的权威,他首创的积分总极值方法推动了国内对总极值的研究,不仅在国内学术界为同行所称道,在国际上也有一定的影响。

郑老师搞科研不分上下班,只要在学校中,即便是寒暑假他也天天到办公室,一呆就是一天,他就是这样一位全身心投入科研并走在前列的好导师。

郑老师的数学基础极为扎实。在我当郑老师的学生时,他教过我概率论、泛函分析、总极值理论和算法等课。授课时他不看讲义,面向学生,随着所讲的内容,一手漂亮的板书快速地出现在黑板上,令学生不得不惊叹于老师对内容的熟悉和讲课的熟练。在我留校走上讲台之前,郑老师要我对讲课内容背得出再上讲台,学生一直铭记于心,努力做到。

对于一个从事科研的教师来说,外语是一个重要的工具,只有具备熟练的外语才能快速地了解国际动态并能作国际交流。郑老师的外语是一流的,每次招新的研究生复试时他亲自对考生复试外语,有时还带我参加。即便如此,在他六十多岁时还早起背外文单词。郑老师就是这样一个终身努力学习的榜样。

运筹学是一门实用性很强的学科,一个全面的运筹学者不仅要做理论上的研究,更要作实际上的应用。积分总极值方法实际上就是很有用的一个方法,他的另一位研究生就跟着他做了很多这方面的工作,而我也曾在郑老师的指导之下参与了照相机光学镜头的非线性优化设计。在电脑房中近一年的忙碌,我深感搞实际课题的辛劳。

我是郑老师的第一届研究生,也是留校研究生中年龄最大的,对我来说郑老师亦师亦兄。因为"文革"的结果,1968年我从复旦大学毕业后先在军垦农场当了半年炊事员,种了一年田,后被分至浙江一个山区小县的农机厂当了两年化验员、六年采购员。当1979年考取研究生时我已34岁并有了两个孩子。当郑老师了解我的情况后,他和他的夫人涂仁进老师一直十分关心我和我的家人,经常询问我家的情况。以后随着我年龄的增大,膝关节有时

---

* 孙世杰,上海大学理学院数学系教授.

感到不灵活,无意中我对郑老师说起了此事,从此以后不管是他还是涂老师只要是去美国,都会替我带回并送给我有利于增强关节灵活性的保健药,多年如此,现在我膝关节不灵活的症状已消失了。

郑老师对我的关心更多的是在业务上。我留校第一年他就把我推上了大四非线性规划这门课的讲台。

1987年,学校给了我系两个参加出国留学人员英语水平测试的名额,郑老师支持我参加了考试。在五月份我得知通过了考试,七月份他又送我去北戴河参加天津工学院主办的为期半个月的组合最优化学习班以扩大眼界。正是在这个学习班上,中科院一些老师介绍了做组合最优化研究所需要的一些基本工具,并介绍了组合最优化的一个重要分支——排序理论与算法的一些研究成果。学习班上所学的知识引起了我的极大兴趣,并决定将自己的研究方向从非线性规划转向排序理论与算法。

孙世杰与郑权(左)

1988年8月,在郑老师的担保下,我前往比利时鲁汶大学公派留学。从1954年发表第一篇排序文章起,到1988年,国外20多种外文期刊上发表了约两千篇排序文章。正是出国这一年半,我浏览了几乎所有这些文章并复印了其中的近五百篇带回国内。回国时我信心满满,因为我已对国外关于排序研究的历史、现状和动态搞得一清二楚。回国第二年我带起了硕士生,在我评上副教授的当年,又以郑老师的名义带起了外国博士生。可以说,正是在郑老师的关切和帮助下,我的后半生走得十分顺利。

郑老师是我的终生导师,如今我已退休十年,仍经常回忆此生的点点滴滴。我的后半生同前半生如此不同,从大处讲是祖国的改革开放政策,从具体讲是郑老师的教育、培养和关心。老师现在身体不太好,祝老师在涂老师的精心照料下一步一步地恢复健康。

2016年7月10日

深切怀念老师郑权教授

周建新*

2020年5月9日下午18:38分郑权老师非常安宁地荣归天堂。当时我虽已有预感但仍觉难舍,依依难舍。

多年来与郑先生相处的一幕幕往事片段常常在我的脑海中回荡。

郑权是我的老师,导师和恩师。我按上海传统尊称他为先生。

我于1973年作为"工农兵学员"进入上海科学技术大学学习,不久便了解到郑权先生和郭本瑜先生是当时上海科技大学数学系的二大台柱。他们都是在文革中带领组织,并坚持举行多种学术研究活动,后来各自成为国内专业学术的领军人物。

(1) 郑先生是我的老师。在我读大学时期,郑先生曾给我们班上过几节专业课。他上课时形式活泼,善于以诱导的方式吸引学生,并着重于思想方法的讲解。这影响了我一生的教学生涯。我为他一手极其漂亮的板书所折服。

(2) 郑权先生是我的导师。我从上海科学技术大学毕业留校工作后,开始与郑先生有了比较亲近的接触。多次聆听他在专业研讨会上的报告,之后,我越来越被他做科研的思维方法、理论与实际应用相结合的方式所吸引,并产生了强烈的兴趣。他当时就鼓励我努力复习功课,准备考他的第一届研究生班。同时他安排我每周一次到上海(漕河泾)自动化研究所去上课,普及计算机知识、编程语言及算法编程。通过考试被录取后,我就在郑先生的门下学习专业知识,走上了在最优化领域做科研的人生之道。郑权教授的一个重要学术贡献就是他提出的求总体极值点的积分型统计算法,及其相应的理论基础和应用实践。这个算法有多个重要的优点:

(a) 求解总体极值点是最优化理论和算法中的重点之重,难点之难。至今几乎所有其它的算法都只能求解局部极值点;

(b) 对目标函数的光滑性要求比其它算法都低,可以接受具有间断跳跃点的目标函数,从而适用性更强;

(c) 算法中计算量增加对于变量维数增加的敏感性比其它算法要低;

(d) 由于是积分性算法,此算法可以按问题不同的实际背景来设计选用相应的测度以便更有效地求解总体极值点,从而增加了此算法的灵活性;

(e) 此算法在平行计算方向上有着巨大的潜力。

我可以很自豪、很得意地宣称,我在这方向得他的"真传",因为作为他的学生,我的硕士论文就是对此算法从理论上进行拓广和在软件实施上进行改进。我在美国工作的早期期间,曾用这个算法去探讨隐形飞机设计中的总体极值点问题,获得很好的效果,论文发表在

---

* 周建新,美国德克萨斯A&M大学数学系教授.

专业期刊上。

(3) 郑权先生是我的恩师。在我成为他的硕士生不久(1981年),他就要求我加强英语学习,准备好去美国留学读博士。这显示出他对国际先进科学技术的洞察力和培养年青科技人员的热诚和前瞻性。没有他指明的人生方向和鼓励,当时的我是不可想象的。他作为"文革"后第一批去美国作学术访问的中国学者之一,一进入美国大学后就开始为我留学美国操劳,与美国教授联络、推荐,并成功地为我申请到了助学金。他还为我到美国大学留学作好了前期的生活安排。这对于我这样一个第一次出国,远渡重洋,人生地不熟,语言不畅,身揣50美元,甚至无钱买到达大学城灰狗车票的人来说是多么的重要和及时啊!

郑先生在当系主任之前和之时,一直对上海科学技术大学数学系有一个雄心勃勃的长期规划——他要创办一个学科完整的应用数学专业。前后多年,他努力为多位年青教师出国留学深造创造条件,并要求他们主攻不同的专业方向,学成归来后要成为这一专业方向的学术带头人。他了解到我曾有专业学习下围棋,并得到过上海围棋比赛少年组第一名的经历,就要求我主攻博弈论,我欣然接受。所以我在美国大学的博士论文就是有关微分博弈的课题。

郑先生作为上海科学技术大学数学系的学术带头人,非常重视组建科研团队。为此他鼓励数学系的其他老师加入其研究课题,协作分享自己的科研成果。

我在美国当教授后,郑先生曾在我工作的大学当访问教授一年。那是我们一起度过的一段最愉快的时光。我们曾一起驾车去参加学术会议,看望在美国的同事和朋友,去旅游。但是那段时间我和夫人刚有了第二个孩子,又各自忙于学校工作,没能有更多的时间陪伴郑先生,这还是给我留下了无法弥补的遗憾。

郑先生不仅数学做得好,在理论和实践方面都能创新做出重要贡献,在生活中他更是多才多艺。他既能高声歌吟,又能谱曲,还能上台指挥大合唱。我记得刚留校时,曾经和郑先生一起代表数学系参加过上海科学技术大学教工运动会的四人接力赛。他还曾在学校的一次文艺汇演中,上台指挥我们数学系的大合唱。

郑权教授一生桃李芬芳,誉满天下。我有幸作为他的学生,回首往事,觉得郑先生对我的人生影响是多方面、深远的,从处世原则、学术方法到人身性格等。当然我只是从他那儿学了部分而学不到全部。

现在当我仰望星空天际时,我会不时想念着在天堂安息的我的老师、导师和恩师郑权教授。

左起:郑权、周建新、纪令克(周建新夫人),1985年摄于美国宾州州立大学

忆郑老师二三事

尹小南[*]

郑权老师和我的丈夫王汉坤有长达 20 多年的师生情谊,他不仅是汉坤学业上的导师,更是汉坤走上成功之路的动力和楷模。

当年在上海,在我与郑老师素未谋面之前,汉坤就经常告诉我他是多么幸运地有郑老师这样的导师,点点滴滴地说着老师的教导和提携。后来郑老师鼓励和支持汉坤去美国宾州大学进一步攻读博士学位。汉坤从求学一直到成为教授后,郑老师和汉坤始终保持在学业上的探讨,互相联系和访问。

郑老师既是汉坤的良师益友,又像是他的兄长,我们的孩子一直称呼郑老师为郑伯伯。郑老师平易近人,关爱学生,待人和善。记得我生下大女儿后,无法从工作抽身的他,特意嘱咐他的爱人涂仁进老师来看望我们。当时汉坤和周建新刚到宾州大学,人地生疏,郑老师也帮助他俩很快地找到了一处方便又温馨的住处,可以无后顾之忧地做学问。

郑老师自己生活很简朴,却很乐意帮助别人。当汉坤去世时,他和涂老师在第一时间发来唁电,并附上支票,在最困难时,给了我们精神上和物质上的支援。从未谋面时汉坤的口中,一直到自己亲身体会郑老师夫妇的照顾,郑老师对我们一家有着不可磨灭的影响,这种影响一直持续到我和汉坤的两个女儿文娃和文妮。现在她们已经长大成人,各自从名校毕业,从事高科技和医生的职业,堪可告慰郑老师的在天之灵。

左起:郑权、王汉坤和尹小楠,1985 年摄于美国宾州州立大学

---

[*] 尹小南,郑权学生王汉坤之妻.

郑 权 老 师

谢志刚[*]

一、序

2013年末冬至那天,我带上回家休圣诞节假期的女儿谢璐到浦东"亲和源"养老社区,去看望我的硕士研究生导师——郑权老师。难得地,让小谢同学看到了我的另一面,更让她终于逮着一次"嘲笑"和"报复"我的机会。

她先嘲笑:"老爹啊,真没想到,你也有如此卑微、马屁和猥琐的一面哈?还以为你从来就不可一世,一直就凶神恶煞,让所有的学生都怕你,让所有家庭成员都怕你。怎么,一物降一物啊,啊?"

我与郑权老师(轮椅坐者),谢璐拍摄于2013年冬至

嘲笑之后还不过瘾,继续报复,对我进行了心理分析,"Dad, you have daddy issues!"虽然我英语不好,也知道这是人身攻击呀!

嗨,没什么!俺走自己的路,让这帮小兔崽子去误会、误解和嘲笑去吧。

不过,这两天休息,正好可以给你们,更是给自己讲讲郑老师的故事,回味一下什么叫做

---

[*] 谢志刚,上海财经大学教授.

好的老师。

本人这辈子运气真是好,从幼儿园的李淑英老师到博士导师 Simon French 教授,个个对我都是鼓励和夸赞有余,而严格和批评则不太足,唯独郑权老师,记忆中他几乎从来没有表扬过我,全都是严厉的批评。

跟郑老师念了三年研究生,其中有两次春节寒假没回老家过年。没回家的这两次春节,郑老师让我年三十去到他家吃年夜饭。

我大约下午 4 点左右过去。哇,郑老师给我准备的第一道"菜",就是列数我期末考试答卷中存在的种种问题,包括其他老师反映给他的问题,一个细节都不放过,绝对让俺无地自容。连师母涂仁进老师在旁边都看不过去,劝了好几次,没用,继续批评。

同学们啦,你们过过这样的年吗?!

仔细想想,郑老师教育我们学生的方法,确实是很值得记录和传承。这样的老师,在今天是很难再有了吧。所以啊,我要回忆、分享郑老师当年是如何教育和影响我的。

二、第一瓢凉水

1983 年 7 月,我考上了上海科学技术大学数学系运筹学方向郑权教授名下的研究生,这可是俺家乡——云南省巧家县历史上的第一个研究生啊,很有点石破天惊的意思,绝对让俺飘飘然,很是得意忘形。整天尽情享受着亲戚朋友的恭维和赞美,那个得意劲呀,远远超过了十多年后我成为巧家县历史上第一个留英博士的状态。

这种光荣伟大和飘飘然的日子,我很是享受了好些天,直到突然收到一封来自上海科学技术大学的信,打开一看,是学校研究生办公室金姓秘书写的,信中说郑权教授刚从美国访问回来,立即委托金秘书给每一位即将入学的新研究生写信,告知开学就要给我们上课,直接用英文上课,请务必认真准备,听不懂自己负责。

我的妈呀,从未听过用英语上的课啊,俺考研的英语成绩就 60 分,一分都不多,而且是拼了老命外加运气不错才挣得这 60 分啊。

还没到上海见面,郑权老师就提前给我泼了一瓢凉水。没法再继续飘飘然了,赶紧找了一本《科技英语文选》猛学英语,尽管很难真正学进去。

三、感受郑权老师的教育理念

毫无悬念,到上海科学技术大学读研的整个第一学期,我完全听不懂郑老师讲的《最优化理论与方法》。

笔记也记不下来。郑老师不仅讲得很快,板书也非常快。

更恐怖的是,课程上到一半左右,说是开始进入考试阶段了,先开卷,课程结束后再闭卷。给了一道开卷题目,是个研究问题,要求自己去研究并给出答案,然后将研究过程和结果写成一份报告,等到学期结束前进行闭卷考试时,将开卷(研究报告)与闭卷试卷一起装订成册,作为评定这门课的成绩的依据,具体分数占比忘记了,好像是五、五开吧。也就是说,学这门课,开卷和闭卷考试两样都要,一样都不能少。试卷订在一起是厚厚的一本。当然,还要求用英语写作。

我的自信心受到严重打击!

我的英文水平，可能是全校各专业这届共30名研究生中最差的，其他方面的基础也很弱，包括政治课程——《自然辩证法》都觉得跟不上思路。我快要完全失去自信了。

于是，我肠胃开始不舒服，睡眠也很不好，要恶性循环了！

鼓起十二万分的勇气，去给郑老师汇报自己的学习状况。

先汇报说，由于自己的基础不好，暂时做不了研究（开卷题目），是不是可以等多学些基础课程，打好基础之后再做研究？

郑老师的回答是："胡说！做学问不是修房子，要先打好基础再建房子，打多厚的基础就建多高的房子。做学问不是这样的！做学问更像植树，树是一边往上长枝干，一边往下扎根，是动态的，是同时进行的，你知道吗？你不做研究怎么打得好基础！"

我再次鼓起超过十二万分的勇气，诉说自己身体素质不太好，尤其是肠胃和睡眠不好，影响了自己的学习效率，进步不可能很快，需要慢慢调养，是否可以让我缓慢一点跟上进度？

郑老师的回答是："胡说！你知道吗，身体不是调养出来的，是练出来的。我以前的身体比你还差，可是我坚持锻炼，坚持游泳，坚持跑步，所以我现在身体很好！"

我滴个娘嘞！非但没有博得半点可怜，只是得到两通臭骂。

没办法了，只好"横竖横"！游泳去，每天一大早天不亮就跑步去体育场露天泳池游泳，从夏天游到秋天，从秋天游到冬天，再游回到春天。当然很痛苦啦，但肯定没有教室里的痛苦来得深重。

贵在坚持，咬着牙，熬过一个冬天就好了。肠胃好了，睡眠也不错了，英语虽然仍不好，但不怕了，有点自信了，做研究也有些感觉了。

这就是严师的风范，现在回忆，真庆幸自己在硕士期间碰上这样一位严师！

四、学术与抉择

转眼之间，几十年过去了，我自己也成了"老教授"。但作为郑老师的学生之一，深感自己在学术造诣上远没达到郑老师的境界，恐怕也难以达到了。我只是运气比较好一些而已，赶上了比较好的时代。

我说的这种境界，可以通过下面两封普通书信来反映。这是20世纪80年代郑老师与他的朋友，光学专家庄松林院士诸多的书信往来之一，不知道现在的年轻人能否想象，那时候的学者之间的相互通信是这样的。

郑老师在最优化领域中开创了一套独特的方法——总体极值的随机算法，并奠定了这套方法的理论基础，在美国和加拿大都出版有专著（注：in Chew Soo Hong 的英文协助以及与 E. A. Galperin 的合作下），发了很多文章。尤其令人佩服的是，他从奠定理论基础架构到编制计算程序包，再到应用于光学仪器设计计算等一整套环节，都是自己一气呵成，这在他那辈学者中也是少之又少的，十分难得。

郑老师曾给我说过，在国外工作期间，他曾希望将那套计算程序申请专利，也找过专利律师进行过咨询，但律师说计算程序软件是难以注册为专利的。

郑老师也曾感叹说他运气不太好，主要指当年在加拿大和美国与他有良好合作，而且特别赏识他的两位大师级人物，都英年早逝，突然中断了相互间的合作，这对郑权老师在北美地区的研究工作极为不利，负面影响极大。是啊，只有成功的科学研究者才能体会，拥有至少一位保持长期合作，而且又互相赏识的研究合作者，对个人的学术生涯有多重要！

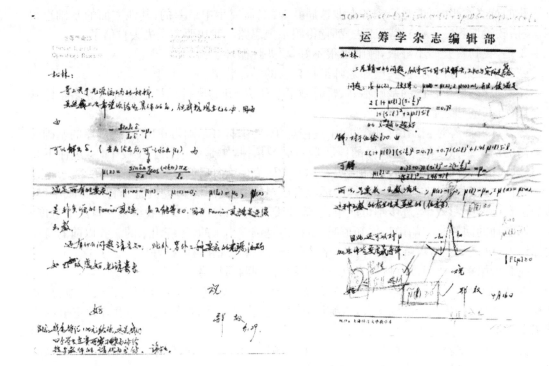

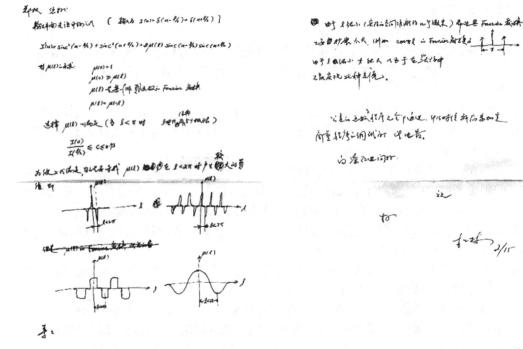

上图中第一行的两页是郑权老师写给庄松林院士的信，第二行的两页则是庄松林的回信

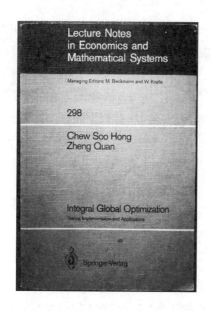
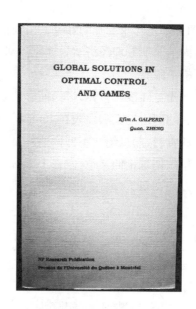

郑权教授在 Chew Soo Hong 以及 E. A. Galperin 协作下分别在美国和加拿大出版的两本专著

要系统介绍郑权老师的学术生涯和成就，也许最合适的人是周建新师兄，他与郑老师的研究领域比较近一些，而且又一直在美国工作，交流机会也多些。我只是说说自己的理解，或可以算作一种补充。

我一直认为，以郑老师的科学素养和长期努力，他应该是应用数学领域中能够发挥重大影响力的人物，我也多次思考这个问题。

先说说我对大多数学者的印象，国内外学者都雷同的印象。

无论在哪里，很多大牌教授带研究生，都会引导研究生沿着自己所开辟的某一研究方向或领域，不断积累研究成果和贡献，这些研究生毕业后，或留校工作，或到其他高校和研究机构工作，便逐渐形成一个不断向外延伸的研究团队，进而成为一个学派或者叫做"门派"也行。无所谓对或错，但自古以来都是如此。

但郑老师不一样，这让我感到很奇怪，很惋惜，同时也很敬佩，很受益。

郑权老师在 1983—1986 年期间指导我们这届四位，以及后两届(1984—1987 和 1985—1988)近十位研究生的时候，应该是他学术研究生涯中处于高峰的时期。如果他那时带领自己的学生和青年教师研究团队沿着总体极值随机算法的路径，继续发表更多的理论和应用研究成果，其学术影响一定会加速上升。这无论对学校的学科建设还是巩固他自己的学术地位来说，都是大大的利好。但他显然没有这样做。

相反，他选择让我们这届四位以及下一届的几位研究生放弃在最优化领域的进一步学习和研究，转而去寻找应用经济学中的研究问题，努力尝试开辟出属于自己的研究方向。

他让张晓东去研究用动态博弈去模型描述经济学问题，让鲁习文研究用计算不动点的方法研究经济平衡点问题，让我去研究风险与不确定性条件下的决策问题。

还有我们下一届的宋学锋、戴万阳等同学，也类似这样。

现在想想，早在 20 世纪 80 年代中期，有几个人能够预测到这些研究方向是 20 年后中国经济金融领域中的热点和重要问题啊！

就我所知，当时国内有类似想法的学者中，有南开大学的史树中教授和中山大学的王则柯教授，两位都是郑权老师的好友。由他们几位老师共同发起，于1985年8月在南开大学组织了国内第一期数理经济学暑期班。郑老师带着我和张晓东参加了这期暑期班，让我俩大大地开扩了眼界。

我自己受益匪浅。首先，自己能够从硕士研究生第二年末，就直接开始阅读美国大学经济系中最新的博士论文和发表在 Econometrica 等刊物上的相关论文，这些都是郑老师从美国背回来的资料，起点绝对不低。或许是为了鼓励和提携我，郑老师还破例与我合作写了一篇综述期望效用理论的文章，发在上海科学技术出版社出版的《自然杂志》上，这应该是我头一次公开发表文章。

关于决策论的基础

郑　权　谢志刚　（上海科学技术大学）

人们时常要在不确定条件下从许多备选方案中决定自己的抉择。随着生产及科学技术和社会的发展，决策问题变得越来越复杂，单凭决策者个人的学识和经验作决策就越来越不能适应了。从而出现了一些科学的决策思想和方法。决策分析就是为帮助人们合理地分析决策问题的结构、选择决策方法和评价标准的一套概念和系统方法，而决策论又是它的理论基础。

本文着重介绍决策论的基本概念和理论基础，介绍这方面研究的一些最新进展，望能引起人们对这方面研究的重视。

结果有78%的学生认为应该执行计划 D。

留心一看，计划A＝计划C，计划B＝计划D，其后果是一致的。然而，决策者的抉择又是如此的不同。可见，人类确实需要研究合理决策和它的基础。

二、决策问题

在考虑决策问题时，其后果不但与决策者的抉择有关，还与外界因素有关。这种外界因素，或者是决策者无法控制的，或者是他作决策时未知的。这种外界因素叫做自然状态（或简称状态）。

这是郑权老师带着我写的介绍风险决策分析的文章，发表于《自然杂志》1989年第3期

更重要的是，因为自己内心充满了对这些新知识的向往、敬畏和自豪，因此愿意整天泡在图书馆阅览室艰难地啃 Von Neumann & Morgenstern(1944)、L. J. Savage (1954) 以及 P. Fishburn(1970——1982) 等英文原著，尽管读得非常吃力，做了大量的笔记，未必真正理解，但非常值得这样付出。估计这些资料也是由郑老师让学校图书馆订购或者他送给学校教师阅览室的，否则学校怎么会想到去收藏这些资料呢。

尤其值得一提的是，我还在学校教师阅览室里读完了后来成为我博士生导师的 Simon French 教授的成名作——Decision Theory: An Introduction to the Mathematics of Rationality (French, 1986)，那也是我第一次知道学术著作也可以采用诙谐幽默的文笔来写，十分喜欢。以至于我后来(1992年)读博士的第一学期，Simon 就觉得我基础蛮好，马上与我合作写了篇文章，还带着我到西班牙马德里参加了一次国际会议，自己顺便看了场西班牙斗牛。这很是让系里的其他博士生羡慕嫉妒，纷纷抱怨 Simon 偏心和不公平。凭这段经历，可以想象，我在英国跟 Simon 读博士并获得博士学位，远比其他同学轻松、潇洒。但这其实要归功于郑权老师当年的教导。

2002年，我陪同郑权老师去中国矿业大学讲学，在徐州与他指导的另一位研究生、我的师弟宋学锋教授合影。宋学锋当年也是剑走偏锋，成为系统科学专家，现为中国矿业大学校长

2002年，我邀请郑权老师到上海财经大学给保险精算专业方向的硕士和博士研究生做讲座

令我惋惜的是,郑老师自己并没有像史树中教授和王则柯教授那样,在国内的数理经济学领域中实现自己的转型并形成较大学术影响。相反,当我们这一届研究生刚完成论文答辩即将毕业时,郑老师又再度赴加拿大访问然后再到美国,加之1989年发生的一些事情等因素作用,失去了在国内继续推动和开辟这些研究领域的机会。

要知道,这些经济学中的理论和应用研究专题,只有在国内才具有开创性,在国外却已经流行多年。而郑老师因为在经济和金融学领域中并没有经过系统训练,没有进入任何门派或圈子,很难在北美的经济与金融圈中依靠这套数学和计算方法立足。

我为郑权老师感到惋惜,也深知,这是选择的代价。

郑权老师当年的抉择,纯粹是做铺路石的抉择。他的抉择对于他所开创的总极值随机化理论方法,对于上海科学技术大学的学科建设以及对他自己的学术影响力来说,肯定是十分不利的。但他在默默无闻的选择中,却及早地推动了国内运筹学界对西方经济与金融学的关注,推动了数学在应用经济学中的应用。

别人的情况我不好评价,但我自己确实是一个实实在在的受益者,当年的训练对我近20年来系统了解一个行业并在精算学领域做些工作有极大的帮助,实现了得心应手的转型。

这是我对郑老师学术生涯和人生抉择的理解,有惋惜,更多是敬佩。

五、多才更多艺

跟郑权老师读硕士那三年(1983—1986),我们同学哥几个根本不敢跟郑老师聊什么兴趣爱好才艺什么的,一方面是学习压力巨大,另一方面是惧怕郑老师。

不过,在私底下,尤其是在其他专业的研究生同学面前,咱对郑老师在学术之外的才华却是非常自豪和津津乐道的,也常常用于内部调侃和私下取乐。

据说郑老师爱游泳,但我们都没有领教和与他比试过。他坚持游了很多年,一直到2011年暑假在上海大学做访问教授期间还每天游,想必是游得不错。

但郑老师最著名的才艺,应该是音乐。

我可以把游泳和音乐两件事串在一起说说,按时间倒序说。

2012年,复旦大学精算中心主任尚汉冀教授告诉我,当年他与郑老师是复旦数学系的同班同学。2010年,他们班搞过一次老同学聚会,聚会中回忆并一起咏唱了他们当年创作的《毕业歌》,也是他们班的"班歌"。很多人都还记得、还会唱这首班歌,也都还清楚记得,班歌的作曲者正是咱们的郑权老师,作词则是尚汉冀老师。

说起来很有意思,按辈分,尚老师算我师叔,但自1997年以来,他一直是我最好的合作者和扶持者,我们一起为推动中国精算事业的发展做了不少事情。

这又让我联想起自己在四川时的几位老师,都是师母涂仁进老师当年在华东师范大学数学系的同学或校友。其中教过我线性代数的陈芝兰老师,当年还与涂老师在华师大住同一寝室,关系很铁。有一年暑假我回四川去看望陈芝兰老师,她开玩笑说我快升级为与她同辈分了,因为郑老师当年也是她和涂老师的小老师,然后她开始"爆料"。

她说涂老师当时是学校里的百灵鸟,很会唱歌,而郑老师是借调到华东师范大学做他们的辅导老师(小老师),也很会唱歌,郑老师和涂老师两人还一起排练和表演节目呢,然后,他们就……就那个了。

"啊,原来是水中桥!"(注:朝鲜电影《南江村的妇女》中的台词。)

六、留在浦东"亲和源"的美好记忆

2013年12月,郑老师和涂老师夫妇打算回上海养老,选择定居于上海浦东"亲和源"养老公寓,一直住到2017年3月17日返回美国哥伦布(Columbus)。

他们夫妇在上海这三年多时间里,再次给我们这帮同学带来许多团聚、感动和美好回忆。

先说团聚。这些年来,同学们各忙各的,见面交流的机会十分稀少,但因为老师和师母的回归,就为我们创造了经常相聚的理由和条件。在上海的同学自不必说,多多少少,一两周就能在"亲和源"里聚一次,如果有国外的比如周建新师兄、张晓东等同学回来,自然也少不了一起去"亲和源"郑老师、涂老师那里热闹一番。

"亲和源"在上海是一家挺不错的养老社区,一区共十幢楼,其中第十号楼用作医院,其它九幢楼是住宅。这里的住户以上海文化教育界的退休知识分子为主,所以社区里组织的各种活动都很文艺,他们哪栋楼一楼都有一个很大的书法绘画厅,墙上展示的作品水平很高,我很有收藏几幅的冲动。

但郑老师、涂老师夫妇使用最多的是乒乓球室、游泳池、电影院和合唱厅,涂老师自然又是合唱团的骨干分子,听她说社区里不止一个合唱团,还分语种,除中文外还有英语、俄语合唱团。

当然还有基督徒组织的许多活动,我和彭建平一家应邀参加过一次社区里的圣诞活动,涂老师在台上领唱,郑老师坐轮椅上在观众席中唱得也特别卖力。

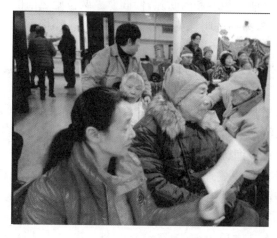

右图中前排左二是涂仁进老师,给郑老师拿着歌谱的是护工小牛

除了在"亲和源"大吃大喝唱歌玩乐以外,我觉得更重要的是收获了许多感动。

首先是感动于涂老师对郑老师无微不至、一以贯之的细心照顾,说实话,我真没有见过如此相濡以沫的老夫老妻,实在是很受教育。

不仅被涂老师感动,还被涂老师的学生们感动。

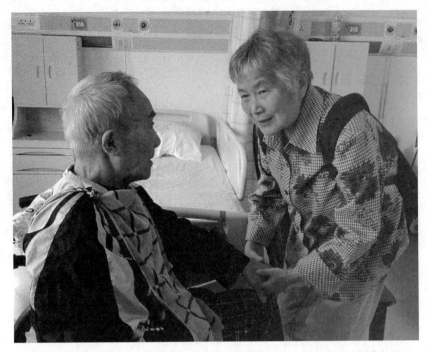

涂仁进老师说她是一个优秀护工教练,不仅培养了几个护工,关键还自己练

涂老师大学毕业后被分配到东北沈阳做中学老师,一做就做了13年,历经磨砺,"文革"结束后还是通过考研究生的途径回到上海与郑老师团圆。但她在沈阳也培养了不少学生,而且这么多年过去了,许多学生都到了退休年龄,竟然还牵挂着涂老师。当他们知道涂老师在照顾着郑老师而且需要帮助时,许多人都自愿要来上海帮着照顾郑老师。盛情难却而且又确实需要时,尤其是在涂老师需要回美国处理一些事务的间隙,便同意了两位她之前的学生轮流来上海替她照顾郑老师,一位叫金玉华,另一位叫金英姿,都挺认真负责,积极配合护工工作,也让我们这帮(郑老师这边的)同学受到了激励和教育。

一不留神我竟然搞起门派来了,区分了"涂门"与"郑门"。不能光涨"涂门"的志气灭了咱"郑门"威风啊!

"郑门"这边,我觉得要数姚奕荣教授的贡献最大。论学历辈分,他还算我师弟,我主要擅长于吃喝玩乐衬托些热闹,要论对医疗系统的了解和护理经验,就远不如姚奕荣了,甚至连涂老师都十分倚重他的经验,大事小事都得咨询姚奕荣的意见。

2016年9月,涂老师需要回到哥伦布市的家里处理一些税务、购药之类的事情,需要离开上海三周左右时间,就把她不在上海期间但可能需要处理应急事项的责任委托给了姚奕荣和我。

那段时间,姚奕荣几乎是每天一大早开车从家里出门,到我家小区门口把我捎上,然后继续向浦东"亲和源"行进,赶在早上医生查房前到达"亲和源"十号楼(注:把郑老师安置在作为医院的十号楼更安全),便于听听医生的意见。然后再返回单位上班,来回大概要三个小时吧。

比较有趣的是,我们每天进出"亲和源"后门的马路旁边,早上有几个村民在路边卖菜,都是村民自家地里种的,特别新鲜好吃,于是我们离开"亲和源"时顺便带些蔬菜回去。很

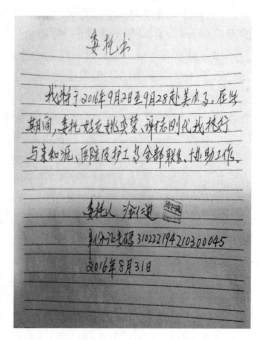

2016 年 9 月，涂仁进老师回美 3 个星期，给姚奕荣和我写了委托书

快,我和姚奕荣买菜上瘾,产生了蔬菜依赖症,觉得其它店里买的菜都不好吃了,就喜欢"亲和源"路边的菜。

涂老师回来以后,我们不再这么早跑过去,也就吃不到这么好吃的新鲜蔬菜了,心里那个难过啊,恨不得每天早上打的过去买菜。

总之,郑老师和涂老师在浦东"亲和源"居住的几年中,为我们这帮同学创造了很好的聚会条件,为我们留下了难忘的美好记忆。

七、与郑老师的两次道别

2017 年 3 月,涂老师告诉我,她和郑老师决定回美国居住一段时间,订了 17 日的航班,至于啥时候再回来或是回不回来,不确定。

我感觉有点突然,也有点疑惑,于是决定去"亲和源"与涂老师和郑老师道别时单独问问郑老师自己的心愿。大概是在 15 日或者 16 日上午吧,我是与彭建平一起去"亲和源"的,细节记不太清,只记得是我推着轮椅上的郑老师出门遛遛弯,在一个凉亭里,只有我们俩的时候,我对郑老师说,我要问你一个严肃的问题,关于你将来的安排,你的归属,究竟选择是在上海还是在哥伦布那边呢?郑老师清晰地告诉了我,是后者。

于是,我也释怀了。这算第一次道别。

第二次是 2019 年 6 月,我和太太陆钦雯去斯坦福女儿那里小住几周。利用这个机会,我们俩一起飞到亚特兰大然后再乘朋友的车到了哥伦布市涂老师和郑老师家,这是我第二次到这里,上一次是 2005 年春天我在亚特兰大做访问学者期间,那时候郑老师还没退休。

可这次不一样了，郑老师住在当地一家医院里，应该是重症病房，一人一间，上了呼吸机，身上插了几根管子，包括胃管、气管、导尿管，神智清楚时能眨眼睛，手指可以有握紧放松的反应，但多数时间是无知觉的，褥疮也比较严重。

涂老师非常辛苦，每天跑医院两个来回，早上是第一次，中午回来吃点东西，休息一小会儿之后下午2、3点第二次出发去医院，然后半夜回来睡觉，天天如此。

我们在这里待了一周左右，我自己每天只去一次医院，离开之前，我觉得自己需要给郑老师作一次告别交流，把我想说的话说给他听，相信他能听得见我说了什么。

也是我们俩单独聊，我讲了半小时左右，讲话的时候我感觉有点激动。现在只记得要点，主要讲了三点吧，简单复述一下。

第一，郑老师你是我的"贵人"，是你在我人生关键时刻改变了我的生活。1983年我报考你的研究生时，考两轮，初试和复试，我初试考分比较高但复试不是很满意，其中犯的一个错误是把手写试卷中的"z"看成"2"或是相反，但我在复试之后给你写了一封信，表达了我对数学研究的痴迷，尤其是表达了我对现行教科书中关于"可测函数"与"可积函数"这两个概念内涵的质疑，并提出了自己的想法，还表达了如果考不上也希望能继续向你请教数学问题的请求。后来你才告诉我，正是我写的这封信让你去找学校有关领导，希望扩大招生规模，把我这种可能有潜力的青年都招进来培养，因此那年运筹学方向一共招了5名（郑老师带4人，张连生老师带1人），而以往的情况是只招收1—2名，而且通常只招本校和名校毕业生。如果不是郑老师你的大度和果断，我将难以成为上海科学技术大学的30名研究生之一。

大约是在1989年，中国运筹学会要组织专家编写一本《运筹学基础手册》，其中关于风险决策分析的内容编写工作，没有比郑权老师与我更合适的人选了，自然成为了我们的工作，经过好几年的努力才完成这项任务

第二,研究生毕业后,郑老师所指导的其他3位同学(张晓东、鲁习文、李珊)都各奔东西了,就我一个人留校工作,而郑老师也一直留在加拿大和美国,这期间(从1986年6月至1991年9月),是我感觉最困惑、委屈和痛苦的几年,完全看不到自己的前途。但也是在这期间,郑老师差不多每个月都会给我写一封信,不断地鼓励我、督促我不能放弃,叮嘱我越是在逆境中越是要努力坚持,一旦机会到来,所有的努力和付出都会获得回报。我至今仍保留着那些信件,因为是这些鼓励和督促陪伴我坚持了下来。

第三,是郑老师你引导我进入了"风险与决策"这个研究领域,虽然我当时并不知道这是经济和金融领域中最核心的议题之一,直到很多年以后我才知道的,但我喜欢这个领域,因为我找到了自己学习和学以致用的圣地,我感觉非常幸福,谢谢老师!

主要就讲了这三点吧。讲完之后,再次感觉释怀许多。

人生能遇到这样的老师,何其幸运,自己能做的,就是像郑老师一样,努力做一个好老师。

纪念我的导师郑权教授

鲁习文*

郑先生是对我人生影响最大的人之一,他虽然已经离开了我们,但他始终活在我的心中。在写这篇纪念他的短文的时候,不少往事浮现在我的眼前。

能成为郑先生的学生是我人生的一件幸事,也是一件偶然的事。

1982年,我大学毕业从武汉到了河南商丘,一时很迷茫,主要是湖北黄冈的生活习惯与河南商丘很不一样,使得我一时生活难以适应,因此我打算回到吃米饭的南方,但那时工作调动很困难,最好的办法是考研究生。当时我的一个同学在上海交通大学,受她的影响,我决定选择报考上海的一所大学。那时我对上海的大学了解很少,想过考复旦大学或者上海交通大学,但担心受挫,因为当时想急于离开商丘到南方,我想还是报考一所把握大一点的学校,自认为考上海科学技术大学,保险系数更大一些。当时心里还有另外一个怪怪的也挺幼稚的想法:我大学读的是华中师范学院(现华中师范大学),当时名称上不是大学,至少上海科学技术大学有"大学"两字,是一所大学。其实那时对上海科学技术大学基本一无所知,连在什么地方都不知道。记得研究生入学报到时,出了上海火车站,一路往嘉定,越走离市区越远,当时想这还是上海吗?好不容易从农村到了城市,好像有一种又从城市回到了农村的感觉。到了上海科学技术大学的校园,感觉怎么校园这么小,远远不及华中师范大学所在的桂子山,说真的,当时挺失望的。

我能成为郑先生的学生,真的是一件幸事。我记得当年研究生入学考三门数学课,我考的还算不错,每门都是90多分。其中高等代数,也可能叫线性代数,记不清了,好像考了96分;但英语考的很差,好像是57分。也许是因为笔试考的还挺好,上海科学技术大学没有让我到学校进行复试和面试。在我研究生入学后,我的同学孙其仁(遗憾的是他英年早逝)告诉我,当初报考上海科学技术大学研究生的人挺多的,参加面试的还有中国科技大学等名校的学生,他们当中有些虽然参加了复试面试,但最后因为名额有限而未能录取。如果我真的参加复试面试,连普通话都讲不好的我,在竞争那么激烈的情况下,我很有可能被淘汰,也就没有成为郑先生学生的机会。现在想起来,我当时真的挺幸运。

我被录取后,在商丘收到郑先生的一封信,我才知道,没有到上海科学技术大学参加面试是郑先生的意思,同时郑先生让我在入学报到之前,认真复习英语。我当时仅仅以为郑先生认为我的英语基础不好,后来才知道让我提前好好学习英语的初衷。我记得研究生第一年,郑先生的专业课程全部用英语授课,再加上英语精读、泛读、口语等课程,几乎所有的课程都是英语,这对英语基础很差的我,一时难以适应。好在我还是熬过了那段艰难时期,挺过来了。那段难忘的经历为我后来的学术发展奠定了良好的基础。

---

* 鲁习文,华东理工大学教授.

郑先生不仅是一位杰出的运筹学家,还是一位优秀的研究生导师;郑先生在优化理论研究与应用方面所取得的成就享誉全国和世界;作为学生的我,始终以他做我的导师引以为自豪与骄傲。他首次提出了全局优化问题的总极值方法。大家都知道全局优化问题至今都是优化理论与方法的难点,郑先生在国内外首次对这一难点实现了突破,正是因为他在总极值理论与算法研究方面的杰出成就,至今仍受到国内外同行敬佩。在我们研究生选题阶段,郑先生为我们几人选择了变分不等式、互补理论和博弈论等方面的问题进行研究。作为研究生的我,当时还认识不到这些领域的重要性,只是后来成为老师和研究生导师后,才越来越体会到郑先生的大智慧和睿智洞察力。他为我们选择的这些研究方向后来都成为国际上热门的研究方向,像博弈论的研究与应用,至今还是运筹学的热点之一。郑先生渊博的知识和指导能力,让学生的我十分地佩服,也是我作为研究生导师的追求目标。

作为学生,我有时总感觉愧对郑先生:1986年研究生毕业的时候,当时郑先生已安排我留校,但我因为女朋友,后来是我妻子的小岳不在上海,我坚持不留校,也不想留在上海。因为毕业分配的事情,既没有按照郑先生的建议去做,也没有实现自己的愿望,当时我的心情很郁闷,对郑先生充满愧疚。最后我既没有留在上海科学技术大学,也没有去成河南的三门峡市,而且自己也没有想到,最后还是留在了上海,来到了华东理工大学,也就是原来的华东化工学院工作至今。如果说世事难料,有时真是这样,人生并不一定总是按照预定的轨迹走下去。尽管在在华东理工大学有过一段一来就生病的困难时期,但总体来说,还是挺顺利的。在我30多岁的时候也成为了教授,那个年代晋升还是不太容易,何况当时我还只有硕士学位。我想如果当初留在上海科学技术大学,在郑先生身边工作,凭借郑先生的威望与声誉,有他的指导与提携,也许我能干得更好一些,当然这只能是一个愿望了。多少年已经过去了,现在想起这事,总是觉得愧对郑先生。我不知张晓东是否和我一样,也有同样的感受,不知在他的纪念文章中是否提到了毕业分配,回顾了当时的岁月。我们两人当时都不听话,真的愧对郑先生对我们的厚爱。

要说愧对郑先生,还有我的普通话经历。在嘉定读书时,郑先生要求我用收音机跟着播音员学习普通话,按照郑先生的要求,我当时努力过,但没有坚持,认为普通话没有那么重要,后来还是放弃了。至今也不过关,真的有点难为情,对不起先生。说真的,我的"蕲春普通话"还是长进不少,少小一直生活在蕲春的一个乡村,到武汉读书之前,从没有离开过那儿,不要说不会讲普通话,平时也不听普通话。刚到武汉市,听普通话都有些困难。大学毕业后,当时就计划回黄冈,也没有打算学习普通话。后来才发现讲不好普通话,在某种程度上,影响了我的发展,当然这是后话。现在人已定型,已经难以救药,是否讲好普通话,真的不那么重要了。想起来我的普通话经历,真是愧对郑先生。

在美国学术访问和开会的时候,我有两次经过或待在亚特兰大,有机会去郑先生和涂老师在Columbus的家。第一次去的时候,郑先生走路已经非常困难,完全离不开涂老师的照顾。在涂老师的帮助下,郑先生还能艰难地扶着房间特建的扶手走路。我记得那天涂老师和郑先生带我和我的同学陈冠涛在Columbus市吃了一顿午饭,当时郑先生吃的不比我少,坐在那里只是说话有些困难,其余都挺好,感到很欣慰。第二次是我和小岳一起去Columbus看郑先生和涂老师,这个时候,郑先生的情况已大不如前,他住在Columbus的一家康复中心,完全依赖涂老师或他人的照顾,当时心里挺伤感的。有这两次短暂相处的机会,眼见涂老师对郑先生无微不至的照顾与关心,心里对涂老师充满敬意,同时看到涂老师那么辛苦,也感到有些无奈。看到涂老师对郑先生深深的爱,我感到郑先生是多么的幸运与幸福。看到郑先生追求生命的坚强毅力,在内心深处对郑先生充满敬意。正是因为两次在Columbus的相见与相处,特别是涂老师谈到那年中国春节时,郑先生为避免摔倒而滑倒在地板上,因无伤害,夜已深,她不愿麻烦他人,而自己又无力将郑先生扶起,故决定用被子垫盖好,两人不得不在地板上睡了一夜,第二天清晨请对门邻居帮忙将郑先生抱起放回床上,听了这事真的心酸与心疼。我后来鼓动涂老师带郑先生回国,便于有人帮助她一起照顾郑先生。我不知道涂老师回国到亲和源是否受了我的影响。但是,在郑先生和涂老师回国后,看到涂老师有时不得不带着郑先生在上海与美国Columbus之间来回奔波,特别是想到涂老师带着生活不能自理的郑先生来回坐十几个小时的飞机,中间还要转机,实在太难了,心里有时候感到后悔,也许我不应该鼓动涂老师带郑先生回上海。如果是因为我的原因,我只能恳请涂老师的谅解,也期望能够获得郑先生在九天之上的理解。

郑先生是一个治学严谨、严于律己的人。他工作勤奋、治学严谨,这是大家有目共睹的,但他做事计划有序、严格要求学生的这一面,可能我比大家体会得更深一些。记得读研的第一年,有一天我们几个同学一起去郑先生和涂老师的家中拜访。由于事先没有约定,让郑先生既感到突然,也有点措手不及。我们唐突的到来,一下子干扰了先生的计划与安排。虽然他当时热情接待了我们,并跟我们聊了较长时间。但后来他明确规定:没有事先约定,不能随时到访。当时我还年少不懂事,心里还不大理解,学生拜访老师还要事先约定时间。人们常说一时为师,终身为父。在我心中,我就是把先生视为长辈,随时拜访先生是自然的事,一时还不理解。后来随着年龄增长和岗位变化,事情越来越多,郑先生的做法也就能够理解了。现在想起来,当时郑先生那么忙,我们这种不约而至的行为肯定影响了他的工作计划,他还不得不舍命陪学生。也可能郑先生感到他对我们的要求有些太严,有些不太符合当时的人们习惯,也就有了后来陪着学弟学妹们一起到浏河等地方的师生集体活动等。当然这只是我的猜测,已经没有机会问郑先生了。看着学弟学妹们与郑先生在一起的业余活动照

左二鲁习文,左三郑权

片，真的有些羡慕。在我的记忆中，我们在嘉定的那三年，与郑先生在一起的时光，只有教学和学术研讨。毕业后，我很少有机会得到郑先生的教诲与指导。在他回国的时候，我与他见过几次面，其中有一次我专门请他到我的家中看看，但也是来去匆匆，每次见面时间都不太长。我记得每次见面时，他经常问我最近在研究些什么，工作情况怎么样。他期望我研究一些大的关键问题，特别是要提出能够受大家关注的问题。想起郑先生的话，我总感觉自己能力不够，努力也不够，离郑先生的要求还相距甚远。只能努力再努力，求得心灵的慰藉，争取做一个不是优秀但能合格的学生与老师。

我的一些回忆

张晓东*

1983年,我在南京大学数学系四年大学生活即将结束,在分配工作和考研之间,继续读研自然是我的首选。

那年,南京大学数学系计算数学专业停招研究生,无法报考本校的研究生。经向系里的孙麟平教授咨询,他向我介绍了上海科学技术大学郑权和郭本瑜两位老师近期很活跃的研究,于是,我和同学曹卫明都报考了上海科学技术大学数学系的研究生,曹卫明考上了郭本瑜教授指导的计算数学方向的研究生,而我则成为了郑权教授那年指导的最优化方向的四名研究生之一,开始了在上海科学技术大学为期三年的学习历程。

我们入学这年,也是郑权老师从美国宾州大学做完两年访问学者刚回校工作的时候。他访学回校的第一件事,就是强化研究生的英文学习和对西方科技文献的直接阅读,上课使用原版教材并完全用英文讲课,一下子就把我们几位研究生带进了现代最优化理论的前沿。

郑老师给我们上的第一门课程内容是关于线性和非线性的优化理论,不仅包括凸优化,各种最优点的充分必要条件的理论推导,对具体的数值算法也有要求。郑老师着重于指导学生从何处获取最前沿的科学理论,算法部分则由孙世杰老师负责,他也是郑老师之前指导毕业的研究生,在系里的计算机实验室里指导我们完成单纯性算法的编程和计算操作。

除了学校和系里安排的教学内容之外,郑老师经常会邀请国外的学者来系里讲学和交流。他不仅安排这些一流学者直接与我们几位研究生进行讨论,还让我们轮流负责接待这些来访学者,以此提高我们的自信心和交流能力。记得有一次,郑老师请来了美国 UT Austin 大学著名的最优化专家 Chance 教授,这位大牌教授与我们几位同学一起讨论博弈论问题,他先在黑板上写了一道题目,然后问谁能上台推算出结果,我大胆上去写出了计算过程和结果,教授十分高兴,马上从包里找出一件 T 恤衫奖励我,让我也倍感喜悦,自信心"爆棚"。

郑老师不仅经常请国外的学者来学校与我们交流,还鼓励和支持我们走出校门去别的学校向其他教授学者学习。记得是在 1985 年暑假里,他安排我和谢志刚去南开大学参加由他与(南开大学)史树中教授、(中山大学)王则柯教授等学者组织的为期一周的"数理经济学暑期班"。这可能是国内第一个用数学方法来研究经济学的学习班,参加这个班的许多人以后都成了这个领域内的著名学者。

受郑老师的引导,我选择了博弈论作为自己的论文研究方向,硕士论文的主要内容还写成了两篇文章在国外发表。特别值得一提的是,由于当时在学校图书馆和上海很难找到相关参考文献,郑老师特意批准和支持我去北京查阅当时稀有的有关博弈论的最新文献,这对

---

* 张晓东,郑权 1983 年招收的研究生.

我完成硕士论文有很大帮助。

除了上述这些直接指导和帮助之外,郑老师对我影响最大的一点,就是要理论联系实际,一定要把最优化的理论模型真正应用于解决工业和社会生产中的实际问题。他以身作则,将最优化原理应用到光学仪器的设计和优化问题,取得了卓越的成就。

正是受郑老师的这些指导和影响,我自己也走上了探索学以致用的人生道路,这几十年来一直从事将运筹学理论方法应用于商业软件的开发工作。

总之,借此机会,作一些回忆,以此感谢恩师对我的培养。

左起:谢志刚、张晓东、鲁习文

纪念恩师郑权教授

宋学锋*

人的一生总会遇到几位对自己成长发展有重要影响的人,郑权教授就是一位对我的成长产生过重要影响的老师。

1985年我从南京大学数学系数理逻辑专业本科毕业,本打算报考南京大学数量经济学专业研究生的,因为入大学后才发现数理逻辑并不是自己喜欢的专业,而一篇"落后就要挨打"的社论,令我萌生了改学数量经济学的念头。但那年机缘巧合,恰逢恢复高考后免试推荐研究生改革的第一年。据说那年郑先生到南京大学开会,向南京大学数学系提出推免二位学生到上海科学技术大学跟他读研。于是,在辅导员老师推荐和劝导下,我和敖大同学一起来到了上海科学技术大学,开始了三年师从郑先生攻读硕士研究生的学习生涯。

坦率地讲,初到上海后的感觉并不好,甚至萌发过不上了,回去重新分配工作的想法。因为当时的上海远没有想象的好,嘉定也很偏远,交通不便。好在正式开学后的体验是好的,研究生处认真负责的沈老师,几位担任主讲必修课程的董炳华和孙世杰等老师,特别是郑先生严谨的治学态度、高超的学术水平和在总极值理论方面取得的领先成就,都令我钦佩和敬仰!后来三年的学习也证明留下来是对的,甚至是幸运的。

郑先生的课程是全英文授课的,这在当时是很超前的,因为,差不多是二十年后教育部才提倡双语教学的。他用的教材、板书和讲授都是全英文,我们的作业、考试答题和毕业论文也都要求是全英文。特别是硕士论文允许全英文撰写,在当时也是罕见的,不过说明当时科大办学思想还是很解放的。郑先生的高标准严要求,虽然一开始令我们学生感到有较大困难,但却令我们的专业英语得到了很大的提高,受用终生。

当时,郭本瑜是上海科学技术大学校长,而郑先生是数学系主任。在他们的领导下,数学系学术氛围十分浓郁。各种学术研讨班、学术讲座和学术活动很多,特别是经常会邀请国内外的学术大咖来校交流。我就曾经被安排接待过一位国外来的教授。郑先生还派我代他参加过中科院系统工程理论委员会会议。也正是在那次会上,刚从美国出访回来的王毓云研究员,介绍了他了解到国际上都在研究的"Chaos",并说以后会成为新的学科方向。也正是这些信息为我后来的博士论文选题埋下了种子。总之,浓郁的学术氛围,严谨的治学风格,既开阔了我的学术视野,又陶冶了我的学术修养。以至于后来自己做老师,也会不自觉地模仿郑先生的治学风格。

郑先生对学生要求是十分严厉的,这在数学系是公认的。在我刚到上海科学技术大学时,就听到过很多传闻。都是讲谁谁被批评,谁谁被"骂"的故事,因此,大家都很害怕郑先生,据说就连系里的教师也都怕他。不过,我很幸运,在上海科学技术大学学习生活的三年

---

* 宋学锋,中国矿业大学校长、教授。

时光,郑先生从没批评过我,而且我还得到了他很多关心和支持。其实,郑先生为人虽然严厉,却也很慈爱宽厚。记得硕士论文选题时,我想选对策论方向,而这并非郑先生擅长的总极值方向,当时我也担心老师可能会不同意,没想到他却很支持!而且还推荐我去调研拜访中科院系统所的王毓云研究员、东北大学的张嗣瀛教授和大连轻工学院的张盛开教授,因为他们几位是当时国内对策论方面造诣最高的学者。那几次调研和拜访对我硕士论文的选题和研究帮助很大,郑先生在论文撰写过程中给予了很多具体的指导和帮助,令我获益匪浅。

最终我硕士论文以(M,N)型主从对策论为题完成并顺利通过了答辩。我把论文的主要成果,写成了两篇学术论文,想与郑先生联名发表,他很支持,把他的署名改写在我的名字后面,并推荐了可投的学术刊物。正是这两篇处女作,为我学术生涯奠定了良好的基础,也是我硕士毕业参加工作后能脱颖而出的重要因素。导师的言传身教,令我获益匪浅,终身受益。我后来指导研究生也都很尊重学生自己的兴趣,从不强加选题给他们,与学生合作发表论文,署名从不当第一作者。

时光荏苒,恩师已驾鹤西去。但郑先生的音容笑貌却时常浮现在眼前。难忘他漂亮的板书,难忘他崇尚学术、严谨的治学风格,难忘他来中国矿业大学短暂相聚的欢乐时光,难忘他在上海"亲和源"与病魔抗争的顽强……

我有时甚至后悔当年毕业时,没按系里意见留校工作。若是那样,岂不是可以和恩师多在一起几年,学到更多东西! 遗憾的是,这些设想都已不可能了。只能凭借这几行文字追思导师的恩情;只能继承和发扬郑先生的治学精神和育人风格,努力工作,为国家和社会培养更多有用人才,聊慰恩师的在天之灵!

宋学锋与郑权(右)

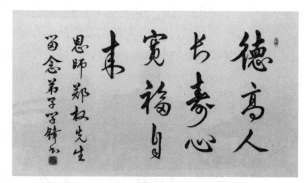

宋学峰作书法留念

我的成功离不开导师的栽培

戴万阳*

本科时,我主要学习纯粹数学,尤其觉得分析学得更有感觉,原准备报考函数论方向的研究生。临报考时,突然发现郑先生的运筹学与控制论方向也主要考实分析与泛函分析,就临时改变主意报考了郑先生,据说考了 90 分,被录取了。

在跟郑先生攻读硕士学位时,我选择了几何控制与随机最优控制作为研究领域,并在随机自适应控制方向上做出了一些成果,也得到了国际出版物的录用,因而得到郑先生的特别批准:作为优秀研究生提前半年毕业,在当时这是一种特许。恰巧,当时南京大学数学系的领导在上海科学技术大学考察毕业生,他们便告诉我郑先生帮我写了一封很强的优秀推荐信,因此,我便得以来南京大学数学系工作。在南京大学工作几年以后,我得到了美国亚特兰大佐治亚理工大学数学学院和工业工程与系统工程学院的同时录取。在佐治亚理工大学攻读博士学位期间,我利用随机分析解决了运筹学排队论等领域中的世界级成果,被冯·诺伊曼大奖得主与世界数学家大会 45 分钟特邀报告者称之为是"同时期相互独立做出的突破性重要成果"。因为是郑先生将我带进了分析与运筹控制等交互领域,一直心存感激,因而,在郑先生 1997 年访问美国佐治亚理工大学时,我便在新泽西工作的美国贝尔实验室向佐治亚理工大学我的博士生阶段的导师发去电子邮件:郑权教授是我攻读硕士学位阶段的伟大导师!

本文作者(中间)和郑先生(左三)及其他弟子的合影

---

* 戴万阳,郑权招收的研究生.

缅怀恩师郑权先生

方敖大*

时间过得真快啊,不知不觉,我硕士生导师郑权先生离开我们已经一年多了。这些天来,师母涂老师、先生的亲朋好友及学生弟子们,正在筹备出版一本纪念他的文集而忙碌着。而我的眼前又不时浮现出三十几年前在上海科学技术大学求学时,他那睿智有神的眼光,精力充沛的劲头,以及在课堂上聆听他谆谆教诲的难忘情境。

我是1981年考入南京大学计算数学专业的。记得大四第二学期开学不久,辅导员李老师找到我说,上海科学技术大学联系系里的何旭初老先生,请他推荐两位可免试攻读运筹学硕士学位的学生,系里研究决定推荐了我与宋学锋同学。听到这个喜讯,真是十分高兴。之后何先生门下的当红弟子孙文瑜(我的学士学位论文指导老师)、孙麟平(我的最优化方法课老师)等知道我要去被他们当时称为全国中青年"优化名宿"的上海科学技术大学郑权教授门下读研,也纷纷替我高兴。

1985年9月开始的三年读研阶段,虽然郑先生当时主持系务工作,科研教学工作十分繁忙,但我们学生还是经常能见到他。印象很深的是他给我们上"最优控制理论"专业课,全英文授课,让我们耳目一新。也是从这门课开始,逐渐地培养了我对最优化方法研究和应用开发的浓厚兴趣,奠定了我一生工作的基础。我硕士学位论文就是有关最优控制的数值方法,以后博士学位论文也是最优随机控制方向。

左起:方敖大、戴万阳、郑权、宋学峰、田蔚文

---

* 方敖大,上海科学技术大学1985级硕士生.

当时读书是刻苦用功的，讨论是激发灵感的。在我们的印象中，先生的面容"严肃认真"居多，偶尔也会"莞然一笑"，虽然对我们要求很严格，但从来没有对我们来过一次厉声呵斥。而且先生也有平易近人的一面，与我们学生打成一片。记得1987年秋季，先生在百忙之中，抽空在一个周末与我们学生一起，骑自行车去太仓浏河长江边一日游。

可以毫不夸张地说，在这三年求学期间，从做学问、做事，到做人，我们深深地受到他的影响，被他潜移默化。

硕士毕业后，当时由于受同乡数学大师华罗庚教授推广"优选法"的影响，更是受到郑先生将优化算法用于光学设计的激励，我进入了华东计算技术研究所，主要参与优化算法设计和软件开发工作，并于1991年获得"国家机械电子工业部科技进步二等奖"。再后来的读博及投入美国工业界的研究院，也是从事与优化和控制有关的企业计划与决策系统分析工作。特别值得追忆的是，十几年前，当我得知他生病，几次打电话问候他时，他首先详细询问的是我毕业后的工作，并给了我很多鼓励，让我深受感动和温暖。当得知我将逐次二次规划(SQP)方法应用于企业计划与决策分析，而且整个项目还得到了公司的最高技术奖(Henry Ford Technology Award)，他很高兴，也很感兴趣，表示这是很实用的方法，要告诉姚奕荣，将这个方法写进正在编著的《简明运筹学》书中。

所以说，郑先生不仅仅是我硕士生导师，更是我一生研发工作的引路人。在今后的工作中，唯有谨遵恩师谆谆教导、殷切希望，努力再努力，方不负郑门弟子之名，来报答先生精心培养之恩，更是告慰先生在天之灵！

于美国密西根州安娜堡市

尊其师,效其行

刘逸明*

我的本科是在上海科学技术大学应用数学系学习的,1985年9月入学上海科学技术大学读硕士学位。我在本科时就听闻了许多郑权教授的传奇故事,也有幸参加过几次郑教授的讲座,领略到了大咖的风采。报考上海科学技术大学同专业的研究生自然成了我当时"不二的选择"。

研究生期间,我终于有很多机会听郑教授授课,参加郑教授的研讨班,耳濡目染郑先生严谨治学、启发式的教学风格,鼓励学生开拓创新,这些"做人做事"的道理对我影响深远,终身受益。

毕业之后,我加入了市经委下的研究机构,运用规划和最优控制技术工具进行产业政策和经济规划方面的研究和咨询。之后,我进入了一家全球咨询公司开始了20多年的战略咨询和管理咨询工作。回顾我的职业生涯,我常常感恩在研究生期间得到郑先生的言传身教,这些"做人做事"道理一直帮助着我建团队、带项目、搞产品,这些道理我也是在工作中慢慢有了越来越深的体会。

寥寥数语无法表达对恩师郑权教授的思念和感激之情,唯有在生活和工作中践行恩师的"做人做事"的道理!

前排右三为郑权,最后一排右一为作者本人

---

* 刘逸明,毕马威企业咨询(中国)有限公司,咨询服务合伙人.

怀念导师郑权教授

姚奕荣*

　　1987年9月,我进入上海科学技术大学攻读郑权教授的硕士研究生,研究方向是积分总极值的理论方法及应用。

　　特别令我深刻怀念的是,自2006年以后,郑老师在上海大学数学系组织了积分总极值方法讨论班。我的一些学生:梁泽亮、陈熙、陈柳、安柳、尹秀秀、王筱莉、张漫利、罗福和于亚茹等有幸在郑老师的指导下学习积分总极值方法中的丰满分析和算法的 Monte-Carlo 实现。

　　积分总极值的理论学习让学生们打下了扎实的数学基础,算法的实现也使学生们实践了计算机动手操作技能,且在现实工作上发挥了积极的作用。

　　在向郑老师学习的过程中,我也领略了郑老师深厚的数学功底和高尚的品德。它使我与郑老师的师生情谊得到升华。正是在这段积分总极值的学习期间,我幸运地结识了既是师姐又是师母的涂仁进老师。令我非常感动的是,2012年3月,我赴美国亚特兰大,飞机误点,抵达时已是半夜。当时,遇上狂风暴雨,涂老师顶着雷电暴雨在漆黑的公路上驱车二个多小时来接我,让我终身难忘!

　　是积分总极值增进了我与导师与师母的友谊,是积分总极值使我的数学理论得到提高,更是我现在从事上海市青少年创新人才培养基地—上海大学数学科学实践工作站工作的理论基础和力量源泉。

左起:姚奕荣、郑权、孙世杰

---

* 姚奕荣,上海大学数学系.

纪念我的导师郑权先生

彭建平[*]

时光飞逝,郑老师离我们而去已经一年多了,但岁月带走的是流年,留下的是记忆,老师的音容笑貌依然那么清晰,仿佛依然和我们在一起。

一、跟随老师读书

1987年9月,我考入上海科学技术大学攻读硕士学位。当时一起入学的有十几位同学,经过一个学期的基础课学习,学院通知我们要选导师了。当时郑老师的名额是两个,选导师的过程是怎么样的?我已经记不清了,只记得,我非常幸运地成为了郑老师的学生,另一位是姚奕荣。

郑老师对学生的要求很严格,除了学术研究上严格要求外,郑老师还要求学生熟练掌握英语,必须用英语写论文。这个要求对于来自五湖四海、英语基础不尽相同的我们来说非常高,但也极大地提升了我们与国际接轨的能力。甚至在后面离开教学研究岗位从事科技管理工作时,英语能力在国际交流与合作中也发挥了应有的作用,受益良多,真心感谢老师的严格要求!

1989年,郑老师离开上海去美国,走之前他对我的论文工作

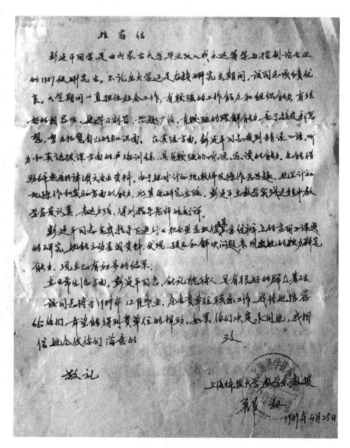

郑权老师给我的推荐信

---

[*] 彭建平,郑权1987年招收的研究生.

做了非常周密的安排,和论文研究领域相关的老师都提前打了招呼,以便我有问题可以随时去请教,并安排谢志刚师兄做我的"小导师",关心指导我的学习。更让我意想不到的,是当时离我毕业还有大半年时间,但郑老师提前为我写好了找工作用的推荐信,老师对学生未来的关心跃然纸上!时至今日已过去30多年,每每想起依然万分感激,谢谢郑老师!

二、与老师重逢

1990年我硕士毕业后去了烟台大学任教,1995年考回上海跟随史定华教授读博士,1998年毕业后留在上海从事科技管理工作,这期间我几乎没有郑老师的任何消息。再次见到郑老师应该是在1999年以后,距我和老师赴美一别已有10年多时间了,那次郑老师到谢师兄工作的上海财经大学作报告,郑老师见到我说,"你会自己画Christmas card"。10多年后再见老师,老师还记得我,心里非常高兴。

人生一路会遇见很多人,也会别过很多人,但如果真的就此和老师别过,真的会是很大的遗憾,因为老师日后对我的影响依然很大。很幸运,我再次遇见了郑老师。

三、向老师学习做人

老师和师母回国以后,他们在浦东的家自然成了我们弟子们的大家庭,是我们周末回家探亲的地方。我们一起唱歌,一起做饭包饺子,用蹩脚的沪语朗读普希金的诗,和老师扳手腕,肚子笑疼了,眼泪也笑出来了……

与郑权老师扳手腕

日常生活中的老师平和自律,令人敬佩。当时老师走路已经很不方便,生活无法自理,虽然身体很弱,但意志很坚强。记得师母每隔一段时间需要返回美国给老师配药,处理一些家事,老师从来都是爽快答应师母的安排,包括最后一次飞行十几个小时不辞辛苦回到大洋彼岸的家。但是有一次师母出发的前一天,老师毫无征兆地突然发高烧,不知这是不是老师的身体对师母出行不舍情绪的偷偷"告发"?老师就是这样,不论自己多不方便,都尽可能不给别人添麻烦，哪怕是家人。

老师后期说不了长句子，但他总能用几个字准确表达他的想法。记得女儿当时在申请出国读研，女儿问老师申请什么学校、什么专业好，老师说没关系，不重要。女儿出国以后的经历确实让我们领悟到老师当时的回答是多么睿智通透，开眼界、长见识、激发主观能动性确实更重要。

还记得有一次我和老师聊天，为了让他多说话，我像个"侦探"一样和老师一起回忆以前的事，比如喜欢做的事、喜欢读的书、喜欢的饮食、喜欢的运动等等，一下挖掘出很多惊喜来。老师是数学大师，还会作作词谱曲，精于研究，运动成绩也很优秀，涉猎之广几乎无所不能！我感叹说："郑老师，您实在太厉害了，是不是特别帅？"老师说，"不厉害、不帅。"，说得那么平常，言语表情没有丝毫波澜。

杨绛先生曾经说过，"洗净这一百年沾染的污秽回家"。我相信这也是老师的状态，不染铅尘，清澈通透。

学生时代和老师学习做学问，现在向老师学习做人。郑老师，您永远是我的导师！

刻骨师恩伴风雨，一朝教诲益终身

梁泽亮*

2020年，我突然听闻郑权教授逝世于美国的消息，心情异常悲痛，受制于新冠疫情，不能前往美国进行悼念也成一生的遗憾。每当怀念起郑老师的点滴教诲，回想他的音容笑貌、渊博的学识、睿智的思维，对待科学一丝不苟的治学精神，都能从他身上感悟良多，对我在生活和工作上都能有持续的激励，回想起在郑老师指导下学习的日子，总是久久难以忘怀。

2013年夏，我作为上海大学数学系2010届本科毕业生，直升了数学系运筹优化与控制论专业的研究生，选择了姚奕荣老师作为导师，并在其指导下对全局优化问题开展学习与研究。期间，恰逢郑权教授回国访学，通过姚老师引荐，我有幸能与郑老师相识，并利用暑假时间，在郑老师指导下开展讨论班学习，系统全面地学习积分总极值方法的理论基础及算法实现，为后续研究生三年的学习研究工作奠定了坚实的基础。

那年暑假，我们在郑老师的带领下，基于郑老师早期的博士论文，深入学习了关于求解全局优化问题的积分总极值方法，通过系统性的理论学习，了解丰满集的理论基础，掌握求解目标函数的极值问题的积分方法理论，证明求解方法的收敛性，并通过计算机利用蒙特卡洛模拟方法实现积分数据计算，从而对各类优化问题的数值案例进行全局最优解的求解计算。讨论班期间，郑老师鼓励我们采用英语进行讲解，通过双语教学更能深理解整套方法论的数学原理，并逐一指导并指正我们在理解知识体系上的不足。通过集中训练与指导，我们对于求解全局优化的方法有了深刻的认识，为我们后续的课题研究奠定了坚实的理论基础。郑老师严谨的教学态度，一丝不苟的学术精神，让人十分钦佩，通过启发式的方式，引导学生自己去发现问题、钻研问题、解决问题，潜移默化地教会了我们如何进行学术研究，也将他的治学精神传递给了我们。从我个人来说，能在刚本科毕业阶段受到郑老师的指点与教诲，实属三生有幸，正是因为熟悉了积分总极值方法论，对于后续研究生期间的课题研究有了极大的帮助，对求解各类全局优化问题开拓了思路，也将该方法应用于实际问题的求解中。特别是在毕业后的工作中，通过应用积分总极值方法，结合蒙特卡洛的计算机实现，在实际工作中解决了一系列优化的问题。如：烟草公司关于烟丝成分优化配比问题、金融机构的投资组合优化问题、资本最优配置问题等，积分总极值算法都能有效求得相应问题的全局最优解，为高效地解决实际问题提供了途径，我也深刻感受到郑老师创立方法论的不易，以及该方法对于学术研究和实际应用的突出贡献。

除了学术之外，郑老师对生活充满热爱，精神上始终保持着乐观与坚强。2015年至2016年期间，郑老师在时隔五年后再次回国，入住上海"亲和源"公寓。此时郑老师健康状况已大不如前，回想当年他精神矍铄、健步如飞的情景，真是让人痛心疾首。再次探望他的

---

* 梁泽亮，上海大学理学院数学系2010级研究生.

时候,郑老师虽已行动不便,但看到我们还是很高兴,依旧那么地亲切和蔼。交谈之中,他仍清楚地记得暑假讨论班的情景,我们围绕在他的身边,向他汇报最近的工作和生活情况,从他的眼神中我们还是能够深切感受到老师对于学生的关爱,希望自己的学生越来越好。郑老师始终把学生当成自己的孩子,真诚地呵护并培育着孩子们茁壮成长。

三尺讲台,三寸舌,三寸笔,三千桃李;十年树木,十载风,十载雨,十万栋梁。有幸认识郑权老师是我一生的福分,能得到他的指点与教诲更是受益终生。近期,得知郑老师夫人涂仁进老师(教授)正在整理他的生前遗作,并将在后续集合成册出版,使得郑老师的研究成果得以传承。作为后辈,略尽绵薄之力,撰文缅怀先师,以告慰郑老师在天之灵。

梁泽亮

缅怀郑权先生

陈 熙*

时间飞逝,郑权先生离开我们已经一年多了。虽然与郑先生接触的时间比较短,也没能有幸正式成为郑先生的学生,但郑先生的教诲,时至今日亦在影响着我。

我是上海大学 2012 届数学系的研究生,师从姚奕荣老师。2010 年郑先生回国,姚老师把郑先生请到了我们研讨班,给我们上课。那段时间只要是郑先生的课,同学们就非常紧张,因为郑先生不仅用英文上课,还会提很多问题。那时郑先生每天从嘉定、宝山校区来回奔波,还没有完全倒好时差,刚回来不久就晕倒在了学校校园,由于没有床位,郑先生只能被放置在医院大门口,涂先生非常担心。那天晚上,涂先生、梁泽亮和我三个人一起和郑先生度过了难忘的一夜。郑先生康复以后,立马又为我们上课,对于数学、对于教学,郑先生永远都是严谨认真、全身心地投入。即使回美国以后,对我的邮件,郑先生也是第一时间给予回复和解答。这些都影响着我以后的工作和学习。

2010 年,正值世博会首次在中国上海举办,由于郑先生身体暂未恢复,原本打算放弃参观世博园的安排。我们研讨班的同学就一起出了一个方案,借了轮椅、推着郑先生去游览了世博园,这是一次非常美好的回忆,值得我们永久记念。

左起:梁泽亮、周广付、郑权、陈熙,2010 年摄于上海世博园

---

* 陈熙,上海大学理学院数学系 2010 级研究生

2013年年底,郑先生回国养病,姚老师和我一起去机场接他去"亲和源",那时候郑先生状态不是特别好。期间我去过几次"亲和源"探望郑先生,在涂先生的悉心照料下,郑先生越来越有精气神了。记得这期间,郑先生、涂先生和我一起去谢志刚教授的家,谢教授住五楼,郑先生刚恢复不久,涂先生搀扶着郑先生爬楼梯,真的可以用举步维艰来形容。但我们能感受到郑先生、涂先生他们那种热爱生活、相濡以沫的精神。

郑权先生是一位杰出的数学家和教育家,虽然已经离开了我们,但他深厚的学术造诣、高尚的品格、乐观的生活态度还在影响着我们。

怀念好友郑权教授

庄松林[*]

郑权教授离开我们已近一年了,我作为他半个世纪的挚友与合作者,他的音容笑貌,睿智的思维,经常浮现在我的眼前,久久不能忘怀。

我与郑权相识在20世纪60年代末,中国"文化大革命"风起云涌之时,虽然那时多数人都投入了轰轰烈烈的红色风暴之中,学术研究受到了极大冲击,但我们几个复旦的学子,包括物理系毕业的严德衎、蒋百川等组织在一起系统学习了"实变函数论"及"泛函分析",而数学系毕业的高材生郑权理所当然地成为了我们的讲课老师。我们将当时光学领域中重要的"自动光学设计"的研究方向之一,作为当时国内该领域的主要开拓方向。我们发展了一种"带迭代序列的蒙特卡洛总极值的求解"方法,在数学上证明了该方法的收敛性及唯一性,论文发表在《应用数学学报》的创刊号上,该方法用到其他的优化问题都有非常好的表现。比如求解实现超分辨光学系统光瞳函数的相位分布,抗反射宽带光学薄膜的优化设计等。在半个世纪前"文革"中要做出这样的工作是难能可贵的。

随着改革开放,1979年以后我们组的成员纷纷去美国学习进修。郑权与我于1980—1983年都在宾州州立大学作访问研究及攻读博士学位。期间宾州大学的中国学者及学生从几个人增加到百余人。郑权一直是我们的带头人,他组织我们在各项研究上做出成绩,周末带领大家运动锻炼身体,在此期间他在统计数学理论、总极值最优化方法等方面作出了特殊的贡献。新世纪以来,郑权教授利用休假,经常回到他曾工作的上海大学数学系指导研究生,开设讲座。也和我们早已回国工作的学者,例如浙江大学的唐晋发教授,中国纺织大学(现东华大学)的潘星辰教授等,进一步将其总极值的最新成果应用于各自的研究领域。

右一:郑权,右三:庄松林

郑权教授学术造诣深厚,品格高尚,是一位杰出的学者和数学家,他的离去使我们失去了一位师长及好友。愿以此文告慰郑教授在天之灵。

---

[*] 庄松林,上海理工大学教授,中国工程院院士.

记与郑权老友共处和合作的几件事

胡毓达*

1978年,停滞了十年之久的中国数学会学术活动,宣布将于当年12月在四川成都举行中国数学会年会。为了选拔有高水平的论文组团参加这次多年未开的重大盛会,上海数学会特地提前于8月份,在上海科学会堂举行了历时3天的1978年年会。在这次年会的运筹学分组报告会上,我认识了久闻盛名的郑权。年会结束后的第二天,上海《文汇报》即报导了这届年会的活动。其中,特别地提到了郑权和我两位当选为上海数学代表团成员的事迹。

1980年初,由中科院数学研究所牵头,在山东济南召开了全国运筹学大会。经过与会代表们的充分准备,决定成立中国数学会运筹学会。在这次大会上,中国数学会理事长华罗庚被推选兼任理事长,郑权当选为全国理事。接着当年6月,由上海数学会运筹学专业组发起,联络了江苏、浙江、江西和福建四省的运筹学工作者,在江西庐山召开了华东运筹学学术交流会。期间,与会的全国运筹学会常务副理事长越民义和秘书长桂湘云认为,华东地区的条件较好,提出是否能承担创办一份综合性运筹学杂志。在我们商议的会上,郑权代表立即十分肯定地表示上海科学技术大学可以承办。回沪后,他一方面向上海科学技术大学有关领导作了汇报,同时联系了上海科学技术出版社,并且很快组建了编辑部。于是,由越民义任主编、郑权和管梅谷任副主编的中国第一份关于运筹学综合性期刊《运筹学杂志》在1982年正式出版。

胡毓达、郑权合译的《最优化理论与算法》,高等教育出版社1983年版

"文革"之后,为了尽快恢复我国的高教事业和科研水平,高等教育出版社聘请了数十位全国有关领域著名的教授和科学家,对反映当代科学前沿的著作出版提出意见和建议。在这次会议上,专家们除积极提出一批建议出版的书籍之外,还提供了10本国外有代表性的近作。1981年底,高教出版社的编辑张小萍找到我,介绍了专家会议的情况。说其他9本书的翻译人选均已落实,只是其中一本由法国Dunod出版社出版J. céa著《Optimisation: Théorie et Algarithmed (最优化:理论与算法)》的专著,尚未有适当的译者人选,肯切地希望我能够承担。我在上大学时学的是俄语,小时

---

* 胡毓达,上海交通大学数学科学学院教授。

学过一些英语,工作后只是自学了英语、法语和德语,为的是能够参考数学文献。鉴于上海交通大学1978年成立应用数学系后,我为青年教师和研究生开"最优化"讨论班时,曾试译了由法国N. Moisseev和V. Tikhomirov合著的《$Optimisation$(最优化)》一书,在上海交通大学油印作为讨论班的参考资料,可能是张小萍编辑知道此事之后找到我的。由于我未正式出版过法文译作,对是否能圆满完成这一任务有些顾虑。1982年初次见到郑权时谈及此事,不料他十分支持地鼓励我应该大胆接受,并表示他可以帮我分担部分工作。为此,我分工给他的部分,他很快赶在2个多月即完成交我,后即赴美国宾州州立大学做访问学者了。在他高效工作的推动下,我加速译完后对全书的文字作了统一整理,于1982年5月便完成交稿。1983年初,我也赴美国哥伦比亚大学做访问学者。由于此书校稿时我们都在美国,校样还是远寄美国,由我校订后寄回北京。此书于1983年10月正式出版发行,这是我们两人很愉快高效率的一次合作。

作为长期的同行老友,郑权留给我印象至深的是:生活简单检朴,治学勤奋用功。我时常怀念他!

深深怀念老师与挚友郑权教授

蒋百川*

我与郑权认识已有半个世纪,他是复旦大学数学系1960年毕业的,我比他晚6年毕业于复旦大学物理系,所以我把他当作老师。我们俩在"文化革命"期间,避开了腥风血雨的政治运动,躲在家里专注于学术研究,并且建立起了深厚的友情,所以他又是我的一位挚友。两年前回上海,与庄松林、李劬、许政权等学长见面时,谈起郑权的病情,大家还相约下次我回上海时,一起再去探望他。然郑权由于病情恶化,于2020年5月便离去了,使我失去了再见到他的机会。现在只能将我心里的郑权,细细地回忆并书写下来,以表达我对他的尊敬。

如何与郑权认识,有一个比较长的故事。我在光学薄膜设计方法上的进展起始于1973年在烟台召开的一次全国镀膜会议。在几天的交流中,最引起我兴趣的,是浙江大学唐晋发老师的关于光学薄膜自动设计的介绍。回厂以后,我就开始寻找这方面的资料加以学习,我初步弄懂这个自动设计实际上是在数学上求多元函数的极值问题时,正好遇到上海科学技术大学数学系的张惠琴老师到工厂里来寻找有关与数学相关的课题。我向她叙述了有关光学薄膜的基本计算公式,以及我需要解决的问题,也向她介绍了浙江大学他们在使用最小二乘法的情况。她一下子便听懂了我的要求,答应帮我编一个程序试试。我乘机提出向她学习编程序和上机,她也很爽快地答应了。那时候提倡知识分子与工农相结合,对于上海科学技术大学而言,我的课题就是一个生产实践上的具体问题,所以很容易得到双方单位的支持。当时上海只有一个市计算中心,各单位要用计算机算题时,凭单位介绍信,去申请使用时间,我们当时称这为"上机"。我们用了约一年的时间,完全重复了唐晋发老师和他的合作者(浙江大学的一位数学老师)已经做过的工作,得到了基本相同的结果。当时薄膜自动设计的一个难以逾越的障碍,是在计算过程中如何从评价函数的局部极小值中脱离出来。张老师是一位非常有耐心和工作认真的人,她将最优化中当时已经成熟的各种方法逐一加以试验和比较。此时我们认识到,当时这些方法都无法摆脱局部极小值。这时候,张老师请来了她系里的另一位老师郑权,我记得那时候他好像是刚从"五七干校"回来。郑权老师在熟悉了我们所要解决的问题之后,经过深思熟虑,提出了他的思路。因为唯一可能摆脱局部极小值的方法,是在多元函数空间中作大量的计算和比较,即通常说的蒙德卡罗方法。但简单地使用这个方法,由于运算速度和时间的限制很难实现。郑权的一个重要的突破是想到用统计的方法通过不断的迭代过程来逐渐缩小搜索区域,从而得以在当时运算速度很慢的计算机上找到极值。当时我和郑权教授两个人的家庭都是分居两地的状态,所以我们平时有足够的时间,不是去计算所,便是去郑权在淮海路附近的亭子间里,日日夜夜都在一起。这样又过了大约半年时间,我们终于取得了不少较好的设计结果。光学薄膜是一种多层的结

---

* 蒋百川,美国佛罗里达州诺瓦东南大学校长杰出教授.

构,每一层膜在数学上可以表达为一个2×2的带复数的矩阵。光学薄膜的设计目的,是希望它的最终的反射率或透射率是入射光波长的一个指定的函数,从这个角度,光学薄膜也可以看作是一个滤波元件。由于它的复杂性,如果这样一个求总极值的方法可以在光学薄膜设计上获得成功的话,那么也预示了它可以应用在许多其他问题上,多年以后的实践表明确实如此。我们在这个方法确立之后,曾写了第一篇关于这个方法的学术论文,投寄并刊登在当时唯一的国家级的数学刊物《应用数学学报》上*。我在1987年到美国以后,与郑权经常有电话联系,他多次告诉我,他还在如何改进这个方法以及扩展它的应用范围,从中可见他在这上面的心血和精益求精的工作精神。

由于最优化方法上的突破,我们决定要将已有的光学薄膜设计方法总结出来。于是,浙江大学的唐晋发,上海光学仪器厂的李夙、许政权,郑权和我有一段时间每星期有半天聚在许政权家中讨论,最后合作写出了一篇长文,在当时北京的一个光学工程刊物上以专辑形式刊出。许政权的家在南市区,是一所老住宅,每次聚会我们一边喝茶、一边讨论,休息时就一起到外面小路上的公共厕所去排队方便。多年以后,唐晋发一度担任浙江大学副校长,李、许两位在1978年一起考进上海交通大学当研究生,然后留校升至教授,最后在上海交通大学先后退休。如今每次聚会时,大家都是非常怀念这段往事。在这样一种讨论交流之中,郑权一方面为我们在数学上把关,另一方面又听取和了解了我们在光学问题上的一些思考。我后来在学校为研究生讲述"科学研究方法"时,讨论过两个不同学科的研究者如何可以更好地合作的问题,我以为郑权与我们的合作就是一个很好的例子,也就是双方一定要进入对方的领域,学会使用对方的语言,只有这样才能更好地相互交流,取得合作的成功。

蒋百川

与此同时,庄松林(当时在上海光学仪器研究室工作,现为中国工程院院士)、郑权和我还在一起讨论其他的课题。那个时候光学富里叶变换、光学传递函数等是光学领域的前沿课题,为了能够在这个方向上做出开创性工作,我们深感过去在物理系学到的一些数学还远

---

* 郑权,蒋百川,庄松林:一个求总极值的方法,应用数学学报,1978,1:161—174.

远不够。郑权当时建议我们学习一下泛函分析,他来当我们的指导老师,当时参加学习的,还有与我在一个工厂工作的严德衍(复旦大学物理系毕业,"文革"后考入华东师范大学的研究生,然后出国)。这样坚持了很长一段时间,每个人都觉得受益匪浅。郑权当时对我们在数学上的帮助,也是我们难以忘怀的。

庄松林、郑权和我后来又用这个求总极值的方法设计了一个消球差的瞳孔函数,这项工作的成果投寄到"文革"后出版的第一期《光学学报》*。写作这篇文章的时候,庄松林和郑权都已在国外学习和进修了。后来有一次我回国遇到庄松林,他告诉我王大珩先生很欣赏我们这篇文章,认为是国内在光学实时信息处理方面的第一篇论文。

郑权是一个十分平易近人的老师,喜欢帮助别人。在与他熟悉之后,许多事情上我很愿意听取他的意见和建议。他很注意锻炼身体,并喜欢长跑,所以身体一直非常健康。大约2010年前后,我去上海见到他,那时候他因为腿关节原因行走已经不便,但他告诉我,改成为游泳在继续锻炼,可见他也是一个非常乐观的人。

郑权教授的一生体现了我们这一代知识分子,在风风雨雨的环境中,不计得失,踏实努力地工作,顽强攀登科学高峰的精神。所以我们永远怀念他,纪念他!

---

* 庄松林,蒋百川,郑权:光学系统像差的实时补偿,光学学报,1981,1:59—66.

深切怀念郑权教授

潘星辰[*]

我与郑权教授相识于1981年,那时我们同在美国宾州州立大学作访问、研究,他是学术研究的带头人。我们敬仰他在数学领域上的深厚造诣,敬佩他对学术研究的执着追求,更赞赏他为人真诚、豁达大度。

在一次学术报告会上,郑权教授介绍了他的新研究成果——总极值最优化方法,获得了众多师生的关注,也给我很大的启发。我和郑权教授首次合作就是采用他的总极值优化方法进行发动机透平结构的形状优化,采用该方法,使计算大大简化,收敛速度更快,并取得了优化目标的总极值。郑教授和我共同署名的论文发表在《计算和数学》国际期刊上。

回国后,随着对总极值优化方法的进一步探讨,我先后将该方法用在带孔结构优化、复合层板优化以及纺织工艺优化等课题中去,都获得好的结果,该优化方法的可靠性和广泛应用性可见一斑。

在郑权教授离开我们一周年之际,我深切地怀念他,一位杰出的数学家!

前排右一:潘星辰,后排右一:郑权,1982年摄于宾州州立大学

---

[*] 潘星辰,中国纺织大学固体力学教研室教授.

与郑老师相识之点滴

金玉华*

金玉华

2015年10月初的一天晚上,我突然接到涂老师电话,说有急事需要我帮忙。我不敢怠慢,因为涂老师不轻易求人,此次必有要事相托。于是,我立刻订机票出发,急速赶往上海。那是我同年第二次去"亲和源",第一次因有涂老师在,所以与郑老师并无太多接触。这一次则不同,我肩负着"使命":在涂老师回美国的一个多月中,我每天负责接待前来探望郑老师的学生、我新结识的老师们;还负责每日巡查护工的工作,并且每天要为郑老师做好早餐(这也是暂时接涂老师的班),更重要的是,我每天必须了解郑老师的病情,代涂老师随时与主治医生沟通。

在这一个多月的时间里,我与郑老师天天见面,他对疾病所表现出的抗争精神,他坚韧不拔的顽强意志,他对弟子们在各自领域做出的工作成绩引以为傲,他对自己相濡以沫的爱人——涂老师殷殷的期盼,以及他们曾经的深情的歌声……这一切无不深深地打动着我,让我感到:为学术而奋斗一生的二位老师,因各自的优秀而结合,也因诚笃的眷恋而不舍;因彼此的情深而忘我,更因事业的功德而灼灼!

当我看到郑老师的优秀弟子们的一篇篇追忆的文章,才知我是多么地荣幸!这一切虽已成往事,然而,那段短暂而难忘的记忆却永远留在我心中!致敬郑老师!您的思想品德和学术精神如烁烁之星,必将永恒!

---

* 金玉华,涂仁进在沈阳工作时的学生.

深情怀念郑权弟弟

郑 栋*

权弟比我小一岁,我们既是姐弟又曾是同学。我的丈夫唐军是他在敬业中学的同学和好朋友。

记得在抗战时期,全家从上海迁至昆明。因为要躲日寇轰炸,郑权、我还有一个姐姐和哥哥被送到乡下。乡下学校很少,当我去读一年级时,郑权也跟我一起去上学。有一次,老师问全班:"你们谁会写唱歌的歌字?"结果全班同学都不会。正当老师失望时,郑权举手并走到黑板前,在黑板上写了一个"哥"字。虽然写得不对,但得到了老师大大的赞扬。

他自幼聪明、好奇、好学。抗战胜利后,全家回到上海,我们俩同上徐汇区中心小学六年级,又在同一个班级。一天,同学们正在听老师讲课,突然教室内铃声大作。大家都很惊讶,不知发生了什么。原来权弟在研究闹钟为什么会在设定的时间响,而弄响了铃声。

在育才中学上初中时,我们同一年级,但不同班级。我属甲班,他属乙班。上了化学课后,他把母亲的银宝塔放入硫酸里试验、观察化学反应。后来我看到他手上、脸上、衣服上、床上都被硫酸弄破、弄坏了。他还积蓄了零用钱买了一架望远镜,晚上在三楼晒台上观察星星。

他不像其他小孩在意玩具、衣装、吃喝,却十分喜欢自己一个人研究、思考,所以家里人给他起了个绰号"小神经"。

他不但专心于科学,而且是个全面发展的好学生。他小时候体质瘦弱,由于长年坚持体育锻炼,后来身体变得强壮。他认为要献身科学,必须要有个健康的身体作基础。他曾有一次告诉我,在复旦大学参加马拉松比赛时,短裤边较硬,把大腿两侧都磨破了,虽然很疼,他仍坚持跑完全程。

他很喜欢唱歌,而且唱得很好。在敬业中学读工科高中时,被选为文娱委员,经常教同学们唱歌。他还曾编写了一个小歌剧参加全校的文娱会演。因为全班无女生,由唐军男扮女装担任女主角。演出时,郑权第一次看到唐军扮的女装时,捧腹大笑而唱不出声了,引起全场哄堂大笑。以后每当他们俩一起回忆当年情景时,都仍会哈哈大笑不止。

他很朴素,从不抽烟喝酒。他的工资,除用于生活必须用品外,都买书了。他的书装满了他的房间。他热爱数学,对数学概念理解深刻。后来我在复旦大学数学系上学时,他十分认真、耐心地帮助我。

我看他二十七八岁还没有女朋友,就有点急了。想替他介绍一下,但被他拒绝。后来他告诉我,他有一个女朋友,名字叫涂仁进,是他的学生,但要求我不要告诉其他人。我答应了,但忍不住。当天在全家人一起吃饭时,就宣布了这个消息。

---

* 郑栋,郑权姐姐.

在上海话中,"涂仁进"与"大神经"是同音的。我们的小妹妹笑着说:"大神经、小神经,真好玩!"郑权恼羞成怒,一把将小妹妹抱起,扔到洗脸间的浴缸中……

当我得到他逝世的信息时,我十分悲痛,往事历历在目。

权弟,你是一个为数学奋斗终身的志士,你已尽力了! 愿你在天堂平安和喜乐!

前排中郑栋(今年87岁),后排右一郑权,1981年摄于家中

怀念我的郑权叔叔

郑 敏*

因工作关系,我常往返于上海市区与上海市嘉定区。每当路过当年的上海科学技术大学时,总是不禁回忆起与郑权叔叔和涂婶婶在一起的往事,让我十分怀念。

1952年爸爸毕业于上海交通大学后,主动要求支援东北重工业发展计划,去了沈阳航空学校(后改为沈阳航空学院)任教。第二年,妈妈从复旦大学毕业后,也去了沈阳市银行工作。1965年,婶婶从华东师范大学毕业,分配到沈阳一所中学教数学。郑权叔叔当时在上海工学院任教,他们俩两地生活。父母常邀涂婶婶来我家度周末。"文革"开始,父母请婶婶将我送回上海,托交奶奶抚养,住在南昌路。"文革"后父亲调至上海708所。刚回沪时,单位没有房子,父母就挤在南昌路的老家。当时,三楼已在"文革"中被抢占。所以,一楼住郑栋姑妈全家四口,二楼住奶奶、小姑姑、小叔叔和我四人,父亲和郑权叔叔分别住在二楼和三楼的亭子间里。因为我有几个叔叔婶婶,父母让我称他们为郑权叔叔和涂阿姨。

爸爸原是上海交通大学的校篮球队员,体质很好。但经"文革"中批斗、挨打、关牛棚、走"五七"道路去荒漠地区的农村劳动多年后,身体变得多病、瘦弱。回沪后,父母工作繁忙、体弱多病,对我学习的指导,已经心有余而力不足了。奶奶、小姑、小叔对我很好,但他们无力辅导我学习。我的学习就靠自觉了。

郑权叔叔和涂阿姨平时住在学校的教工宿舍,周末回家。他们很关心我的学习,经常帮助、督促我。有一次,我在家做功课、读英语。趁人不备时,偷看在课本下藏着的世界名著,一边心不在焉地时不时读着课本上的单词"announcement",叔叔听到我断断续续地重复着同一个单词,觉得奇怪。他走进我的房间,发现我在看小说。叔叔笑着对我说,学习要专心致志,做事都要一心一意。这一句话,语重心长,我记了一辈子。在我的生命中起了极为重要的作用。

我高中毕业后,郑权叔叔和涂阿姨将我接到嘉定,住在他们新分配的房子中,复习、备考。我看到他们满屋的大书架和大写字台上堆满了很多中文、外文图书和杂志,叔叔总有看不完的书和写不完的东西。涂阿姨一边上班,一边帮助我准备各科目的考试。我们一起去学校食堂吃饭,晚饭后一起去散步。夏天,他们经常去嘉定的一条河边,从船上为我买新到的西瓜。并说:"备考辛苦,慰劳你一下!"我很感动,对他们说:"等我长大了,挣钱后,一定要请你们吃一千个大西瓜!"他们笑着说:"西瓜倒不必了,你好好地学习就行了!"

郑权叔叔和涂阿姨非常好客。来访的客人和学生很多。常听到他们在亭子间里传出的欢声笑语。当时,因为人多、拥挤,厨房和菜柜小,加上涂阿姨不喜欢吃剩饭菜。所以每当需要留客人在家吃饭时,叔叔会预先说明,并逐个询问每人的饭量,而后他们两人一起定量做

---

* 郑敏,上海派普诺管道检测科技发展有限公司董事长。

饭菜,一顿吃完,不多不少。我们大家都笑说,郑权叔叔不愧为数学家,连做饭也把握得非常精确!我们共同生活在南昌路多年,从来没有看到他们夫妻两人吵过架、红过脸。他们志同道合,十分恩爱。郑权叔叔性格爽朗,对晚辈和蔼可亲、百般疼爱。涂阿姨活泼开朗,热情大方。我们都很喜欢他们。

郑权叔叔是我特别尊敬的长者。与他一起生活的时间虽不长,但却在我幼小朦胧的心中留下了不可磨灭的印象。我对学习的兴趣,也源于他的潜移默化。

我们家后来也搬出了南昌路,住到708所分配的房子去了。郑权叔叔和涂阿姨经常来看我们。爸爸住院后,他们也常去医院探望。后来郑权叔叔与涂阿姨都去了美国,与他们见面的机会少了,我更想念他们了。每当叔叔回国或他们同时回国来探望我们全家时,我都非常兴奋。叔叔与父母一起聊天,我总喜欢坐在一旁,听着叔叔聊着在国外生活和工作的每一件事,都让我感到津津有味。

听到郑权叔叔去世的消息,我非常悲痛,心中时常怀念着他。悠悠往事,依然温暖着我的心。

前排左起:钟琴倦(郑敏母亲)、郑楠(郑敏父亲、郑权哥哥),后排左起:郑敏、涂仁进、郑权,1981年摄于上海家中

相惜相知六十年

涂仁进[*]

一、相惜

郑权与我1960年相遇于华东师范大学数学系。当时我是上海工学院数理力学系第一届学生。由于上海工学院师资力量不足,学院与华东师范大学领导协商决定并向我们两个班约六十几名学生说明并保证:华东师范大学数学系代培后,回归上海工学院分配。郑权从复旦大学数学系毕业,刚分到上海工学院,就成了派往华东师范大学的五位教师和政工干部之一,担任"数学分析"课程的助教。他住在男生寝室,既是老师,又像学生。他送女生一幅居里夫人画像、男生一幅爱因斯坦画像,鼓励同学们要为祖国的科学事业而努力。

每次进教室,郑权从书包中拿出一个小闹钟,放在讲台上,然后开始讲课。他讲课深入浅出、思路清晰、形式多样,深受同学欢迎。一次他组织讨论极限概念,先由各小组内讨论,然后派代表到大班交流。"数学分析"课代表与我分在同一小组,她很聪明,基础又好,理当小组代表。可是她害羞,求我代她去大班发言。我当时无知无畏,便答应了。每个小组代表站在原来的位置上发言后,全班同学,包括老师都可提问。轮到我发言,郑权问了三个问题,我答了。接着问第四个问题,答不出;又接着问第五个问题,问题答不上来,眼泪却掉下来了。下课后,他把我叫去办公室,问:"为什么哭?"答:"我没哭,只是掉泪而已。"又问:"为什么?"答:"生气!"还问:"为什么?"反问:"作为老师,是否一定要把学生问倒,才能显示出你的水平?"答:"不是。我只想帮助学生加深对重要概念的理解。"我无言以对,随即沉默。我正要起身向外走,大概为缓解紧张气氛,他看着办公桌上的作业本说:"你的作业本很特殊,挺好认。"我说:"家里穷,那是我利用家中废纸,自己用线缝制的。"然后问:"作业本的质量影响作业对错和课程的成绩吗?!"说罢,我就不辞而别了。

第一学期近末,郑权和我们全年级学生由学校安排赴崇明,挖河泥、筑堤坝、围海造田。我们割芦苇做床垫,很多人挤睡在同一个帐篷里。早上起床,把脚硬塞进了冰的鞋里,然后敲冰取水,洗脸刷牙,匆匆吃了早饭后,便去海边筑坝。由于天冷、风大、潮湿,加上饥饿,不少同学病了,我得了风湿性关节炎。元旦放假一天,学校要求我们就地搞庆祝活动。政治指导员找我谈话,要我与郑权合作出一个节目,我作为学生代表,他当教工代表。那可能是指导员考虑到我当时是华东师范大学歌剧队队员,而郑权曾是上海市大学生合唱团团员吧!于是,我们对唱了一首当时流行的电影插曲《敖包相会》。此后,有人传言,郑权与我,因歌而恋。虽不属实,却也有因可循。

---

[*] 郑权夫人,美国哥伦布州立大学数学系教授.

1962年夏季的某一天,郑权找我谈话,说:"我很快要回工学院了。×××同学看出我喜欢你。希望以后能与你交个朋友,保持通信联系。"我懵了!不知如何作答才好。想了一下,就坦言道:"你是一位德智体全面发展的好老师。我对你印象深刻。但由于家庭原因,我不相信婚姻,不想恋爱、结婚、生儿育女。"(最近读到一篇文章才知,原来,这是一种名为"恐婚症"的心理学疾病,多发于父母离异的女性)他说:"我要为科学而奋斗终身。恋爱结婚、生儿育女,太浪费时间和精力,我并没有这种计划。"他又说:"跟你说话,我感到很开心。所以希望能与你交流工作、学习体会。"我告诉他:"我自幼散漫成性,好玩不好学。我很笨,基础差、字潦草、速度慢,不会写信。再说,学生生活单调,没有什么值得写。"他说:"不要紧,试试看吧!"从此,他用日记的方式写了他的工作与学习。每周一封,很有规律。他字体工整优美,语言简朴。他写得多,却收得少。但是,他不计较。

后来发生的几件事情,促进了我们关系的发展。

首先是政治指导员找我谈话。她说:"据同学反应,郑权与你通信频繁,你了解他吗?"见我没有吱声,她接着说:"郑权在'反右'中,犯有严重的政治错误,你要认真考虑你的前途。"见我仍无任何表示,她就说:"你回去好好想想吧!"后来,我将她的话向郑权复述了一遍。他沉默了片刻,告诉我:"1957年我与另外三位同学一同去劝一位年轻的物理老师,希望这位老师能检讨过关。因为这位老师非常聪明有才,不但物理强,数学也精,深受大家喜爱。后来,这位老师成为'右派',我与其他三位同学犯了'右倾错误'。因为我是系学生会主席,所以受到留团察看的处分。"我同情他的处境,理解他的心情。我不懂政治,年轻而逆反。我说:"好坏对错有时需时间考验,才能辨真假。古今中外,好人受屈、坏人得势的例子并不少见。你的信,对我的学习有很大的帮助。我们继续通信吧!"

1963年,郑权报考浙江大学数学系陈建功教授的研究生,他对考试胸有成竹,但结果却未被录取。后来听说,陈教授去复旦大学抱怨道:我要的,不给;不要的,硬塞。闻讯,郑权深受挫伤而郁闷,但未失勇气而更加努力。我对他说:"我相信,以你的聪明、能力和毅力,即使没有导师,你自己也能闯出一条路来,你的理想一定会实现。"

1964年,郑权下乡,参加"四清运动"。临行前,我去看他并带去一条新棉被。我说:"乡下冷,营养差,易得病。这是我母亲特意请人用新

郑权指导我学习

棉花弹的被子,非常柔软暖和,你带去吧!"他说:"我身体好,没问题,你有关节炎,自己留着吧!"但是,他拗不过我,我们就交换了棉被。"四清运动"结束回校后,他就把被子还给我了。

郑权非常热爱生活,他坚持长跑、游泳,在大学时代,他曾参加过马拉松长跑比赛。他游泳姿势正确、速度快。他教我蛙泳和自由泳。我们一起游泳时,他一入水,很快就把我远远地抛在后面。他熟知几乎所有科学家的传记,如数珍宝,津津乐道。我们还经常一起唱些中

国民歌,他也教我唱一些外国民歌,有时他还会为我唱一些外国歌剧中的选曲。

我过去对学习不求甚解。上课抄笔记,下课看笔记、看书,参照例题做作业;把作业做对,考试成绩得"优"作为奋斗目标。他认为,这样的学习目标和方法都是不对的。他认真地分析了产生这些错误的原因,并引导我深入思考、理解主要概念和理论本质,培养我独立提出问题、分析和解决问题的能力。在我选专业时,他详细地介绍了各专业的特色,并指导我如何选专业方向。他的指导,对我读大学以及后来读研都有极大的帮助。而且在以后的工作及生活中,仍有深远的影响。他是我的第一位导师。

那时候有人说闲话,说我跟郑权交往的目的是为了留在上海。在毕业分配填志愿表时,我只花了几分钟,全填了外地,就交上去了。他听我介绍后说:"你的志愿应该完全出于自己的内心,不必顾忌他人的说法。让别人去说,走自己的路。"他还说:"无论你的选择是什么,我都会尊重你的选择。"

在与他交往过程中,我觉得自己与他相差甚远。他有远大抱负、富于创造、惜时如命;他还很耐心、谨慎和大度,我却不然。好在我们"三观"一致,又都喜欢唱歌。另外,我们还有一些共同点:生活简朴、真诚善良、知足感恩。我们互相信任、关爱、包容。

毕业时,我被分配到沈阳。毕业后,他向我求婚。他问:"我们结婚吧!好吗?"我答:"好。"于是各自去单位开介绍信,我们同去民政局。郑权交了二角钱,我们领到了结婚证书,他就成了我的丈夫。婚后第三天,他送我到火车站,开始了我们长期两地分居生活的序幕。

二、相知

1965年我大学毕业,被分到沈阳,就遭遇了"四清运动",并从患肺结核病的房东大娘处染得肺结核病。1966年,在第二期"四清运动"中,因家庭和社会关系中有多人被批斗关押,我因此也受围攻,得了严重忧郁症,几近精神分裂,生不如死。郑权出"牛棚"后得知此事,劝慰我:"凡事要想开,我们都还年轻,要有信心,等待黎明。"我们相互安慰并约定:无论发生什么,一不自杀,二不发精神病。每当离别时,我们同声高唱语录歌:海内存知己,天涯若比邻……,我们的心是连在一起的。我们之间的革命的战斗的友谊,经历过疾风暴雨的考验!

1967年,我被分配到沈阳市第85中学当数学老师,当时学校停课"闹革命",上班时搞"大批判""大颂扬""唱语录歌""跳忠字舞"。有时半夜被叫醒,集合起来,上街游行,敲锣打鼓,高呼口号,步行来回十几里路到市"革命委员会"大楼去报喜、贺喜。后来复课"闹革命",带领学生到工厂去学工,到农村去学农。在沈阳13年,真正教数学课的时间不到2年。这个中学校址原是沈阳市教师进修学院,图书馆里藏书不少,我向管理员借书作为写"大批判稿"的参考资料,她将钥匙给我,让我自己去选。在这期间,我读完了《鲁迅全集》,也借机看了不少其他书籍。

郑权一直希望我能抓紧时间,继续学习数学和英语。可惜,我没有听取他的忠告,目光短浅,随波逐流,白白浪费了青春年华。1978年恢复招收研究生时,郑权鼓励我考研究生。为了解决两地分居问题,以便返沪团聚,我只得临时抱佛脚,抓紧时间进行考研前的复习准备。

他却不然,不论周围条件如何,即使被批斗、关押了两次"牛棚",去了两次"干校",他也从不放弃学习和研究数学。明知不可为而为之,我欣赏他的执着。

沈阳当年物质供应很差：每人每月有三斤细粮，其余为粗粮、三两油。不少人浮肿，得肝炎及其他疾病。我很幸运，每年寒假回上海得到休息和补充。暑假时，他还为我当运输大队长，补充供给。有一次，他坐轮船经大连转乘火车到沈阳，为能多带一些大米和面条，他用扁担挑着大包小包入校门，经学校的主要通道到位于最后一排我的宿舍过程中，很多师生目睹了。2010年，我邀几位当年在沈阳的同事来沪，参观世博会，谈及此事，他们说："过去我们见证了郑权对你的关爱，现在看到了你对他的照看和护理，很感动。你做得对，也应该！"

有一年寒假回上海探亲时，他建议我们一起骑自行车去郊游，对我进行体力测验。我们清晨五点起床，简单吃了些早点，就出发了。一路北上，经嘉定、罗店，一切顺利。中午吃了一碗面，就返程了。可回程时遇上了大风，无法骑车，只好下车逆风推车而行。直到进入市区才能再骑车前行。我咬牙坚持着，到家时，几近瘫倒。他说："今天体力测验你及格了，你辛苦了！"他又说："你先去休息一下，今晚我来做咸肉菜饭。"等饭好了，我刚尝一口，立即吐出，因为咸得发苦。他连续加水改做了菜粥，尝了一口，说："怎么还是这么咸？我再去加点水，煮一下吧！"原来，他只用冷水简单冲洗了一下，咸肉里的大盐块并没被冲掉。看他辛苦、耐心，我很感动，说："今天就随便吃一点吧，你也辛苦了！"

1978年，我36岁时，成为上海科学技术大学第一届研究生中年龄最长者，压力很大，尤其是英语。我们从字母开始学了一册教材后，就不分基础，全部并入一个大班，一起读一本字体很小、纸质又差、颜色发黄的科技英语教材。每篇课文，我需用字典逐一查出一二百个生词。终于，我流产了、失眠了、视力模糊，看不清教材内容。我几乎丧失了学习的信心。郑权那时工作极其繁忙，又要准备出国。但他还是耐心地鼓励我，要树立信心、坚持努力、克服困难。他用大字体把教材内容抄在大白纸上，让我读。每天中午，他都先买好了饭菜在食堂等我下课，一起吃饭。晚餐后，陪我在学校附近的田埂小道上散步。在他的精心呵护下，我的失眠很快好转，视力逐渐恢复。

1981年，在我毕业前，他被派往美国当访问学者。出国后，他一如既往地以日记的形式，每周一封信，详细地描写了他在美国的生活。据说，人在国外，很容易孤独。那时我回信及时且详细，除了写信，我也曾录制了一盘磁带，详细地描绘了周边情况及我的生活，我还录制了一首自己唱的《小河淌水》请人带给他。

硕士毕业后，我留校任教，被分配教"概率统计"课程。1983年郑权回国后，建议我自费公派去美国开阔视野、参观访问，为期2年。我对他说："我知道你是一片好心，但我在沈阳13年，读硕士3年，我累了，哪儿也不想去了。再说，我们新分的房子，需要装修，家务一大堆。你工作忙，我来搞后勤服务吧！"可是，他一直坚持他的想法，不断地鼓励我学习英语。最终，于1987年5月，我以自费公派访问学者之名访问美国宾州州立大学数学系，同年8月随陈巩教授去德州农工大学访问。

到达美国后，前上海科学技术大学研究生室友罗自平，几乎每周从加州打来长途电话，鼓励我在美国读博士。但我觉得自己年龄大、基础差而没有信心。当时，为了提高自己的英语水平，我去学校的数学实验室当义工。在那里，认识了一位年长的美国学生。有一天，从校报上看到一幅他的照片和一篇报导。文中介绍了这位73岁的机械系硕士生，曾是二战中的飞行员，复员后在波音公司任职，退休后来校读硕士。文中还介绍他准备继续读博士，并有争取获诺奖的雄心壮志。我问他："校报上对你的报导是真的吗？"他回答："关于诺奖，是他们瞎吹的，别的都是真的。"看着他，我真正地懂得了"活到老，学到老"的意义。我终于决定试一下,如果不行,对朋友和自己都算有了交待。我写信征求郑权的意见,他回信答复道:"作为系主任,我不同意你在美国读博士。你访问2年,到时回来。作为丈夫,我尊重你个人的选择。"后来通过考托福、GRE,我在1988年成了美国堪萨斯州威奇塔州立大学数学系概率统计专业的博士生。

1989年5月下旬,郑权赴美参加国际数学学术会议后来看我,并讨论我的回国日程。我当时刚完成第一学年的课程。我说:"你当访问学者时省吃俭用,为让我自费公派来美参观访问、开拓视野,时限2年。现在目标已完成,时限已到。我非常知足感恩了。我们结婚24年,却长期分居两地17年,相聚仅7年。我已经47岁了,我想回家。拿不拿学位,无所谓。"他看到我当时学习主动积极、兴趣盎然、成绩优秀,英语也有了很大进步,便说:"我当然喜欢我们现在就一同回去。但是,如果我现在先回去,你拿到学位再回去,对我们系今后进一步开展概率统计方向的教学和科研有利。这也是一种选择。"

正当我们在讨论这个重要抉择问题的时候,那个震惊中外的事件发生了。前车之鉴,令人悲伤惶惑。我们能做的唯有希望和等待。

此后,郑权分别在加拿大和美国几所大学做访问教授,与多位教授合作写论文、出版论文和书籍,并一律以中国上海科学技术大学数学系署名发表。1992年郑权57岁时,他用了一年时间,获得美国克莱姆森大学的数学博士学位。

1996年,上海大学数学系主任来信,告知郑权:"运筹学与控制论"博士

外出合影

点得了"黄牌"警告,并希望他速归,这使郑权寝食不安。我理解并赞同他立即回国的决定。他马上准备行装和有关资料,只等学校批文下达,即飞上海。但此事后来没有下文,成了郑权的终身遗憾!

2002年至2010年,在时任上海大学数学系主任王翼飞教授的努力下,郑权被聘为上海大学数学系的第一位外籍(加拿大)自强教授,终于圆了他报效祖国的梦。为了一生热爱的祖国,为了数学,他从朝气蓬勃到风烛残年,鞠躬尽瘁。那美好的仗,他已打过,他已尽力了!

当郑权得了帕金森病后,他的行动能力逐渐下降。他的游泳从遥遥领先于我到相差无几,再到比我慢,最后他不能游了,但他仍不放弃,坚持在水中行走锻炼。有不少人,因得病而怨天尤人,性格变得消极自私,但他一直保持坚强乐观的精神。有一天,当我推着他一起唱完了《草原之夜》后,他说了一句:"发个伊妹儿就行。"我当时没反应过来,以为他要我给谁发伊妹儿,就问他:"发给谁?"他说:"不是没有邮递员吗?"我这才恍然大悟,那是他对歌词中"可惜没有邮递员来传情"的幽默响应,于是我们一起哈哈大笑起来。郑权对所有的医护人员,都表达了他的尊重和感激,他的乐观与坚强也给他们留下深刻的印象。多年来,很多亲友、同学、同事及学生们的热情探访和帮助,使他感受了人间的关爱和温暖。

2020年5月9日,郑权告别了人间旅途中所有的悲欢与奋斗,解除了一切病痛,平安地

美国乔治亚州Callaway私人公园，摄于2002年10月

回归永无疾病的天堂了！与郑权相惜相知的60年间，由于种种原因，我们断断续续两地分居约30年。他从来没有对我说过，他是多么地爱我。但他的行为彰显了他的爱是那么真挚、深远、恒久！我感谢他对我的理解、关爱和指导。他是我永远的导师、知心的朋友和亲爱的丈夫。他拓宽了我的视野，启迪了我的智慧，改变了我的人生。

有什么能使两颗相知相爱的心隔绝呢？患难吗！距离吗！！死亡吗！！！

郑权墓碑

感恩与鸣谢

首先要感恩郑权和我的父母,他们都历经抗战的艰辛和社会变迁,也都能竭尽全力让他们的子女受到良好的教育,并维系相互间的骨肉深情。

感谢郑权的复旦大学老同学和校友们。陈铿夫妇、吴立德、吴霭成、陶宗英、周慰因和邹悦都曾去上海亲和源公寓看望郑权,邹悦、俞丽和还组织联系了老同学。写文章纪念郑权的,除了她们,还有陶宗英、程沅生、尚汉冀和沈海华等。沈海华还曾从美国纽约特地赶到哥伦布市看望在康复院中的郑权。

非常感谢原上海工学院老同事张宪荣特地为郑权而作了墨宝对联。郑权在上海工学院的生前好友还有施惟慧、梁兆荣和张玉藻等人。

真诚感谢原上海科学技术大学数学系的领导和同事对郑权工作的理解和支持。黄育仁教授是上海科学技术大学数学系的元老和系主任,为上海科学技术大学数学系的建设起了开创性的作用,1983年他力荐郑权当系主任并全力支持郑权开展工作。柯寿仁先生是一位有远见的伯乐,他对郑权的超前认知和支持,为他创造了发展空间,使郑权在教学科研、评职晋级、学科建设、获得殊荣等方面都得到了极大的帮助。特别要感谢汤生江先生,在他和郑权分别任上海科学技术大学数学系党总支书记和系主任时期,他们相互信任、尊重、理解和支持,大家都心情愉快,工作卓有成效。上海科学技术大学的老同事郭本瑜、张荣欣、杜卧薪、茅德康、贺国强、史定华、邬冬华、陈民仪、颜珍棣等人都曾去亲和源看望郑权。衷心感谢汤生江、盛万成、张荣欣、陈民仪、许梦杰、李志良、朱国勇和邬冬华等人还为本书深情撰写纪念文章。

1981年郑权受美籍华人陈巩教授之邀,成为美国宾州州立大学的访问学者。陈巩教授和郑权长期合作探讨研究,共同发表论文,成为好友。

加拿大蒙特利尔魁北克大学数学与信息系教授 Efim A. Galperin 也曾邀请郑权访问他所在的学校,开展学术交流、合作发表论文和出版书籍。

美国克莱姆森大学数学科学系教授 M. M. Kostreva 是郑权的论文合作者。经过他的努力,郑权与校方取得协议,允许郑权免除英语考试和免修大部分博士生的必修课,但需完成教辅工作、博士资格考试、博士学习程序中最后一年的全部课程和博士论文及答辩。郑权以优异的成绩完成了全部要求,成为该校史上第一位在一年之内取得博士学位的人。没有 Kostreva 教授对郑权的充分了解和信心,这是不可能的。

史树中、庄松林、蒋百川、唐晋发、潘星辰、胡毓达等皆是各自领域的专家。他们因工作、学习、研究而成为郑权的挚友。每次郑权回国,无论多忙,庄松林和夫人史以珏必亲自来访。史以珏是瑞金医院神经内科的专家,她对郑权的诊断和治疗起了极为重要的作用。潘星辰也曾多次随访郑权。

罗自平曾是我在上海科学技术大学的室友。她以一个初中毕业生,于1978年被上海科学技术大学破格录取为硕士研究生,1980年又被美国普林斯顿大学破格录取为博士研究生。后来与丈夫张永锋博士,在洛杉矶共创了一家制药公司。她的真诚和不懈的鼓励,开启了我人生的新篇章。每当郑权去美国西海岸时,他们夫妇总是抽空与郑权相聚畅谈。为了本书的出版,她提供了很多重要建议并详细地修改了我与其他不少人的文章。

刘薇青于1982年获上海科学技术大学计算机专业硕士,2013年获UCLA生物统计专业硕士,毕业后留校做研究工作。丈夫关存厚博士是洛杉矶市政府所属单位的工程师。他们曾接待、陪同我参观了美国两个海岸的多个主要景点。2013年,郑权和我去圣地亚哥开会时,关存厚夫妇特意从洛杉矶市远程驱车来看望我们,并开车陪同我们参观圣地亚哥。

李兴中是中央华盛顿大学英语系教授,1993年他和我分别在美国卡罗拉多州Adams State College的英语系和数学系任教。他曾帮我改写过我亲属来美的英文邀请信,郑权逝世后,他对墓志铭的文体作了专门的研究,为郑权的墓碑设计并定稿了墓志铭。我的大学同学张小萍,曾是高等教育出版社的编审;顾荣佳是我在沈阳的同事和好友刘芝芬的丈夫,他曾是《辽宁大学学报》主编。三位老朋友对我的纪念文章都作了认真的修改,对"小传"和"感恩与鸣谢"也提出很多中肯的意见。

邓百樵曾是我同事、邻居和朋友。他的夫人张之玮在亚特兰大CDC从事研究工作。他每周往返于来亚特兰大与哥仑布市。20多年来,他经常帮助我们从亚特兰大代购中国货物并送货上门。当我们回沪时,他代我们收信件并处理有关事务。平时需要帮助时,总是随叫随到,完全像一位家人。

江擎旗是一位医治癌症的专家,他对我们的健康非常关心。每当郑权住院时,他每天都去病房查访,包括重症监护室。2020年疫情严重时,他和夫人鲁丽娅经常来看望我并送来口罩、食物和自制的各种点心。当我得了带状泡疹,他送医送药上门。2021年年初,他为我登记并送我去注射了防治新冠病毒的疫苗。

王轶恩曾是位钢琴演奏家,不幸手指得病,医治康复无效后,攻读电脑博士学位。她和丈夫葛韬一直对我们非常关心,去年疫情严重时,他们主动购物并送货上门。为配合本书中郑权的复旦大学老同学尚汉冀写的一篇纪念文章,她花费不少时间精力,帮助寻找并下载简谱软件,为那首由郑权谱曲、尚汉冀作词的歌曲配上了电子文版。

最令人感动的是郑权的学生们,他们不是亲人,却胜似亲人!

孙世杰是从生活上对郑权和我帮助最大、付出最多、历时最长的一位。几十年如一日,他不辞辛劳地帮助我们处理嘉定的一切事务。我们嘉定的房子在五楼,没有电梯。他自己膝盖有病,但他从付账、订杂志、整理房间、经办各种手续,到最后帮我们卖掉嘉定的房子。事无巨细,尽心尽力,做了我们两家任何一位亲属都做不到的事。

多年来,我在美国一直受到王汉坤、周建新的关照和帮助。他们有求必应,亲如家人。对王汉坤的英年早逝,郑权和我都非常悲痛,并时常念及他。最近,为出版本书,王汉坤夫人尹小楠花了不少时间去实地拍照,只是为了验证郑权一张照片中的信息。周建新对本书中的"小传"和"感恩与鸣谢"也提出不少积极建议。

2007年,崔洪泉邀请郑权和我去崇明岛旧地重游。看到崇明岛发展迅速,引发了我们对1960年在崇明一起围海造田的亲切回忆。

2010年,郑权第一次在上海大学发病昏倒时,陈熙、梁泽亮陪我上救护车,并帮忙办理有关医疗事项。医院当时无床位,只得在走廊中等待,我与陈熙、梁泽亮三人在厕所旁守护郑权一晚,彻夜未眠。第二天一早,姚奕荣不顾自己90多岁高龄的老母亲病情危急,闻讯赶到,经他努力,将郑权安排入病房医治。郑权住院期间,很多同事、朋友、学生前去探访。出院后,考虑到郑权实际情况,我们决定放弃参观正在上海举办的世博会,可是同学们却不肯放弃。陈熙、梁泽亮、周广付、安柳和王筱莉做了细心周到的安排,帮助郑权和我参观了所有的展馆,包括当时最热门的"中国馆",那是当时最难看到的展馆。

谢志刚、鲁习文、姚奕荣都曾来美国访问我们的家,或去康复院或去医院探访郑权。鲁习文首先提出建议:希望郑权回沪养病,以便于大家一起帮助照顾郑权。郑权入住上海亲和源后,他自己经常忙中偷闲,去亲和源看望郑权,还带去不少礼物,包括他家园中自产的水果。

2013年12月6日,那天上海雾霾特别严重,能见度极差。当郑权和我到达上海浦东机场出口处时,姚奕荣、陈熙、张曼利、陈思豪和曾丽媛等人和涂颂华早已等候在机场。他们艰难、谨慎地开车,将我俩送至亲和源老人公寓的医院门口。

2015年夏,郑权入瑞金医院重症监护室。王翼飞、姚奕荣、谢志刚每天相聚在医院与我共处一个小时。出院那天,王翼飞从清晨就到瑞金医院,并随救护车送郑权到亲和源。直到下午近五点,看见一切安排妥当后,才放心回家。

2016年3月,我返美为郑权取药。我在沈阳的40多年前的学生金玉华专程来沪帮助联络。在近一个月时间中,她每天将郑权的所有情况向我和姚奕荣、谢志刚等汇报。而姚奕荣则每天清晨开车从普陀的万里小区去杨浦双阳北路接上谢志刚再同去浦东亲和源,与医生探讨有关郑权的病情和治疗方案,确保安全后,再各自去上班。操心费时,实在辛苦!

张晓东、宋学锋皆远道而来到亲和源看望郑权。韩伯顺夫妇、彭建平夫妇也是亲和源的常客。

2017年当郑权和我返美时,我在沈阳的前学生金英姿从沈阳专程来沪,并一直陪同我护送郑权到美国。

俗话说,人一走,茶就凉。然而郑权杯中的清茶,却几十年未凉。君子之交,淡如水,却深似海。

上海亲和源老人公寓的工作人员,都很热情尽责。邻居相互关心、友好。有位入住亲和源的诗人,看到我推着坐在轮椅上的郑权同声边走边唱后,由感而发作诗赠送我们以资鼓励。在美国的小区,邻居们也都很关爱郑权。看到郑权行走不便,有一位近邻来家帮助安装室内设备以防摔跤;两位动过关节置换手术的邻居,一位在郑权手术前,上门向他介绍经验;另一位在他手术后,去病房为他介绍术后康复体会。还有一位邻居在郑权出院前,用了一天时间,开车陪我遍访了市内所有的康复院;每当救护车来家时,小区主任(义工)会主动陪我去医院。小区义工办的仅一页的月刊简报,对小区内的逝世者,一般会用一句悼念语句提及。郑权逝世后,竟用了近半页的篇幅,表达了深切悼念。另一位邻居还送来了两大盆栽鲜花以示安慰。

当我回美为郑权取药时,上海亲和源教会中天天有人为我们祷告,有人去医院为郑权唱圣诗,有人送给郑权很多精心制作的食物。在美国教会的一位姐妹,用了两天时间开车带我在全州范围内找寻最佳康复院。郑权逝世后,教会几位姐妹上门送花、送卡,以示关爱。一位姐妹几乎每天打电话来安慰并询问有什么需要帮助,长达一年半之久。

衷心感谢本书的所有撰稿人,感谢你们的深情回忆和宝贵时间!你们对郑权的为人、处